I0786905

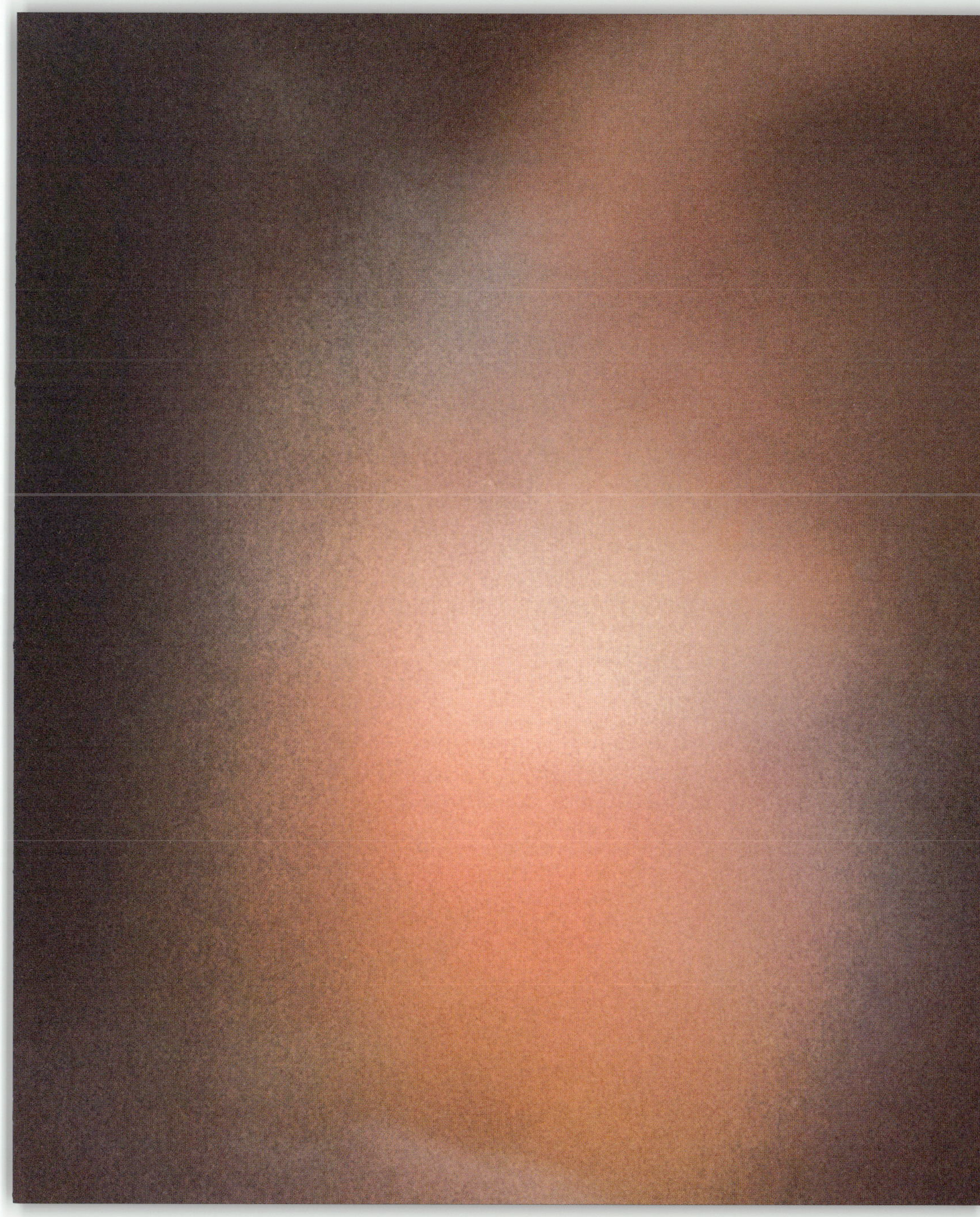

When the days get dark and the things that are hard start to overshadow everything else...

These are the moments when it's easy to lose sight of yourself.

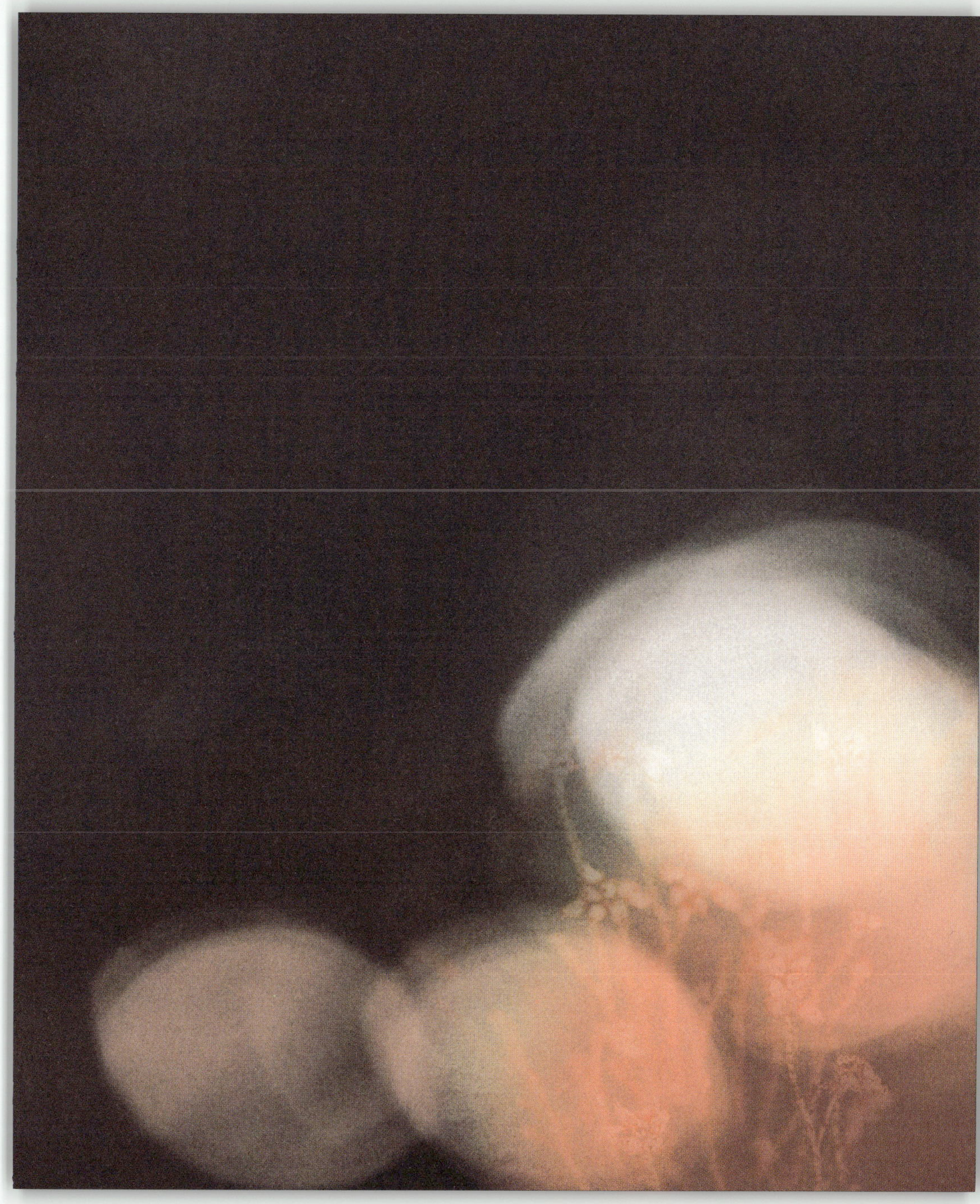

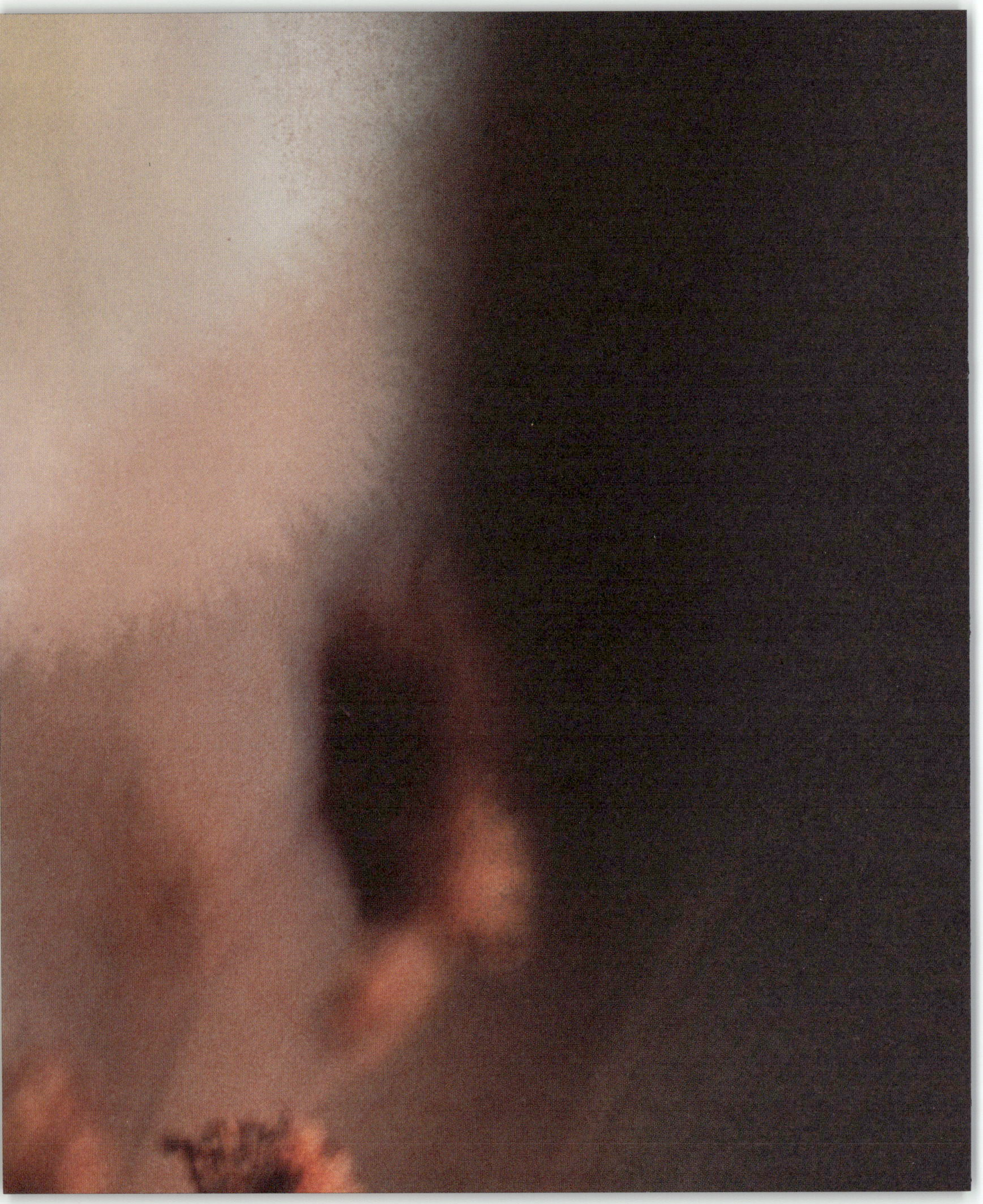

So if, at this moment, you have forgotten
who you are—if you have forgotten the spark
that is yours and the goodness that is yours,
and all the things about you that are
wonderful and true...

I'm here to say: *I remember.*
I remember, and I want to remind you.

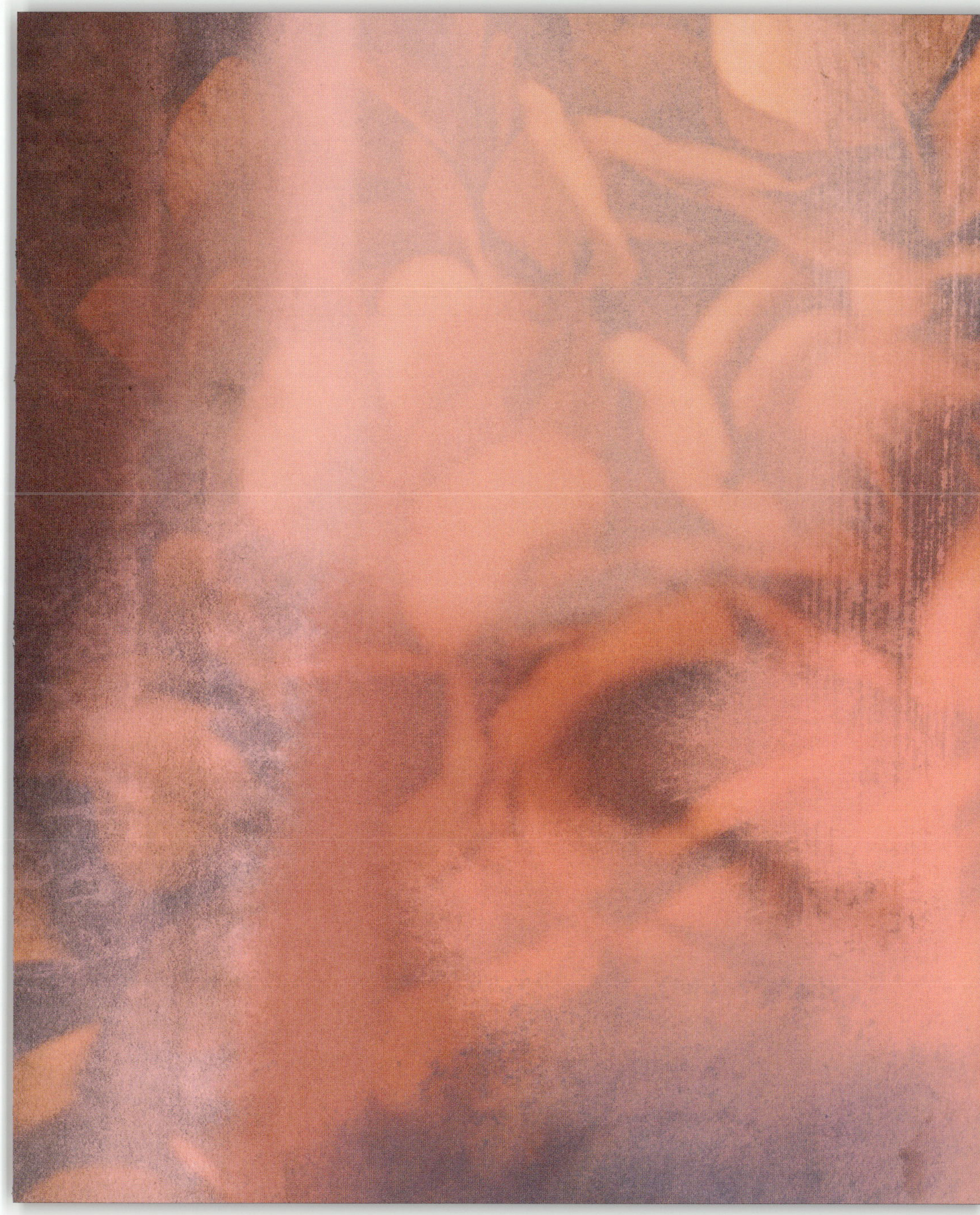

Because I have watched you
go through challenges before.
I've seen what happens when you do.

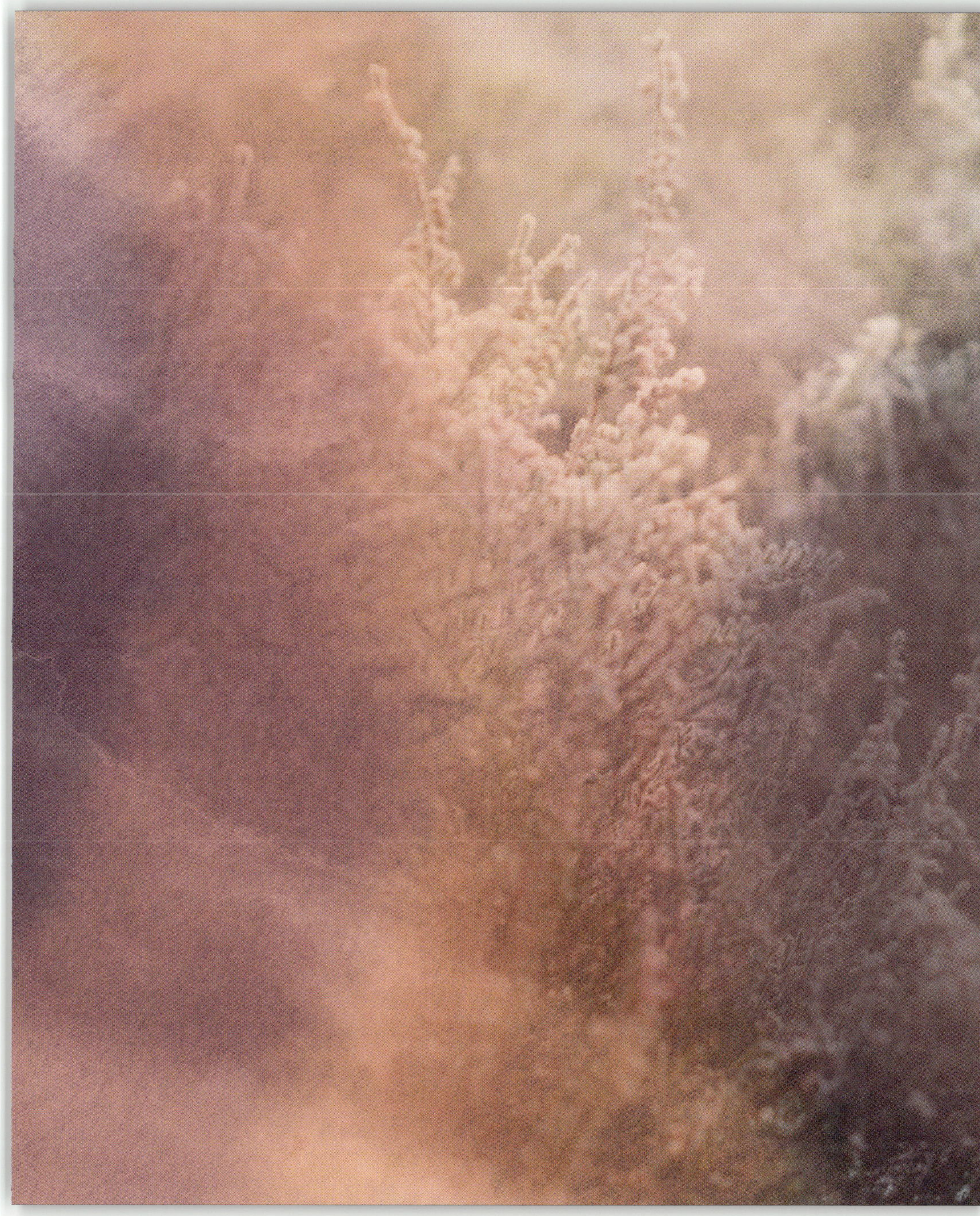

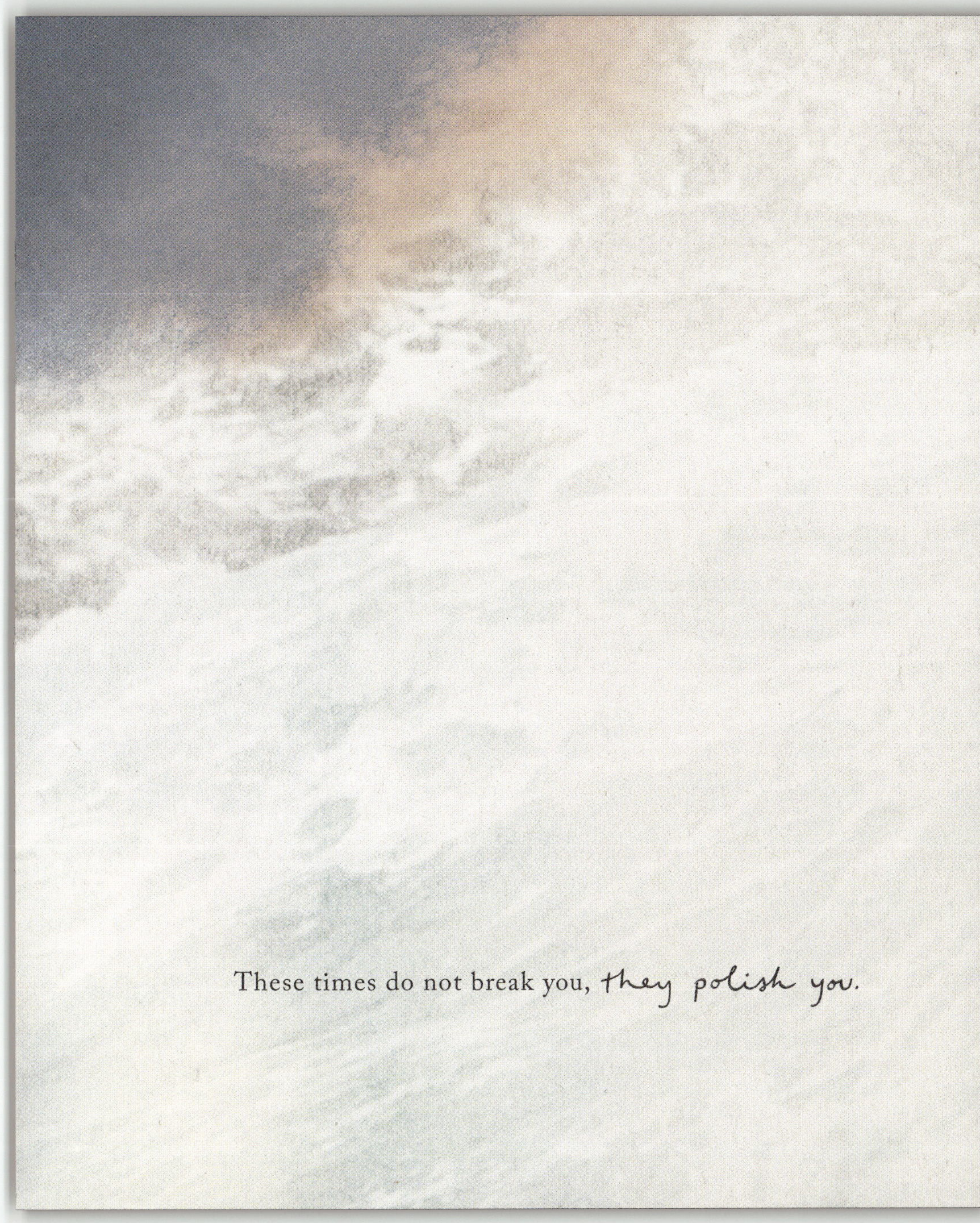

These times do not break you, *they polish you*.

And the strength that is yours comes out.
And the light that is yours switches on.
And you meet the moment with a power
that's incredible to see.

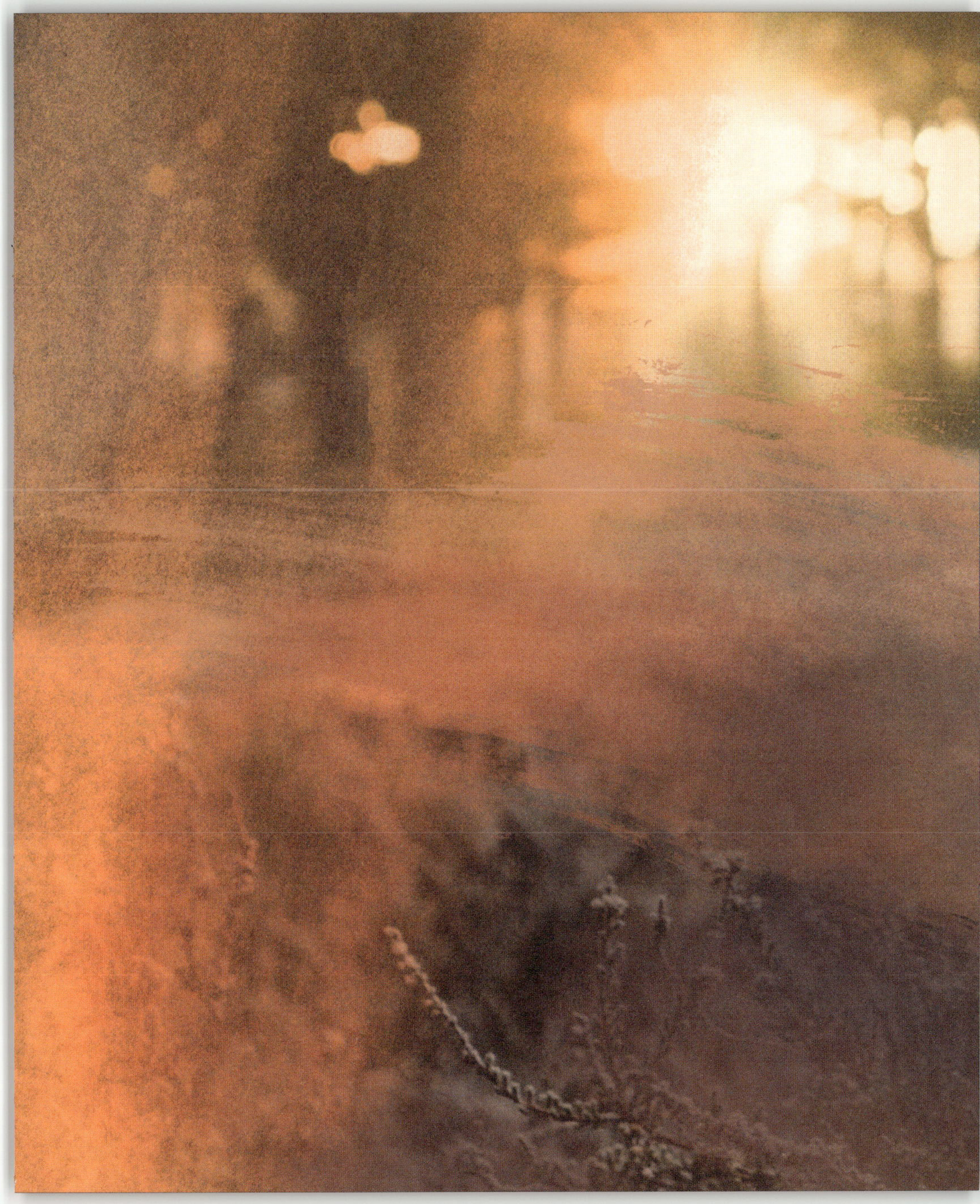

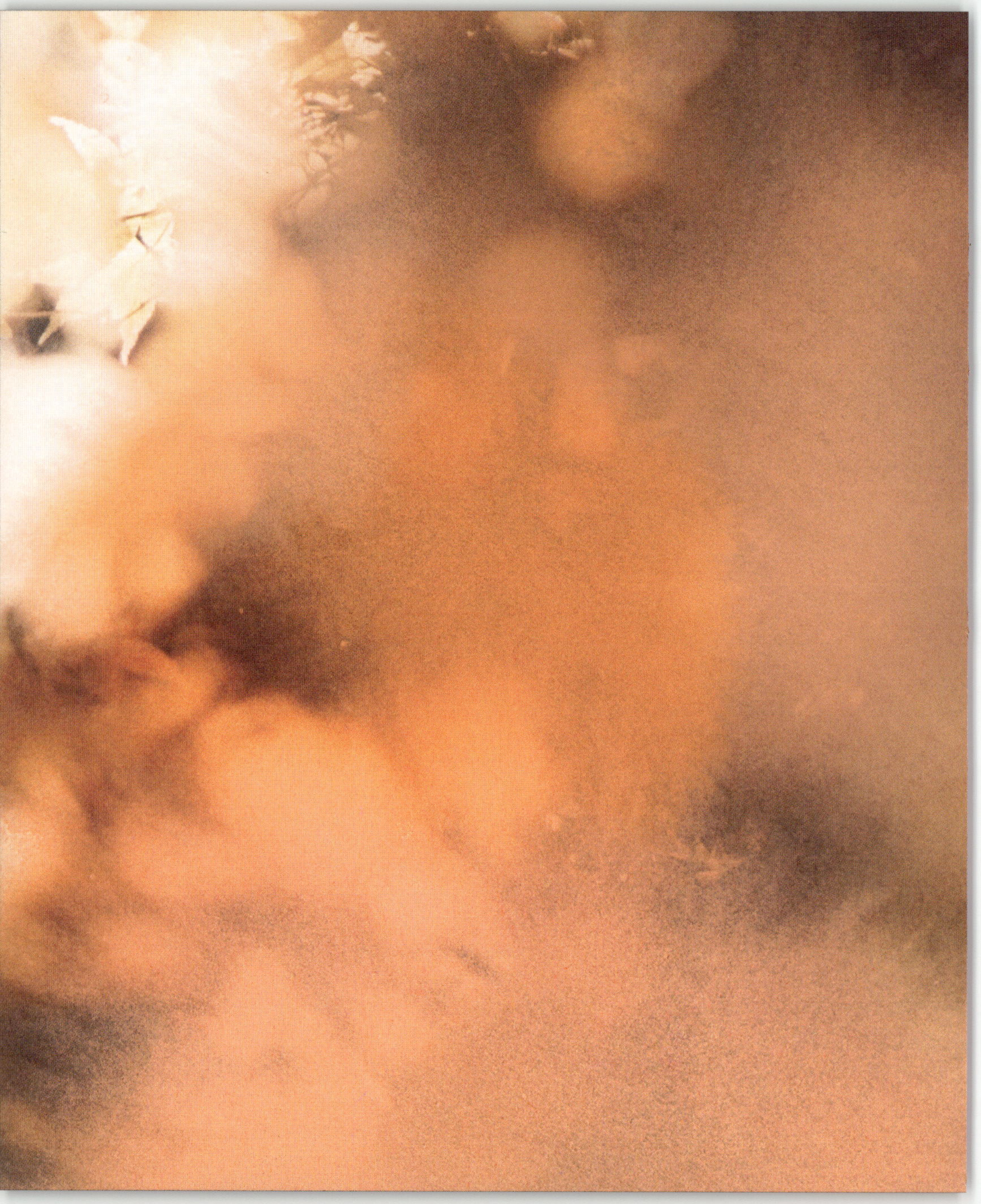

This is a beauty all your own.
It's a kind of *alchemy*.

And I wish I could quiet the waves for a moment.
I wish I could get them to end.

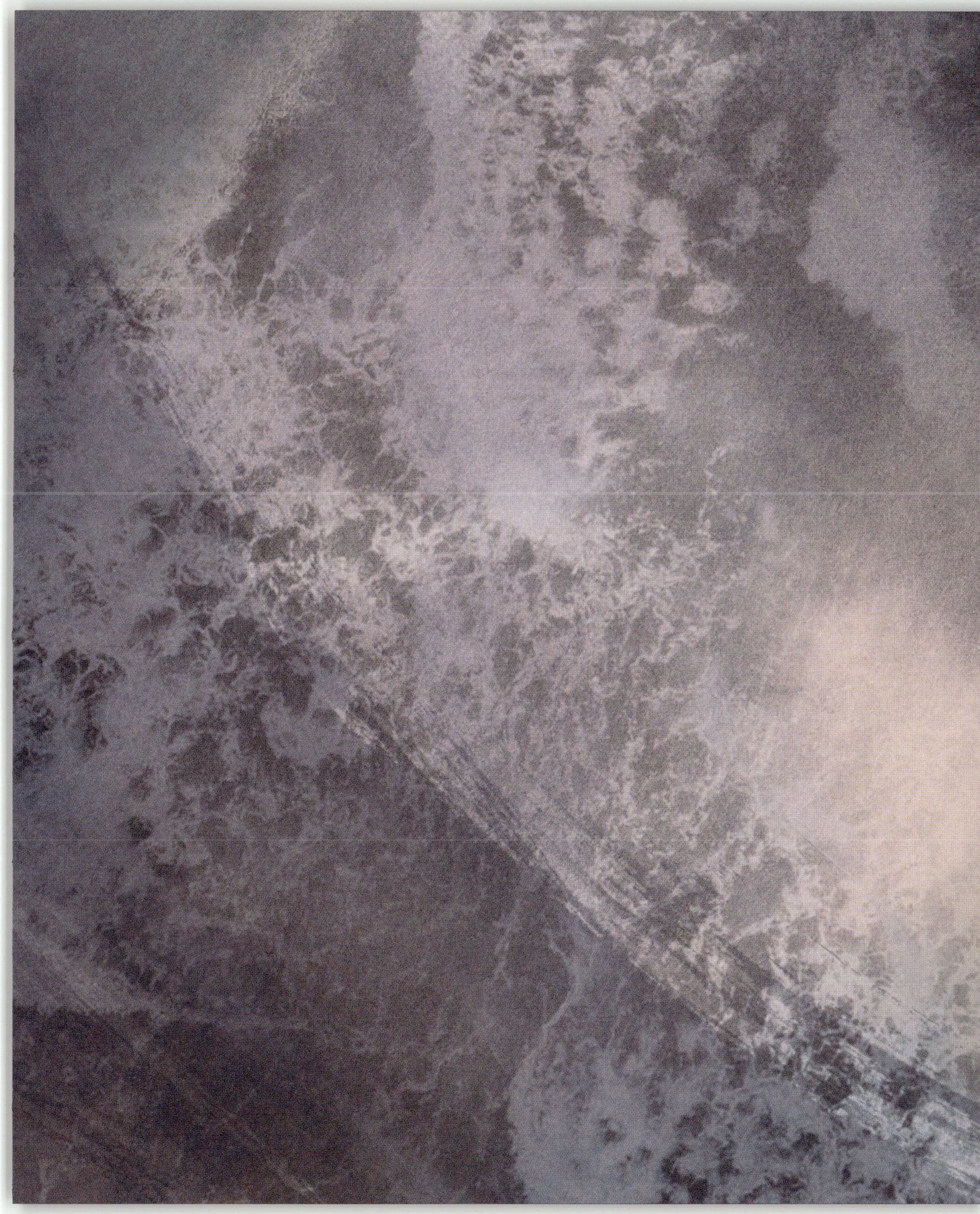

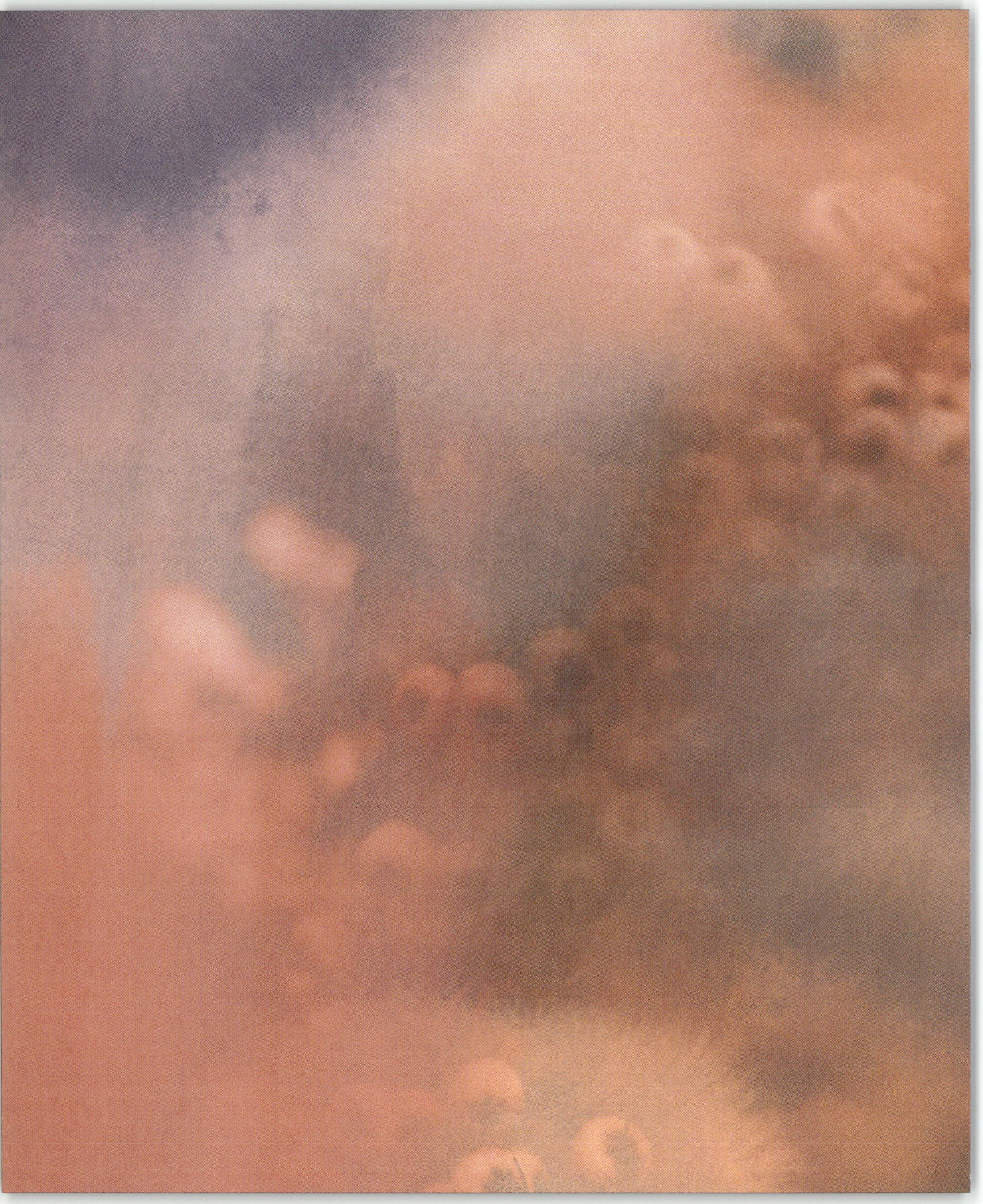

But since I can't do that, I'll remind you of some things that I've learned from being your friend...

I'm here to tell you that gentleness and fierceness can coexist.
And I'm here to say that *you've taught me this.*

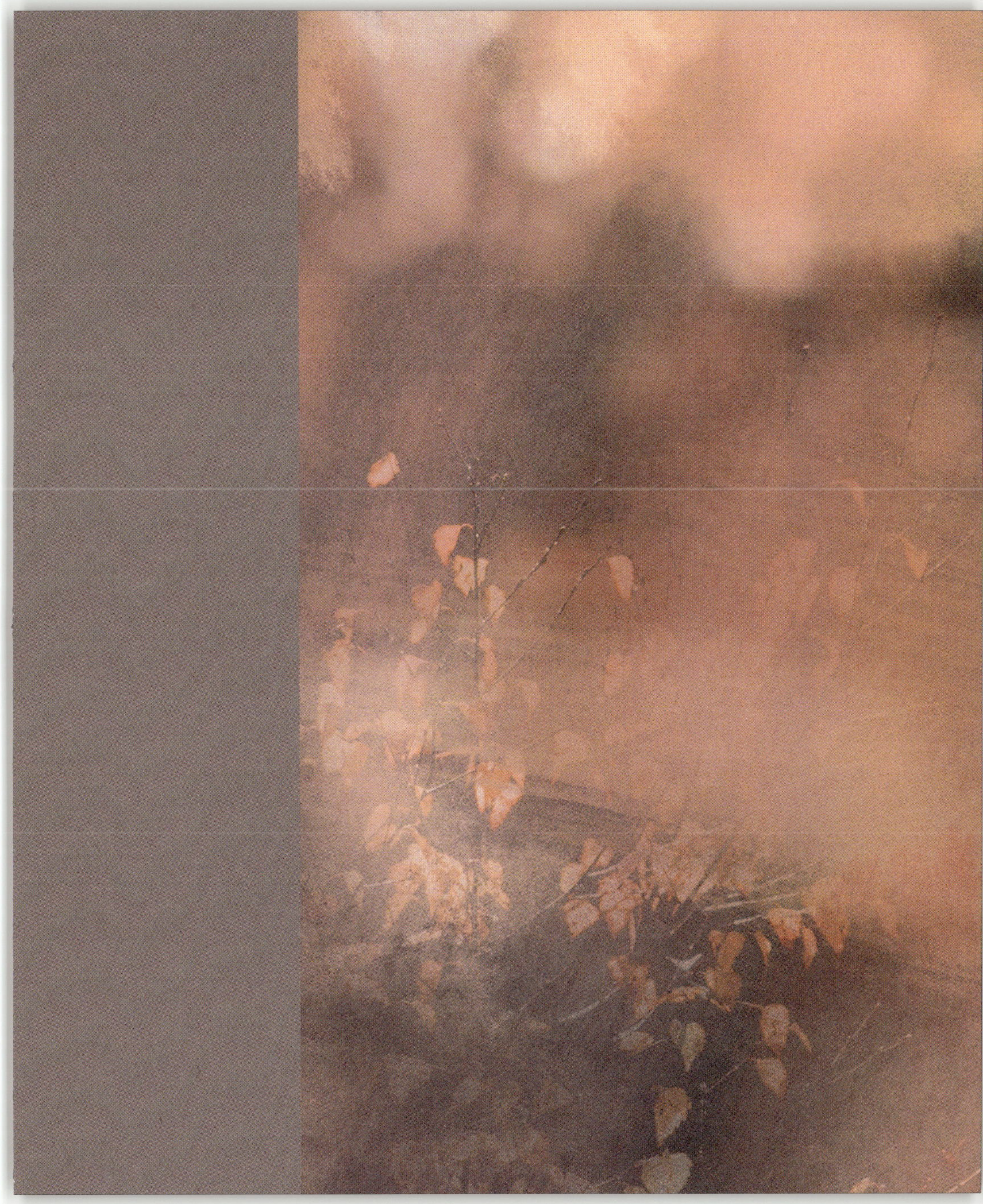

I'm here to tell you that it is possible to shape the world as much as the world shapes you.

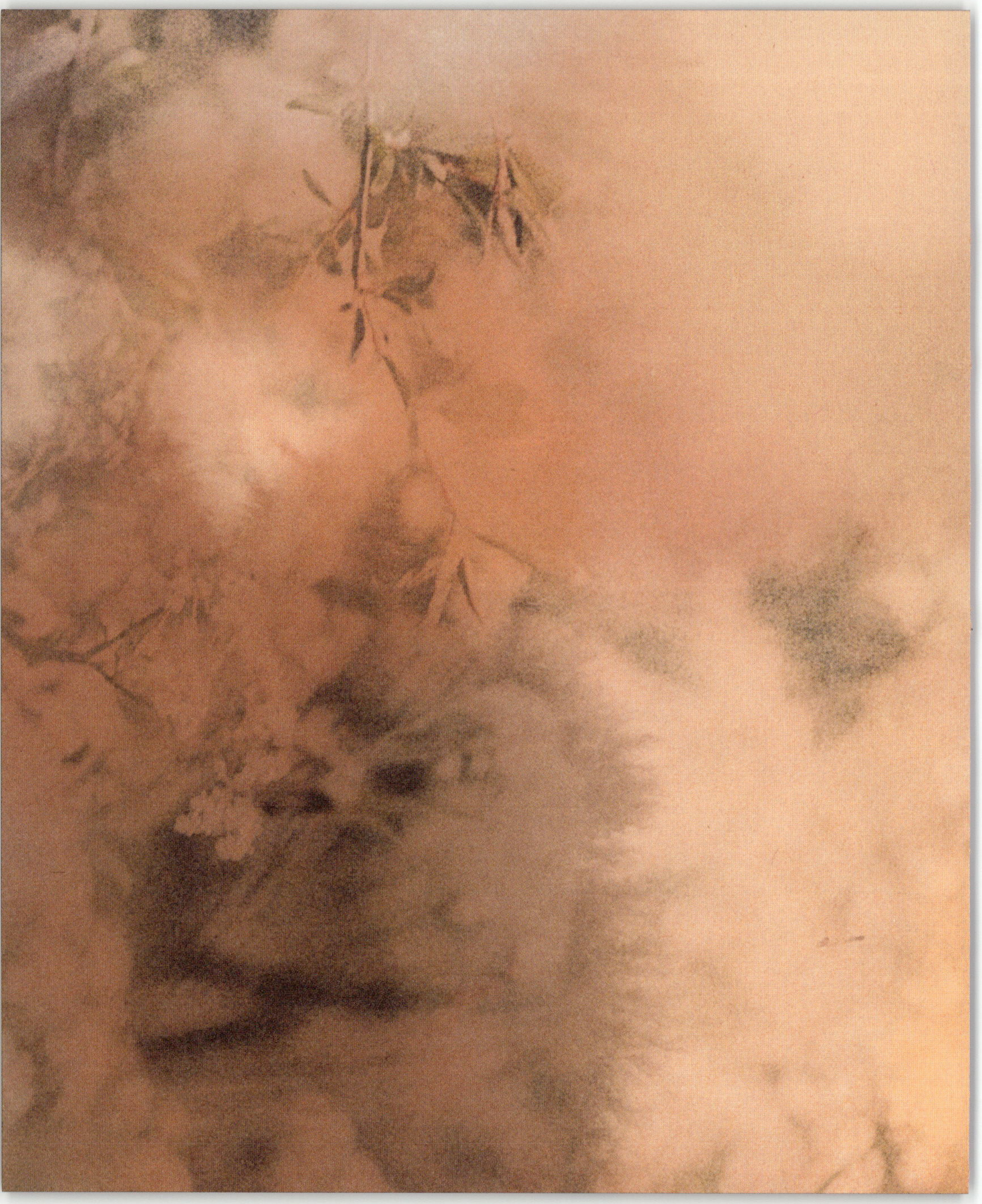

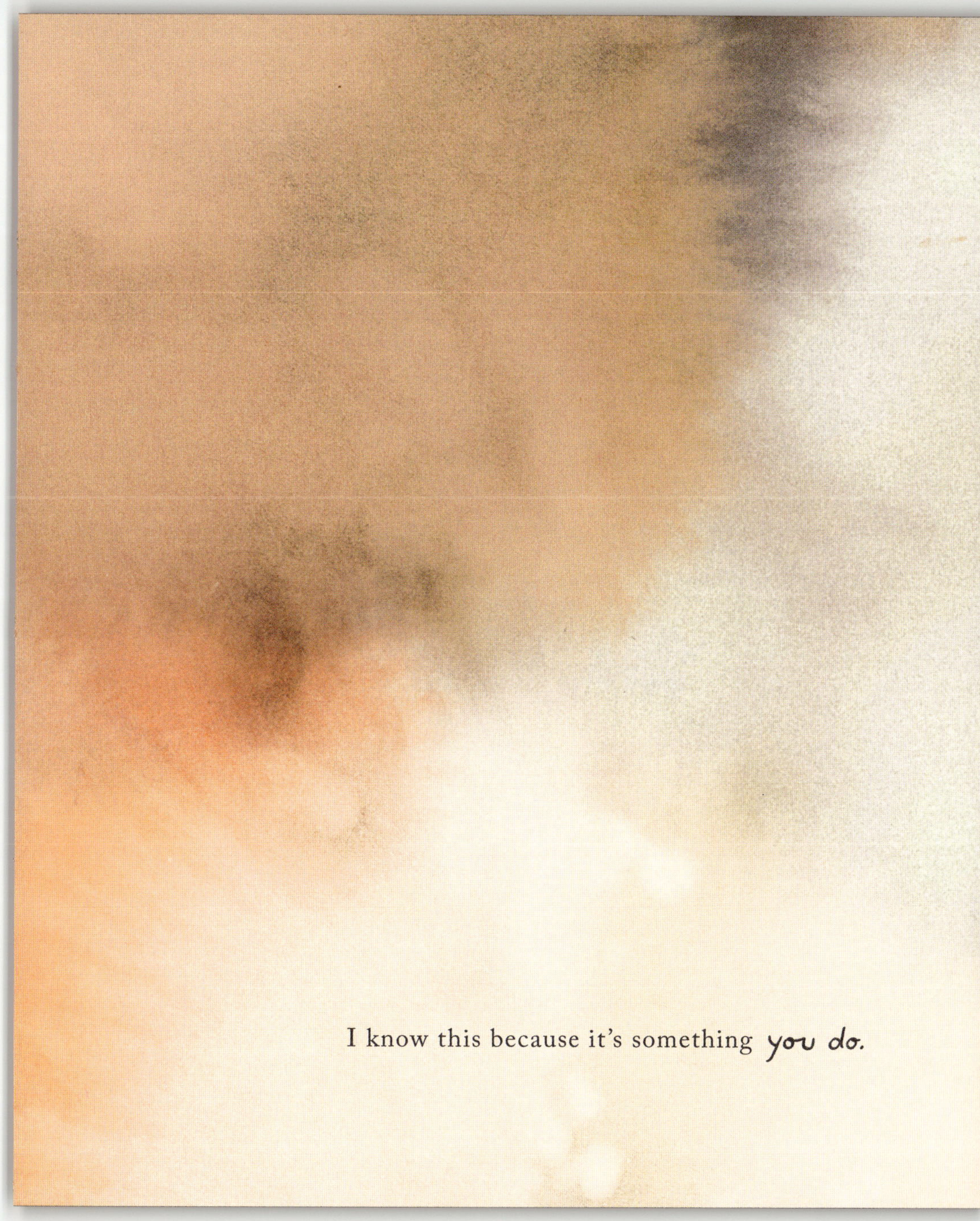

I know this because it's something *you do.*

I'm here to tell you there is beauty in changing.
In knowing your work is not done.

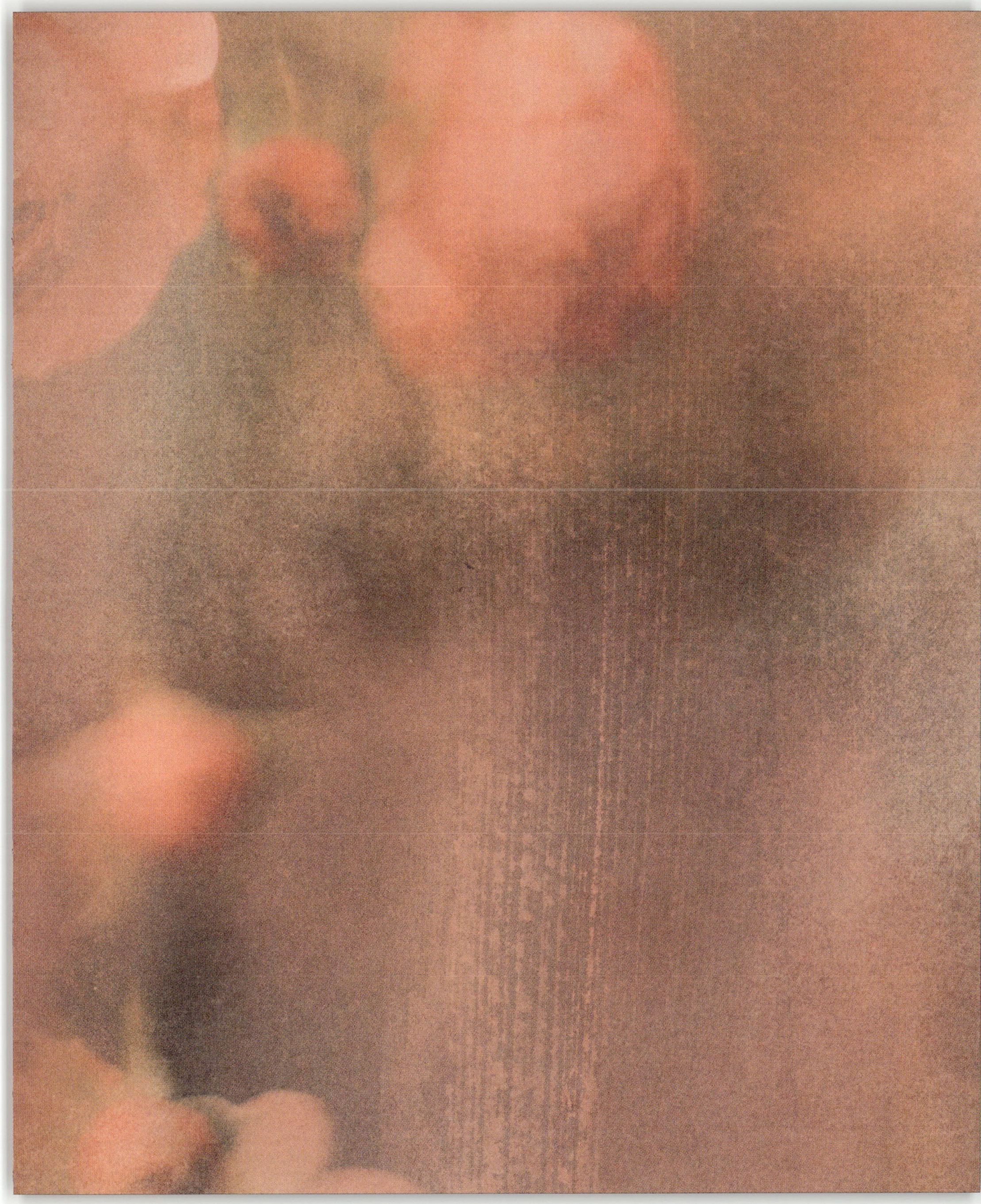

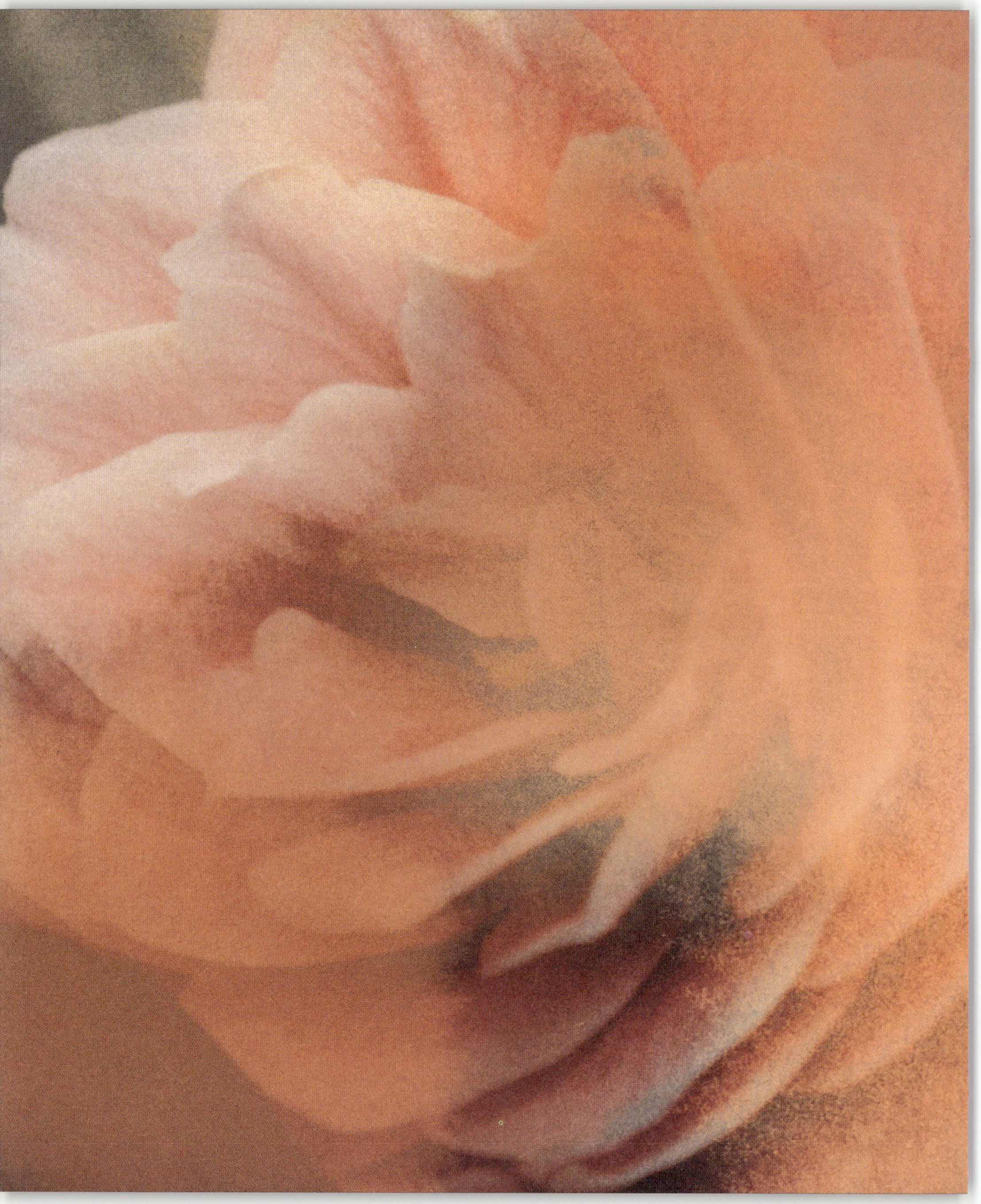

I know this because I'm in awe
of all that you've become.

I have watched you do the hardest things with grace.

And I have watched you do the hardest things with grit.

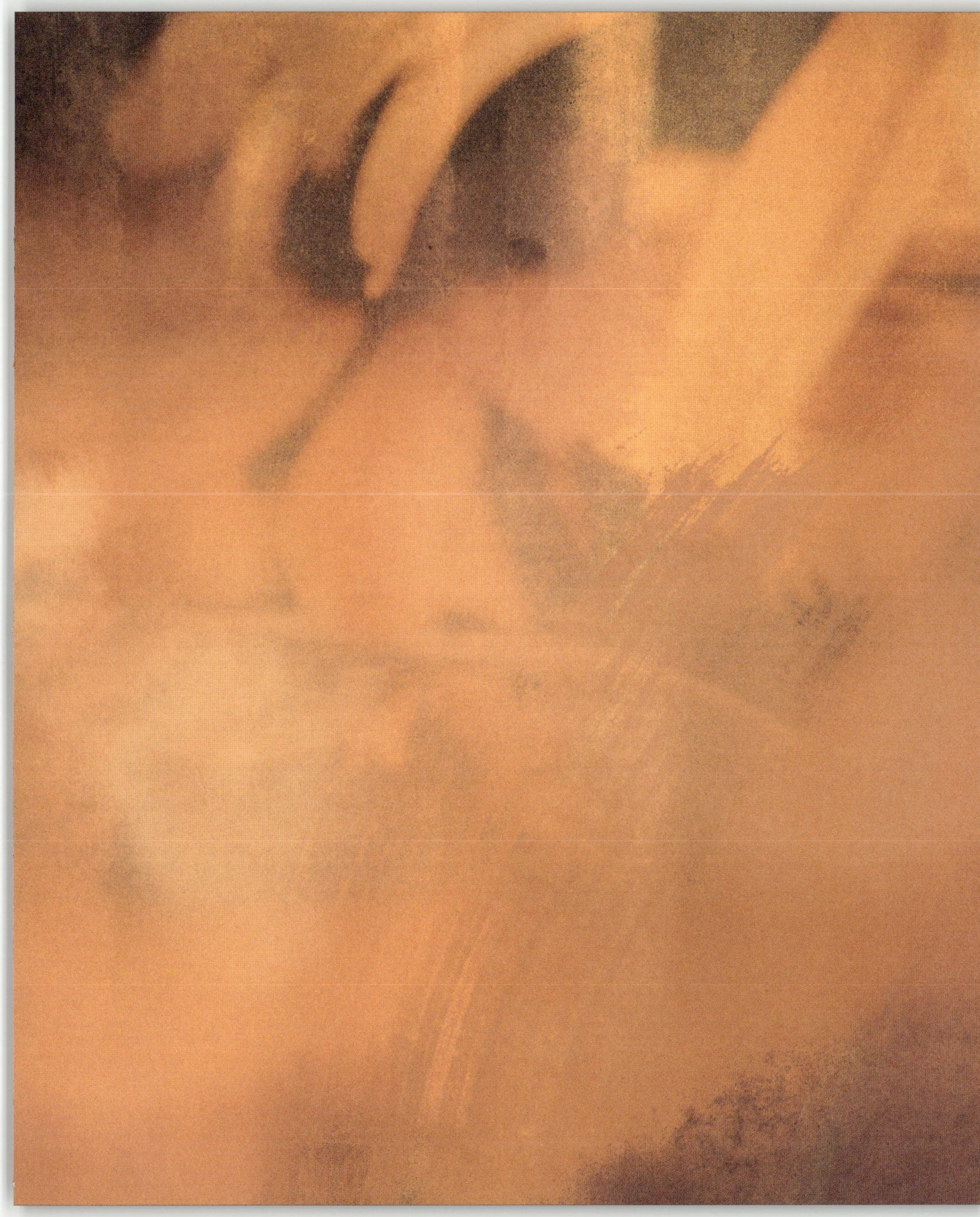

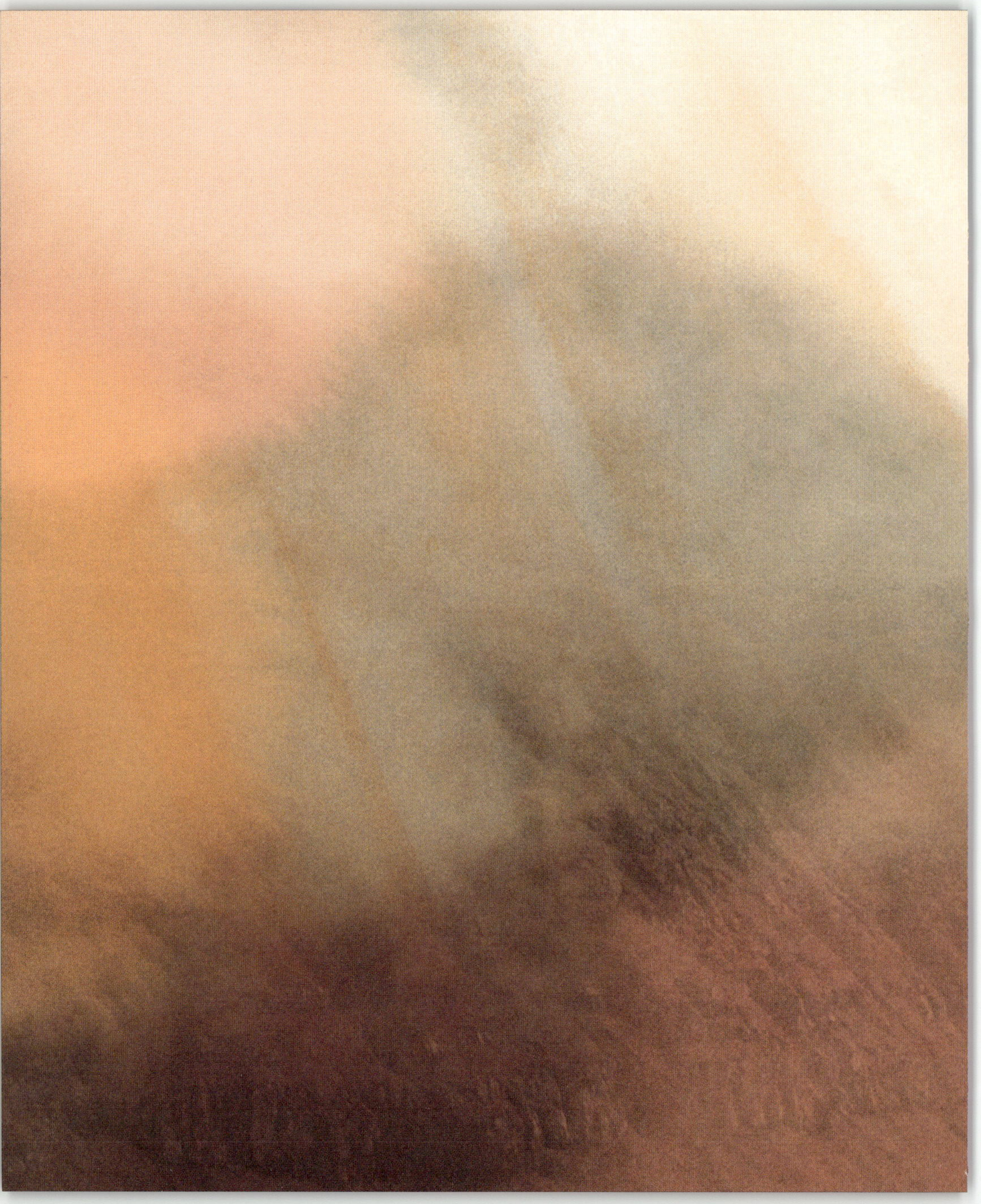

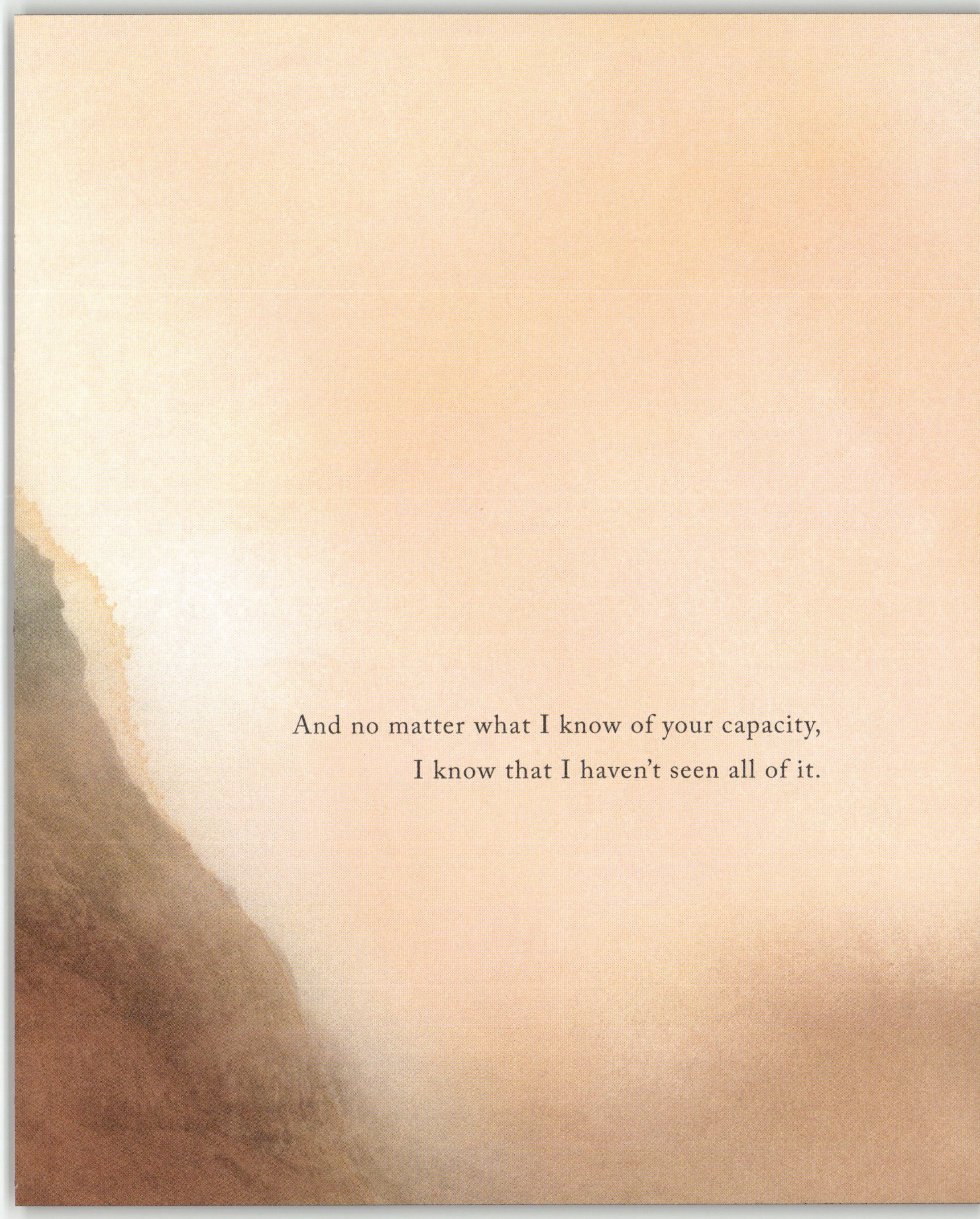

And no matter what I know of your capacity,
I know that I haven't seen all of it.

I've watched you emerge
from so many storms stronger.
More full. More capable.

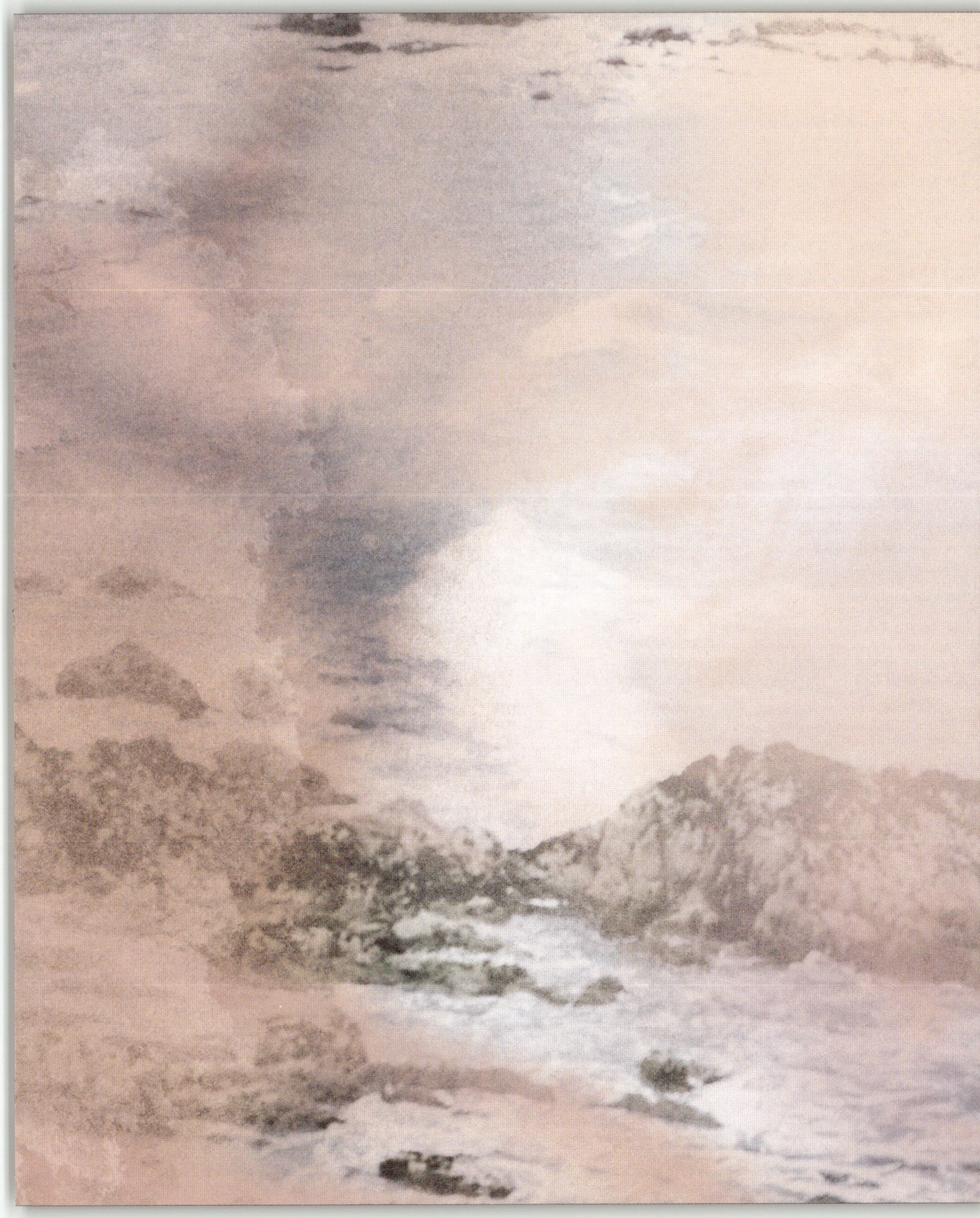

And I want to say that even now, I see you.
You are undiminished.

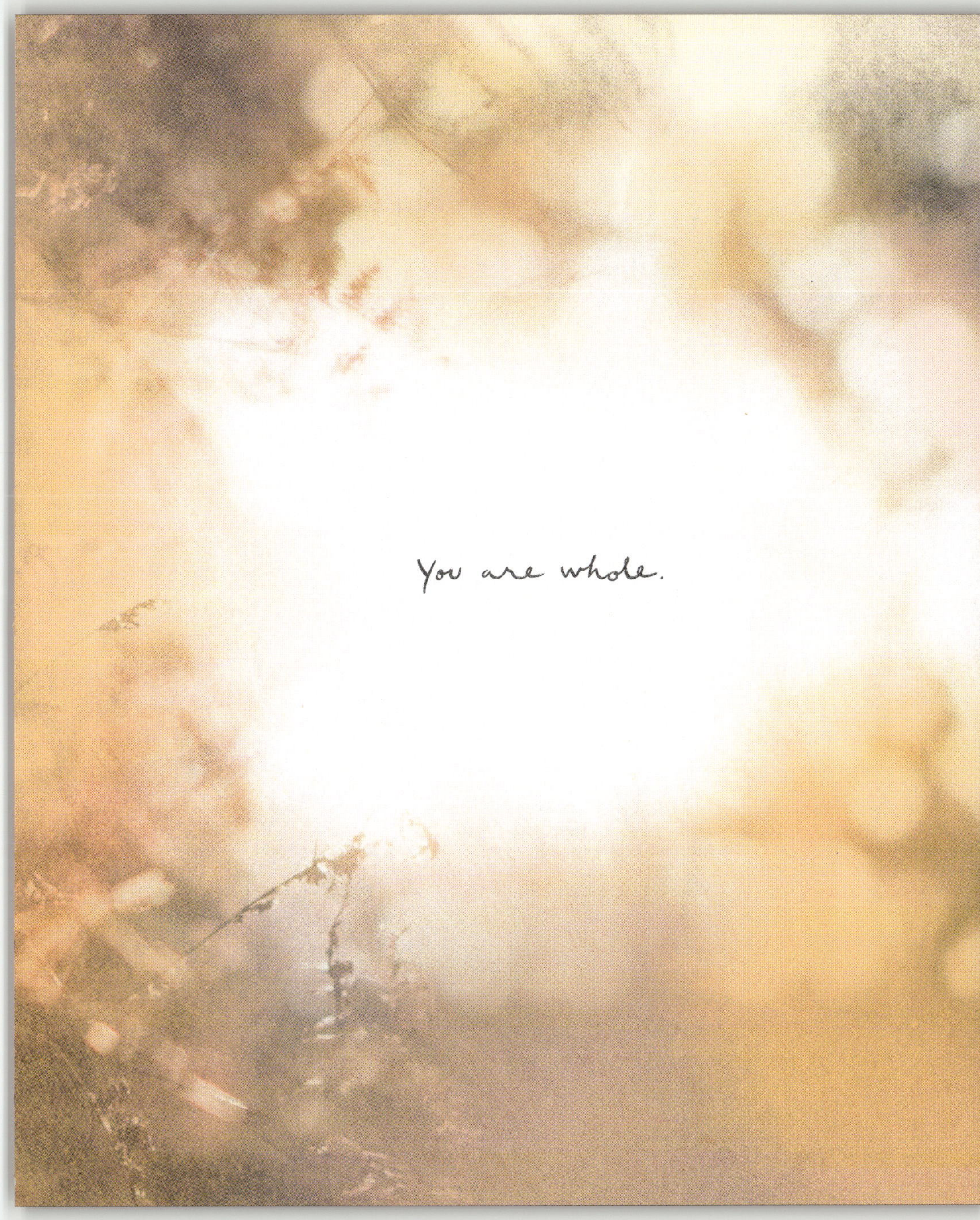
You are whole.

And if, right now, these things are difficult to believe...

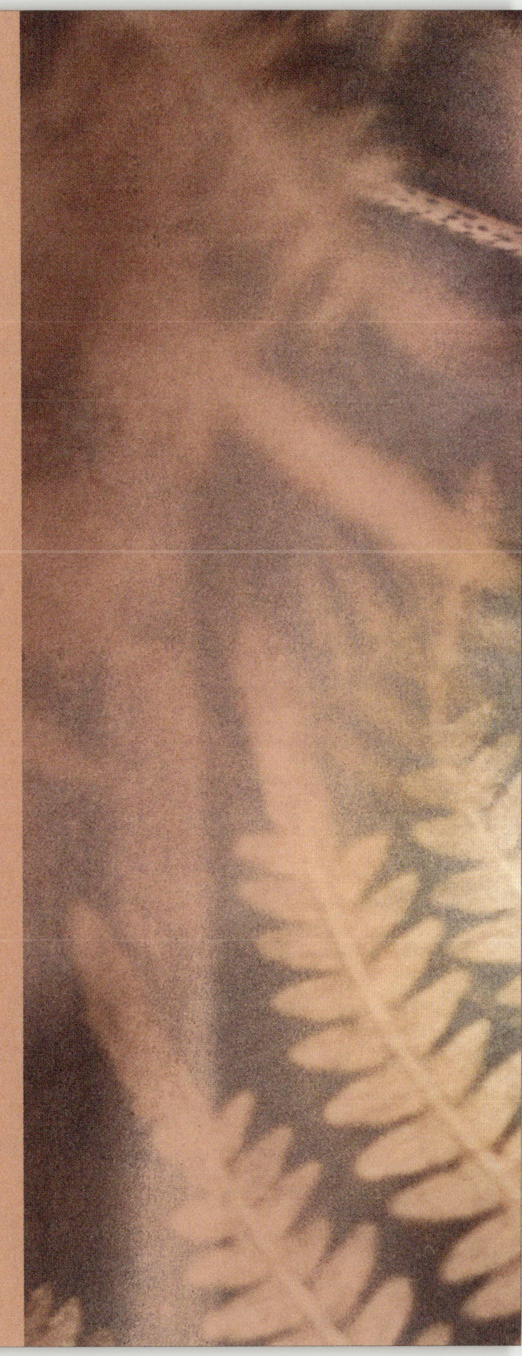

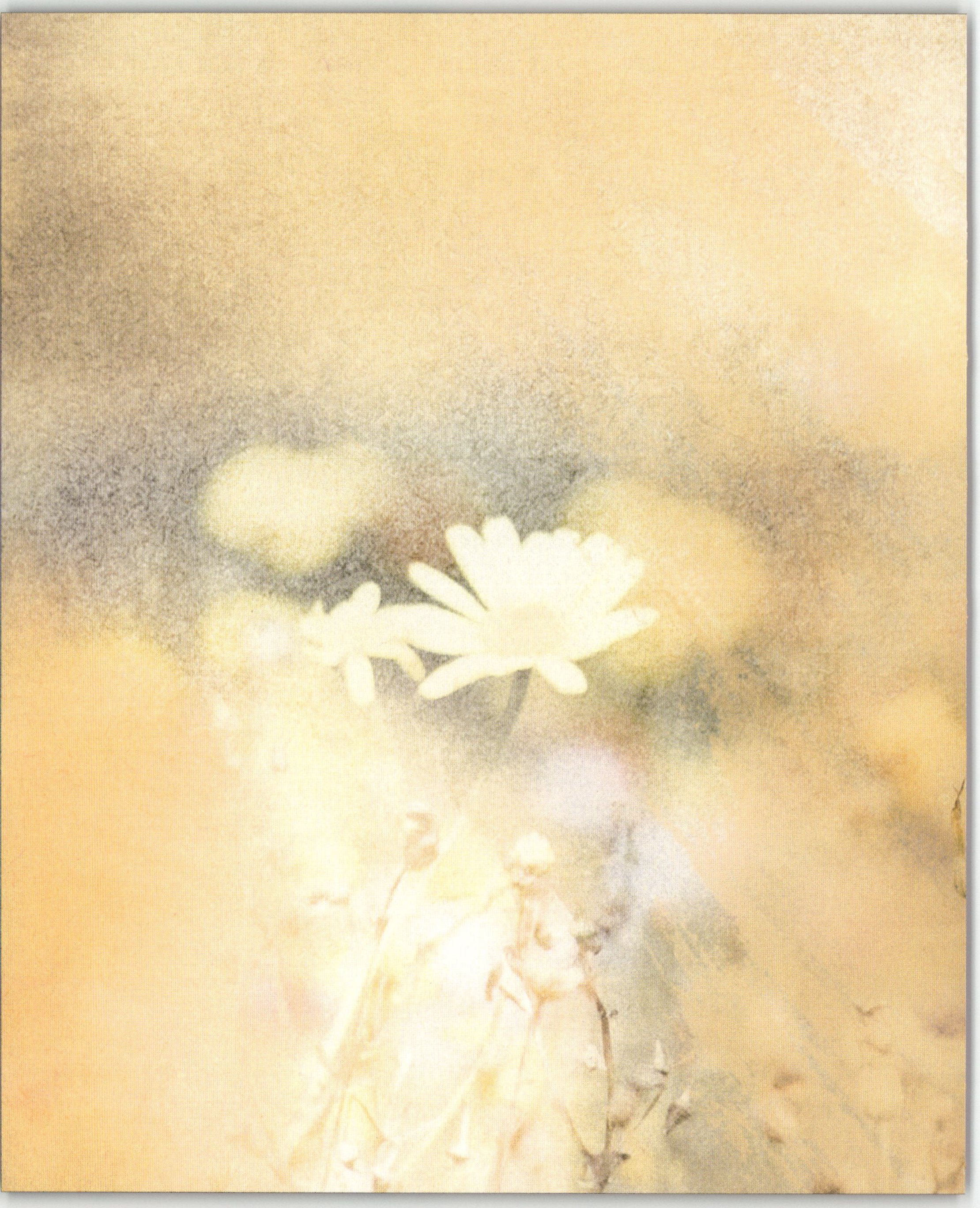

I hope you can hold them for even just a moment.

Because they are so clear to me.

I am hugely and wholly and completely
on your side. Through this moment,
and all that comes after.

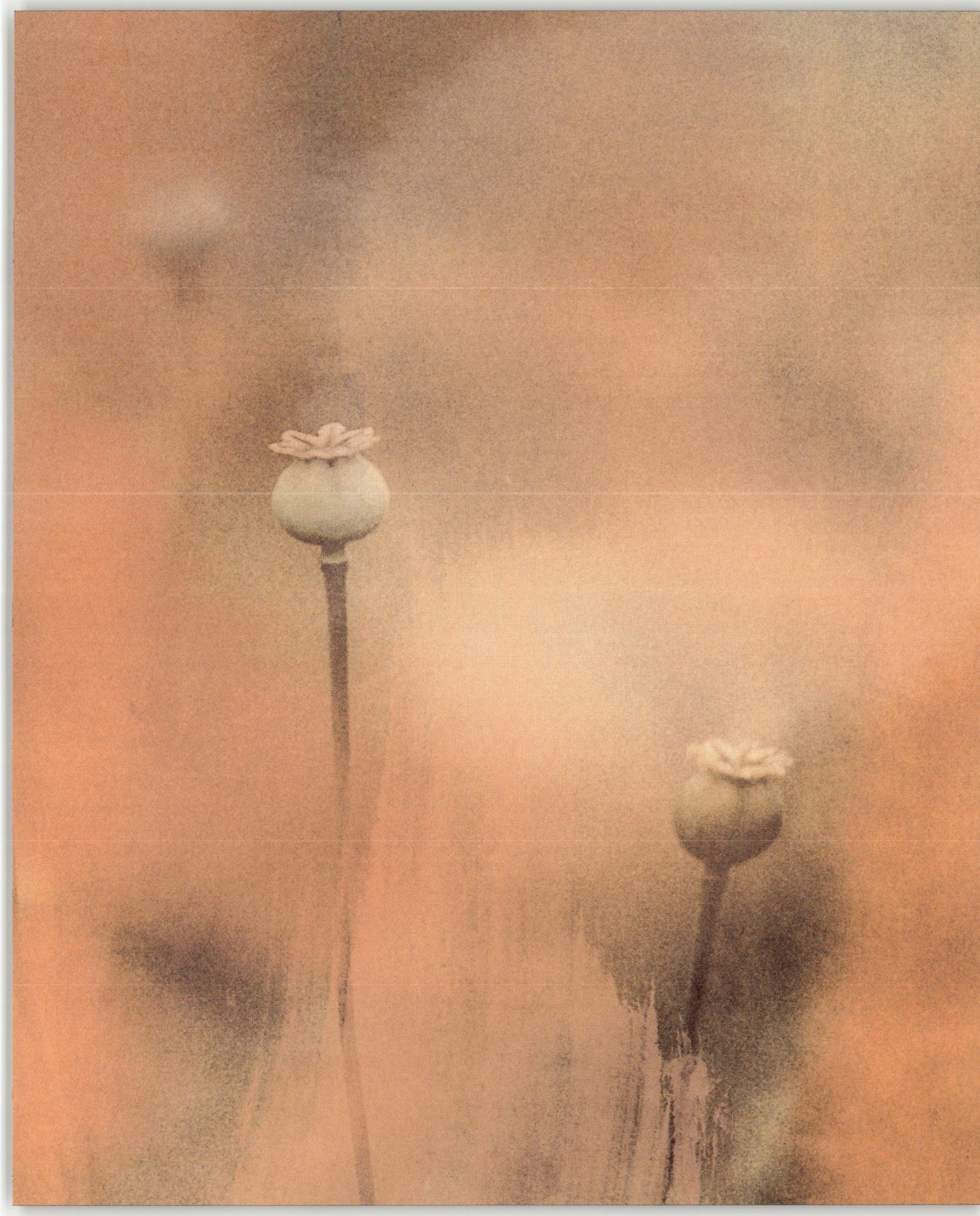

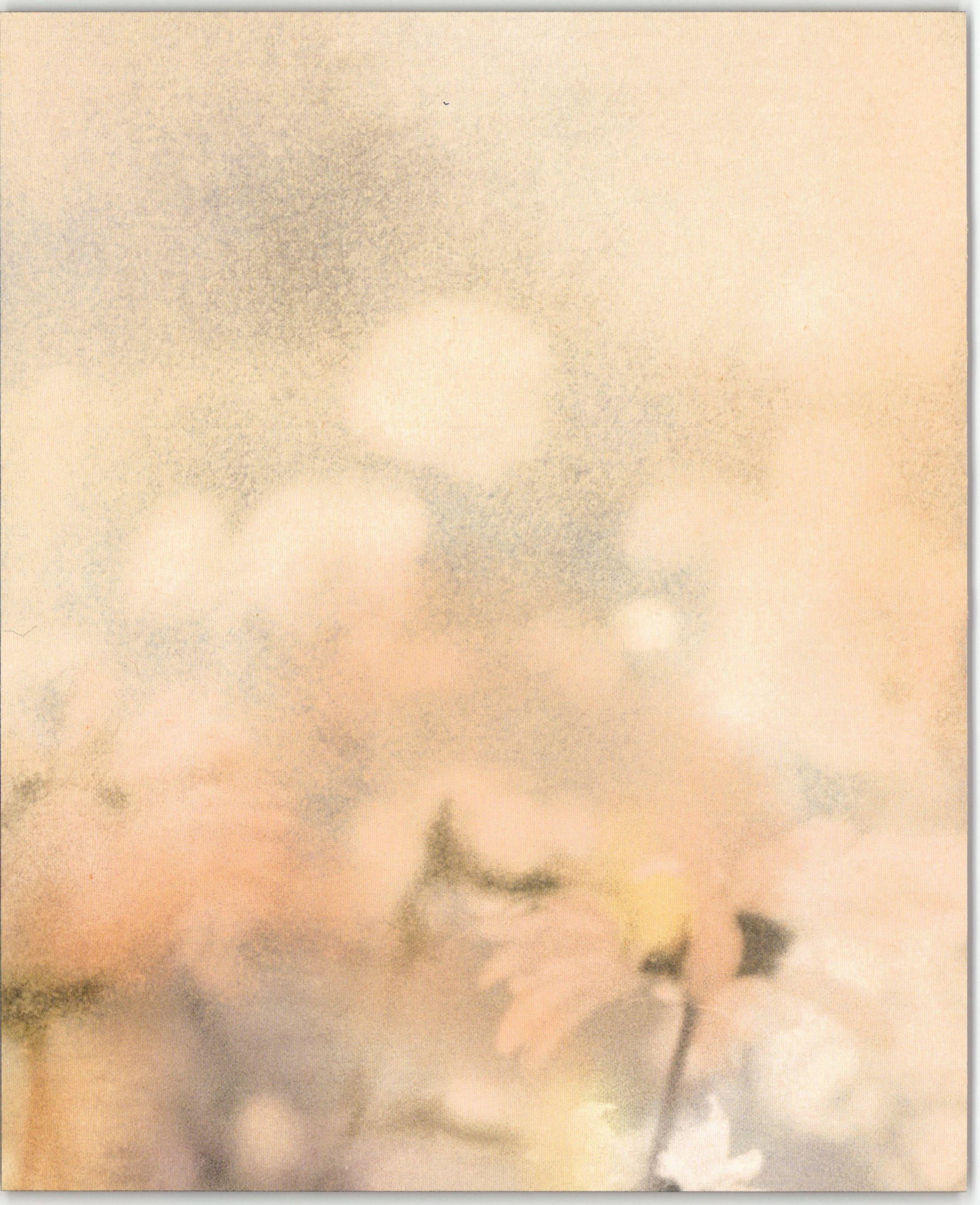

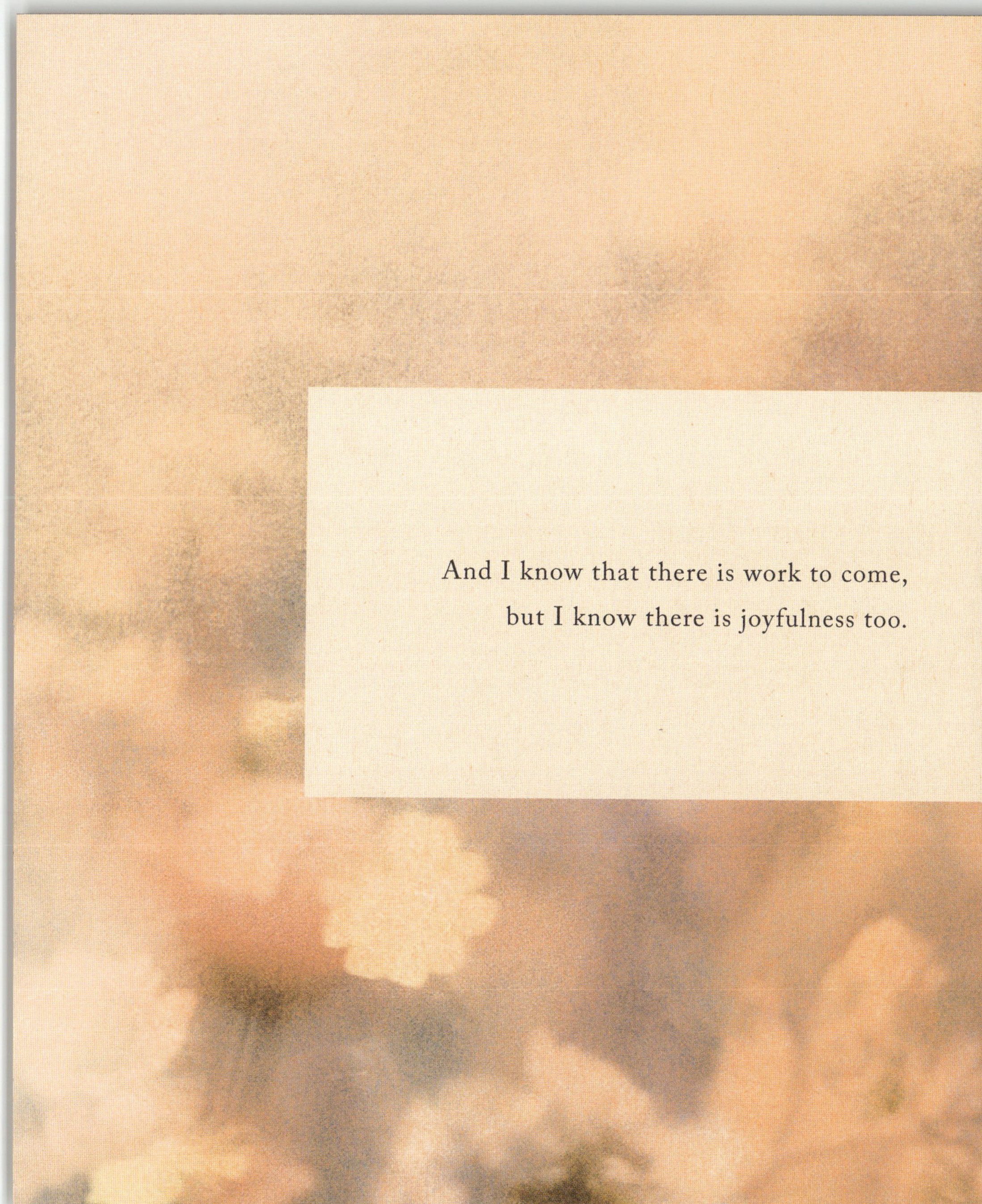

And I know that there is work to come,
but I know there is joyfulness too.

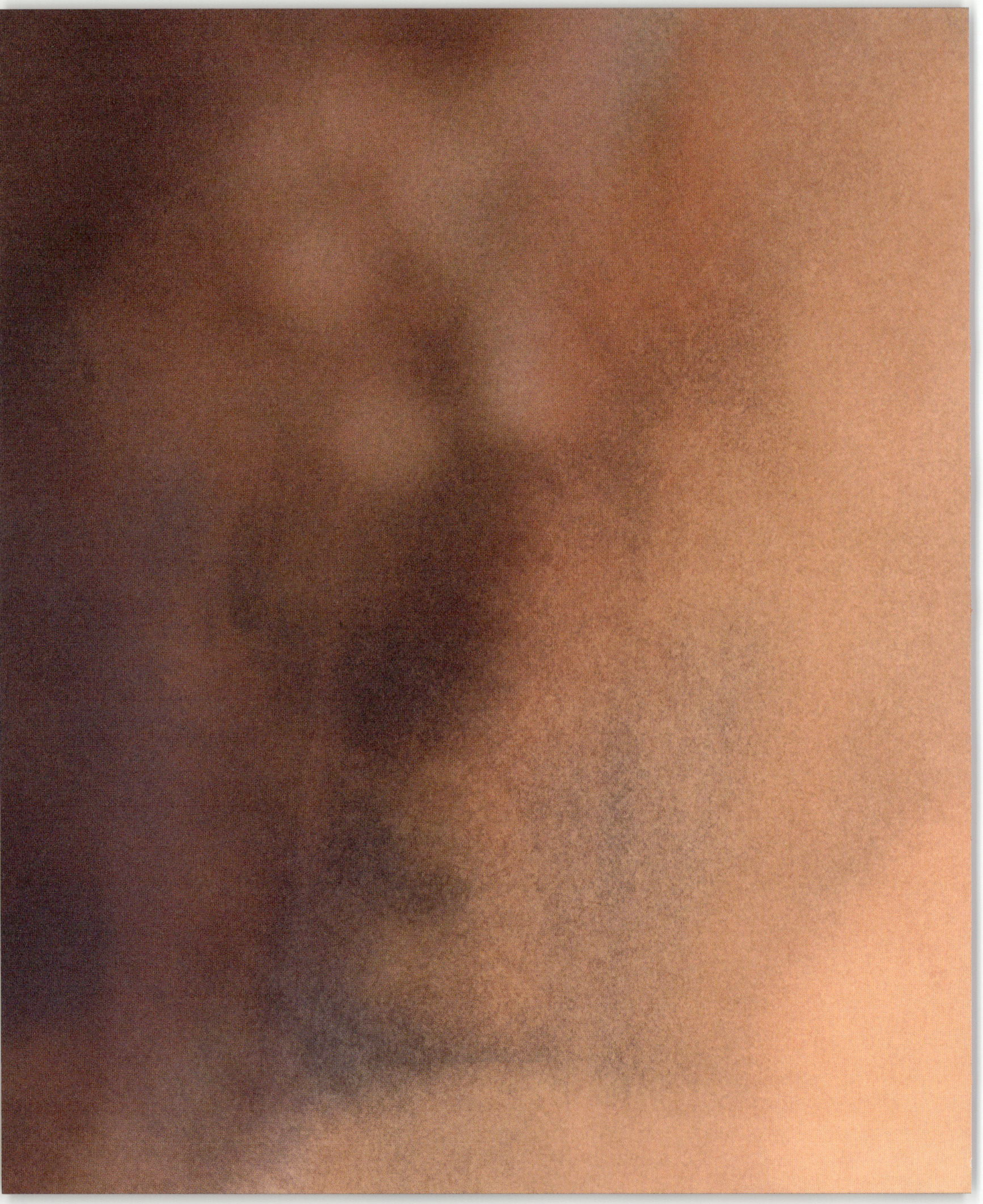

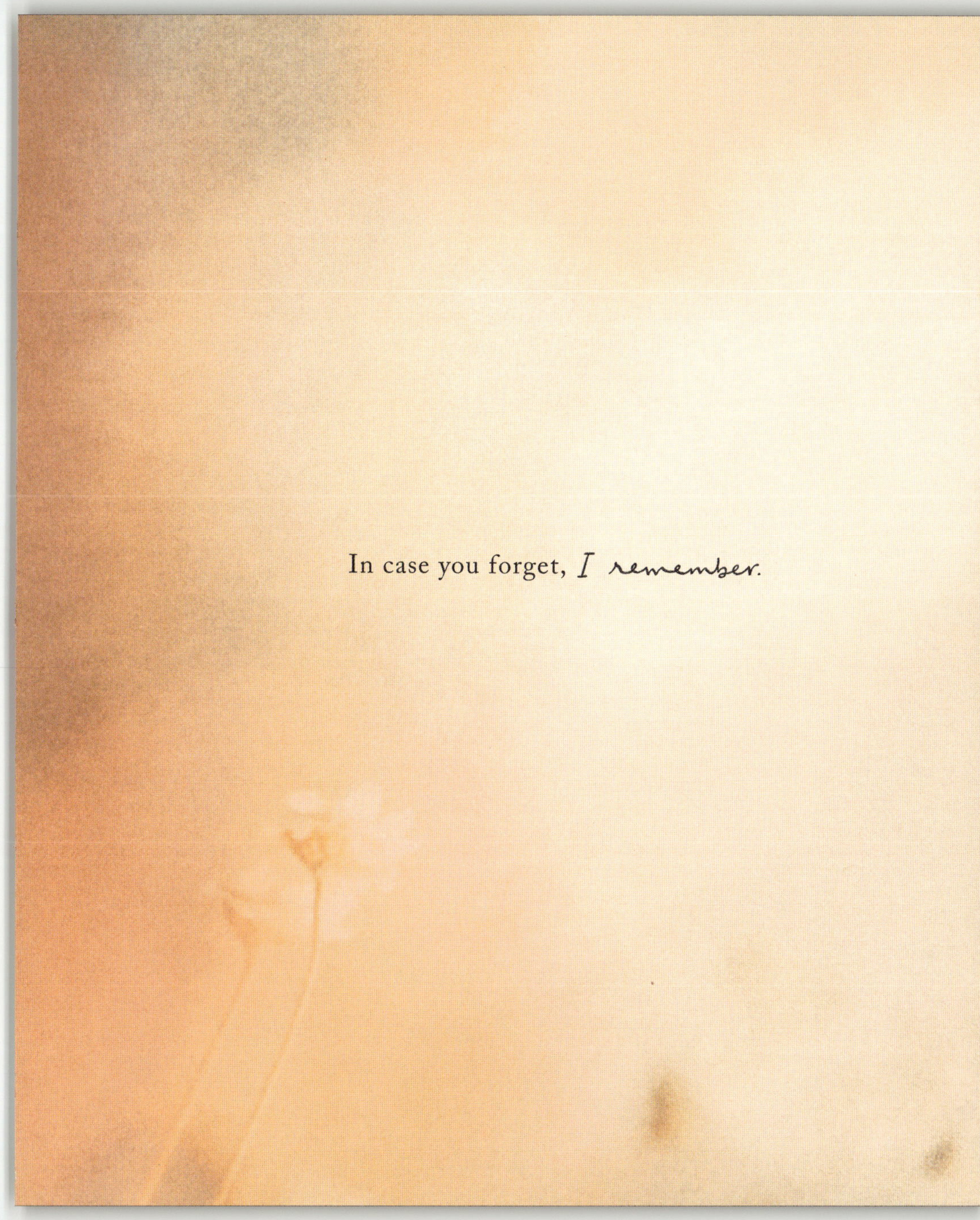
In case you forget, *I remember*.

And I will keep reminding you that you turn even the hard times into substance. And you always end up with *more beauty*.

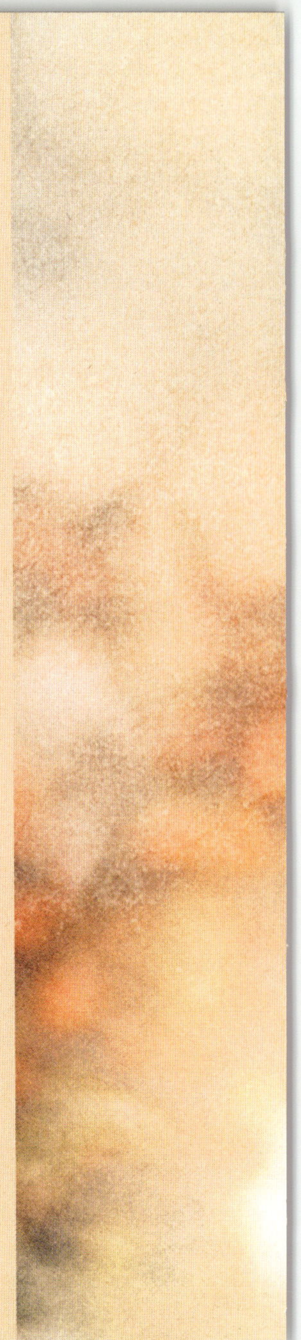

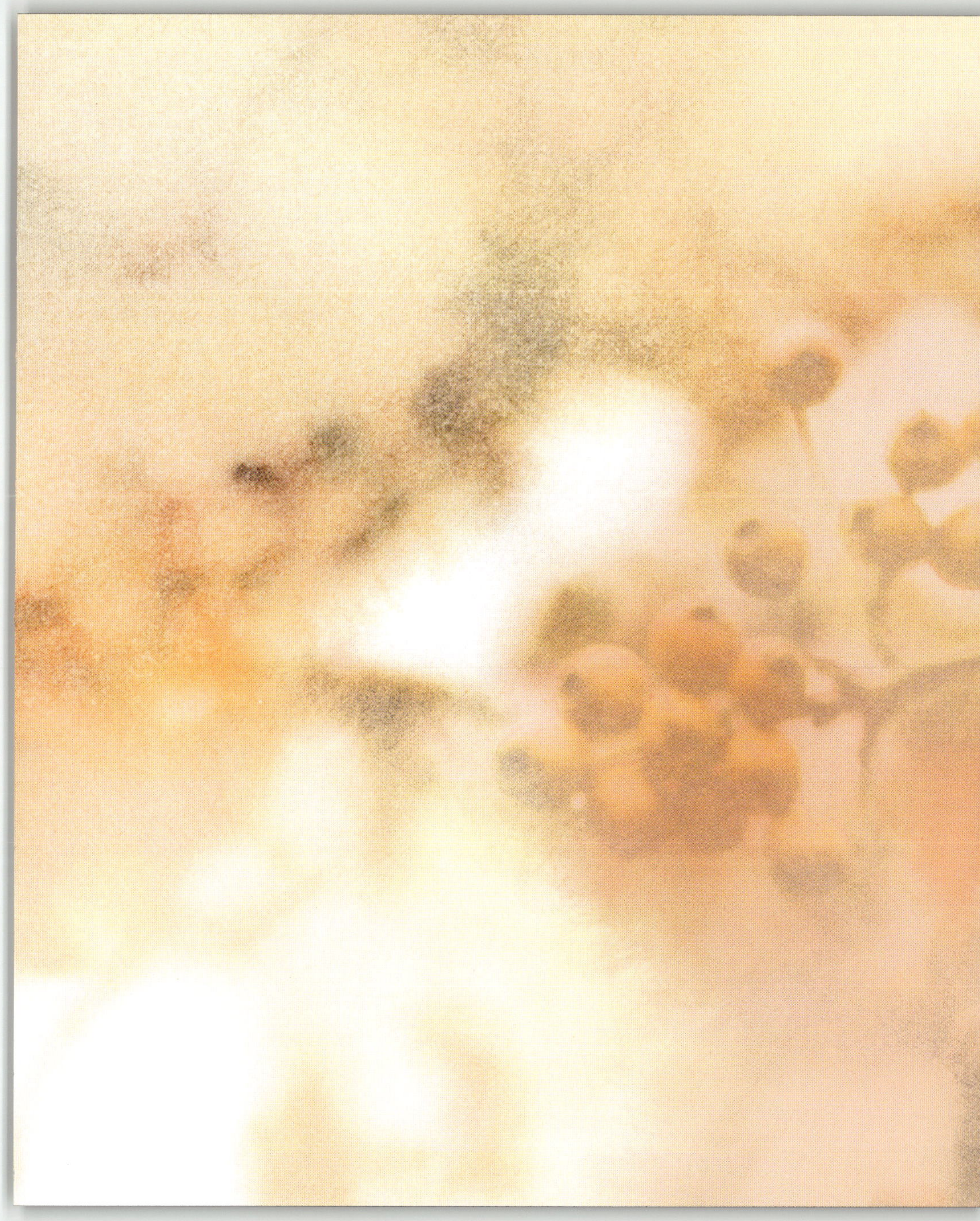

And I hope that you can hold these words,
not just because they're true...

But because they're what the world gets to see, *each day, in you.*

COMPENDIUM.
live inspired

Written by: M.H. Clark
Designed by: Jessica Phoenix
Edited by: Kristin Eade

All photos by Annie Spratt from Unsplash.com.

Library of Congress Control Number: 2021931698 | ISBN: 978-1-970147-54-4

© 2022 by Compendium, Inc. All rights reserved. No part of this publication may be reproduced or transmitted in any form or by any means, electronic or mechanical, including photocopy, recording, or any storage and retrieval system now known or to be invented without written permission from the publisher. Contact: Compendium, Inc., 2815 Eastlake Avenue East, Suite 200, Seattle, WA 98102. *In Case You Forget, I Remember*, Compendium; live inspired; and the format, design, layout, and coloring used in this book are trademarks and/or trade dress of Compendium, Inc. This book may be ordered directly from the publisher, but please try your local bookstore first. Call us at 800.91.IDEAS, or come see our full line of inspiring products at live-inspired.com.

1st printing. Printed in China with soy inks on FSC®-Mix certified paper.

Create meaningful moments with gifts that inspire.

CONNECT WITH US
live-inspired.com | sayhello@compendiuminc.com

@compendiumliveinspired
#compendiumliveinspired

CW01640837

The A to Z of Victoire de Castellane

THE A TO *Z* OF VICTOIRE DE CASTELLANE

DIOR JOAILLERIE

Texts by Olivier Gabet

RIZZOLI
NEW YORK
New York · Paris · London · Milan

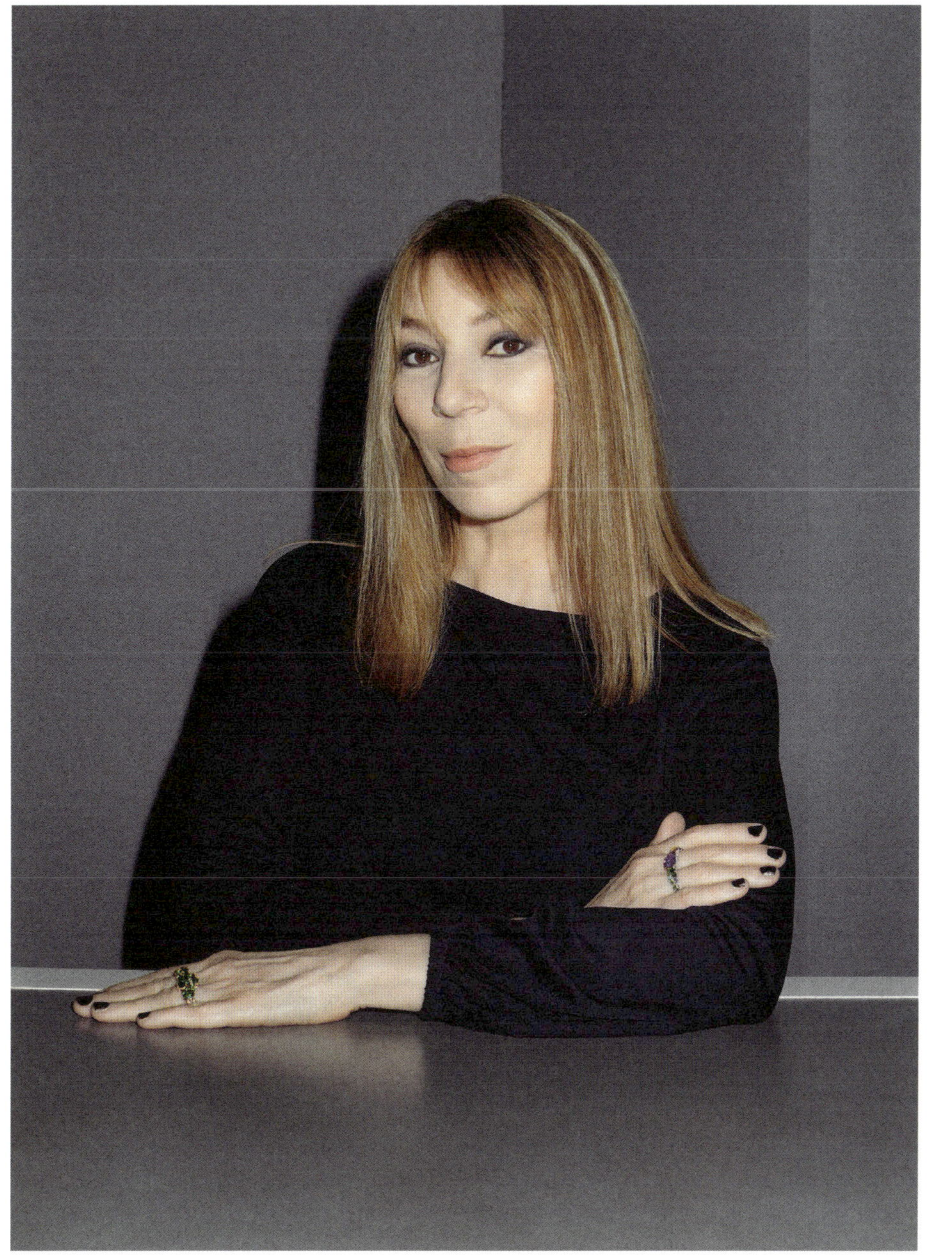

Victoire de Castellane

In the world of luxury and creation, being the art director of the same house for more than twenty years has become a rarity, an exceptional phenomenon, and a luxury itself. When, in 1998, Victoire de Castellane met Bernard Arnault, they shared their enthusiasm about creating *haute joaillerie* for a house that had just turned fifty. Christian Dior, both house and name, had already gained legendary status in the history of fashion. How could Victoire have known then that this adventure would be imbued with thousands of creations, and so much more?

It is always difficult to summarize in a few pages or a few words a body of work that has found depth over time by weaving the narratives of the imaginary stories that Victoire adores. Similar to the branches of a vast family tree, there are resemblances and complicity, collections that lead to others, elective or intuitive affinities, and a game of many happy families. For Victoire loves unions and family resemblances, like the instinctive associations created when a shape or a stone leads the imagination to a new jewellery set or a new jewel. She loves words, too, and the evocation of a single word. Words again.

And so, almost one hundred and sixty words have been chosen, brought together, dissected, loved, and examined from every angle, like the many facets of a diamond. Others disappeared as the book progressed. With little evocative power, occasionally charming and seductive, but ultimately rather irrelevant, they were withdrawn, for Victoire does not like needless furbelows, no matter how meaningful they might be. The epic inspiration of the retrospective was passed over in favor of the A to Z, which reconstructs each defined word with a moment, a perspective, a flash of brilliance, or an episode. For the woman who chose, in 2007, to present the incredible *Belladone Island* collection against the backdrop of the sublime *Nymphéas* of the Orangerie Museum, that Sistine Chapel of modern art, there is nothing more legitimate than the impressionist touch of each word, in an eclectic palette, which, from afar, reconstructs a sensitive and balanced vision, and close up singles out revealing details.

This A to Z was composed like a rhapsody, in the most Greek sense of the word, by sewing words together, altering them, and establishing a connection between them, with some words echoing each other and others bringing opposites together. There are jewellery words and design words naturally, and others linked to the vocabulary of haute couture, or even architecture, but there are also more abstract, more subjective words. There are the names of people, too, in Proustian splendor, those linked to the epic of Christian Dior, which runs to the house and the archives. Each of these words was like the crystallization of twenty years of dreaming, imagination, and stories. A word would spring forth from the list and Victoire would pluck it out of the air, making it her own, with both reserve and clarity, like all those people whom we tend to think of as voluble, but who are in fact taciturn observers. As we turn the pages, we are struck by the spirit of continuity given to these words by the richness of time, by spontaneity, and candor, and by the "great freedom" that makes this book not just another book, but rather a dictionary of feelings and love, a very personal A to Z, and a new letter from Victoire de Castellane to Christian Dior.

Olivier Gabet

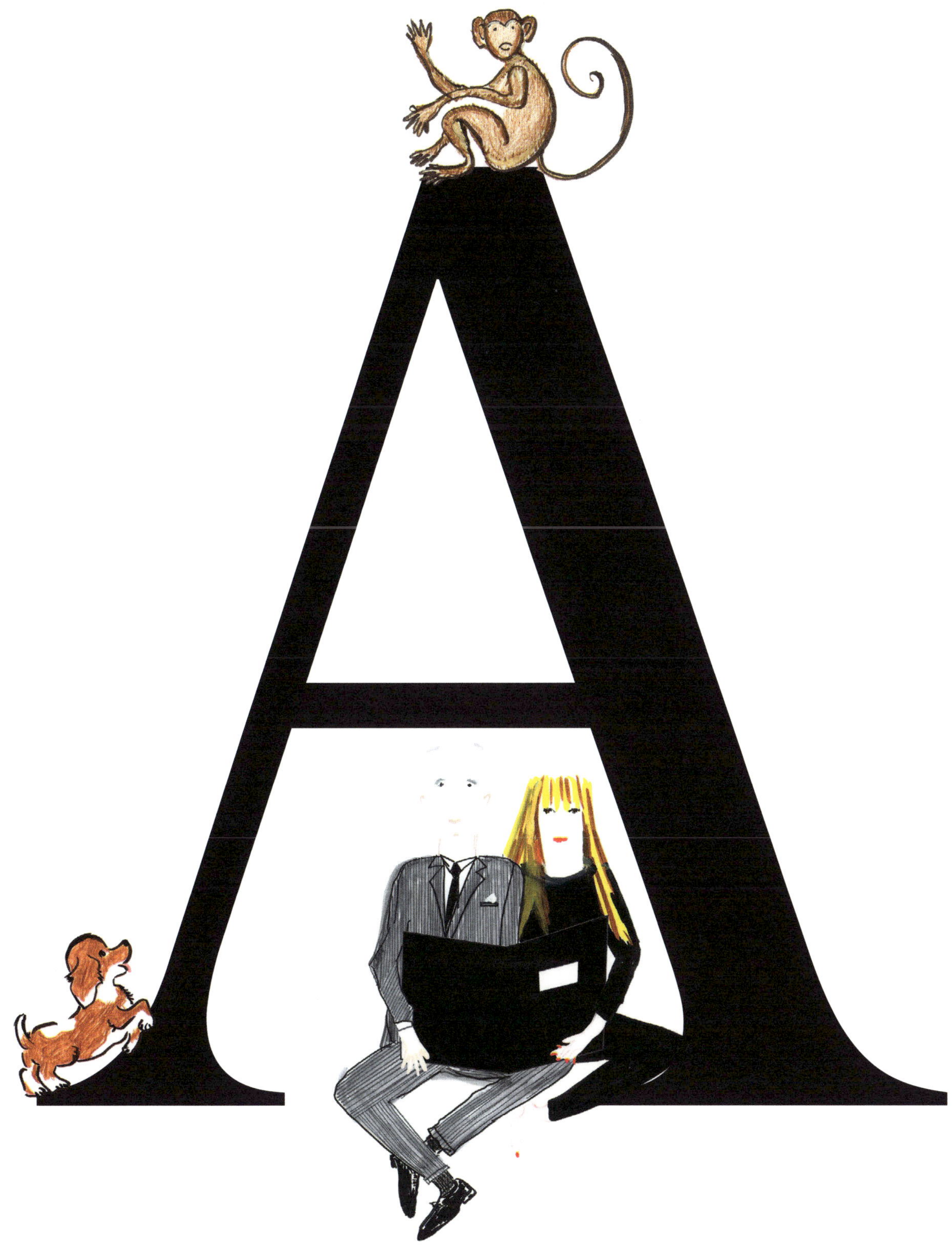
A

A TO Z

"As a child, I loved dictionaries." This is a dictionary of choices, containing the words we want to explore, some of which reveal vast territories, others which reveal smooth surfaces and almost technical precision. There are obligatory words and other, unexpected ones. There are names, too: family names and place-names.

This one-hundred-and-fifty-eight-entry A to Z volume gradually paints the portrait of Victoire de Castellane, a woman who has worked for twenty years in creation, with thousands of drawings and sketches, hundreds of jewels, some discreet, others indiscreet, at the heart of a house which, under the name of its founder Christian Dior, symbolizes elegance, style, couture, and a certain idea of women throughout the world. Each entry was chosen by Victoire, and it is all her own words that appear here in quotation marks—and all of her secrets too.

ABSTRACTION

"When you think of my work, the aesthetic notion of abstraction probably isn't what comes to mind." Victoire never tires of creating new jewellery adventures. In 2019, with *Gem Dior*, she delivered new inspiration in wonder, taking the abstract path for the first time: "I realized that there was also a sensual element in the abstract, and as someone who loves colors, they can seem even more dazzling. It's like an organic abstraction, where all of a sudden it isn't that I no longer want to tell stories, but that the stones are telling stories on their own, through a play of form, clashes, and simple forms." It is then that you feel just how poetic and playful the jubilation born of abstraction can be, for the woman who has explored so many possibilities.

ABUNDANCE

"Abundance is in no way obligatory, but it is true that the very idea of abundance, in jewellery, contributes to the pleasure and the jubilation it can evoke. Jewels always profit from giving off an impression of generosity." According to Victoire, generosity is conveyed by the volume of the jewel, its composition, the quality of its stones, its colors, and also, above all, by the manner in which the jewel tells a story, its own story, which is the element to which she is deeply attached.

ANIMAL

"It's a cliché, but animals are wonderful subjects for jewellery, I love working on fantastic animals with opals, which lend themselves perfectly to the subject." Although she uses the animal repertory both in compositions and as ornaments, Victoire never goes too far. She recognizes that this is a source of inspiration that might, at first sight, seem banal, or even common, but never really is, and it holds fine adventures in store for the imagination and the talents of the ateliers. See *Bestiary*.

APOLLO

Since Nietzsche, we have known that life is just an oscillation between the Apollonian—that which brings us order, measure, and structure—and the Dionysian, which is related to the emotions, the intangible, spirit, and madness.

For Victoire, Apollo reflects Versailles, as the radiant figure of the young god of the arts expresses the spirit of the place so well, like the pond and the baths that bear his name, and in the majesty and reigning order of the classicism that embodies the château and its gardens. The name serves to designate certain jewels that Victoire created, inspired by Versailles, through a play on memory and memories: "For these collections based on Versailles, images that I have had in my mind since childhood nourished my inspiration rather than the walks I took with that specific aim in mind." In her creative process, she "always likes to work with the memory of something, of a feeling, or a place," from which she will "then extrapolate." "These three successive collections," she says, "stemmed from my idea of Versailles rather than any specific visit in every detail." See *Versailles*.

ARCHI DIOR

"I wanted to design a collection that would evoke Christian Dior's passion for architecture, looking at the details of certain very structured suits and dresses from that era to express them differently in metal and to study them, play with them, and turn them into the principal, essential shape of the jewel," Victoire explains. And Victoire's quest is a reminder that Christian Dior dreamed of being an architect, loved architecture with a passion, and often spoke of his work as a couturier by borrowing terms from architecture, citing the relation with couture. "The idea I had was to design and to work in metal on the most difficult elements of these Dior dresses—the flounces and pleats, everything that is obvious when drawing or designing in fabric becomes an amazing feat when you apply it to jewellery."

Archi Dior (2014) is like a subjective précis of architecture and couture in the service of jewellery, nourished by the vision and choices of Victoire, who recognizes that her architectural sensibilities do not come from academic knowledge but from her own visual knowledge of architecture, gathered throughout her travels and wanderings, which replace the well-trodden paths of art history.

"In my approach to architecture I am moved only by pleasure and intuition—what my mind retains, and sensations, even fleeting ones—that's what it's all about for me." Like Christian Dior, after all, Victoire plays with architecture through impressions, nuances, and details. *Archi Dior* is probably one of her most graphic collections, a series of lines that she captures in a movement or a gesture: "Certain pieces imitate the hemline of a dress moving as a woman walks." Here, jewellery pays tribute to the birth of couture according to Dior. The narrow waist of the 1947 *Bar* suit from the *Corolle* line, inspired a *Bar en Corolle Émeraude* bracelet, where the wasplike waist becomes a slender wrist. The illustration of the 1949 *Junon* dress, from the *Milieu du Siècle* line, is transformed into diamond earrings, like the 1950 *Francis Poulenc* dress from the *Verticale* line. This delicate and sensitive translation from one domain to another seems perfectly natural.

ART NOUVEAU

The art nouveau aesthetic movement, which blossomed around 1900, decorates the artistic digressions of the name of the Siegfried Bing contemporary art gallery on the rue de Provence in Paris. The ornamental style has sometimes been associated with Victoire's jewellery work, as she likes to take inspiration from the movement's reigning floral and plant motifs, although the reality is more nuanced. "As a little girl, I was very frightened of art nouveau objects, which I found disturbing, as they made me feel very uncomfortable."

But over the years, Victoire's tastes changed: "I learned to love art nouveau, and I think Lalique was an incredible artist, with complete freedom and a love of free-form. In his work, the extraordinary aspect prevails over the disturbing." The decorative repertory of René-Jules Lalique certainly contained worrying references. "The dragonfly woman is actually quite disturbing, and as a child I didn't understand the dark, even tortured aspect that could even seem malevolent with regard to women." But this somewhat "seedy" aspect, and the impression of unease are, however, transcended by some art nouveau works, which for Victoire, and rightly so, "have to be excellent to be beautiful," in an artistic domain where the average is horrible, and the "bizarre aspect of some of Alphonse Mucha's motifs, or some of Émile Gallé's more unfortunate colors," is present.

Victoire cleverly speaks of the "border with ugliness, with which art nouveau often flirts, when it reflects a dusty old-fashioned image." The designer has a sensitive understanding of the history of style, in the manner of someone like Philippe Jullian.

ASYMMETRY

"Working on asymmetry is much more difficult than symmetry, although they both fascinate me, like opposite and complementary poles, but from the start, the play of asymmetry is much more alive," Victoire specifies. She has created entire collections through the prism of Versailles, which is associated with great French taste and classical forms, where a type of regular rhythm goes hand in hand with symmetry, and yet she has never derided her leanings toward asymmetry, once again, in the spirit of the game. "One of the games that amuses me the most is finding a balance, a different harmony, in the precariousness of asymmetry," she says. Victoire evokes in *Versailles* (2016) or in *Gem Dior* (2019) the effect of irregular cascades, random sequences, and the hazardous accumulations that her jewellery compositions give rise to. This vision of asymmetry is a form of humanism. "We are all asymmetric," quips Victoire, who is taken with asymmetrical faces.

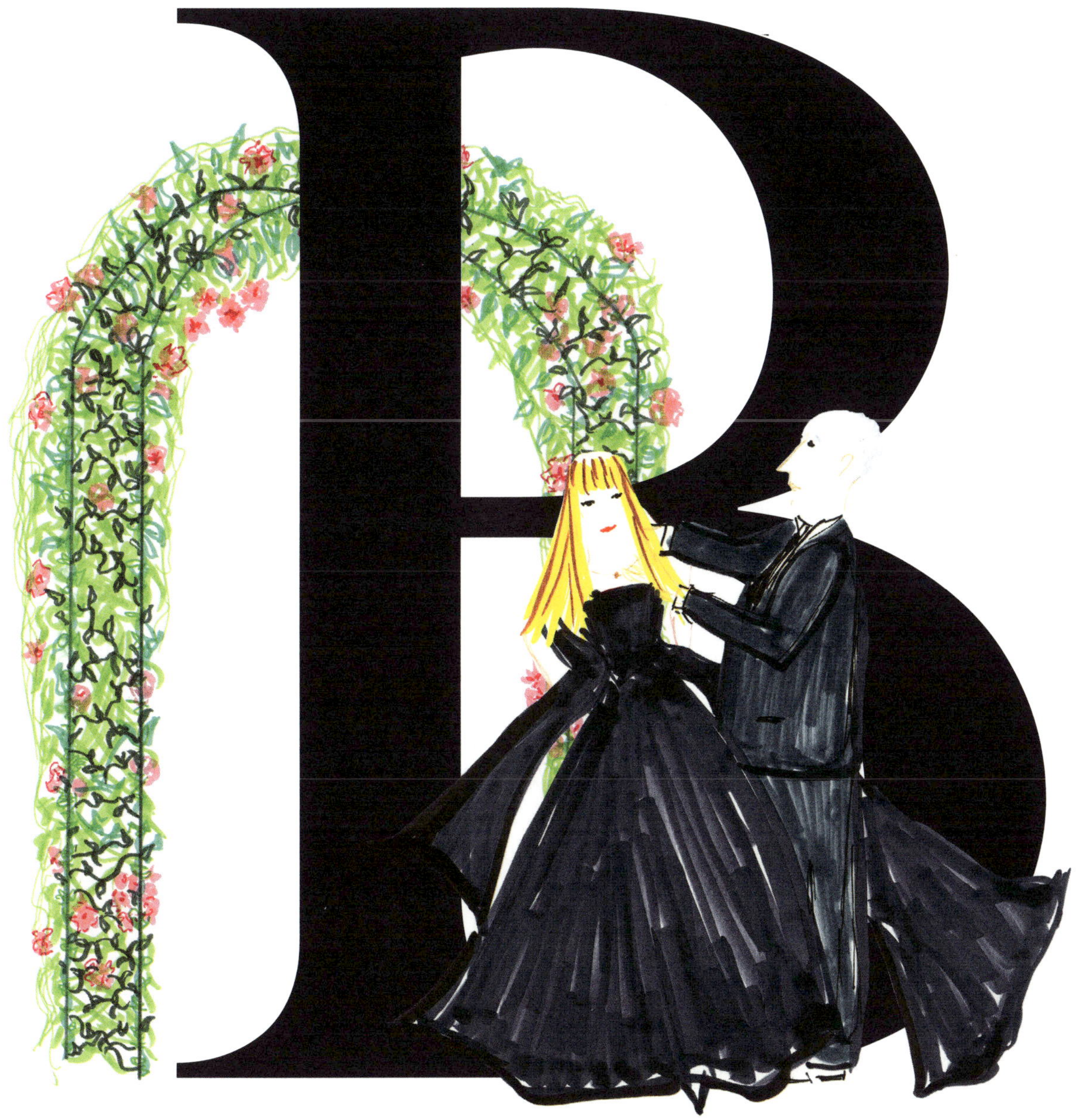
B

BAGATELLE

"Bagatelle is the park par excellence, the garden of roses—the first flower that comes to mind as soon as you think of Christian Dior—and also a place of calm, where no tragedy could ever happen," recalls Victoire, evoking her childhood walks, where her first memory echoes "the immense aspect that feels small, whereas its scale is successful, like a perfect model, and an idea of delight." From the Comte d'Artois' mad construction of a château in record time as a bet with Marie-Antoinette "for a *bagatelle*," which was then occupied by Lord Hertford and the Wallace family as well as British aristocrats and enthusiastic eighteenth-century collectors, Victoire has not necessarily retained the neoclassical aspect, but rather that unity with her childhood neighborhood. This sense of precision and happiness can be found in some of Victoire's creations bearing this very name (2000).

BAL

"As a young girl accompanying my uncle, Gilles Dufour, I attended balls, real balls, where, through the hosts and their guests, I could still imagine the balls given in Christian Dior's day. These balls demonstrated what the grand balls of the twentieth century had been like, they followed in their footsteps, with the same idea of something gratuitous, of balls given for the sole pleasure of giving them, balls held by people for their friends." There is something slightly nostalgic in Victoire's voice as she defines what the very Dior word "*ball*" means to her. She emphasizes the "joy of going, of getting ready, and of having fun," and the "true generosity of those who created them to enjoy themselves and dazzle their guests."

This world of balls, which has inspired many of her creations, in particular the *Bal* collection (2011), isn't something Victoire has seen through the filter of Instagram. She has specific memories of her own that have nourished her imagination and the creative impetus under which she created these jewels. "The guests at these balls attended for an almost elementary form of joy. I remember a red ball given by Nelson Seabra, a Brazilian billionaire, for his seventieth birthday, where people were so happy, from Mick Jagger to Ines de la Fressange, and all the real jet-set socialites," such as the legendary industrialist Paul-Louis Weiller. "I was sixteen years old, and Paul-Louis Weiller seemed old to me, but he was so amusing, so generous, and so innately well-mannered, that was my introduction to the culture of balls."

Far from the sets designed by specialized agencies, Victoire remembers incredible decors, with some incredibly extravagant private homes, and "that obsession with prior preparation, where everything was essential, and the game became a life philosophy, an almost vital element of seduction."

Around the same time, at the Bains-Douches and Palace nightclubs, Victoire also learned about other parties, which were different and yet comparable in their brilliance and liberty. And a good many jewels, created in the thread of these memories of unforgettable parties, have been designed by Victoire to show the glamour and magnificence of these balls from the past.

BARBARA HUTTON

"Barbara Hutton had a bright green Rolls-Royce." Victoire, as we know, has great color sense. "In fact, I don't believe I ever saw her, but I heard so much about her in my childhood that I probably persuaded myself that I met her, although I doubt that I actually did." A dramatic turn in the course of the conversation, as articles about Victoire de Castellane frequently cite Barbara Hutton (1912–1979) as a reference in her artistic childhood. "But I realize that what I know of her comes from my mother's memories, her Japanese palace in Mexico, and witty stories from my family."

A socialite with a storybook destiny, Barbara Hutton was known by her contemporaries as the "poor little rich girl," an orphan left loveless in an adult world. She was married seven times—three princes, including one fake; a German count with a long, complicated name; a baron; and male icons of the twentieth century, Cary Grant and playboy Porfirio Rubirosa. Her list of conquests recalls that Diana the Huntress could, in fact, be a prey herself. From New York to Tangiers via Paris, Barbara Hutton crossed the century with her elegant style, a thoughtful air, a slight pout, a hesitant smile, a beautiful expression of a certain voluptuousness of melancholy.

Gems and jewellery distracted her from nostalgia and her path led her to the Place Vendôme for spectacular purchases and orders: historic pieces like Marie-Antoinette's famous pearls or the Pasha's diamond were combined with sometimes disconcerting, almost radical tastes, as seen in her incredible jadeite necklace with perfect spheres of green beads against the skin or the tiara with the almost strict design, created by Cartier in 1947 at her request, using the staggering emeralds of the Grand Duchess Maria Pavlovna. "I know her life through her jewels, which, like Hansel and Gretel's pebbles, are strewn throughout the portrait I have created of her."

In life, Barbara Hutton's best friend and partner in crime was Sylvia Hennessy, Victoire's grandmother. Women dressed in the style of their era had men come hurrying. Like a Proustian madeleine or the crystallization of childhood, the enchanted, almost magical vision of these women of the world nourishes Victoire's imagination: they did not wear their jewels as trophies, but as natural accessories, knowing that pearls would tarnish and die in the darkness, and that the raison d'être of diamonds was to sparkle in the light. Life was more beautiful than a showcase. "My grandmother wore her jewellery every day: she was always ready and would get dressed even when she wasn't going out. I can see her doing her embroidery, with all her charms tinkling. She wasn't a grandmother; she was an apparition, and watching her, I said to myself that growing old wasn't something sad." (*Madame Figaro*, interview with Aurélia Lebailly, May 2, 2010)

Victoire remembers, "Barbara Hutton was the crystallization of all the women who made an impact on my childhood whenever I was with my mother. Her chauffeur had married Irène, covered in jade, who was a florist on the boulevard Flandrin; Michèle, the perfumer on the rue de Longchamp who lived with her mother, wore impeccable red nail polish, dressed in black with a leopard-print toque, and her big charm bracelets, buddhas and bells, and the divine sound of these bracelets when Michèle wrapped a gift. If that shop were still there I would go back every day and sit and watch her." Barbara Hutton is something of all that, in the way that jewellery associates itself with people, and vice versa, to create long-lived memories.

BELLADONE ISLAND

February 2007: the possibility of an island. Working closely with Eric Troncy to present her new collection called *Belladone Island*, among Claude Monet's *Nymphéas* at the Orangerie Museum, Victoire made a splash in the world of jewellery by overthrowing the canons of the time. Not without wit, and with her own vision of Christian Dior heritage, she launched a presentation revealing an ensemble of seventeen flowers and butterflies, set on petals, like a flight of honeybees. *Belladone Island* was instantly applauded for its salutary extravagance, having overthrown the habits of the jewellery world, which is frequently obsessed with its own historicism and an inclination for self-reference. It majestically combines various inspirations with an obvious jubilation for the off-piste to express a totally originally idea.

The magical, almost incantatory presence of this ensemble impressed critics and the public with the ambition of the project, the feeling of something monumental—vivid colors, multiple stones, the joyful prospect of the possibilities of lacquer, and the charm of a naturalism fully transcended by an irrepressible creativity. *Haute joaillerie* can tend toward the commonplace, ready-made expressions and the ordered tracks of expertise. With *Belladone Island*, Victoire seemed to own the fundamental phrase of François Rabelais, "Science without conscience is but the ruin of the soul."

Victoire has shown in her previous collections that she has perfect technical mastery, that she knows her repertory of forms and her history of Dior heritage, but the experience of risk is related both to life force and a taste for the unknown. Resigning oneself to making only pretty, previously mapped out designs has no creative interest. *Belladone Island* is related to Sursum Corda, the lifting up of our hearts cherished by Tacitus, and the challenge taken up for oneself with panache, with full awareness of fantasy, and with the freedom to dream and imagine. It is without a doubt that all of this together gives the pieces presented an alchemical presence, and therein lies a blend of seduction and repulsion, the sublime and the monstrous, where we are as close as possible to what art is.

With the distance of time, almost twelve years, you can feel how far this collection was a flash of brilliance destined to last, and we seem to make out a sort of liberating force and a moment of grace. There is a joyful erudition in the work, along with more mysterious nuances, an *oeuvre au noir* as Marguerite Yourcenar might have described it. The virtuosity of this collection is dazzling, in the service of unusual imaginary worlds in jewellery, where the notion of *a work of art*, as delivered by the goldsmiths and cabinetmakers of the ancien régime, is a way of establishing your position in a profession, by surpassing your abilities to the point where you surprise yourself.

By botanizing a mysterious island, whose position on this earthly planet—if it actually exists on earth—has been forgotten by geography and cartography, Victoire scorns naturalism and ventures off into other worlds and other eras, when nature was not the pretty, easy thing that we believe we understand and love, but something that inspired fear, or even terror, when visited. You can imagine Victoire drawing these flowers and insects like Captain Cook exploring primitive forests in the eighteenth century, recording the strange, then unknown flora, and a wild nature that was both generous and hostile, like on *Belladone Island*.

In this latter collection, certain stones even evoke these faraway adventures in uncertain natural climes, with emeralds from Sandawana in Zimbabwe and tourmalines from Paraïba in Brazil. The spirit of the collection evokes the introspective force of those who sought to understand the still unclear frontiers of the world and of the living, from curiosity cabinets to natural history museums, between the sixteenth and the eighteenth centuries.

Victoire harvests the zeitgeist with enthusiasm and freedom. And this freedom is affirmed in the titles given to each of her pieces, taking pleasure in the Renaissance science of Latin denomination, from an era so attached to naming the world. With puns, double entendres, and nods to the initiated, here it seems to reinvent the family tree: *Reina Magnifica Sangria* necklace, *Ancolia Veneinosa Pop* ring, and the staggering, *Grani Opalia Devorus* ring. Victoire seamlessly compares these wild and defensive flowers to women whose freedom is questioned by a world that remains widely aggressive and hostile.

But what remains of *Belladone Island*, so vividly in our minds, is a strangeness that cannot be reduced to any given adjective, for none of them, neither surrealist nor fantastic, can aptly characterize it. Or perhaps, to quote André Breton, "Beauty will be convulsive or will not be at all" (*Mad Love*, 1937). This beauty makes you stare wide-eyed in stupor, with an effect not unlike the belladonna plant that dilates the pupils, or like the Marquise Casati, the Medusa, without fear of attempting artificial paradises.

BESTIAIRE FANTASTIQUE

"The fantastic bestiary is not that of Christian Dior—we're a long way from Milly-la-Forêt here—but animals that transcend the imagination. They are not all fictional. Some of them, like salamanders and jellyfish, actually exist, but our imagination gives them an additional, dreamlike dimension; while others, like chimeras and dragons, are born of stories and myths handed down to us."

BESTIARY

"It is the bestiary of Christian Dior that I am surrounded by, which inspires me the most, with its insects—ladybugs and dragonflies—that you come across in countryside gardens and on rural lanes." Victoire creates a sensitive and humble parallel with the fruits and flowers of Milly-la-Forêt, loving "the almost childlike aspect, in the prettiest sense of the word, of what Christian Dior loved, of this childhood bestiary, on a childhood scale, forming a perfect, protected world." Victoire recognizes that this bestiary grows like a family, with other species that are stranger, more exotic, sometimes more majestic, sometimes more dangerous, such as Mediterranean jellyfish and seahorses, or panthers and big cats for their patterns and their allure. "And then the industrious bee, the emblem of the house, because in the past twenty or so years, our view of the animal world has changed profoundly."

C

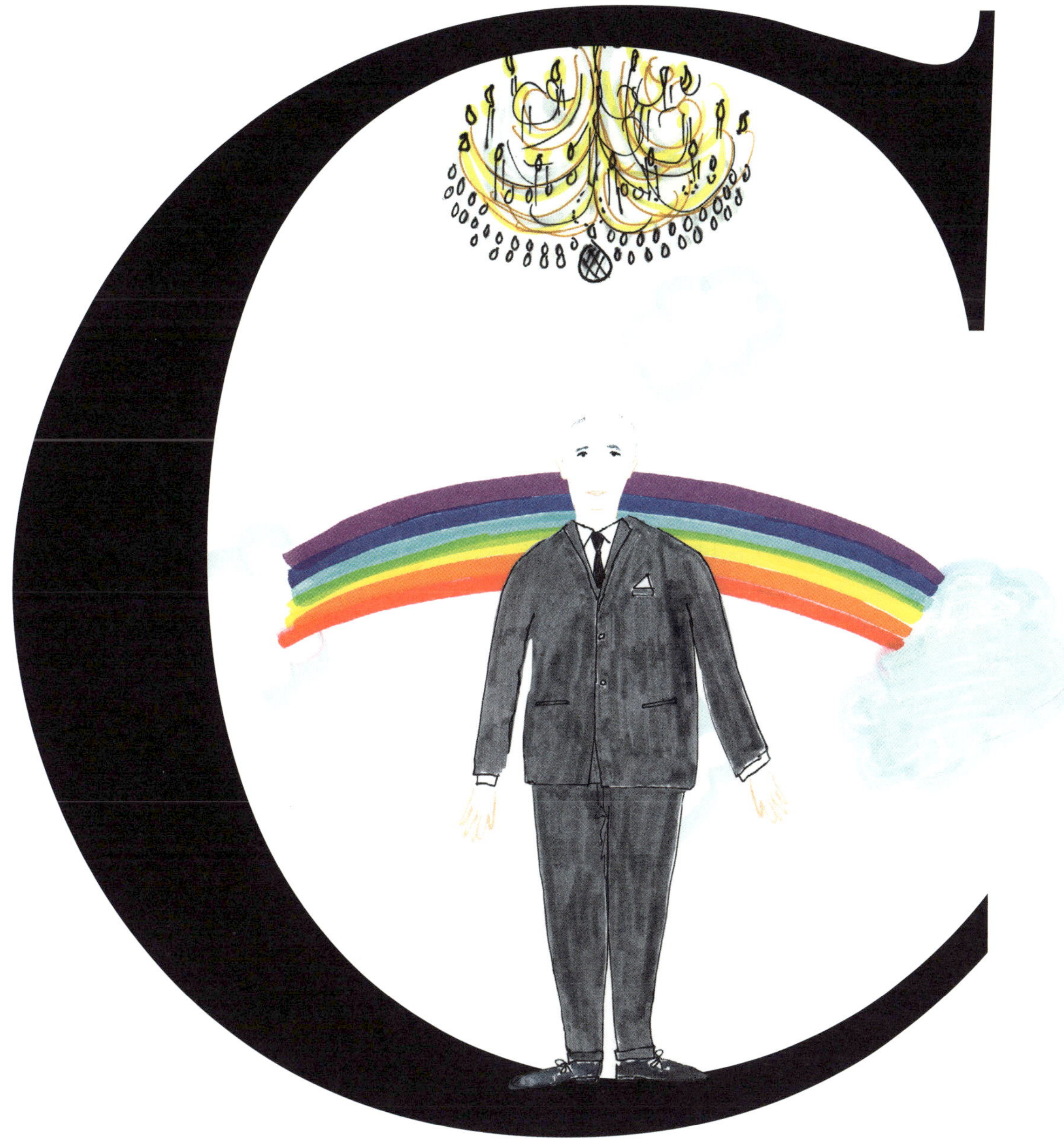

CANAL

"The word and the idea of a canal, of the Grand Canal fascinates me—as do those ornamental ponds at Versailles and at French châteaux, and then I adore the effect of gardens, of shimmering water, seen from an airplane, like little models." Victoire finds that this perspective also owes much to the reign of symmetry, and likes "all that you take in with a single look."

CANEWORK

"The canework motif provides a beautiful effect with a very couture feel, and is somewhat the privilege of the very couture, very Dior chairs and armchairs," recalls Victoire. Used in the classical French furniture that Christian Dior admired and collected, canework is a weaving technique using rattan canes that was developed during the Regency and the reign of Louis XV. As such, it provides an endless stretch of a pattern where the weft and warp are clearly visible. "I thought this motif was worthy of being reproduced in jewellery, as if I were cutting out a piece of canework and transposing it as a decoration, in a very literal way, onto a jewel, like woven golden straw in which, thanks to engraving work, I can blend polished and matte gold."

CARNIVORE

"It's strange, these carnivorous plants are always disturbing; nature isn't necessarily kind," as the *Milly Carnivora* pieces (2008) see it bloom, unsettling. "For me, they were like the continuation of the *Belladone Island* story (2007), they were the daughters of *Belladone*, for whom I wanted to work in fluorescent colors, as though they were children, because I often see things as a family story, I didn't want to draw unique pieces, but rather create midrange jewellery pieces that were more approachable."

And speaking of family is more charming, and more elegant than to speak of lines, another word now overused in the fashion and luxury worlds. "Depending on the volume of the jewels, they are parents or grandparents, while little jewels are like newborns; all these jewels are like characters to me," Victoire explains. And then, the obsession with carnivorous flowers is a delectable evocation of *Little Shop of Horrors*, in whose terror we finally delight.

CASTELLANE

"Castellane is my name, it's the name of my father, Antoine. Over time, you realize how far some memories affect your vision of things, and it took me some time to understand the influence of my father, a whimsical artist, a painter who, with a type of audacity and great freedom, would wear Mexican medallions, bracelets, and no aristocratic signet ring but thick bands with stones, and some kinds of vaguely Indian torques and breastplates. They might have been the first jewels to make an impact on me, who knows?"

Castellane (phonetically the dental "t" is emphasized) is a small town in the Alpes-de-Haute-Provence. A travel guide would describe it as "charming." At the edge of the sculptural Verdon Gorges, the town nestles in a more than spectacular landscape, a rocky equilibrium brimming with the sublime, in the pre-romantic sense of the word. Alas, no famous *vedutisti* have immortalized it. In the great armorial of French nobility, Castellane (and here, by a magic that characterizes family names and place-names, which enchanted Marcel Proust, the dental "t" is elided in favor of an elegant glide) is the name of French nobility of ancient lineage, feudal, to be precise.

We will spare you the details of a family tree with its glorious branches: nine bishops and archbishops; a hundred-odd knights and commanders of the Order of Malta; a Marshal of France; a cousinship with the Countess of Grignan—the recipient of so many wonderful letters from her mother, the Marchioness de Sévigné in the seventeenth century; a dandy and connoisseur collector in the person of Boniface de Castellane, whose first name is a tradition throughout the descendants; and a jewellery creator, Victoire de Castellane.

The heraldry specifies, like an engraving or a setting, the description of the coat of arms: a crenellated castle with triple towers of masonry sand, the middle tower higher than the others, so ruby and gold are already sealed, like fate. The motto, in Provençal, "May d'hounour que d'hounours," means more honor than honors, and is a relevant match for the lives of the family members. This dynastic and aristocratic information was considered largely sufficient, as the essentials truly lay elsewhere.

CHANTILLY

Chantilly is the name of a château, a textile technique, and a gastronomic term. For Victoire, the obvious link is that of the fabric known as Chantilly lace, made according to a traditional ancestral technique, which has become a symbol of skill in the fashion world and is the key to complete refinement.

"For the *Dior Dior Dior* collection (2018), I wanted lace. I had imagined reworking all the different types of lace—and there are many—kept in the Dior archives, and thereby creating something like a repertory of gold netting." As is often the case for Victoire, inspiration becomes an ongoing game of shapes and exploration by renewing links with a certain form of tradition. "Lace always represents a form of absolute, it has both a very old-fashioned and a very couture side to it." It is also the graphic dimension that appeals to Victoire: "Lace is a work of transparency. It composes designs that sometimes repeat themselves and also leaves the skin visible, so you can make it out."

Chantilly and lace is a combination of sensuality and "something of a very French skill," which is the perfect source for Victoire's creative curiosity.

CHER DIOR

"*Cher Dior* (2013) is the name of a collection, but it is also something more than that. For twenty years, it is as though I have been holding a conversation with Christian Dior. That was my line of action in the beginning, and I have stuck to it," Victoire confides.

By launching Dior Joaillerie, Victoire set off on an adventure that had no other basis than the history of the house of couture and that of perfumes. The outlines of the empire built by Christian Dior held no previous experience in the highly subtle world of jewellery. It did not only mean becoming the *haute joaillerie* designer for a house that itself embodies fashion, it also meant starting from zero, with a certain humility, and from a central question: "What would Dior jewellery have looked like if Monsieur Dior himself had designed it? This is the question I was asked, although this approach of mine might seem crazy." As the collections evolve, this attitude has probably grown more nuanced, but the direction of this secret, ongoing dialogue, like an exchange of letters with Christian Dior, has been maintained: "I find it quite respectful to not forget the person who founded the house we work for."

CHRISTIAN DIOR

"I was already fascinated by the name of Christian Dior when I was a little girl, and the fascination never ended. I think of nothing else but the contraction of *diamant* and *or* (diamond and gold), and I see the perfect couture name." Where Jean Cocteau had stopped at *Dieu et or* (God and Gold), Victoire goes further with this nod to jewellery.

As a child, she would go to the Montaigne Avenue boutique with her mother and grandmother: "Back then, there was still a mixture of clothes and accessories, and the smiling, scented, well-mannered sales attendants who handled all the social codes with dexterity. It was magical, an enchanted world, with perhaps even a hint of the *Bonheur des Dames* (the department store from Émile Zola's eponymous novel), it was about assuaging desire. There was nothing blasé about it."

Christian Dior also means the powerful images seen on posters in the streets, magazine photographs, and shots that appealed to roving eyes: "There was already something mesmerizing about knowing which celebrity was dressed by which house; we would flick through *Vogue* and admire the stunning Princess Grace, and later Caroline of Monaco, radiant in Dior, I loved the house of Dior advertisements. At the same time, Charles Jourdain was making shoes for Dior, and he commissioned Guy Bourdin's completely crazy photographs for his own ad campaigns, and everything was merged together—it made quite an impression..."

The years passed, and Victoire started working at Chanel on accessories and jewellery, alongside Karl Lagerfeld. "When I started working in fashion, Christian Dior was the other couture house, which seemed far from my reach because of personal things in my life. I would go out in head-to-toe Chanel, although with Azzedine Alaïa I gradually liberated myself from that, and in fashion, all of a sudden, other characters appeared, like Jean Paul Gaultier, with a different type of inspiration." And then, in 1998, Christian Dior, a further house away, became hers. "I met Bernard Arnault, and it was a real meeting of minds, where we found a shared desire to imagine what a Dior Joaillerie might one day be. Each of us had an idea, an intuitive feeling, and the adventure began with that challenge." In January 1998, Victoire officially joined the house of Christian Dior to work on the first *haute joaillerie* collection, which was revealed in spring 1999. It was twenty years ago.

CLASSICISM

"Obviously this might be surprising to some people, but the notion of classicism appeals to me, as there is something very French about it, with the idea of the right balance and perfection. And as someone who doesn't really create things that are, strictly speaking, classical, I do, however, always seek out this form of balance and proportion." In this spirit, Versailles, a fundamental element of the visual and artistic culture of Christian Dior, was quite an obvious source of inspiration, to the point that it led to three collections that were all memorable for their richness and inventiveness: *Dior à Versailles* (2016), *Dior à Versailles: côté Jardins* (2017), and *Dior à Versailles: Pièces Secrètes* (2018). "The word *classical* could be seen as slightly pejorative, or dowdy, but that's just a received idea. Christian Dior is a great classic in the same way as a timeless literary masterpiece is, and from that point of view, classicism is inexhaustible," explains Victoire.

COCKTAIL

"I might as well say that for me, cocktail evokes what we called cocktail rings in the 1950s and 1960s, following the Roaring Twenties." This type of ring very soon seemed to Victoire as fabulous grounds for exploration. "When I arrived at Christian Dior, I looked around me, and I found that jewellery had grown terribly bourgeois and had lost its sense of joy, freedom, and lightness too."

In this moment of realization, the reinvention of the "cocktail ring" immediately appealed to Victoire as grounds for weaving together the stories and threads of her imagination. "Why not make rings like dresses, on the same scale and with the same extravagance that John Galliano gave free reign to in his haute couture collections?" This was also a way of renewing the links, at a jewellery level, with the true creative folly that appeared with the New Look in 1947, with excess and abundance. Victoire elaborates, "To make rings as crazy as those cocktail dresses, with their almost endless, excessive lengths of fabric, the way Christian Dior created them in 1947."

COLORS

"Colors form the basis of my work. They provide complete freedom, and every shade in the world is found in stones, so why deprive myself?" Color is like a manifesto for Victoire, and a spontaneous motto: color! "It's what I liked most as a child, and a box of Caran d'Ache pencils was the most extraordinary gift that I could receive." And although certain shades, such as ocher yellow or khaki green, are drab, each of them has its own place. "I like to make them live together. I love the idea of bringing a beautiful jewellery design to life with color—you have to give every hue a chance!" This almost consuming passion, the gluttony and the joy that color evokes, once led Victoire to note a frustration that was quickly swept away: "One day, I was thinking that it really was a shame that there weren't more gold colors, and so I started to work with lacquer, and fluorescent hues, in an almost endless field of possibilities, where new tones joined existing ones, and gold could be fuchsia pink." Color is a signature—that of Victoire. See *Lacquer*. See *Monochrome*.

COROLLE

"With the *Archi Dior* collection (2014), I enjoyed emphasizing words and expressions that recalled some of Christian Dior's haute couture collections, and corolla was one of these words." And Victoire sees this as an echo of both the flower and the first collection in 1947 originally called *Corolle*, before Carmel Snow's finely polished New Look slogan established its place in the history of fashion. "The corolla is a very gracious form for a jewel, as it creates a soft, happy, and feminine effect."

CORRESPONDENCE

"Every collection since 1999 has been a form of correspondence between Christian Dior and myself." And for twenty years, nothing has interrupted that correspondence, which has a Baudelaireian feel, as jewellery according to Victoire, makes feelings, sound, scent, and taste communicate so well. "My collections are not unimaginative, I create these collections as though I am writing letters to Christian Dior. And he doesn't need to answer me."

COUTURE

"It goes without saying that when you create a jewellery collection for a house like Dior, you think of the word *couture*, and I have always linked it to Christian Dior's couture." Victoire's statement gets straight to the point, claiming her primary source of inspiration and the basis for games to come, like a main theme in her work and her own leitmotif. "I realize over time that I have continued to rework couture terms such as ribbon, bow, lace, embroidery, cut, line, and corolla, at a jewellery level—it is one of the obvious sources of inspiration in my work." For twenty years, Victoire has nourished close links with what takes place in couture, while maintaining a free space, indicated in her approach to the art of jewellery as not merely an annex of the fashion world. She carefully evokes "the exuberant era of John Galliano, the more design-centered, radical time of Raf Simons," and she discovers affinities with Maria Grazia Chiuri over the personal, ultrafeminine, and sometimes superstitious nature of jewels, "for which we share the same fascination."

CRYSTAL

"In the collections dedicated to Versailles, I loved playing with the possibilities of rock crystal," Victoire specifies. Often found in Renaissance curiosity cabinets, but also in royal collections and in the crown jewels of which Louis XIV was so fond, for Victoire crystal is the "perfect material for expressing the transparency of water, and it also has frosted effects that I find magnificent and which contrast with the purity of diamonds." Crystal is also represented by the great candelabras, girandoles, chandeliers, and wall lights that flood the Versailles galleries with light, offering shimmering reflections echoed by jewellery sets worn next to the skin.

CROWNS

Victoire naturally dresses her *Reines et Rois* (2009) in crowns, the royal insignia of which her series of *vanitas* pieces is deserving. "With the *Fiancée du Pirate*, and my *Reines et Rois*, I had fun with various versions of the memento mori. I went for a walk in the very impressive Capuchin Crypt in Vienna, where bronze skulls decorate the tombs and coffins." From hard stone *vanitas* pieces with regular features, Victoire created new dynasties and hitherto unknown families. "I wanted to create regalia, jewellery sets with every sort of diamond, like crowns from imaginary kingdoms." Queens decorate rings; kings, pendants; and couples are ready to ascend their ghostly thrones. "Diamonds lend themselves so well to the spectral aspect of these apparitions, there was nothing heavy about it; quite the opposite, and everything seemed evanescent." We are indeed far from the imperial weight of the Schatzkammer (Royal Treasury) next to the Capuchin Crypt. "I wanted to compose new headwear and ruff collars."

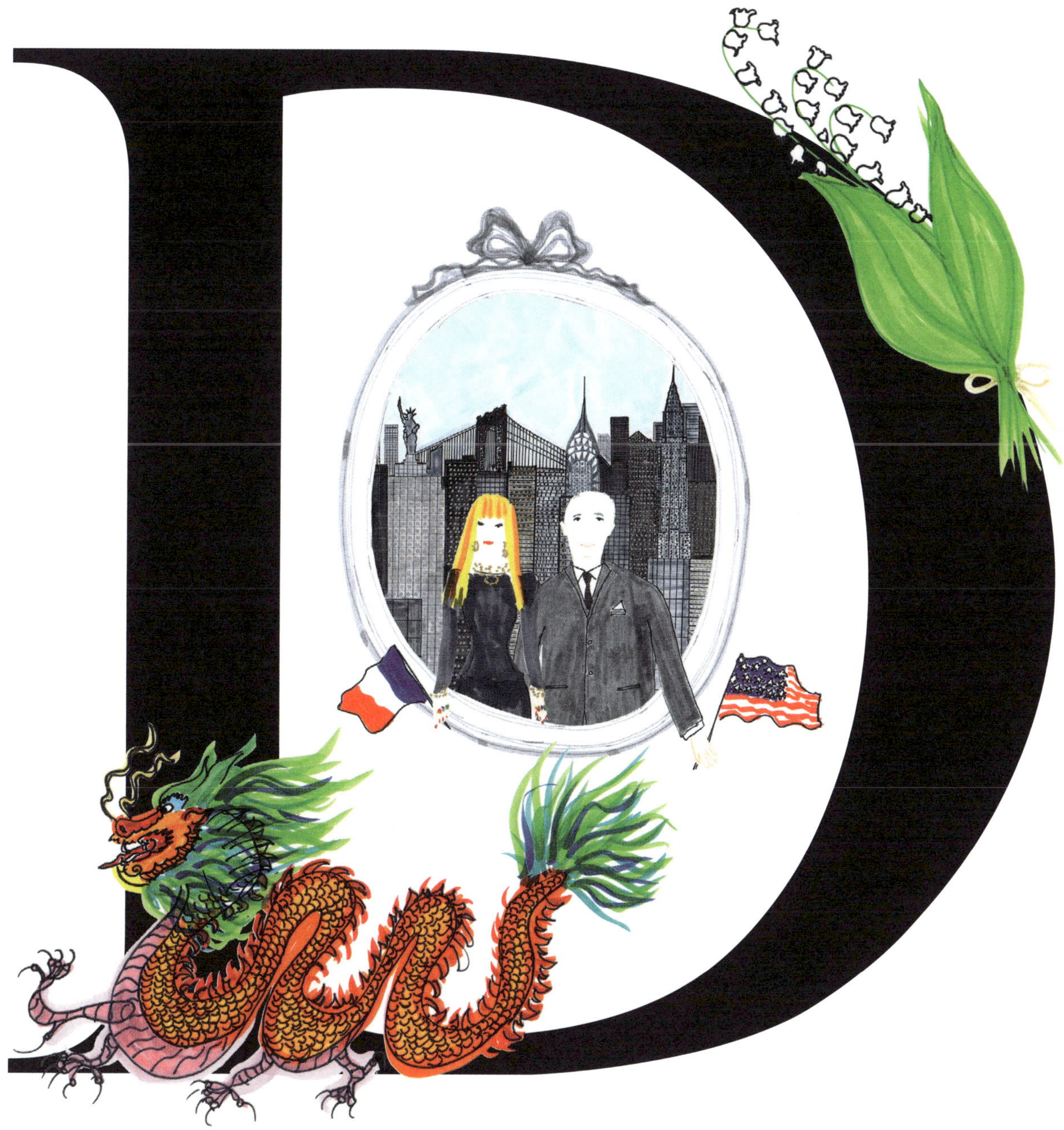
D

DEAR DIOR

"*Dear Dior* (2012) is the idea that I continue to correspond with Christian Dior, but with a cross-Channel or transatlantic feel, because Christian Dior was also a great traveler." When she presented this collection, Victoire admitted that it was less narrative than previous ones and that she was moving into more abstract terrain. In a tribute to the couture jewels of the 1950s, the collection features bright colors, voluminous forms, and generous stones subtly combined with colorful audacity, such as the sublime opals that light up numerous pieces, in stylized creations that relinquish plant, flower, and animal forms. Victoire explains, "Once again, I wanted to give equal consideration to the visible parts and the backs of the jewels, which are all designed as gold lace, reproducing the embroidery patterns drawn from the Dior archives and reworked."

DECOR

Victoire doesn't hold forth on the idea of decor, and once again this is evident in her work, as she confirms that "the word has no negative connotations to my mind, quite the opposite." In jewellery, according to her, "it is the setting that contains the decorative aspect. It is the setting that tells the story of the ring, or the story of the jewel, with motifs and ornaments."

DETAILS

Details are always revelatory, of course, but they also craft excellence, in both couture and jewellery, and Victoire emphasizes this. "As with an haute couture dress, in jewellery, the internal and external details are equally important, and for me, the technical, or even mechanical work of a jewel denotes a sense of detail as crucial as the drawing of a visible ornament, like the seams of some dresses." This is the key to understanding Victoire's attention to detail, which means that the jewel will be worn with pleasure, and that you might, by chance, as seen in the *Cher Dior* collection (2013), glimpse a beautiful gold netting at the back of a piece.

DIAMOND

Of this "very difficult stone," Victoire immediately says that she likes them "aquatic," and she uses them flat like mirrors, in simple, almost humble shapes, rendering them limpid and discreet, for "a diamond is extraordinarily powerful, it can annihilate the personality of the woman wearing it by drawing other people's attention to itself instead of to her."

In the *Gem Dior* collection (2019), Victoire states that she has absolutely "no fascination for complicated multifaceted cuts, which are there only to catch the light, and cast the wearer into the shadows. That's why I like free shape diamonds so much." On the other hand, she also creates masterpieces of jewellery, where diamonds are cut like a mirror, smooth-surfaced, "the only white stone which, cut in this way, takes on an incredible, poetic dimension."

DIORAMA

Now here is a very nineteenth-century word that frequently turns up in converstions about Christian Dior. "Have I made a collection called *Diorama*?" questions Victoire, when we ask her about the word. "Yes, I have (2015)! But the diorama is above all a process of showing or presenting something, like a great ancestor of the cinema, with which I have played to shift people's perception of my jewels." Very soon, Victoire took up both this visual and scenographic method to "create another view of my collections when I presented them in the windows of our boutiques, as a way of bringing them back to a more balanced scale, and of telling a story, their story."

DIOR DIOR DIOR

"For this collection, I immersed myself in the Dior archives, and I was particularly curious about lace. I found it interesting to reproduce some of the designs and compositions, and to cut out certain patterns to make jewellery, bracelets, and rings."

Victoire likes to relate precisely how a collection is born. Sapphires, pearls, diamonds, tsavorite garnets and emeralds seem set in webs of lace, reproducing the undulating patterns of guipure and organza with ethereal grace. The jewels seem ultralight, like a precious flight: "Cut out in this way, the pattern itself looked, in places, as though it had been drawn straight onto the skin."

DIORETTE

"Beyond the obvious rhyme with *pâquerette*, a simple fresh wildflower, very Christian Dior in Milly-la-Forêt, it is also a name that I find modern and old-fashioned at the same time, and which appears in a collection from Christian Dior's era." (Spring-Summer 1948, *Envol* line).

Like a rhapsody, Victoire's imagination weaves a story around this daisy or *pâquerette* motif, with countryside gardens "like little bouquets," she says. Like a botanist, Victoire seems to create a new floral species, scattered across rings in infinite color variations thanks to the playful use of lacquer. *Diorette* (2005) has become something of a watchword and is one of biggest success stories in contemporary jewellery.

DIORISSIMO

"As someone who doesn't wear perfume, *Diorissimo* is my favorite scent, as one of my mother's friends wore it. It is a fragrant sensation from my childhood." From this fragrance with its extraordinary nuances, it seemed obvious that Victoire would invent a no-less-extraordinary necklace, like an immense stem of lily of the valley, curling around the neck of a stylish woman. "Yes, it was an obvious thing to do. It was in 1999, my early days at Dior, and the beginning of a secret correspondence, like a tribute, with Christian Dior."

DRAGON

"The best of art nouveau lies both in the floral reign and the imaginary and fanciful bestiary, and in that oeuvre, the dragon is what fascinates me the most, even though I haven't actually explored it very much," states Victoire, who loves to be precise. "Fantastic animals go hand in hand with fantastic stones." And the most fantastic stone, the "queen of stones" as she likes to say, is the opal. Thanks to the opal, the dragon becomes "fundamentally benevolent."

DRAWING

In jewellery as in a good many creative fields, drawing is like child's play. Victoire loves to draw, it is like an absolute for her: "I love to draw on Post-its, so I create small-scale drawings that I explain to the studio, who then convey my original idea to the atelier."

The process is set down with simplicity and efficiency by Victoire, who doesn't trouble herself with lyrical flights on the art of creating. "Before I start drawing, I have an idea of what the final jewel will be. And so I draw everywhere and in a very spontaneous way. I tend to draw an idea, which has nothing to do with the precise, detailed jewellery drawing in the classical sense of the word." The method has to be constructed. A collection is composed almost two years before it is revealed to the public. It is a balancing act of anticipation, which Victoire willingly and frankly recognizes: "The full difficulty lies in knowing whether this drawing will still be something I like two years later."

Although Christian Dior would go to Milly-la-Forêt to draw his collections in his garden, Victoire likes to say that she "needs to be in Paris" when she draws, to be "rooted in life." Through her drawings, she expresses more feelings and sensations divided between anxiety and fascination than if she had allowed chance encounters or the discovery of a subject or work of art to do so. "My inspiration is born from a sort of self-protection; I protect myself enough to always keep a certain freshness and a form of distance, which can, alas, wrongly be taken for indifference. Above all, I do not look to be absolutely carried away by things I may have seen."

It takes real strength to admit in our time that you haven't created a collection because you have discovered a place or an artist or an exhibition you like, something which is increasingly popular and has become banal in the fashion world. On the contrary, in an almost literary way, Victoire is nourished by faraway and more personal inspirations: "I picked up a lot of things as a child, from which I still take sustenance, and which continue to inspire me today!"

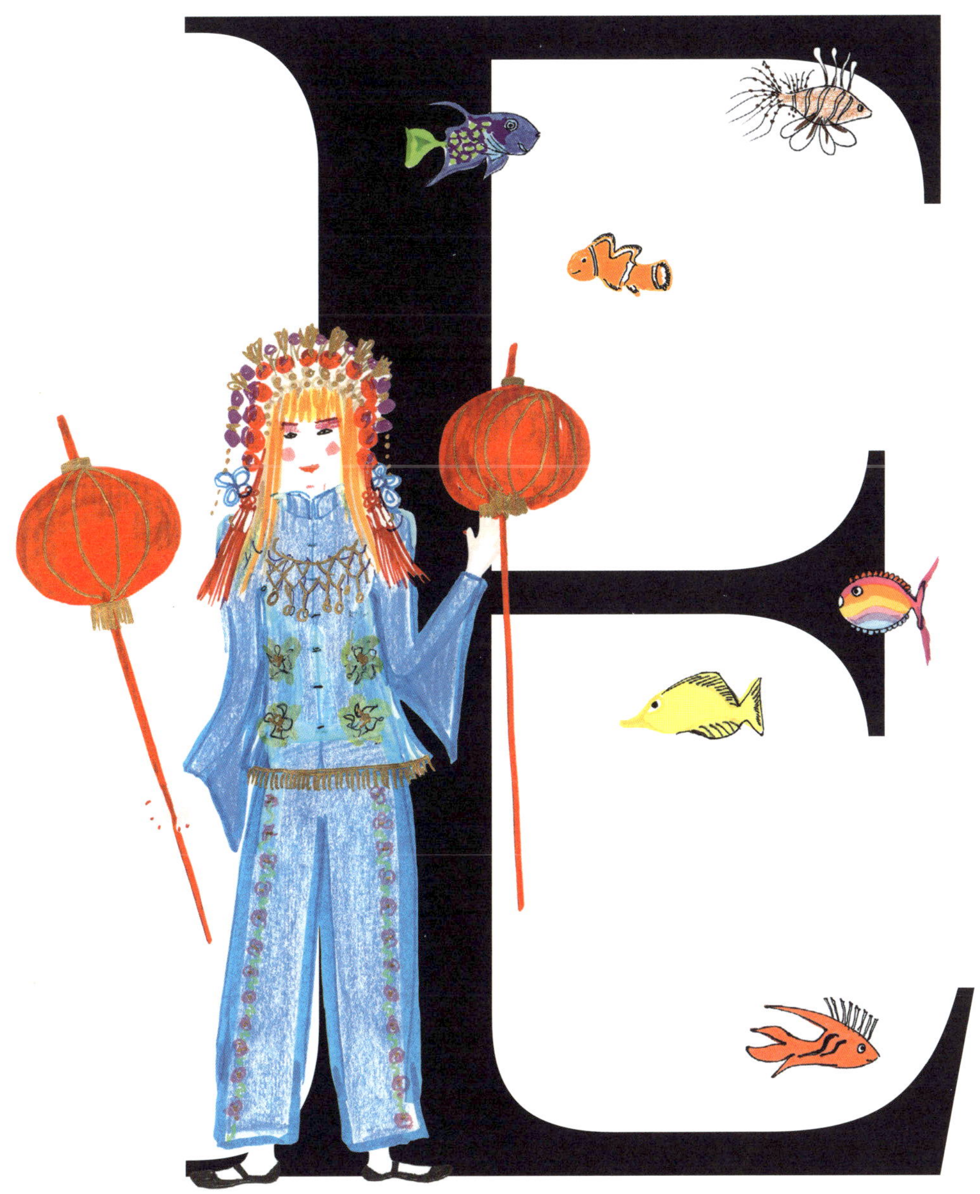
E

ECCENTRICITY

"It's a word I have heard a lot, heard too much perhaps," murmurs Victoire. "For a long time, I have been judged as eccentric, but I confess I am not convinced that the word corresponds to me, and I don't like being associated with it." For Victoire, semantic precision very quickly ends tired debate. "It is a fundamentally pretty word, but it's a bit of a shame, it's a bit short, it doesn't mean much anymore." I acquiesce, for it is certainly true in fashion: "Eccentricity is a bit like luxury, too hackneyed, it doesn't mean anything anymore."

EMERALD

"I always like to imagine that stones have a taste. And when I see an emerald, I think it tastes like mint, like mint cordial," says Victoire dreamily. The twenty years of *haute joaillerie* designed by Victoire are strewn with emeralds, including her most personal collections, *Belladone Island* (2007) and *Milly Carnivora* (2008).

In the *Bal des Roses* collection (2011), emerald is naturalist in style, with leaves in a chlorophyll-green-veined richness that serves as a showcase for the rosebuds. In the incredible *Bal de Mai* necklace in particular, emeralds are treated in every possible different way, with ultrasimple cuts and baguette cuts in settings from the most elementary forms to the most precious facets.

In the *Archi Dior* collection (2014), emerald figures greatly among the stones used, but in a more abstract way, like a chromatic expression of ornamentation, underlining the construction of the jewel, like the teardrops on the *Corolle Jour Émeraude* necklace and earrings. It is majestic at the center of the *Envol Drapé Émeraude* ring and presents a contrasting palette in the *Ailée Diamant* ring, where emerald juxtaposes green tourmaline in a play of subtle green nuances.

Even more majestically, emerald radiantly punctuates the finest creations of the *Dior Dior Dior* collection (2018), pampered in its solid purity by the lightness of a lace jewellery setting, like the *Dentelle Velours Émeraude* necklace. She likes to gently set these emeralds, which are so strong and so incarnate, in the lace and guipure settings of several of the pieces in this collection. See *Ruby*, *Sapphire*.

EROTIC

"Wearing jewels is erotic, but the jewels themselves are not," according to Victoire. Like the sixteenth-century poets Clément Marot and Maurice Scève, who so beautifully evoked the "blazons of women's bodies," Victoire draws a geography of the body where the jewellery eroticizes the spot it is worn on—necklaces and earrings at the neck and the nape, the décolleté and the bust, and the wrists to which bracelets cling. "Personally, eroticism is always present in my mind in the inspiration for a collection, by a movement that the jewellery implies or a gesture that it will add sparkle to and make important; jewels can never be dissociated from anatomy. And Victoire notes just how far "people tend to forget the seductive or erotic power of a jewel, whereas for me, that remains very powerful, as much for a man as for a woman, in fact."

EXOTIC

"Exotic? To me that means almost everything that isn't Parisian, and that isn't pejorative in any way. It's a word that we avoid more and more, as it too has been overused. Something exotic is what marks an otherness, and therefore takes me out of what I see every day."

EYES

"In jewellery, the eyes are your first work instrument and your most indispensable. It is a profession of meticulousness, of details that count down to the last tenth of a millimeter, and of an observation of materials and techniques. We never work at full scale when we make a jewel, we look into the material, and we put the reality under a magnifying glass, enlarging it."

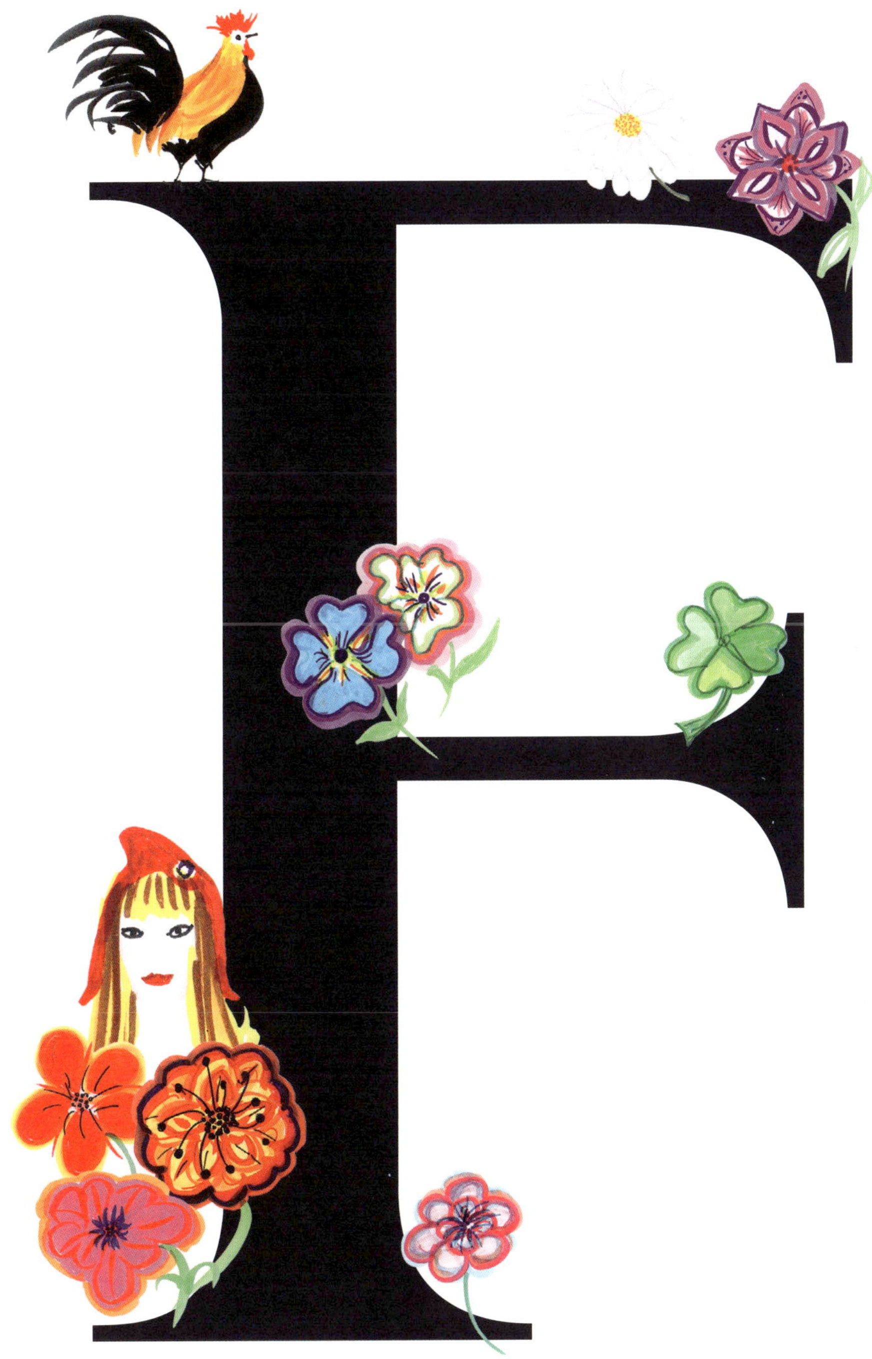
F

FAIRIES

"Fairies aren't my thing! I don't believe in them."

FAMILY

"Desperately seeking a family—that could be the central theme of my jewellery stories." It is probably the most personal aspect in Victoire's work, a form of quest that is expressed in creation and in drawings: "I am always seeking to recompose a family through my jewellery. I project that onto these objects, but always in an idealized way."

For Victoire, "jewels compose an ideal family, where everyone gets along well, without suffering about anything, without being crushed by anyone." From one collection to another, or within the same collection, she likes to invent kinships and cousinhoods, where certain ornaments, certain stones, converse, evoking resemblances, where there are grown-ups and little ones, parents and children. "In my choice of stones, I don't want one of them to be crushed by the others," she explains. It is a magical world that opens up, anthropomorphizing jewels into an ideal family, all loved equally. "I want each stone, each jewel, to have its chance, and none of them to be killed by another."

FANTASY

"Like eccentricity, the magnificent word *fantasy* is often ruined by our preconceived idea of it. And in the gem and jewellery world, it was long considered that fantasy jewels could not be precious jewels." Word and things, this inclination to find exactly the right expression is always striking in the work of Victoire, who loves this incessant balancing act. "But how to you add fantasy to a precious jewel?" It is a question that seems to have permeated her twenty years of jewellery creation at Dior. "When you go over the edge, it lapses into kitsch," she warns, which is without a doubt the absolute worst and something her talent has protected her from.

FAUNA

"Fauna is certainly a vast domain, but it seems to me that there is a Dior fauna—little insects, very happy, harmless insects that you would find in the garden at Milly-la-Forêt." See *Animal, Bestiary*.

FIANCÉE DU VAMPIRE

"The collection *Fiancée du Vampire* (2002) arose from my desire to create a romantic story, a crazy love story, one of eternity too, and so there's nothing like a vampire falling in love with a young girl." Victoire loves to surprise us by telling us her stories, and she is a talented raconteur. "When you talk about haute couture and Christian Dior, you can't help thinking about him, yet in fact we know very little about him... What did love mean to Christian Dior in 1947?" That was the question she had in mind when this collection was created. "We know that Christian Dior was a homosexual in an era that didn't allow it. His professional milieu probably did, but not his social milieu, no more than French society of the era. So, I wanted to glorify his probably tormented love life with a perfect love story. I wanted to give him the great love story he deserved." Against this incredible and moving backdrop, Victoire composed a series of jewels representing the different moments in this love story, in a nod to the sentimental jewellery that people were so partial to in the eighteenth and nineteenth centuries. These took the shape of diamond crosses, without the element of being religious jewels, or hearts: "It was rather a romantic idea of absolute love that moved me as well as the element of immortality provided by the jewel."

FLOWERBED

This word, borrowed from the gardening world, comes up several times when Victoire's work is spoken of, particularly when she is delightfully exploring the realm of possibilities that is represented by Versailles. The graphic rigor of the château gardens—which we are a little quick to call French-style gardens—inspires the refined composition that is enamored of symmetry of some of Victoire's jewels. But the idea of the flowerbed is not limited in her ever-free imagination. "For me, certain jewels, through their composition and the color of their stones and enamel, are like the flowerbeds of certain châteaux seen from the sky as you look out of the window of an airplane," she confirms. "As you fly over, the relation between the jewel and landscape is total, like rivers of diamonds, and perfectly describes the visual impression of the sun glimmering on the water or the cities that you see from a plane at night, like molten metal, or as if all of a sudden you had zoomed-out on a set of jewellery." In short, the art of jewellery reflects the art of landscape.

FLOWERS

"This motif is a natural partner for many of the collections I have designed for Dior Joaillerie in the past twenty years; there are wildflowers from *Milly-la-Forêt* (1999) as well as exotic flowers and carnivorous flowers." Victoire understands that ever since ancient times the floral palette has always been closely linked to the very idea of a jewel. She adds, however, her sense of narration and makes the motif come to life; it is not simply set down as a decoration: "When I created *Bal des Roses* (2011), I had in mind the idea of roses getting dressed to go to a ball. There were images that came to me from the ball scenes in *The Leopard* by Luchino Visconti, where Claudia Cardinale is stunning in her crinoline. Like the corolla of a flower, each of these flowers had to have a dress color of its own."

FONTANGES

Mademoiselle de Fontanges, the short-lived but madly loved mistress of Louis XIV, is still known today for her grace and elegance; she even originated a hairstyle that bears her name, "*à la Fontanges*," in which the hair is put up into a sophisticated composition of curls and ribbons. In the collection dedicated to Versailles, Victoire plays with this motif: "The Fontanges bow is a ravishing shape that lends itself perfectly to the design of a jewellery piece."

FRANCE

"I absolutely love France for its craftsmanship, its couture, its classicism, its landscapes and geography—it's an extraordinary country, isn't it? And I am a city girl who loves the sea." We discover an unexpected side of Victoire, who is as fascinated by far-off waters as she is by the land. "The best of nature is to have both of them, the sea and the countryside," according to Victoire. She loves coastlines both here and elsewhere, like the one seen from the clifftops of Granville, where the Dior family villa, like the prow of a ship, whose vast garden had a staggering view of the Channel.

FRUITS

"Fruit offers inspiring shapes, but not really exotic fruit, which is much less Dior... no, the fruit of Milly-la-Forêt, French gardens, and the countryside." Incorporating these fruits—raspberries and cherries—Victoire created exquisite jewels, to which she then added vegetables like turnips and peas from local markets. Playing with small stones and sowing rubies like you would scatter seeds, she again invents family stories, like in botany: "I thought it was wonderful to once again evoke babies with these mini-fruits; I was thinking of harvests, of that idyllic image of Christian Dior going into his garden to pick fruit, fruits of the forest as well, to serve for dessert at a lunch in the country."

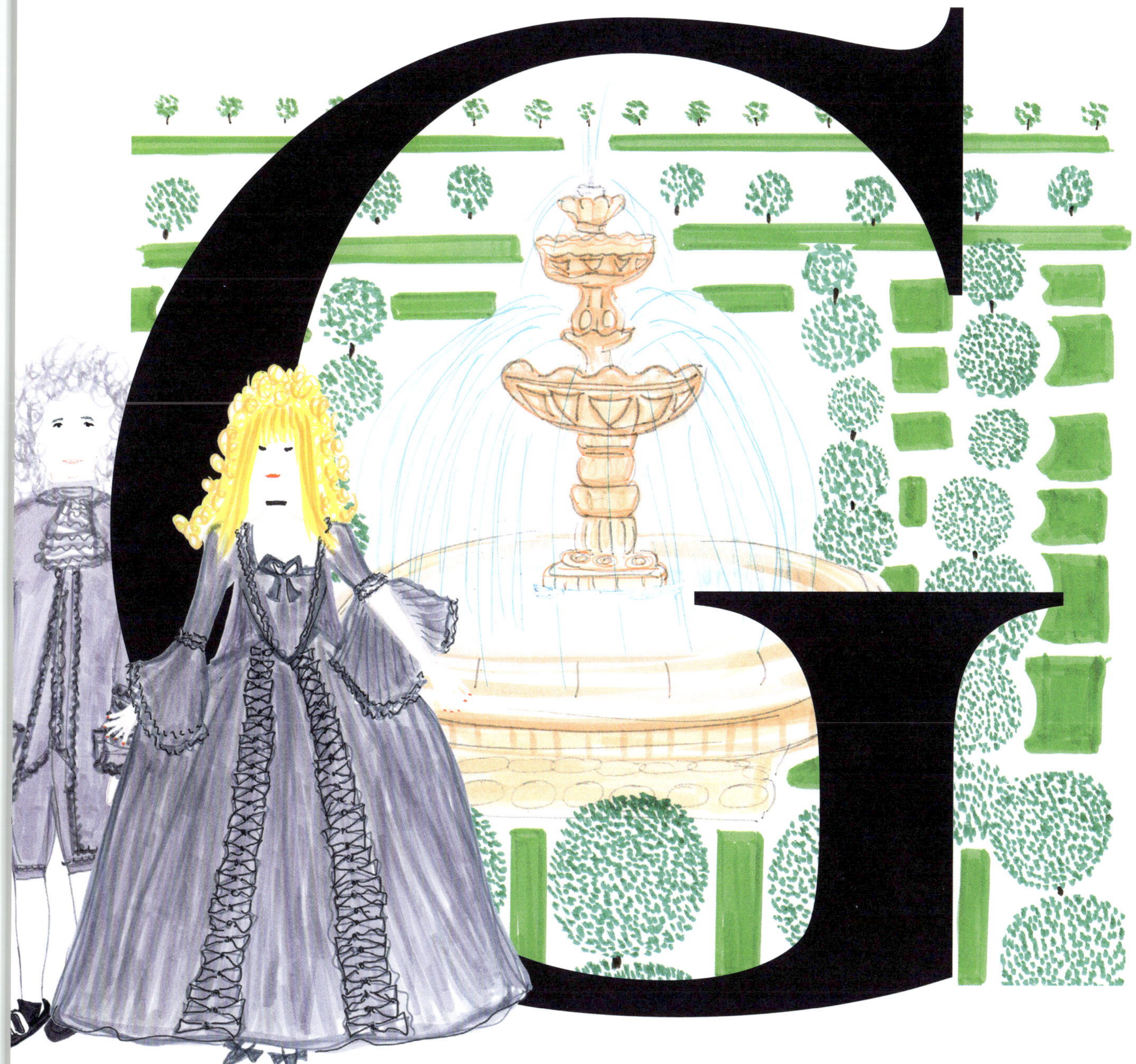
G

GEM DIOR

"In 2019, for my twentieth year working at Dior Joaillerie, I wanted to create a collection leaning toward the abstract, a first for me. It's like an organic abstraction, with nothing arid or dry about it, and it plays with simple shapes, putting them together and taking them apart."

The colorful and visual power of this collection is seductive, conferring an almost cinematic aspect on it. "I wanted to play with the idea of pixelization, as if you were zooming in on the surface of the jewel and obtaining a kind of pixel of the gemstone." The collection is once again a wonderful manifesto for color, for color without the artifice of a setting to protect it from an immediate, direct look. "It's as though I had mixed all my most figurative collections together in a cocktail shaker and they had all come out like this, reorganized and rejointed differently." It is the art of decanting.

GEMS

"Indispensable!" is the first word that comes to Victoire when we talk about gems. "In jewellery, it is all about gems, as much for their form as for their color." When designing, Victoire starts from an idea that she sketches, but she willingly admits, "Even if I never start out with a stone, and depending on my idea, I do sometimes base things on a stone, and sometimes I might even take the color of a stone as a starting point." Gems are simultaneously a passion, a seductive appeal, and the almost secret material behind the creative alchemy.

GENEALOGY

"One day, we will be able to trace the family tree of my jewels, with its roots, its branches, its sets of siblings, all the ancestors and all the descendants. It's an idea to which I am very attached." See *Family*.

GEOMETRY

"I admit that I was rubbish at math at school, and geometry was a closed world to me," laughs Victoire, who has never yet designed purely geometric jewels, even though she has, bit by bit, come to favor simple shapes, cleverly articulated in their design. "In *Gem Dior* (2019) I started to create more abstract forms, and that was a first step."

GIFT BOX

"The gift box reminds me of cases filled with precious objects, stones, and jewels, like the ones you see in films; the box is also what you take away with you—a portable treasure." For Victoire, the gift box also inspires a certain way of working, "a way of offering jewels without enclosing them into a particular theme . . . of creating something at random with a stone that appeals to me or a drawing that comes to me without necessarily feeling the need to include them in an entire collection." A form of liberty, and generosity, too.

GLAMOUR

"I don't often use this word, although it was very important to me in the 1980s, a time when the idea of glamour was everywhere. It was the fashion word par excellence and the perfect adjective," explains Victoire. It is also a word that reflects a bygone Hollywood era of the 1940s and 1950s, when actresses had a certain presence, with innate or very calculated attitudes. "Glamour in 2019 is almost a pastiche—you read the word everywhere, but it doesn't mean much anymore."

GLORY

"What is glory? The honor you gain from it?" asks Victoire, who confesses to being "not very sensitive to honors," preferring to believe that she is the one to confer them. The glory of the vain is not for Victoire, and she almost sees in the word, "something very personal, when I'm happy with a collection, with what it finally represents after months, even years of work. If I think it's good, I feel satisfied, a feeling of glory for myself, it's nothing external at all." In the thread of the conversation, Victoire laughs about it, saying, "I don't think I was looking for glory, or maybe I was after all, a bit, but with my name, it might well be subconscious!"

GOLD

"The finest medium and the most beautiful material for creating a jewel. I love it so much that I have given it every color." See *Lacquer*.

GOURMETTE CHAINS

"One day I wanted to use the gourmette chain motif, but to rethink it, as much for bracelets as for rings." This is also a way of revisiting a neglected type of jewellery by breathing modernity and nobility into it. The principal challenge for curb chain jewellery lay in providing a new vision for the plaque that decorates it: "I wanted to engrave a description of every object, to show every element in the jewel with a precise description, just like the names that used to be engraved on the curb chains."

A colossal task carried out for every piece, making each one of them perfectly unique: "I had them engrave what is usually hidden, the hallmark, the stamp, the figure 750, which signifies 18-karat gold, the finger diameter for the rings, and the serial number." A piece of pure jewellery, like a personal, private reference number, embodies the art of objective description, like a *nouveau roman* text. "It was a genuine production challenge for the ateliers, creating similar pieces that were differentiated from each other by some tiny detail." Luxury, as it were.

GRAND SIÈCLE

"An expression that I like a lot. It conveys in itself glory, but also a sense of balance and of harmony, characteristic of the seventeenth century. It is also the art of French gardens that are still a source of fascination, related to architecture." See *Versailles*.

GRIS-GRIS

When she talks about her work at Christian Dior, Victoire likes to recall the designer's superstitious nature—the little symbols, gris-gris, compass roses, and bees that she enjoyed transforming into charms. She often evokes the protective, benevolent value of jewels: "In my opinion, a jewel is already such an ornament, a sort of protection, to see them and hear them chinking together even has a certain charm."

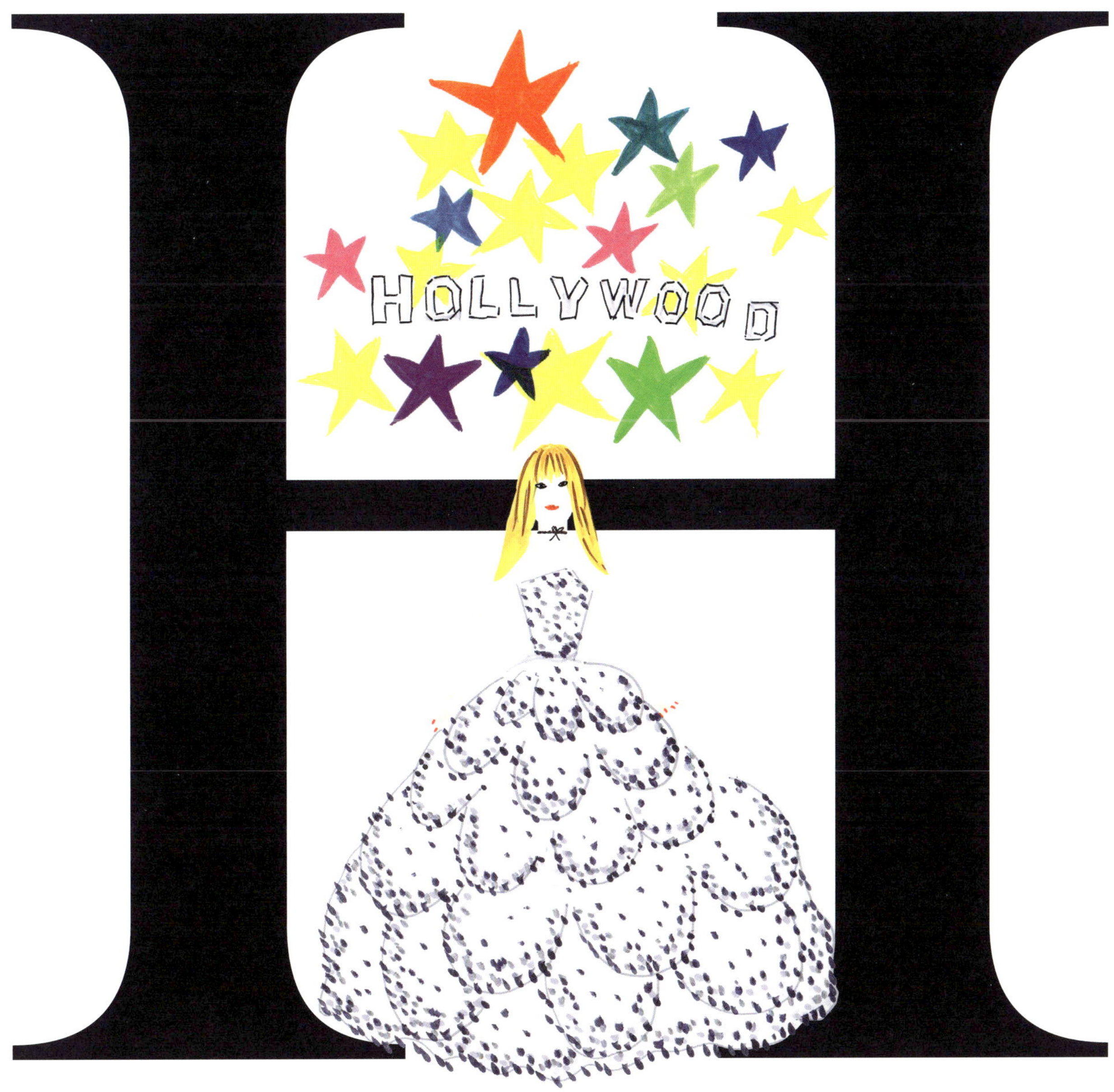
HOLLYWOOD

HAMEAU DE LA REINE

"The *Hameau de la Reine* (the queen's hamlet) is the idea of nature left to its own devices, and that's what I like." At the time of the collection dedicated to Versailles, Victoire liked to draw on them for "a rustic and simple inspiration, full of joie de vivre, and a carefree spirit, beyond the clichés associated with the very image of Marie-Antoinette." Keen on botany and highly observant, she believes that "such a place creates a desire for jewels blended with floral references, easy to wear, bathed in natural light, but with no heady flowers under any circumstances." See *Marie-Antoinette*.

HAUTE COUTURE, HAUTE JOAILLERIE

For a long time, these two words managed without the adjective "haute," which was probably added over time by designers who had no place interfering in these two areas. For Victoire, the best definition is crystal clear: "The idea of a unique creation, where the sense of detail is complete, the lining perfect, is where the work that remains hidden is as elaborate as that which is seen."

In a parallel between haute couture and *haute joaillerie*, the former often highlights the notion of the client, a member of a reserved elite, riddled with codes and secrets. Victoire nevertheless considers that the idea of a typical or regular client for her is "a more fluid category" than it probably is in couture: "I don't necessarily think of clients; in fact, that's why none of my collections resemble each other. I don't believe in the ideal client who has a profile destined to buy my creations."

Similarly, *haute joaillerie* probably does not go out of fashion in the same way: "In an haute joaillerie collection, there is a truly timeless aspect. A fine jewel carries so many feelings and stories that eventually it generally transcends the very idea of being dated; moreover, my collections are not presented with their dates, but with their titles."

HOLLYWOOD

"When I think of Hollywood, the first thing I see is saturated color—Technicolor, musical comedies, and films from the 1950s—along with something naive and innocent, even though there's nothing innocent about Hollywood," recalls Victoire.

Christian Dior loved film and the actresses loved him. They made his dresses into a signature look that remains unchallenged. In Christian Dior's day, the Hollywood stars who shaped the imagination of cinephiles and forged their culture were Marlene Dietrich. Ava Gardner, Olivia de Havilland, and Rita Hayworth. They all soon became clients of Christian Dior, some as early as 1947, the year of the New Look. A knowledgeable cinephile, Victoire does not hide her fascination for the universal imaginative world that Hollywood represents: grandiose destiny, the ups and downs, the commotions, the red carpet, and the spectacular entrances of dethroned screen queens like Norma Desmond, for whom *Sunset Boulevard* (1950) was a painful postscript.

A feel for narration lies at the heart of Victoire's collection for Dior Joaillerie, with its series of fade-outs, tracking, freeze-frames on a detail, and cleverly orchestrated scenarios that bring about surprise and intrigue. Wearing her jewels, women slip into a role without putting on an act: love, passion, irony, drama, and lightness are all played out, depending on whether the characters are mysterious or radiant—whether it's Christina, Queen of Sweden or Cleopatra, a pirate's fiancée or a boisterous agitator, Elizabeth I or Scarlett O'Hara. Describing the *Bal Bleu Nuit* ring without getting lost in a mineralogical description, Victoire narrates the scene: "This ring evokes a situation from a film in which the heroine is running and then grabs her dress to go and meet her lover; she is Scarlett O'Hara."

The power of evocation and the universal appeal of film enables each person to find the right vision. Each precious gem is an exotic journey in itself, whether it is the lost mountains of South America or Asia or torrid mines in Africa: each jewellery set is an adventure into which the woman wearing it leaps. Hollywood is above all the idea that we make of it—the stars, the destinies, the femmes fatales—and this metonymic shift implies both a filmography and a showcase, with Elizabeth Taylor leading the way. More glamour than love. It is also excess, a *Great Gatsby* extravagance not from a distance but on a daily basis; it is a form of familiarity, like the imagined conversations of legendary drama and humor between Victoire's grandmother Sylvia and Barbara Hutton.

A confirmed cinephile, Victoire has fun with the graceful, very Hollywood limit that exists between kitsch and taste—not "good" taste, which should be proscribed, but taste in short, which requires an ounce of bad taste in order for it to touch the sublime. She uses as examples the famous Palais Rose of Boni de Castellane and Anna Gould, which contained works of art by masters, rare pieces of furniture, monumental marble, all with the slight faux pas that appeals. "A touch of tackiness is healthy," stated Diana Vreeland, and her canonical quotation comes down to the same thing: too much good taste can be boring. Hollywood combines high and low for the sake of it, and from this fluctuation stems glamour and chic, style codes that Victoire's attentive and amused eye pierces perfectly.

HUMANISM

"It is impossible for me to detach the human dimension from my jewellery. This type of humanism is a requirement in the very design of the jewel."

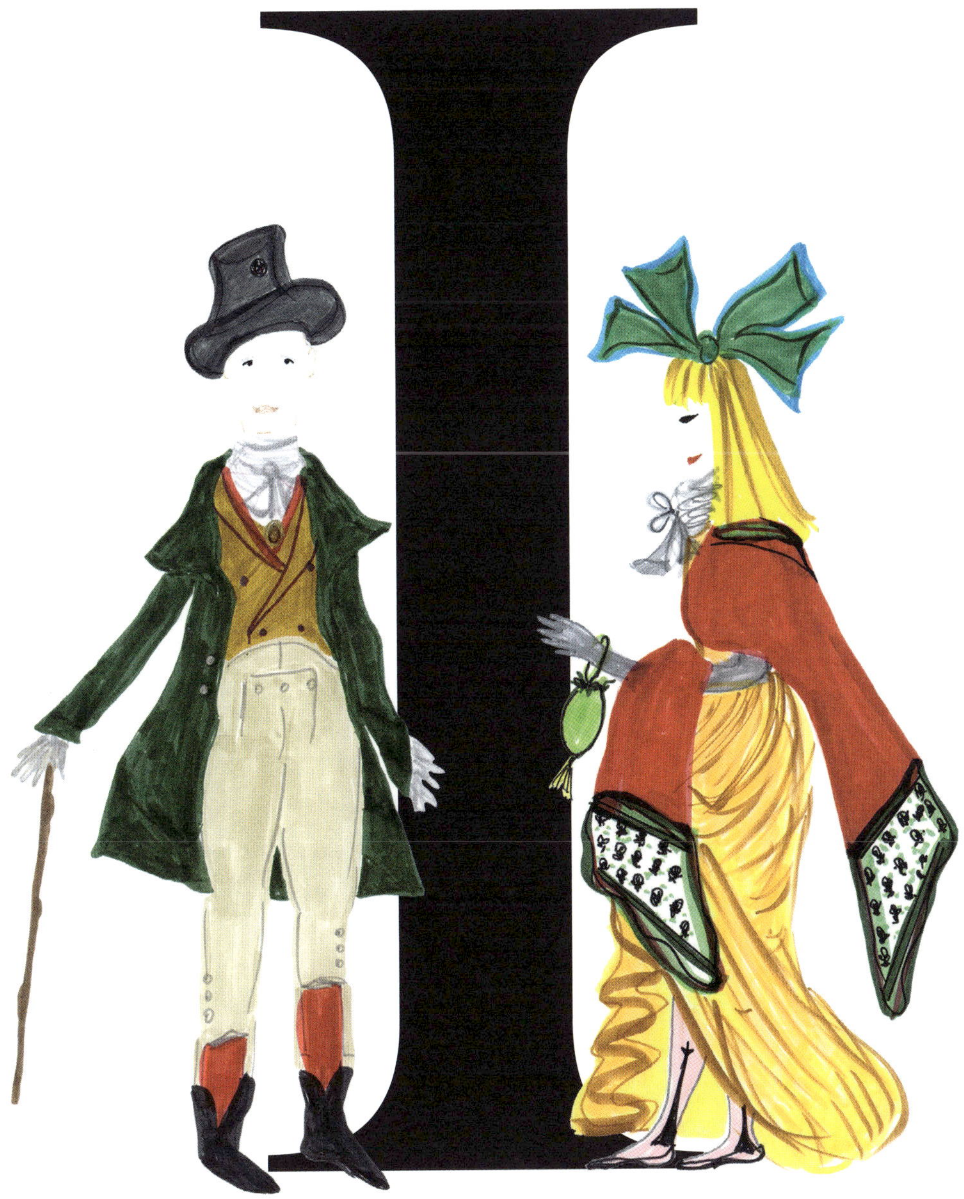
I

IDYLLE

"*Idylle* (2009) is the name of a collection in which I imagined that seven bracelets were given to one and the same person, and that each bracelet was designed in connection to a country she had arrived in." A love idyll is always about travel for Victoire.

ILLUSION

"The illusion setting enables me to value a stone that isn't necessarily important or big in size, but which catches the eye anyway." A master in the art of jewellery, Victoire loves playing with those "things" that enable her to augment the effect of a design, a stone or a setting, and the impression the jewel gives off. Nevertheless, she says, "I don't use optical illusions too much." But this is not for reasons of truth, she is more intelligent than that, instead she says, "I already like to escape from reality. I like to subvert situations and ideas, and so illusion alone doesn't necessarily appeal to me."

IMAGINATION

"The imagination? It's my driving force," states Victoire. "It is powerfully invasive, which probably has a lovely side to it, but it's exhausting, too, because it solicits me all the time with obsessive waves." Any moment her mind is empty mind, it is immediately filled. "The second of boredom is instantly filled in by my imagination. Incessant ideas strike each other, aided by the power of projection. As a result, the imagination is so strong that it doesn't always seem to reflect reality. It is often so much more captivating than reality, that the latter often seems disappointing to me in the end."

Victoire does not deny the salutary aspect of an imagination that enables her to flout ambivalent aspects of life, or of good and evil. The imagination is a narrow escape. "It prevents you from being in the present moment," she says. Victoire remembers having been a "very dreamy child, always in a story that I would tell myself to avoid a reality that saddened me." For a long time, this melancholy of hers has been transcended by her vivid imagination, by these images that are born and give rise to the utmost inventiveness in her jewellery work.

INCROYABLES

The *Incroyables* and the *Merveilleuses* represent two of the most fabulous moments in fashion history, when French society decided to drown its sorrows in splendor and extravagance after the horrors of the Reign of Terror. "The *Incroyables* were jewels, rings in particular, whose dimensions were inspired by the cocktail rings of the 1950s. In a reversal of scale, they reveal a desire to play with exaggeration, excess, and the hierarchy of values." At the same time, John Galliano was delivering couture collections in which bustiers, capelines, and dresses took on monumental dimensions worthy of the fashion excesses of the *Merveilleuses* in 1797–1799. "I said to myself that this excess, this way of revisiting the dimensions of a piece of clothing had an echo in the history of jewellery, and this collection was brimming with folly and a carefree attitude."

INSPIRATION

"It is always difficult for me to describe my inspiration, or my inspirations. It's a driving force within me, related a lot more to feelings than to factual things." Victoire admits, moreover, to the very limited impact of the latter as a source of inspiration. There are of course triggers—"obviously visiting a museum, Gustave Moreau for example, with the sensuality of the faces, those accumulations of chains and necklaces, but in the end it is always highly filtered, never literal. I see an artwork, but that passes and its role is often very limited."

INTERIOR

"The interior of a jewel is to my mind just as important and just as noble as what you can see of the same jewel; it is what comes into contact with the skin, which is also precious, so there is an element of intimacy. In jewellery, it is the appreciable parallel made with couture," recalls Victoire. She is faithful to the idea that frequently comes back to her during the conversation: in an exceptional register, every aspect counts, including what you can guess at and what is hidden, as well as what you can see, and as such, the interior gains her full attention. See *Recto-verso*.

IRIDESCENCE

Once again, Victoire associates this wonderful French word with her favorite stone, the opal, which displays "all the fire of color, a mother-of-pearl element and shell-like iridescence." The light, a subject of constant concern for Victoire, plays a crucial role here: "I am fascinated by the idea that the effect of light, and therefore the stone itself, are never exactly identical." See *Light*, *Opal*.

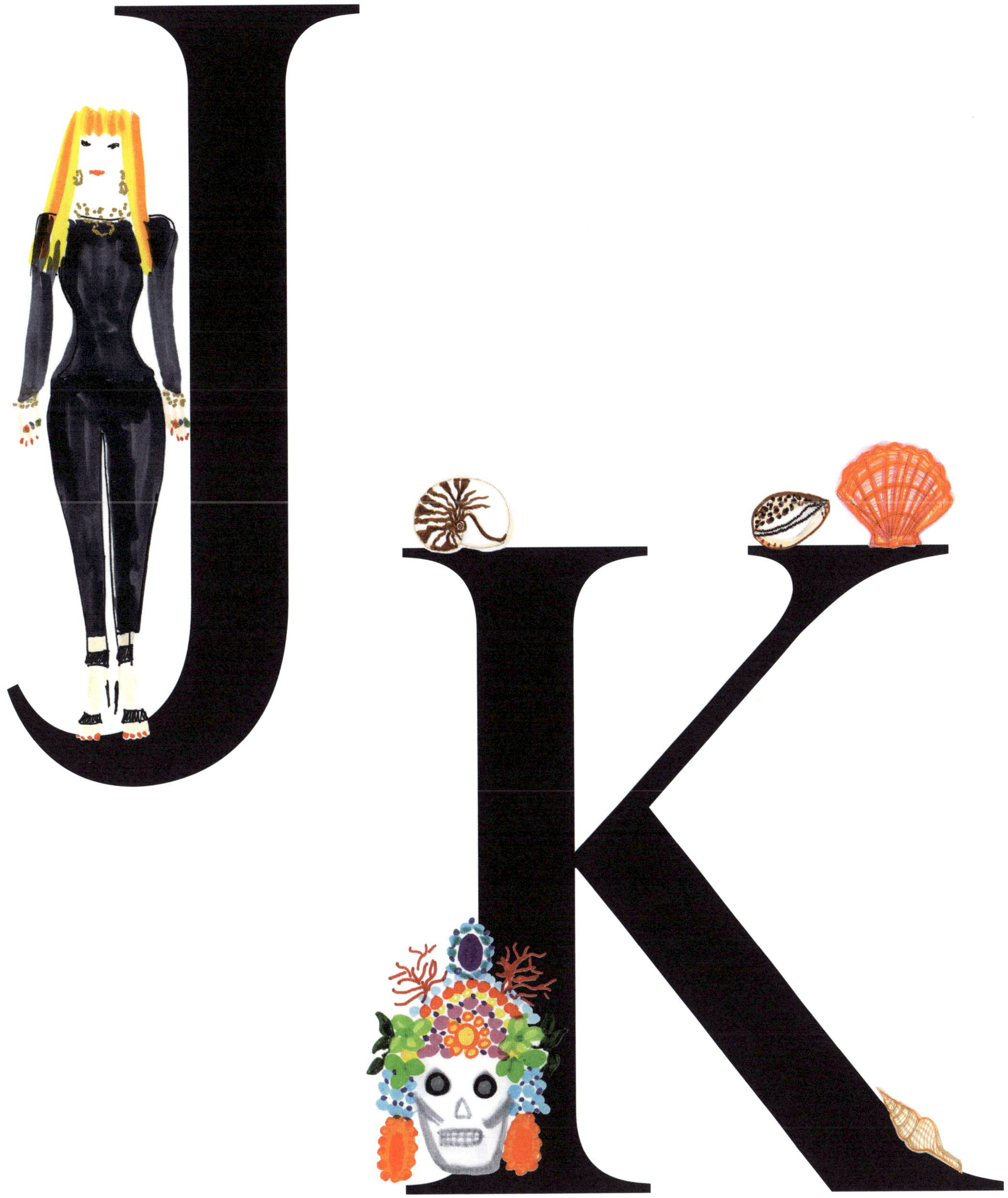
J
K

JEWELS

"Joyful jewels," exclaims Victoire. The word *jewel* is so suggestive and evokes so many images, including the crown jewels, precious stones and jewellery handed down from one French king to the next—even including emperors—which can be drawn on to once again create new jewellery sets and new jewels, the traces of which can be found in Apollo's gallery at the heart of the Louvre museum collections. "*Jewel* is the jewellery word par excellence, but I also love making jewellery that isn't just about inaccessible jewels. And in jewellery I like to explore all levels, from the simplest to the most exceptional." In short, jewels for everyone.

JOAILLERIE

"In a word, jewellery for me is a way of joining together all the lines, the pleasure of creating jewels by playing with all the possible elements. Obviously, jewellery encompasses very technical, complex things, but for me, from the beginning of this adventure, it was the principle of pleasure in creating that motivated me.

KUNSTKAMMER

Wonder rooms, cabinets of curiosities, and natural or artificial treasure rooms, *Kunstkammer* have fascinated connoisseurs since the Renaissance. They were a powerful influence in shaping a major part of European humanist culture, appealing to collectors and to great decorators. The word naturally comes to mind when invoking Victoire's early inspirations and collections. "When I arrived at Christian Dior, I wanted to create jewels without linking them to a specific collection or a particular story." Claiming a terrain of freedom and curiosity, Victoire plays with rare and precious materials. "I created jewels based on cameos, exotic woods, shells, and old things I picked up at flea markets, creating a very personal sort of collection composed of completely unique pieces."

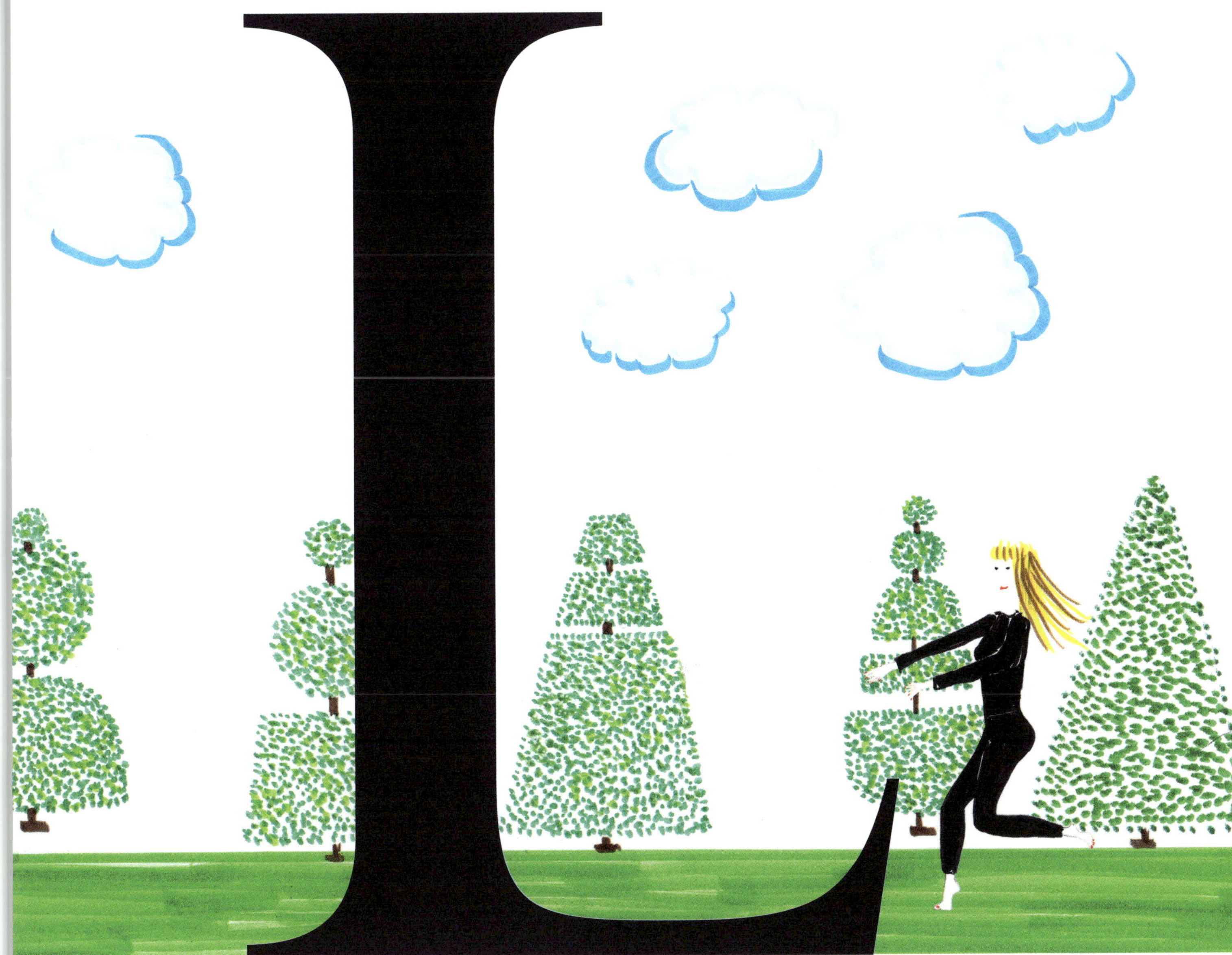
L

LACQUER

"Lacquer for me is the fourth gold color, in other words, all the colors of gold at the same time." For Victoire, lacquer symbolizes her sassy and relevant consuming passion for color. "It was as if I were frustrated at not finding any other gold colors, and so I said to myself that I just had to paint gold to have an apple green gold or a fuchsia pink gold."

A certain classical vision of great jewellery long promoted the primacy of the monochrome, of the white or transparent, depending on your point of view, that characterizes diamonds. Naturally, rubies, sapphires, emeralds, and semiprecious stones also added color to jewellery; while in the nineteenth century in particular, the art of enamel gave rise to other chromatic opportunities. In the space of a few years, supported by research in the Dior ateliers and the enthusiasm of craftsmen for finding new areas for experimentation, Victoire managed to make lacquer into a liberating infrangible technique that enabled her to use an almost unlimited color range. She has currently developed over a hundred shades that she uses with unfeigned joy.

For Victoire, creation is a way of reinventing herself and never tiring of a routine which, in essence, should always be the exact opposite of jewellery. Whereas enamel confers a delicate fragility on a jewel with its translucency, lacquer plays with the opacity of the material and the imperturbable polish of the surface, allowing for daring color palettes. Lacquer's density, which comes from a succession of layers, affirms the fiery colors and inserts them precisely into the composition: it is the long-awaited combination of color and design that closes a lengthy quarrel which began, it is said, with Rubens and Poussin. Lacquer reconciles the two and means that nothing is done inadvertently.

Loved by creators from the 1920s and 1930s, lacquer returns to boundless inventiveness, flirting with illusion and letting us admire spontaneous wild blooms in the *Diorette* (2005) or poisonous ones in *Belladone Island* (2007). It is also freed of all realism, with colors ranging from delicate shades of Louis XV green or antique rose to the most daring fluorescent hues, electric pinks and blues in a post-Warholian riot of color. Both in Pop Art and in New Realism, we know how magnetic the lacquered effect was in sculpture, from César to John Chamberlain. By covering gold or eluding stones, lacquer reminds us that, in the direct lineage of art nouveau, what is precious isn't always a question of rare and costly materials. Lacquer is "color for everyone," detaching itself from the limits of a unique piece. For Victoire, who loves color as much as words, lacquer is a favored field for exploration and challenge.

LE BAL DES ROSES

Along with lily of the valley, the rose is the Dior flower par excellence. "*Bal des Roses* (2011) explores an invented story as, again and again, the Roses go to the ball, dressing up to make their appearance. The settings of these *Bal des Roses* rings are like dresses, and it's as if each dress were designed by Christian Dior for each Rose." The art of jewellery raised to the heights of pure magic. This absolutely splendid collection sees *Bal Vénitien*, *Bal de l'Opéra*, and *Bal Champêtre* wear dresses draped in chrysoprase, chalcedony, and opal.

LE NÔTRE

André Le Nôtre was undoubtedly the king of gardeners as much as the gardener to the king. Victoire was fascinated by the seventeenth century and in her 2017 collection *Dior à Versailles, côté Jardins*, she created several discrete tributes to Le Nôtre. From the monumental to the miniscule, her designs go to great lengths to capture his sense of perspective and graphic love of symmetry—the "very reassuring (aspect) of nature's mastery." On the scale of a jewel, the drawing plays the same crucial role in the composition and structure.

LIGHT

Like a painter, Victoire pays constant attention to the light, judging and gauging its effects to see when it enhances a jewel or when it kills one. Above all, Victoire likes to see "sunlight on jewellery. Light without the sun is always melancholic, and although the light of a cloudy gray sky can look very beautiful on certain sapphires, there's nothing prettier than Mediterranean light on gold jewellery."

LIGHTNESS

"Lightness in jewellery is not only a sensation, it is one of the most difficult aspects of this art—giving shape to a drawing and constructing it in metal without it being weighty." For Victoire, lightness is not an attitude, but a technical concern, that of creating a jewel that will let the skin breathe and the heart beat.

LUXURY

"I still like to think that luxury should be synonymous with quality and rarity, and that luxury is above all a space of liberty, the best of mankind and its skills," says Victoire. The words *fashion*, *haute couture*, and *jewellery* all seem to have been swallowed up by the total and absolute term of *luxury*, an economic reality that is often substituted for a type of lifestyle and type of creation that, since ancient times, has reflected some of the rarest and the most exclusive concepts. "I work in luxury in the most noble sense of the term. The word is very overused these days, but my own luxury is to think that I am in it in this noblest sense."

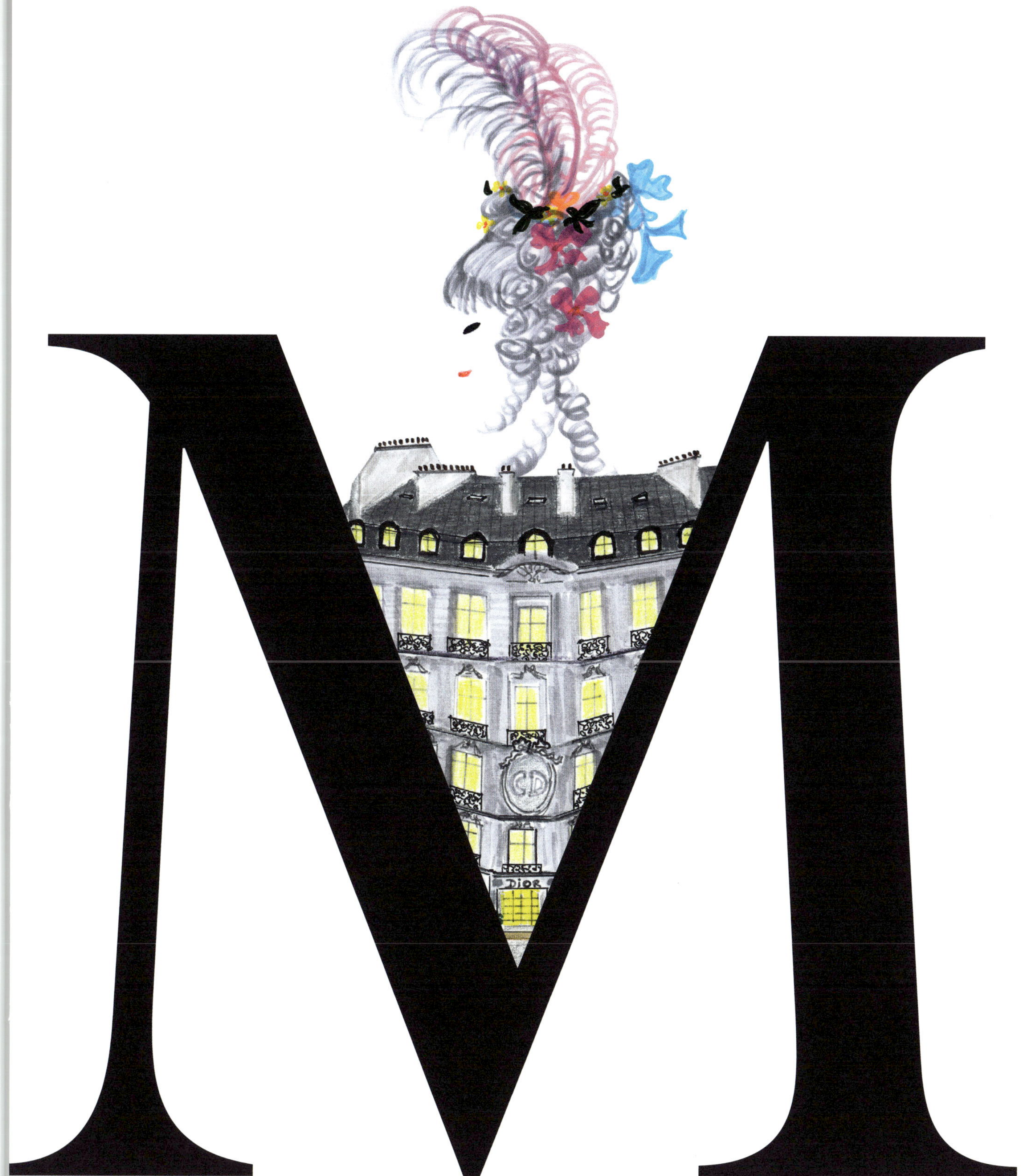
M

MARIE-ANTOINETTE

"I have no particular fantasy in relation to Marie-Antoinette, and I have never been fascinated by the queen," confides Victoire, who had a walk-on part in the 2006 eponymous film by Sofia Coppola. However, the image of the queen is in fact present, and her shadow hovers over certain collections, in particular those inspired by Versailles. Once again, the explanation is crystal clear: "The eighteenth century remains a prime reference and playground—after all, it is a sublime artistic era, so it is true that when I create a collection or design jewellery for a house founded by someone who was fascinated by Marie-Antoinette, it seems obvious to me that I have to take that into consideration in one way or another."

In fact, Christian Dior's fascination with Versailles and for the eighteenth century was very real and deep and nourished a good many of his creations, and so a tribute in jewellery is a natural consequence. With a sparkle in her eye, Victoire says, "It was Marie-Antoinette, so it's there, in the history of the house, but it could have been Sisi."

MARQUETERIE

"Wood or stone marquetry is an absolutely fascinating artisanal technique, and it is related to architecture, decor, and furniture, which really appeals to me." In the collection dedicated to Versailles, it becomes a marquetry of precious stones, revealing the mastery of the ateliers and the craftsmen.

MAXIMUM

"The maximum? For me it doesn't exist, for there are no limits." See *Minimum*.

MÉLANGE

"Personally, the idea of a mélange is the very idea of creation," admits Victoire, who likes ideas that get mixed up, giving rise to other creative sparks. Above all, isn't a mélange a blend of elite taste and popular culture, of high and low? "The ideal mélange is one of stones that look like a bouquet of flowers. It's above all a mélange of colors, like boxes of Caran d'Ache coloring pencils or toys jumbled up in a toy box."

MERVEILLEUSES

"The *Incroyables* and the *Merveilleuses* (French dandies of the late eighteenth century) are intertwined, both in history and in my jewels, with audacity, exaggerated sizes, and a feeling of freedom and humor that brims with life." See *Incroyables*.

MILLY CARNIVORA

"*Milly Carnivora* (2008) are the children of *Belladone* that I created six months after the *Belladone Island* collection (2007), like the children that would have grown up in a greenhouse of carnivorous flowers in Milly-la-Forêt," points out Victoire. The collection houses strange sibling flowers with vivid colors, shimmering lacquer, and astonishing organic shapes, as well as with the *Poisonus* earrings and necklace like splashes of incredible vegetation. Victoire plays with magic gemstone seedlings of tsavorite garnets, rubellites, citrines, amethysts, peridots, and yellow tourmalines. And her humor runs through the delightful names she calls her pieces: *Milly Carnivora, Egratigna Angélique, Chipie, Mangatus Pistache Fraise,* and *Orange Réglisse*. The carnivorous flowers, opening and closing, then eat little insects as they move. "Creating them in jewellery required the use of discreet, secret mechanisms to make the jewels mobile," Victoire elaborates. It's enough to entrap your heart.

MILLY-LA-FORÊT

"The name of a fairy tale," responds Victoire without a moment's hesitation. This little village in the Île-de-France region, a few leagues from Fontainebleau, with its châteaux and its rocks, is associated with Christian Dior, who in 1947 purchased a house there, the Moulin du Coudret, with the fruits of his early success. Here, one cannot forget his friend Jean Cocteau, who discovered and decorated a wonderful house that is now a museum. "Milly-la-Forêt has a carefree feeling, an idea of friendship, an idyllic vision of happy weekends in the postwar years spent playing cards, reading, enjoying the gardens, and nature left to run free. This spirit of freedom and lightness inspired many of my collections for Dior Joaillerie, the floral repertory, the wildflowers, and certain fruits from countryside orchards or market gardens that have no exoticism."

And as so often for creatives, the idea that you have of a place is more essential that the place itself, as Victoire mischievously confesses: "Milly-la-Forêt? I've never been there. I saw a sign on the road indicating the way, and the idea is enough to inspire me. For me, it's one of the magical names that composes the final very short story of Christian Dior. Ten years, like a magical parenthesis of lunch with friends, echoes of Venetian balls, and later the home at la Colle Noire." For Victoire, the very Proustian poetry of place names, means associating Milly-la-Forêt with "the best of that era."

MIMIOUI

"*Mimioui* (2001) is the smallest ring in the world, a miniscule diamond worn on the finest possible chain, designed as a lingerie-jewel, one that you could even slip on beneath another, dressier ring." And as we know, Victoire likes a family story, so she couldn't help but create *Maxioui*, "as her older sister, with a bigger diamond."

MIMIROSE

"*Mimirose* (2019) is the younger cousin of both *Mimioui* (2001) and *Rose des Vents* (2015)—it's another family story," laughs Victoire, making use of a metaphor that is not just anecdotal. *Mimirose* borrows features from each collection, taking the slenderness and color effects of *Mimioui*'s precious stones and the beaded settings of *Rose des Vents*. *Mimirose* is like the continuation of this light spirit that Victoire is fond of above all else.

MINIATURE

Victoire likes to think that "jewels are little miniature treasures that you can take with you." Far from being pejorative, it's the word that, in her opinion, defines the meticulous and precious work involved and is the impression of containing the world in a few millimeters of beauty and jewellery, in numerous dreamlike materials that you can admire yourself."

MINIMUM

"I don't know who decides on the minimum, it's ultra-subjective and too reductive," says the woman who dares to do everything in jewellery. She rightly emphasizes that minimum and maximum come together both in their radical aspects and in their excesses. "You can be a maximalist with a single jewel," Victoire reminds us, "and you can be less than minimum and completely insignificant with many jewels." And as with anything you are looking at, it's a question of point of view. "Whether minimalism or maximalism, it always worries me that people take these words literally to define their style or their lifestyle. After all, that only gives rise to conformism." See *Maximum*.

MITZAH

"To have one day said, 'My florist is Cartier,' is already genius in itself, isn't it?" Victoire had to meet Mitzah at some point in time. Bathed in mystery, Mitzah Bricard was one of history's major fashion muses. During his pioneering years, she accompanied Christian Dior with panache and brio, helping him craft the house's image. She and Christian Bérard formed a mischievous artistic duo, surrounding the couturier with their advice and enthusiasm.

Staggeringly elegant—described in a Parisian idiom of the day as "filthy chic" in a fine oxymoron that has barely been bettered since—Mitzah Bricard was a fairy with the name of a French locksmith, who knew how to open every ultrafeminine secret of the New Look. Christian Dior had complete trust in her sense of style and saw her as the most apt person to detect chic, or what he called "that indefinable, somewhat old-fashioned thing." "I love the idea of these women who were completely obsessed by the idea of chic, and that chic was like a continent that you instinctively explored," says Victoire.

What she likes about Mitzah "is the very couture spirit of the 1950s, always concerned with elegance and detail at any time of the day." Mitzah knew how to add a killer accessory, emphasize a look with a revealing detail, or strengthen her appeal with a graphic makeup look. Louise Dahl-Wolfe and Cecil Beaton immortalized her in astonishingly similar poses: regal bearing, chin up, neck majestically offered, ready to welcome rows of pearls. For her hats and coats, dresses and stoles, she had a predilection for leopard print—the taste of audacious women.

"In a René Gruau illustration of Mitzah, I always liked the detail of her hand on top of the animal's paw. A leopard-print silk square worn as a bracelet, to hide a scar, so they said, and so a secret or a mystery. I love wild animals and big cats, for the mesmerizing aspect of watching them in movement and their protective side too." In a shift characteristic of fashion, it is as much the woman in the flesh as the slender-fingered hand of René Gruau's drawing that have gone down in posterity, with this hand confidently and seductively placed on the spotted paw of the feline. For this now-legendary hand, Victoire de Castellane created her own variations in honor of Mitzah, in the polysemic claw that sets a citrine or an amethyst on a ring, the surface of the stone making the gold-spotted, fur-print enamel even wilder. The *Mitza* collection (2003) is a masterful and metonymic work in which the feline, under the influence of a spirited drawing that has no cause to be jealous of René Gruau's earlier work, is summed up with two of its body parts: the paw ending in a lacquered black tail whipping swiftly through the air like a comma. Two parts making a whole. "You can never fully describe the physical perfection and the absolute beauty of these big cats," recalls Victoire, who knows better than anyone how predators covet beauty.

MONOCHROME

Following a new path in her work toward a type of abstraction, Victoire's most recent collections for Dior Joaillerie jubilantly venture into monochrome territory, with, for example, *Gem Dior* (2019), which marked her twentieth year of creating for the house. "Each piece becomes a color in itself," she says, which led her to be "even more exacting about the quality of the stones and to find perfect stones to brave the radical aspect that monochrome color imposes." In this new vein, the stone has to provide the ideal surface and depth for the density of a single color, "and there, once again for me, it's about playing, even in this work of patience and research, which is both graphic and chromatic, my work is motivated by this game over and over again." See *Color*.

MONTAIGNE

"For me, it's Christian Dior Avenue," exclaims Victoire, summing it up perfectly. It is the legendary address par excellence, where Christian Dior established the house when he launched it in 1946 at number 30. It was the birthplace of what would go on to become an empire, with its neoclassical decors thanks to his friend Victor Grandpierre, its ateliers, and the salons where the first show was held for the New Look in 1947. This discreet, perfectly proportioned building sums up Christian Dior's style, his culture, and his sense of beauty. "There isn't a Christian Dior street in Paris is there? It makes you think…" recalls Victoire, a stone's throw from the avenue that nevertheless bears the name of the writer who best defined friendship as "Because it was he, because it was I" (*Essays of Michel de Montaigne*, 1580).

MUSEUMS

Victoire is a curious person who likes to roam. A traveler at heart, too, of real countries and imaginary ones. Museums lend themselves to nourishing visits: "I like certain museums that house wonderful collections of jewellery, especially antique jewellery." Although the prizewinners do not hold any meaning for creators who know how to make honey from any discovery that makes an impression on them, Victoire nostalgically remembers the former Acropolis museum, nestled among the majestic ruins. "I have always enjoyed walking around the galleries of certain museums, the Musée des Arts Décoratifs in Paris for example, or the Victoria and Albert Museum in London. I am fascinated by the Museum of Natural History in New York, with its impressive minerology collections, or the labyrinthine Archaeological Museum of Naples, where the refined and archaic aspect of the collections appeals to me." And then there are the great classics, too, "with a predilection for period rooms, those bubbles of time, like the decor of the room from the Palazzo Sagredo, conserved at the Metropolitan Museum, and where the mind is free to dream."

MY DIOR

"This collection (2012) takes up the canework motif, like a golden mesh," says Victoire. The interlaced motifs perfectly express strengthening links. "I also play with the homonym, *My Dior Maille Dior*, in a very light way." See *Canework*.

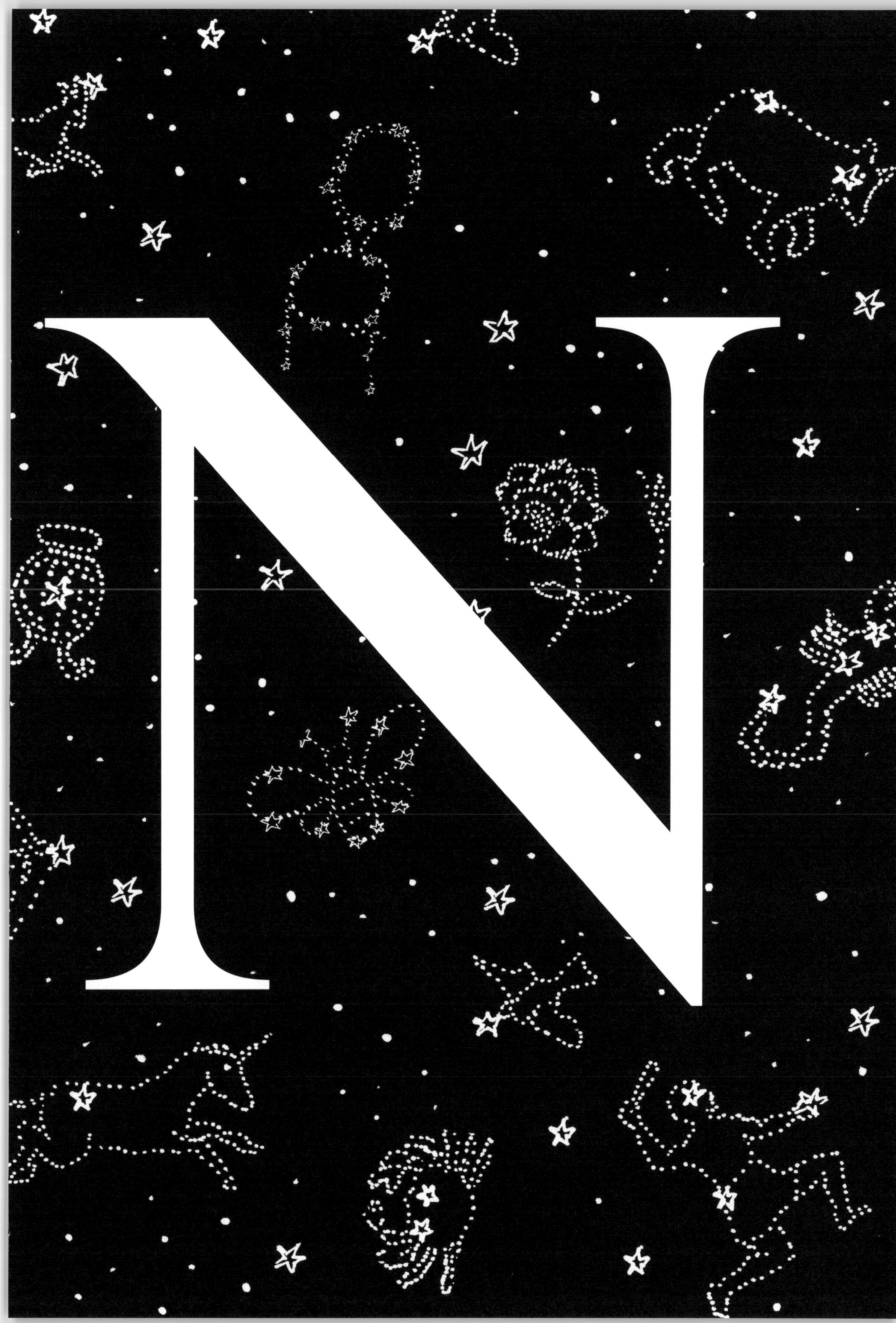
N

NARRATION
"As a child, I loved having stories told to me, so I would listen with my full attention and even now, I have the impression that it is the only time that I am able to concentrate for a long period of time," confesses Victoire, who in her work, however, demonstrates outstanding concentration. Narration serves both to inspire and to relate the process that leads Victoire to create a collection or a new chapter in a long adventure. It is also a gift, and each collection weaves a story, with suspense, diversions, happy conclusions, and mysterious developments. "Yes, I love stories, I get lost in them when I'm creating my jewellery."

NATURAL
"Natural stones are a passion for me, and the essence of my work lies in the mineral kingdom in all its splendor or its modesty. Working with natural stones is like a gift from nature, the height of luxury in jewellery."

NEW LOOK
On February 12, 1947, when Christian Dior presented his very first haute couture collection, the expression "New Look," exclaimed by Carmel Snow, editor of *Harper's Bazaar*, was immortalized. In two words, she had embodied the revolution of form and fashion.

"The New Look was the idea of a new silhouette and a new style, with this excessive use of fabric, tens of yards of it, just after the war. From my early collections I wanted to create my own New Look in jewellery, like a new silhouette for jewels, with exacerbated volumes, substituting gold and the generous use of numerous stones, for the textiles of Christian Dior's era. And to return to a comparable freedom of form."

NIGHT
"I always notice that jewellery settings, even the most sumptuous ones, disappear when you look at them at night. The night gives stones their full place. Depending on the light, or lights, stones reveal a changing personality."

NO
"A word I never hear in our jewellery ateliers, for everything is possible there." See *Oui*.

NOCES DE SANG
"In the *Fiancée du Vampire* collection (2002), I wanted to create a necklace of roses and thorns that would enlace the neck in a very romantic way, like the forest of thorns that the prince has to confront in *Sleeping Beauty*," Victoire tells us. The necklace is definitely romantic; it even has a gothic tone, in the Gothic Revival sense, like something evoked by the English gothic novel, by Mary Shelley or William Beckford, or the most disturbing fairy tales. Although Victoire can express her art in an extremely precise and specific naturalist register, *Noces de Sang* stems from a design that has a degree of austerity, where leaves and rosebuds are evoked in a highly elliptical manner, making the branch from which thorns are almost absent, exquisitely strange. The rosebud is echoed by a ruby tear, like a drop of blood blossoming from a secret wound. This is one of Victoire's most emblematic pieces of the work, showing that she is capable of taking inspiration from a narrative while sidestepping the tale to provide a necklace without flourishes or trivial details.

NOUGAT
In our minds and in literature as well—Balzac and Baudelaire, Maupassant and Fitzgerald—gems and jewellery are often associated with a fondness for food. With her *Nougat* (2003) Victoire goes even further, fascinated and amused by the idea of obtaining the impression of "molten gold that runs into soft and generous forms, working with it as though it were always molten, giving this formless feeling to jewellery form." Humor is never far away from Victoire's attention, as she seeks new forms by letting her mind

wander and play, always play, even evoking, in the very rare art of a successful alliance between luxury and visual culture. For her, it is "the golden and appetizing honey of Winnie the Pooh in the cartoons."

NUIT BLANCHE

"It's the romantic pendant from the *Premier Bal* necklace, as if you had changed your outfit in the middle of the night, and the necklace has a bow that has come loose, undone—is it due to fatigue, the dancing, or sensual abandon? Anyway, the *Nuit Blanche* necklace, one of my first couture jewellery necklaces, evokes a moment of letting go and of sensuality during one of these balls that I like to imagine in their splendor and their surprises."

NYMPHEAS

The *Nymphéas* par excellence are those of Claude Monet, and in 2007, the rooms at the Orangerie museum in Paris served as a showcase for the *Belladone Island* collection (2007), under the leadership of Eric Troncy. The exhibition made an impression. "When I see the *Nymphéas* collection, I think of that fascinating blue opal. There was nothing gratuitous in the choice of this place for me, as the opal, my favorite stone, is an impressionist stone." See *Belladone Island*.

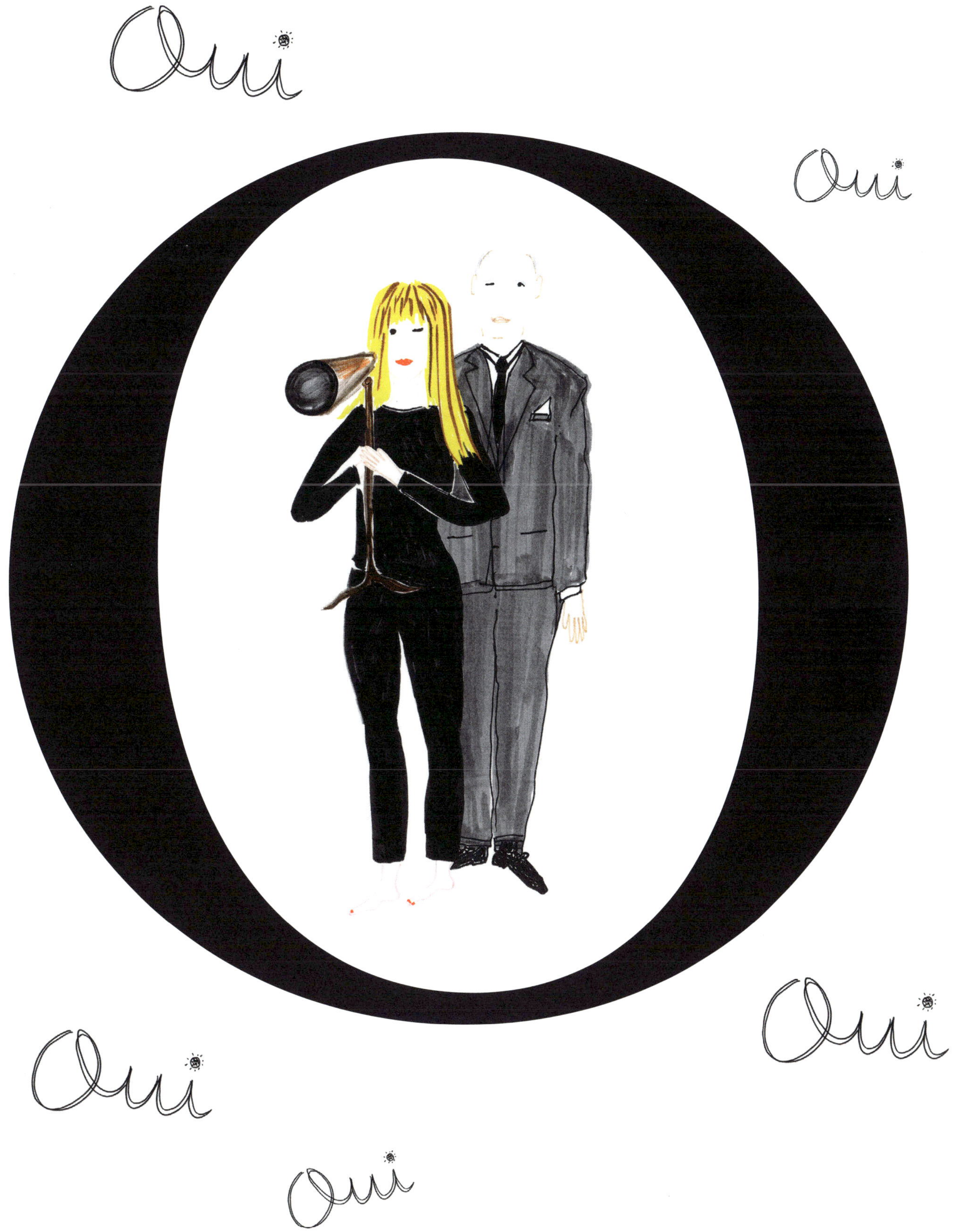
Oui
Oui
Oui
Oui
Oui

OBSERVATION

"I spend my life observing others, observing places and situations. In general, I prefer to observe than to speak." This manner of defining herself, in all honesty, echoes concentration, another aspect of her profession in which "we are obliged to concentrate on every detail to avoid any irreversible mistakes." Is Victoire part concentration and part dissipation? "Observation and concentration are quite the opposite waves of imagination that constantly assail me." See *Imagination*.

OPAL

"Every stone in one stone, it's an ideal form," is how Victoire defines the opal, *her* stone among stones, "as though all the art of nature was crystallized in one stone." The opal represents iridescence and the nuances of the oceans, punctuated by green islands, pieces of land seen from the sky, forest foliage and the undulations of giant trees in Amazonia. "This stone was long scorned, through fantasy and through a mistake of appreciation, it was the object of powerful and superstitious rejection in certain cultures." This very fragile stone is difficult to cut, so opal is little used. "For me, the opal embodies absolute fascination for a stone, it is elusive, mysterious and changing, between pure artifice, and the most remarkable nature."

ORGANZA

"It's the couture material par excellence," says Victoire about a fabric so delicate it needs to be used with subtlety. In the *Archi Dior* collection (2014), she remembers playing with the affinities between couture and architecture—something that Christian Dior was so fond of—to create a jewellery collection under the elementary and audacious motto of "Let's make it as light as organza!"

ORNAMENTATION

"The decor is the freedom that we give the setting," and ornamentation is its consequence. In the drawing, ornamentation is also a field given over to innumerable details, but Victoire admits that ornamentation has to be controlled, especially as, with the passing years, she is more willing to take an abstract path. See *Abstraction*.

OUI

Over the course of a few years, the *Oui* ring (2005) designed by Victoire has become a legendary wedding ring. "What always fascinated me about seeing someone wearing a wedding ring was the thought that this person had said Yes." And so the word inspired what she prettily calls "a ring for love" and, she says, by writing these three letters "it was the power of this word that I wanted to emphasize."

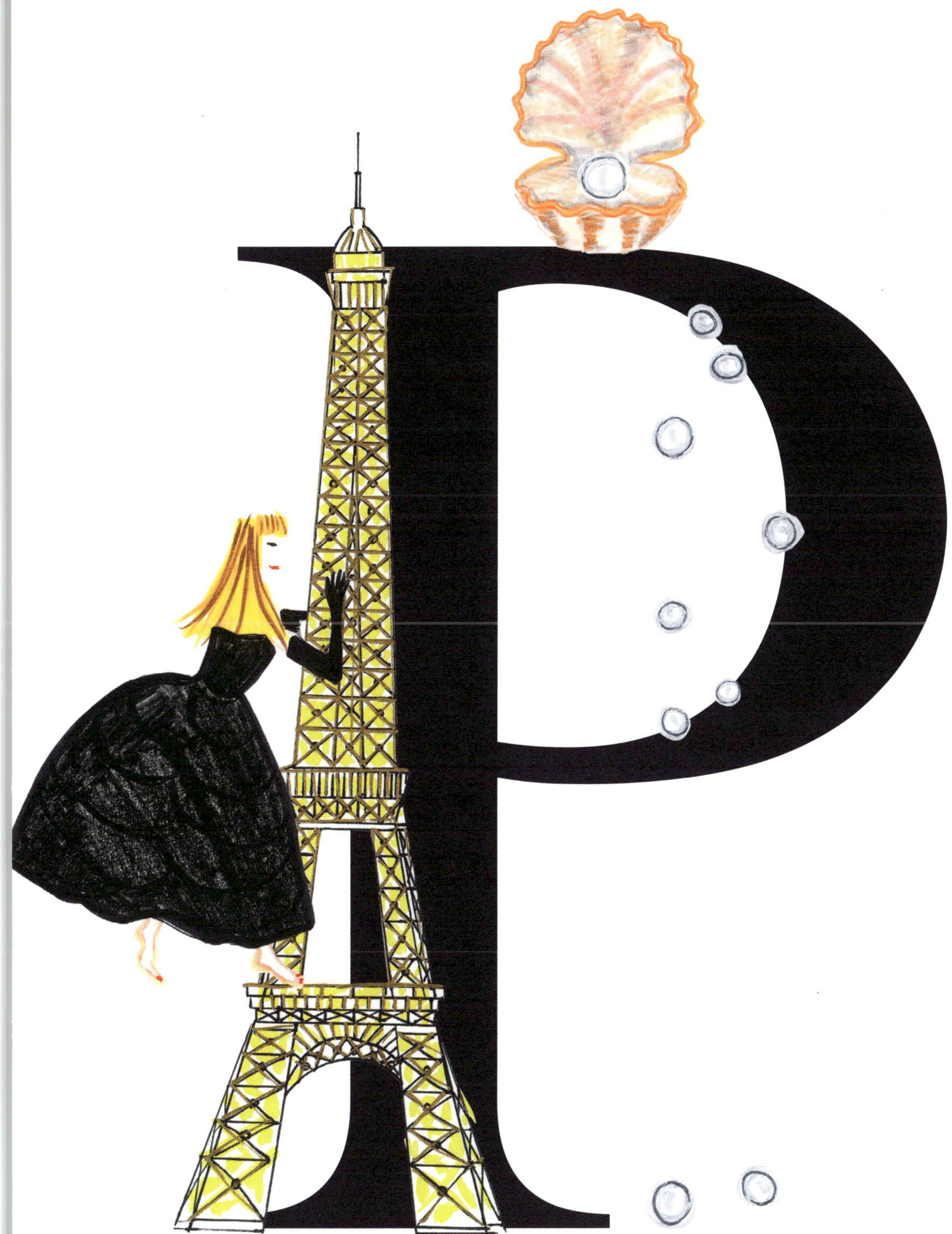

PARAIBA

"In the early 2000s, when this exceptional tourmaline was discovered in a mine in Brazil, I was instantly captivated." Victoire doesn't hesitate to classify Paraiba tourmaline alongside opal, in the category of stones that she likes to use more than any other. "Paraiba looks like a would-be transparent turquoise, it's like an idealized sea color, and its neon blue effects are incredible. It's the color of freedom," she admits. "I use it whenever I can, for its unique, fascinating color."

PARIS

"Paris is inextricably a city of creators. I have never lived anywhere other than Paris," notes Victoire. "In my opinion, Paris truly lends itself to creation. Perhaps that's changing a bit, but for a long time Paris was the city that had the time to create, to wander around, and I still believe that the city fully lends itself to that, it's where I draw and imagine things, and my spirit roams."

PEARLS

"I adore pearls, all pearls, not only the perfect round ones. I love them all, from the most sophisticated to the least polished." Victoire says this hungrily, and you feel that pearls are important to her among the most spontaneous of crazes in the vast world of gems and jewellery. "The tears of Venus are fascinating, their interaction with the skin, and the immediate sensuality of their seductive appeal." This fascination leads her to unearth pearls in painting: "Vermeer, Caravaggio, in all the paintings of the old masters, pearls are like magnets, and my eye has fun finding them. It's a rare pleasure for me to find them in paintings by Ingres for example." His portraits of women fulfill Victoire's appetite for the history of jewellery in every aspect: "The way in which his models wear the jewellery is very modern, I love their hands covered in rings on every finger." "Then, this sensual aspect of pearls seems to appear in certain paintings where they themselves don't actually appear, such as the *Demoiselles des bords de la Seine,* by Courbet." We examine the painting: no pearls, only a gold bracelet that shines at the wrist of one of the two courtesans, but their pale, pearly skin is painted like the surface of a pearl.

An anecdote tactfully tells of Victoire's love of pearls: "I made myself a very large ring in the shape of a heart made of pearls—it was really simple, a really simple ring. And then I had to let it go. I found out later that Yves Saint Laurent had bought it and then given it to his mother. I was touched by that."

PERFUME

"I never wear perfume," specifies Victoire, although some of her jewellery creations give off such a heady sensation that one might, for a moment, have thought the opposite. In the register of Baudelaireian correspondences, however, perfume and jewellery are not necessarily dissociated in Victoire's mind. "Wearing perfume is like an additional gesture, it's almost one step too far, and my last gesture in the morning is to choose the necklace or bracelet I'm going to wear for the day, it's never applying perfume. Perfume can in fact often be harmful to certain precious natural materials, certain stones or pearls for example. For some women, a touch of femininity lies in a drop of perfume applied to the nape of the neck, or behind the ear, whereas I still prefer to hang a pair of earrings there." Metonymy has never before been handled with such charm in carrying out certain gestures: "For me, a jewel is a perfume like any other."

PLEATS

The subtle pleats of the *Archi Dior* collection (2014) mark the collection with a lightness brimming with ease that characterizes Victoire's art. "The pleats are always easy to draw, but much harder to work with, especially with gold, which definitely isn't the best material to use." This decorative motif is among those delightfully borrowed by Victoire from the couture repertory, in a very subtle, graceful correspondence that seems natural between fashion and jewellery. "I played with the models created by Christian Dior based on some of his dresses from the very beginning, the New Look, and I decided to work only on this detail, like an architectural ornament." Victoire often creates her jewellery collections in the same way that a musician has fun with scales on a musical riff, searching through it and varying it.

PLUMETIS
In the delicate register of transposing a technique or a visual effect from couture into jewellery, *plumetis* is a raised satin stitch in embroidery that creates subtle reliefs through padding. "*Plumetis*, in my jewellery creations, is above all a play on the texture of tulle, like the *Dior Dior Dior* collection (2018), but also in certain linings of pieces from the *Cher Dior* collection (2013), like little dots on embroidered tulles."

POISON
"Although *Poison* is the name of a Dior perfume, for me it evokes *Belladone* (2007) above all, with its poisonous, dangerous flowers. But they don't contain mortal poison, as jewellery clothes them in other qualities, like a love potion." See *Toxic*.

POLYCHROMATISM
"With hindsight, over almost twenty years, it seems obvious that polychromatism is one of the leitmotifs of my collections." And when talking of color, Victoire seems to evoke an alchemy like the creation of a recipe, speaking of it in precise gastronomic terms: "I dose the colors to find a balance that won't cancel them out, but which will, on the contrary, heighten them all. It is continually evident in my work," she says. Concluding, she asserts, "I don't deny myself anything in color."

PRECIOUS
"Precious, like precious stones. The *Précieuses* (2006) form a sort of classic, where I used four center stones as strong, generous values with very couture-style settings inspired by Christian Dior's garden," Victoire tells us. In doing so, she has invented a suite of mini-*Incroyables*, a collection that makes use of key Dior references.

PREMIER BAL
"The *Premier Bal* necklace corresponds to the idea of a necklace with a perfectly tied bow in a very classical style. Here, a ribbon bow is created by a little trompe l'oeil effect, with the red satin of the ribbon seen through a ruby lining—it's a feat of jewellery." See *Nuit Blanche*.

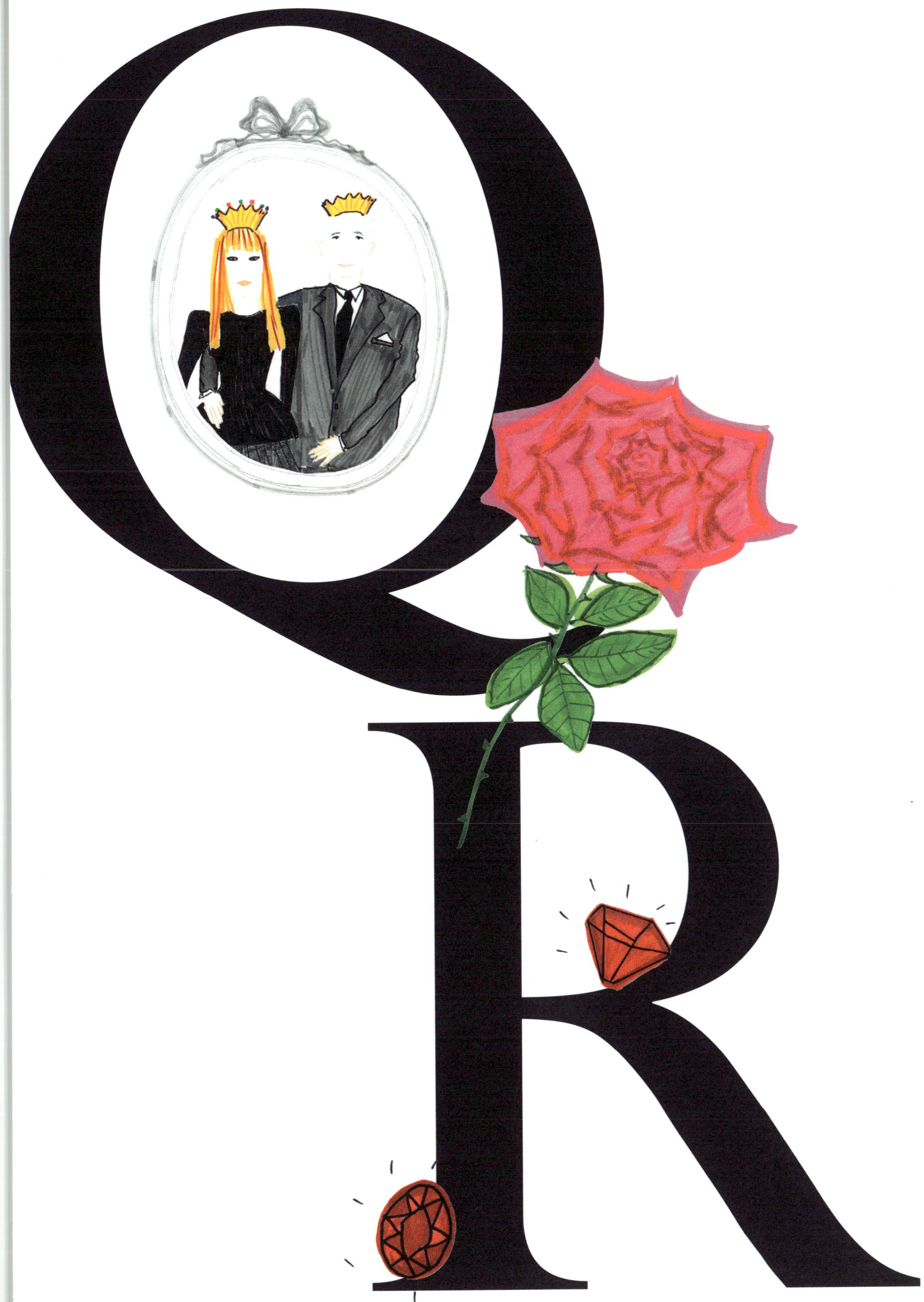
Q
R

QUALITY
"Quality is *haute joaillerie*'s obsession, the quality of the stones and materials used, the quality of the designs, the quality of the execution and finish, the quality of the jewelers' and ateliers' work," Victoire emphasizes. The word is everywhere, to the point where it is a given, and there is no longer even any need to mention it. "For me, it's intimately associated with the pursuit of that perfection that's the object of all our desires."

QUESTIONS
"When starting any new collection, I always ask myself what is, to me, the ultimate question: 'Will this piece still appeal to me in two years?'—which is the amount of time it takes to produce a collection, from the design to it being finished in the ateliers. It's almost as important as the question of whether it will appeal, full stop," Victoire underlines.

In a creative world of which we may sometimes wonder whether it is asking all the (right) questions, Victoire seems to forge ahead by asking herself the most basic questions, the ones that allow her to create in a spirit of freedom and calm. Asking yourself questions often allows you to eliminate them as you go along. "It's also what means that you stop asking them, the work is finished when I don't have any more questions, because I've asked myself all of them before."

RECTO-VERSO
"As yet, I have never made a jewel that can be worn on two sides. It's an extremely difficult exercise," says Victoire, "but I like the idea of working on a pendant which, as it moves with the body, means that it often needs to be beautiful recto-verso." Victoire is often moved by the idea that the underneath, the hidden and secret face of a jewel, should be as beautiful as that which is offered up to the eye, a principle shared with the world of couture. In addition to the sense of sight, we can consider that of touch. The idea of a recto-verso includes a tactile, sensual dimension. Victoire explains that "a jewel is looked at and touched before it is even worn or displayed."

REINES ET ROIS
See *Crowns*.

RIBBON
"As a little girl I hated wearing ribbons, but I have to admit that playing with ribbon is quite marvelous and the motif has given me true freedom in my search for shapes. There is something very graphic about it that I find amusing to draw," emphasizes Victoire, who several times has created variations on ribbons in pieces like *Dernier Bal* and *Nuit Blanche* (1999). The element of fun lies in the fact that the ribbon can also be untied and abandoned—the subject of stories she loves. For Victoire, a woman who loves finding traces of jewellery in paintings, the ribbon at the neck of Édouard Manet's scandalous Olympia, which even inspired Michel Leiris to write a book dedicated to it, leaves nobody indifferent. The ribbon, like an ancient jewel, is linked to popular cultures as well as to an entire tradition of classical jewellery.

ROCOCO
Although the neoclassical imprint is deeply etched within the historical heritage of the house of Dior, rococo is more like a disheveled, turbulent cousin. In the eighteenth century in particular, the style was a house reference, and it provided Victoire with a range of sources and decorative ornaments that punctuate specific pieces, especially her more unbridled floral designs. "It isn't necessarily my most frequent source of inspiration, but the word has always appealed to me. It's an amusing word, one that you could almost pronounce in a cheeky way, like Arletty would. I like its very popular resonance, the rock music side of the thing and the stony side, too." Victoire remembers, "When Karl Lagerfeld spoke of it [rococo], it meant nothing to me at the time.

I was living in the present, with the 1980s rock of Blondie, Depeche Mode, and the Pet Shop Boys. I'm more rock than rococo."

ROSE

"Without any doubt, this is the flower par excellence, the absolute Dior flower," says Victoire. Aptly, the rose was the flower that Madeleine Dior, Christian's mother, acclimatized on the windy clifftops in her Granville garden. Victoire has handled the rose numerous times in her collections, renewing it each time, in either a realist or idealist style. "The rose is the emblematic flower of the house, and it was in some way, inescapable. But it can be worked on in a thousand ways, as there are a thousand species of rose. There are aspects that are seductive to explore; antique roses, for example, are never banal. And then I adore the thorns, which are in themselves a decorative motif."

ROSE DES VENTS

"Engraved in the floor of the Dior family home in Granville is a compass rose and it was this rose that struck me immediately." From this compass rose, Victoire created a mélange of this family inspiration, a recurrent theme in her ornamental work, with jewels as numerous points of reassuring reference. "The compass rose instantly imposed a very pretty idea of a journey. For me, the creation of a jewel or a piece means going to the end of something, whether it's the wind, or it's elsewhere, or like a guide showing the way." Available in nearly endless variations, the compass rose star motif appears on rings, pendants, and bracelets, a continual play on the family's history.

RUBY

Haute joaillerie can be a form of gastronome, and Victoire excels in the game of making Baudelaireian connections. "I like to associate the colors of stones with candy or syrup, and ruby is often like a pomegranate syrup for me, diluted with water for either a light effect or a richer, deeper one."

The collections created by Victoire never focus on one particular color or stone, as she likes color too much to be able to exclude the others in favor of just one of them. Therefore, like emerald and sapphire, ruby has been used in numerous collections over the past twenty years, and like these other precious stones, it is never cut in the same way or using the same technique.

It is fun to look at Victoire's creations over the years to notice the use of ruby variations in *Exquises* in the *Cher Dior* collection (2013) that are placed at the heart of settings rich in diamonds, pink and yellow sapphires, and spessartite garnets. When she feels nature is at its most inspirational, Victoire becomes the most realistic, combining rubies with neighboring stones on the red-pink spectrum—red spinel, rubellite, and pink spinel—which provide the subtle variations of gently contrasting pictorial strokes, in an almost impressionist style. A different vision of the ruby can be seen in the 2019 *Gem Dior* collection, where, in a resolutely contemporary abstract vein, the ruby is treated as a cascade of different shapes, often angular and geometric, often with a softer, more organic motif. Ruby appears either as a dash of red in tune with other colors or is deployed across the entire jewel in an absolute monochrome. Here, one no longer thinks of impressionism, but rather of the luminous deep red found in the soft-edged squares of certain paintings by Mark Rothko. See *Emerald*, *Sapphire*.

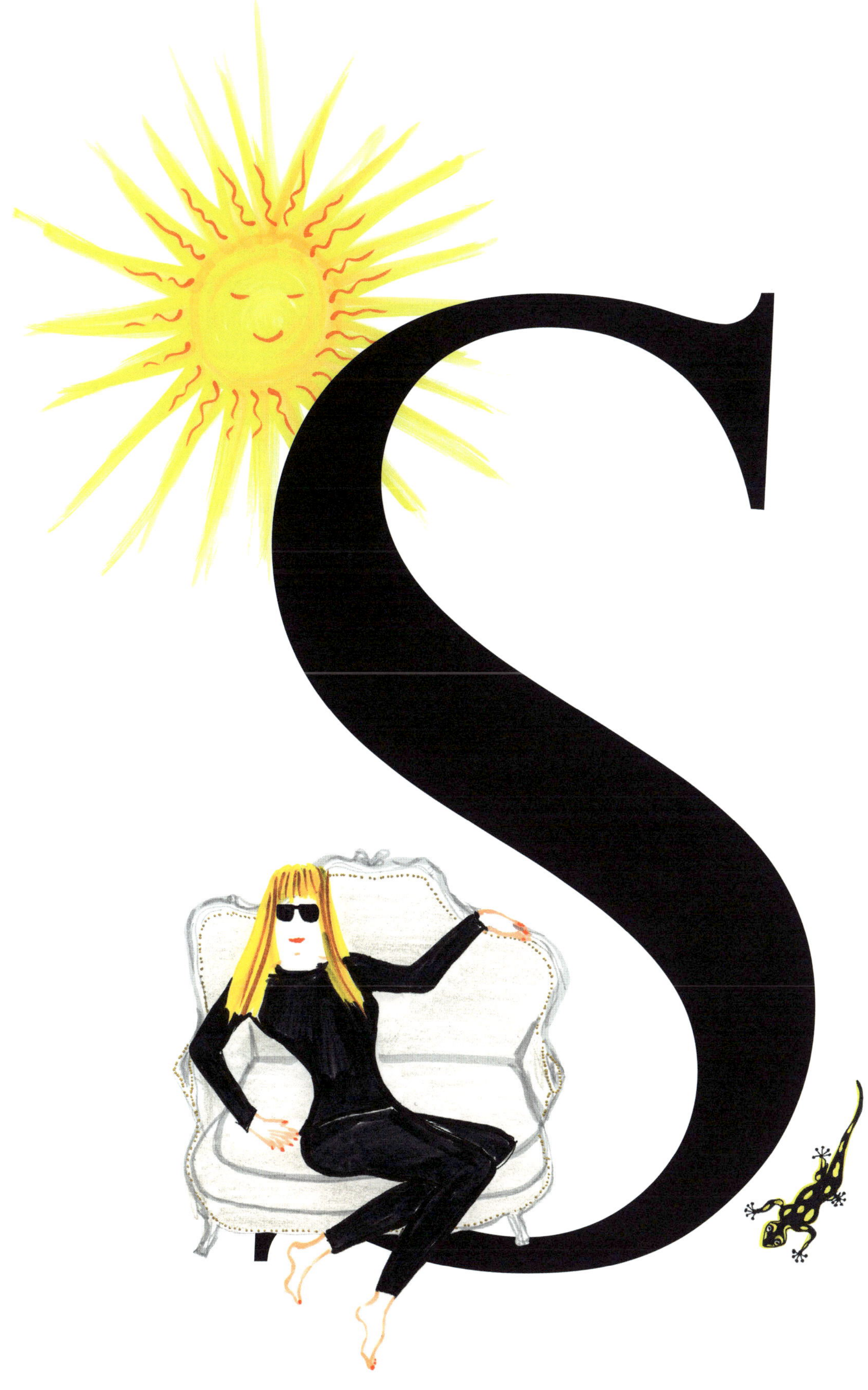
S

SALAMANDER

"The salamander is the very idea that I have of a fantastic bestiary," reveals Victoire. The salamander really exists in nature, and is a small, strange amphibian, in particular because it has perfect night vision. "The salamander is the symbol of François I, and when I used it as a source of inspiration, it was my nod to rue François I, which crosses avenue Montaigne along the house, and which is closely linked to its history." But seen through the prism of Victoire's imagination, the reinvented salamander of the nineteenth century is what inspires her, as they are seen throughout the château de Chambord and other châteaux of the Loire Valley.

SAPPHIRE

"Among the precious stones, sapphire doesn't evoke flowers or nature, but rather the elements—the deep blue of the oceans, the blue-green of the Mediterranean, or even the azure or cerulean blue of summer skies," describes Victoire.

The actual field of the sapphire's expression means that it is not floral or naturalist, but rather abstract by definition and reflecting the purely ornamental. Sapphires are thereby present among the most wonderful compositions of the *Gem Dior* collection (2019), like the drop earring that moves like an unruly cascade of endless blue. Like emerald, sapphire occupies a choice place in a collection like *Soie Dior* (2015), as the center stone for certain pieces titled *Galon*, but also cut in fine baguettes drawing the central framework of *Gros Grains*. In the *Cher Dior* collection (2013), Victoire enjoyed using shades of blue in a palette ranging from the palest blue to deep violet. And then blue also goes perfectly with the effect of fabric—silk and velvet as well as more universal materials—and Victoire likes to remind us that "certain Ceylon sapphires are the color of blue jeans, or even chambray," which gives them a more modulated, almost graphic light. As Victoire's work is also characterized by a tenacious ability to let her imagination run free, so she does not hesitate to free herself from the shackles of realism. For the *Bal des Roses* collection (2011), for example, she designed the *Bal Bleu Nuit* ring with a midnight-blue rose, where sapphires are made even more dazzling by the chromatic association with gray diamonds, blue chalcedony, and tanzanite. Fascinated by color, Victoire has mastered blue, the coldest of them all, making it a realm of aesthetic exploration like any other. See *Emerald*, *Ruby*.

SECRET

"For the first collection based on Versailles, I enjoyed designing secret rings, echoing those secret pieces that punctuate the royal wings and apartments of the palace." Making use, in her own way, of the fantasy that associates Versailles with corridors of intrigue, Victoire avoids the pitfalls of the commonplace: she loses herself in the hidden chambers behind the reception rooms, in boudoirs, secret passages, concealed staircases, and doors hidden in the woodwork. Once again, as often in her creative process, nothing is literal. And the idea is, of course, to not only take up the well-rooted tradition of secret jewellery, but to go further with it, taking inspiration from the spirit and genius of the place. About secrets in general, Victoire says prettily, "I have a secretive side, yet I detest lies."

SENSUALITY

Here is a powerful word that is not always associated in our minds with jewels. It is a word, however, that suits Victoire well and assumes a unique, even personal interpretation in her work. "Working on sensuality in jewellery is something I have really enjoyed doing, although less so now." It is true that in twenty years of designing, certain themes and stories are more propitious than others at evoking sensuality. We can see this in the flowers of *Belladone Island* (2007) first and foremost, as well as in certain other collections that weave a more obvious link with couture and, consequently, with the body. "It's obvious that over time a part of my work has moved toward the abstract, which isn't an aesthetic category that one intuitively links with sensuality."

The notion of sensuality approaches another kind of immediacy that is clear for Victoire: "For me, a jewel is sensual, after all, as soon as you wear it next to your skin." And through the history of a jewel, Victoire pertinently notes that "certain jewels have no sensuality, often those in the Art Deco or modernist style, with ball bearings and angular forms; on the other hand, the idea of sensuality does come to mind when you think of art nouveau jewellery." In this story about sensuality in jewellery, a special place is reserved for Suzanne Belperron, for her "sense of soft, round shapes." Naturally, designing jewellery often involves making it agreeable to wear and she has often been motivated by "the idea that a jewel could blend into the skin, never clashing with it or constraining it." Something that is not that simple to achieve because, as Victoire emphasizes, "Stone equals mineral," a world in which sensuality is relatively rare. For example, pearls are sensual, as are opals, and are primarily treated as sensual cabochons. She is particularly fond of these two materials, saying, "as for precious stones, the way they are cut goes a long way toward giving them a certain sensuality."

SOIE DIOR

"Personally, I'm not that keen on silk, as I don't find it a particularly easy material, but silk is such a constituent element in the very idea of haute couture, that the parallel with jewellery was a must." Victoire created an entire collection when she was inspired by silk, both for the implication of its construction and its texture and surface effects. "*Soie Dior* (2015) was a tribute to this indispensable aspect of a certain idea of couture in Monsieur Dior's era, a way of playing as much as possible with couture and therefore using the most Dior fabric possible. I wanted to give it the grace of ephemeral silk shapes, flat pleats, frills, braid, flounces, and raised satin stitch."

Soie Dior is one of Victoire's jewellery collections that plunges the precious object into the world of fashion and couture, bringing the professions together with shared inspirations. The play on ribbon is a recurring shape in the collection, where it lends itself both to moments set in time and to the delights of fleeting movement, which are crystallized in gold and precious stones, retaining an emerald or sapphire. Each jewel is a soft, gracious shape that follows the random gestures of the hand wearing the ring or the swaying of a wrist. "*Soie Dior* is also a homonym for *Sois Dior* (Be Dior), so it's like an invitation, the expression of which I wanted to be as close as possible to what a Dior woman is."

SUN

"The sun is a motif I have sometimes used. In the very beginning, in particular, I created a *Roi Soleil* necklace (1999)," in a nod to Versailles and its close link to Christian Dior himself and the balls where Sun-King costumes were all the rage. Thus it was, in 1951, at a masked ball given by Carlos de Beistegui at the Palazzo Labia in Venice, Christian Dior appeared dressed as a simple domino, in contrast with the radiant splendor of rival courturier Jacques Fath's Sun-King costume. For Victoire, the sun evokes light above all. "The most beautiful light for jewellery is none other than that of sunrays, whereas people generally seem to think it's the opposite." Sunlight, or its absence, depending on the season, creates a different impression for Victoire: summer jewels are lighter, and allow gold and other less noble materials to triumph; winter jewels are often less numerous and involve "heavy pieces, a very large ring worn alone, and massive brooches pinned to thick fabrics."

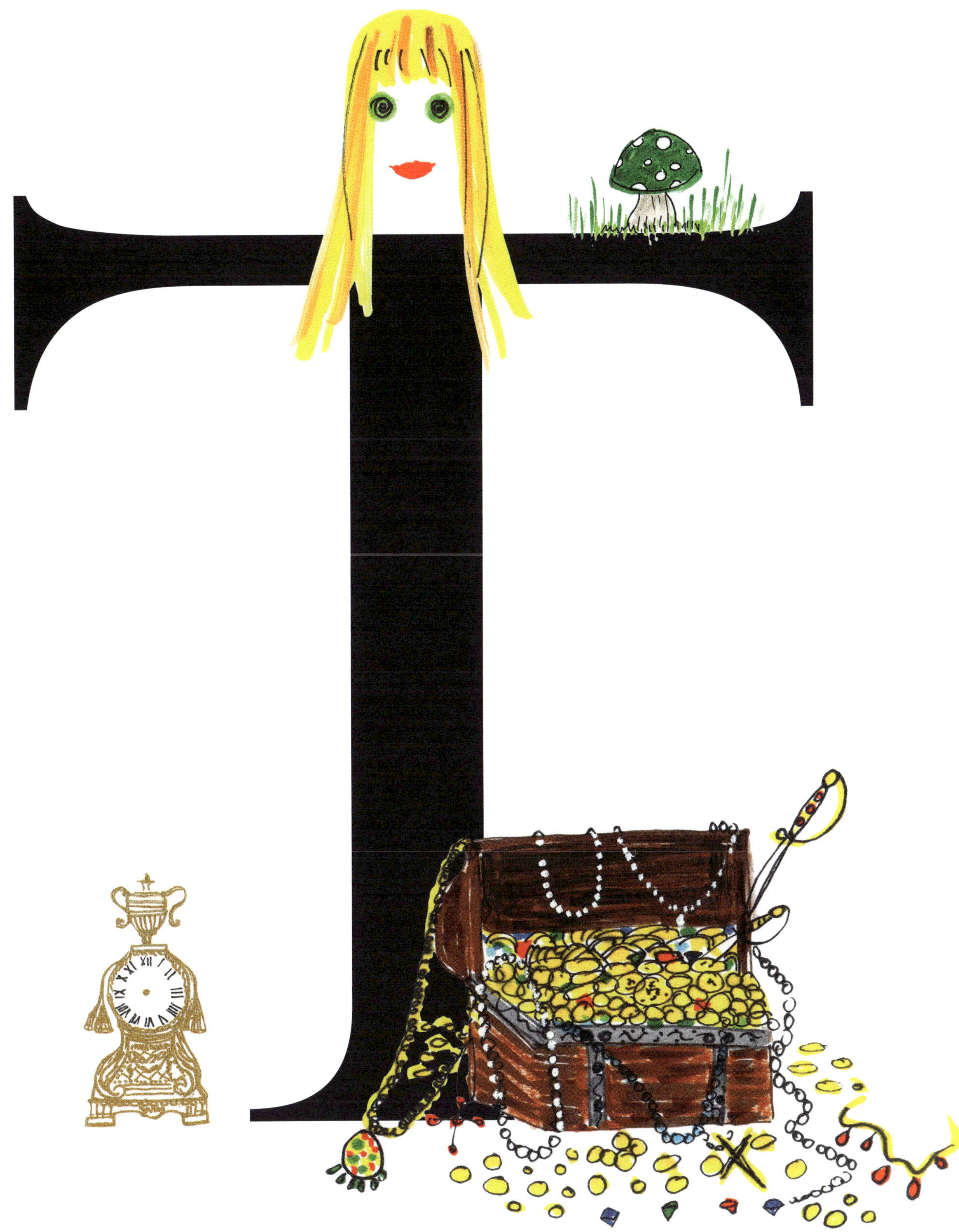
T

TECHNIQUES

"There is nothing simple about jewellery techniques, and I learned a lot when I arrived at Dior," says Victoire. At a time when luxury puts itself before skill and the transfer of traditional techniques and their contemporary renewal, Victoire does not hesitate to affirm that she is not "someone who likes to learn instantly, and especially in this very specialized, very particular profession." If one is too keenly aware of the technical process, it can hamper the imagination, which Victoire wants to protect: "I like the idea of keeping a space for inventing, for being free, really free, rather than taking technical considerations into account and filling my mind with them."

As a result, in this world, Victoire claims both the freedom and the privilege of experience and intuitive learning. "I have learned all these things in spite of myself, and anyway, I don't like the idea of knowing everything. I prefer that the ateliers retain some of their mystery for me." Although Victoire is enthusiastic about working with them, what makes her even more enthusiastic is that the ateliers "deliver something that remains mysterious, even magical... I love to discover, with a certain degree of modesty, the fruits of their work and of their actual creation. I always expect an element of surprise and knowing everything would spoil that." This should not be seen as indifference, only that Victoire prefers to follow the work of the ateliers without actually tracking them, which would reveal a lack of trust on her part. We see this in the relationships of Wiener Werkstätte in 1904, and how designers like Josef Hoffmann and Koloman Moser had faith in the ateliers and craftsmen who produced their designs. Victoire states that she "respects a bit of distance, thereby preserving my freedom and theirs." And then, the technical constraints for certain pieces, or the impossibility of producing this or that aspect of certain jewels, are not incidental: "These technical impasses or difficulties encountered act as a recall to reality, and I like to bear in mind the possibility, at any moment, of this recall to reality."

TIME

"You need to learn to play with it," admits Victoire, straightaway, "and I'm very impatient by nature." A possibility arises: what if the incongruity of these opposites was the secret to the beauty of Victoire's creations? "The issue of time is a painful one, as jewellery is a profession where you need to be able to take time and to let time pass between the drawing, which is an imaginative time, and the creation, which is the production time. For me, because I am so impatient, waiting has also been a real learning curve." In contrast to the rhythmic pace of couture, which we like to imagine as nocturnal madness with designs perfected on the eve of a show, Victoire's collections are not created in a hurry. On the contrary, they are the fruits of work carried out in advance, a year or more prior to presentation, giving them time to decant and rest, so that choices can be made and specified. For a woman who describes herself as impatient, this working time was undoubtedly an exercise in linking essential elements, explaining that "time, to tell you the truth, is the essence of luxury, and there is no better way to define it."

TOXIC

"Toxic? The word is disturbing. For me it characterizes the *Belladone* (2007) and *Milly Carnivora* (2008) collections, with this idea of plants and flowers, which, like nature, are not always harmless, and if mankind touches them they can even become dangerous," Victoire tells us. Like certain venomous animals, insects, or reptiles, the vivid lacquered colors of the jewels in these collections are not made to be reassuring. Heady and intertwined like nets to capture and imprison, certain necklaces give the impression of biting and being poisonous. And yet, the truth is otherwise, especially in jewellery: "Jewellery freezes the living, whether plant or animal, and toxic flowers are never harmful in jewels, where they even become a protective antidote."

TREASURE

"As in films or in comics, the very image of treasure is extraordinary in itself. Pirates opening chests filled with jewels—I love that." Victoire has her own accumulation of precious pieces. "I love a jumble of jewels; previously I kept my jewellery in bags, in chaos, like real pirate or buccaneer treasure. Now I put them away and protect them." In Victoire's treasure chest there are 1940s bracelets, Indian jewellery, coral, cameos, *boulonnais* pieces, and jade necklaces all jumbled up together.

TRIANON

"In the collections inspired by Versailles, I paid special attention to the Trianon, a world of its own in the realm of the château, with that perfect balance between nature and architecture."

TROMPE-L'ŒIL

"Trompe-l'oeil, for me, proves that realism does not prevent imagination." It creates relationships of scale, illusion, and optical effects and, by playing with perspective, it also allows relief and distance; in short, it is what "brings the jewel to life." With the use of lacquer and color, Victoire brings nature to life, confusing our sensations, even more so when she brings the feeling of something monumental down to the tiny dimensions of a jewel. See *Illusion*.

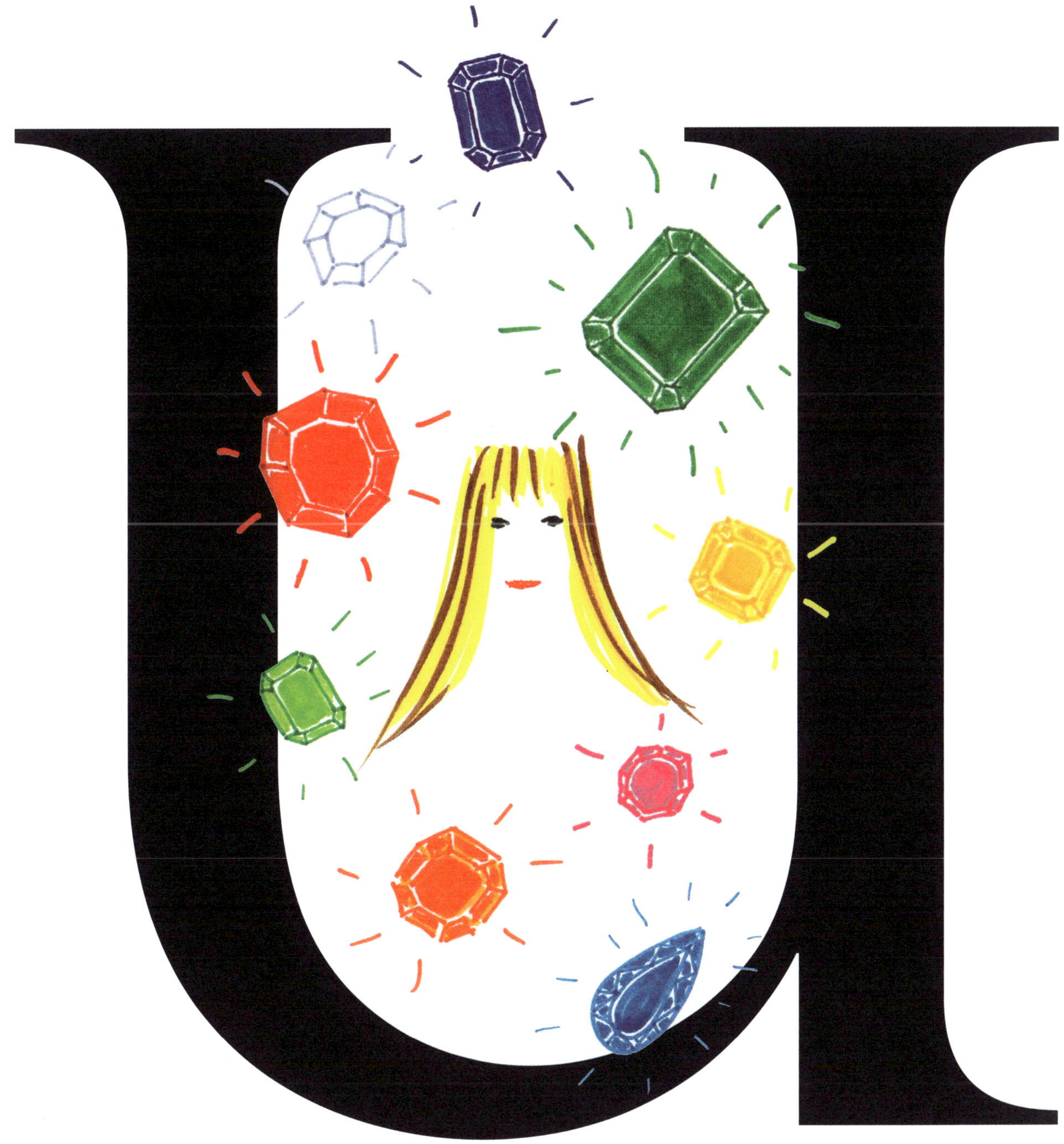

ULTRA

Without getting deeply into Latin etymology, where the word means "beyond," this elegant prefix characterizes many aspects of *haute joaillerie* work, just as it does in haute couture: "Going beyond is like a watchword in my profession, that idea of pushing the boundaries, exceeding what has already been done, surpassing the limitations of what's familiar, always being new and original. Going beyond is also what we always ask of the workshops, for every new collection," remarks Victoire. Jewellery requires its designers to surpass themselves, and in Victoire's case, her abundant imagination seems to push back any notion of "déjà-vu" a little further every time, because she enables the "jamais-vu"—the never-seen-before.

UNIQUE

"'Unique' is the most vital adjective, I'd even say it's the overriding principle that's at work in any *haute joaillerie* collection," underlines Victoire. She has taken all sorts of ranges in her stride, from the infinitely unusual to the most accessible, but with a shared sense of preciousness, and has created in effect a network of genealogical branches between the families that her collections constitute.

What sets *haute joaillerie* apart here is this almost consubstantial idea of a unique creation. De facto, it expresses the jewel's exceptional character; everything contributes to it: the rare stones that never produce the same color or reflection effect; the composition or line, varied by the imagination; the idea that has suddenly and spontaneously taken root. The idea of uniqueness is dizzying, it gives every item in an *haute joaillerie* collection an extreme power, pure originality; but on closer inspection, it also offers each creation a sort of febrile fragility, its fleeting radiance is preserved in your memory or on the photograph, but the jewel is given away, it disappears, it gives delight to a woman who in most cases remains unknown, and you wait anxiously for it to reappear one day, by chance, or perhaps never. "Since every piece is unique, it's a challenge, I might never see it again..."

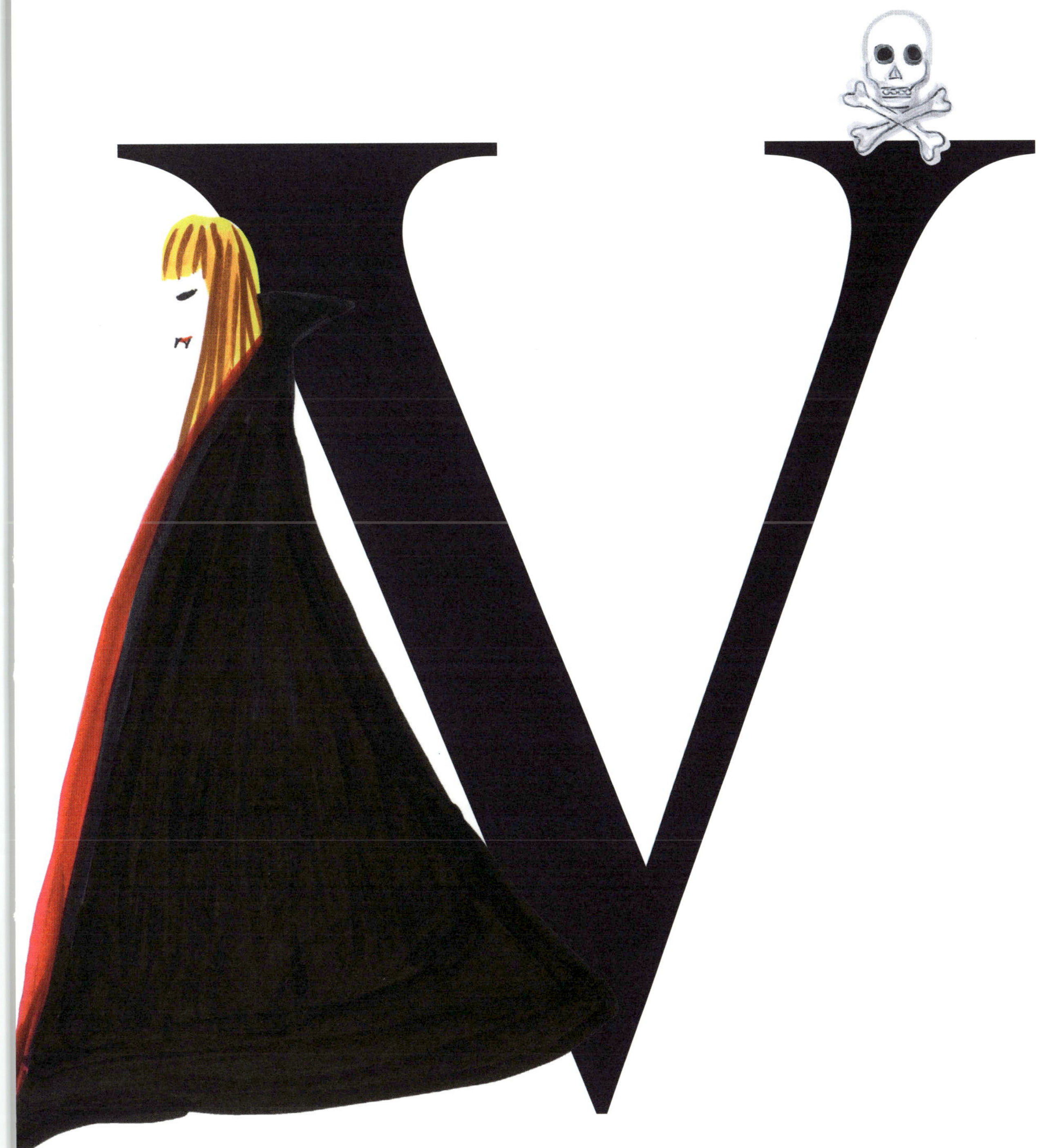
V

VAMPIRE
See *Fiancée du Vampire*.

VANITAS
"The theme of *vanitas* symbols is such a great one to work with in jewellery. I love bringing them to life, adorning them, emphasizing them, decorating them, and crowning them like I did for the *Reines et Rois* series (2009)." The *vanitas* works, which have fascinated the Western world since the Middle Ages, form a bridge to primitive art, with its emblematic skulls from tribal cults and rituals. These *vanitas* are found in curiosity cabinets and in old paintings, in the crypts and cathedrals of Europe, and in macabre dances in country churches. *Vanitas* represents the power of the memento mori. According to Victoire, while it is an exhortation to "remember that you are going to die," it is also an invitation to dream and to take imaginary journeys. Victoire gives these symbols a contemporary and personal vision by decorating them with her fantasy ideas, and she says she can "understand that one might want to collect them," and go beyond the bizarre.

VENOMOUS
"Jewellery has the gift of transforming dangerous animals, those whose bite is fatal. These animals can then be worn, without them being hostile, as though jewellery had tamed them."

VERSAILLES
"The place is certainly historical and mythical, but I enjoyed working on these collections dedicated to Versailles like a narrative in three chapters," Victoire recollects. We know how attached Christian Dior was to Versailles, with its innumerable sources of inspiration represented by every detail of the château and its gardens. We know that the history of Versailles inspired entire sections of Dior's couture collections between 1947 and 1957 and then continued to inspire his successors, including John Galliano, Raf Simons, and Maria Grazia Chiuri. In an immediate way, Victoire sees this jewellery tribute as a sort of trilogy, where the profusion of three successive collections enabled her to take advantage of an endless source of images and ideas. "It was a way of visiting it all, even if you never really visit all of Versailles." One after the other, the three collections explore first the interior, "with details of the ornaments, elements of the decor and furniture, but always seen through the filter of the imagination, never literal, and moved by the impression of jewels lit by candlelight. The diamond was best adapted to produce this sensation." Second came the exploration of the outside, where "natural sunlight, the very colorful aspect of nature and gardens, and therefore a confirmed polychromatism of stones," and then, finally, the secret rooms with their "openings, hidden staircases, and passages." This trilogy leaves no one unmoved and draws an elegant, distanced tribute to the most famous château in the world, but without forced references to historical characters. Instead, it favors an almost abstract vision of both great history and the small story, with a reading of the place's architecture that is both symbolic and anecdotal. These three collections are a triumph.

VICTOIRE
"Victoire is my first name, it's also the name of a model, Christian Dior's favorite model. Moreover, my mother adored Victoire de Montesquiou. I owe this name to her."

VIRTUOSITY
"Virtuosity is found first of all in the ateliers, in the hands of the craftsmen and the technicians working there; it would be impossible to achieve such a level of quality without them," Victoire admits. "I see them often, once or twice a week, and these are my favorite meetings." It is in some ways a meeting of two worlds, where the realm of

dreams converses with the technical realm, where the meandering meets the precise. "The stakes are always the same: how to produce and materialize an object that has been dreamed up? This way there can never be any lassitude." See *Techniques*.

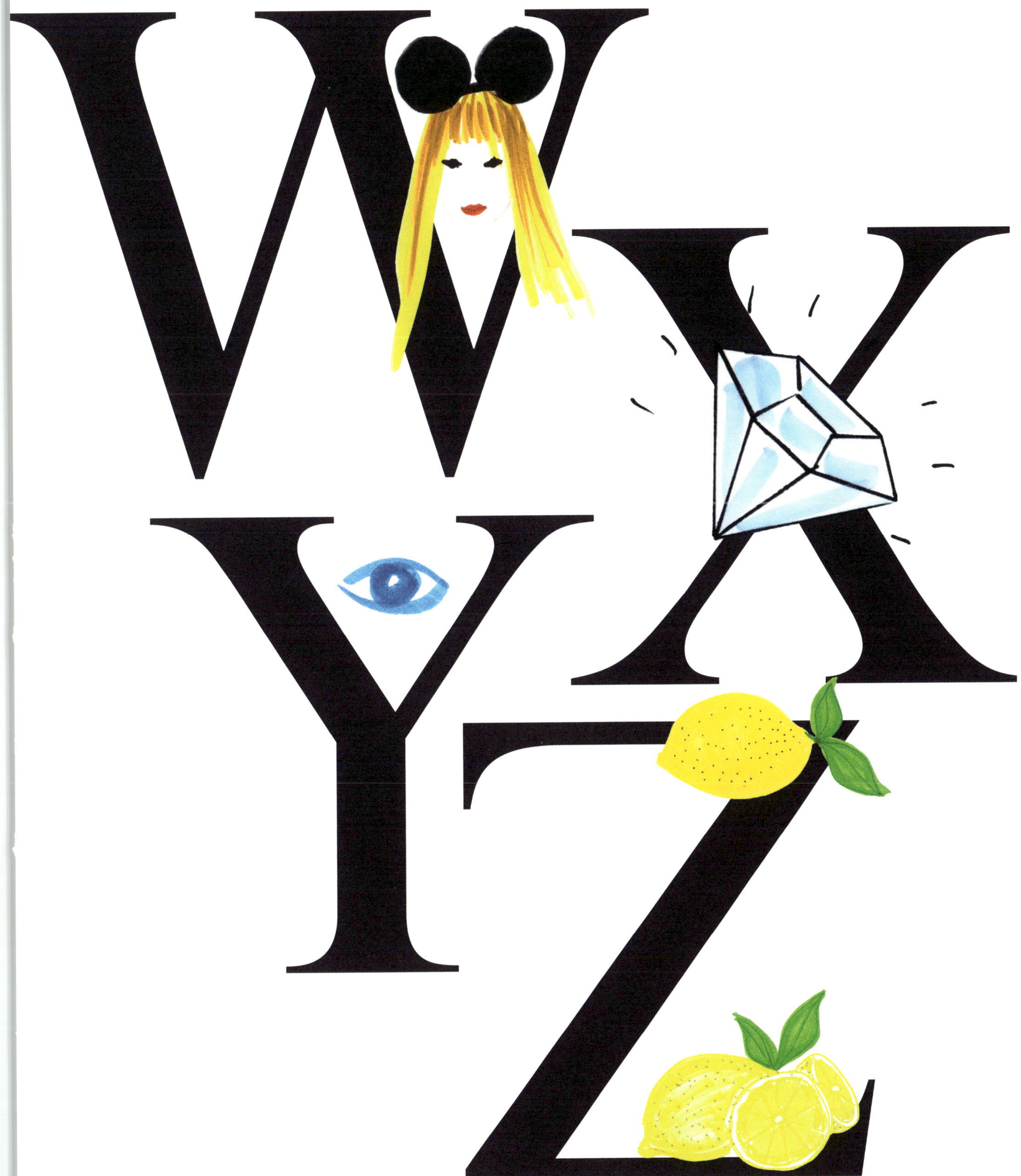

W
X
Y
Z

WALT DISNEY

"I adored Walt Disney's cartoons. I have often said so," states Victoire. She says that there was a time, in the 1950s and 1960s, when these cartoons were truly brilliant. Those are the ones she watched as a child. "For me, the world of Walt Disney is the enchanted world of the flowers in *Fantasia* and those found in *Alice in Wonderland*, and then also the stardust scattered by Cinderella's fairy godmother. I saw it as diamond dust. As a child, these magical, fantastic moments were like a suite of aesthetic shocks." Cartoons were ideal terrain for detecting the tiny, evocative details that later enchanted creators. "In my childhood, for me, the most beautiful cartoon was, and still is, *Sleeping Beauty*."

XXL

"Size variations in jewellery are one of the most exciting things. When I started at Dior, I immediately wanted to make use of the whole range, from the extra small to XXL, and show that every volume was possible, from newborn to grandfather." For Victoire, a family story always appears early on and is a leitmotif that nourishes her method of creating collections and of talking about them. In the sculptural work of these volumes, the passage from the miniscule to the monumental is imperceptible. Seen close up, a ring can become a gigantic architectural structure in the imagination. "Obviously, one of the major stakes in the art of jewellery is the weight of the pieces, so that they rest pleasant and are light to wear. But what's exhilarating is to be able to take a jewel from one extreme to another, from XS to XXL."

ZEST

"I love the acid yellow color of certain diamonds, which reminds me of lemon zest, with its light, acidic aspect," recalls Victoire. This brings to mind the radiant yellow diamonds that heighten the *Dentelle Guipure Yellow Diamond* bracelet in the *Dior Dior Dior* collection (2018), but also several jewels from the *Archi Dior* collection (2014), such as the *Verticale Plissée* or *Envol Drapé*, which take on a citrus flavor when the yellow diamonds are illuminated by orange and pink diamonds.

ZIGZAG

The word *zigzag* refers in particular to a line from one of Christian Dior's collections (Spring–Summer 1948), which was like the fruit of an energetically drawn sketch. "I have a rather linear life, I really don't think I have a zigzag-shaped life, but I like to zigzag back and forth between periods and sources of inspiration with complete freedom."

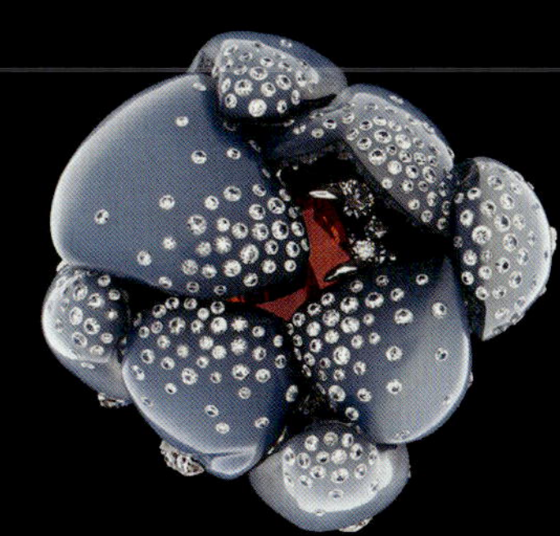

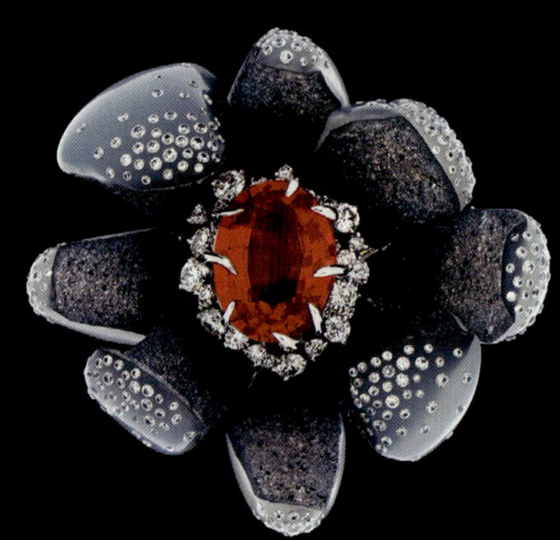

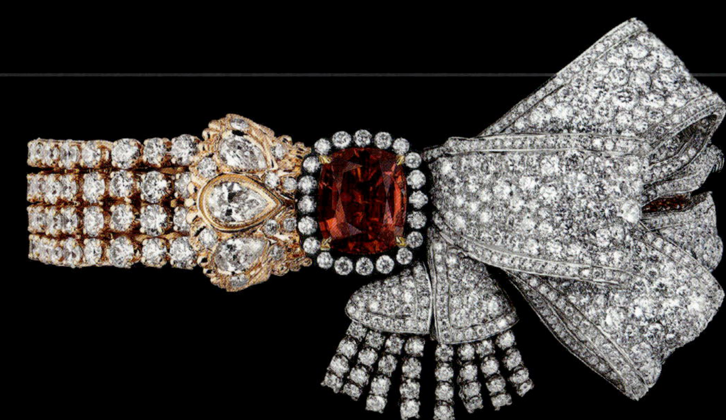

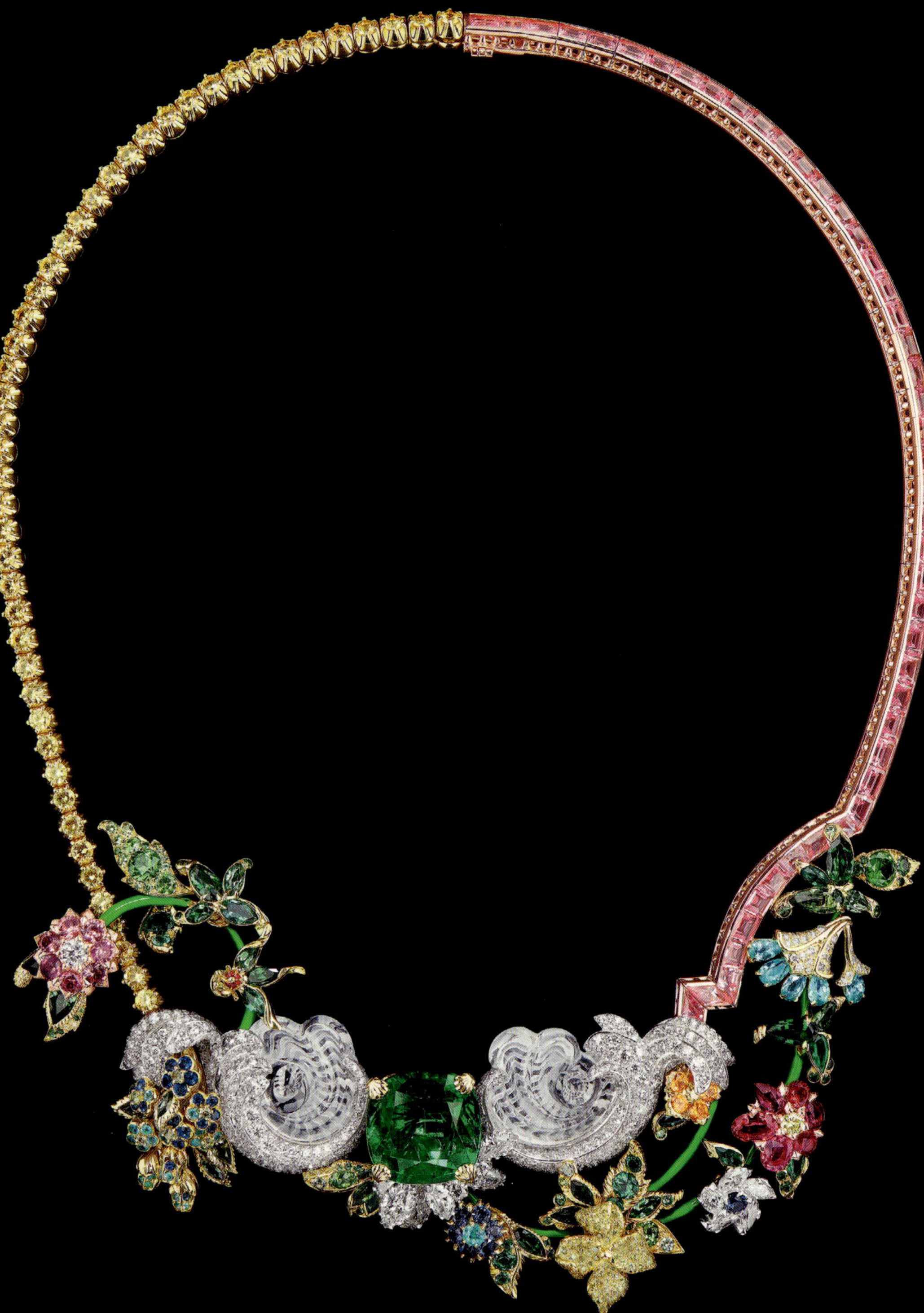

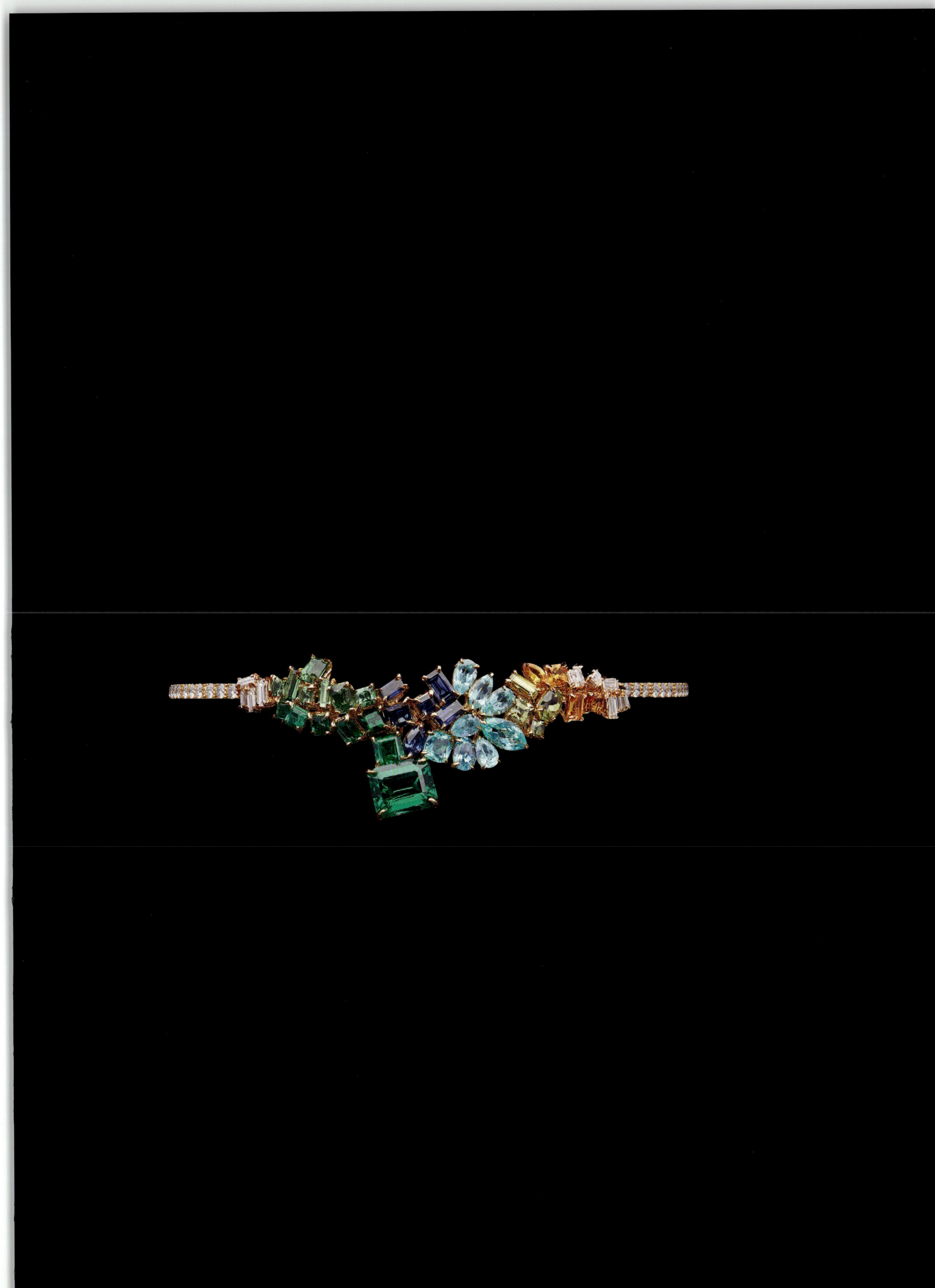

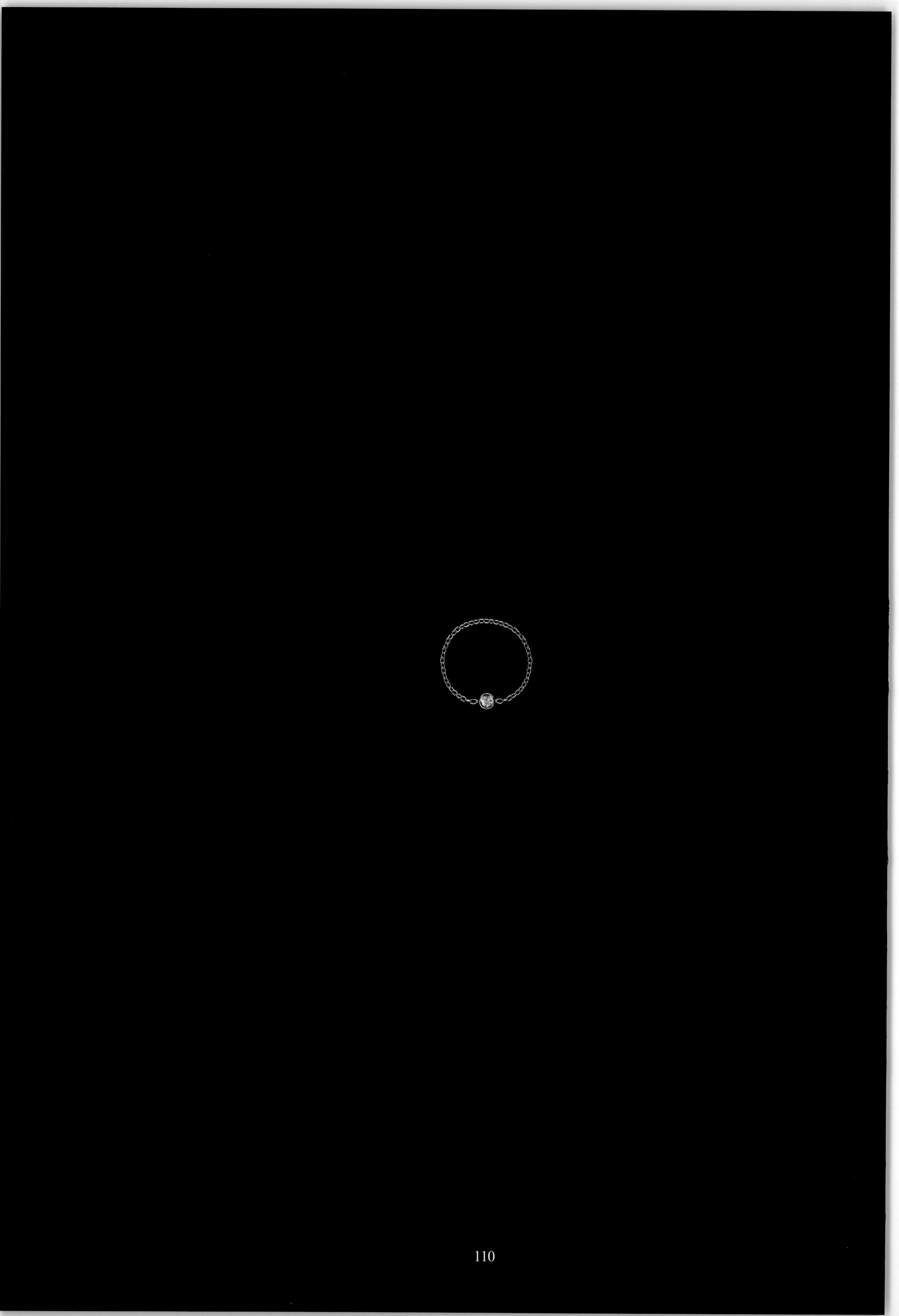

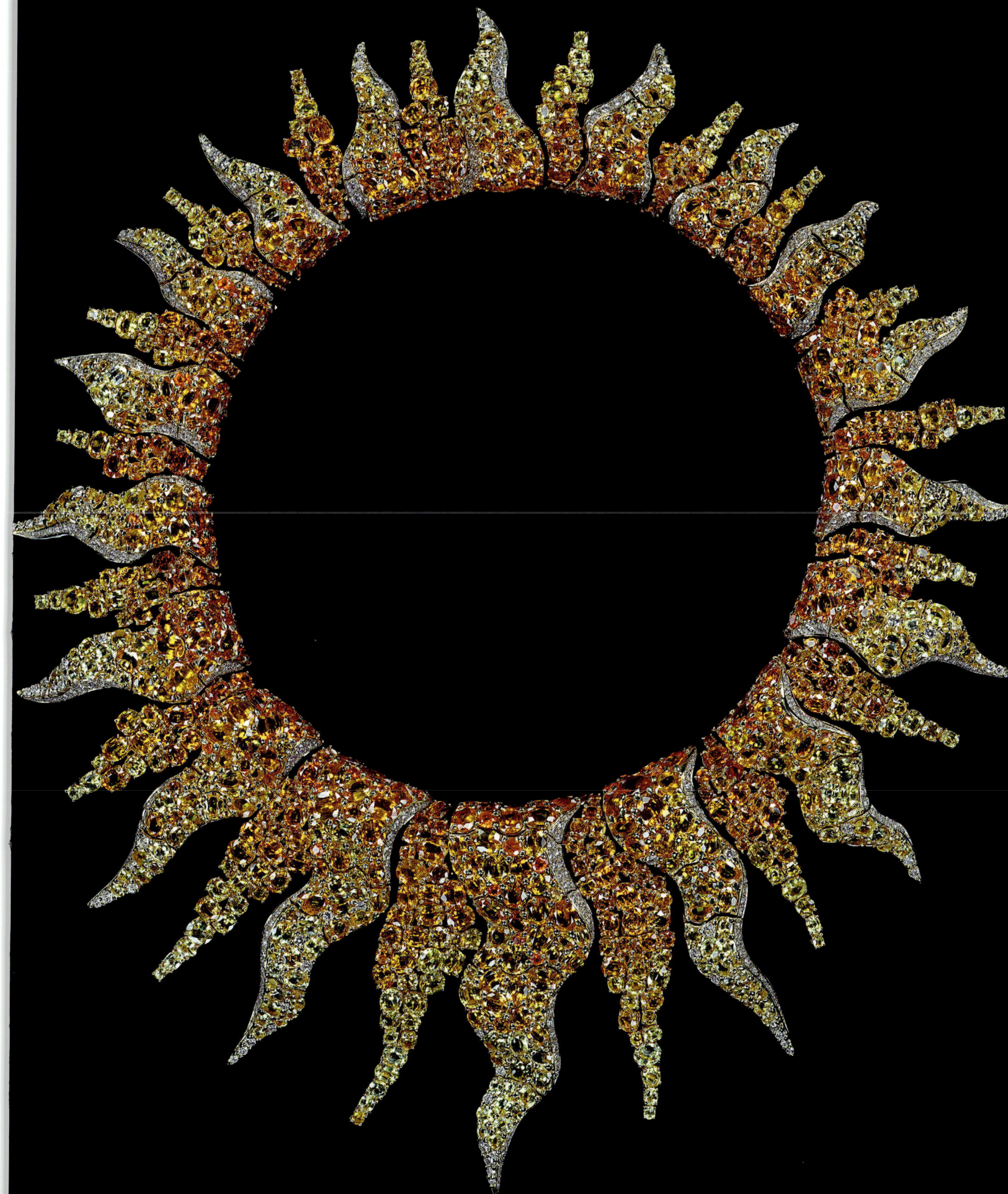

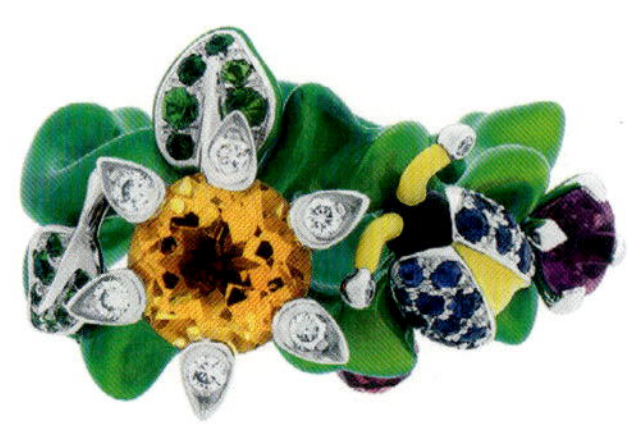

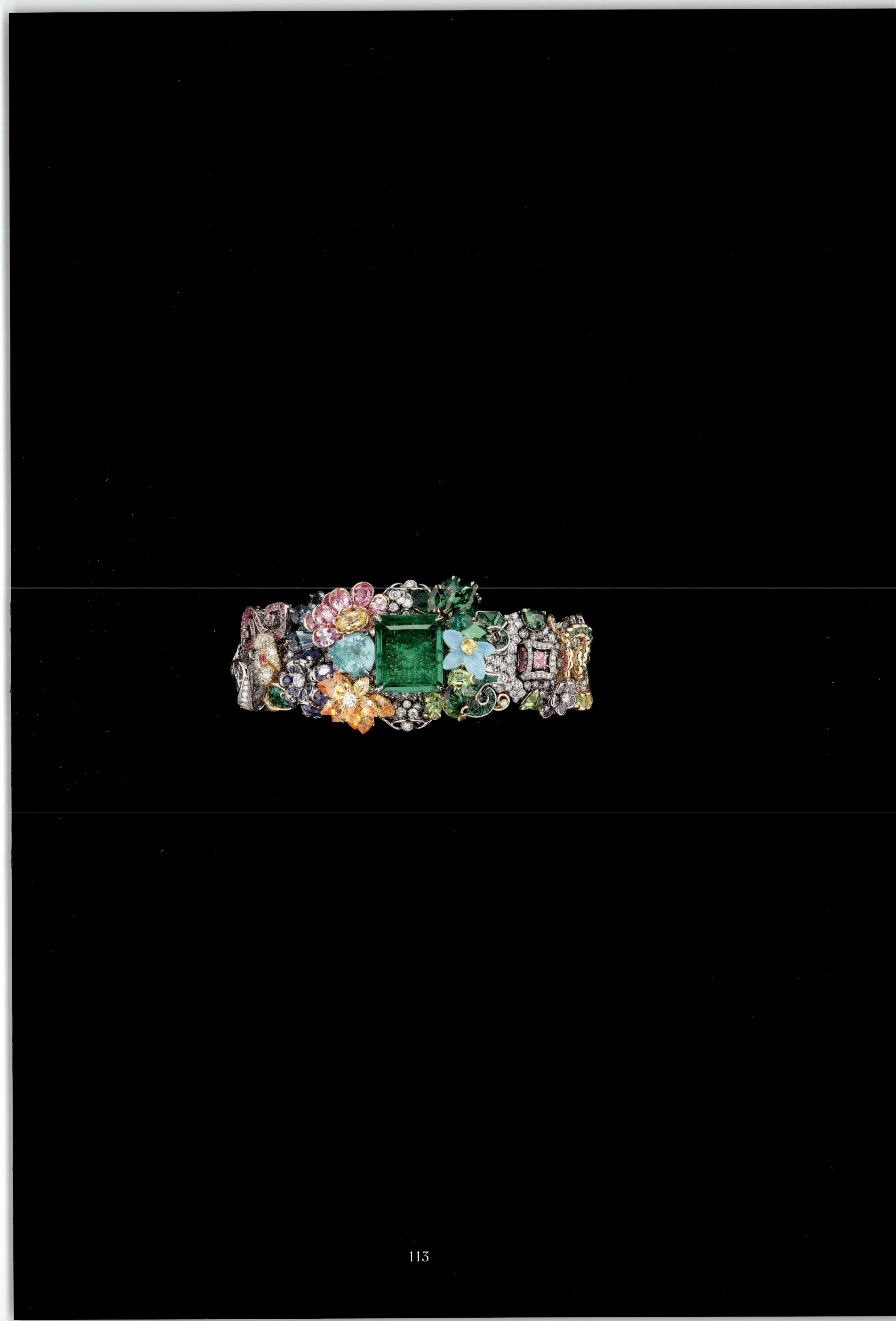

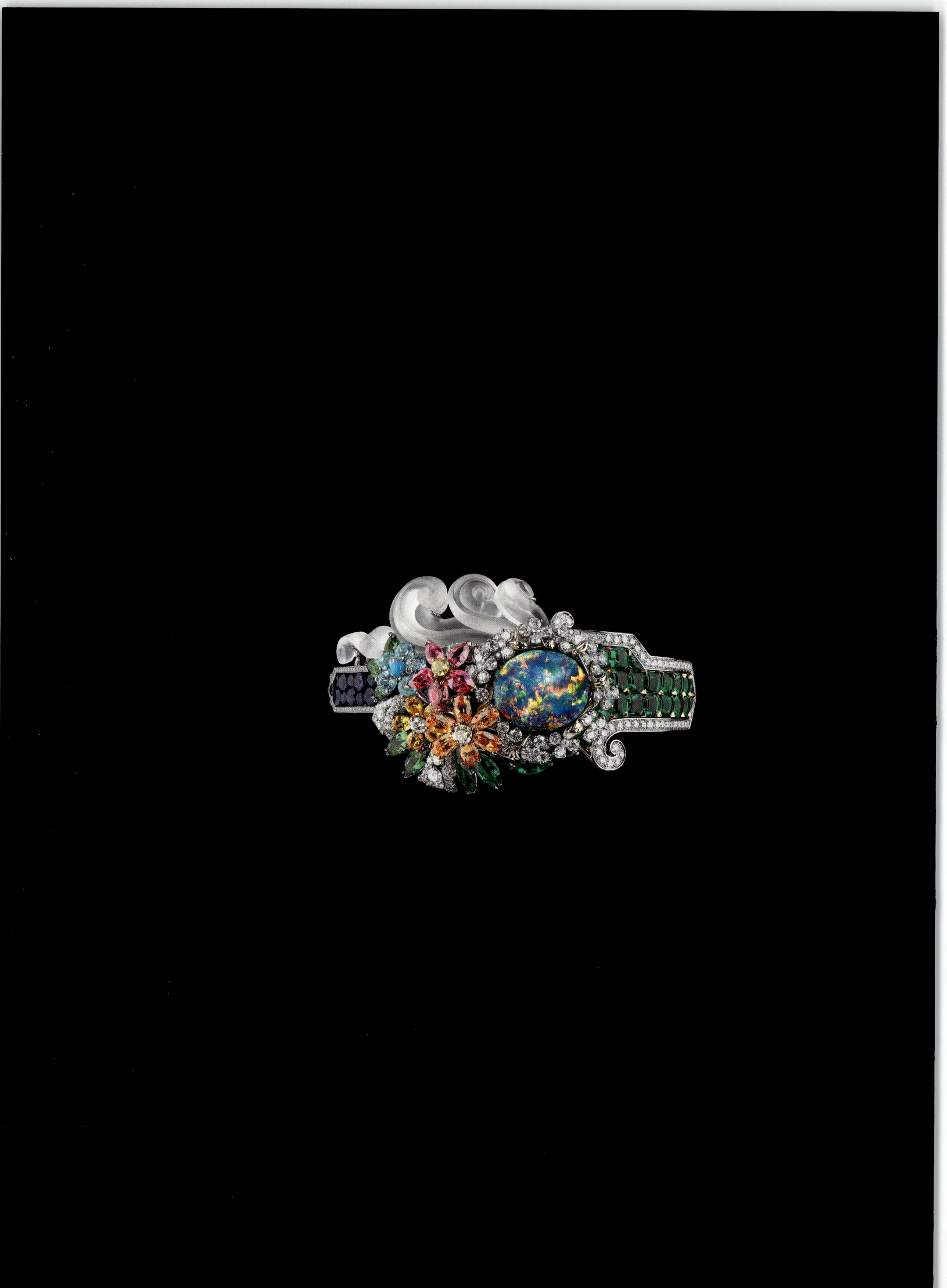

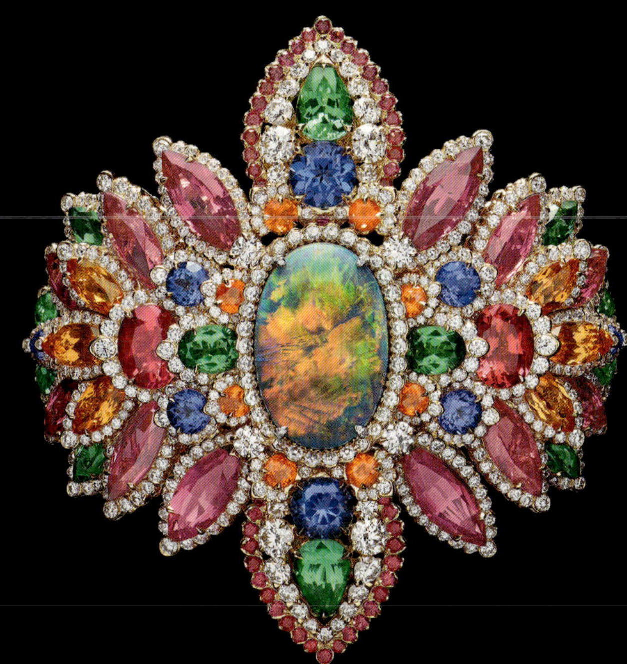

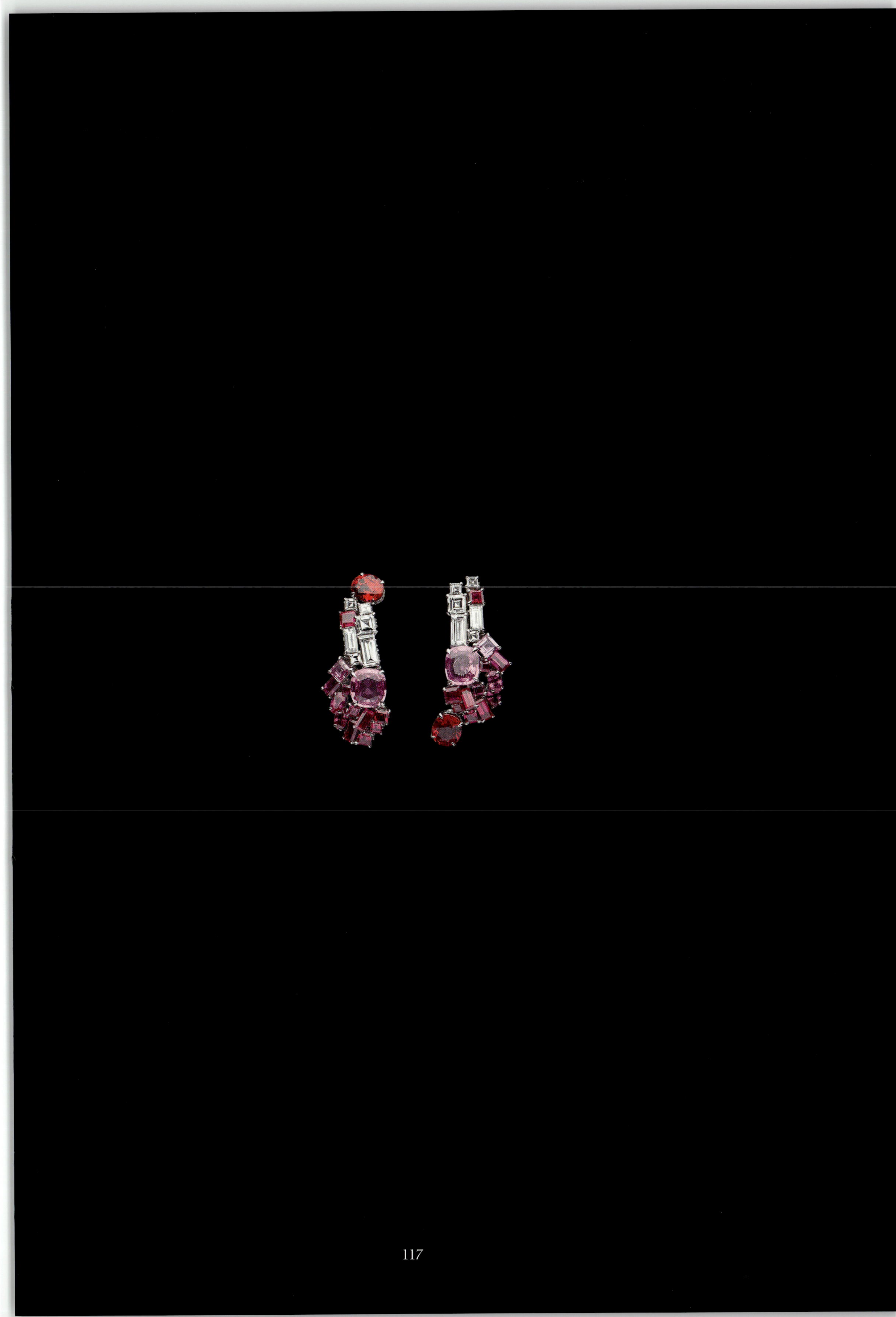

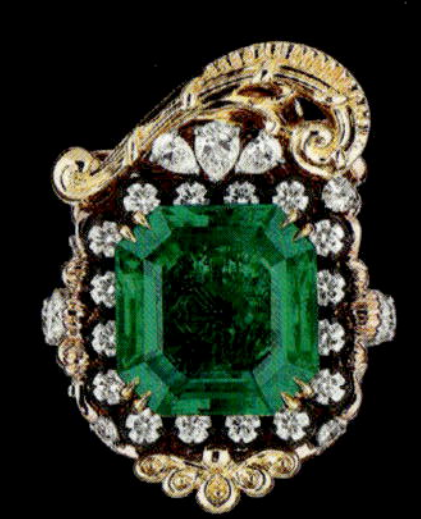

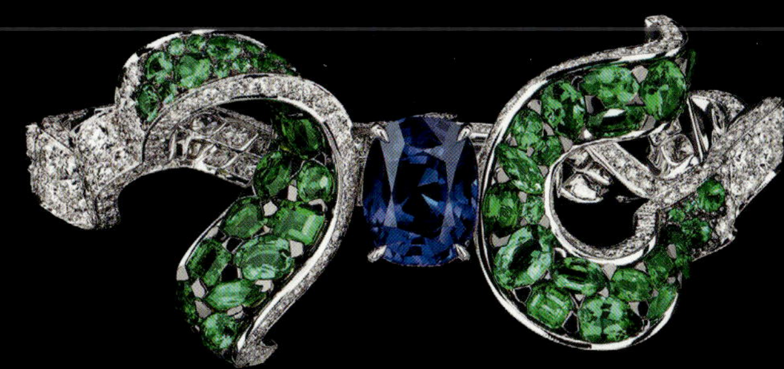

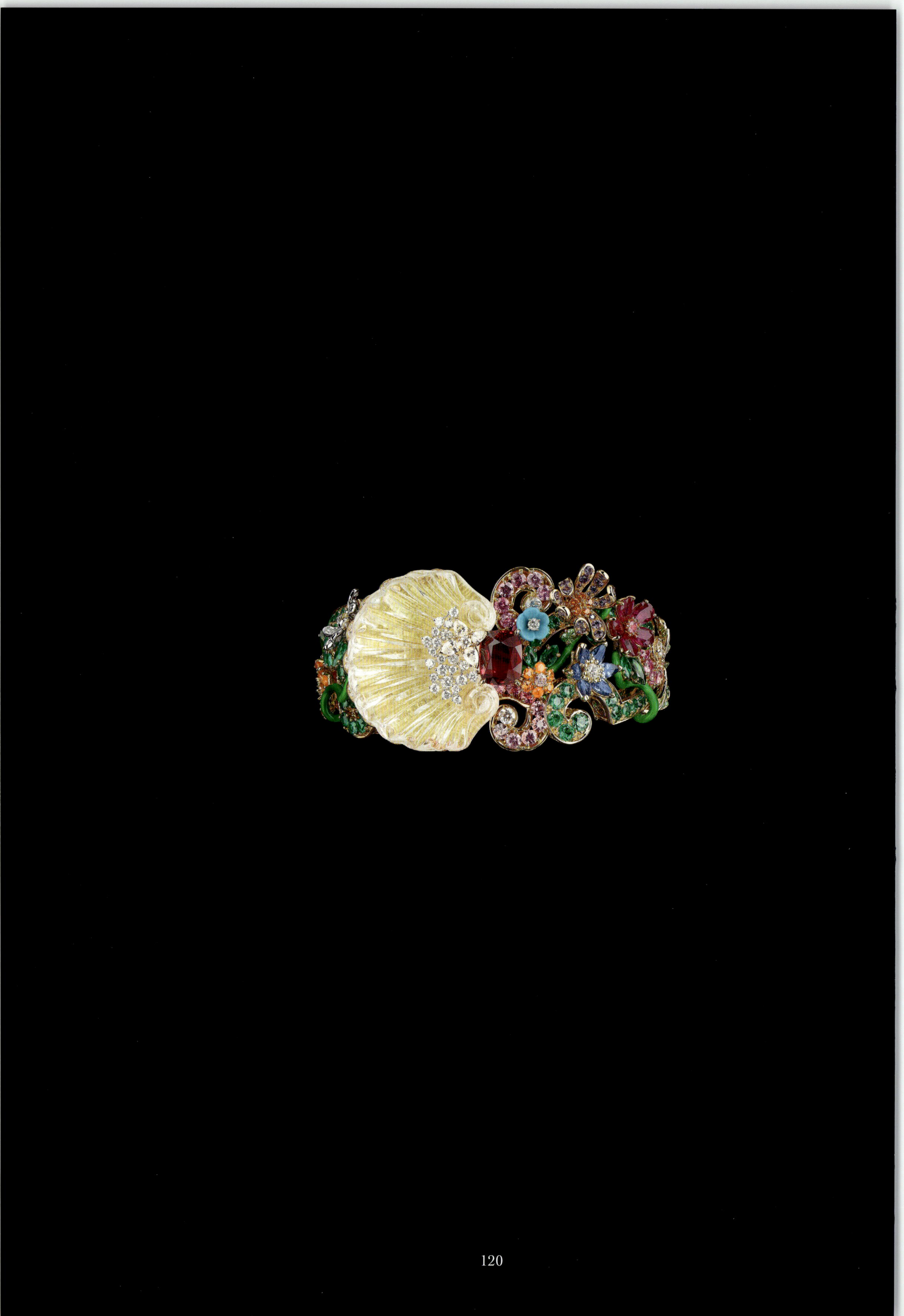

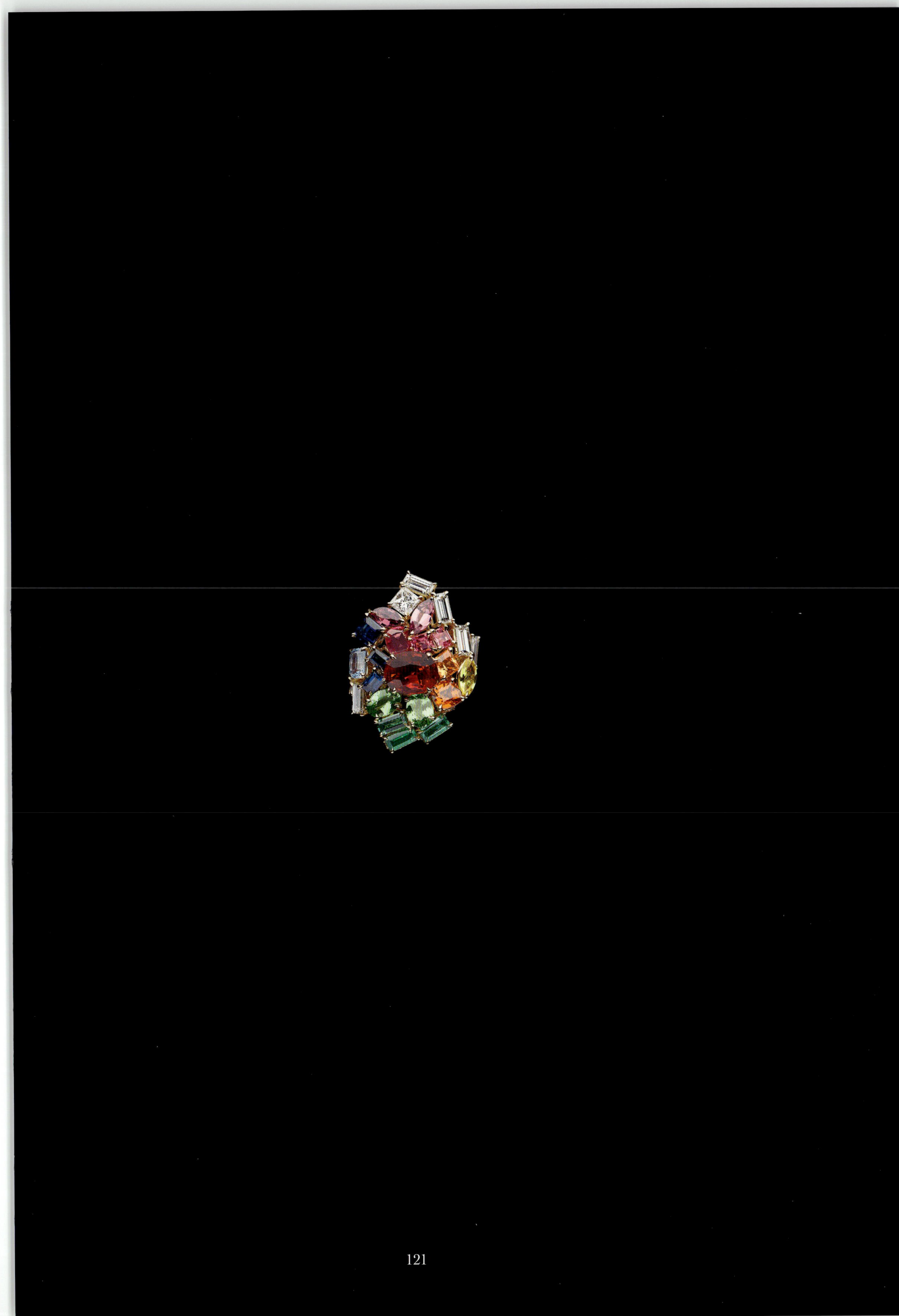

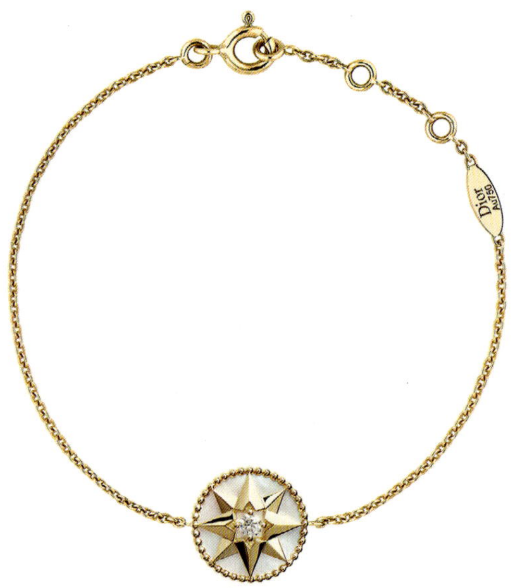

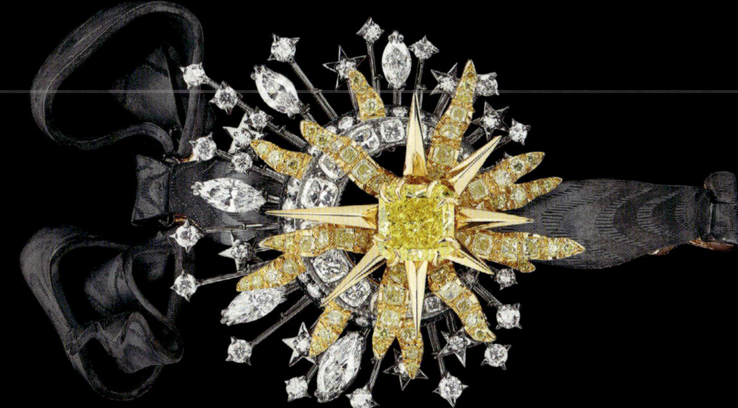

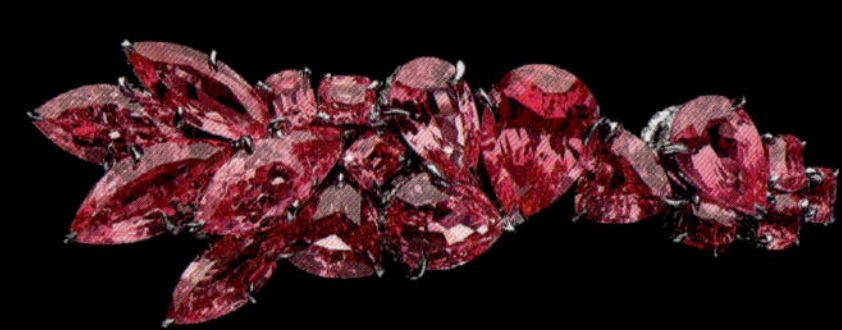

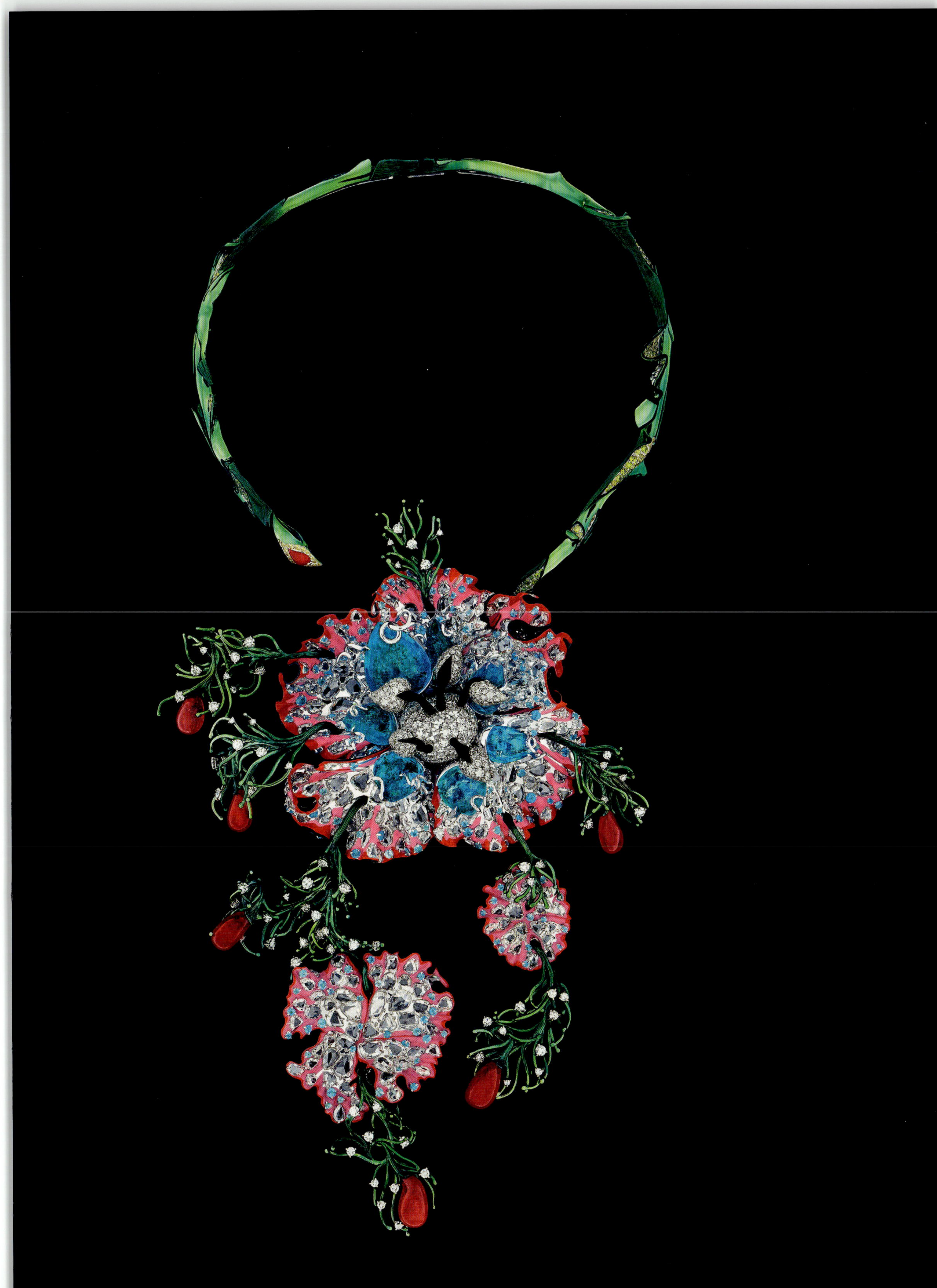

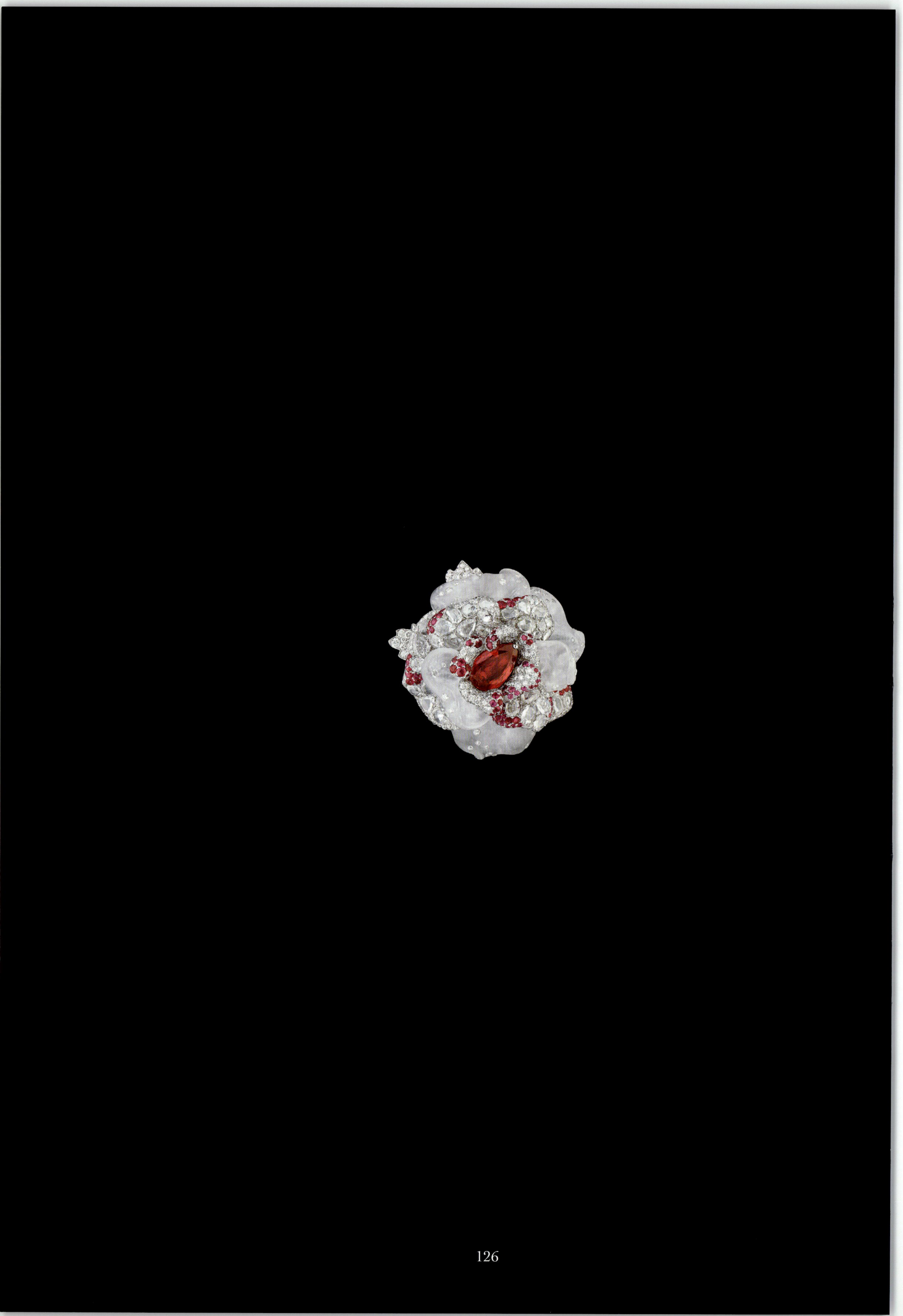

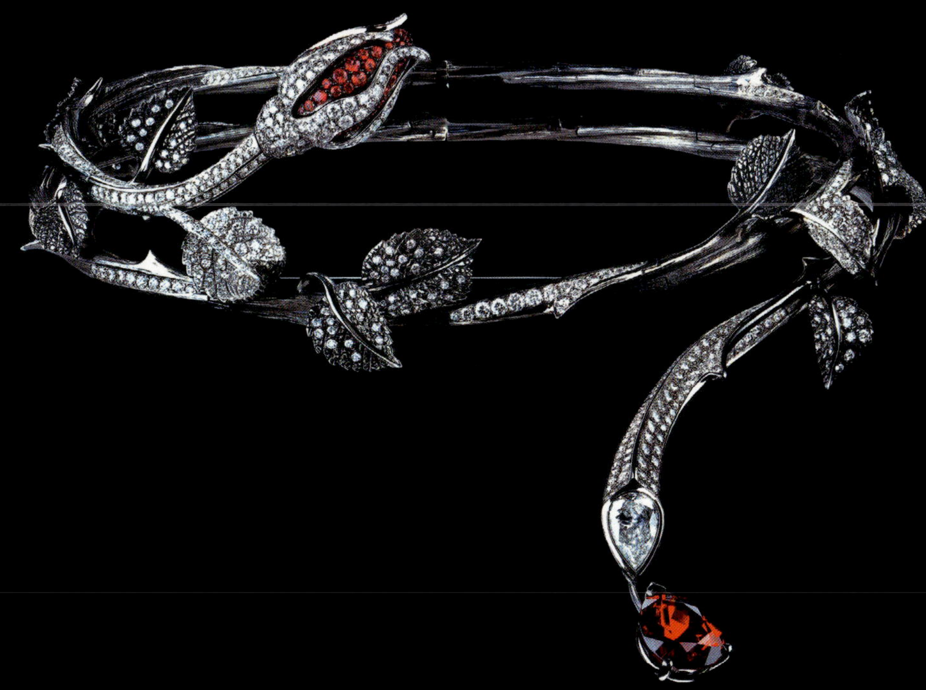

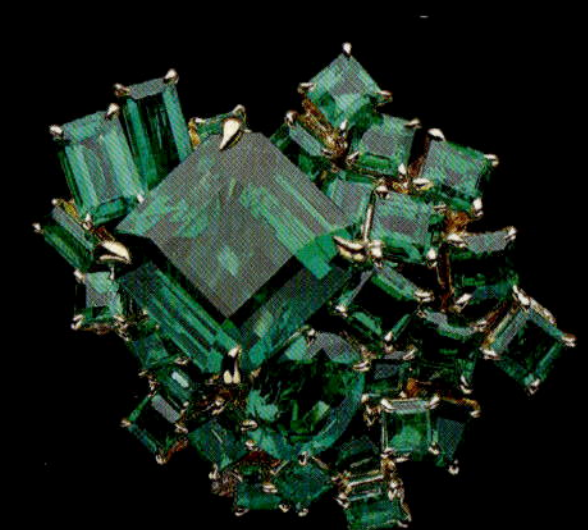

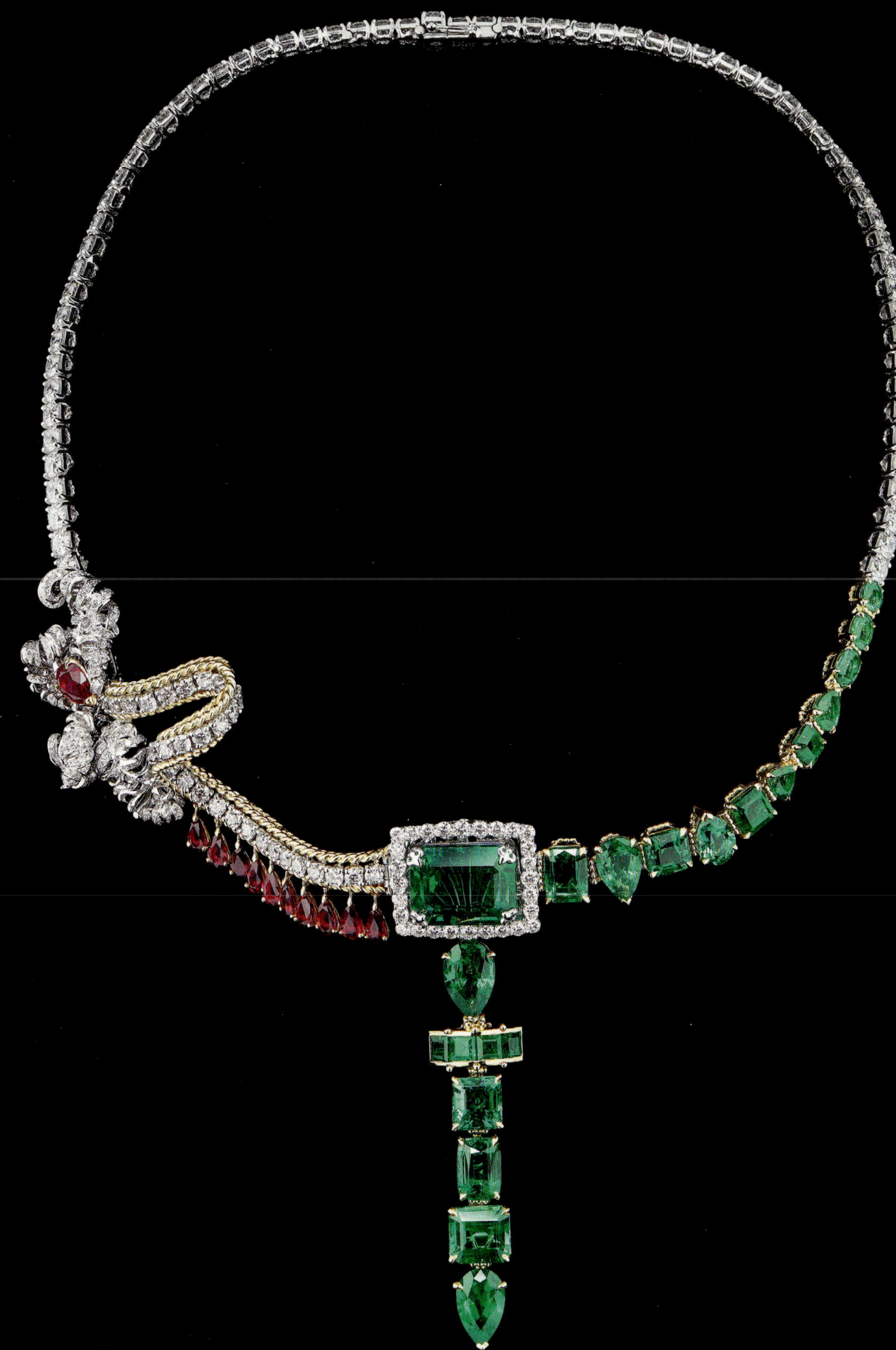

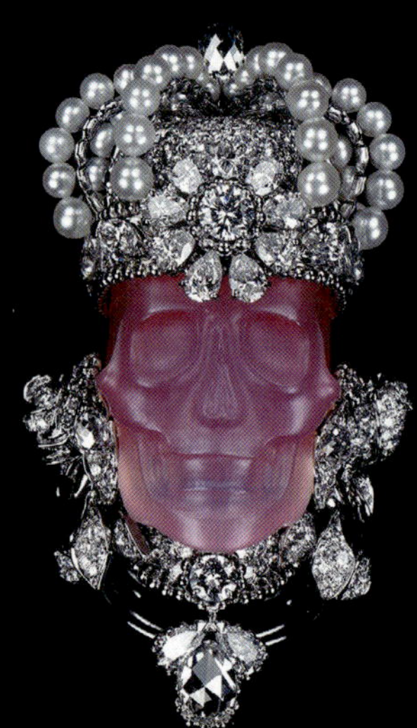

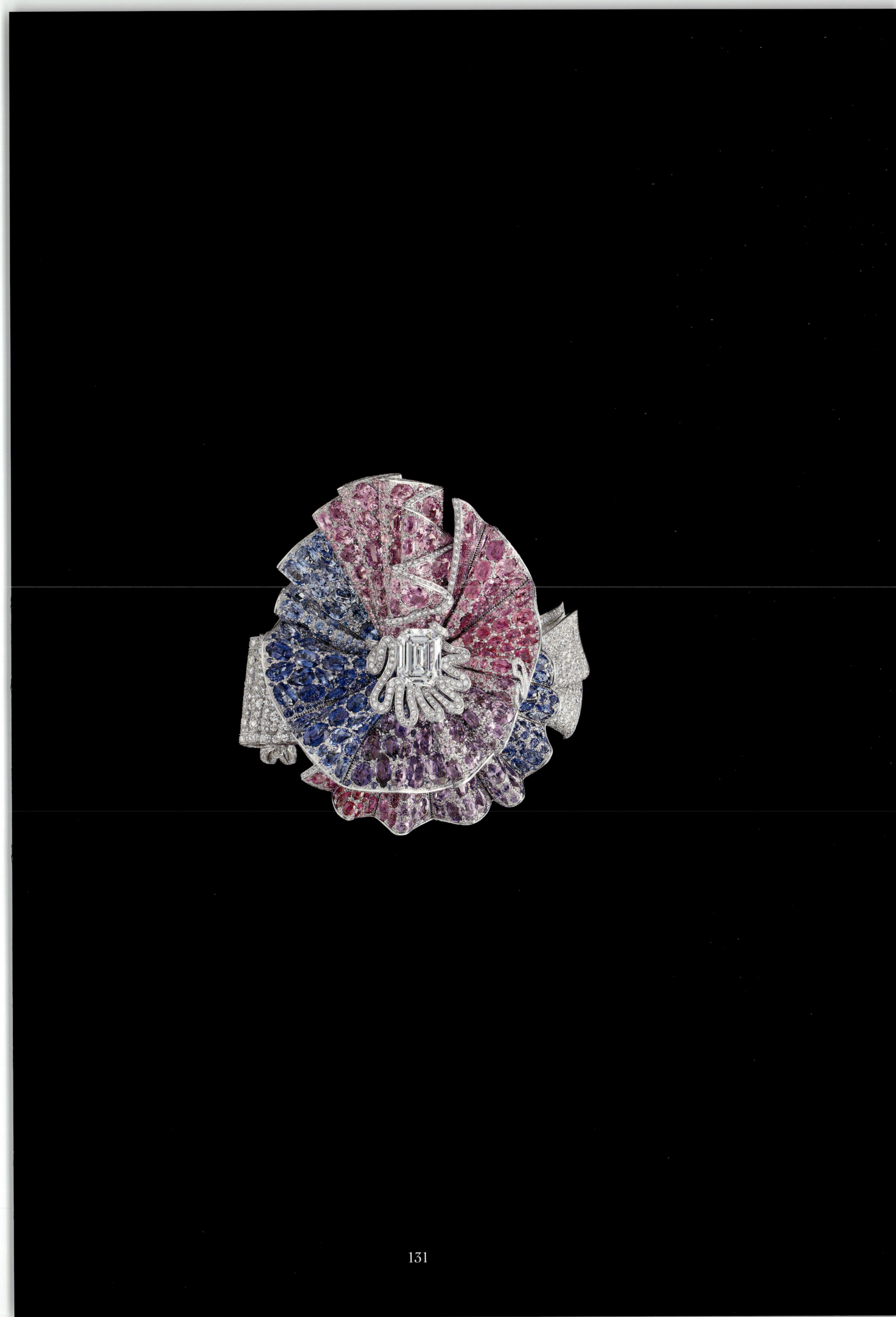

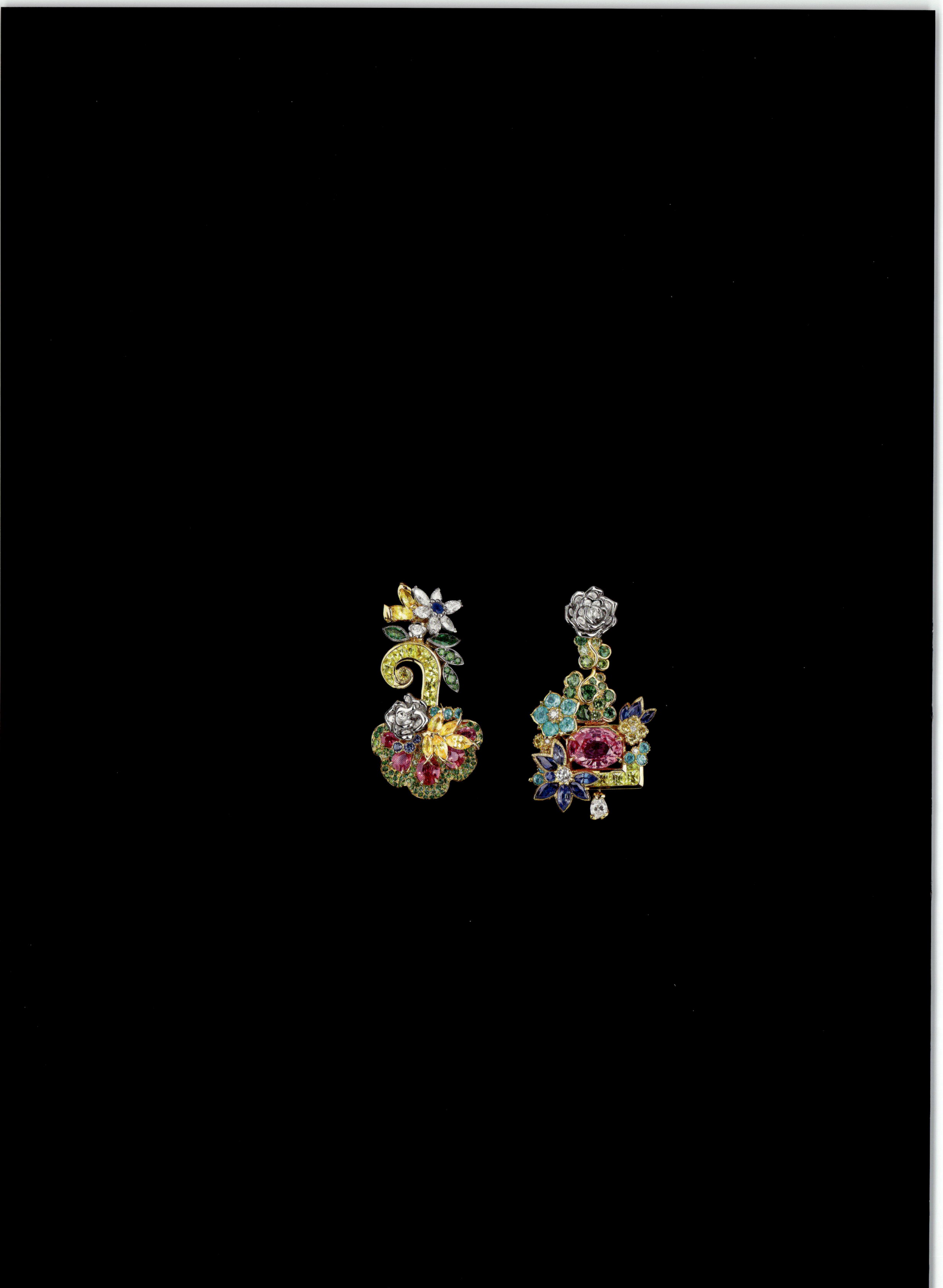

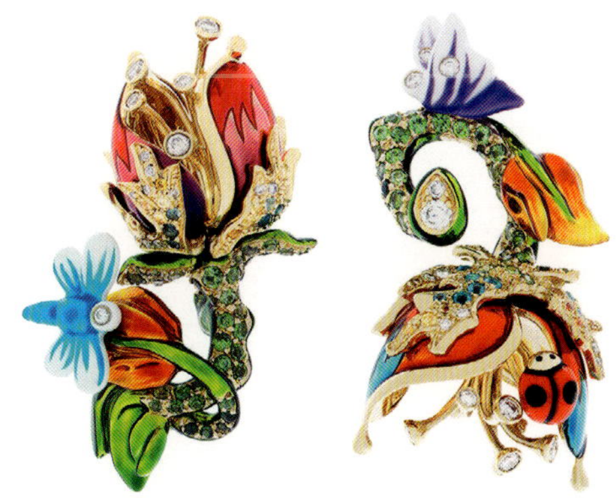

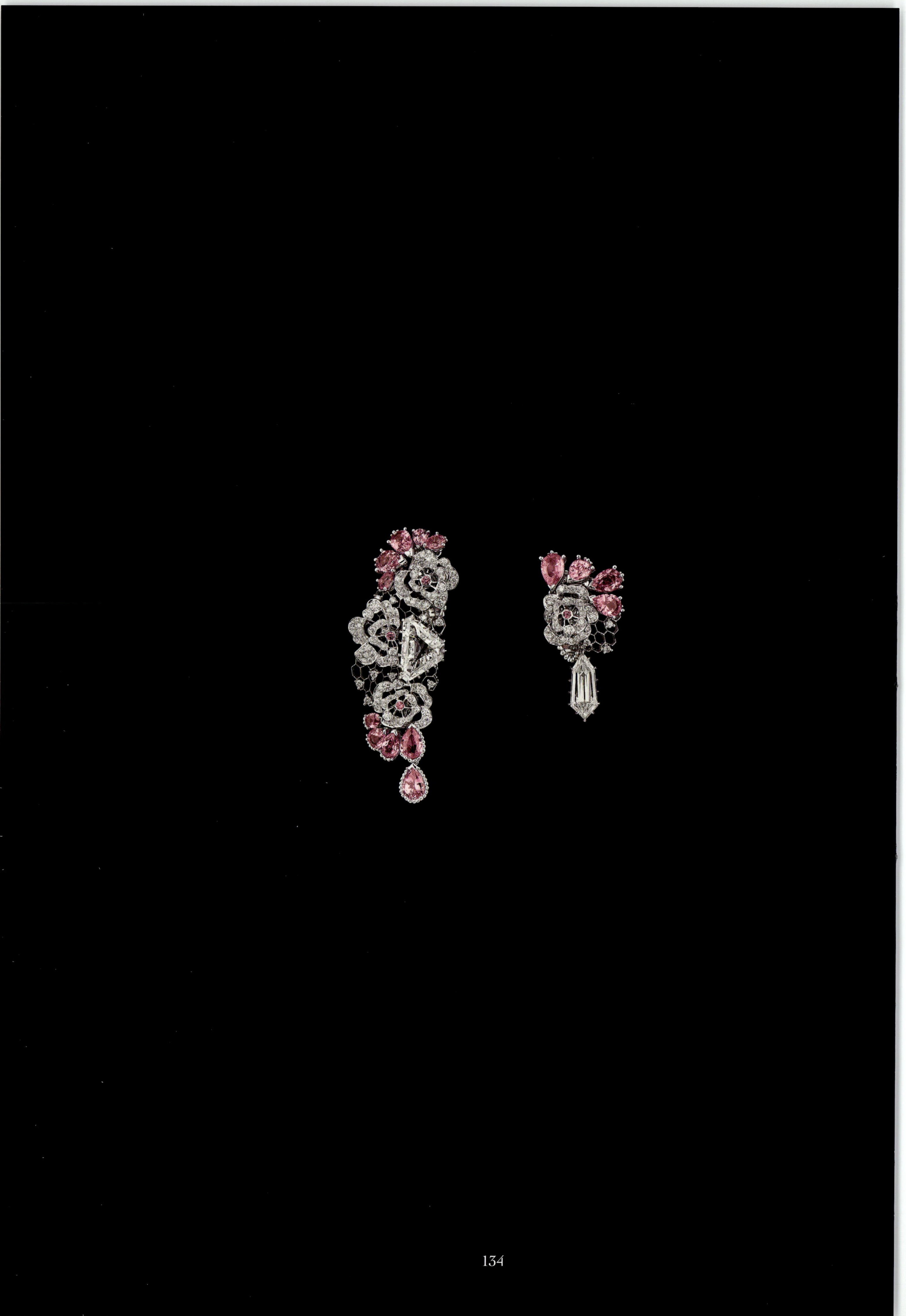

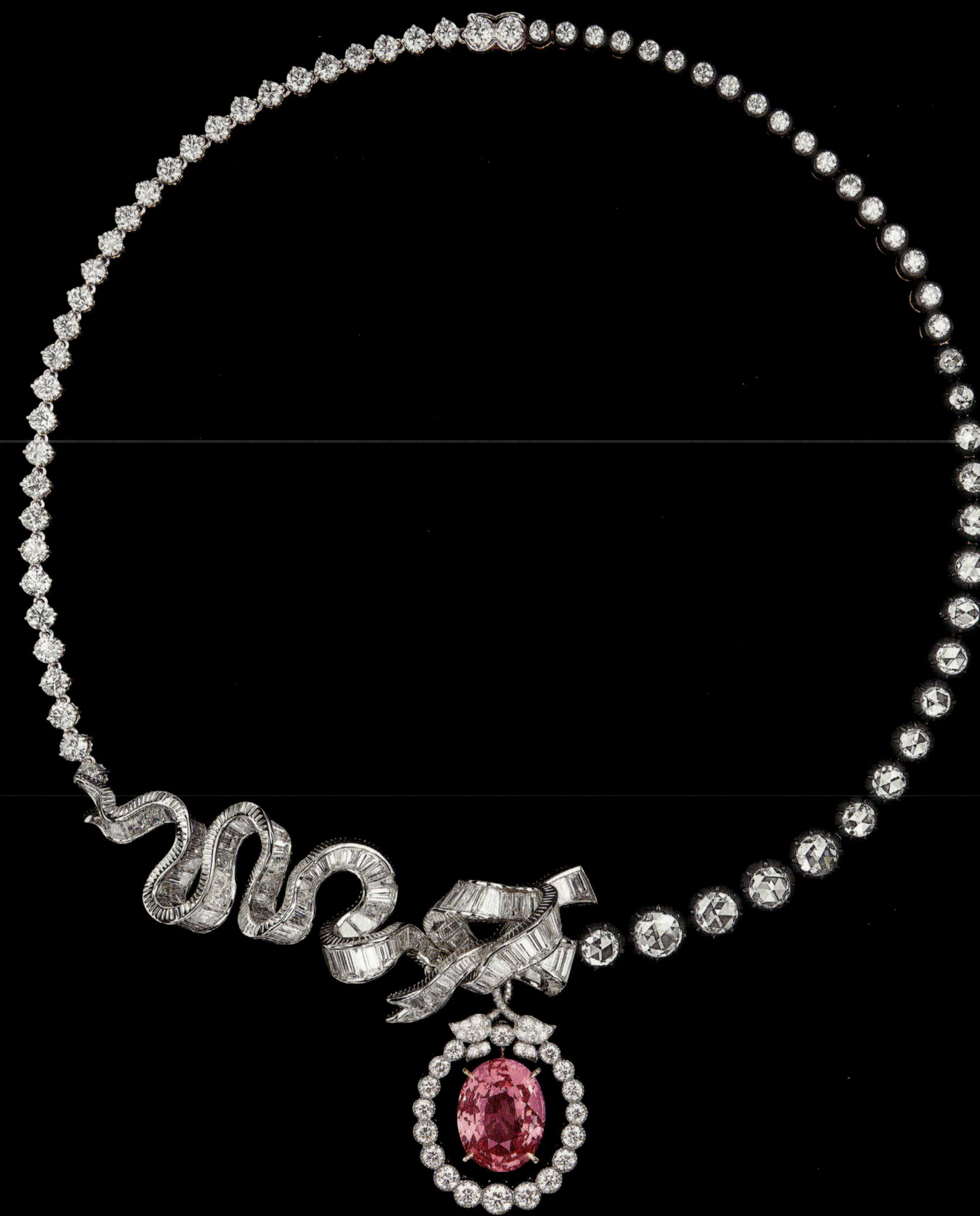

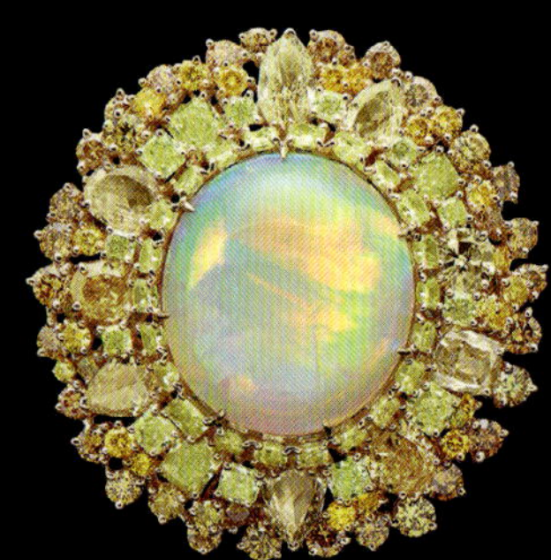

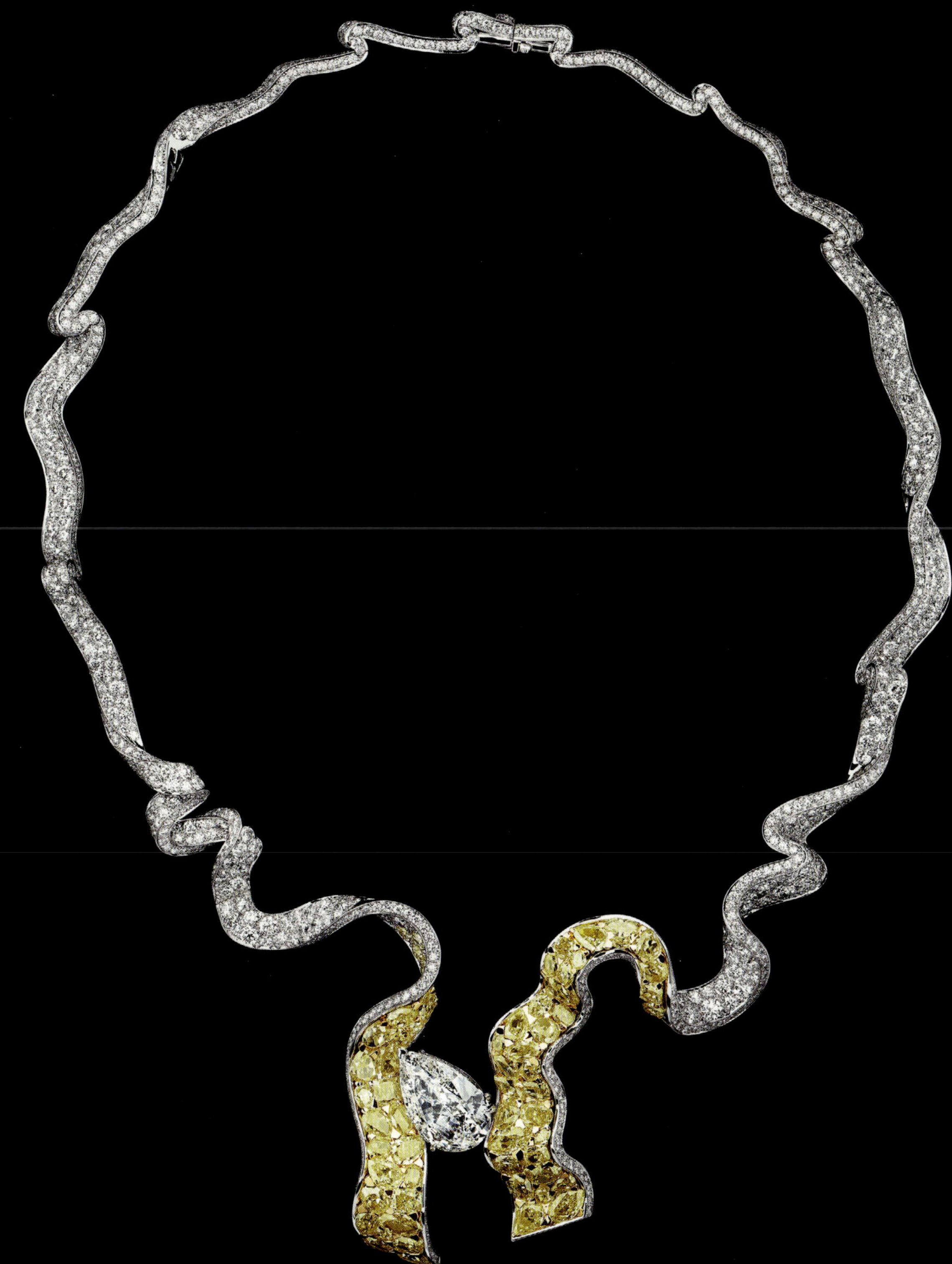

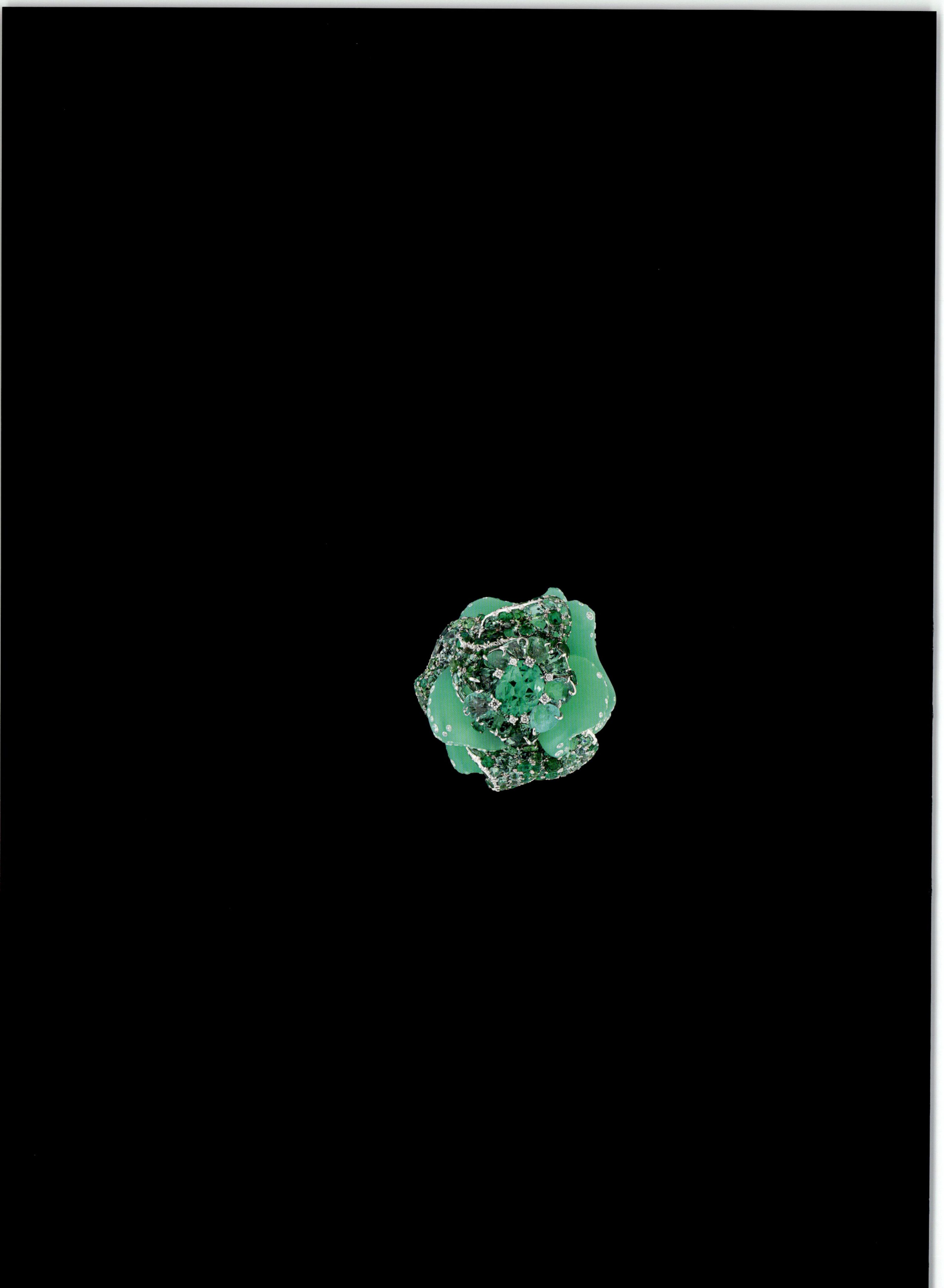

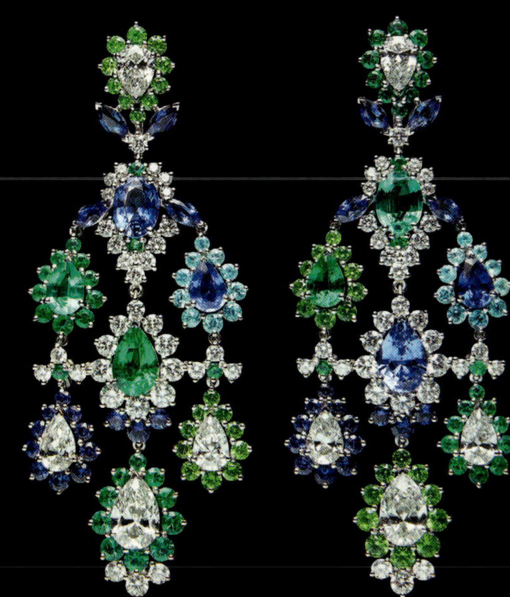

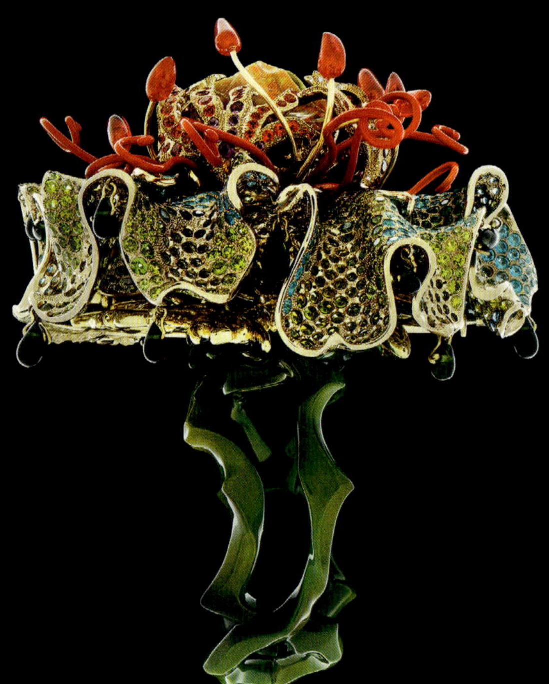

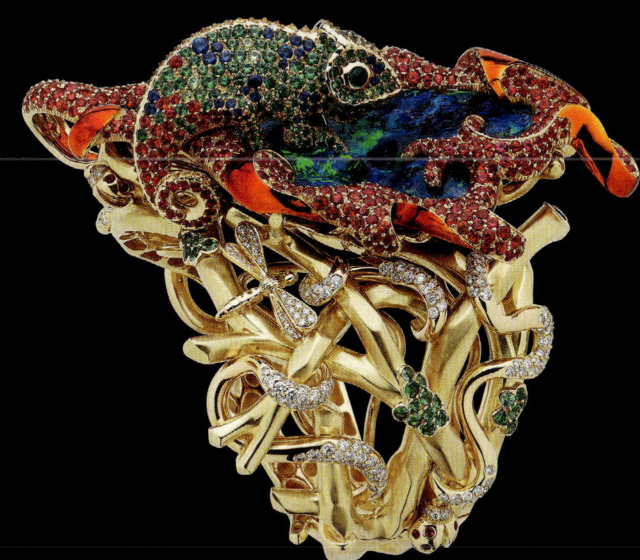

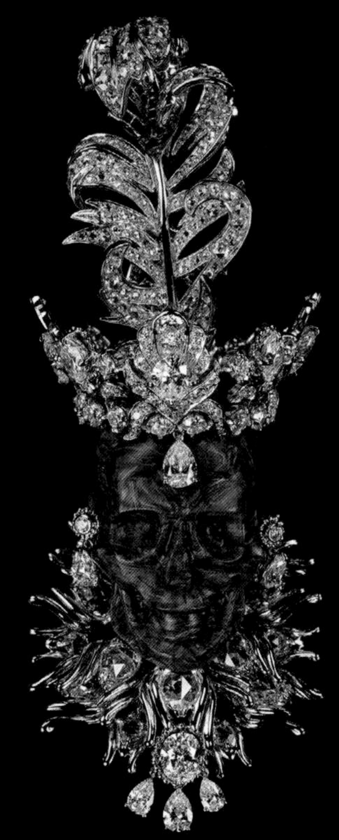

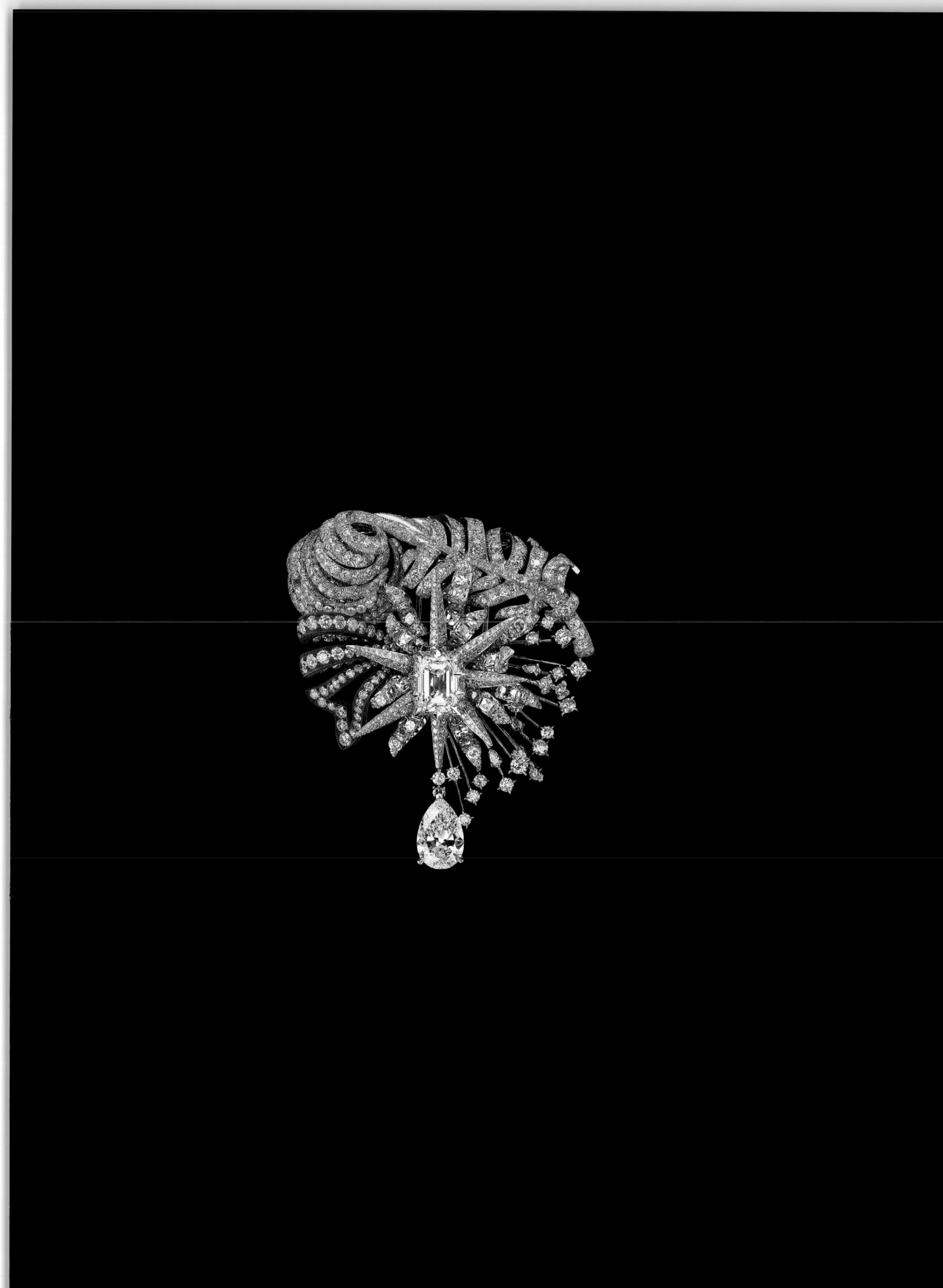

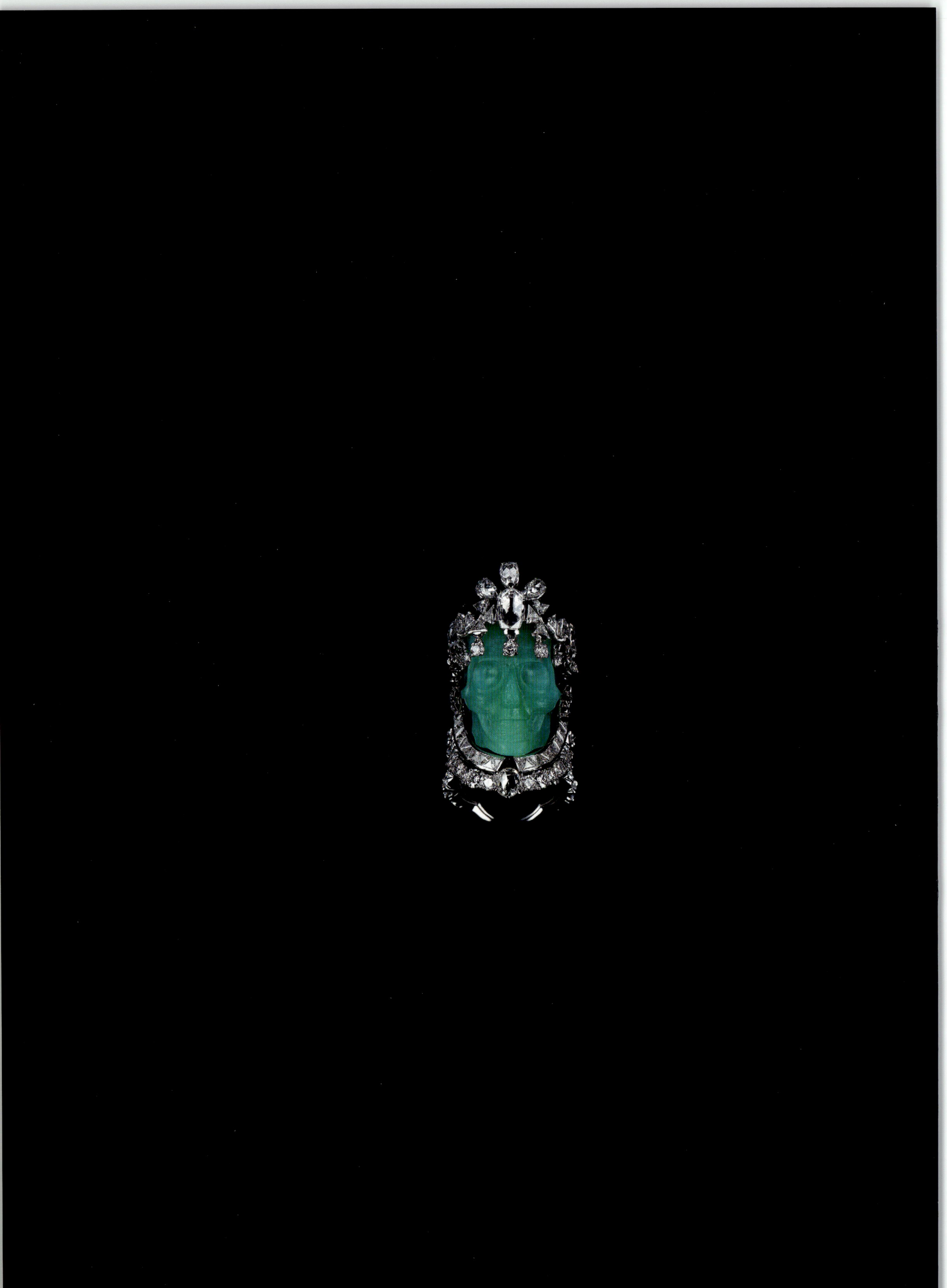

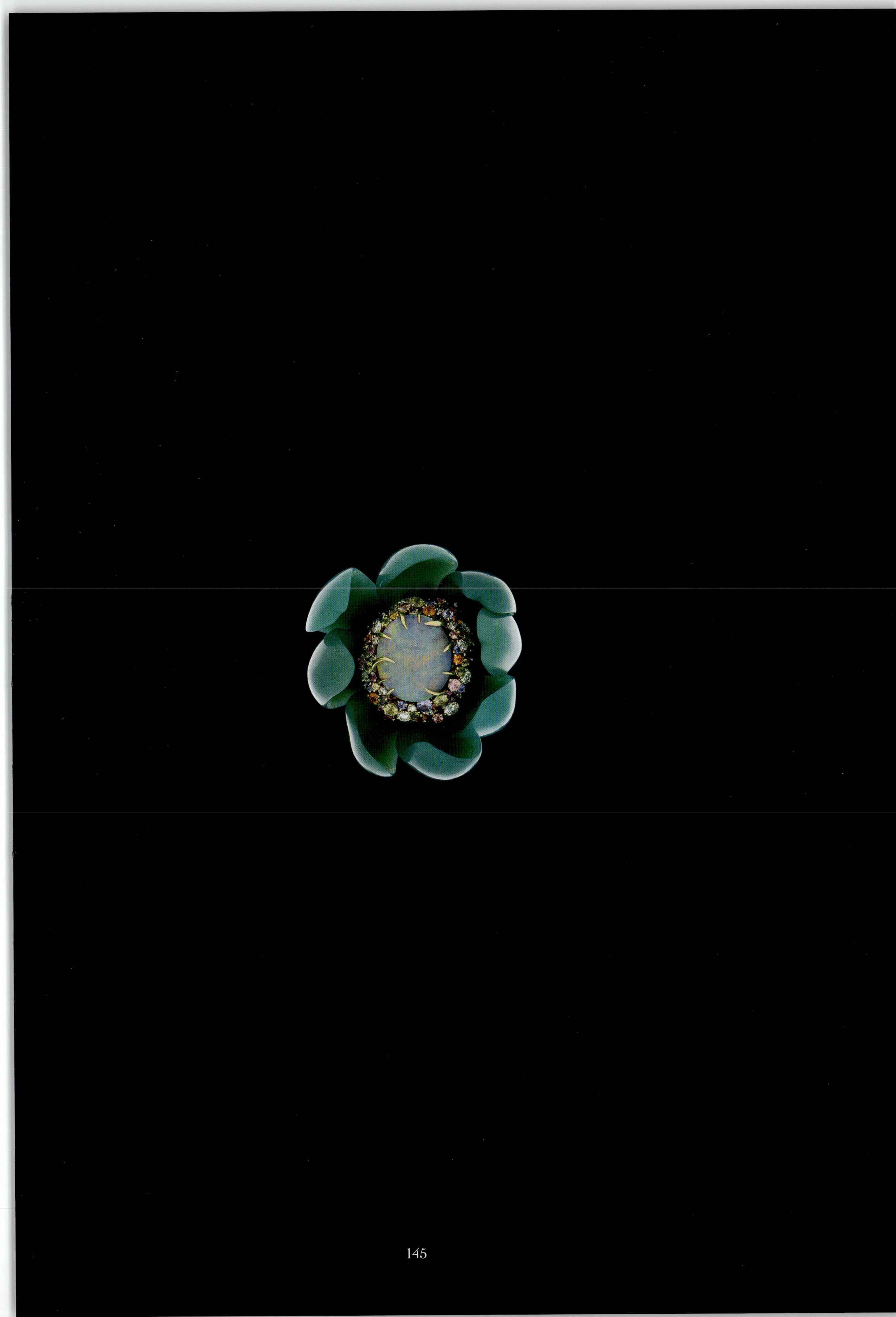

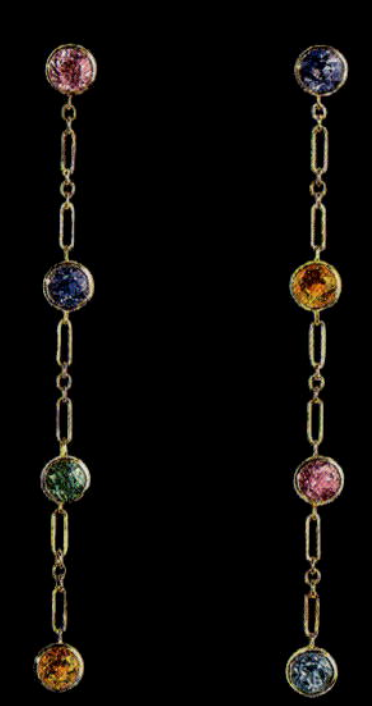

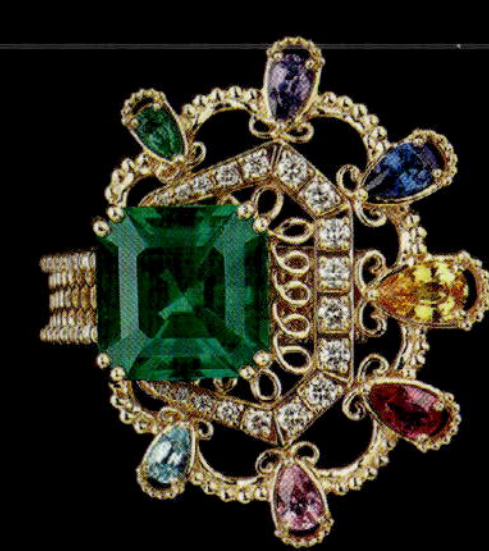

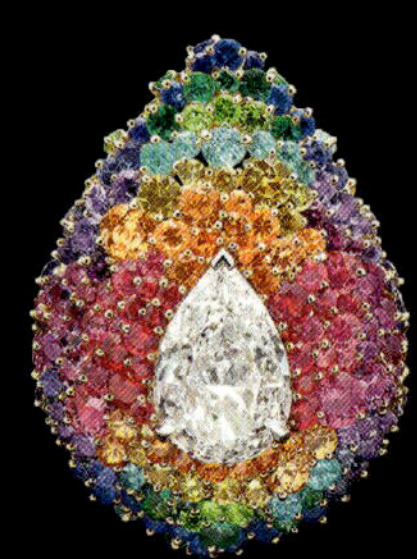

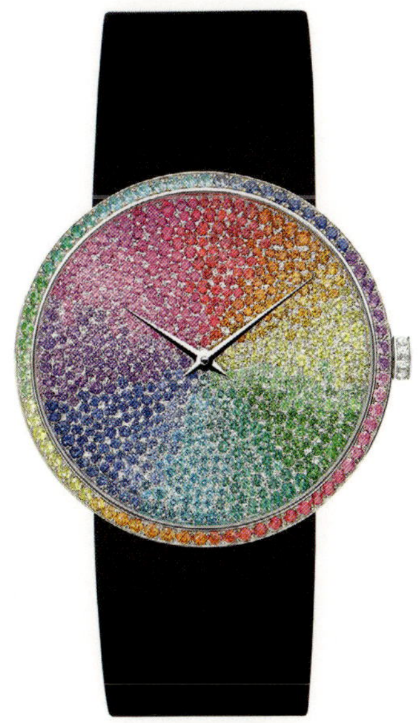

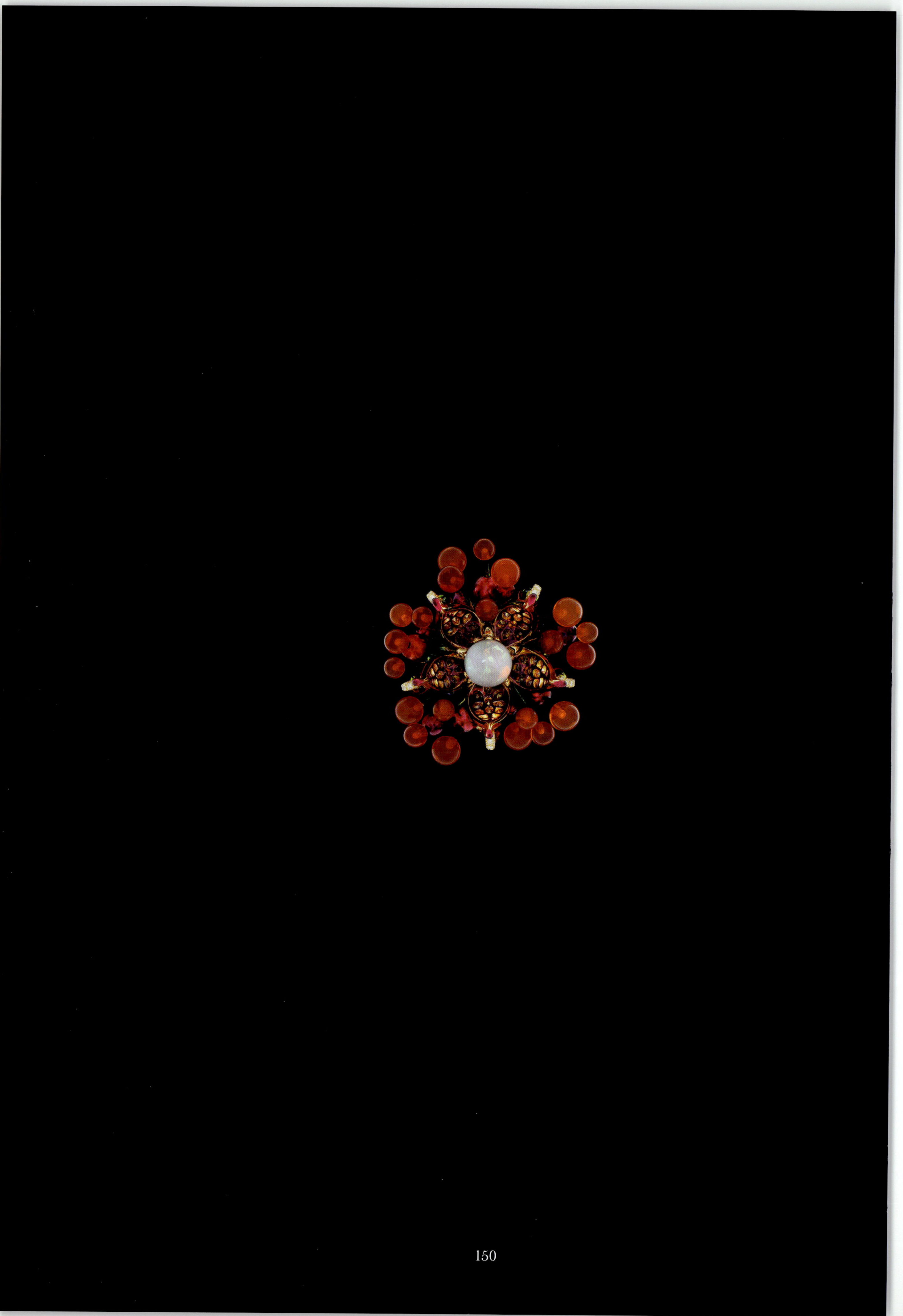

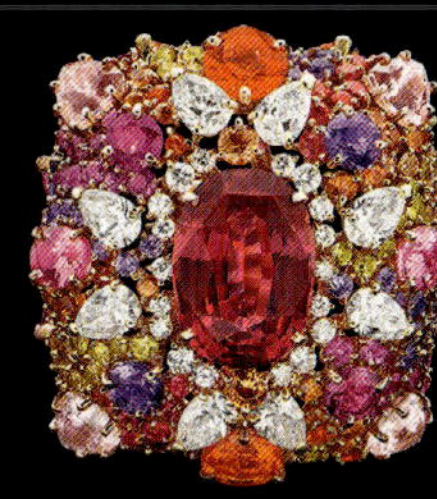

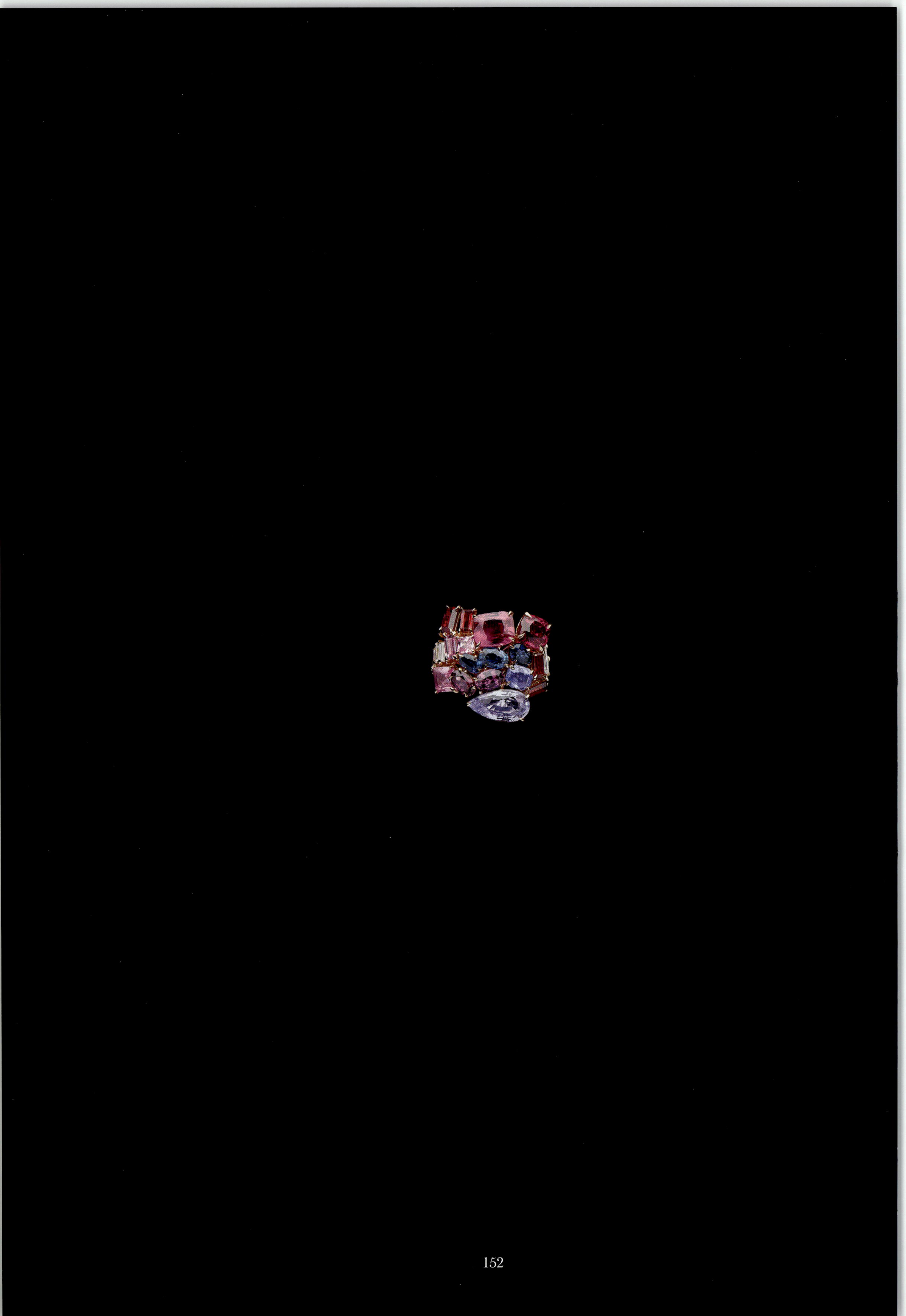

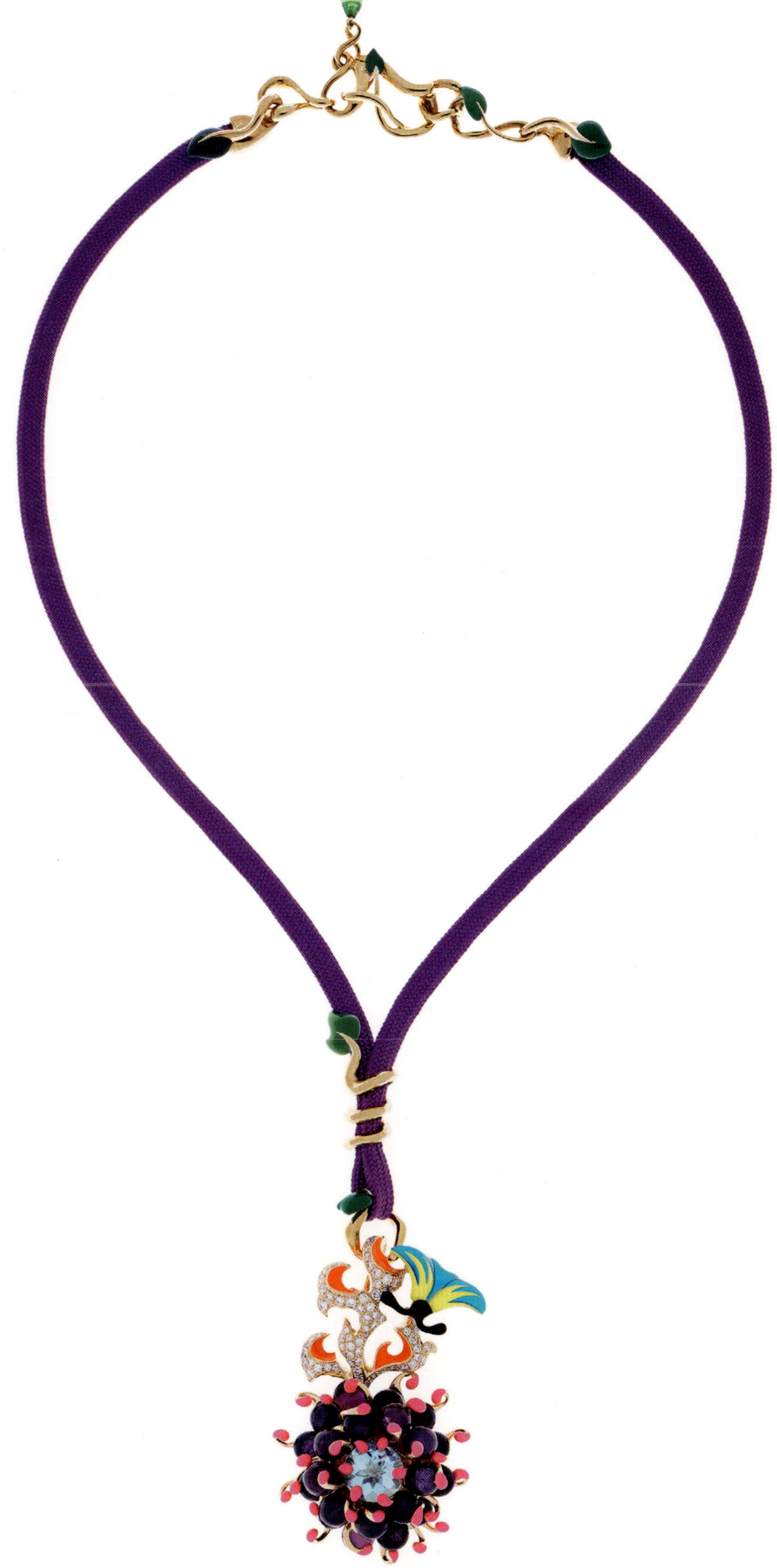

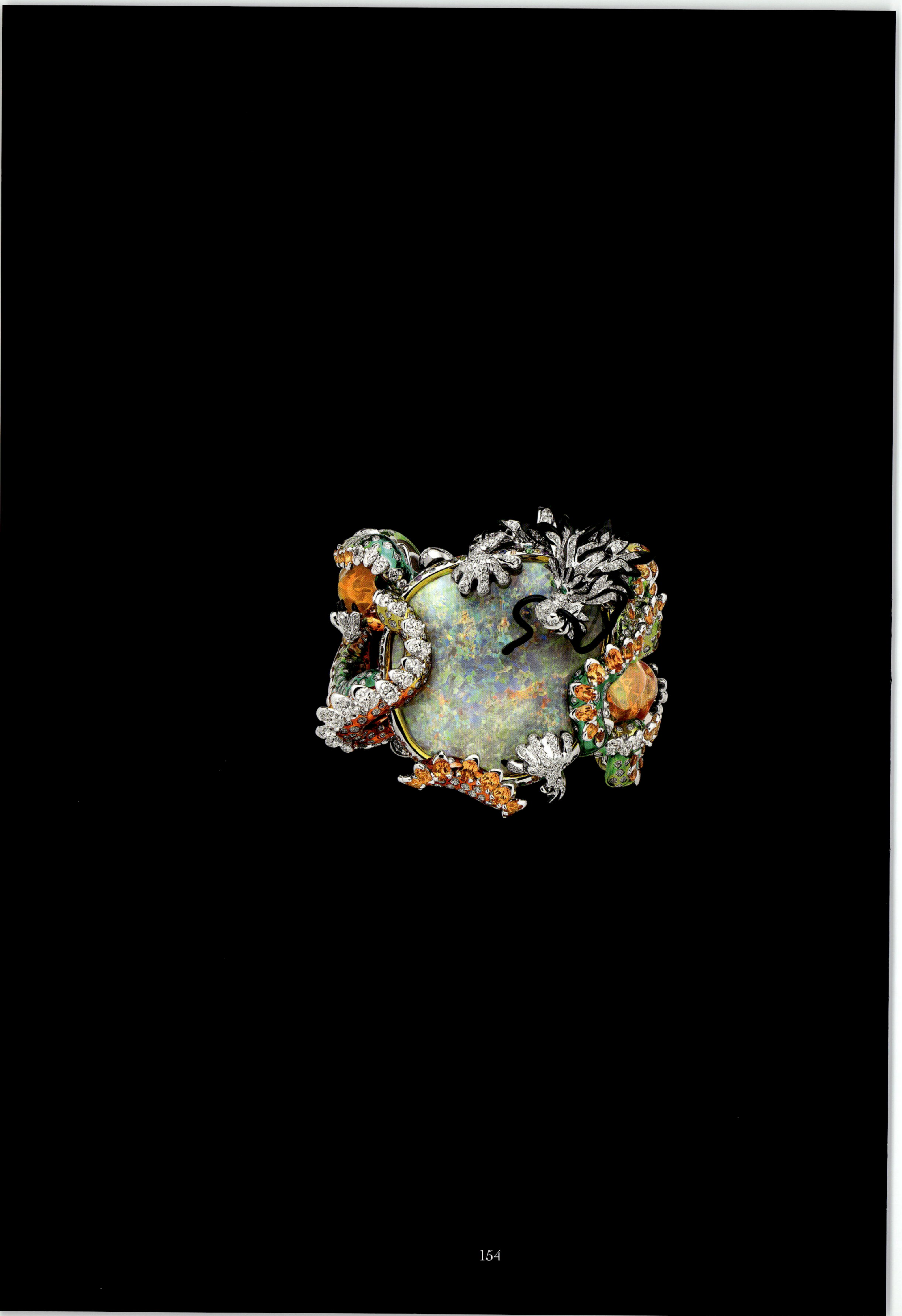

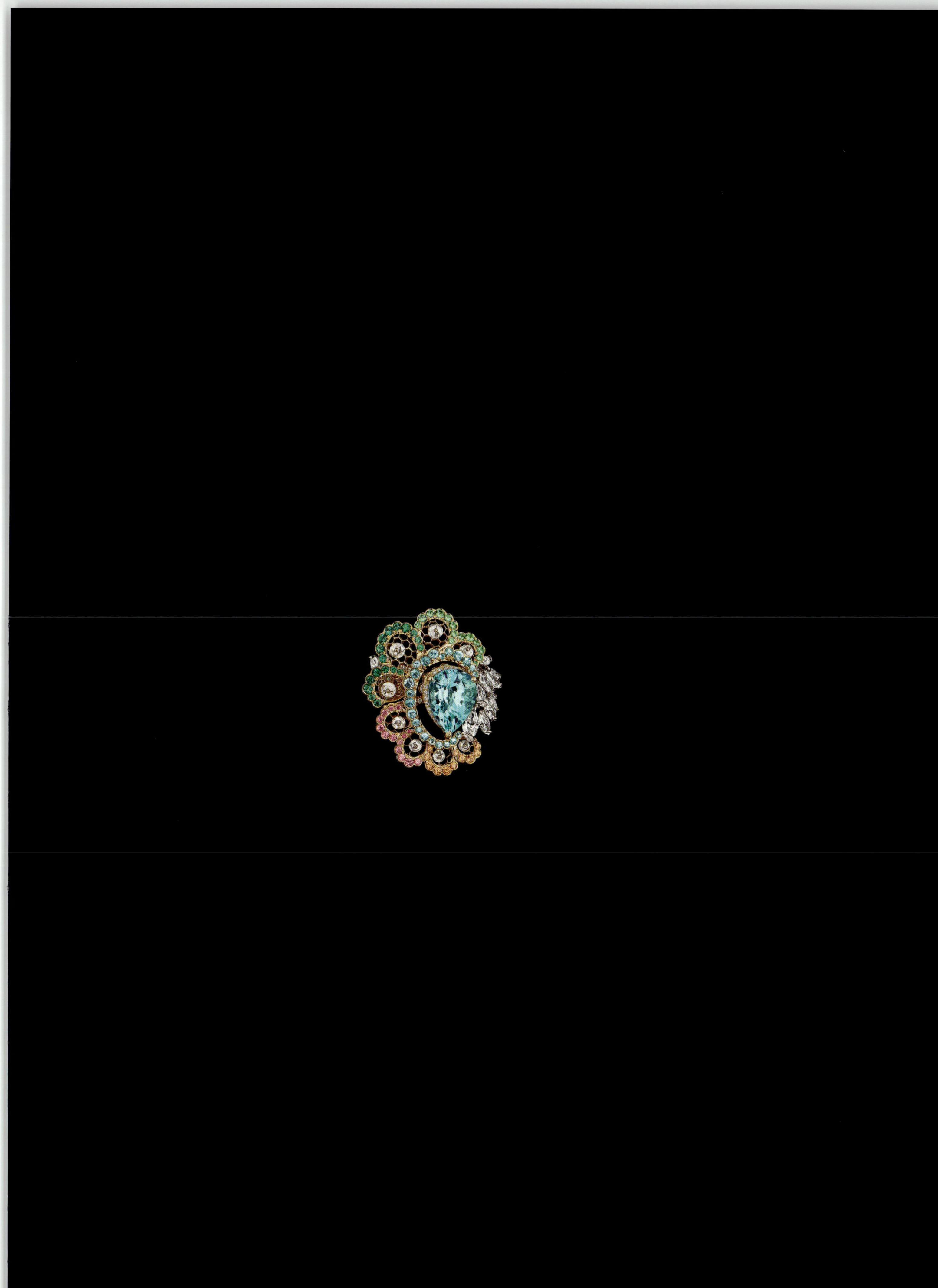

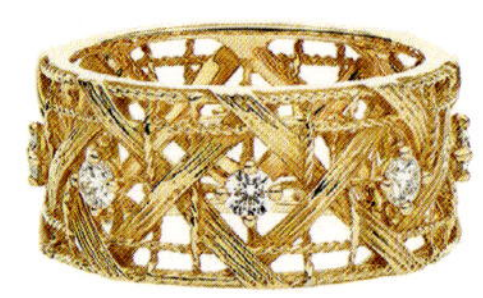

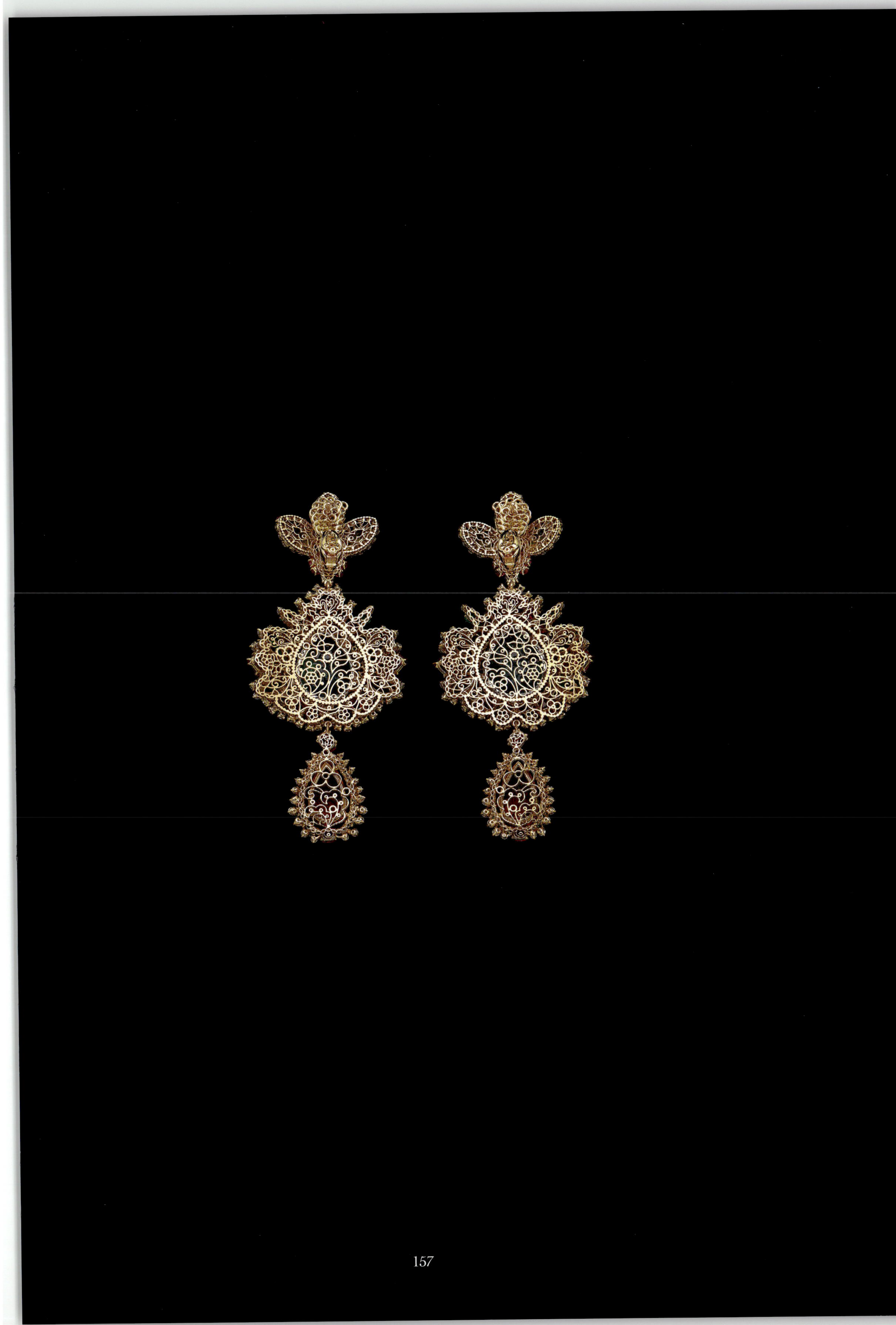

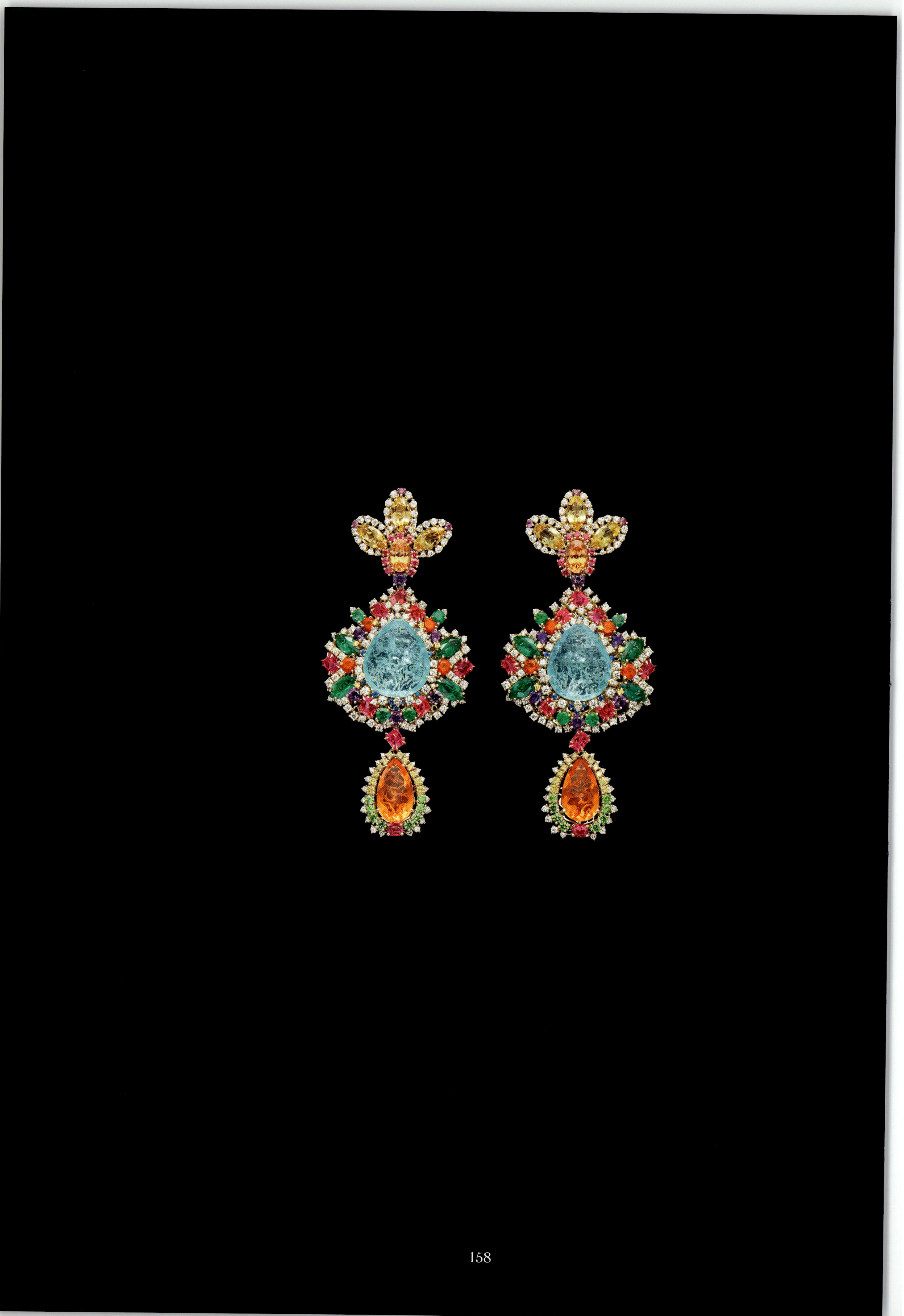

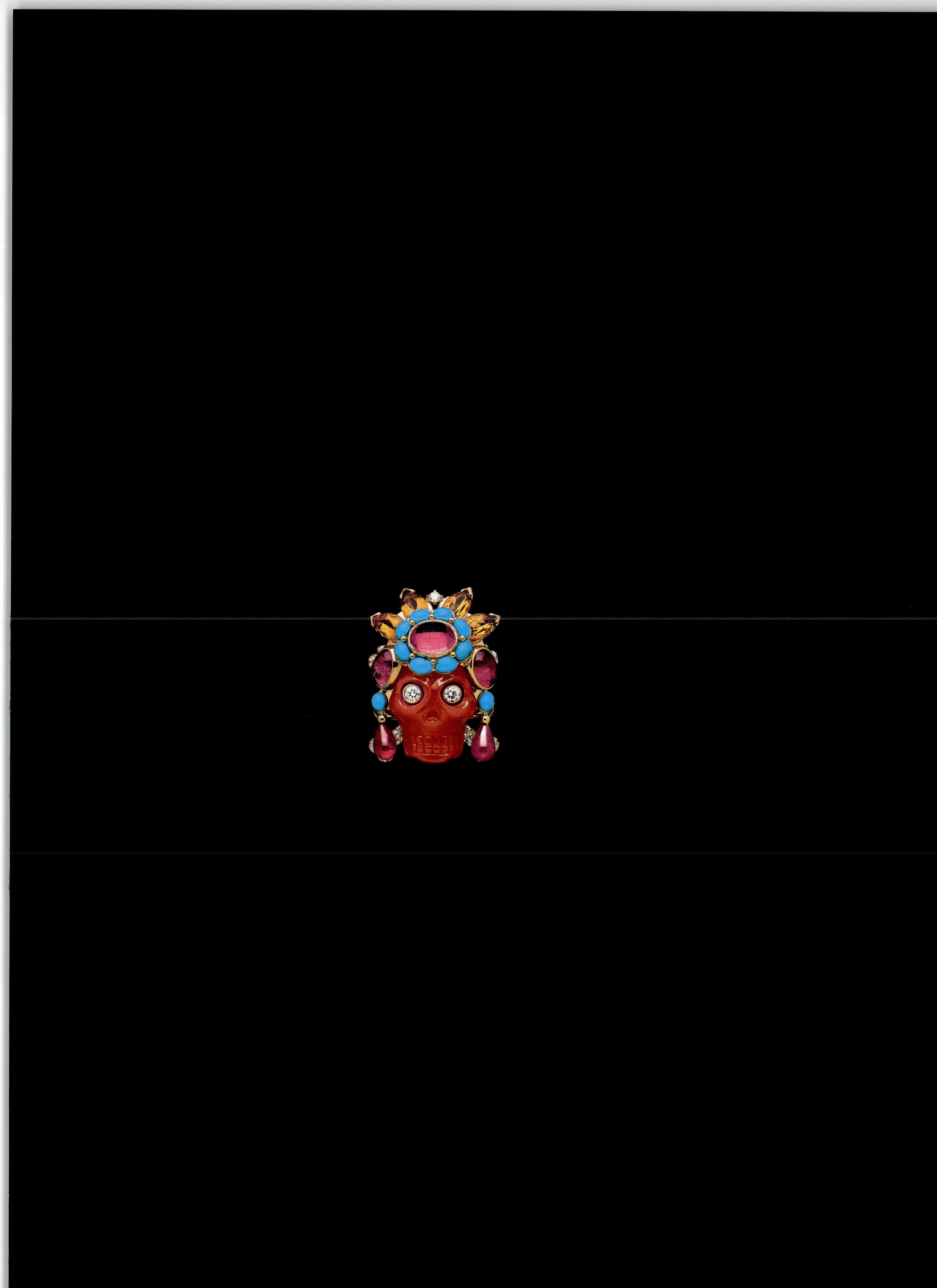

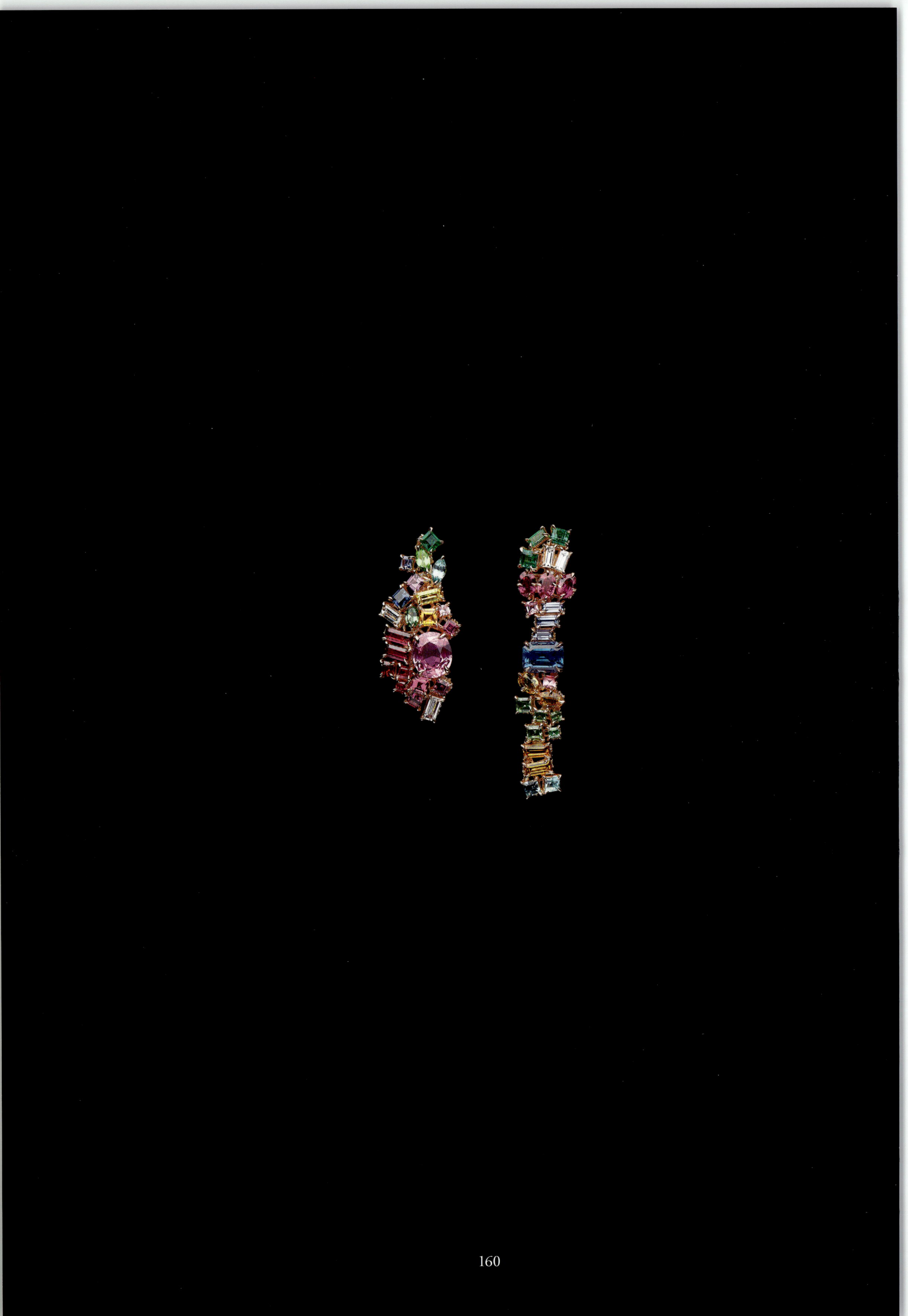

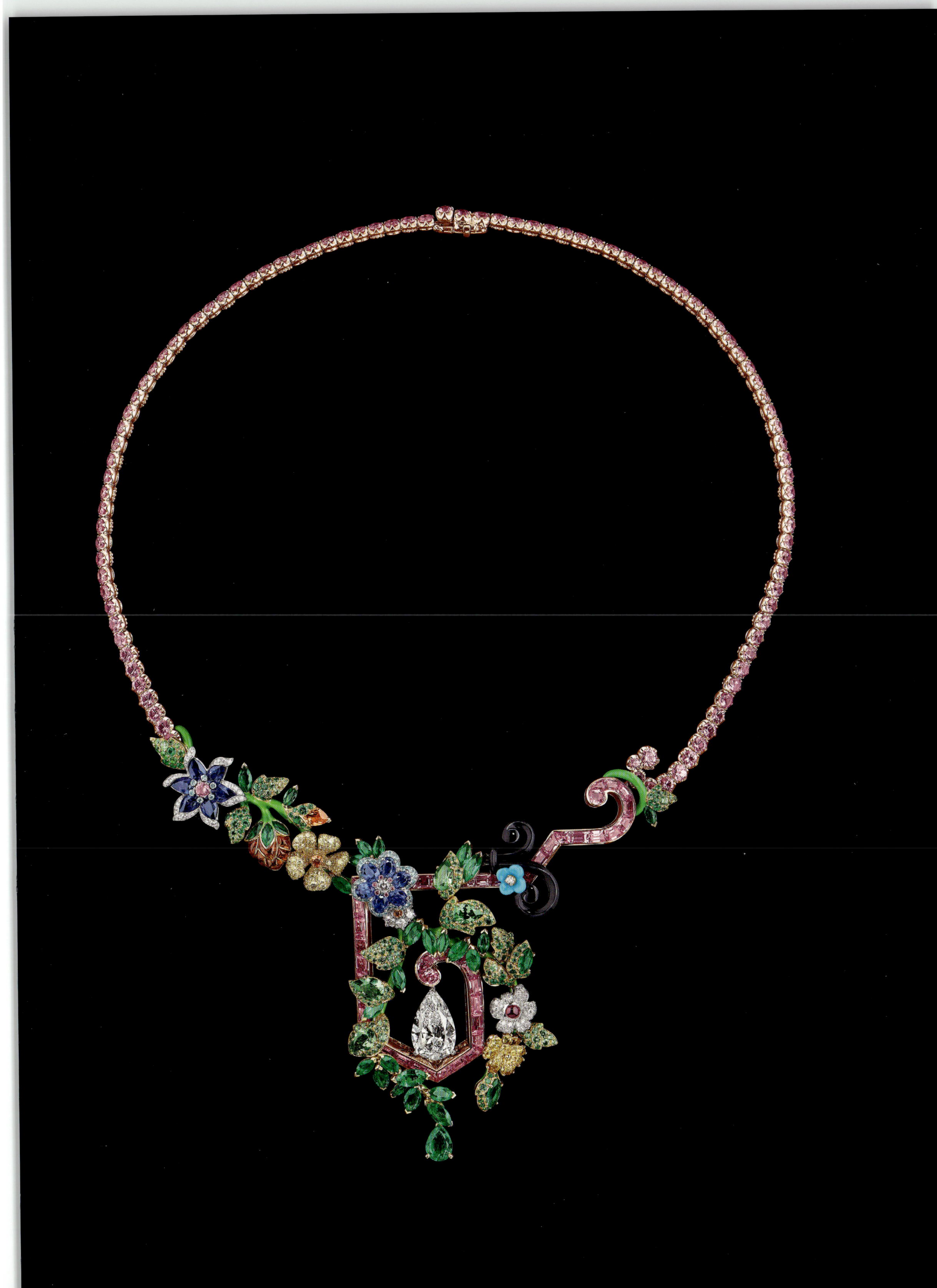

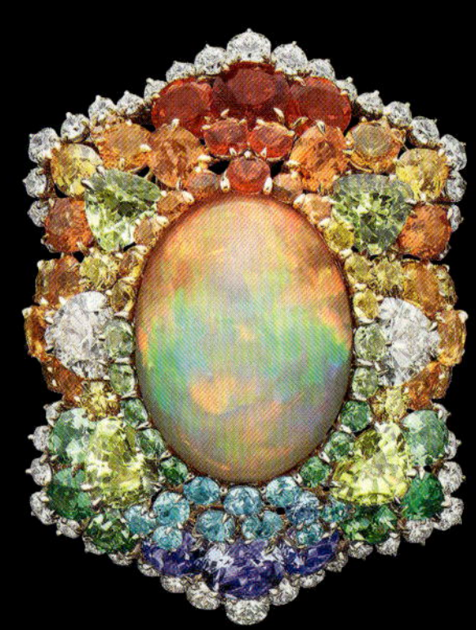

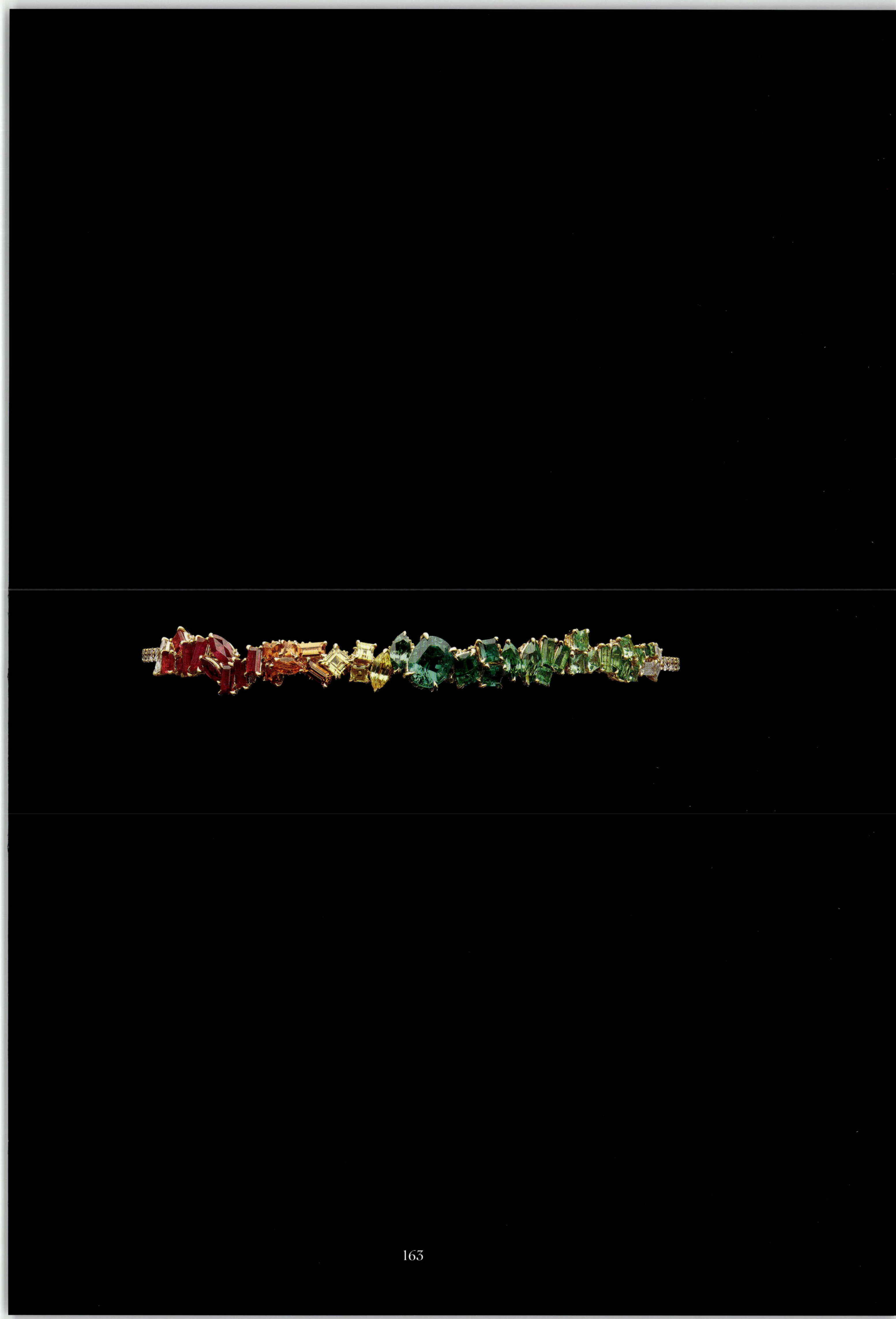

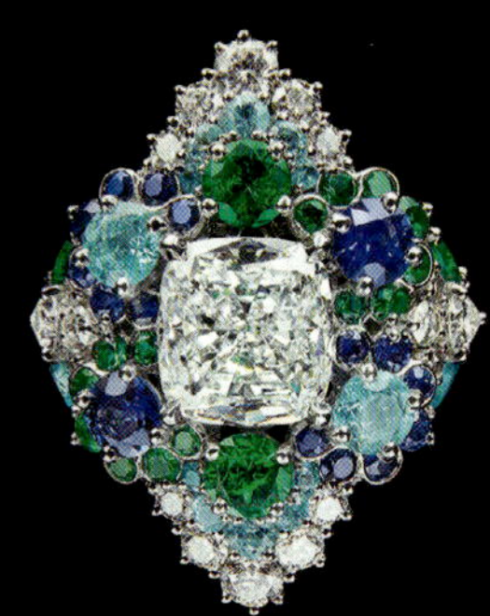

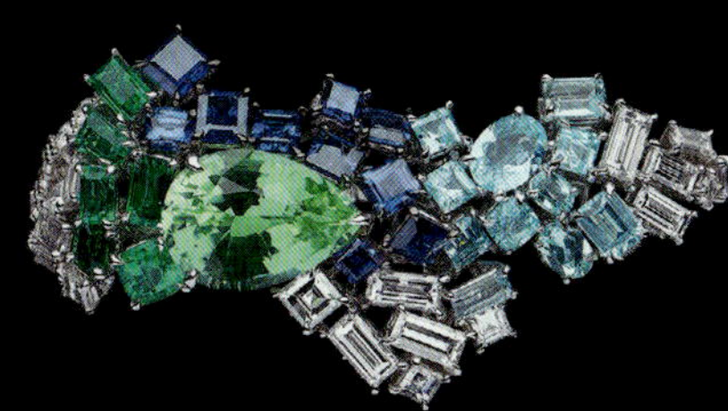

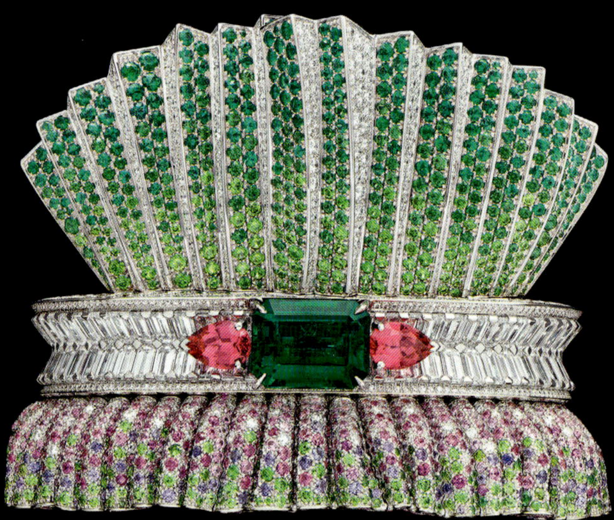

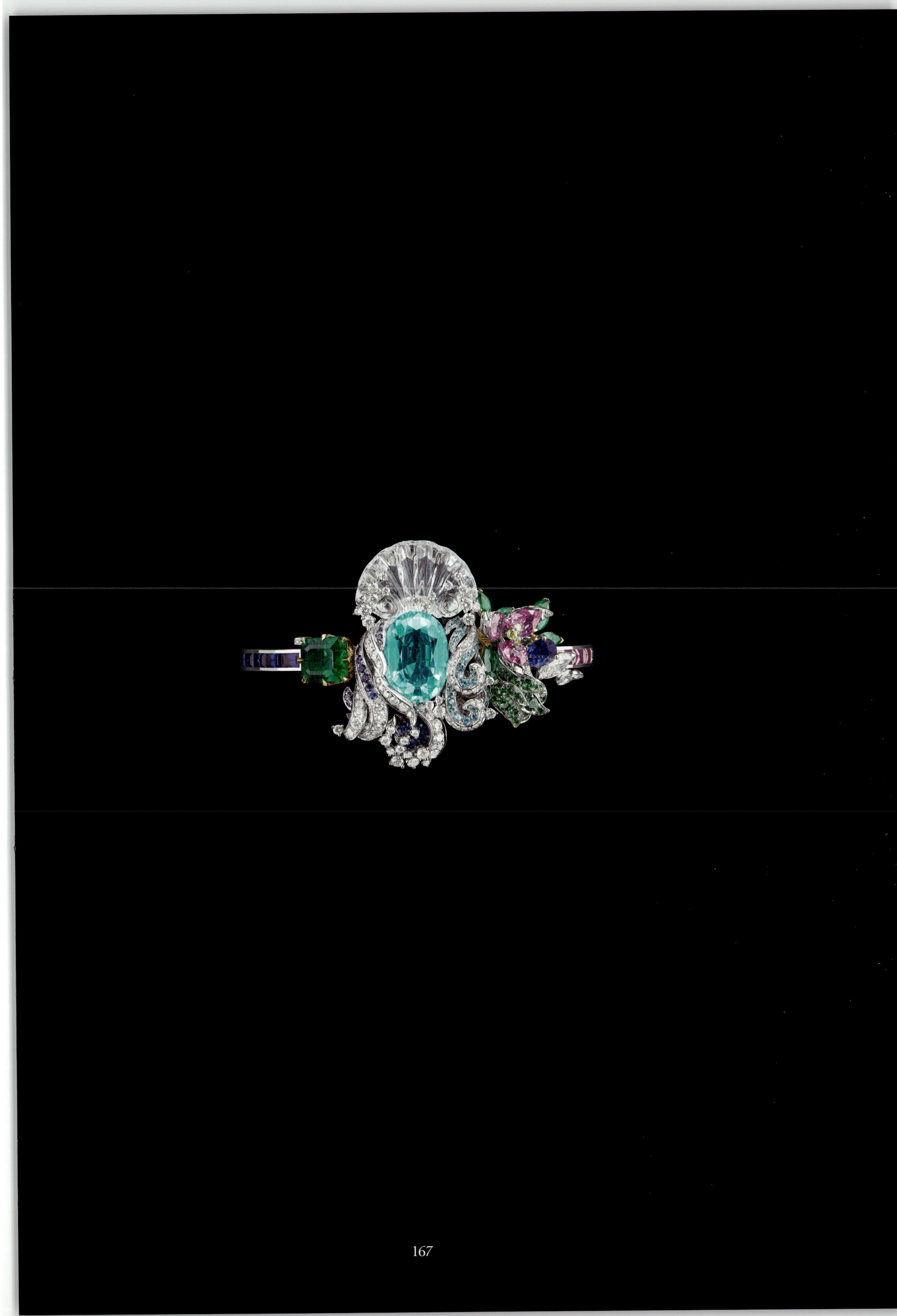

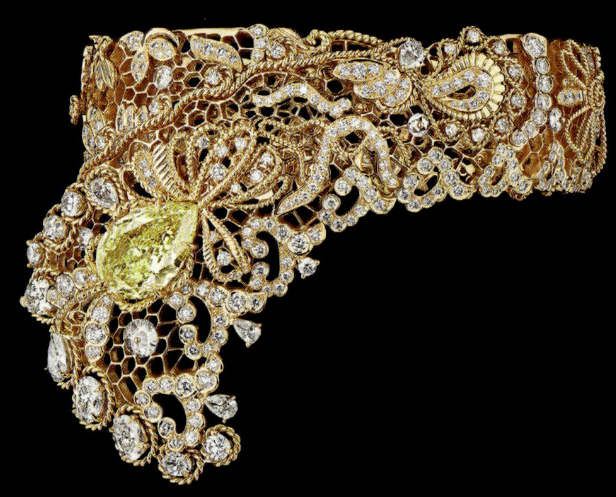

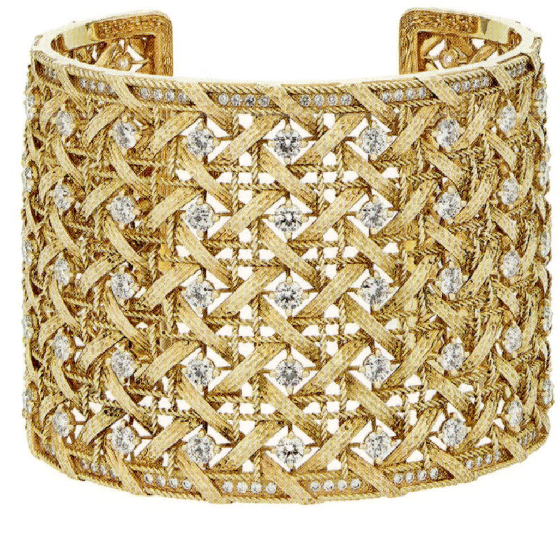

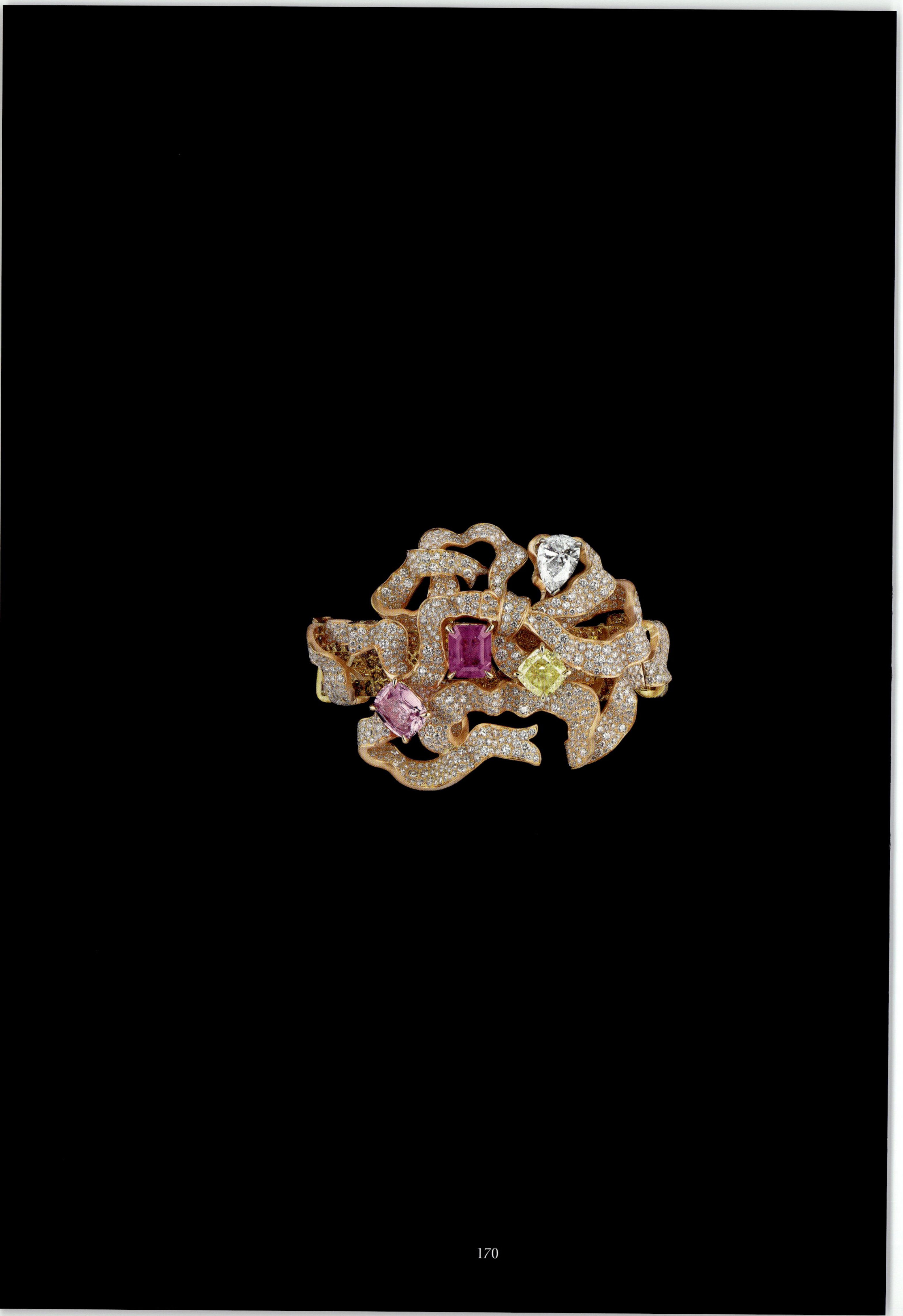

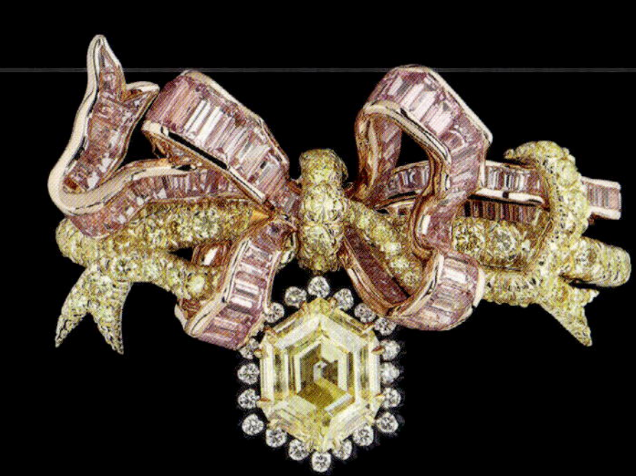

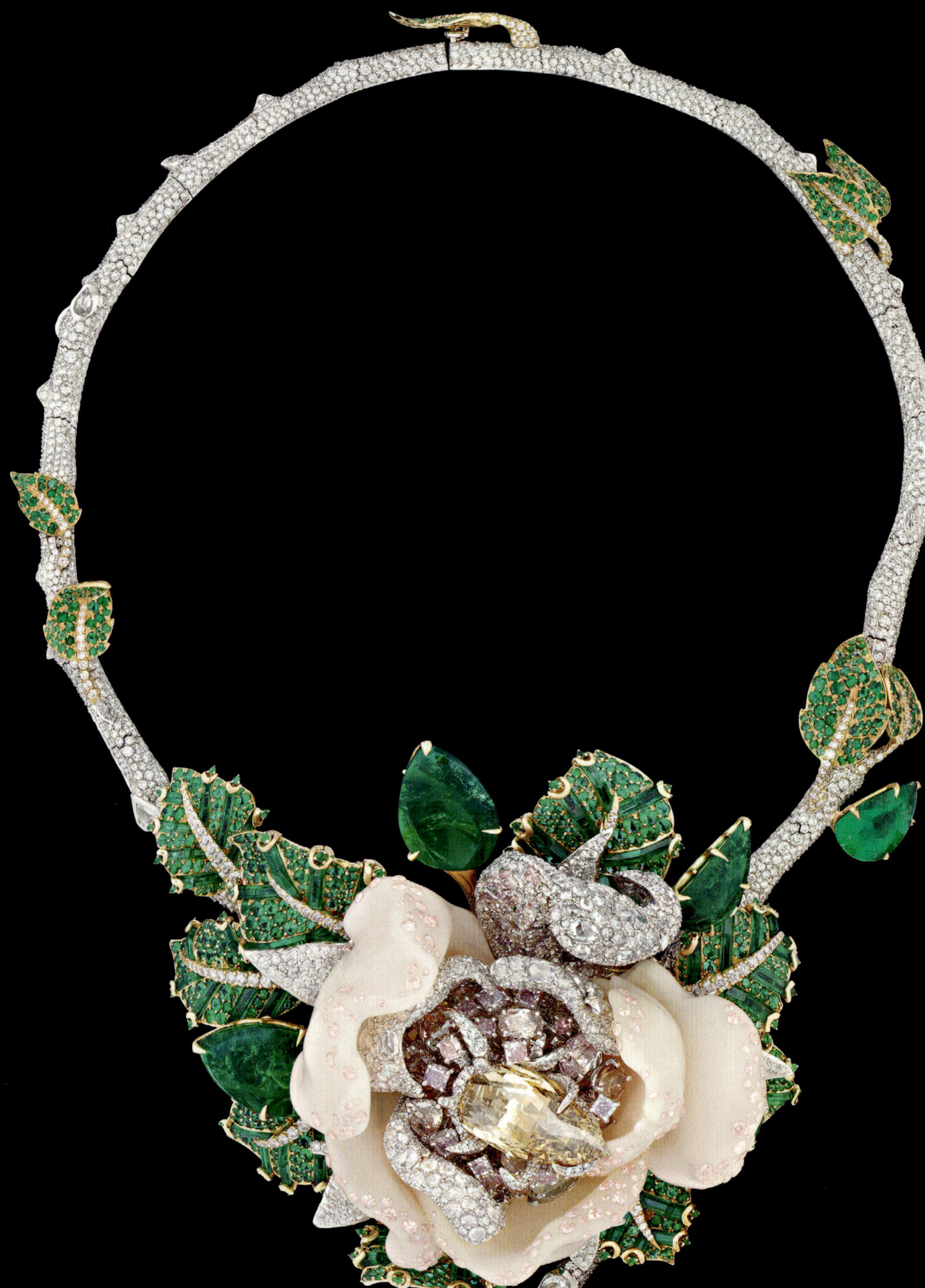

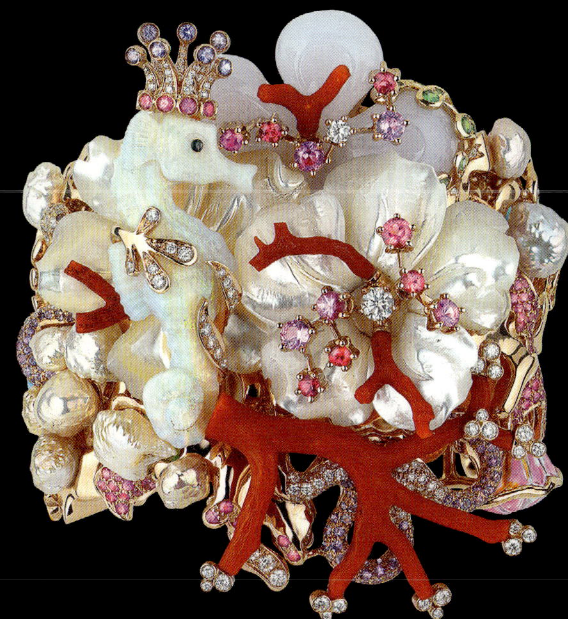

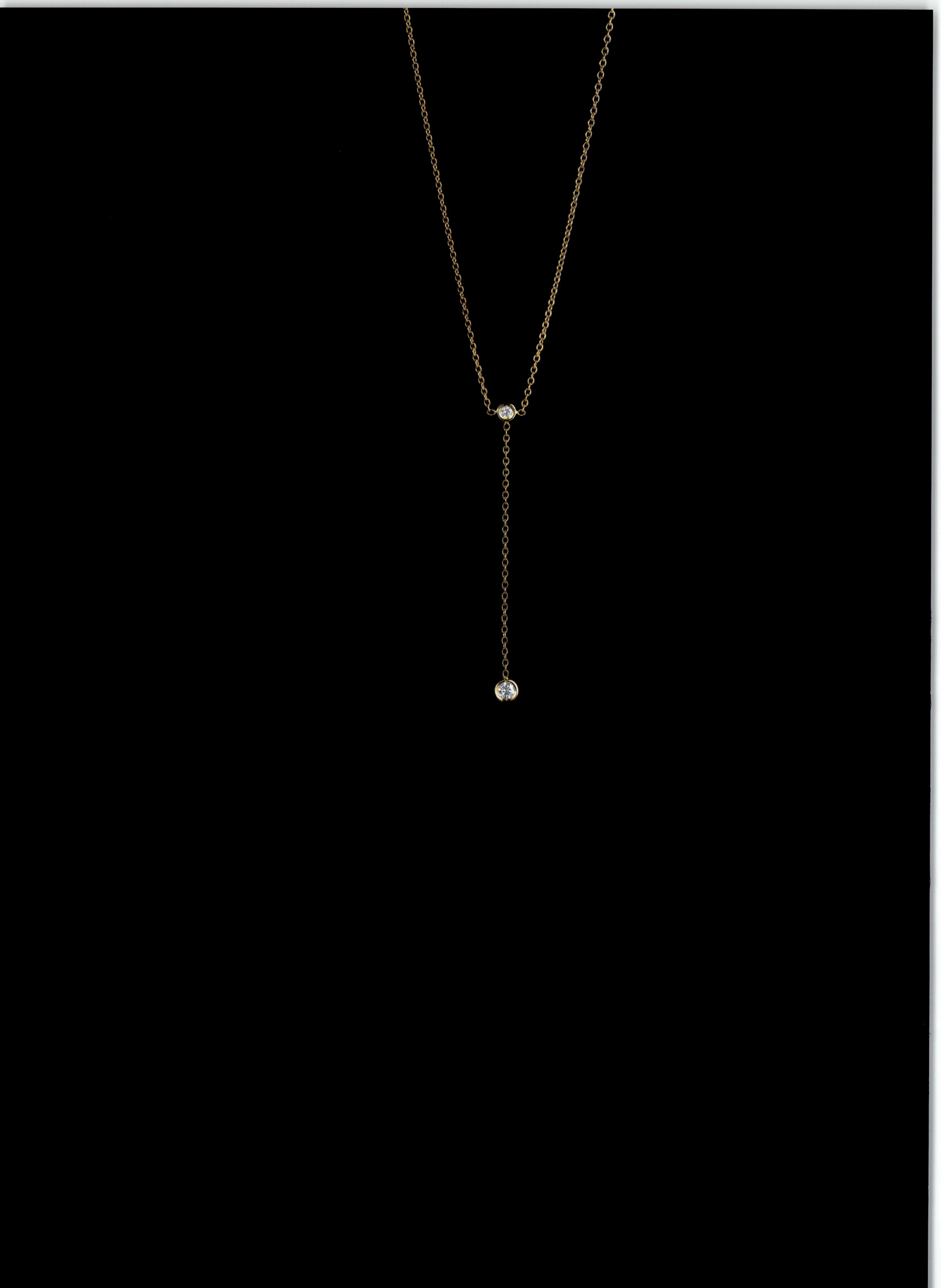

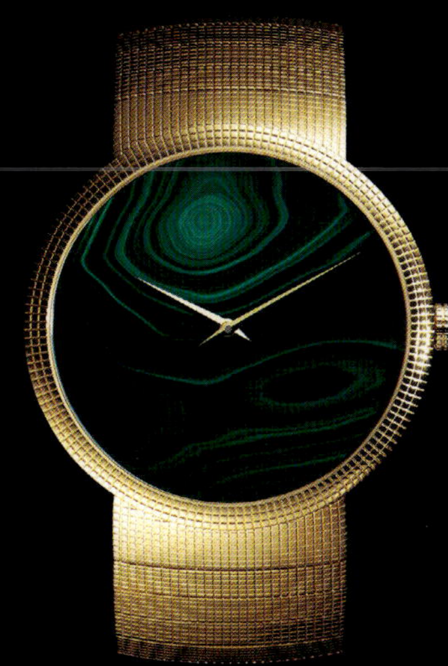

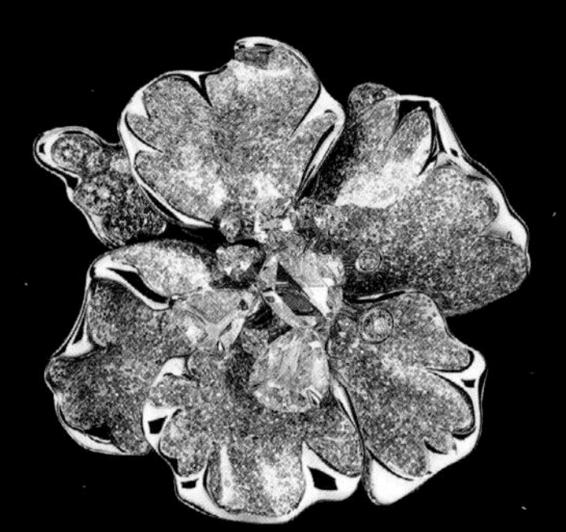

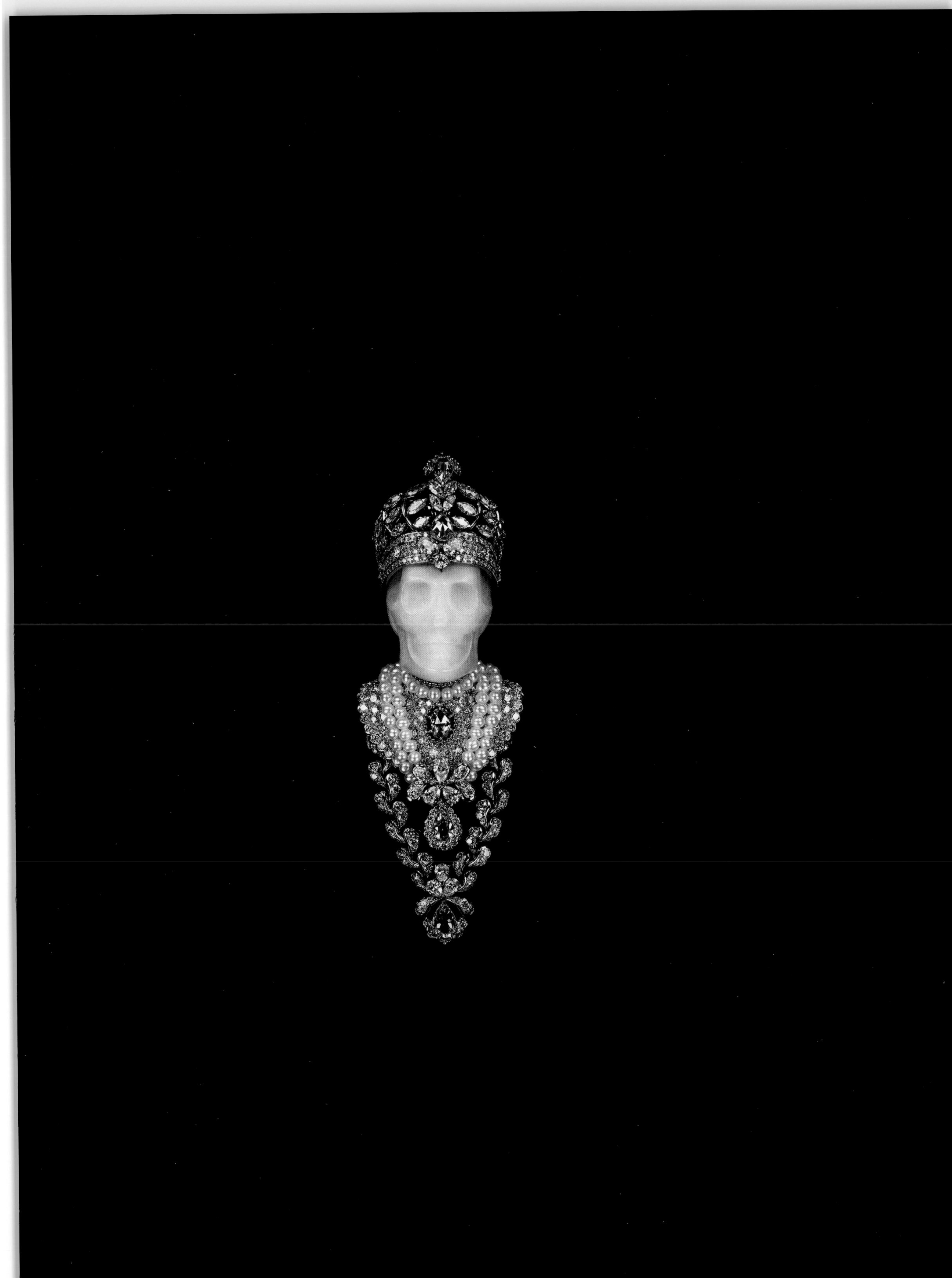

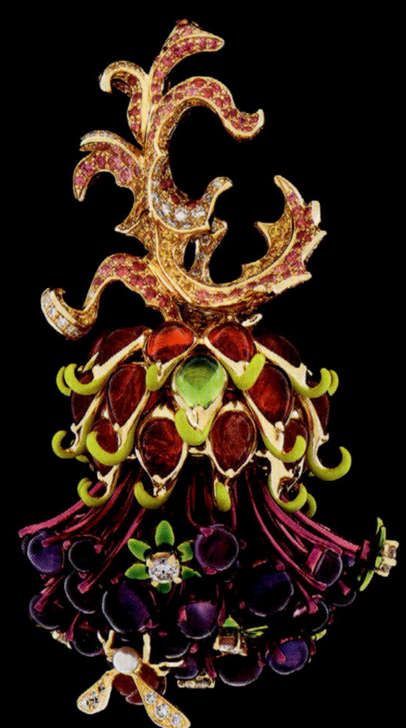

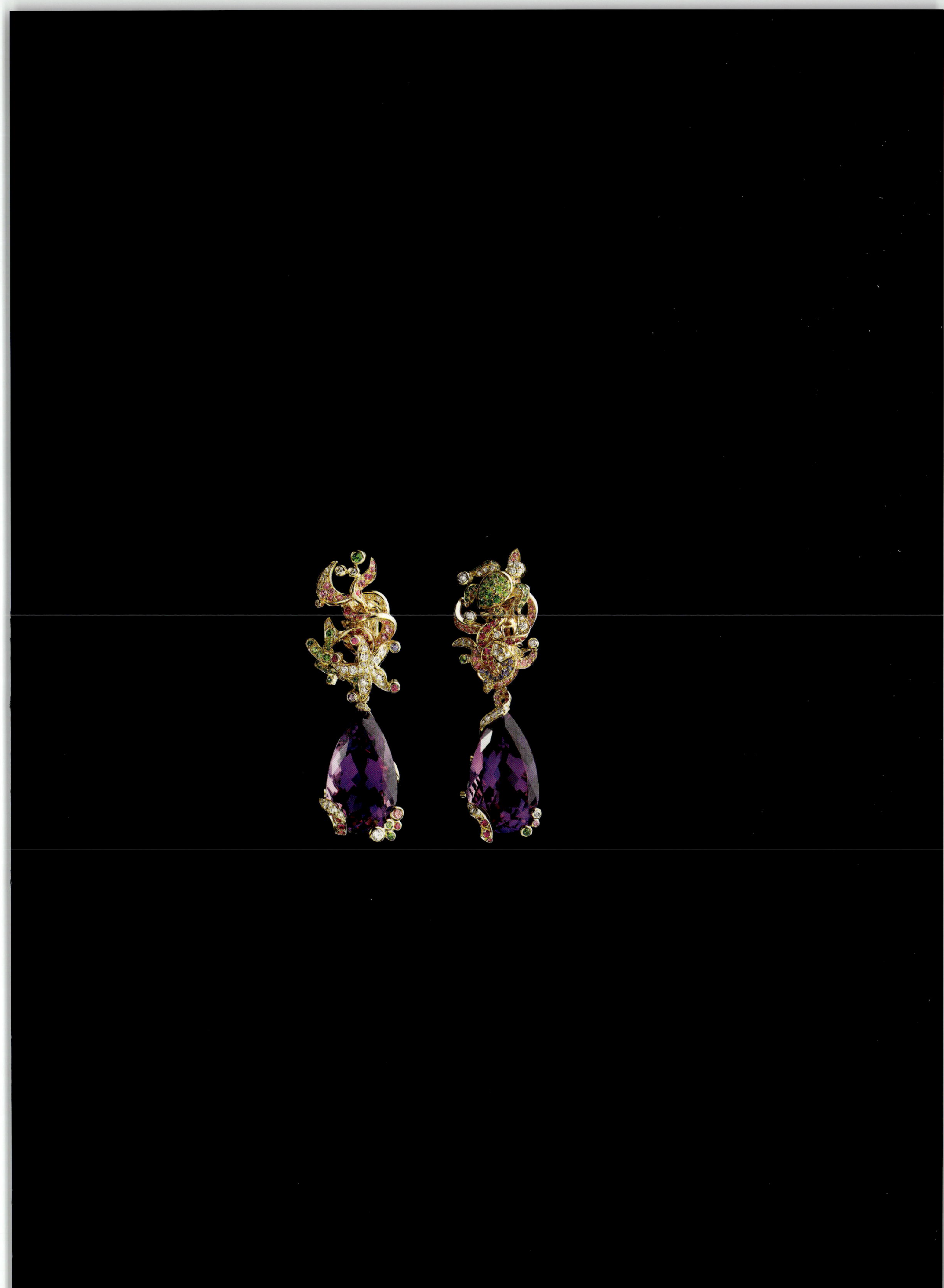

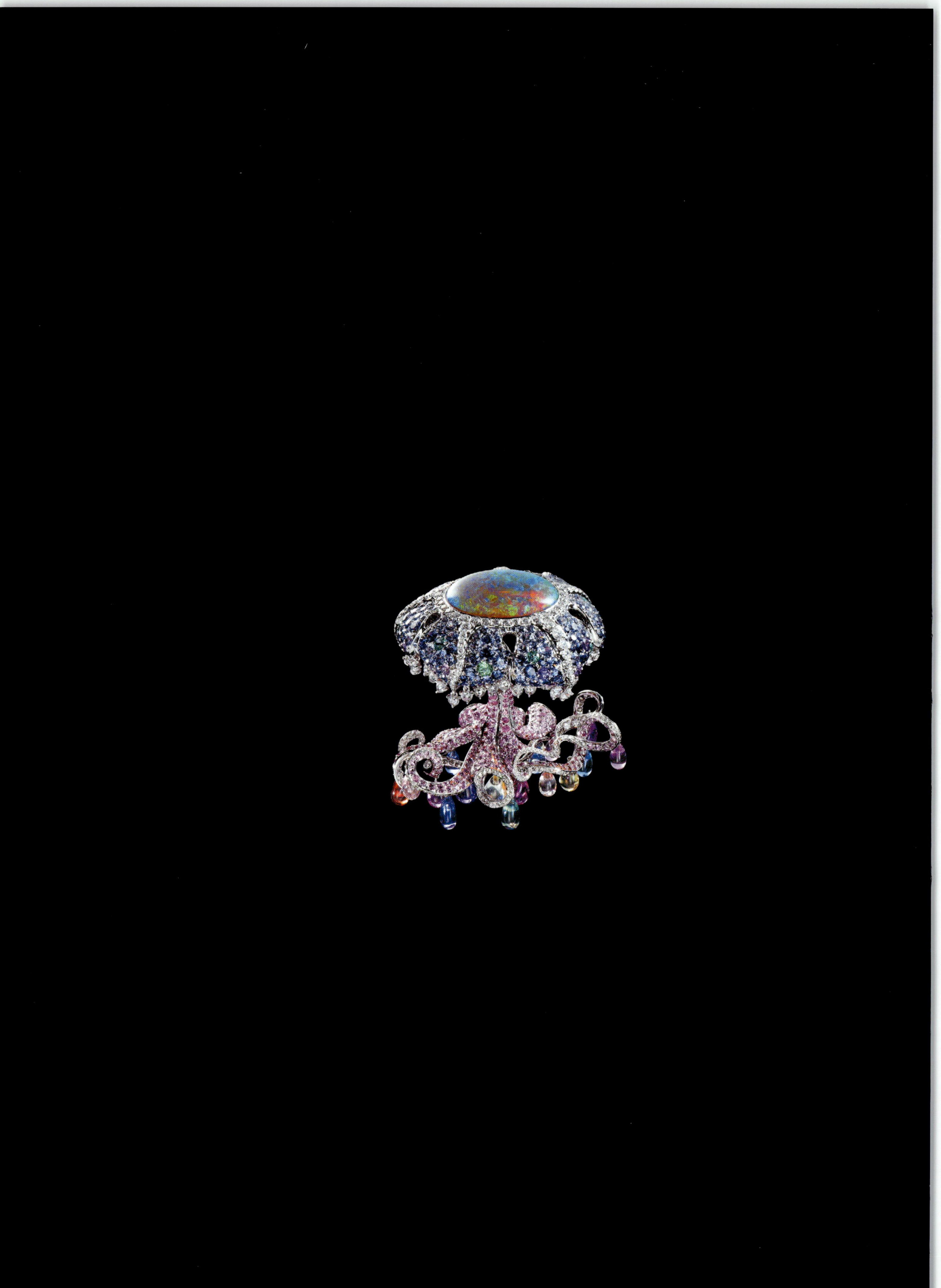

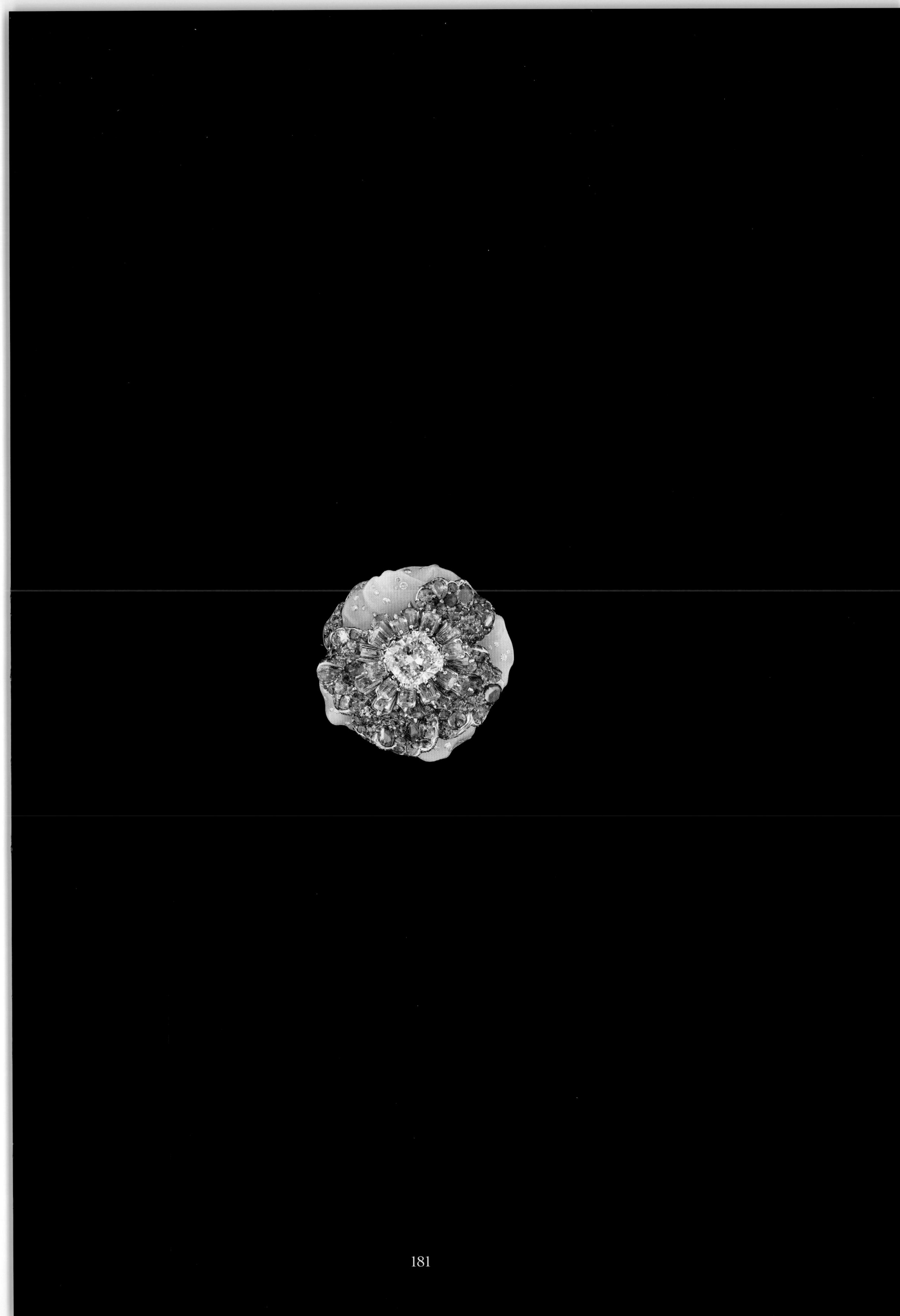

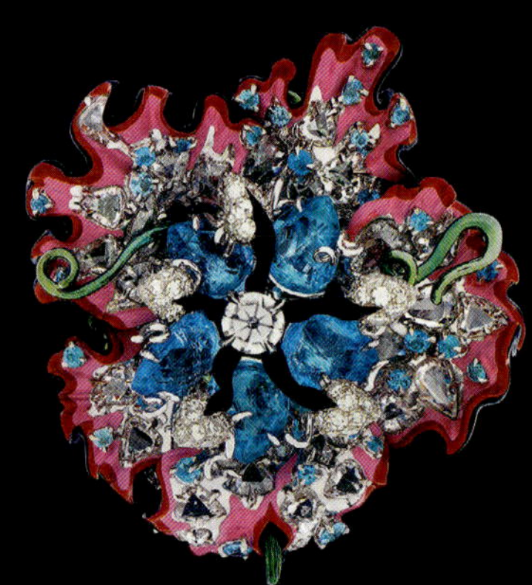

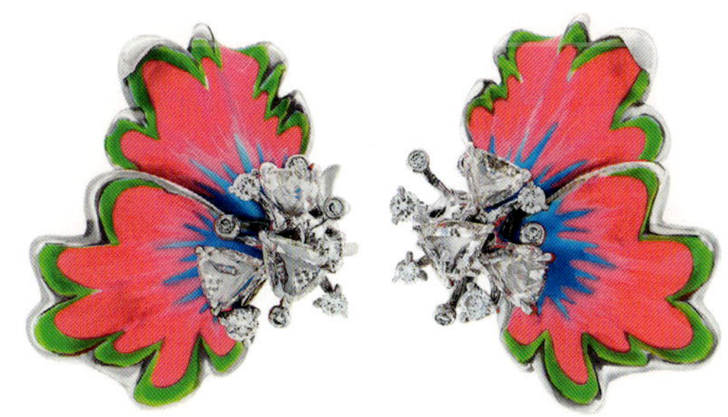

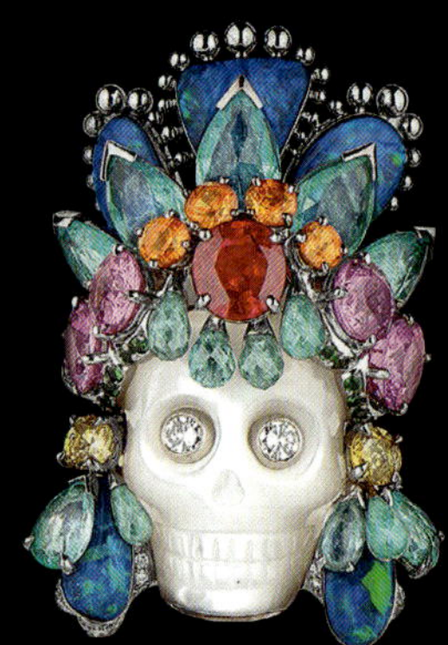

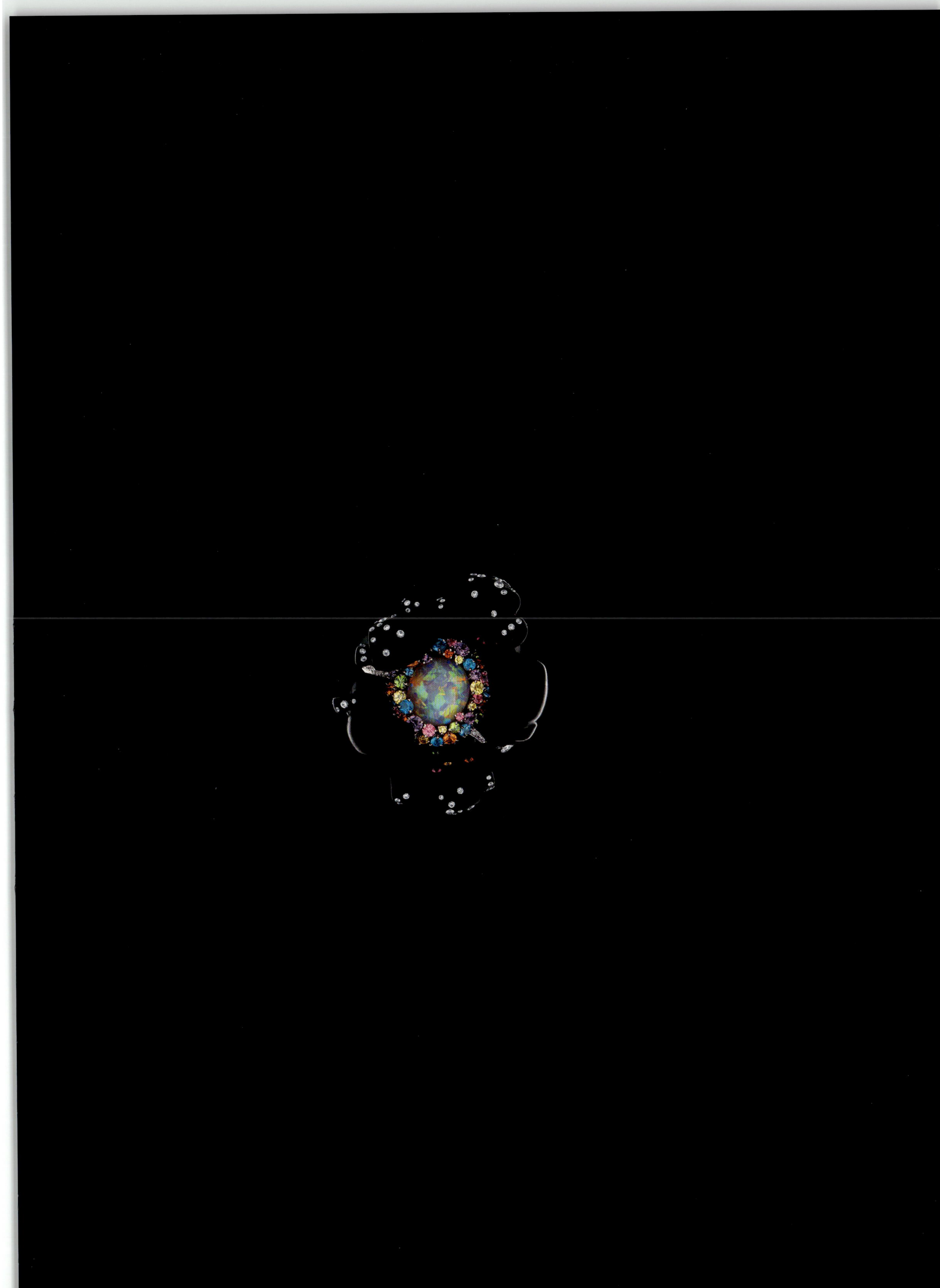

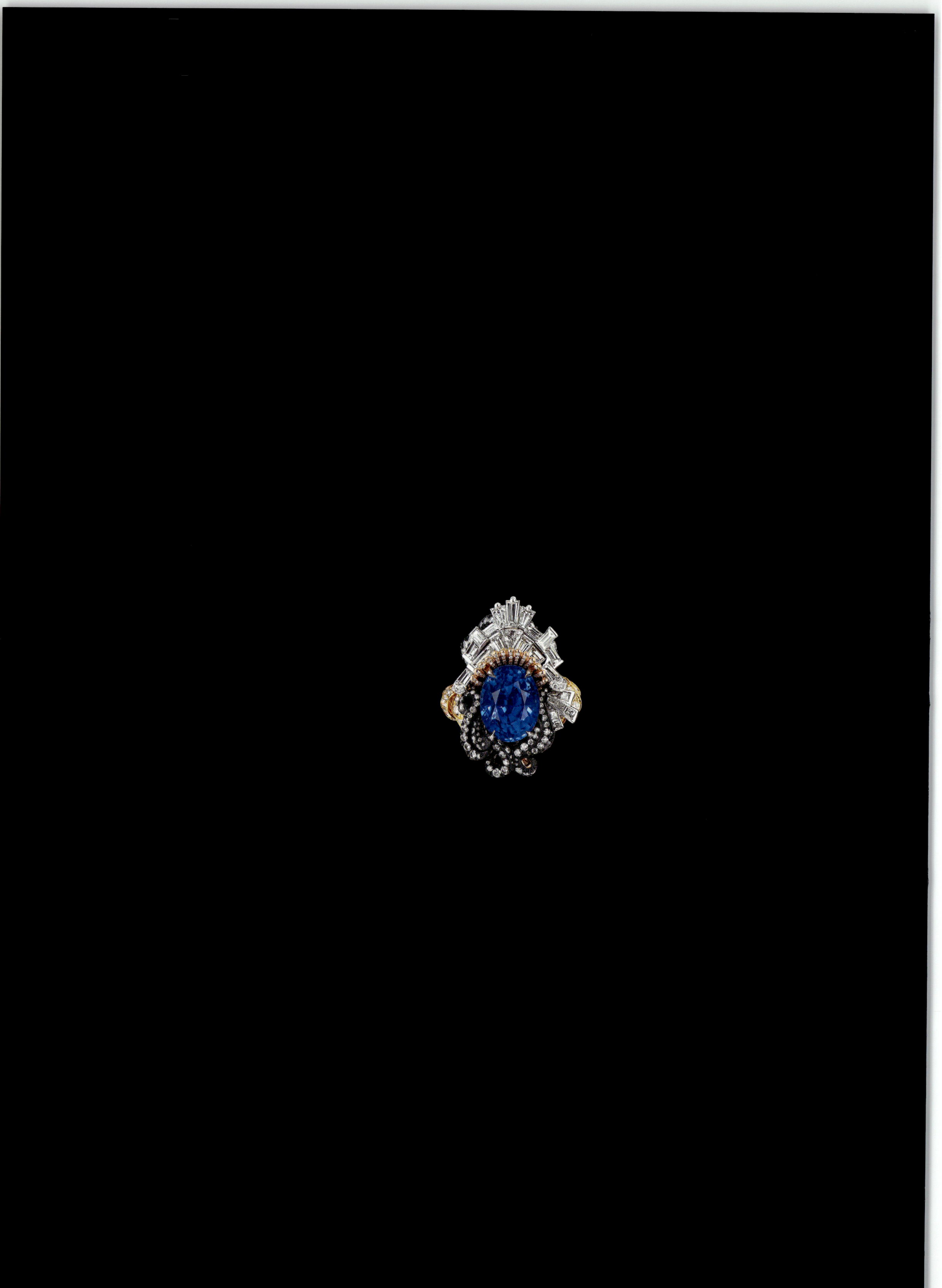

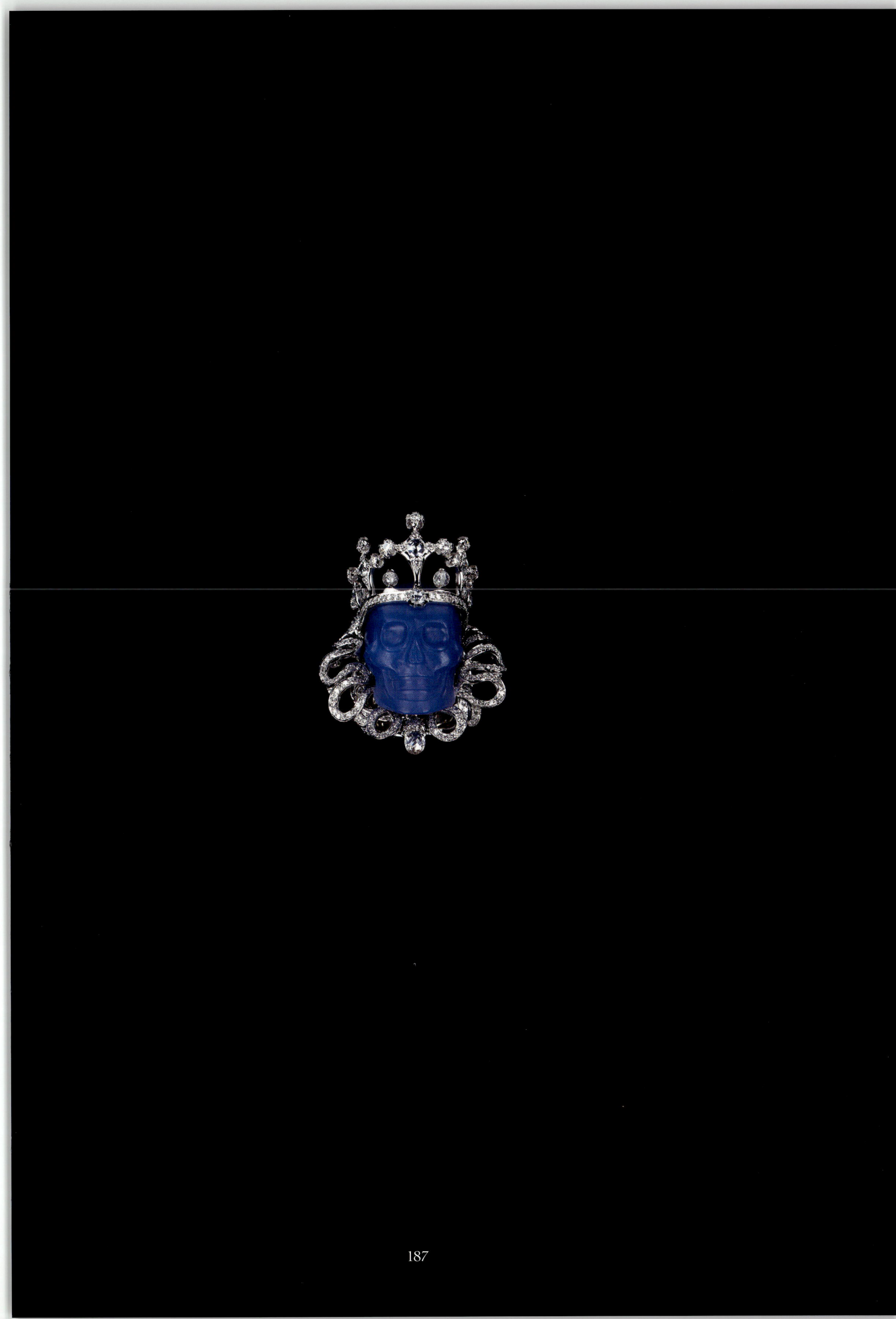

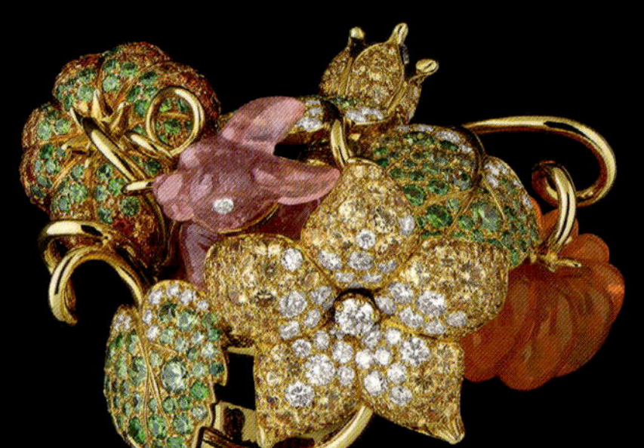

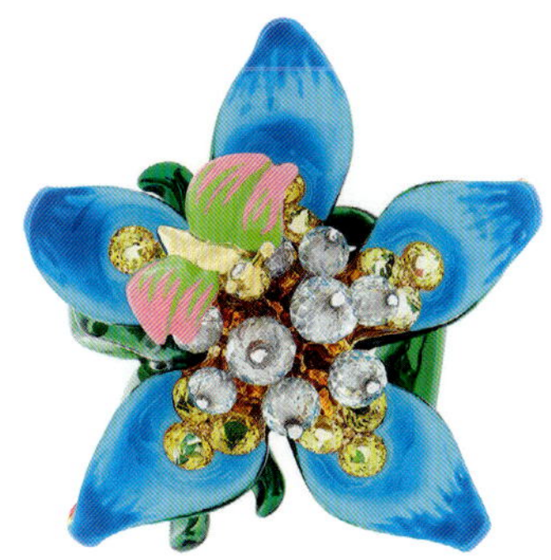

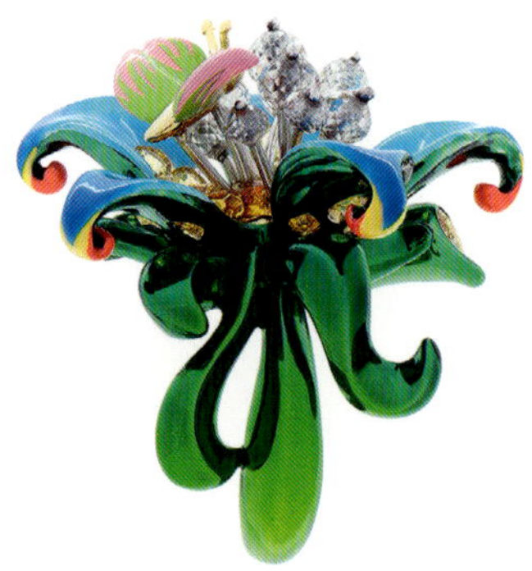

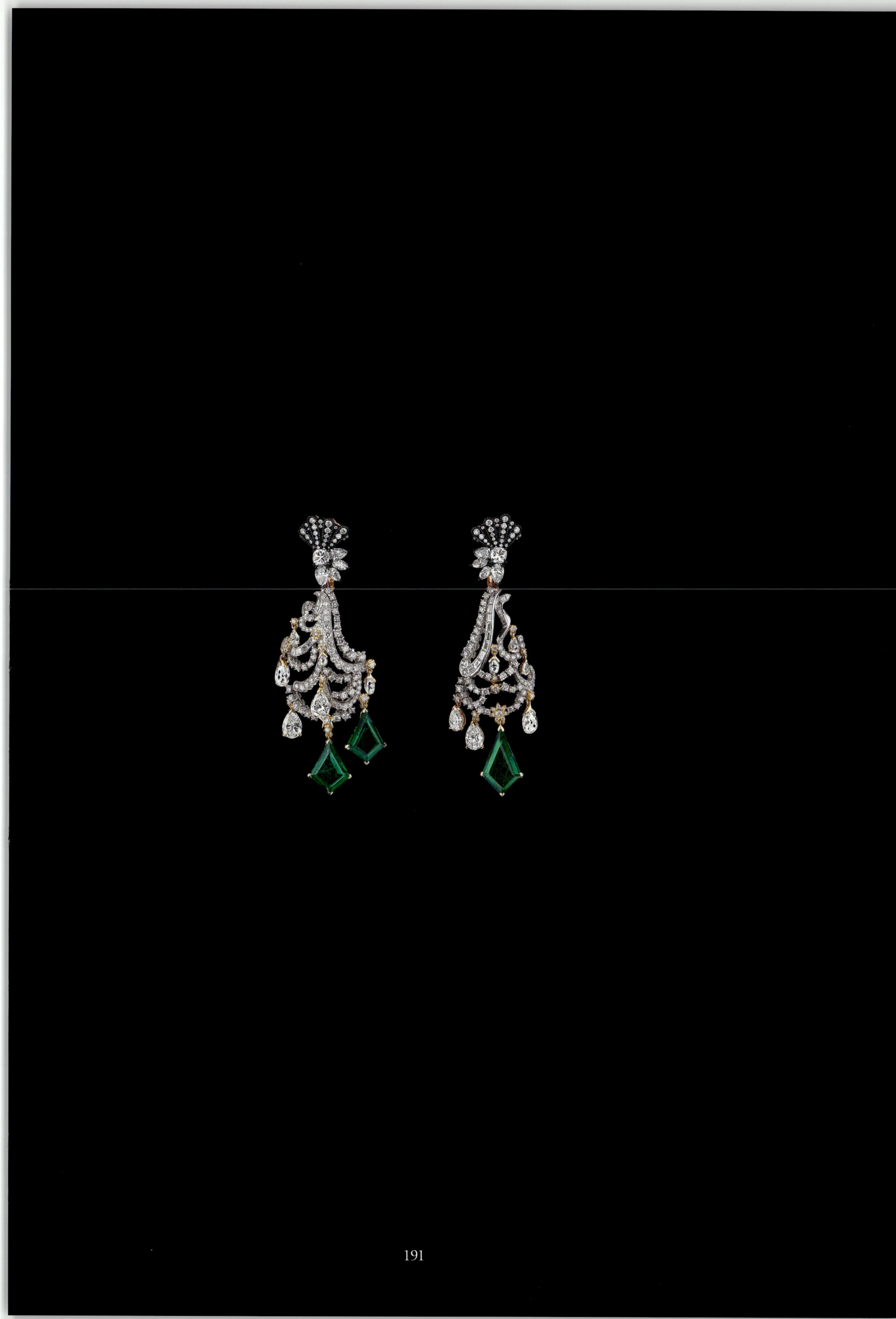

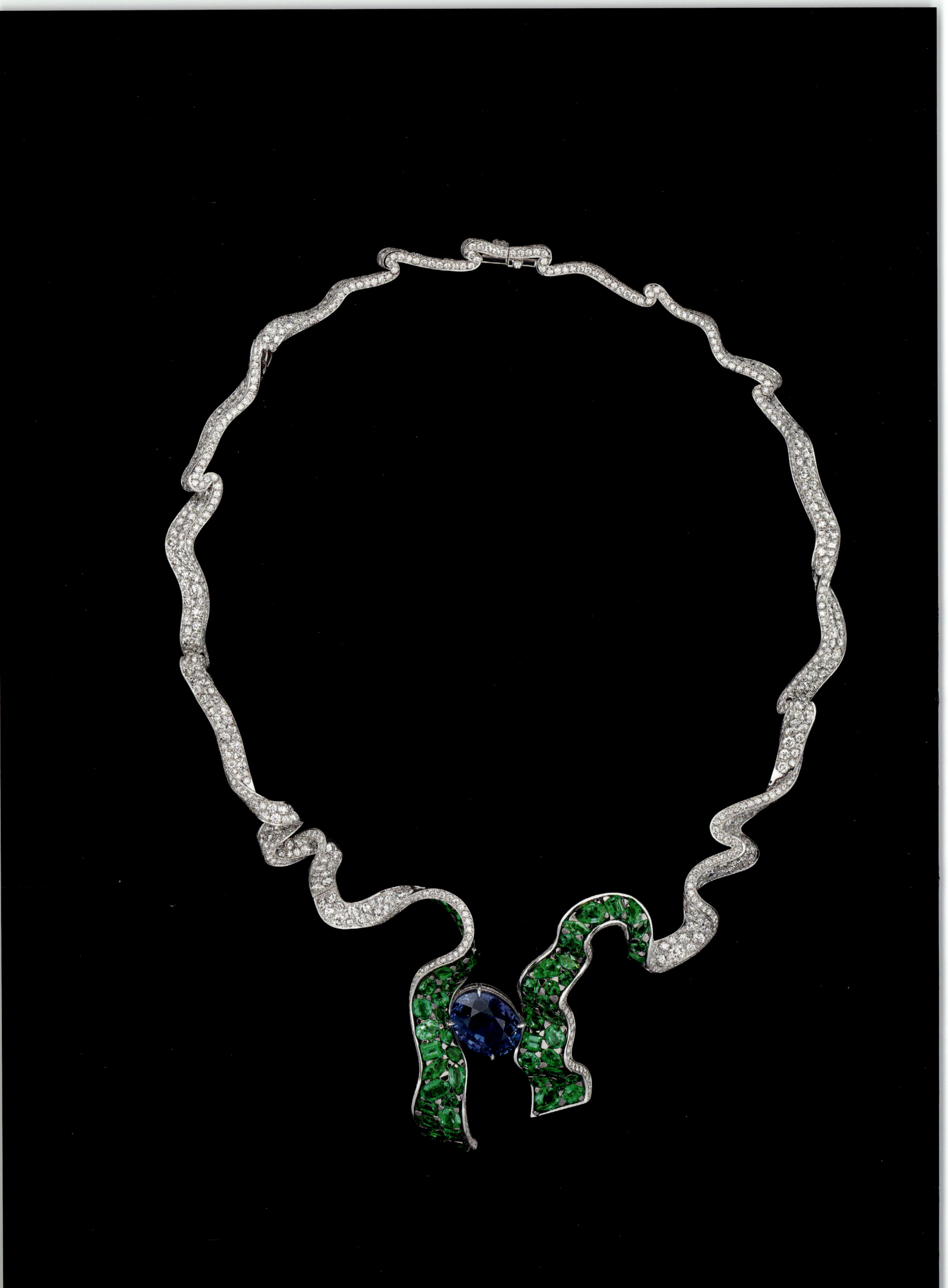

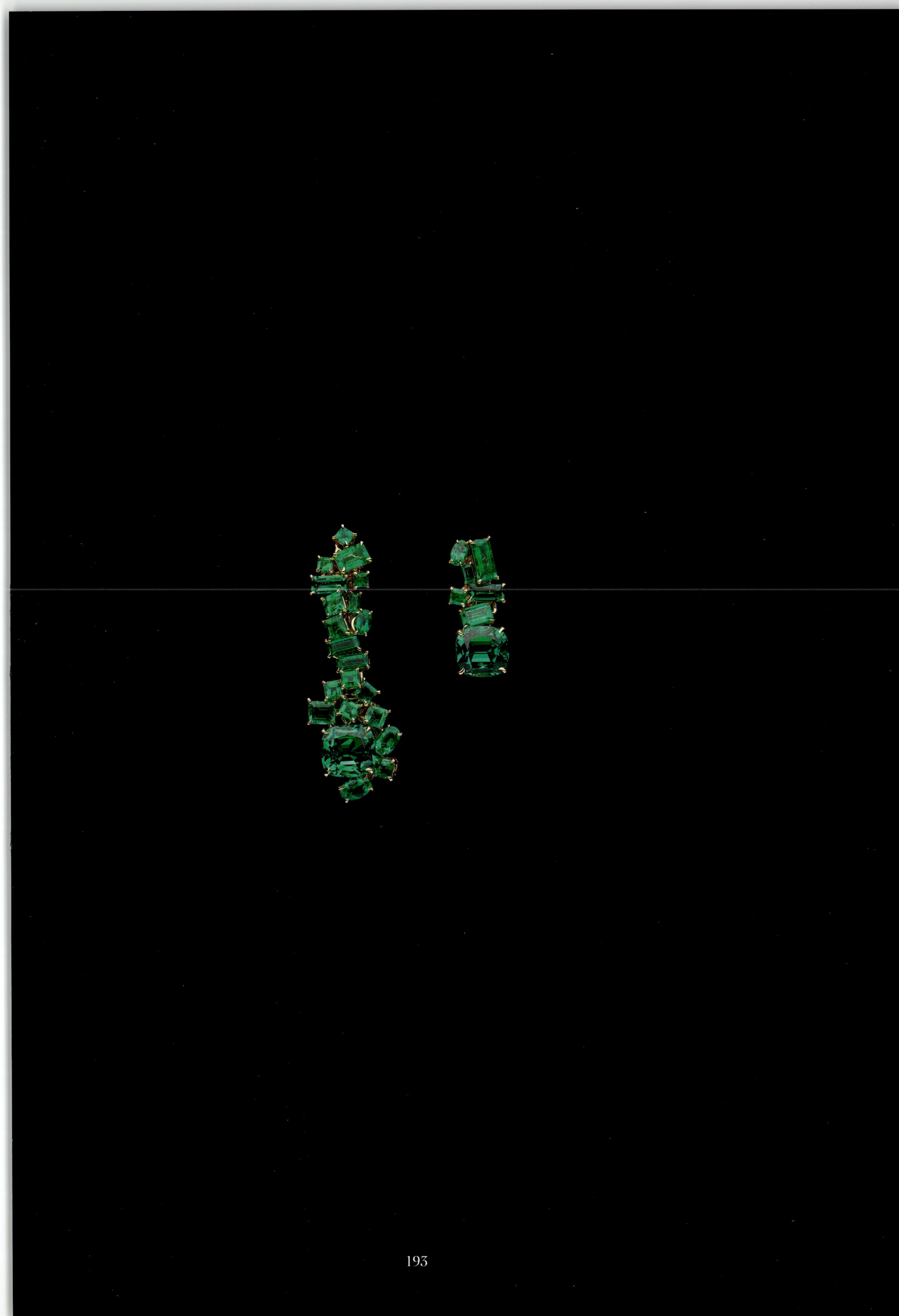

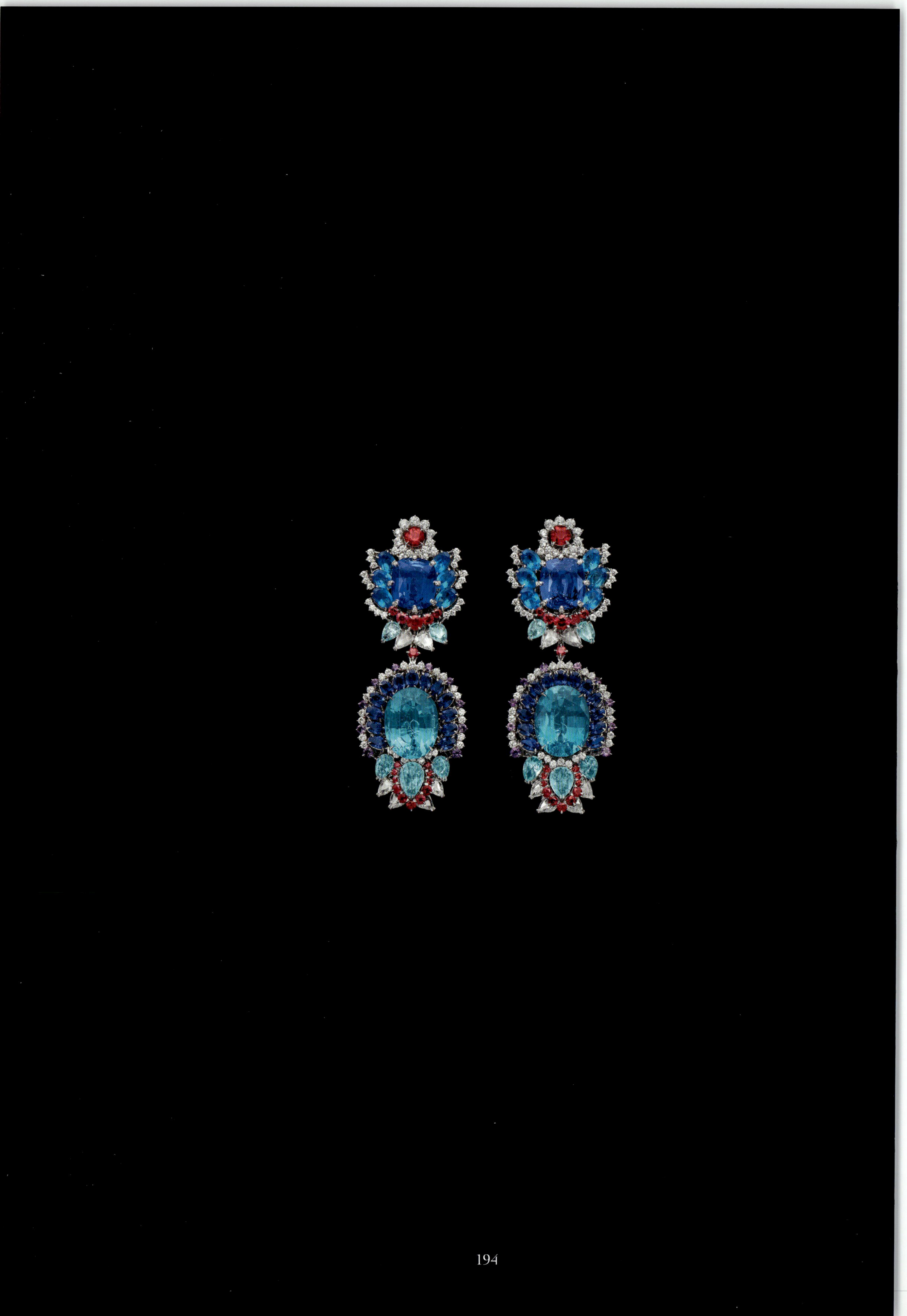

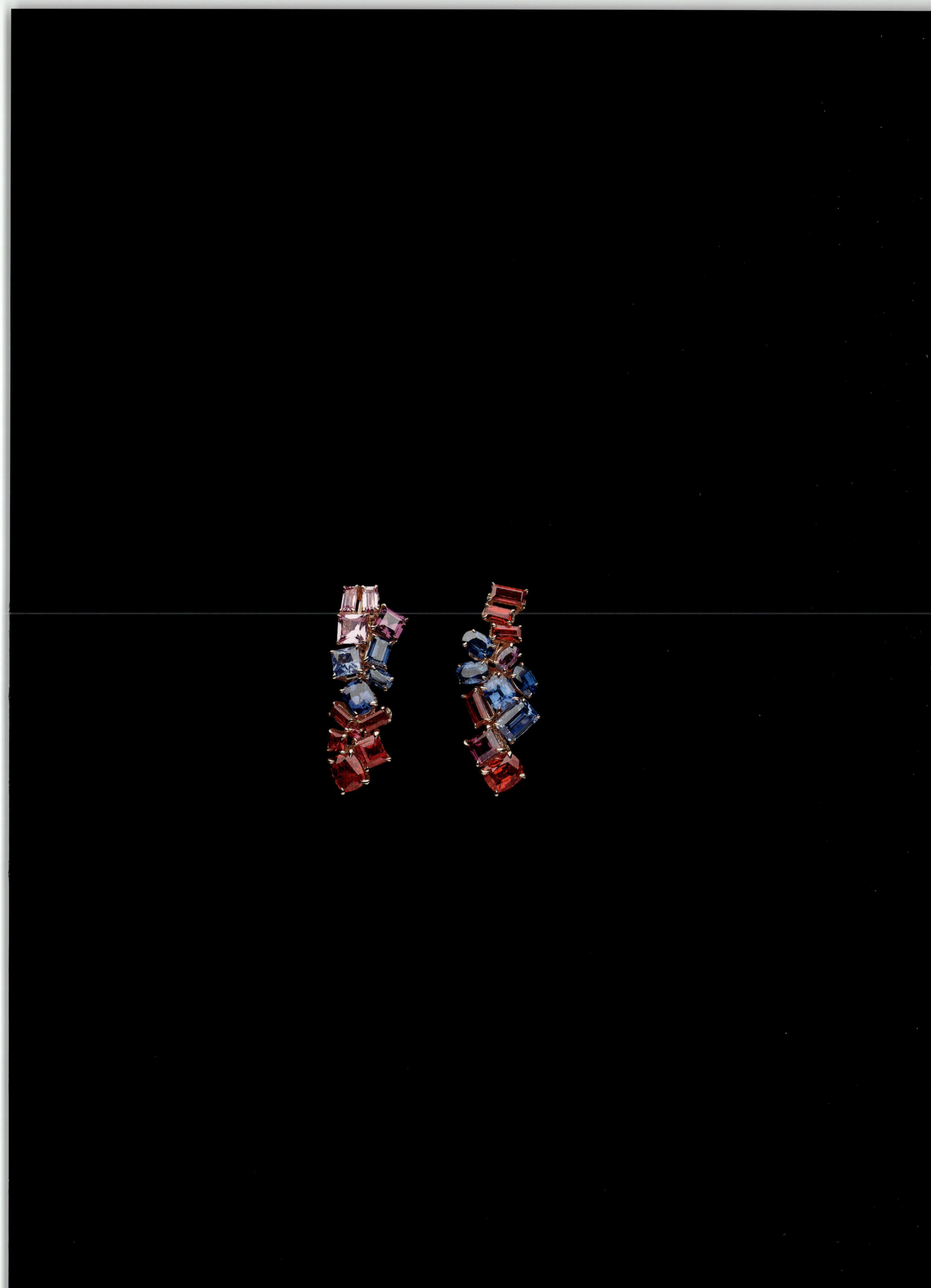

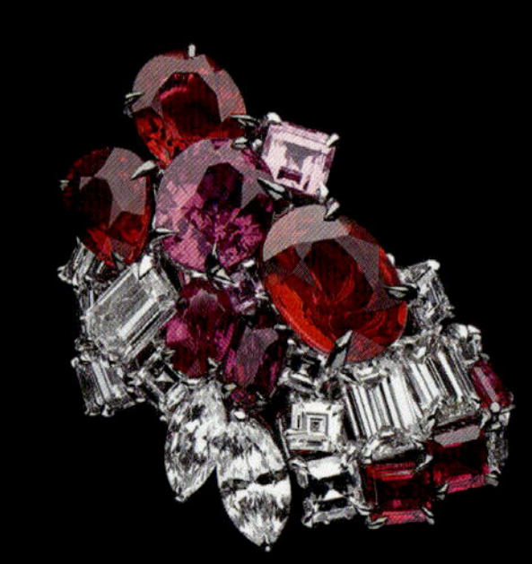

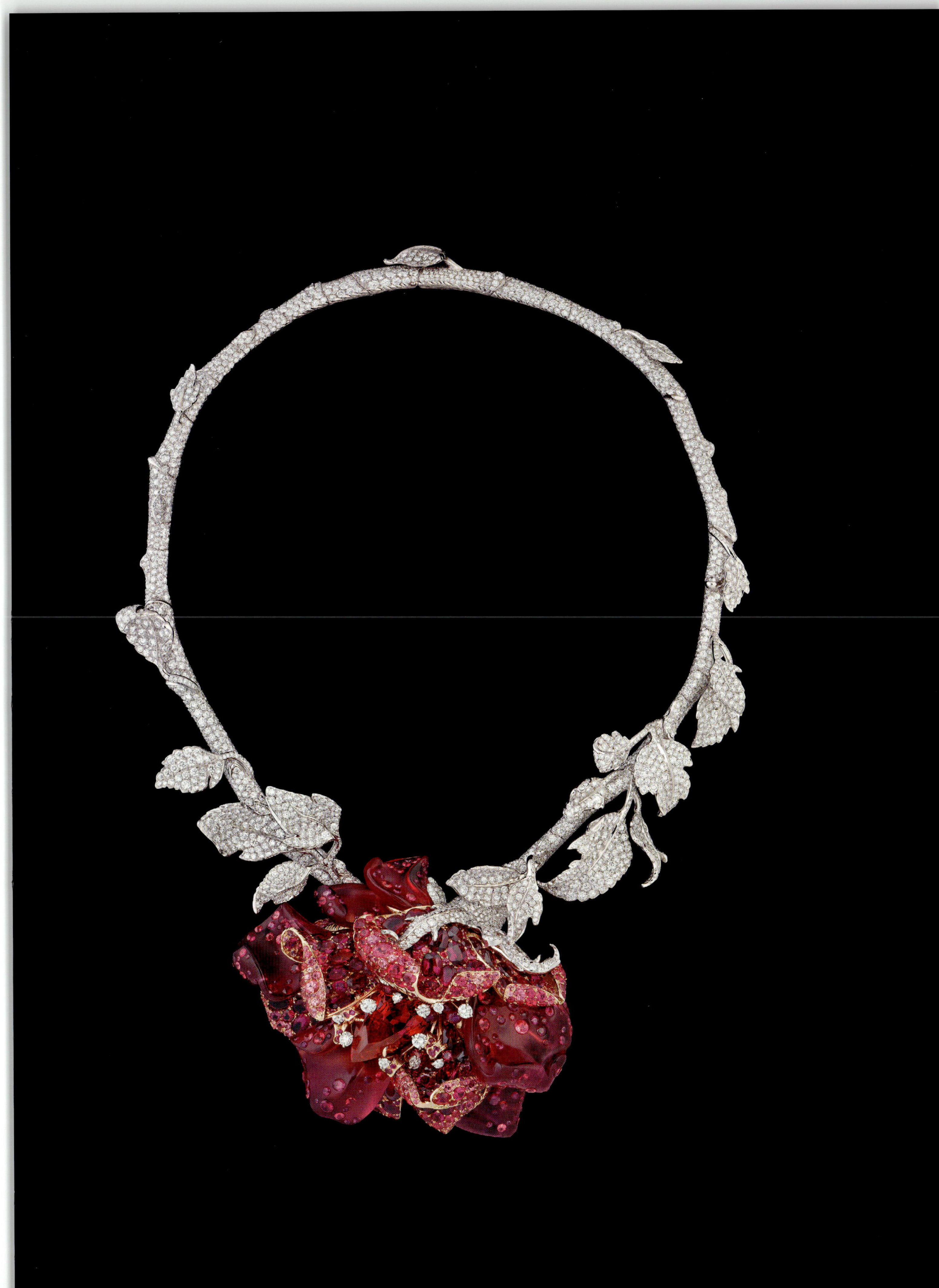

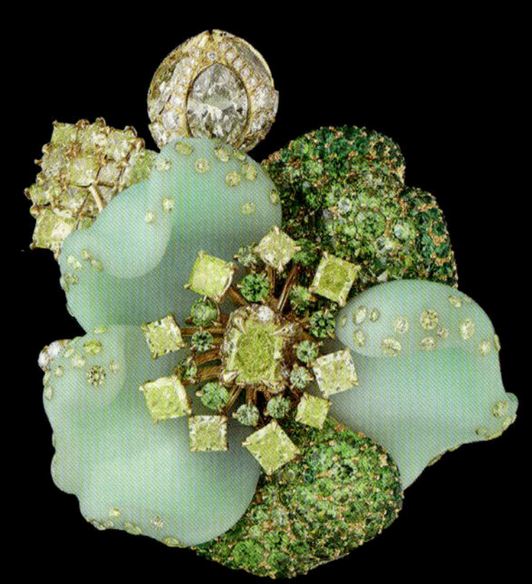

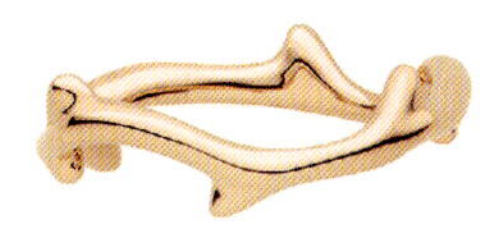

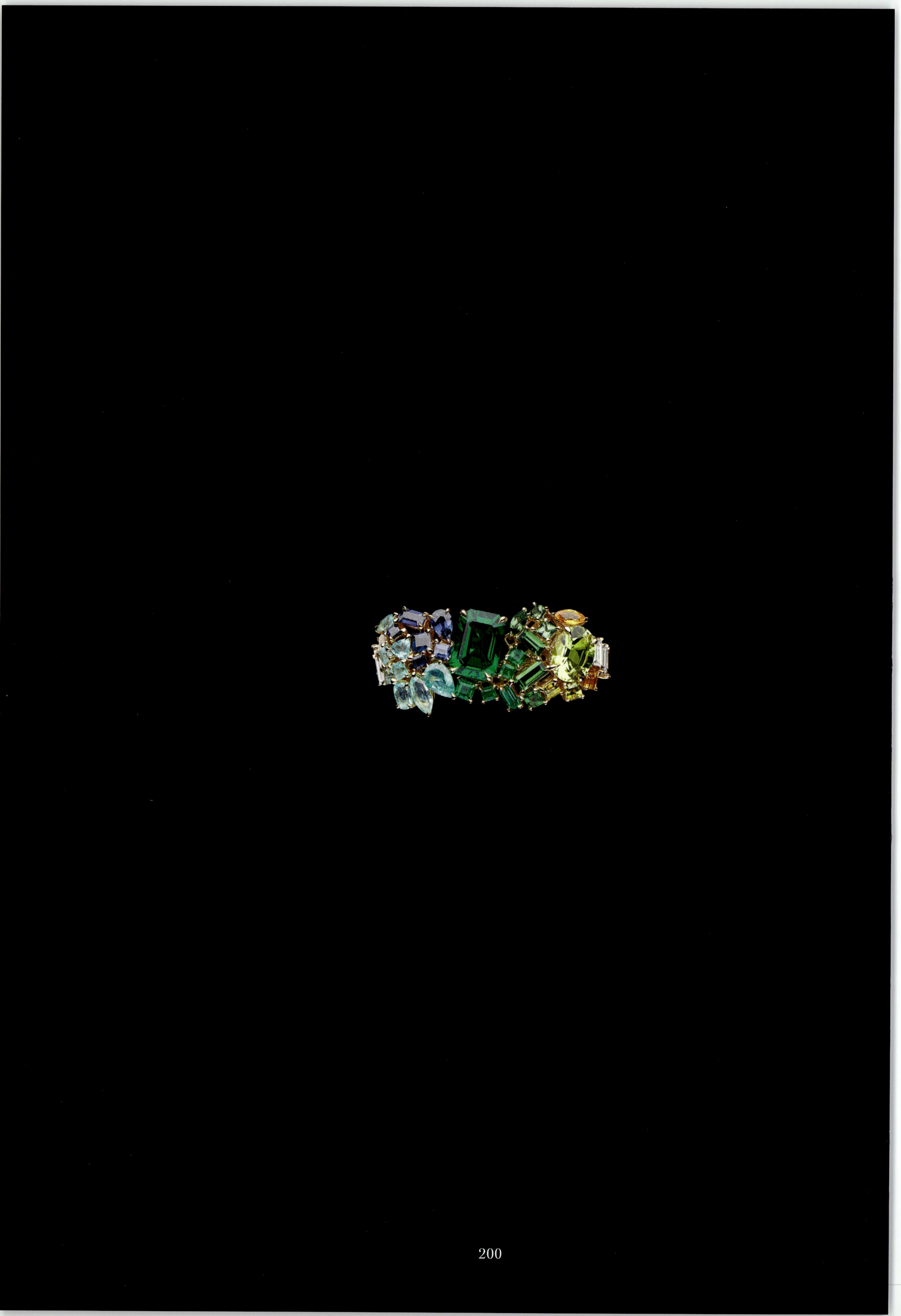

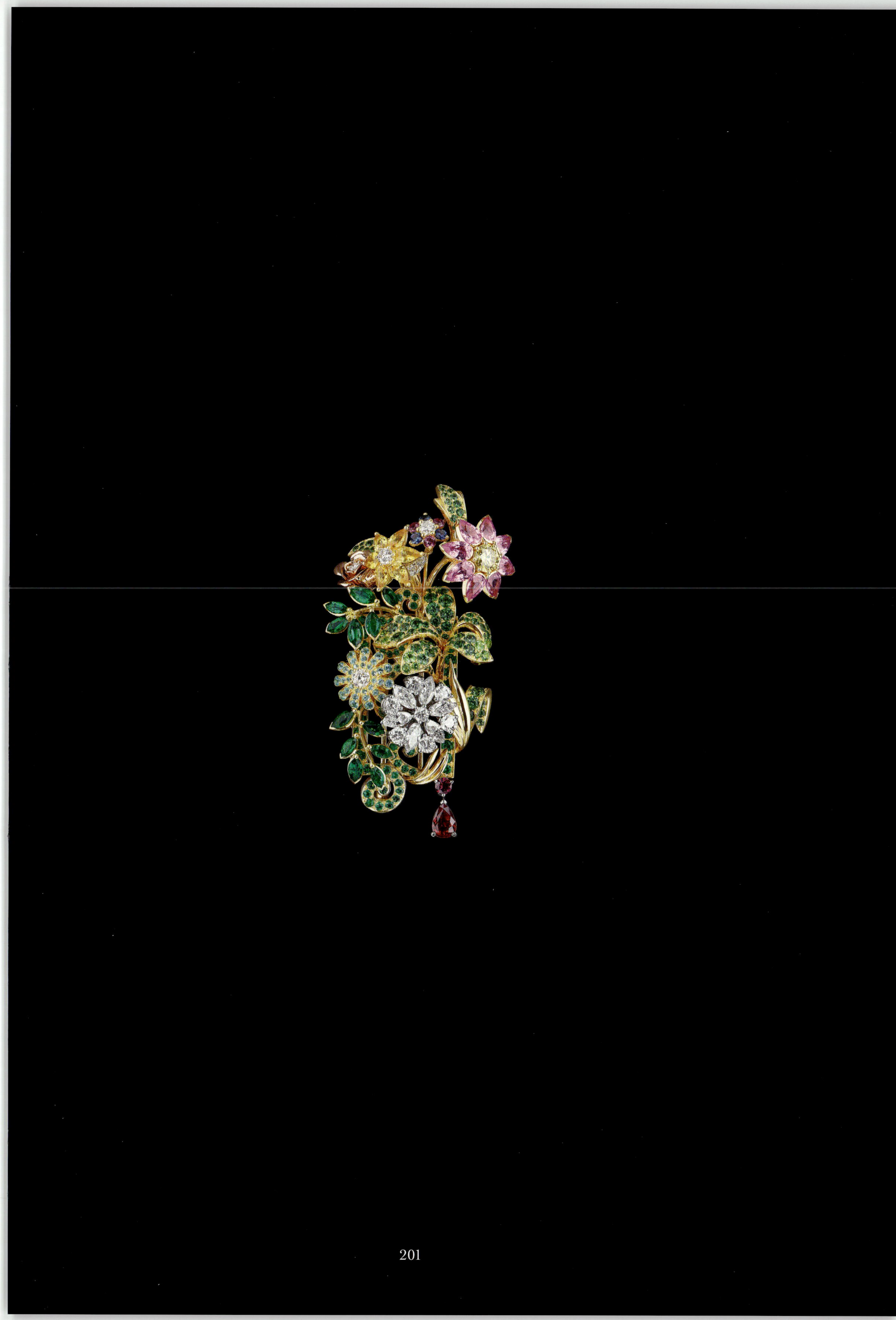

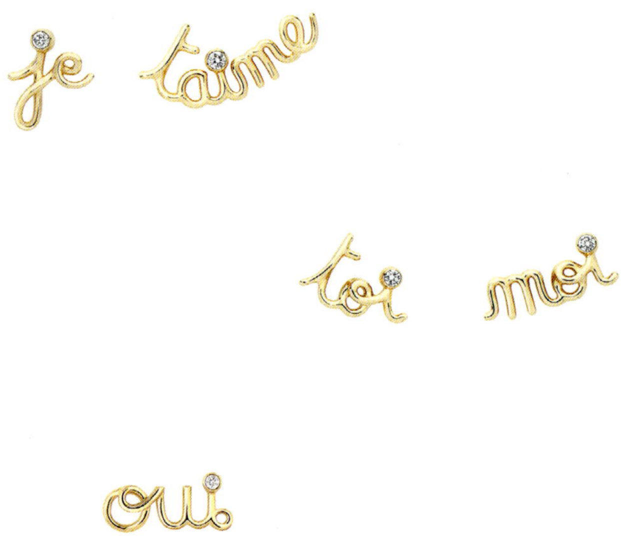
je
taime
toi
moi
oui

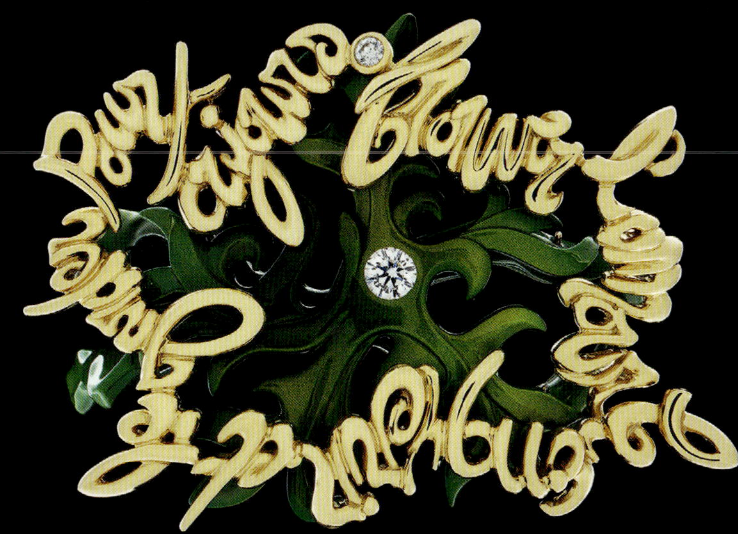

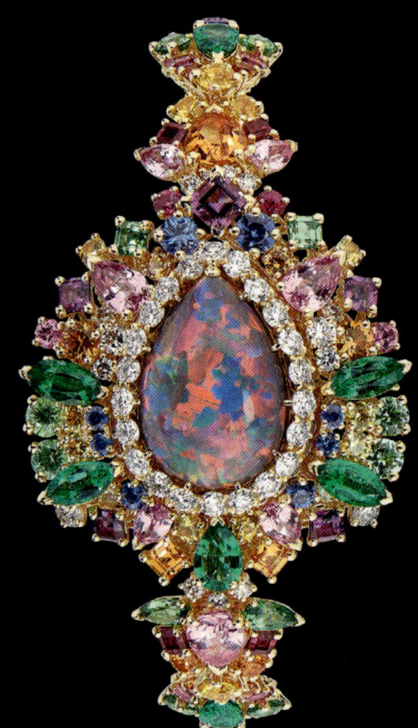

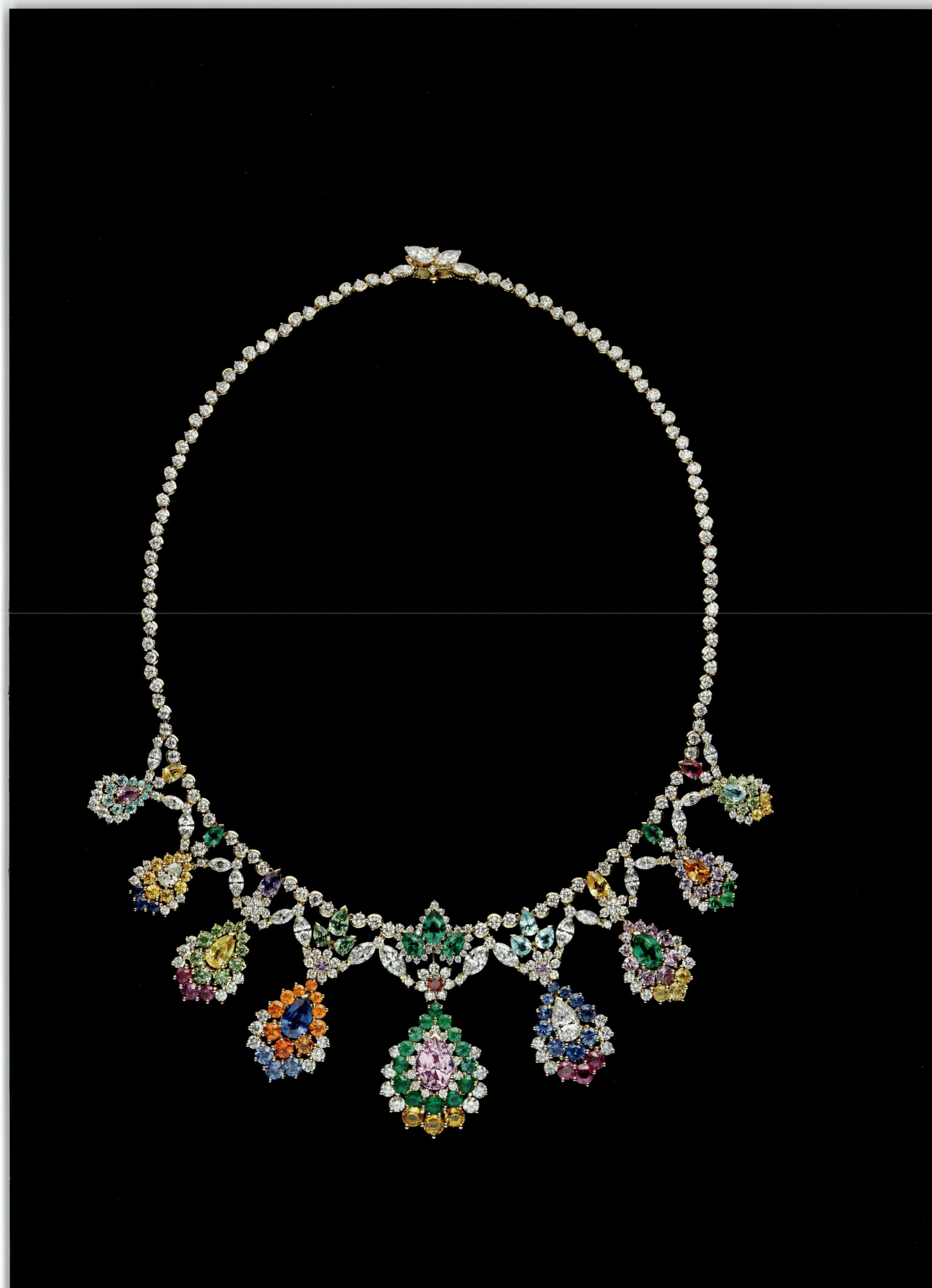

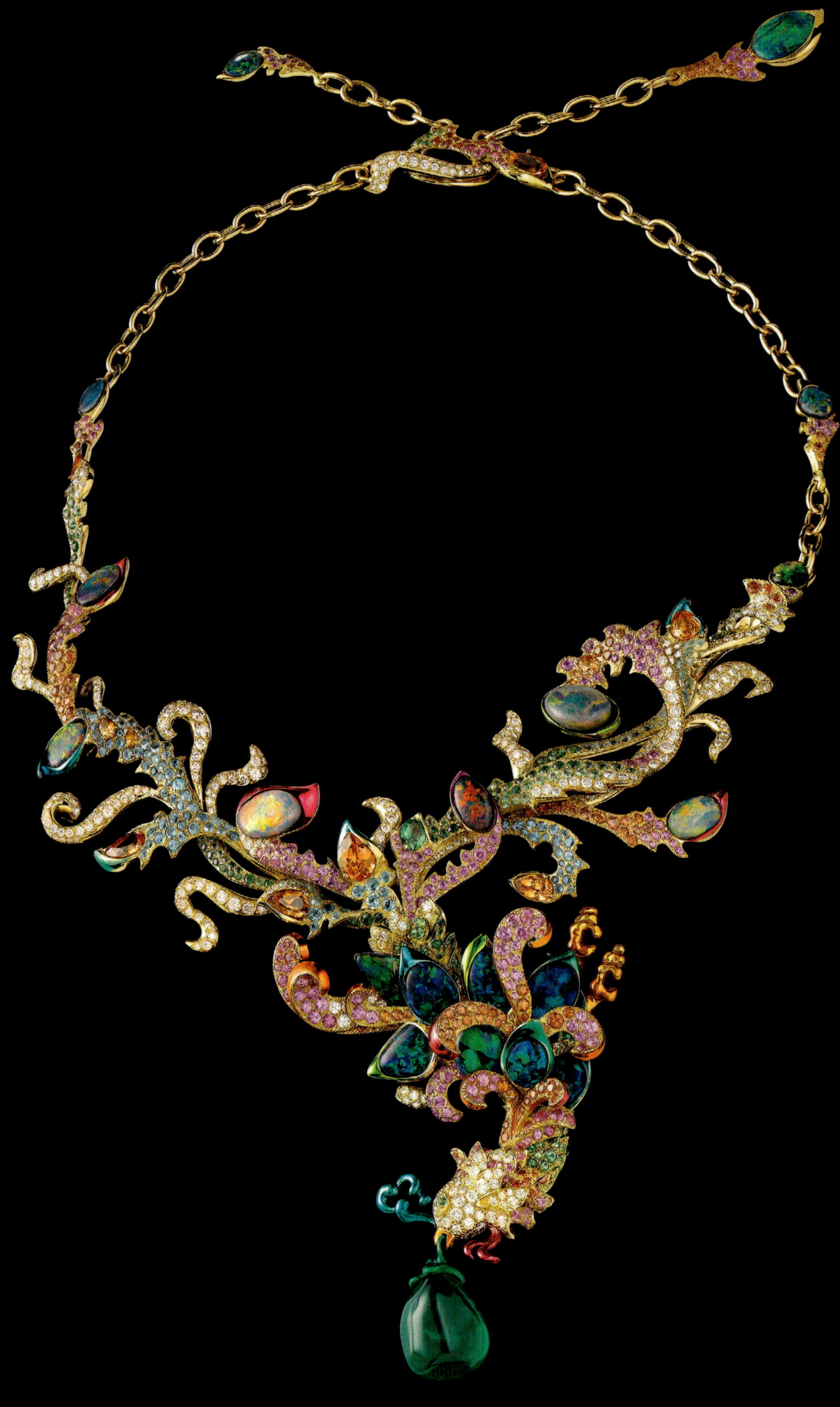

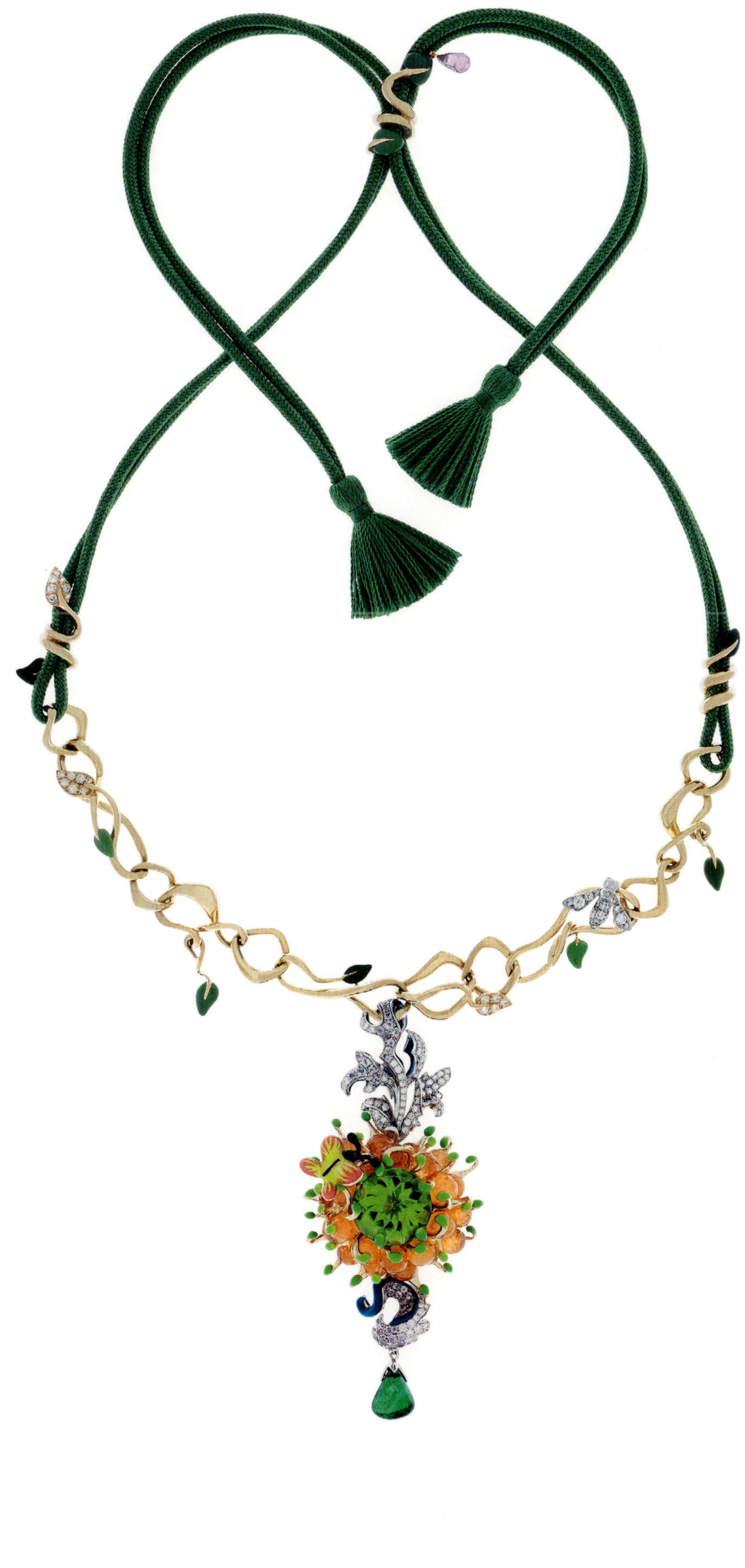

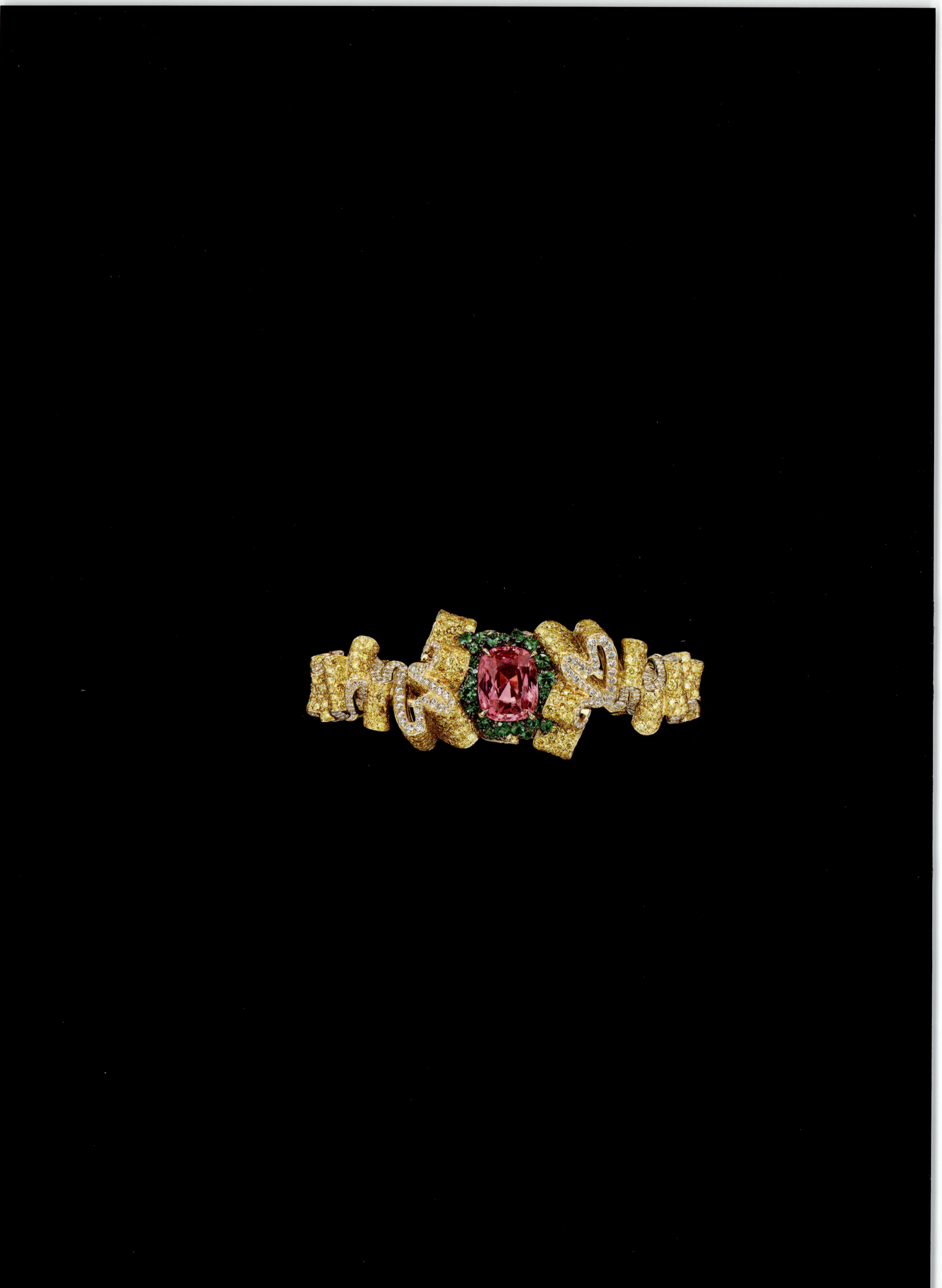

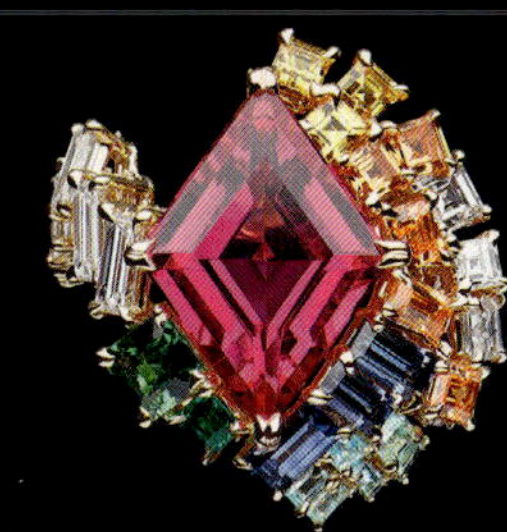

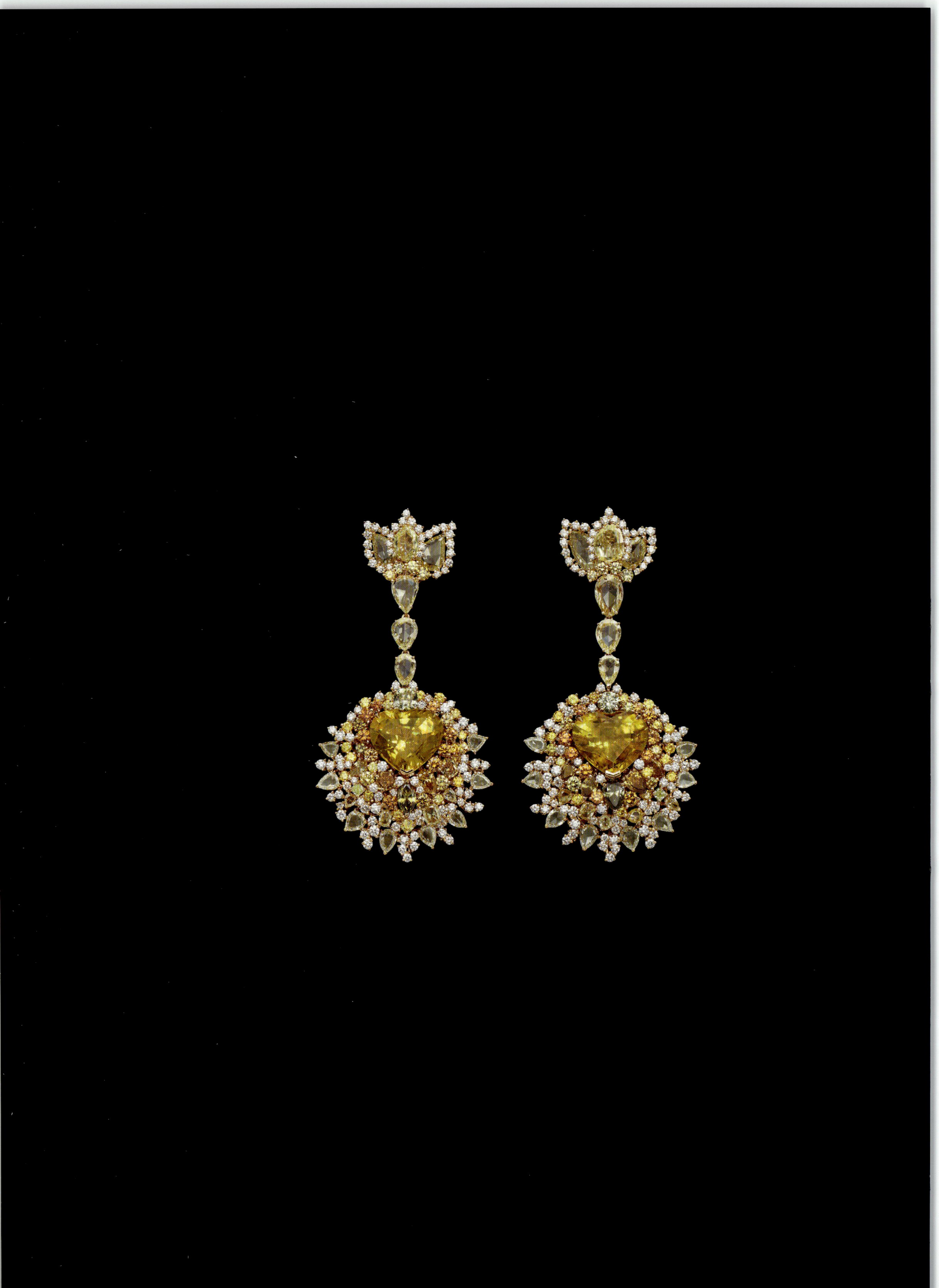

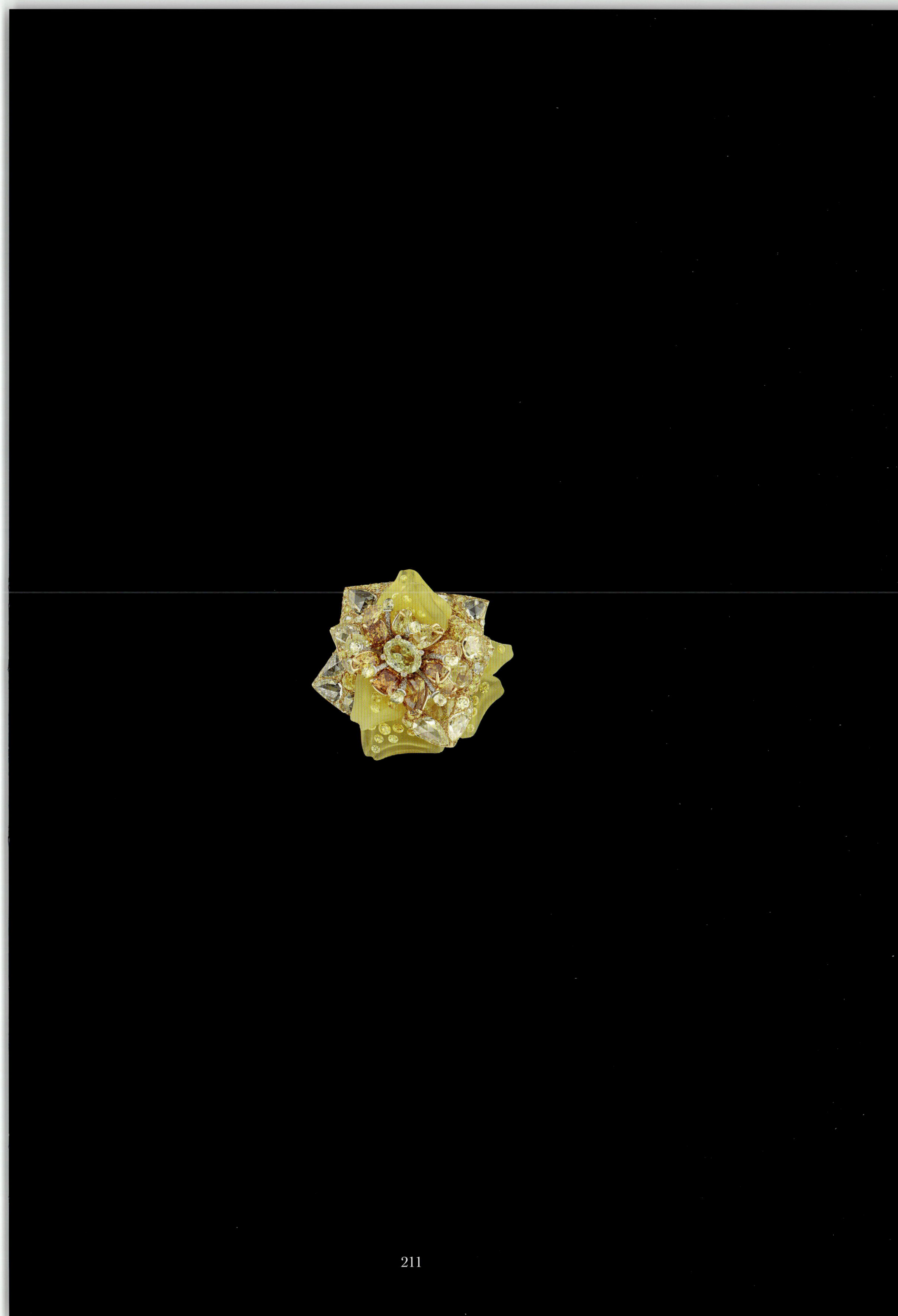

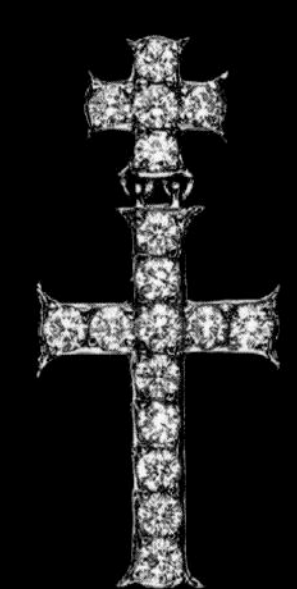

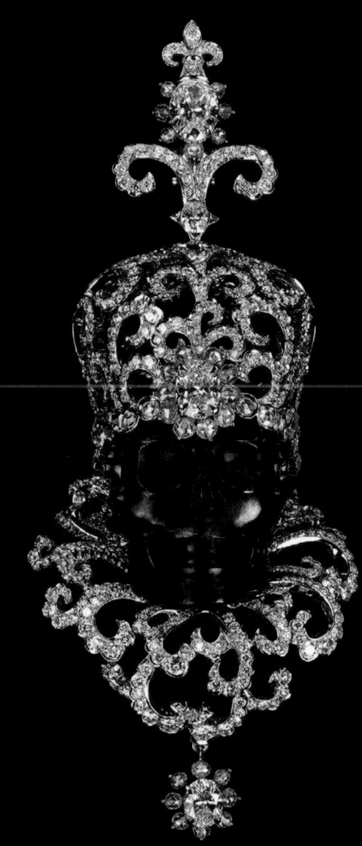

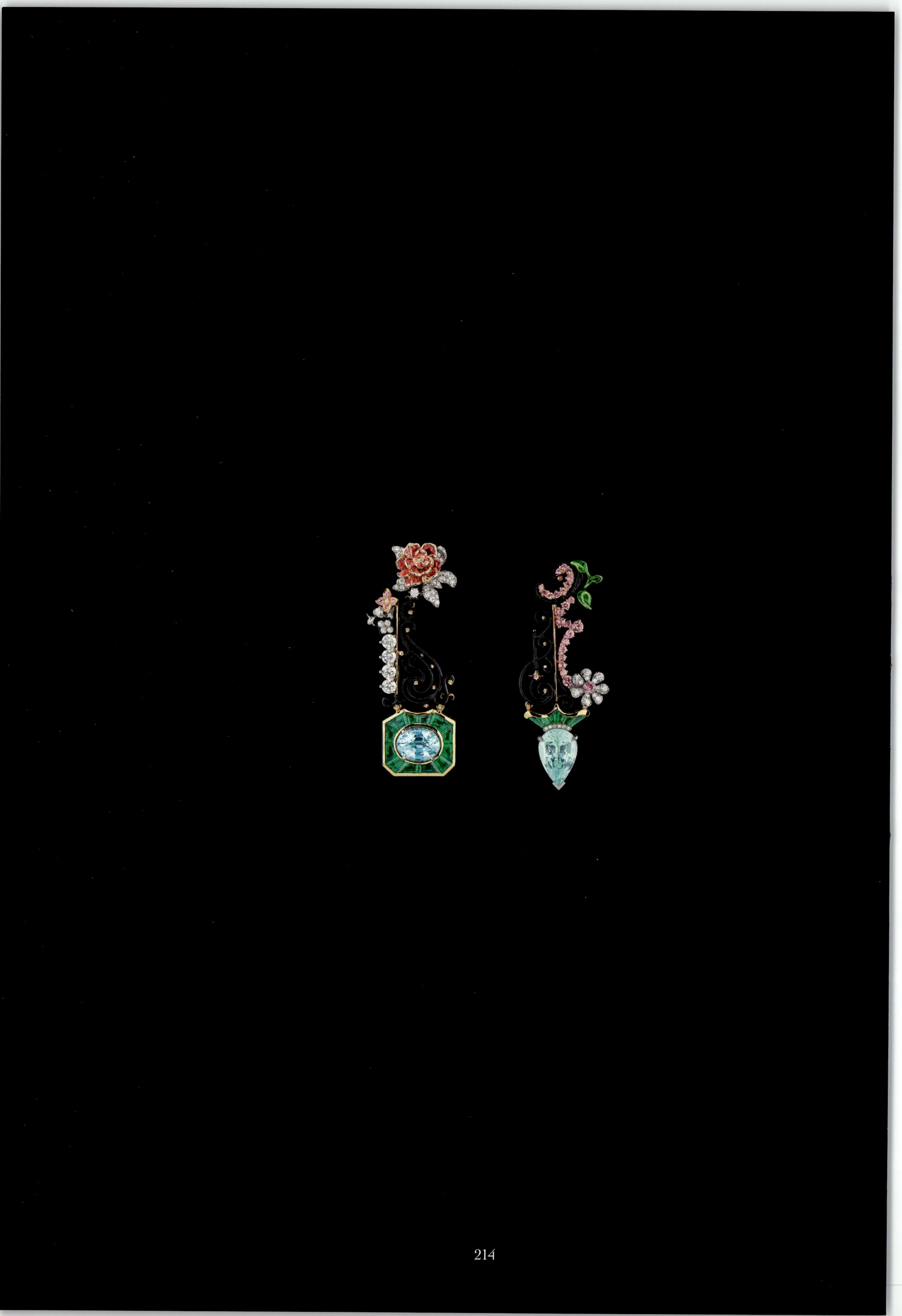

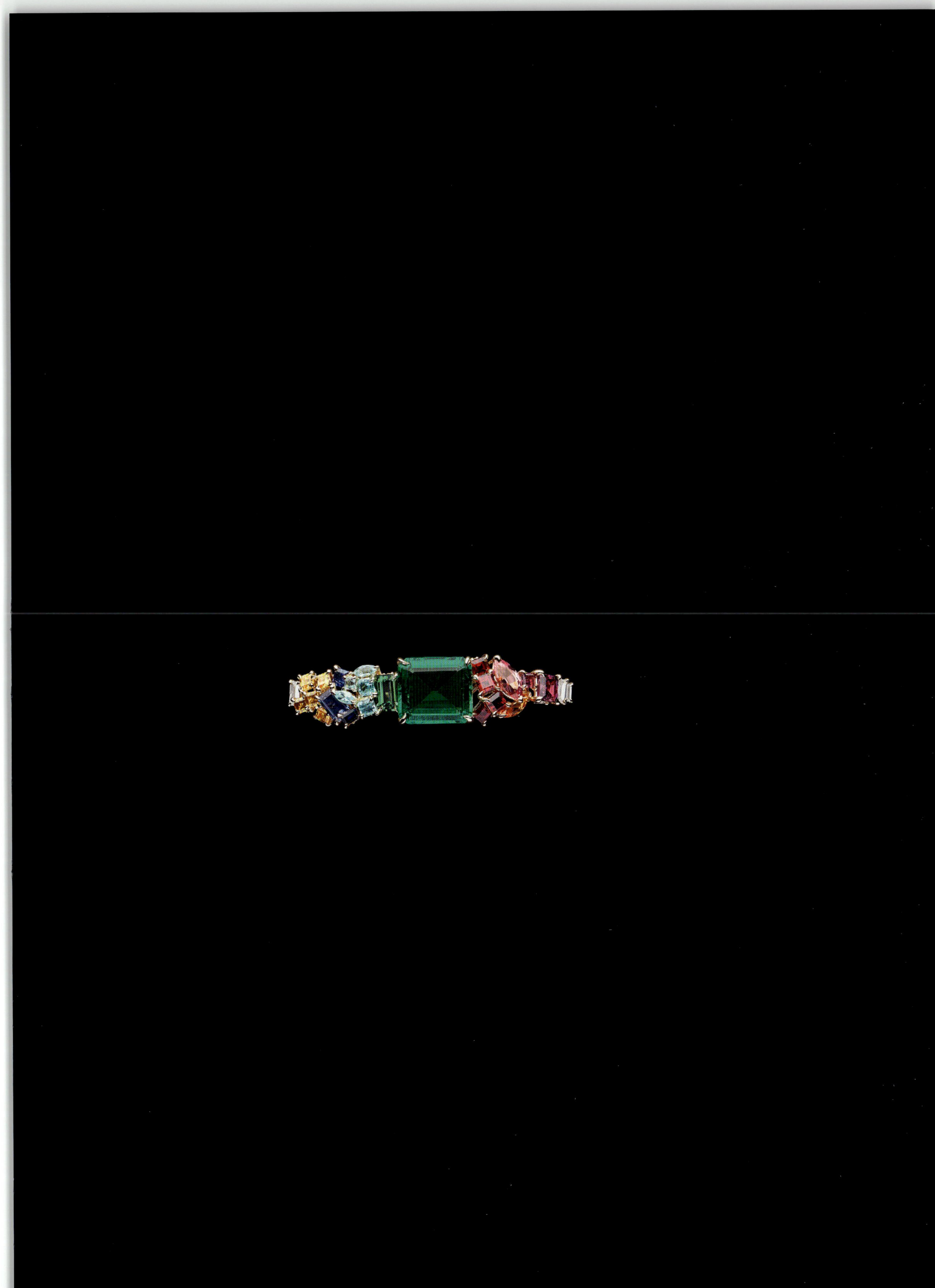

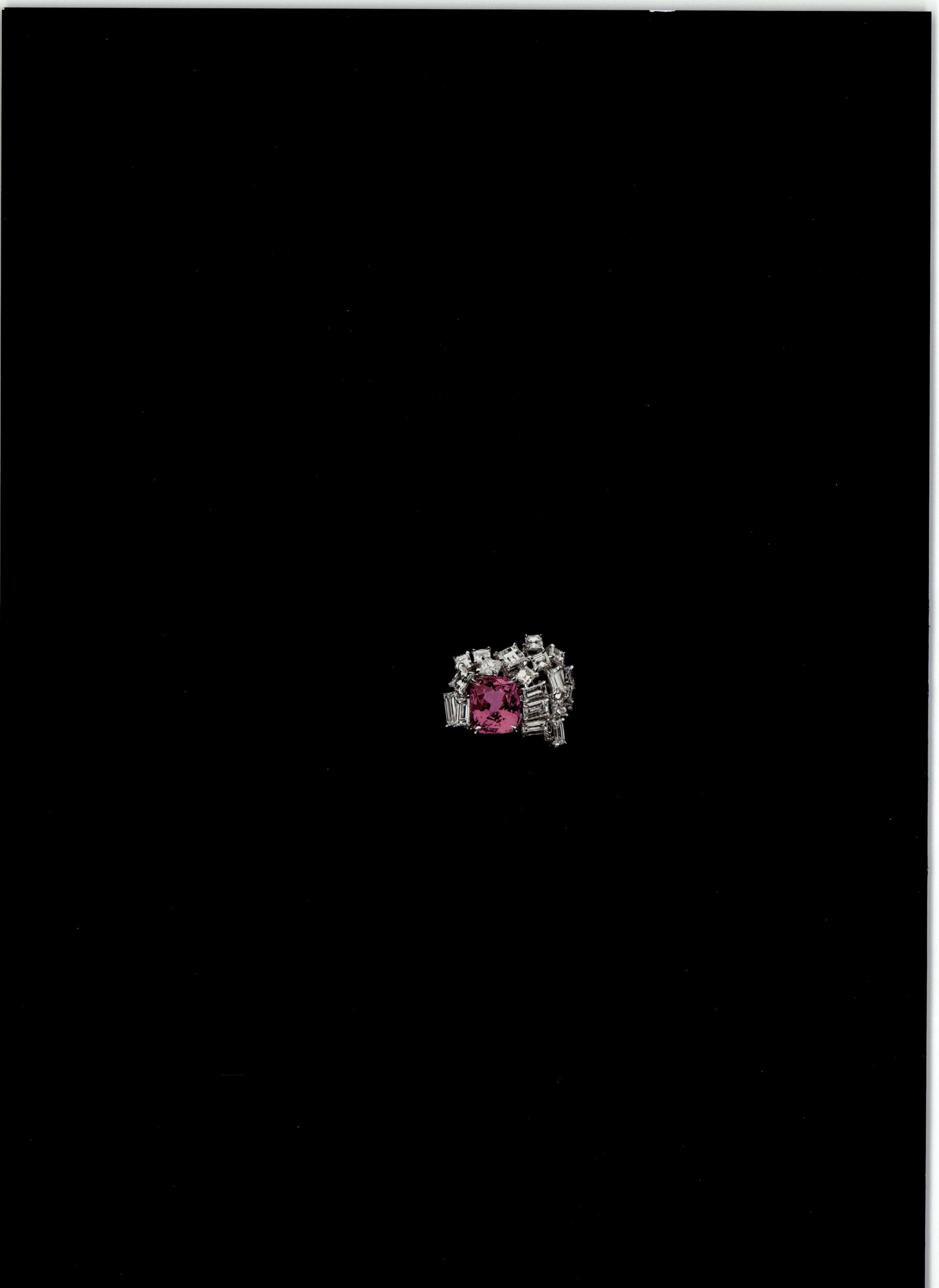

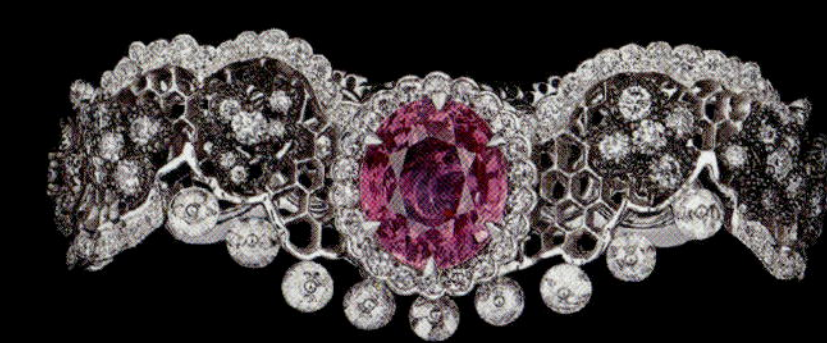

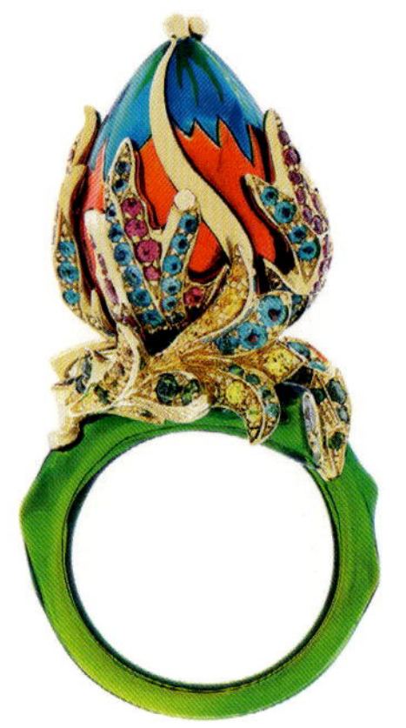

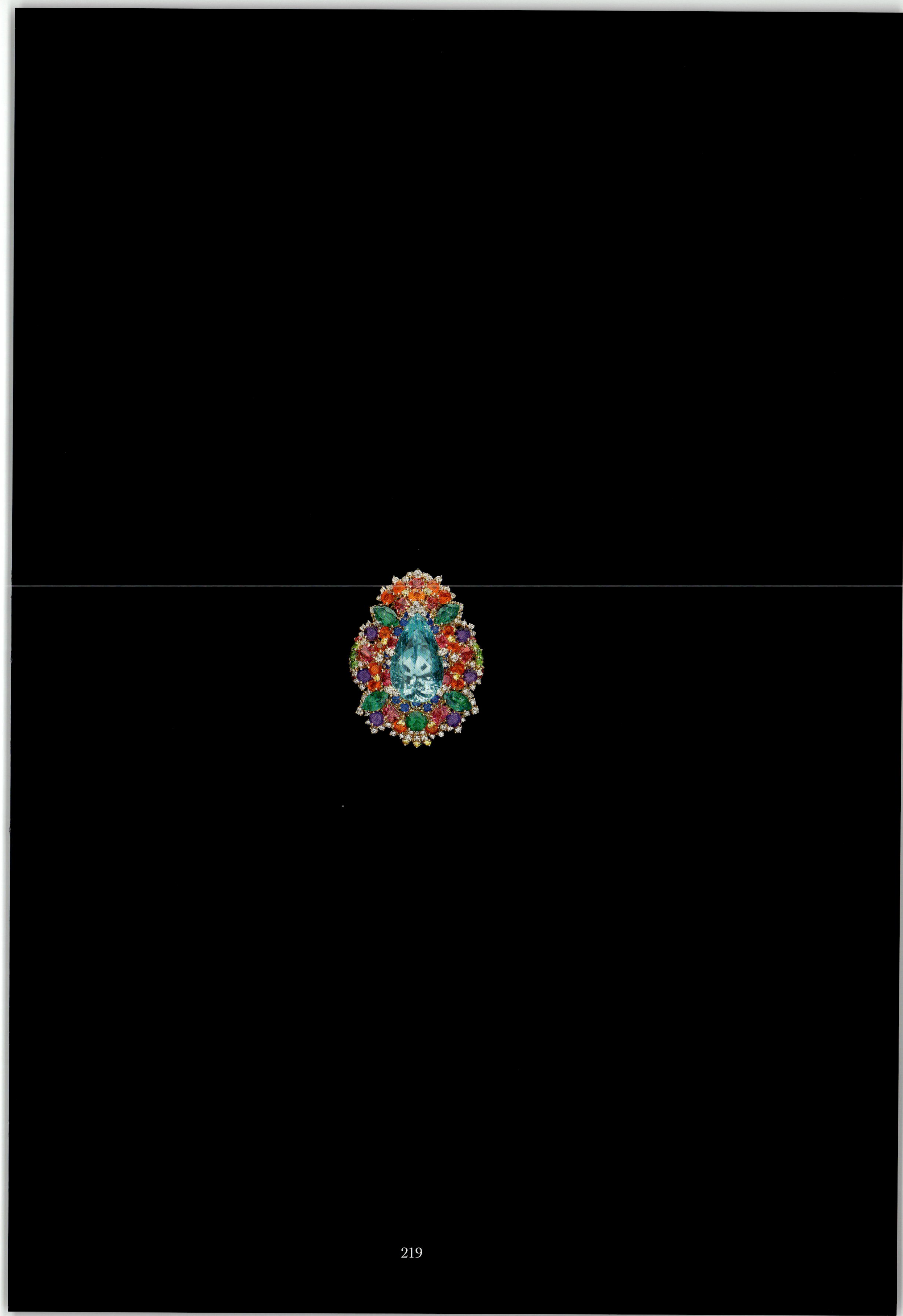

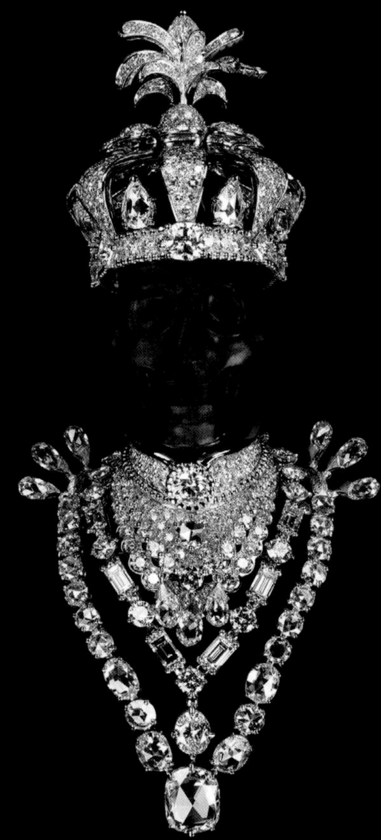

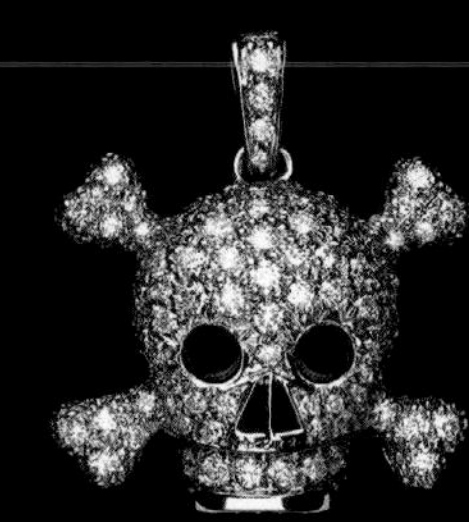

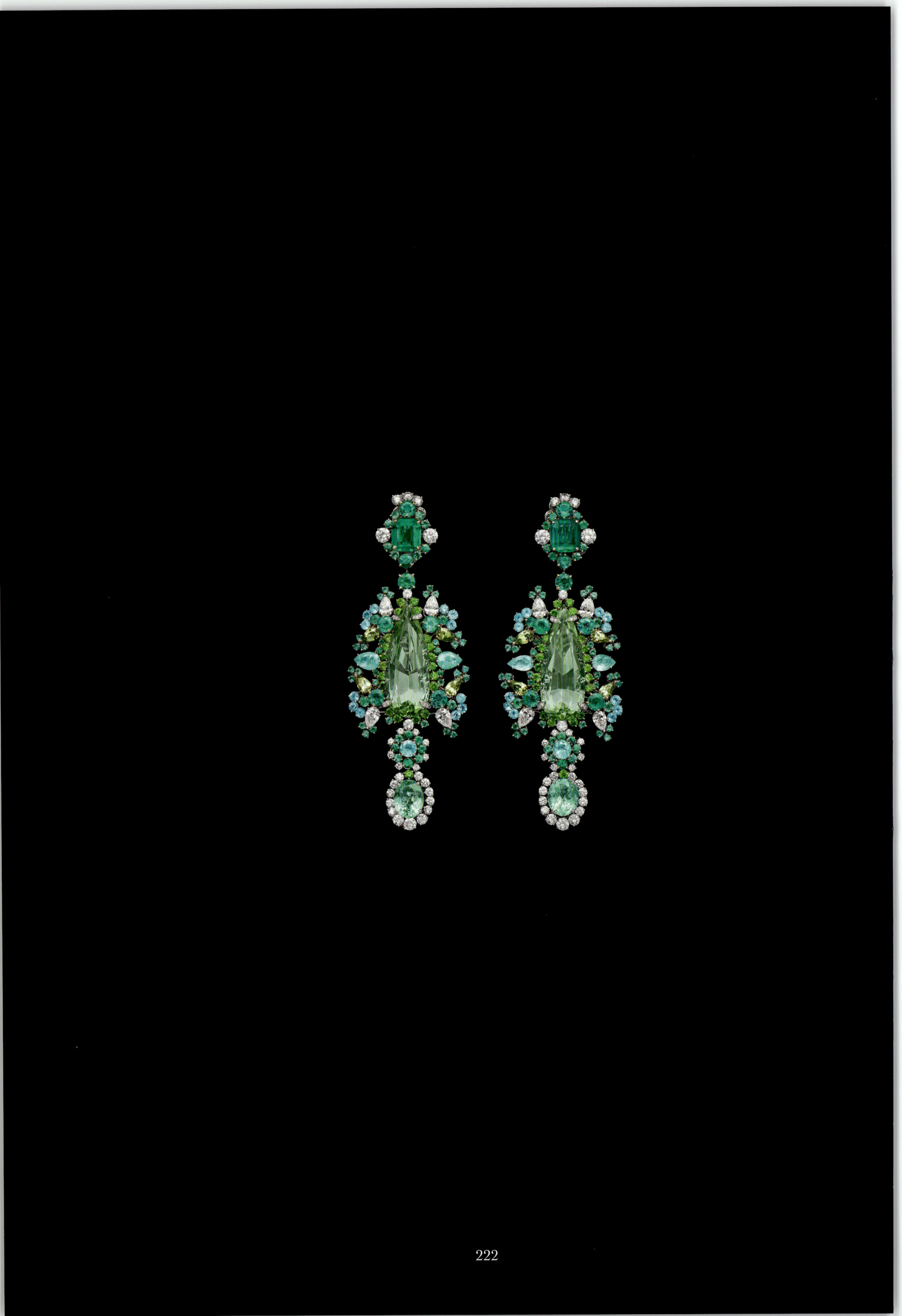

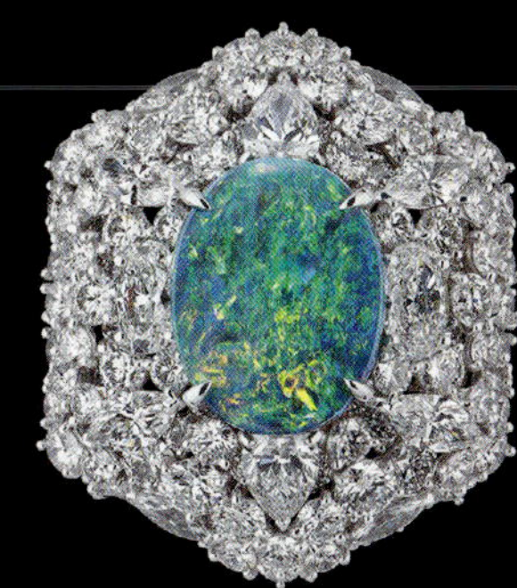

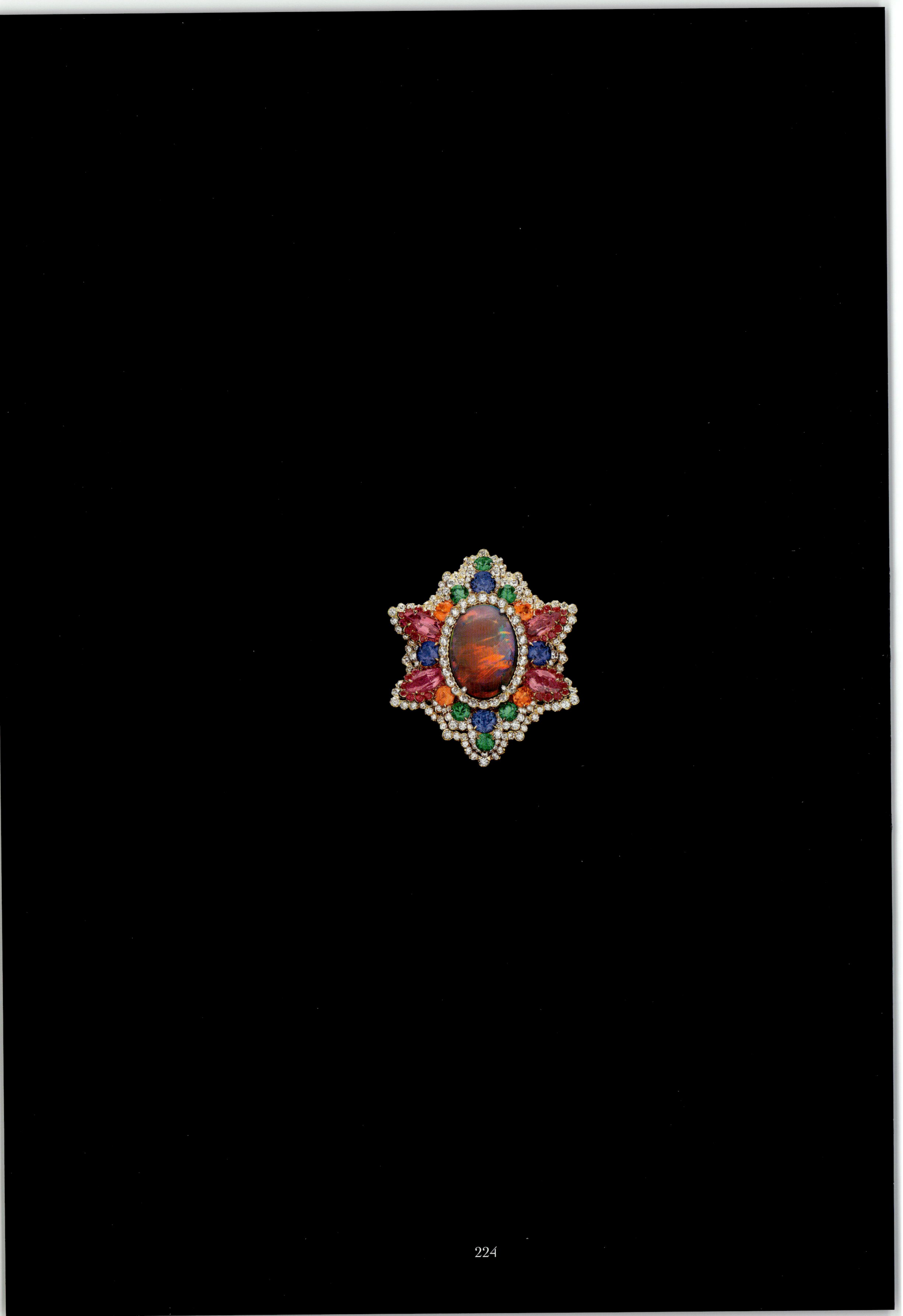

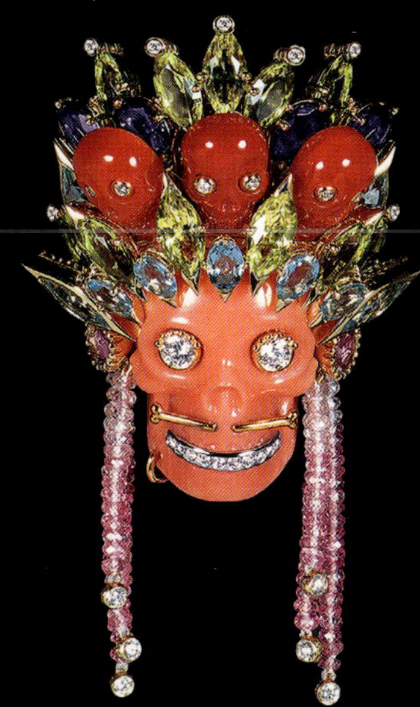

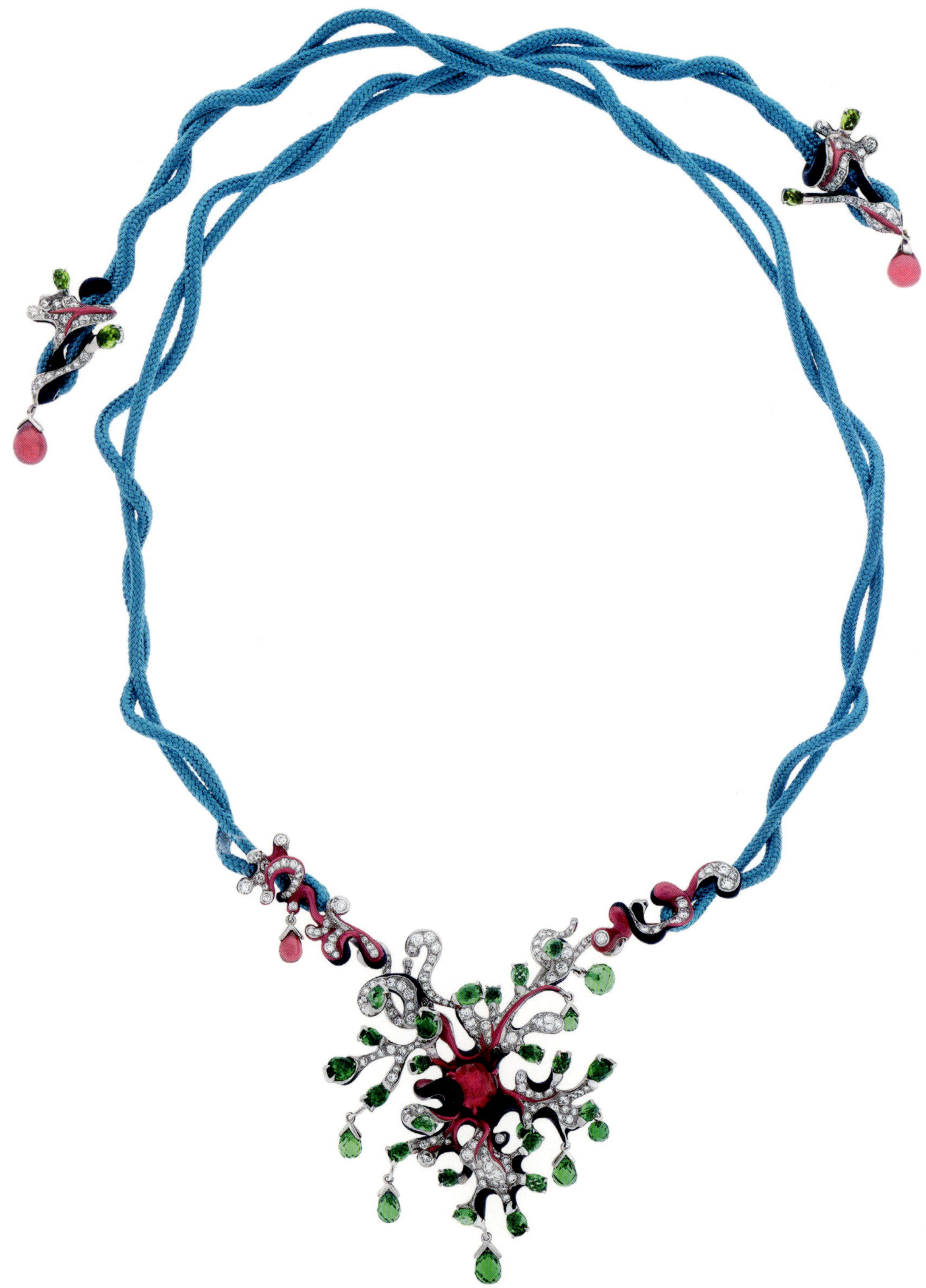

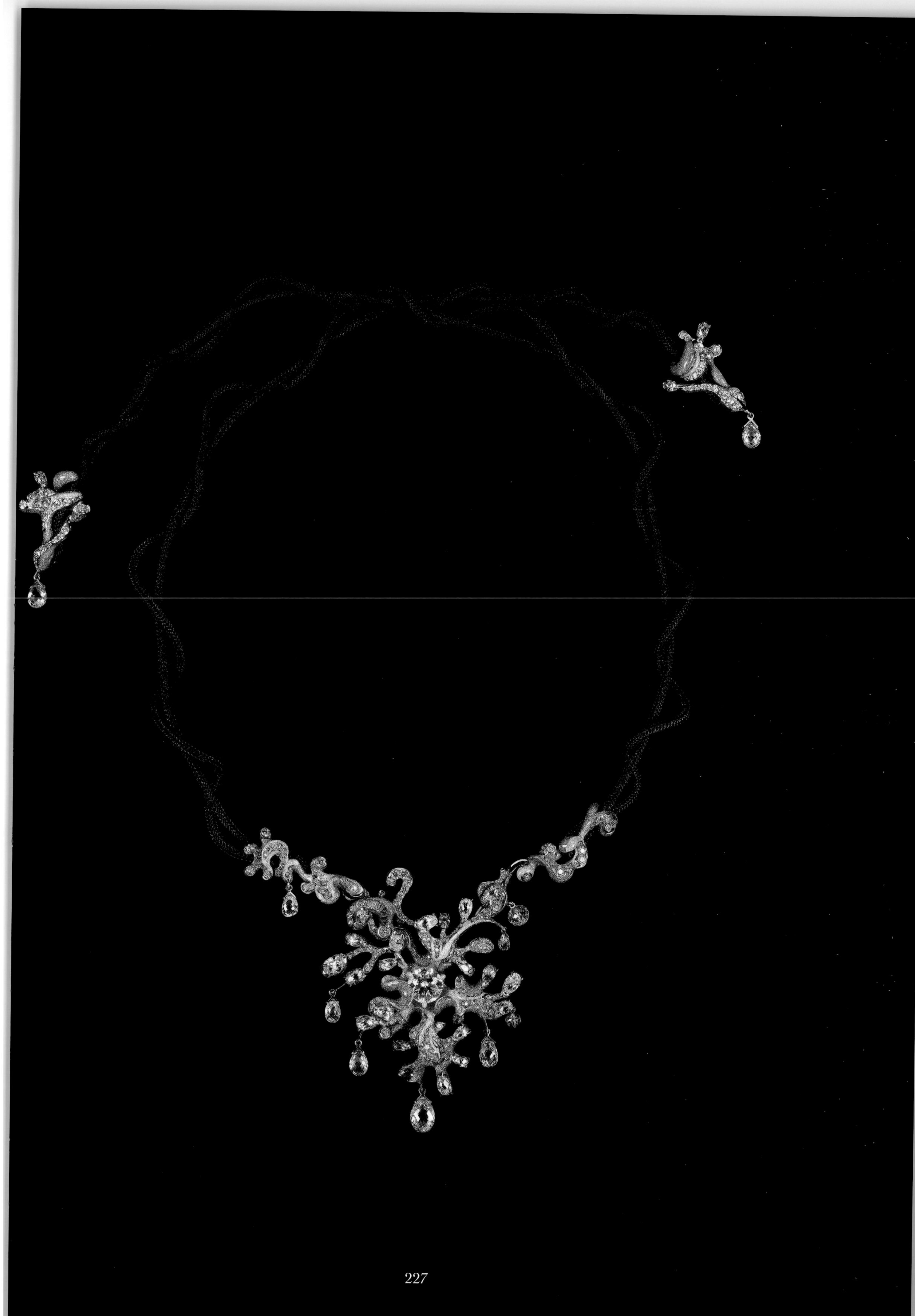

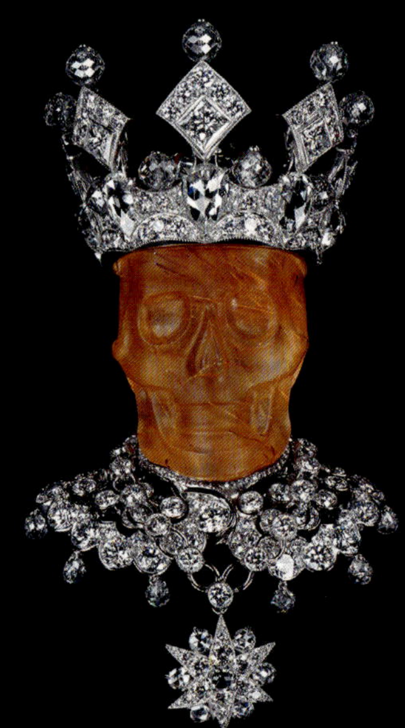

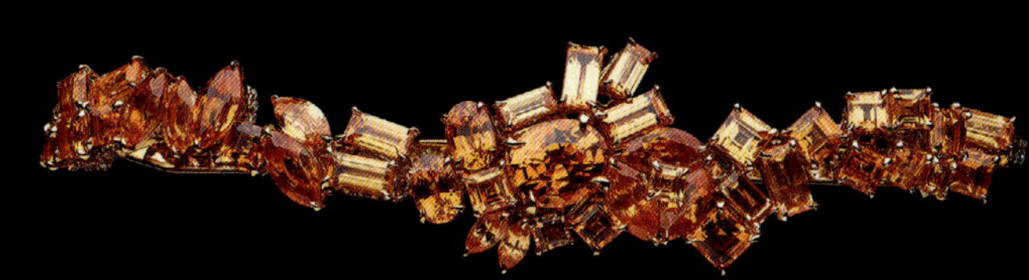

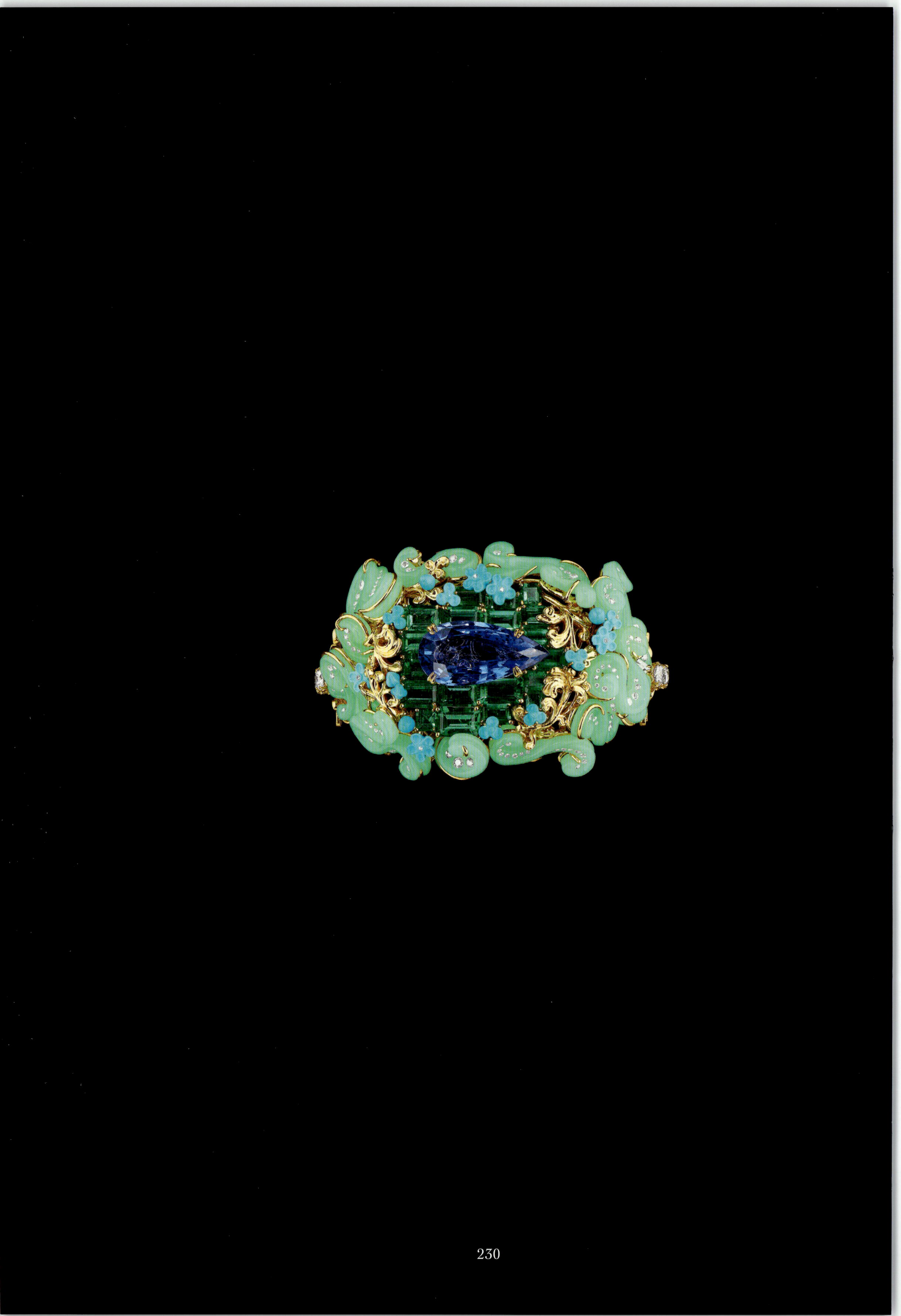

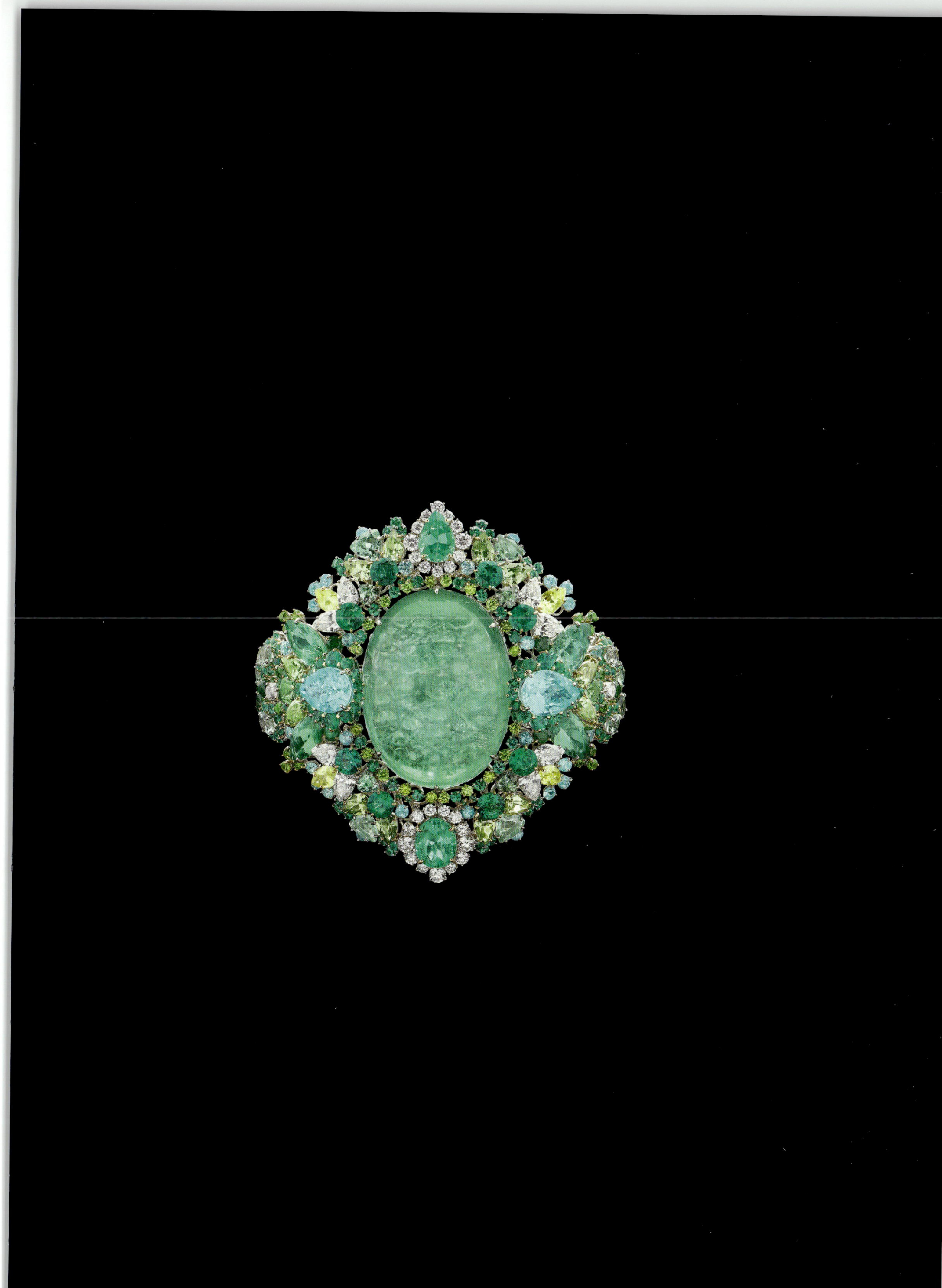

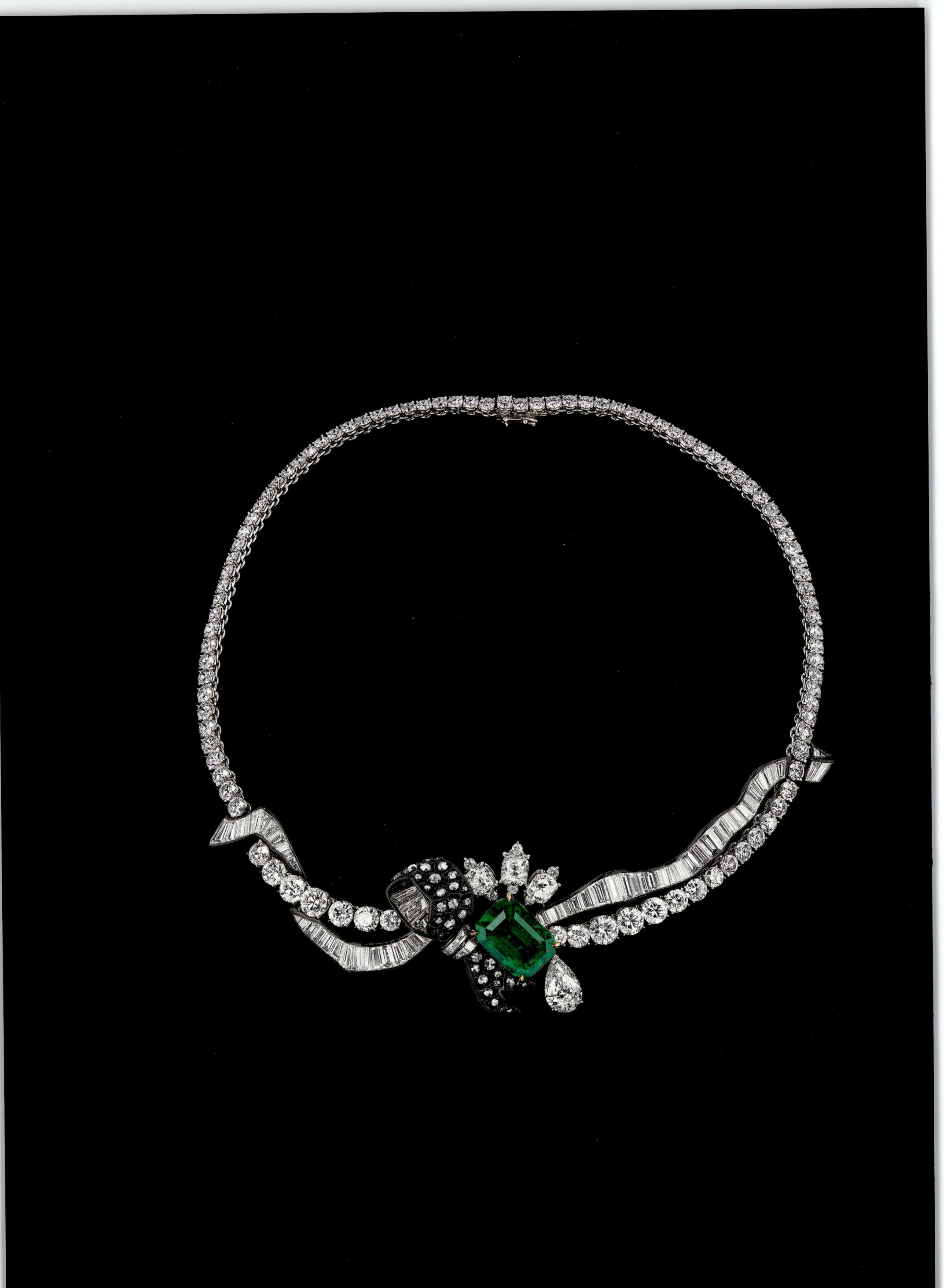

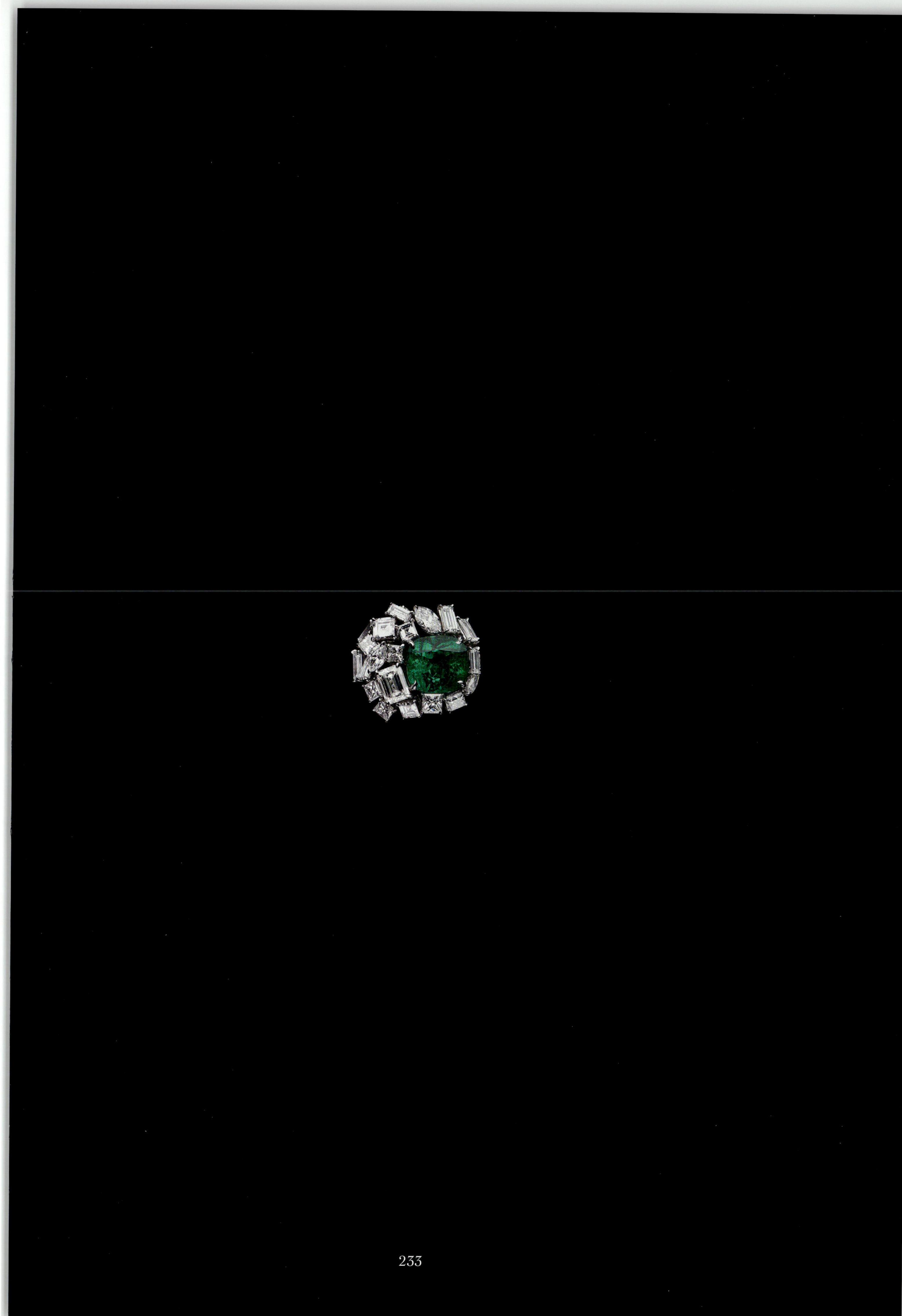

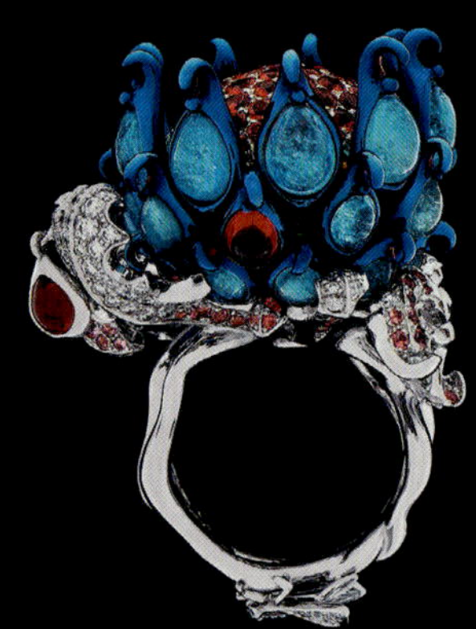

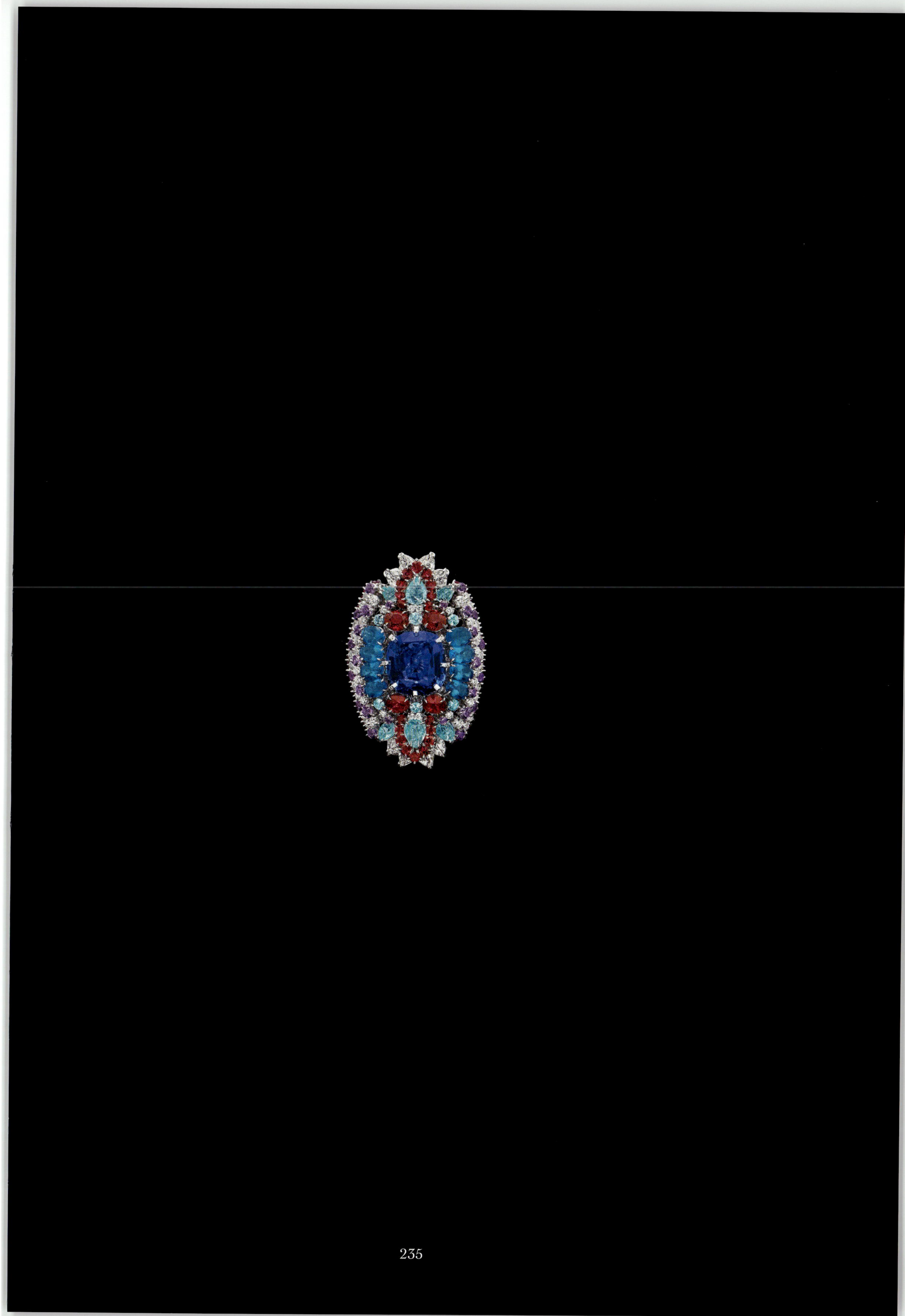

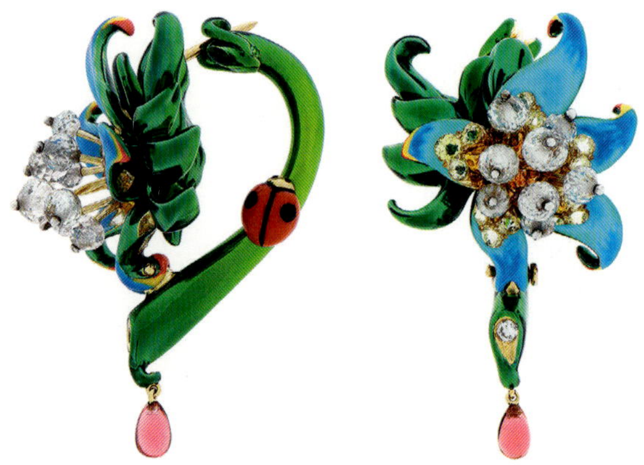

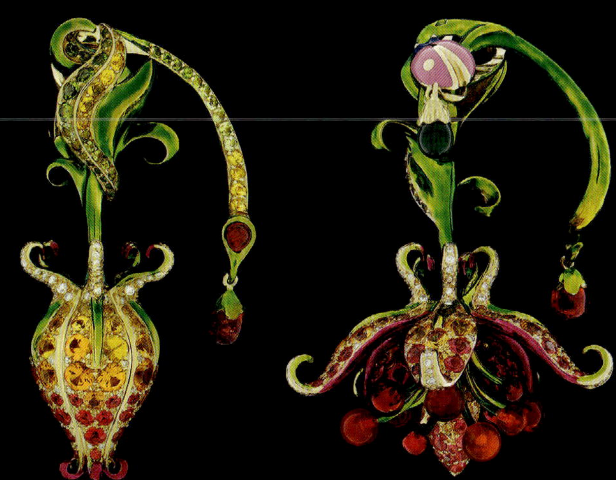

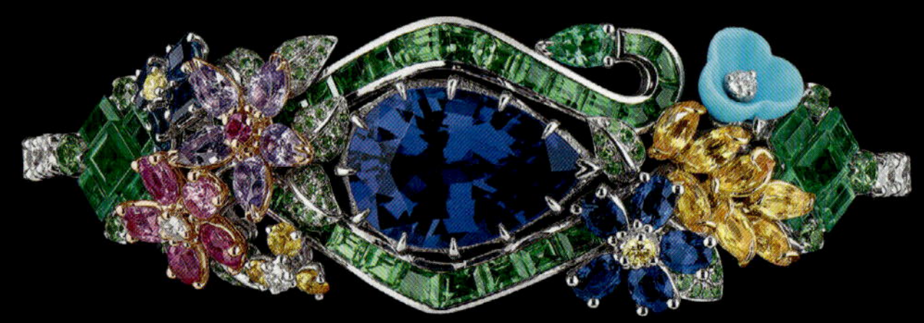

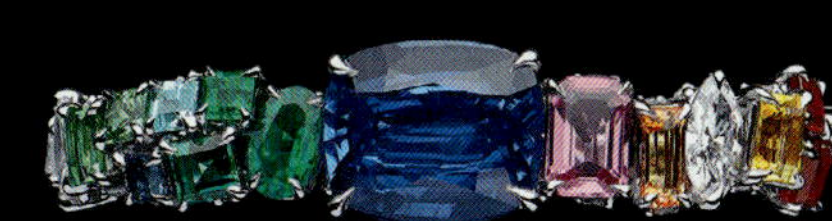

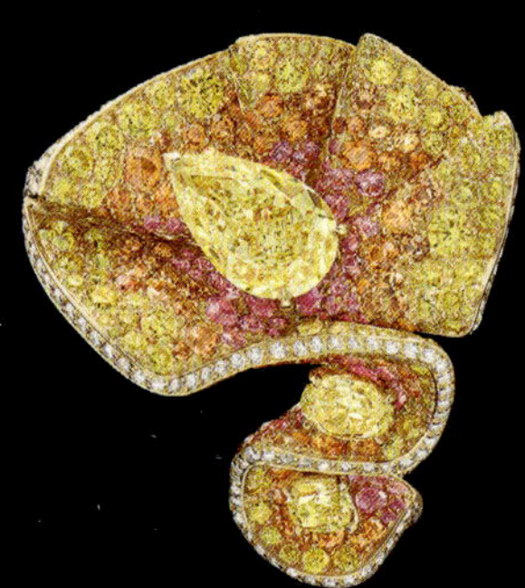

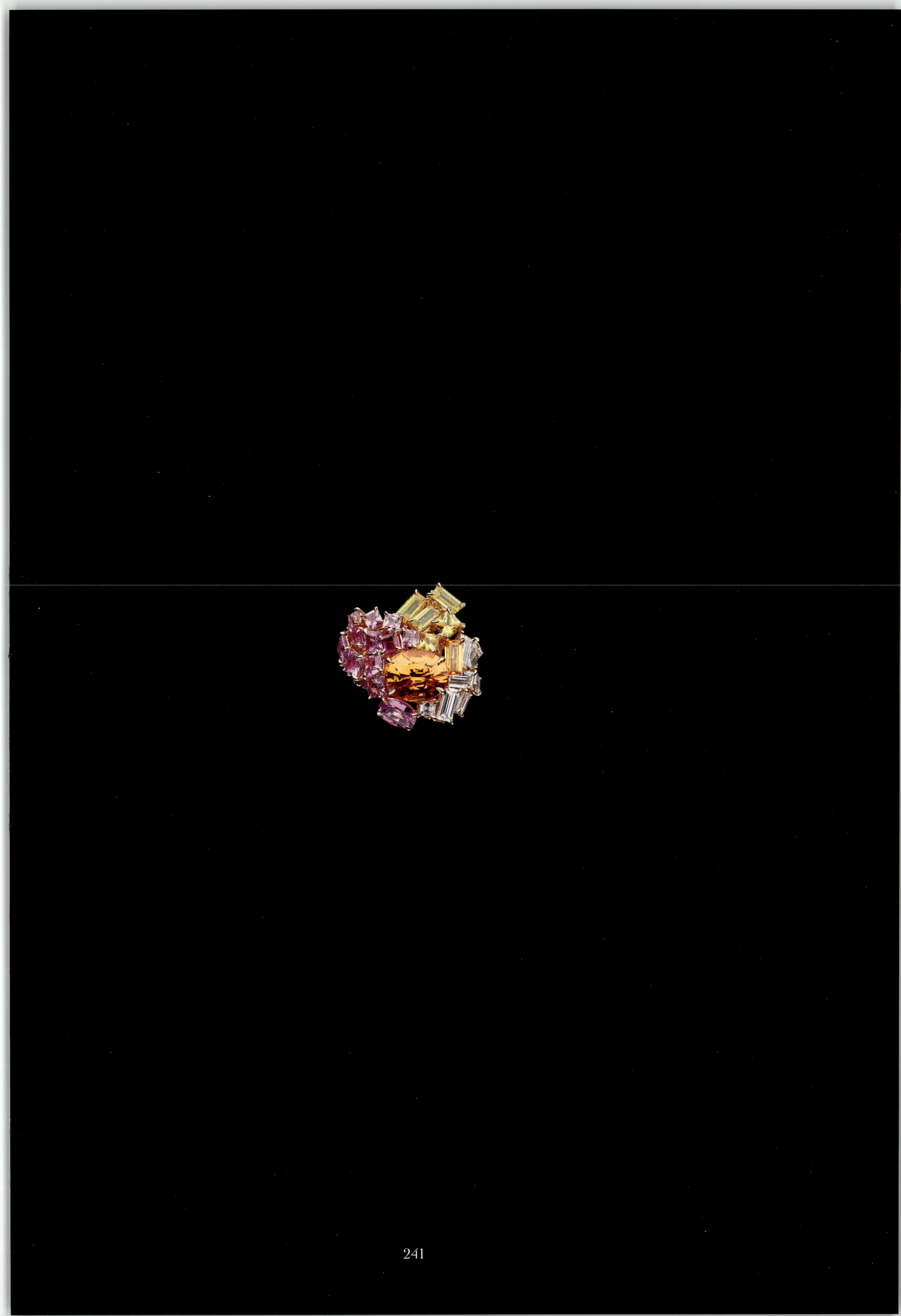

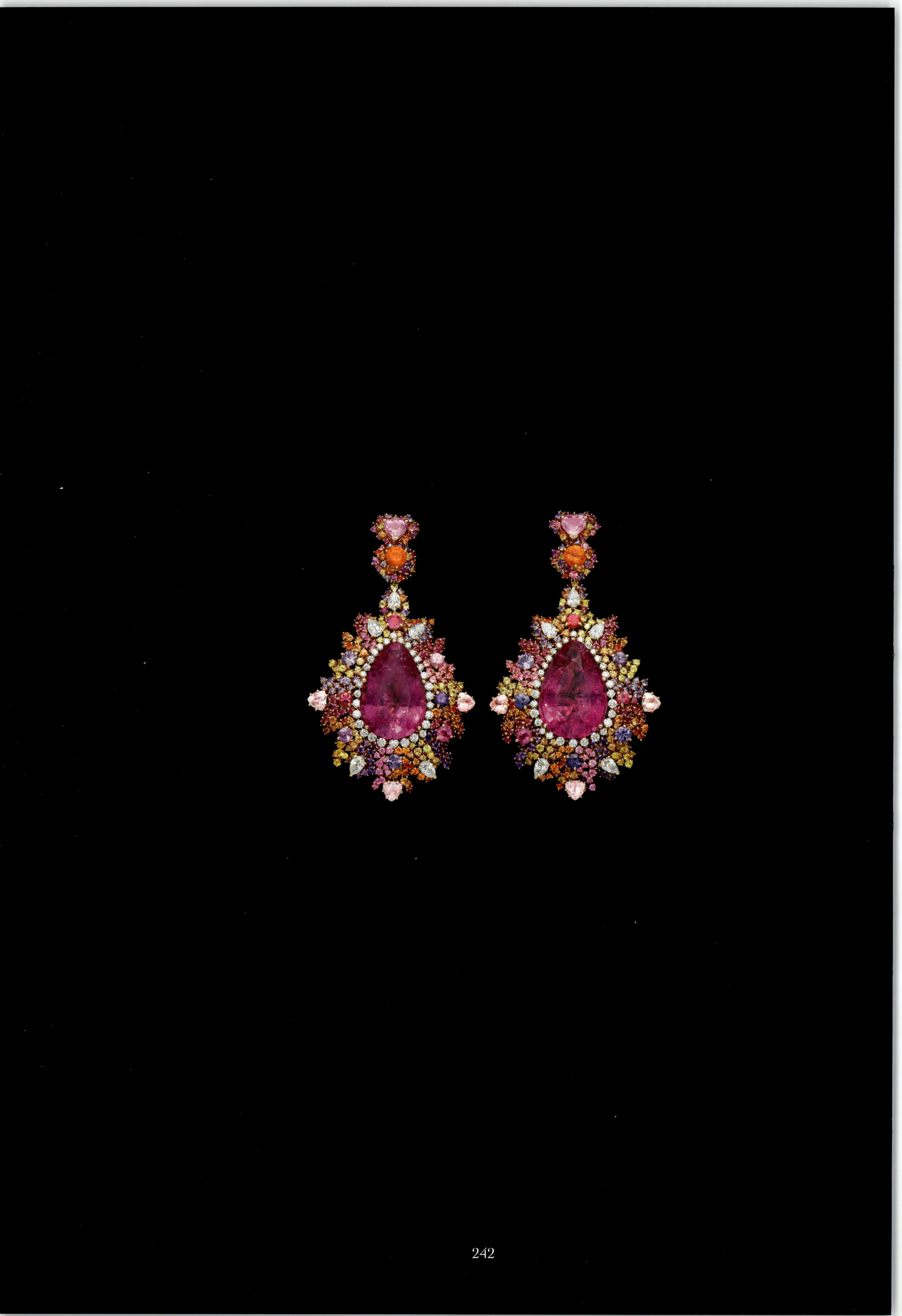

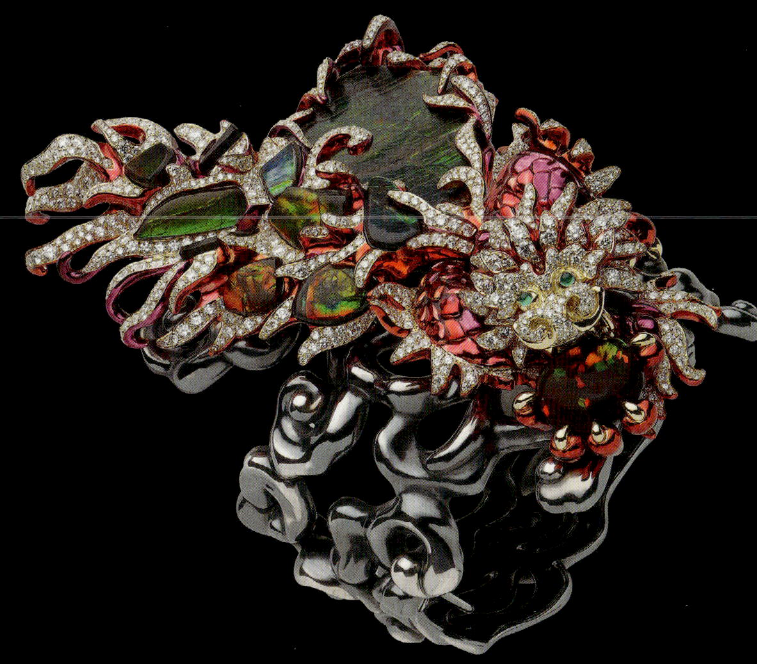

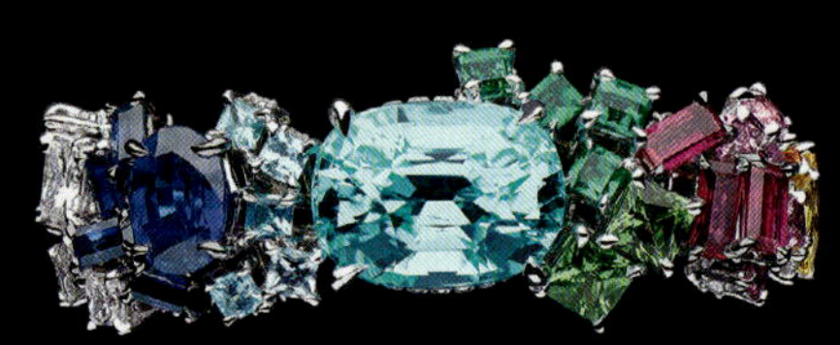

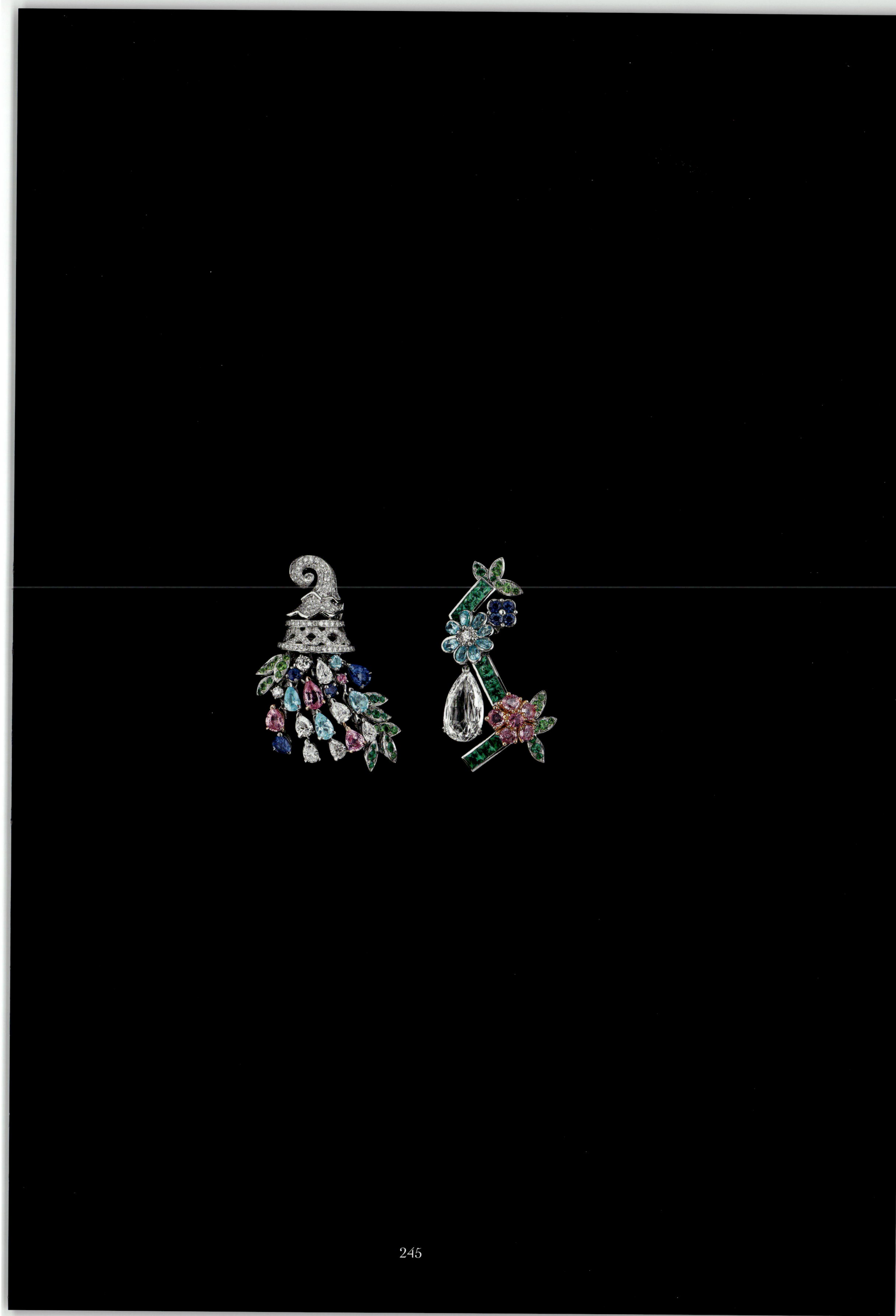

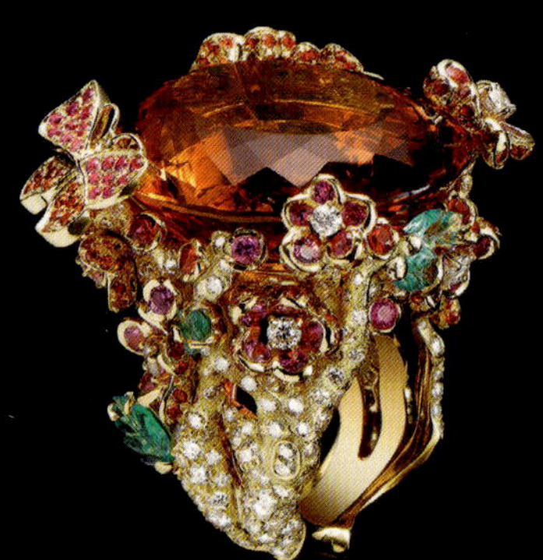

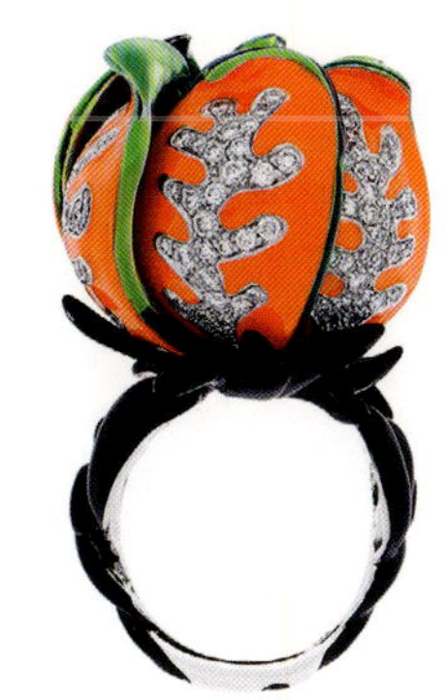

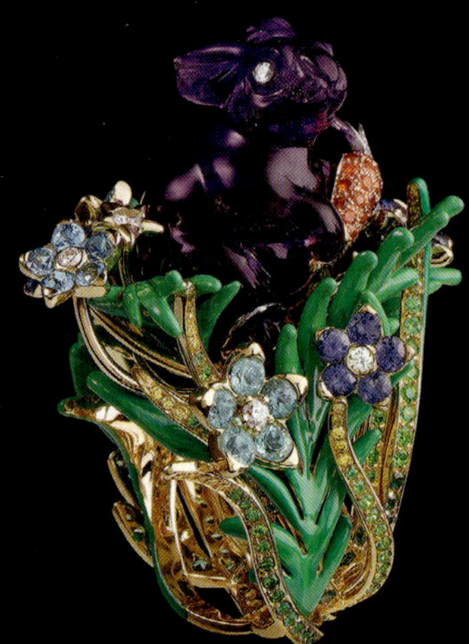

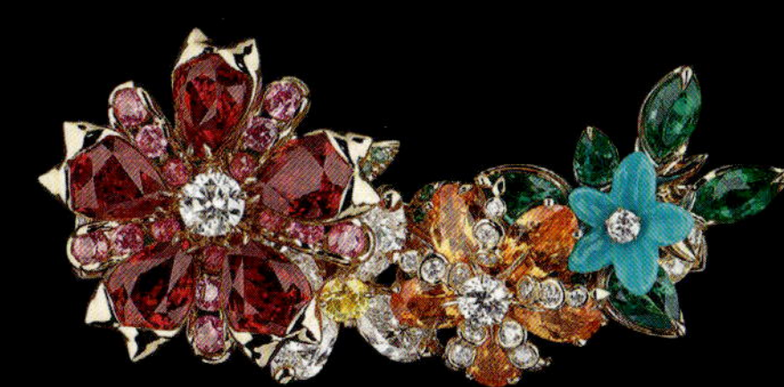

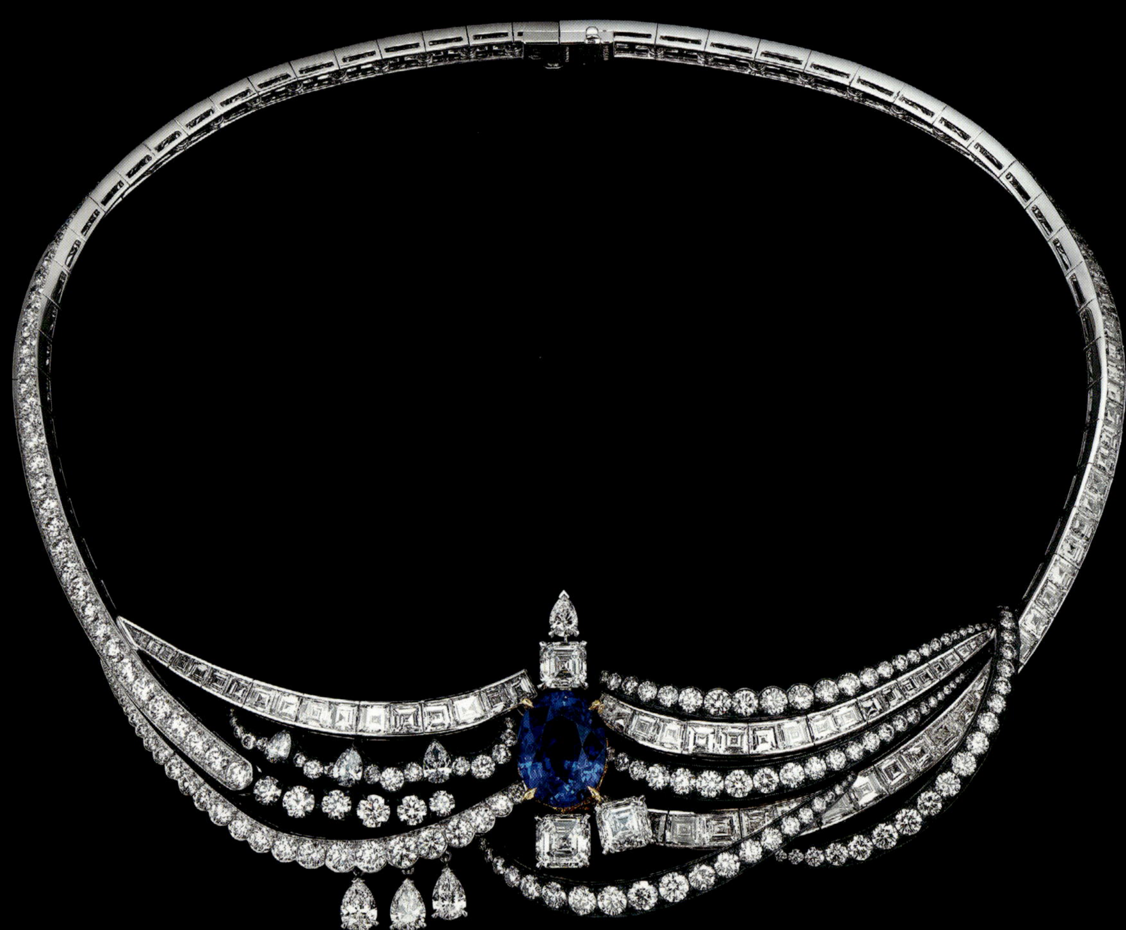

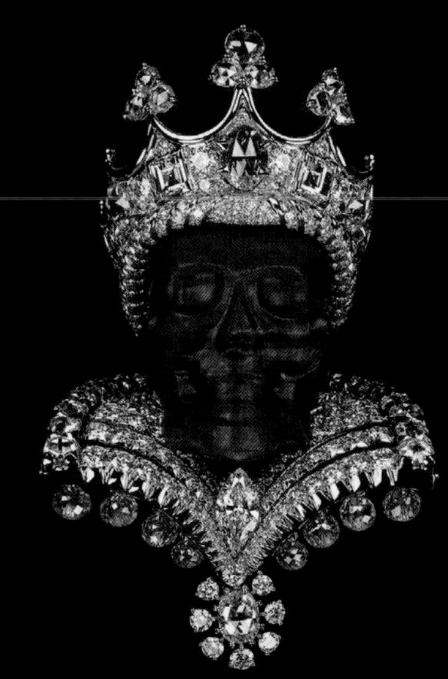

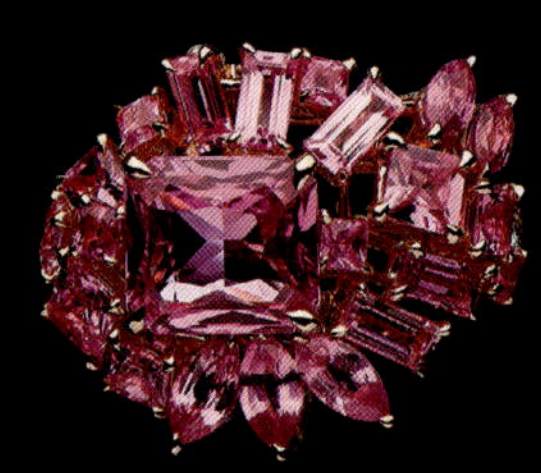

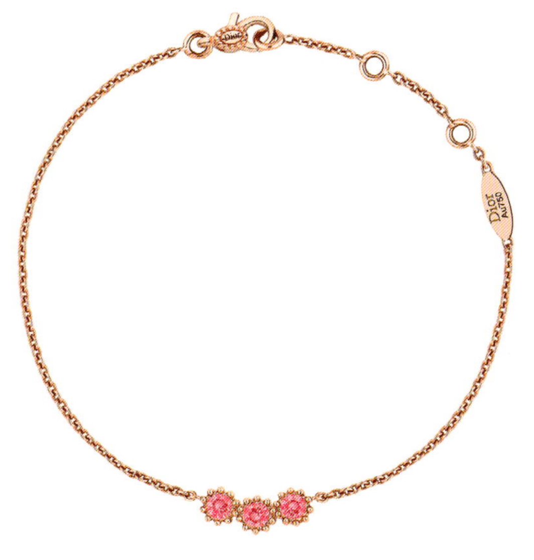

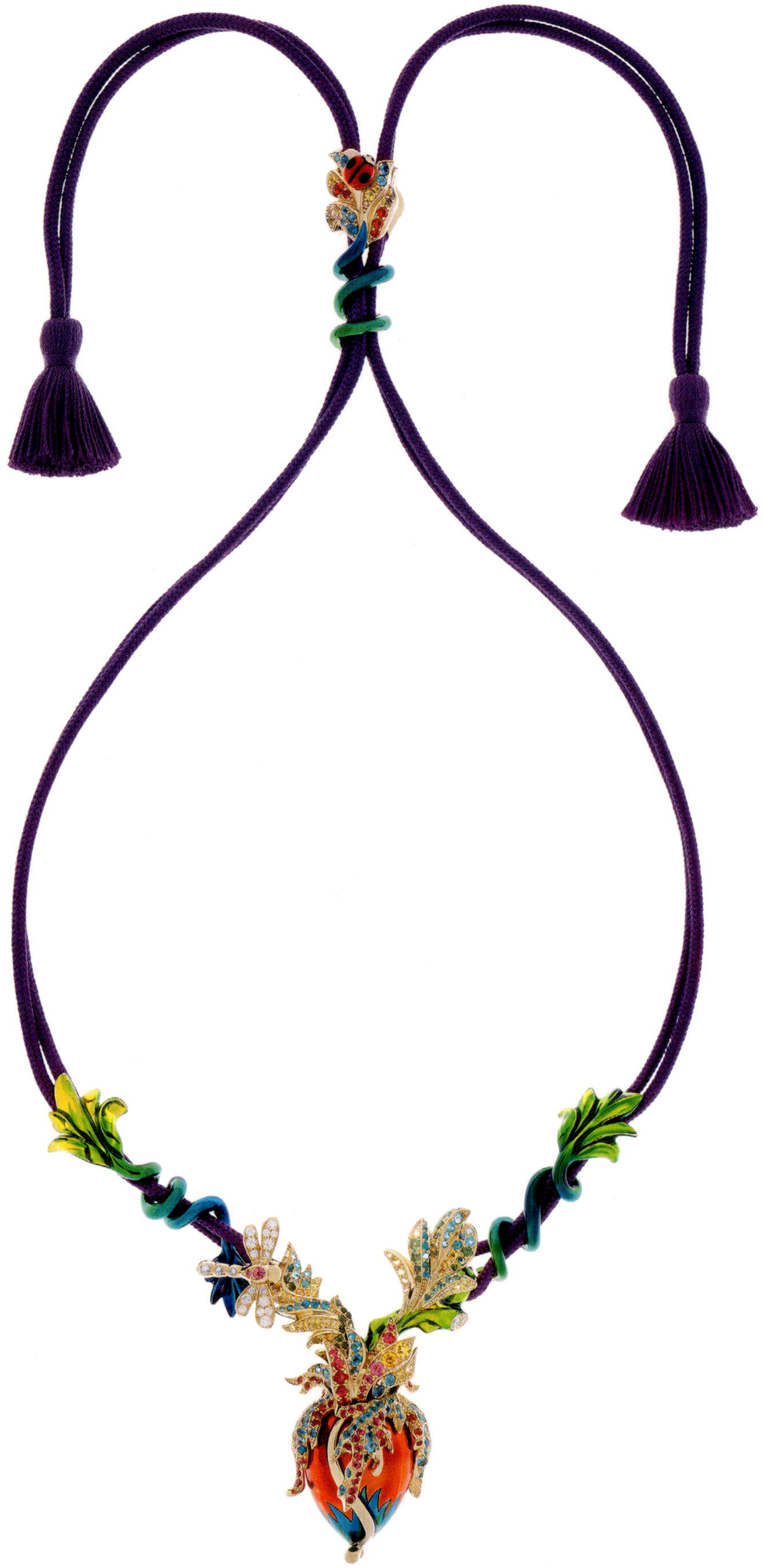

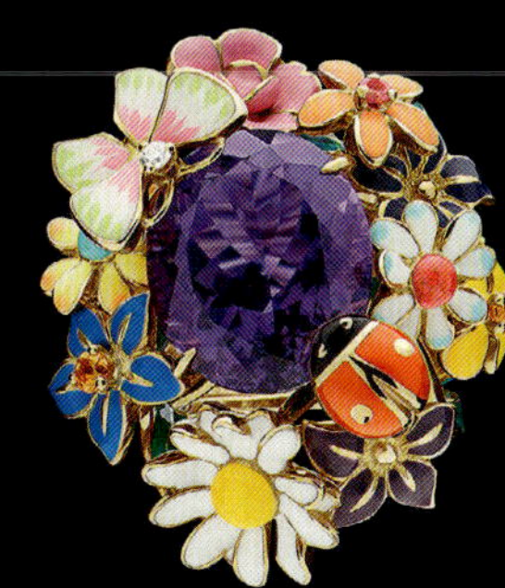

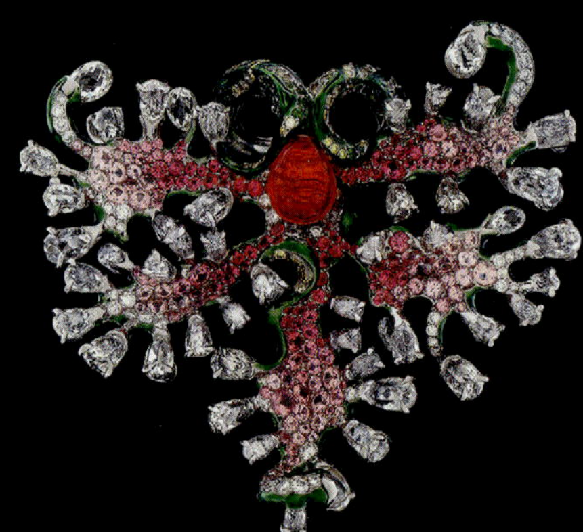

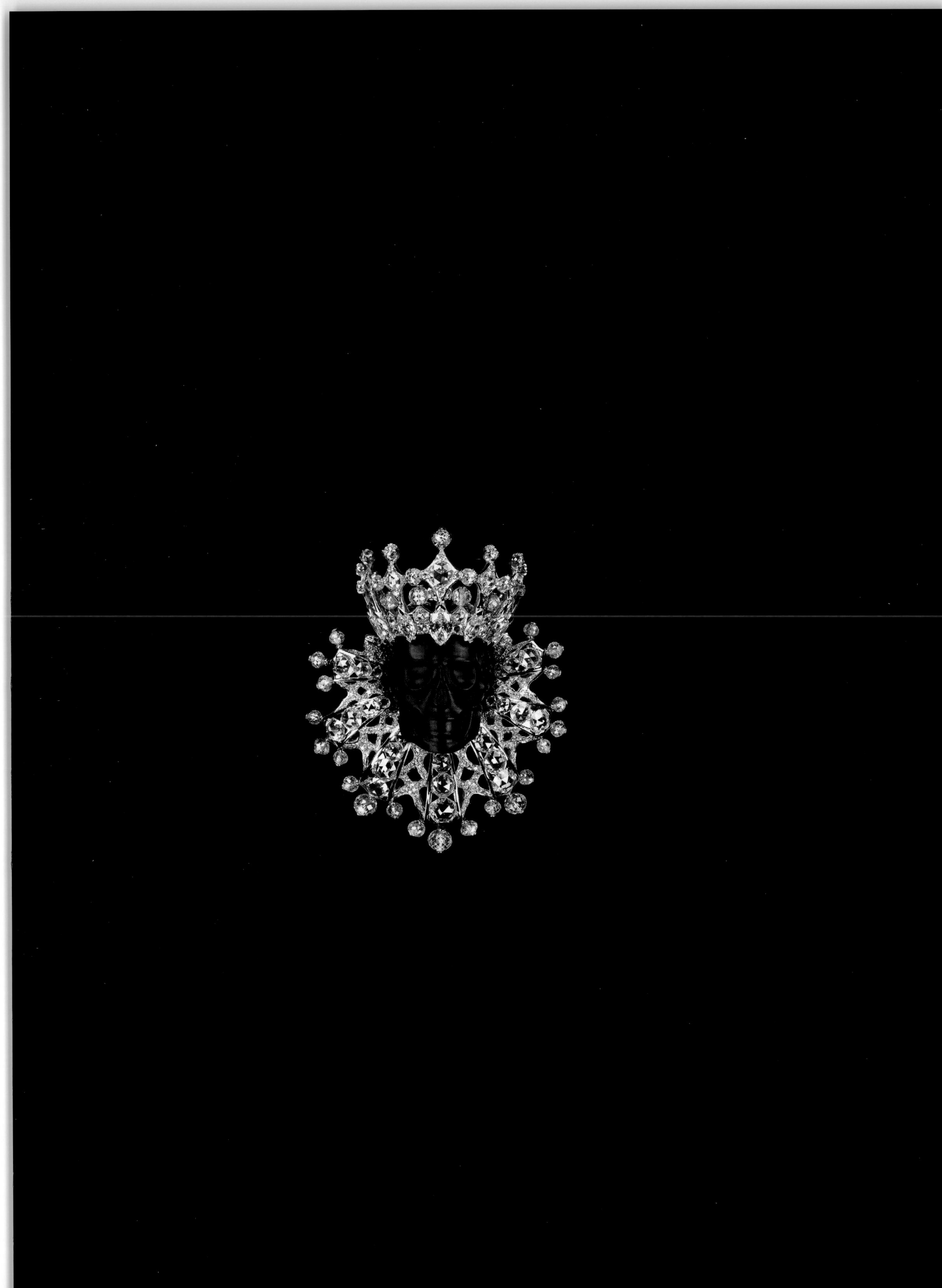

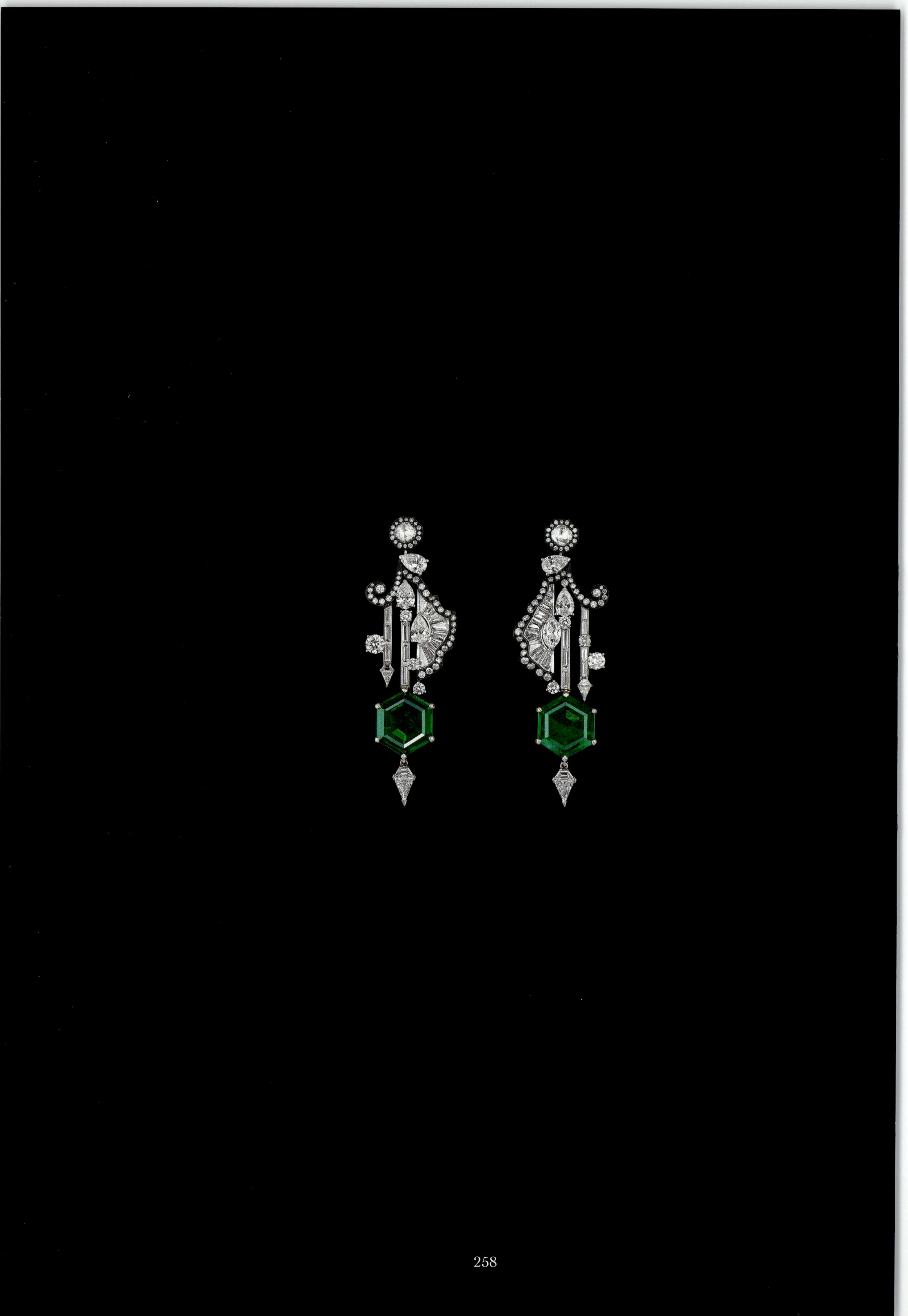

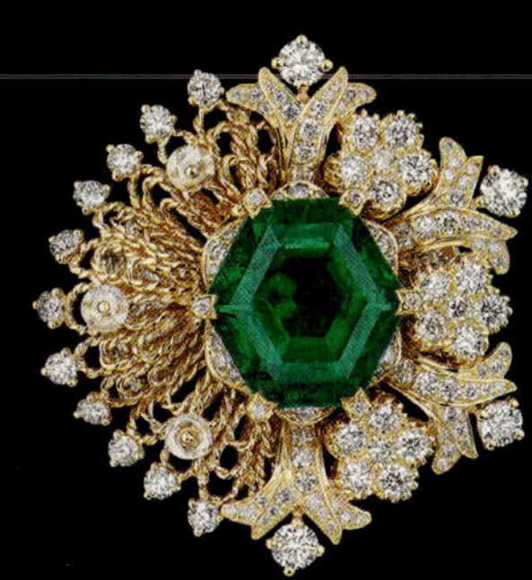

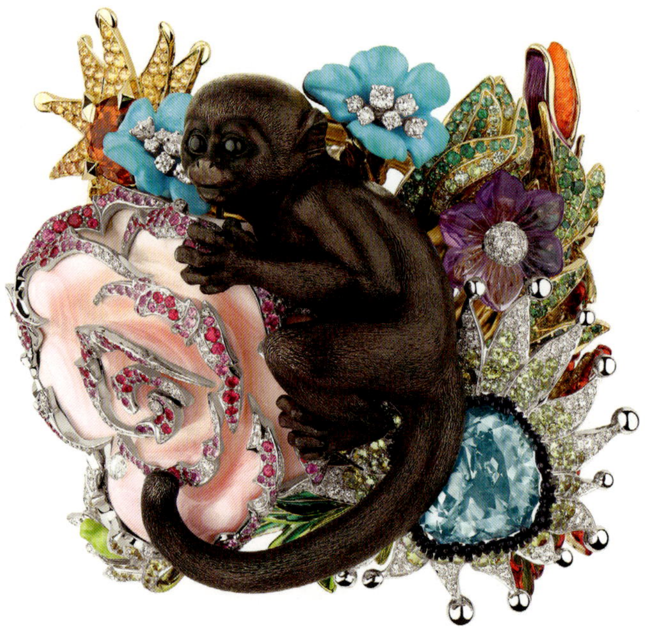

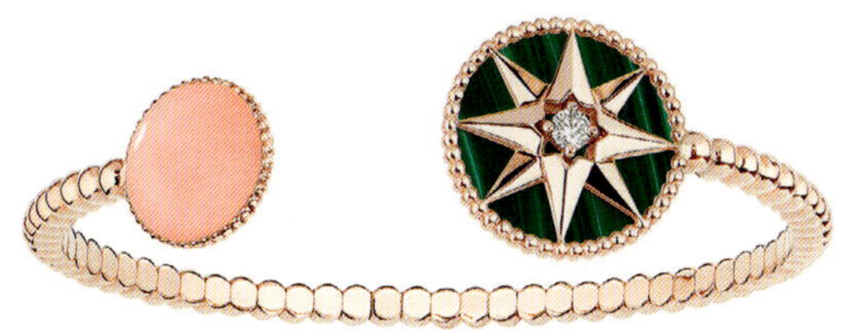

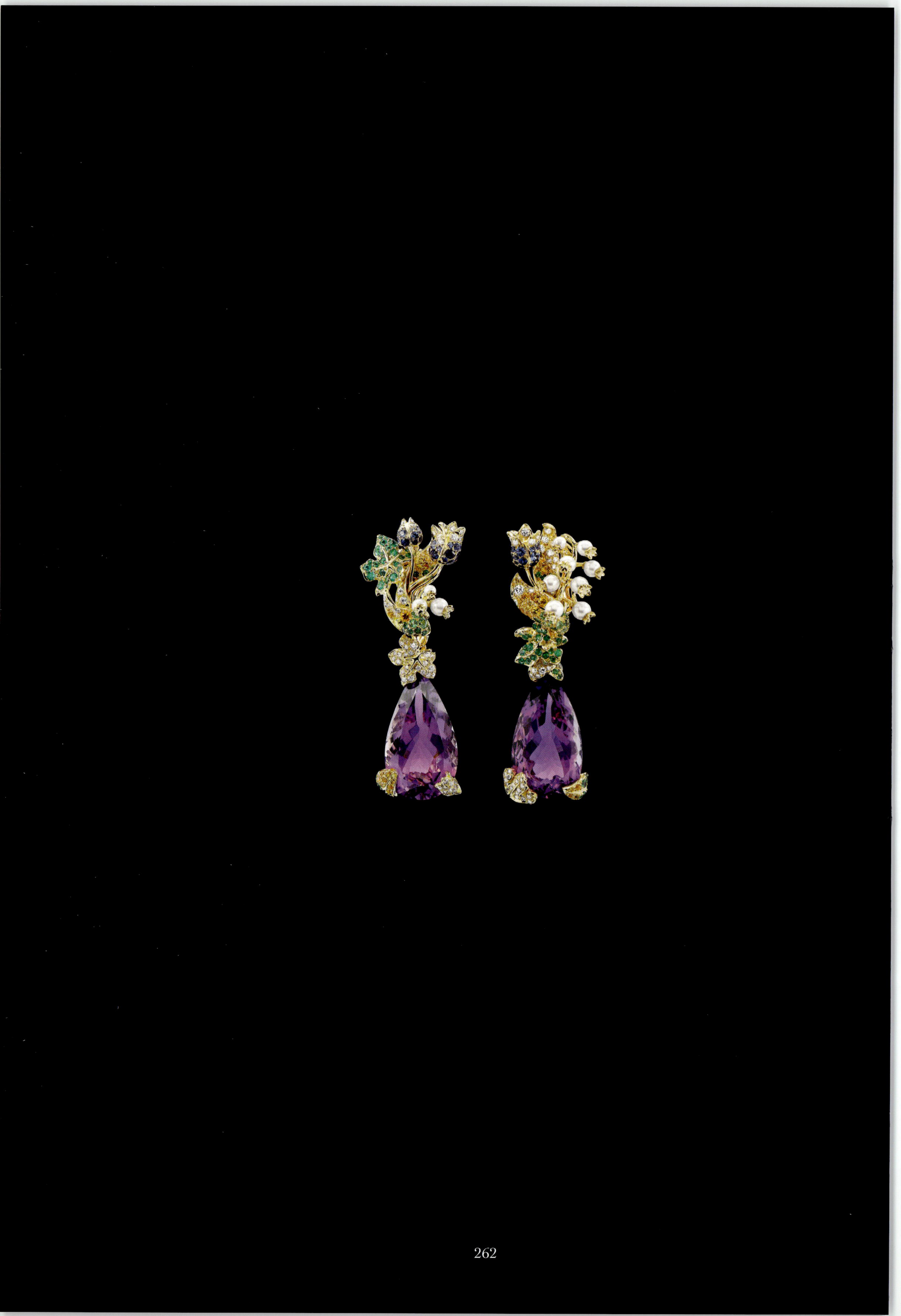

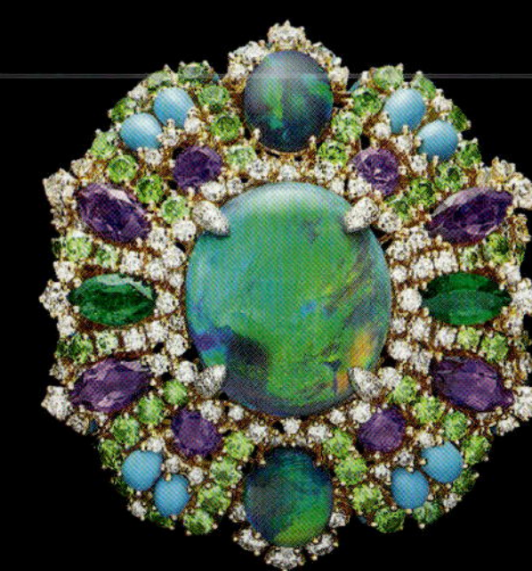

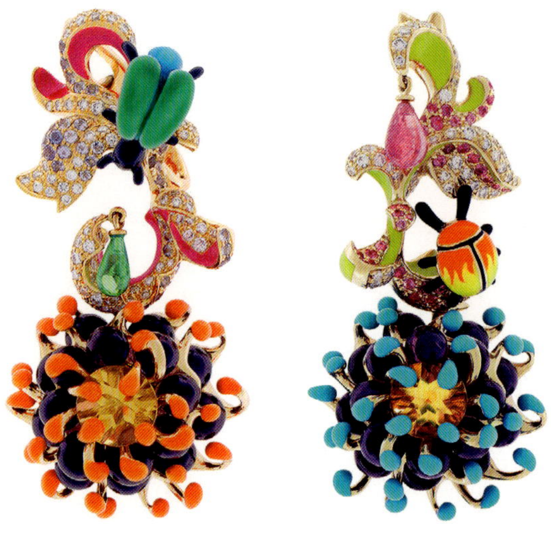

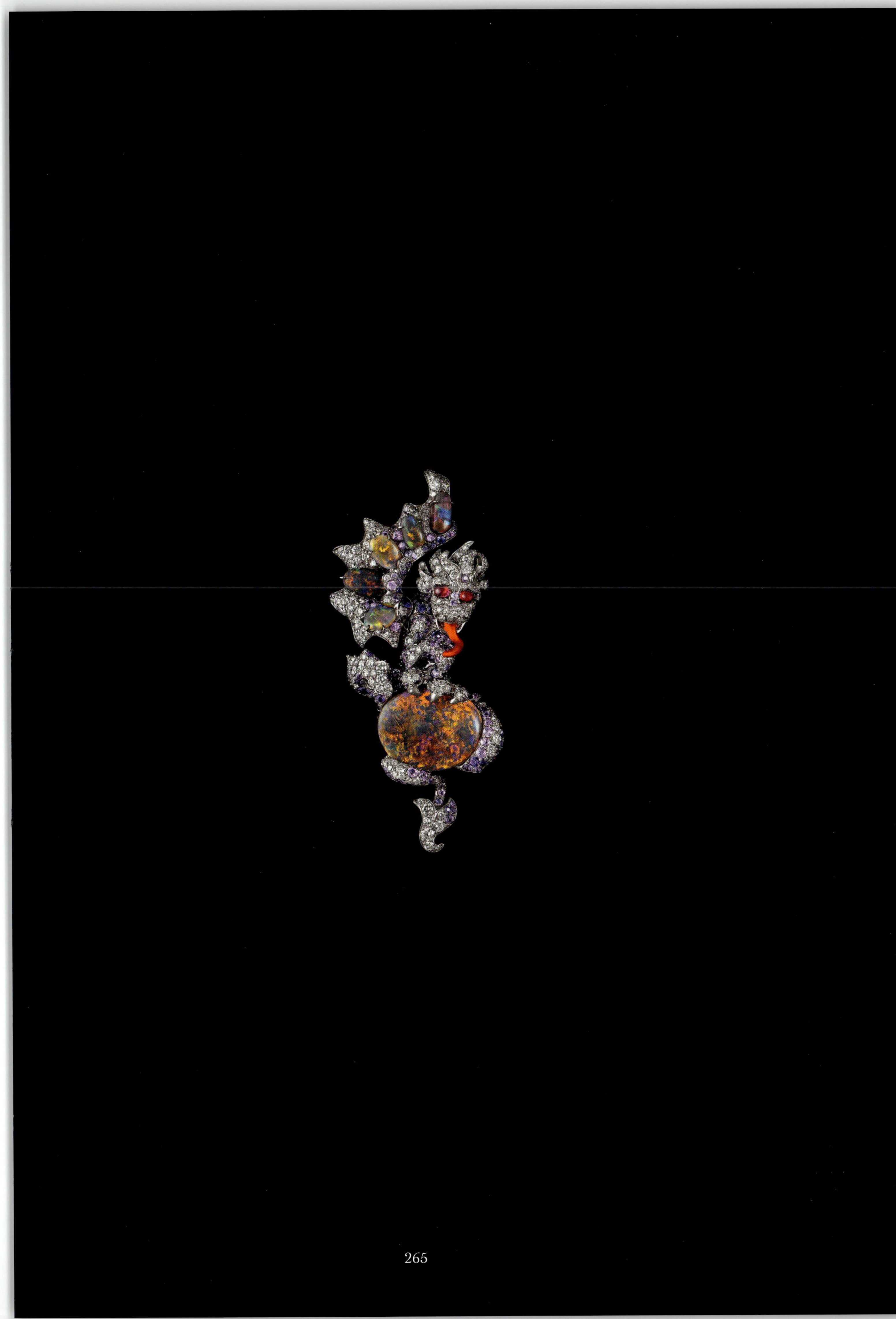

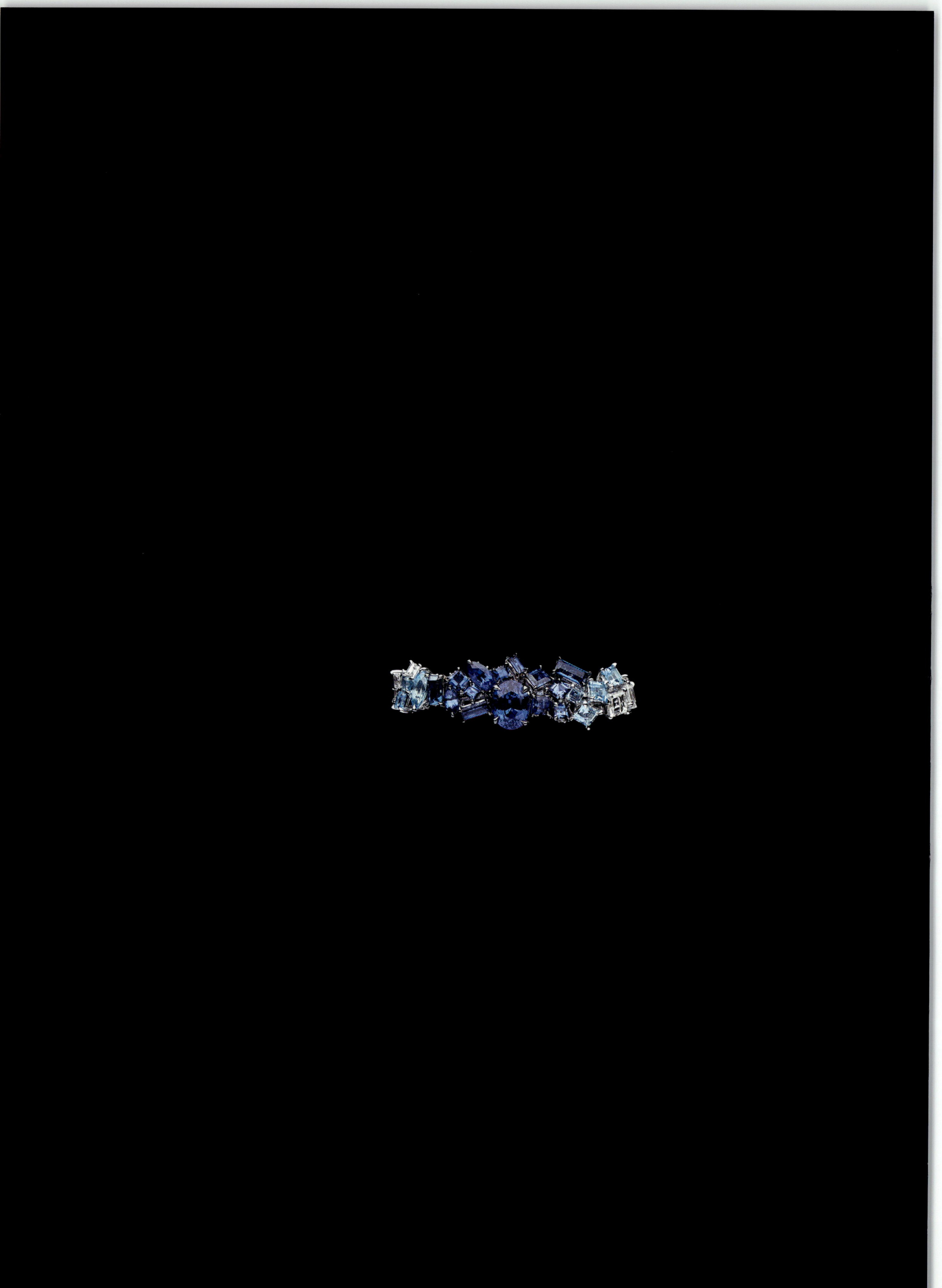

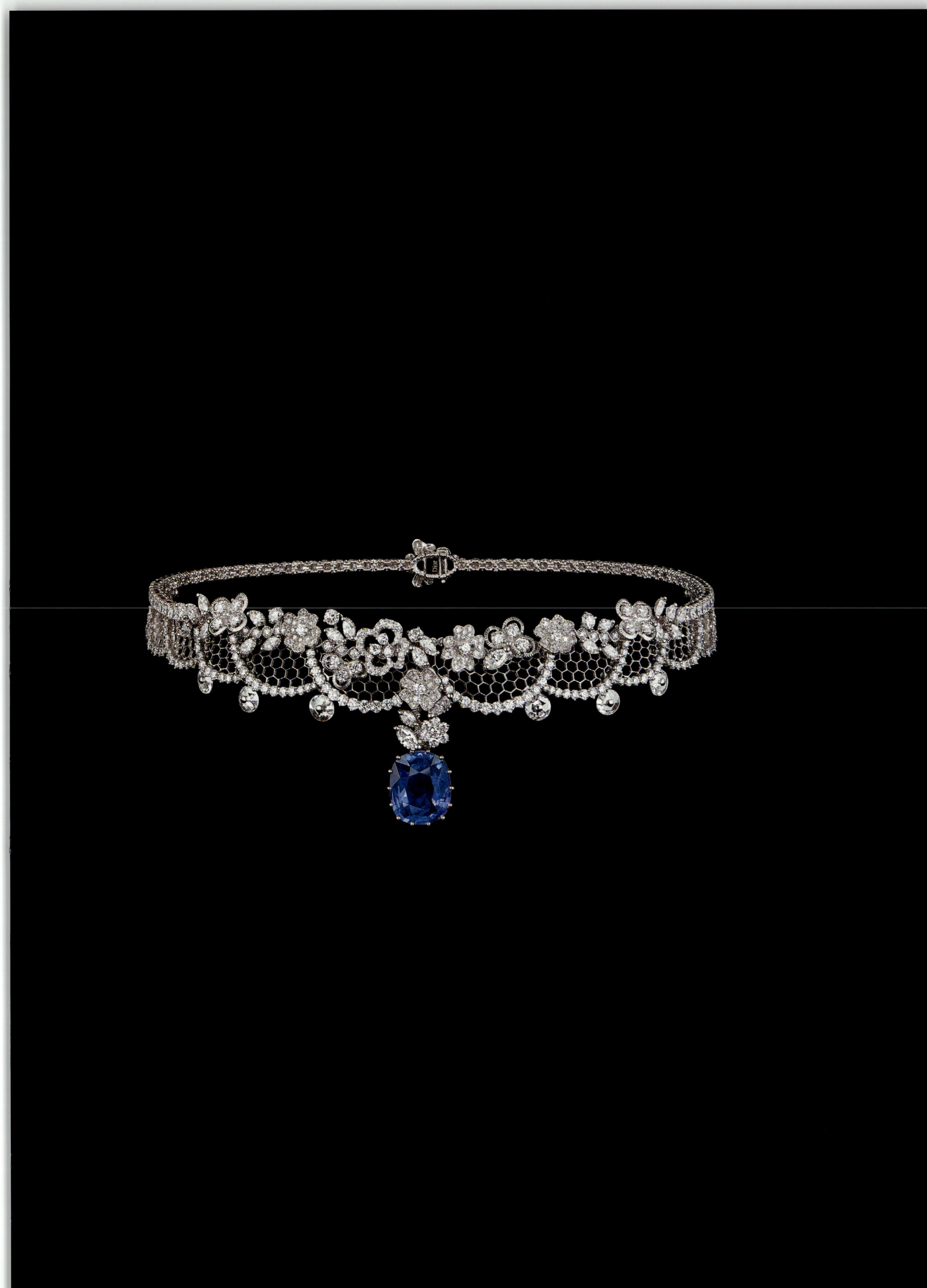

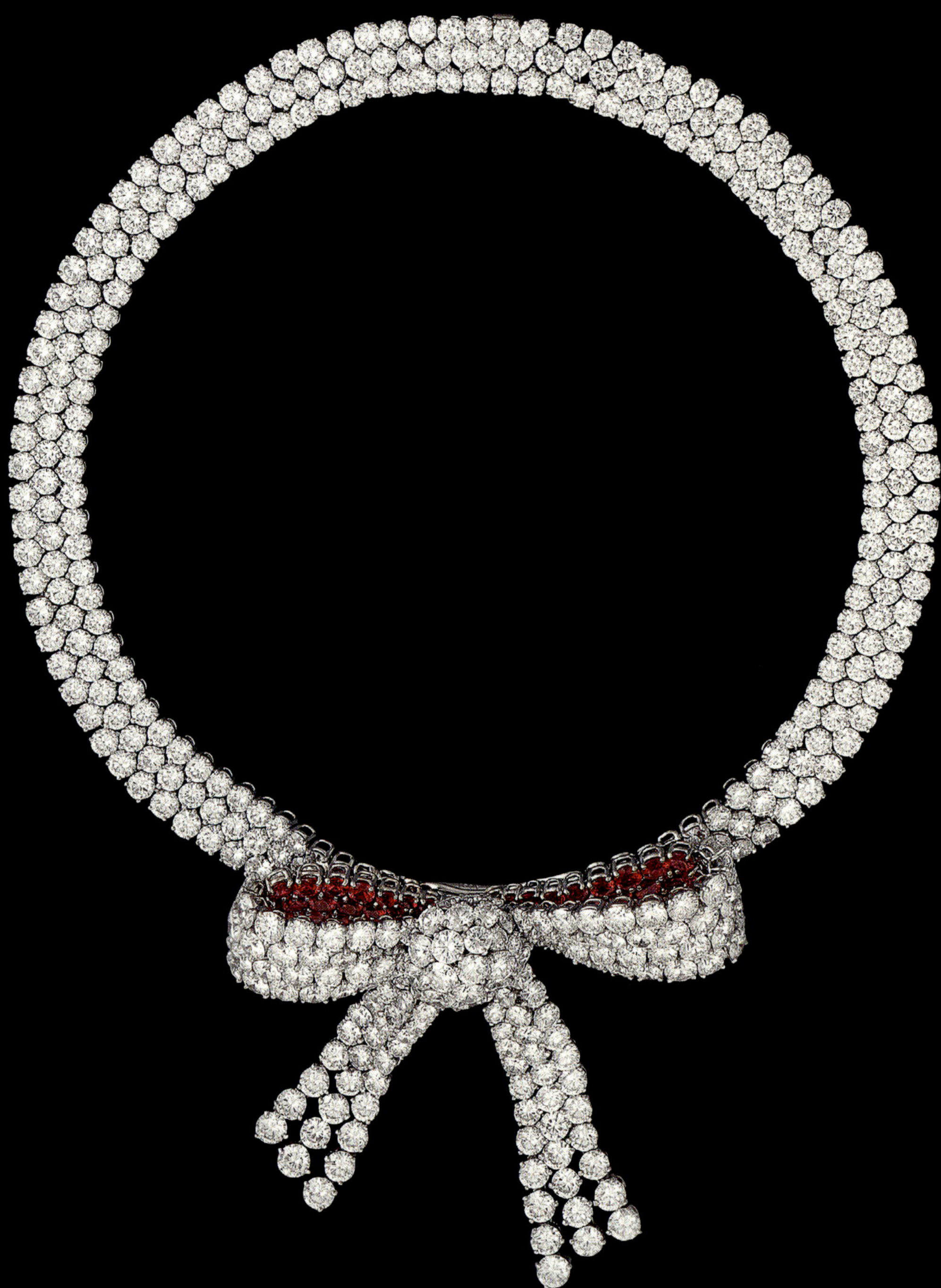

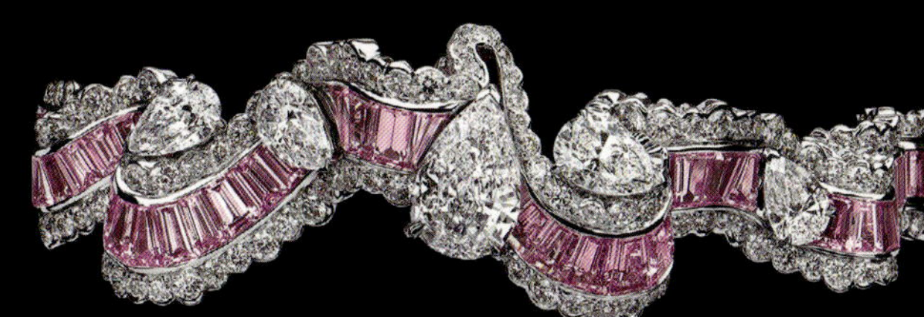

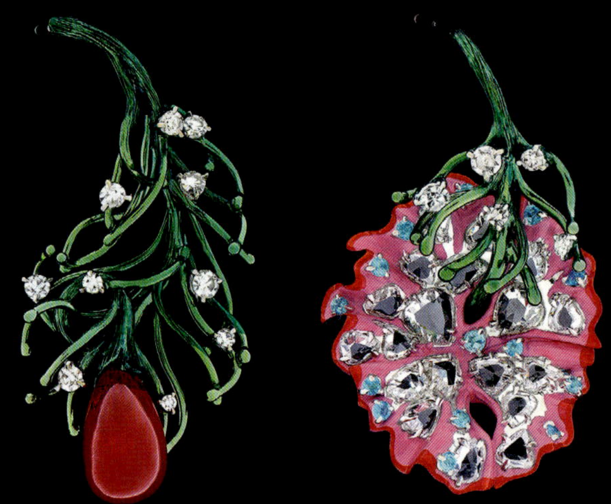

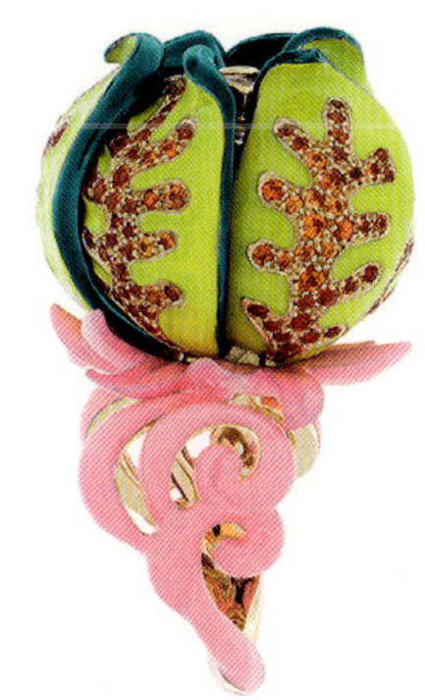

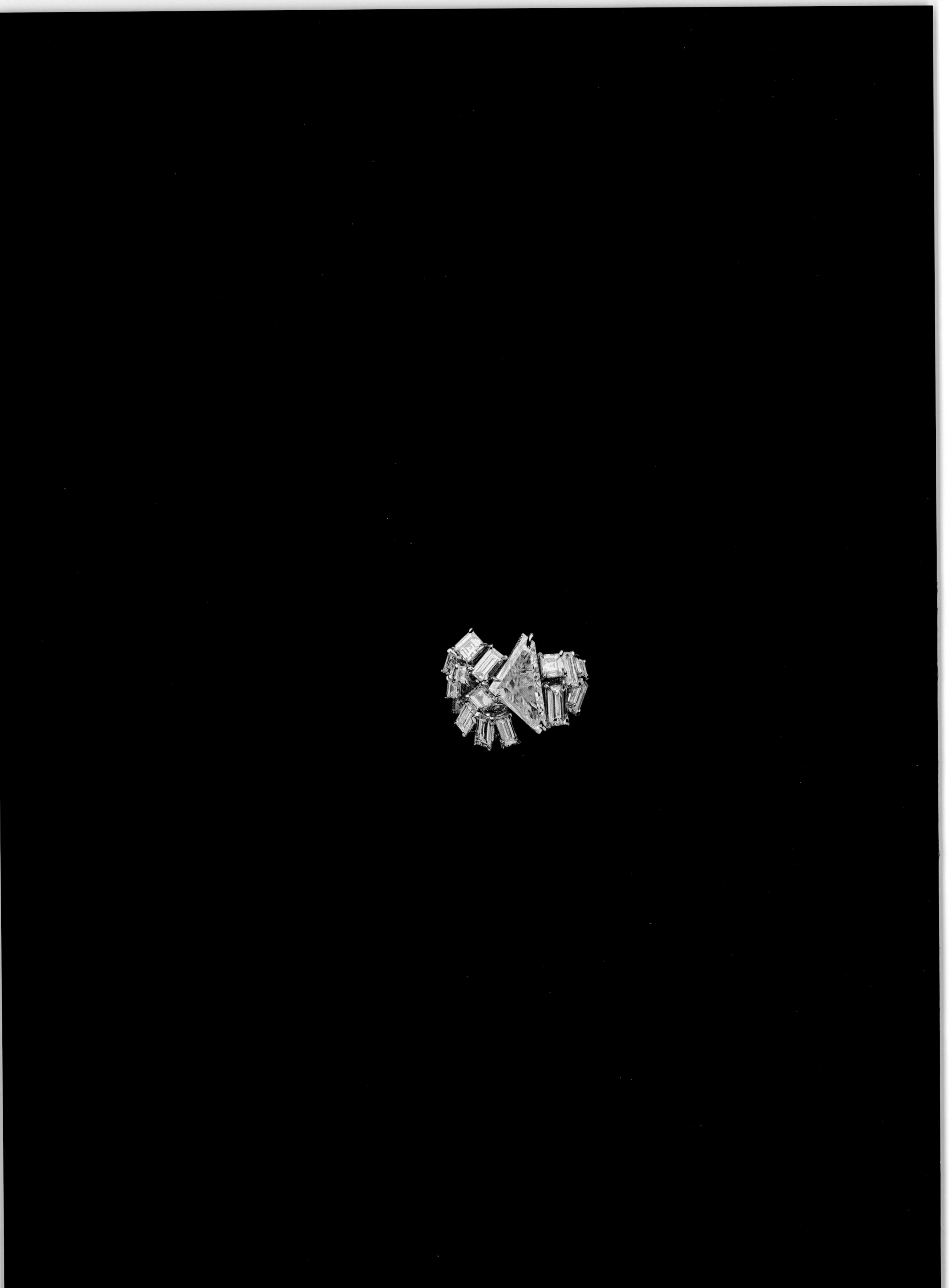

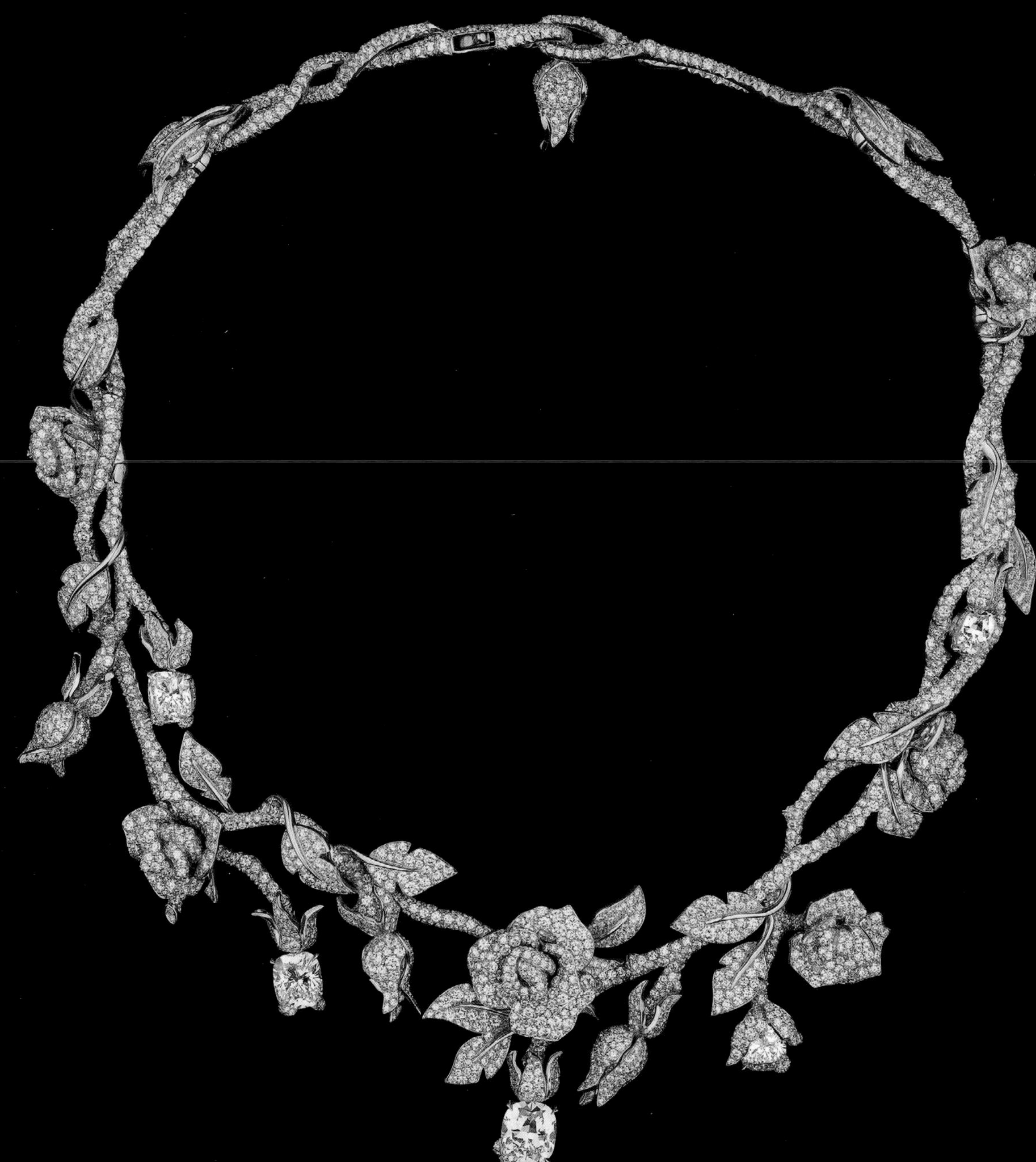

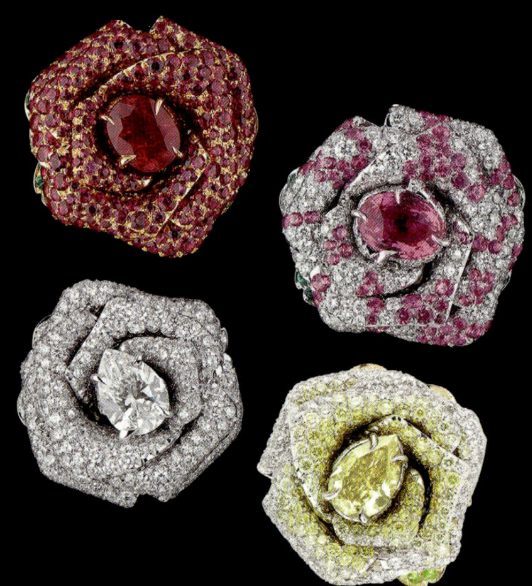

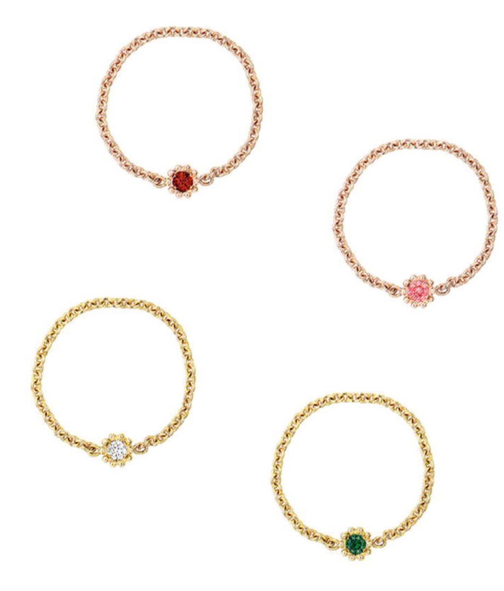

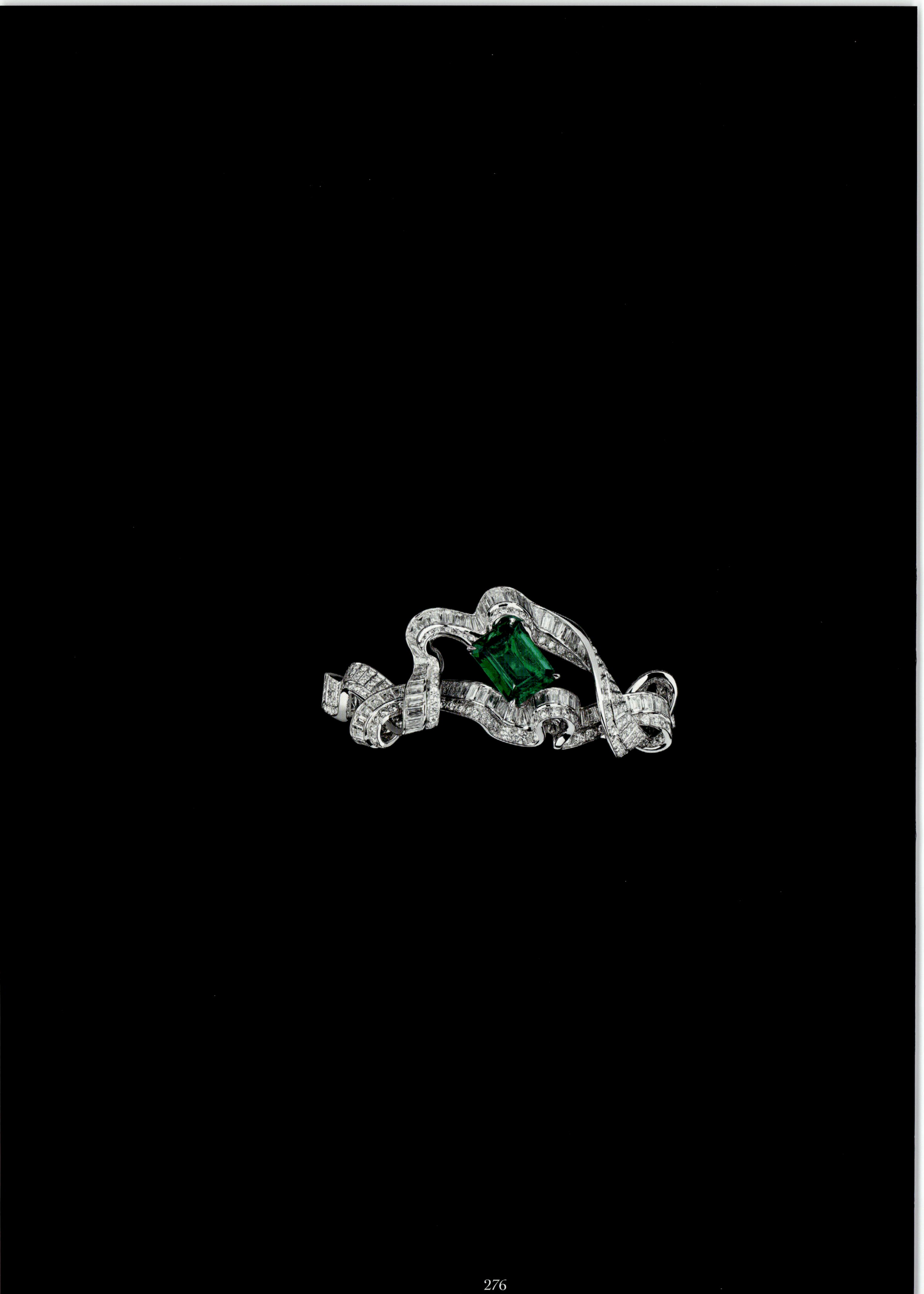

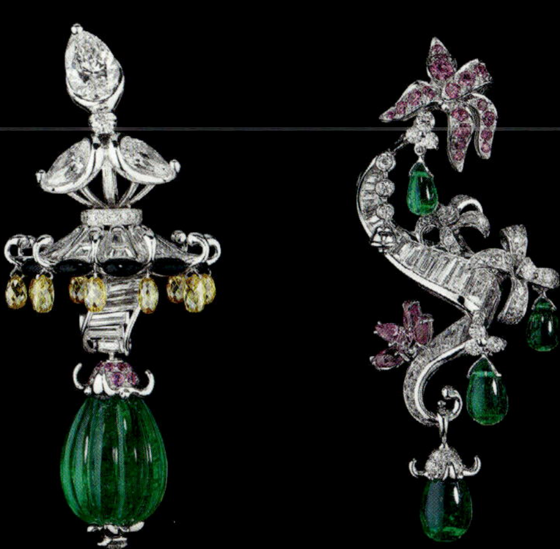

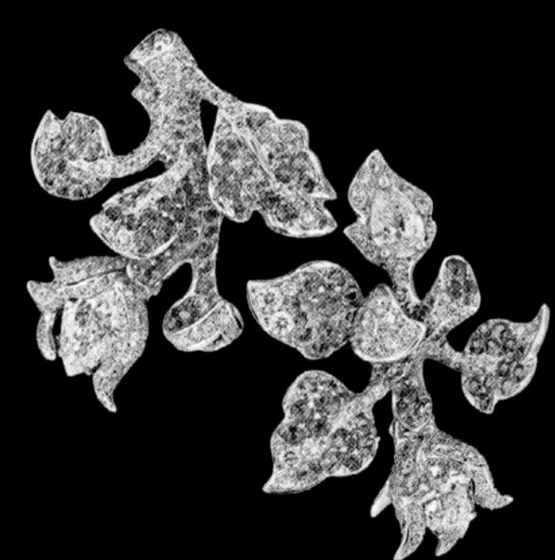

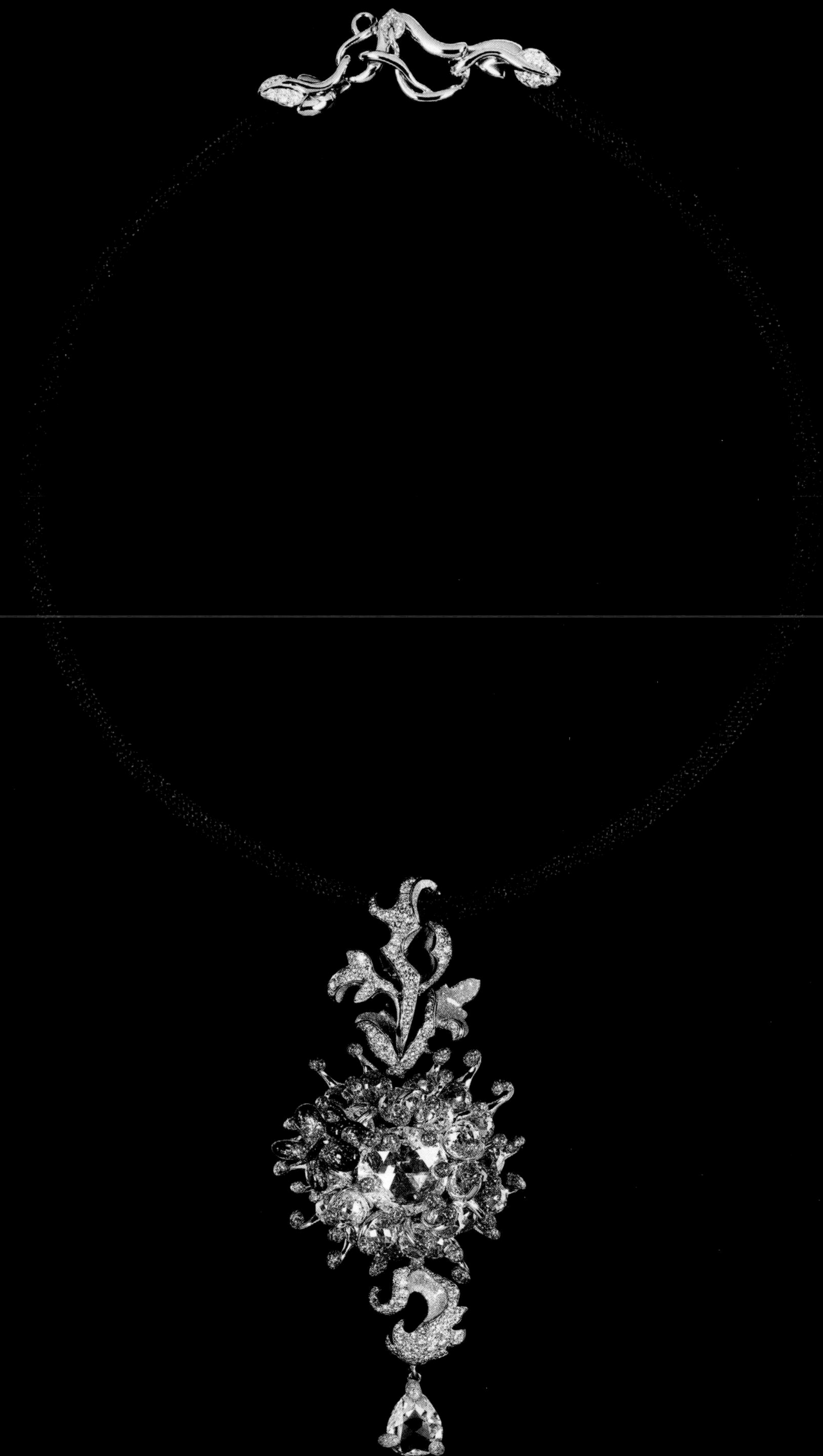

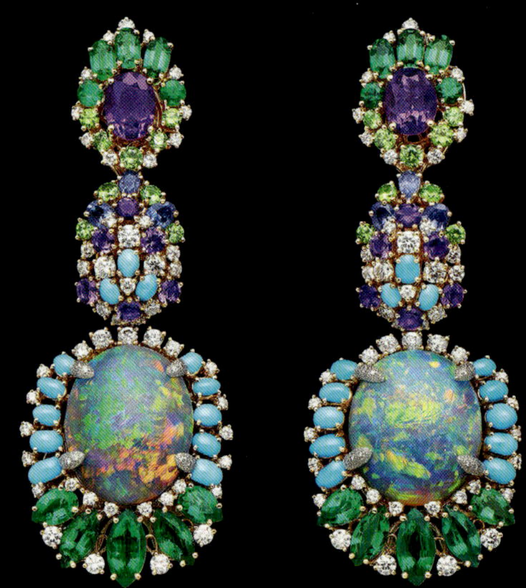

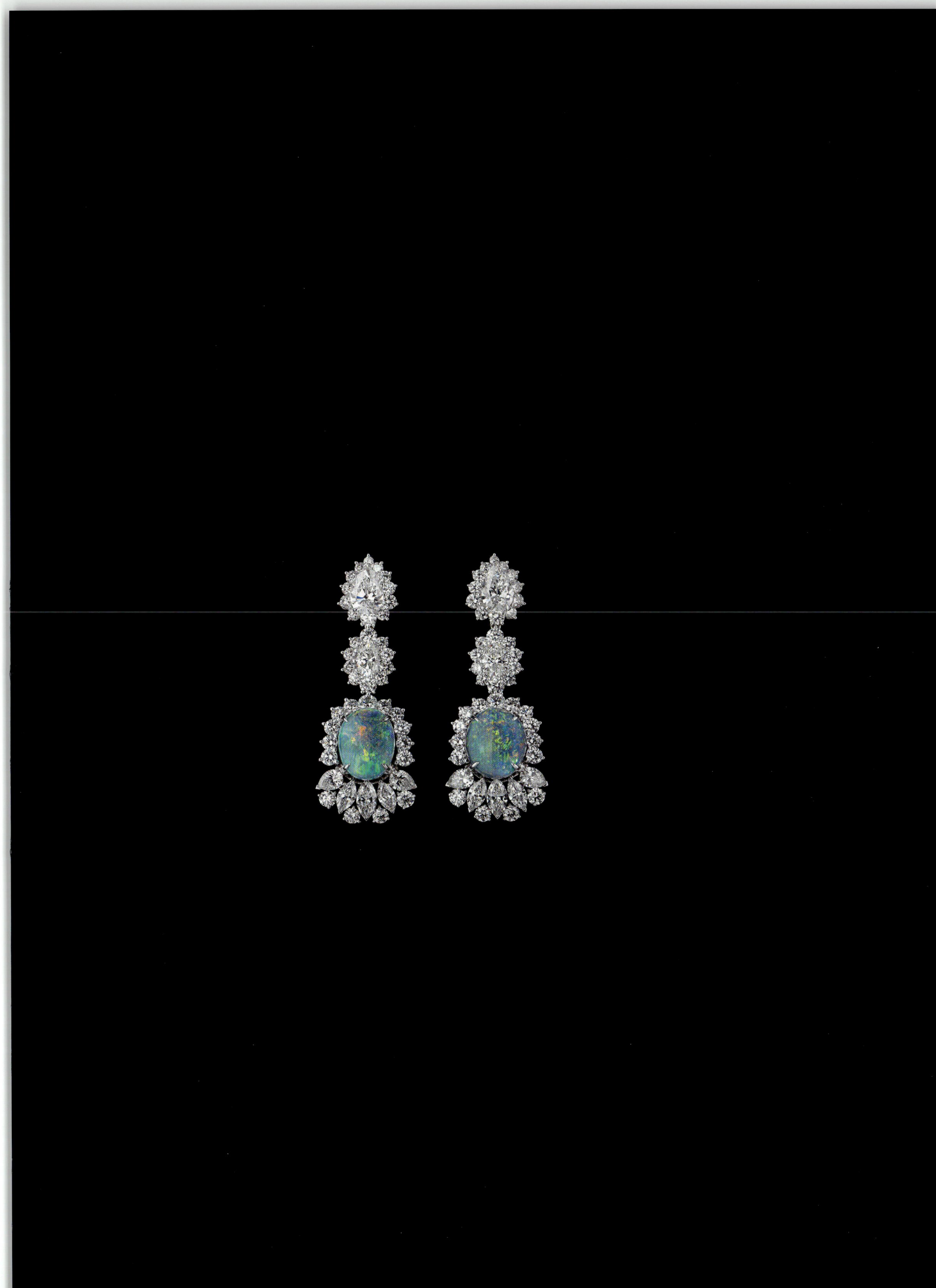

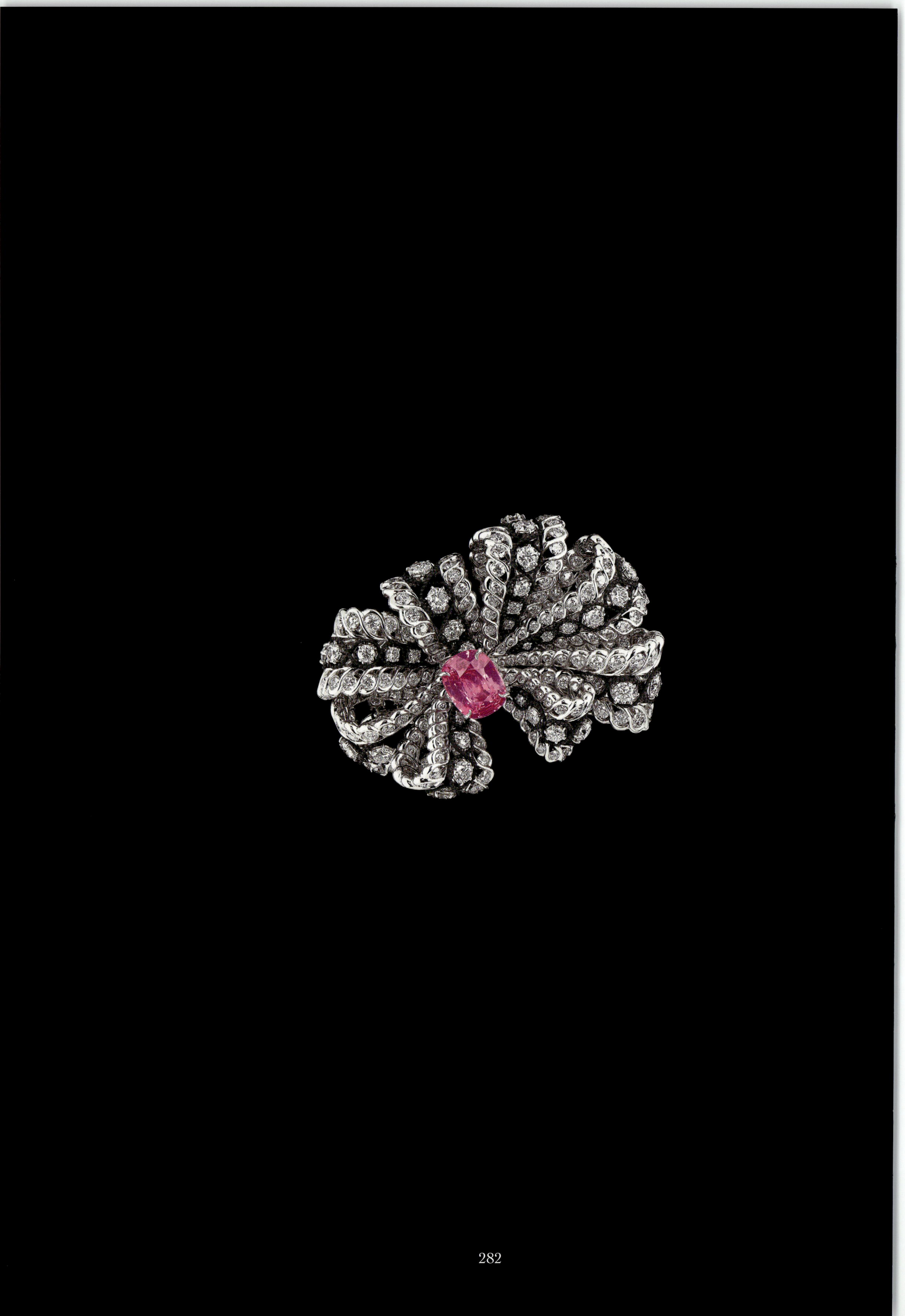

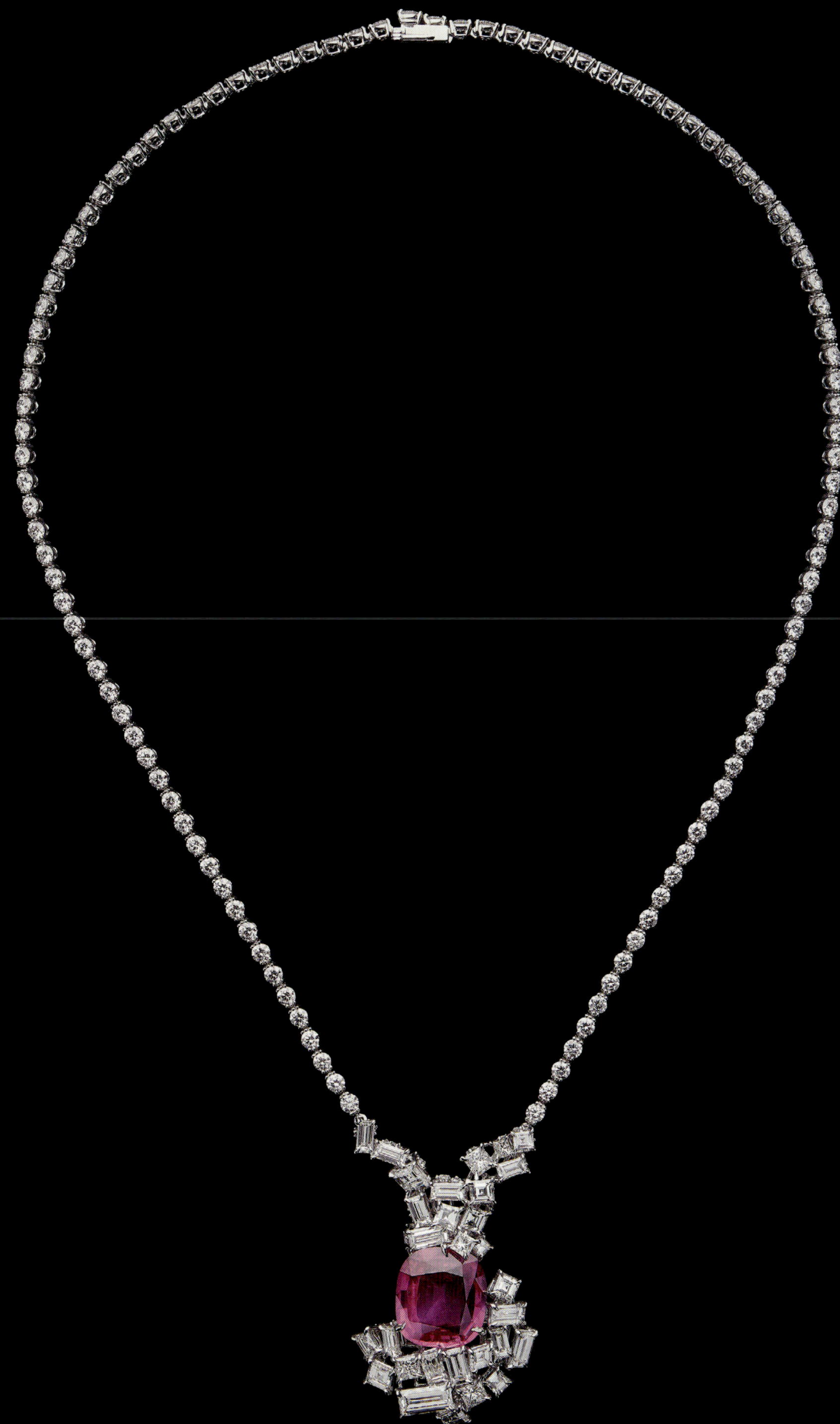

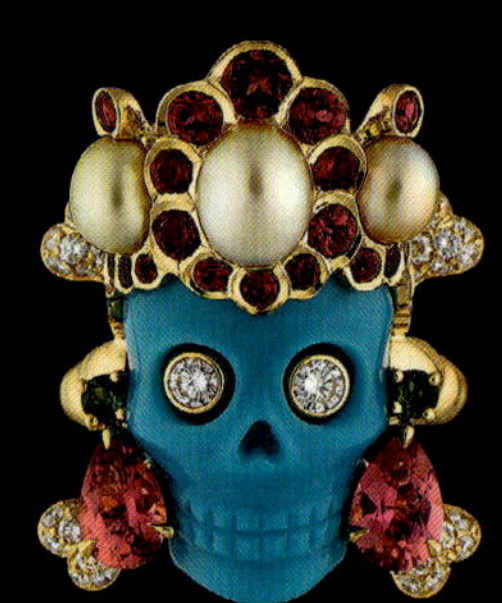

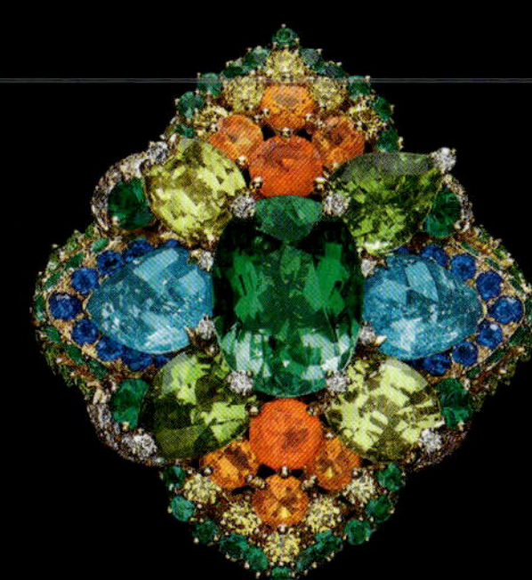

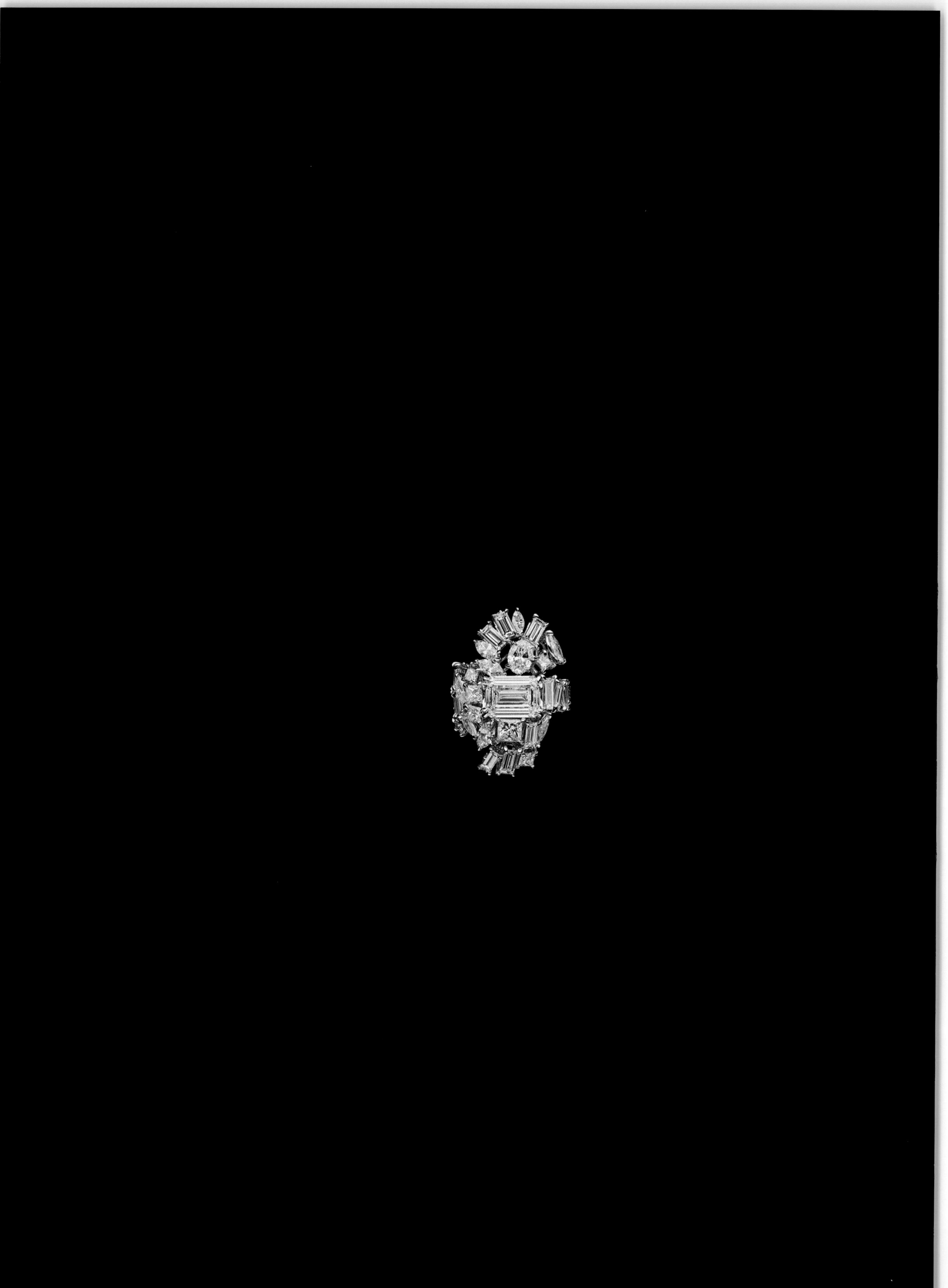

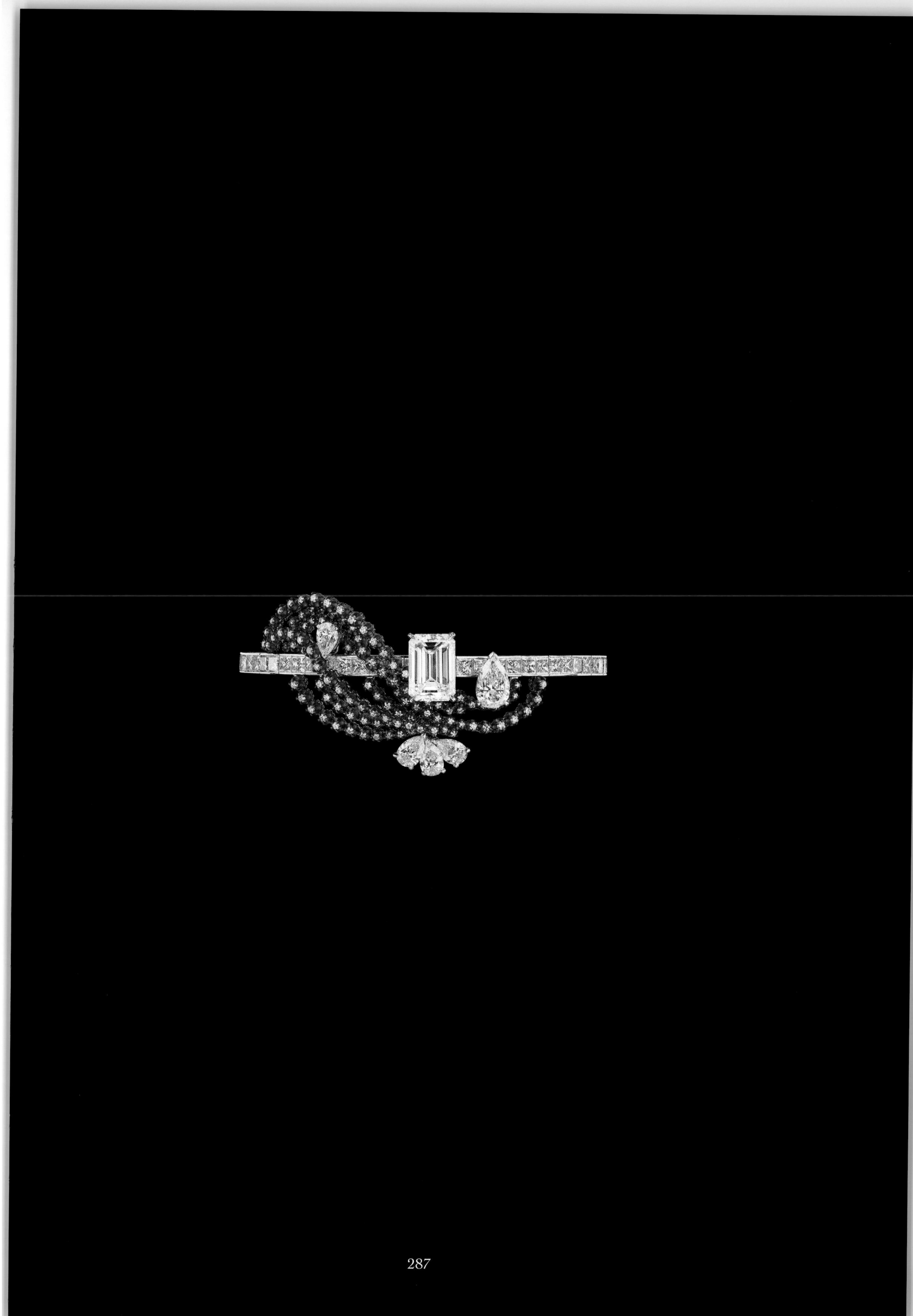

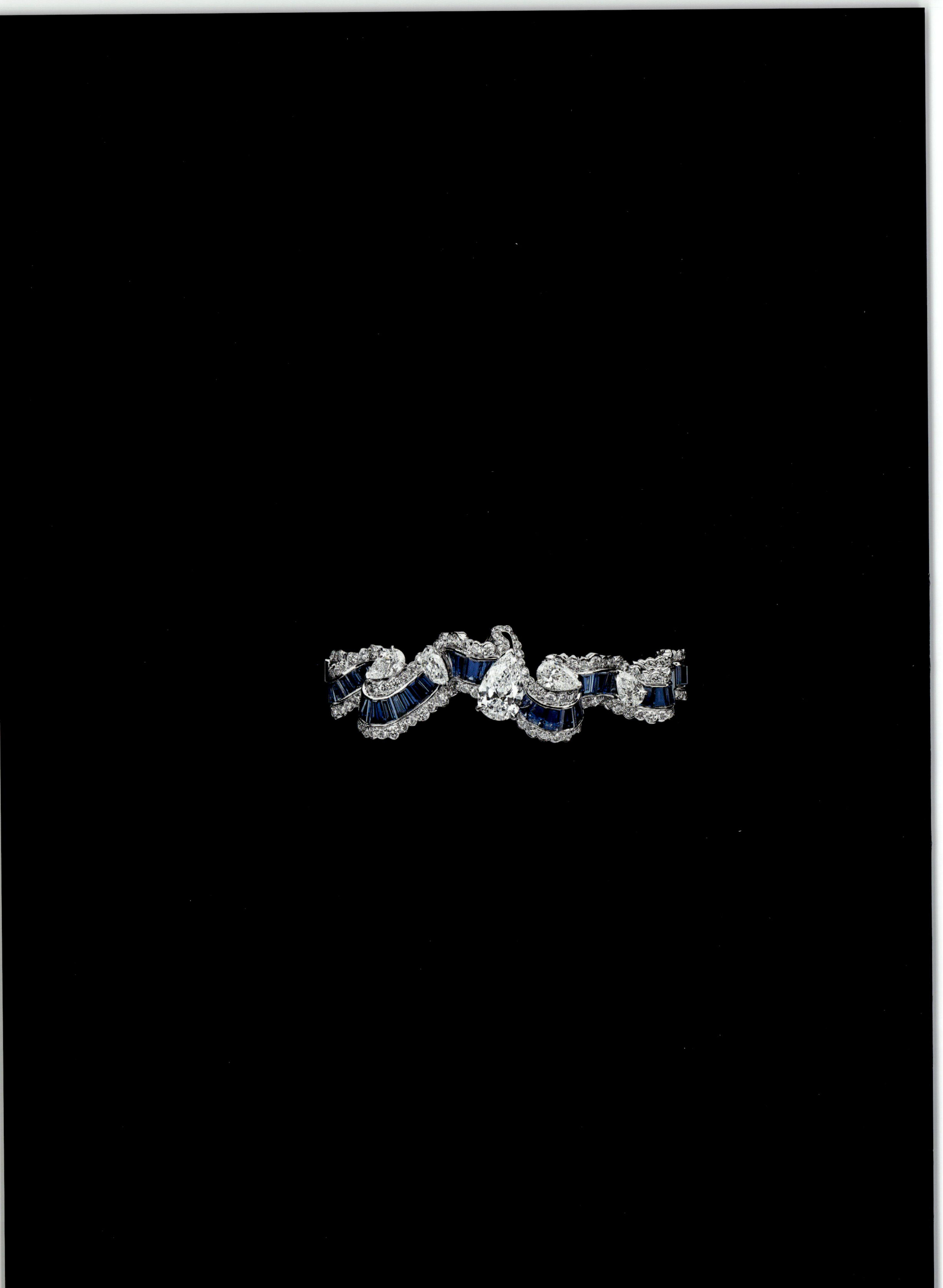

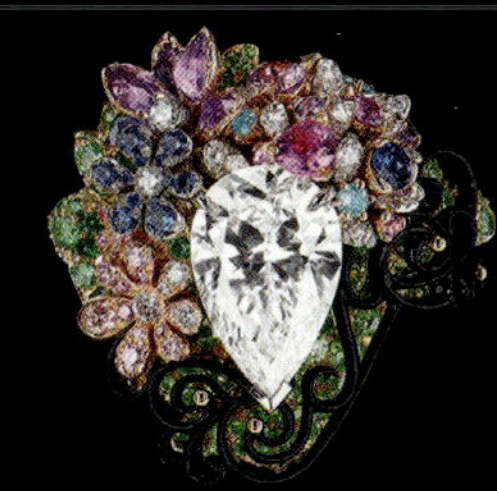

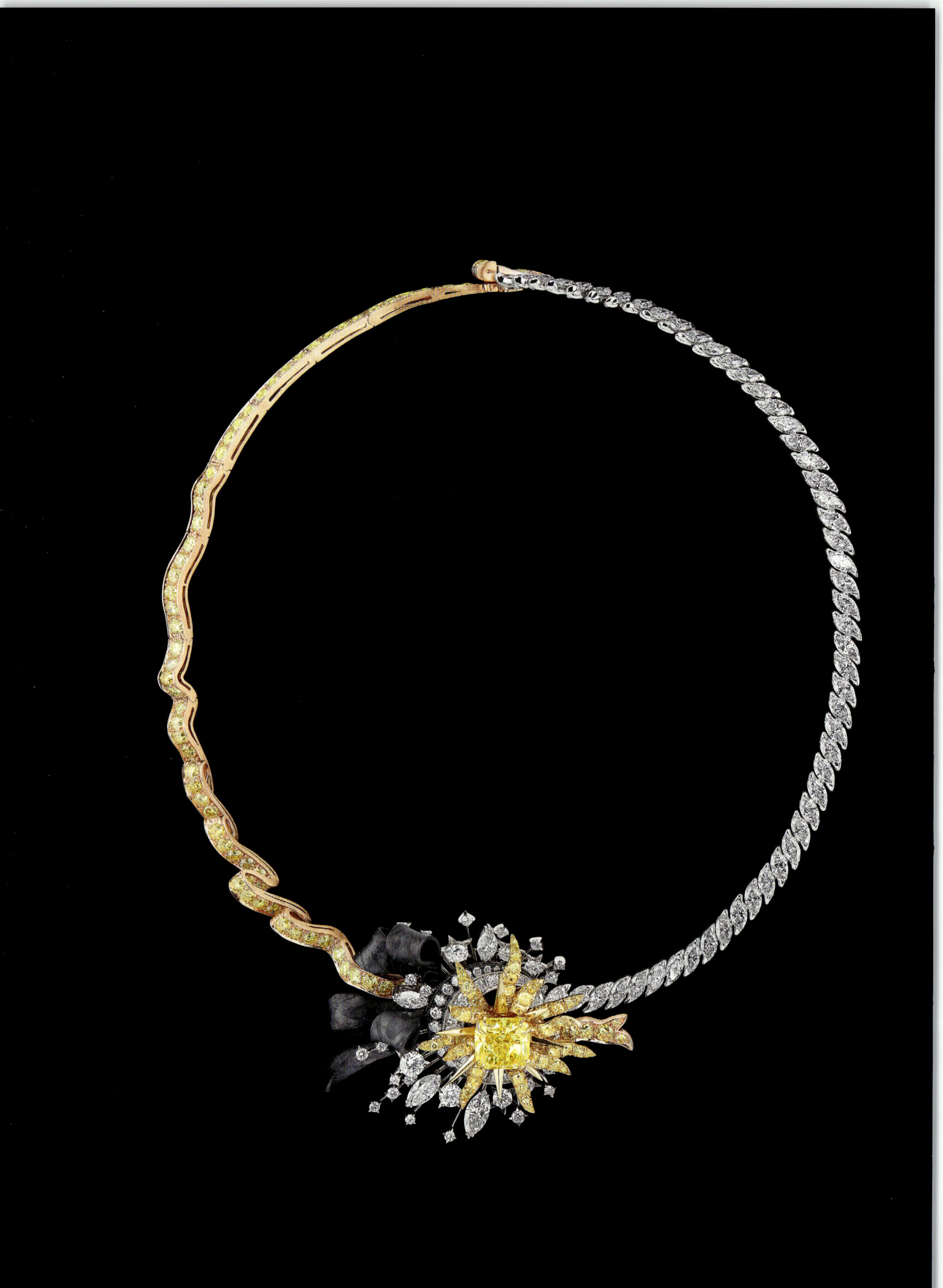

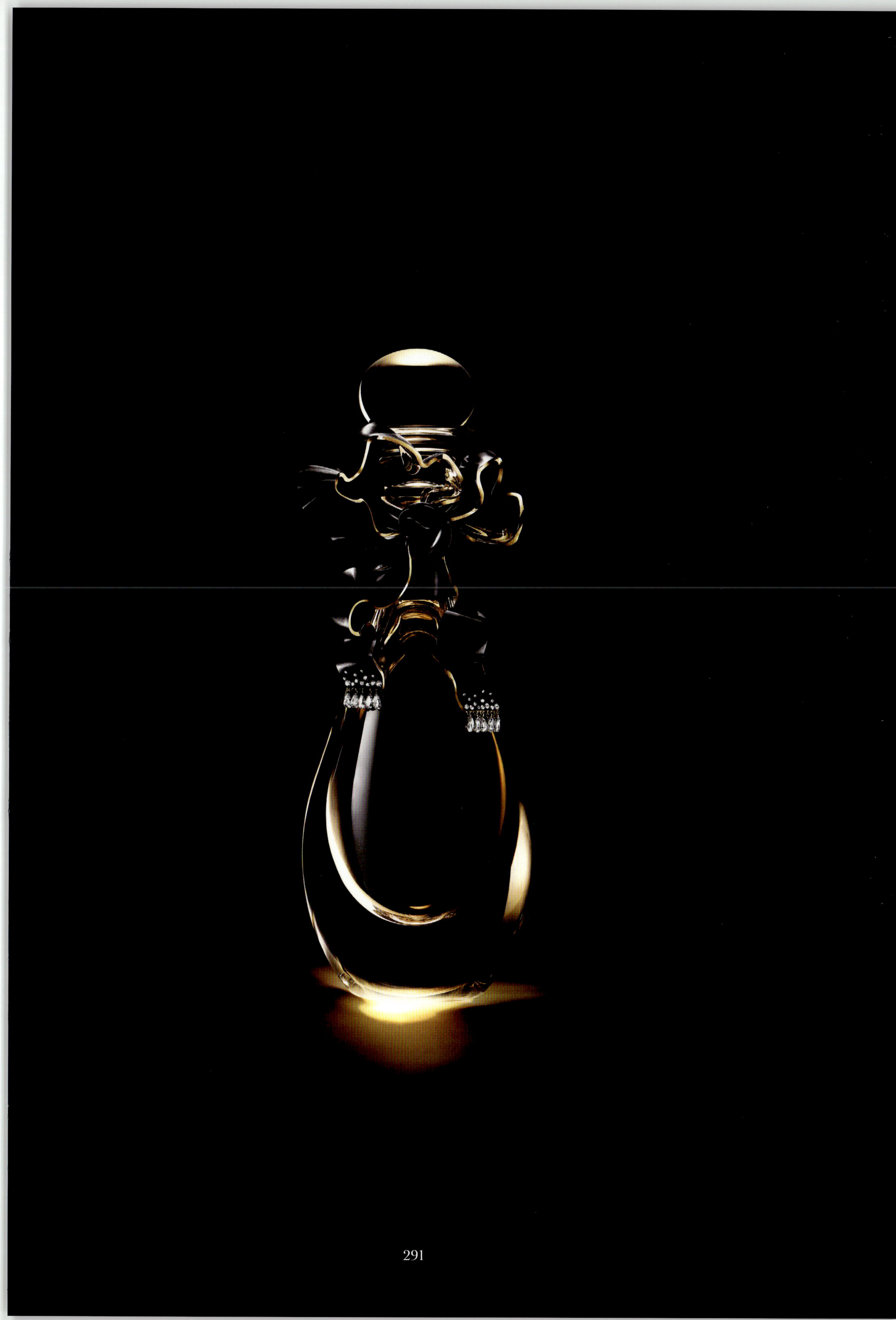

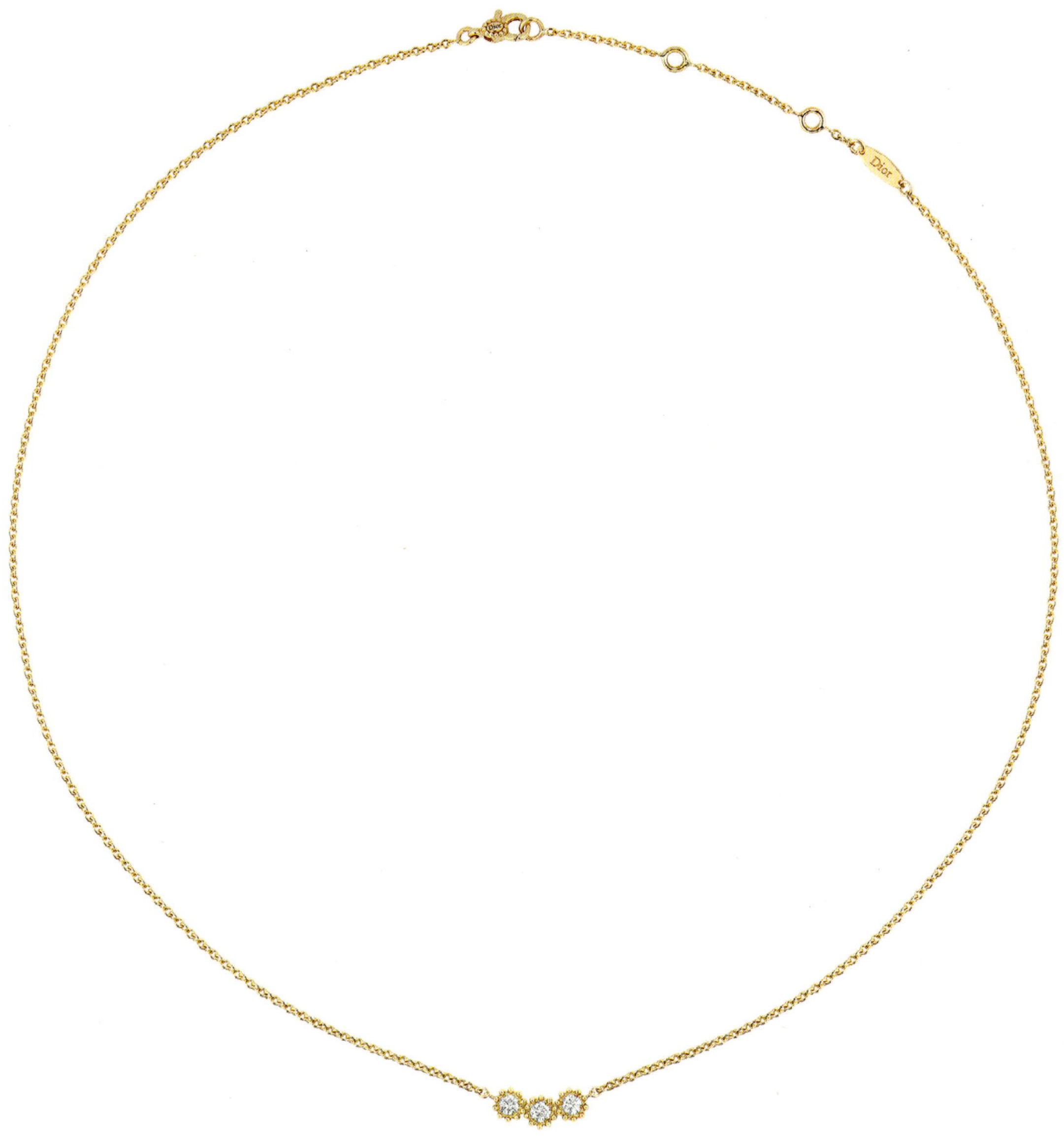

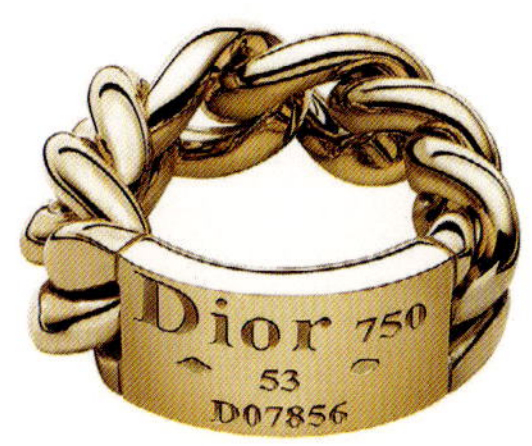
Dior 750
53
D07856

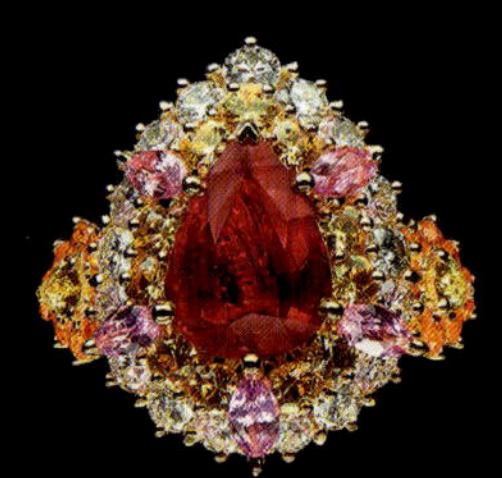

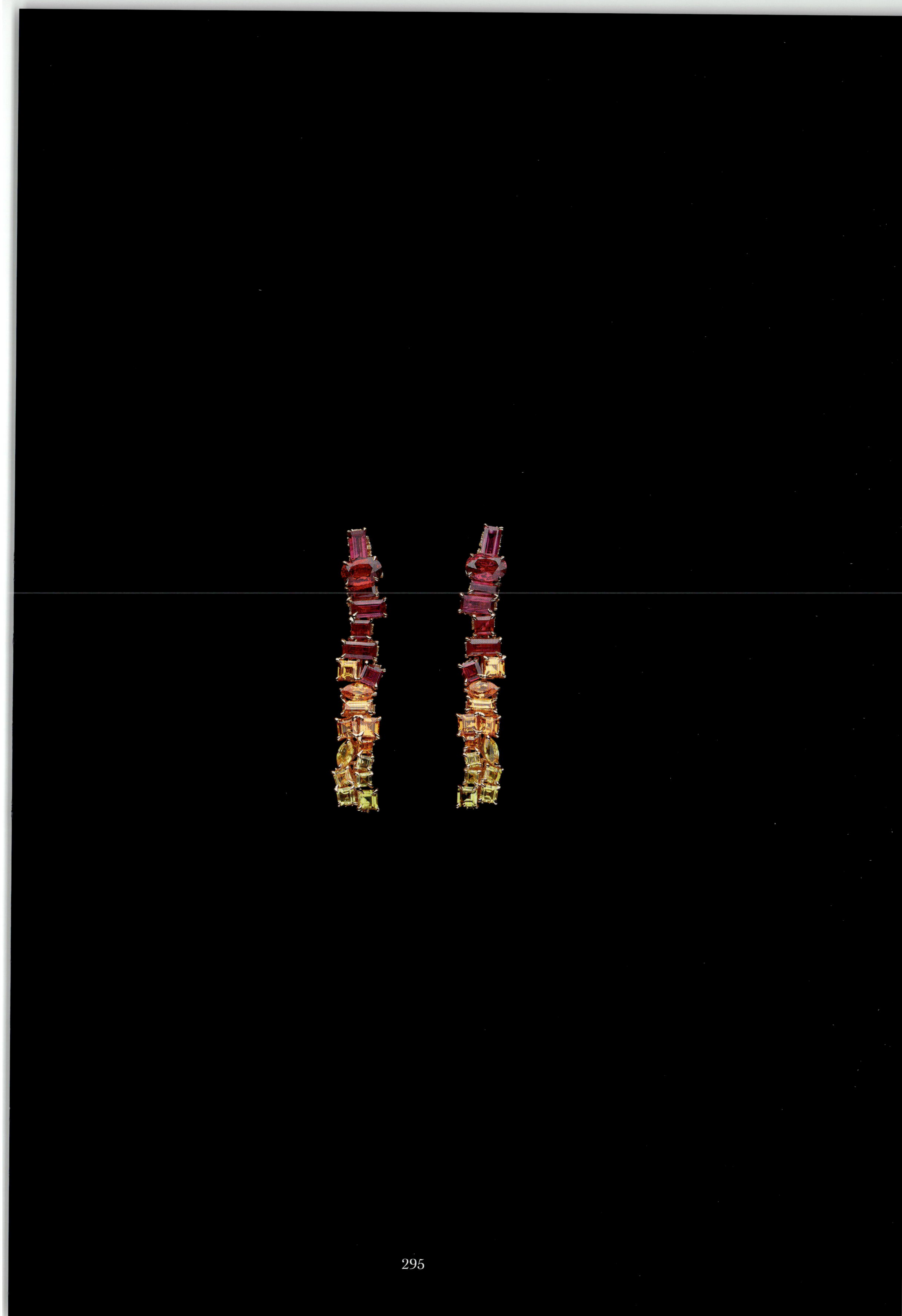

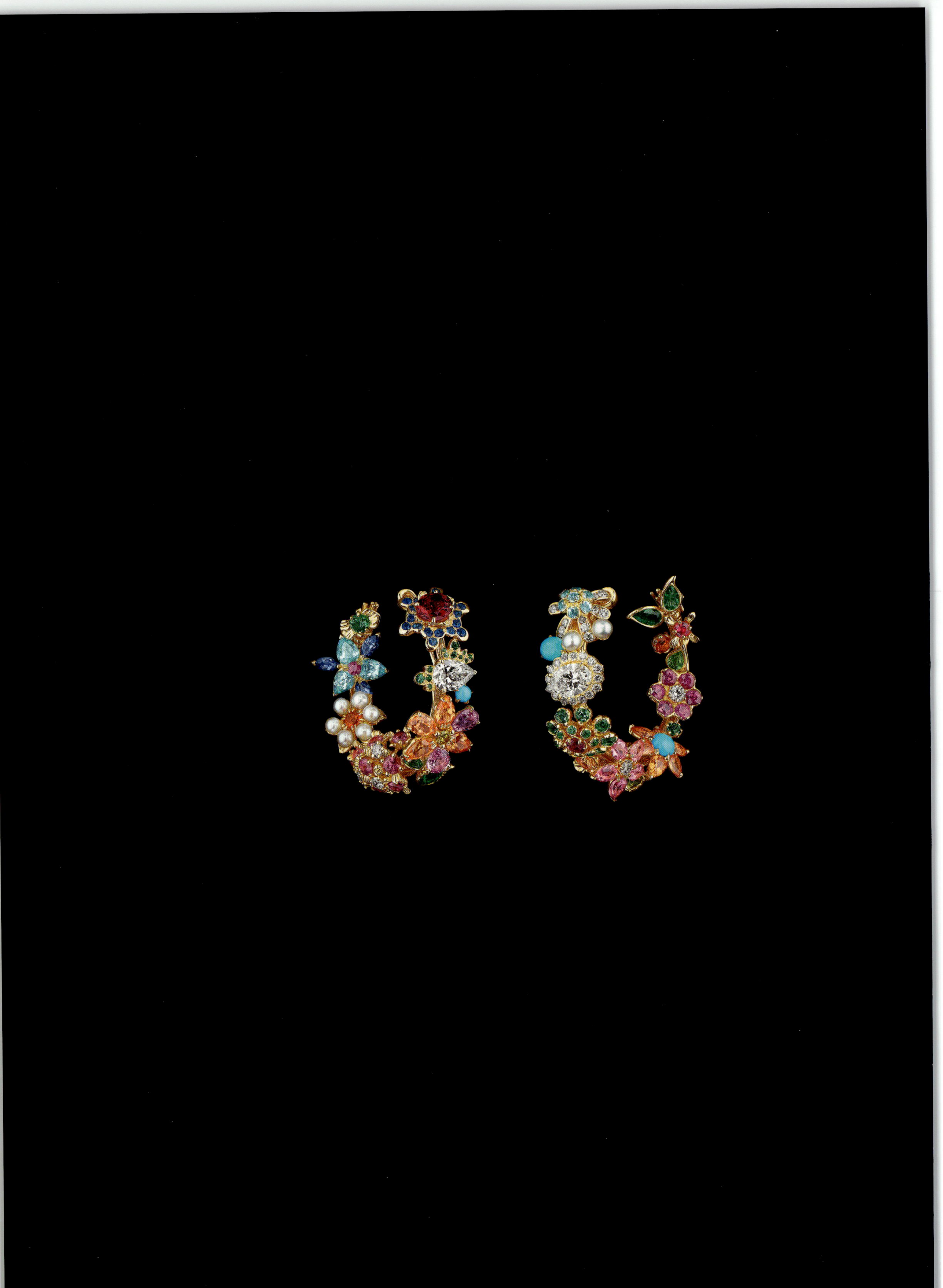

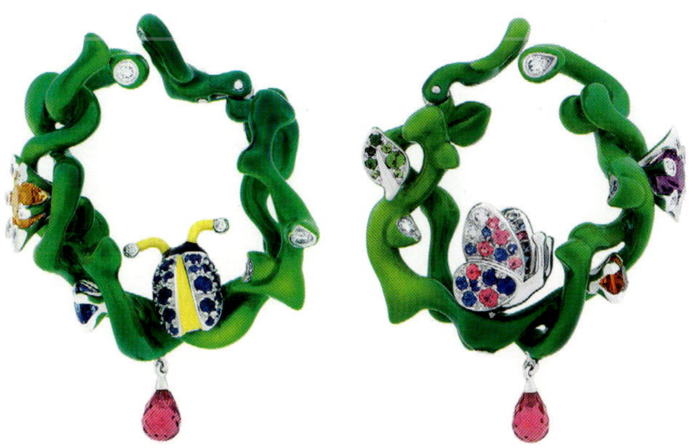

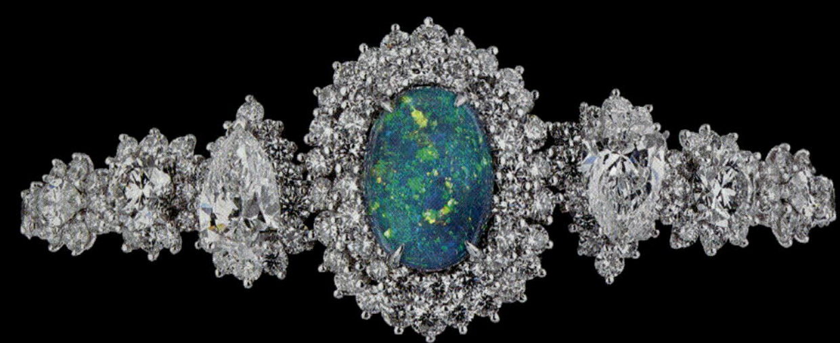

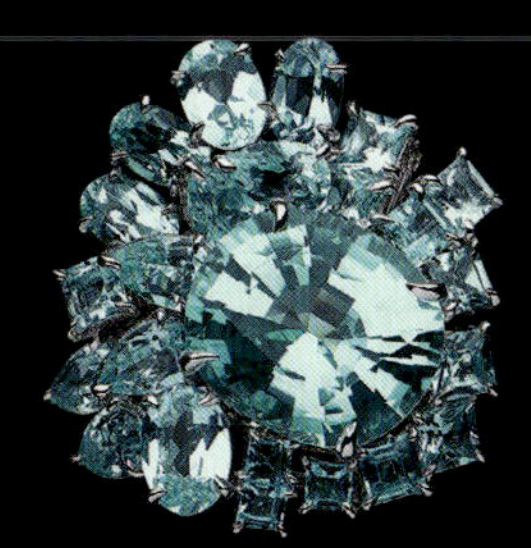

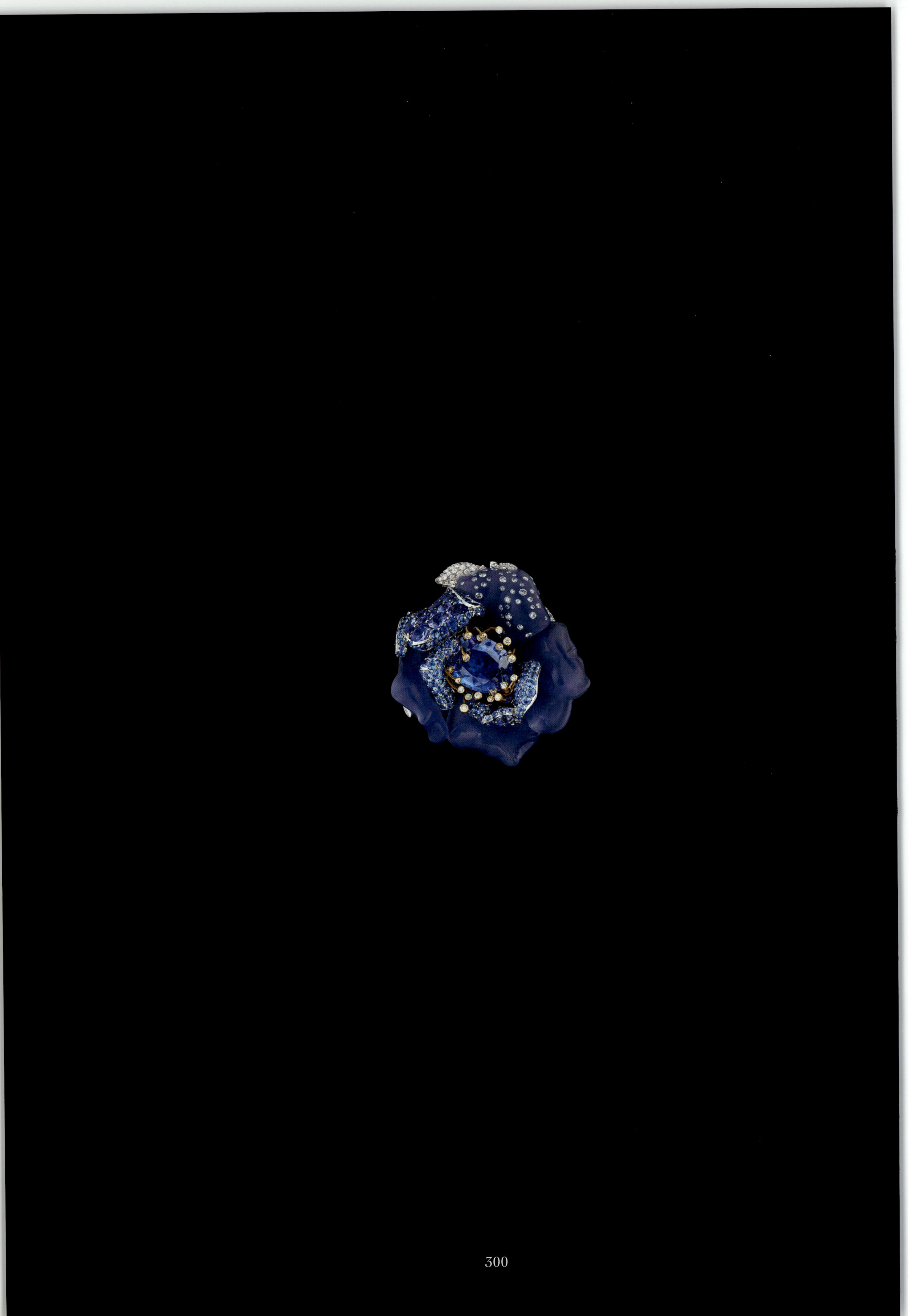

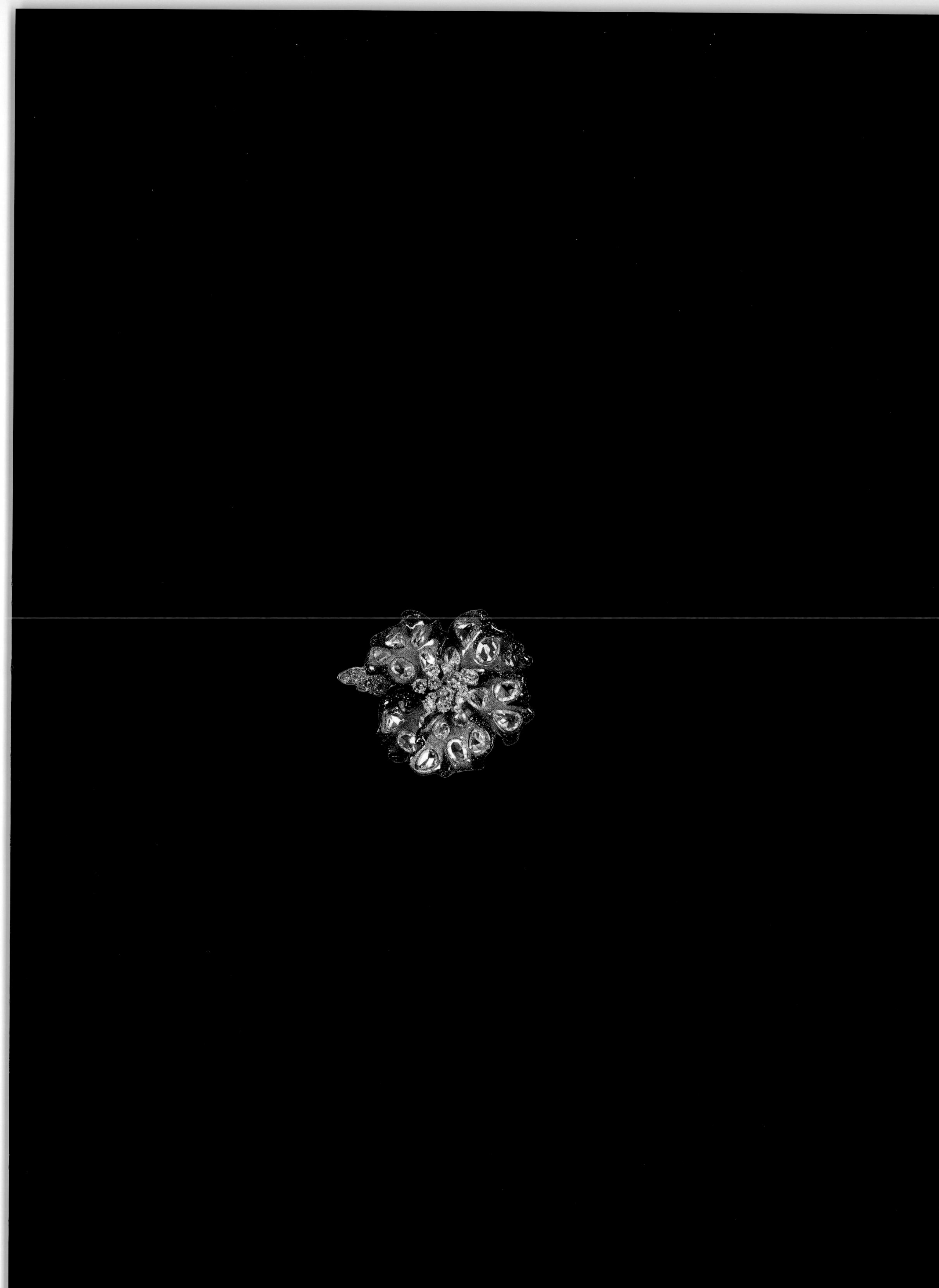

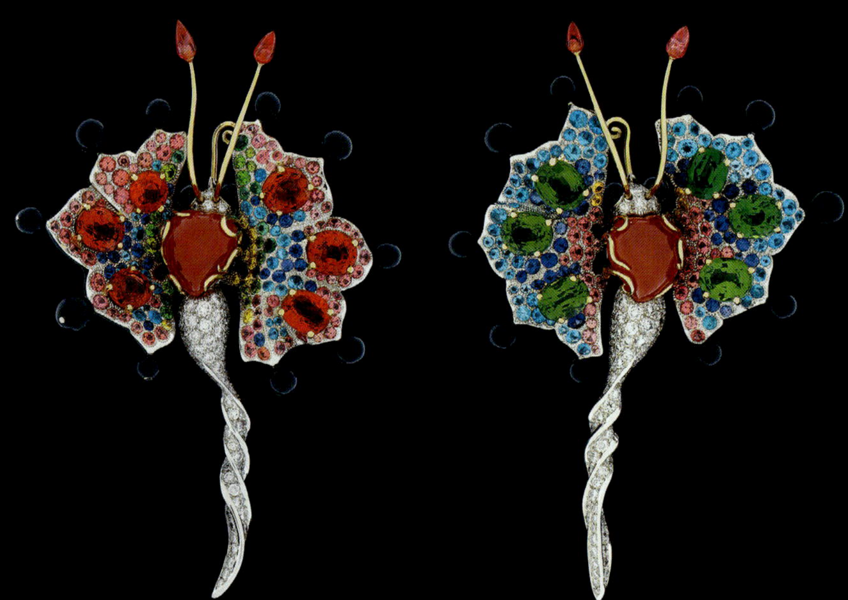

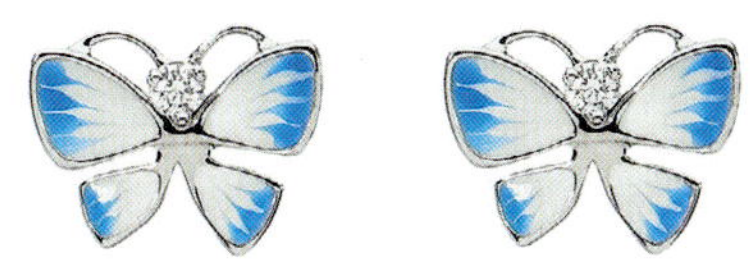

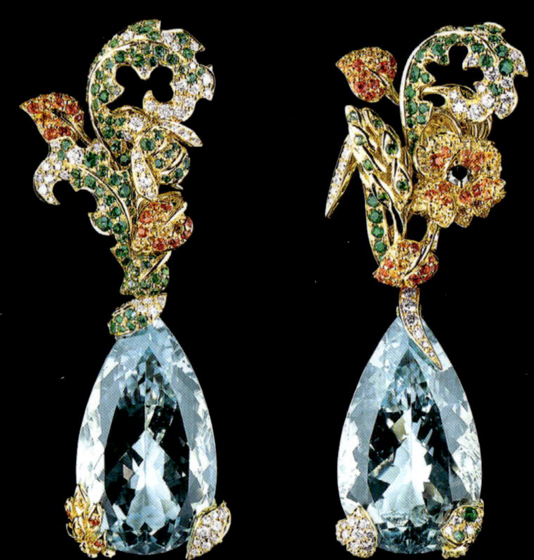

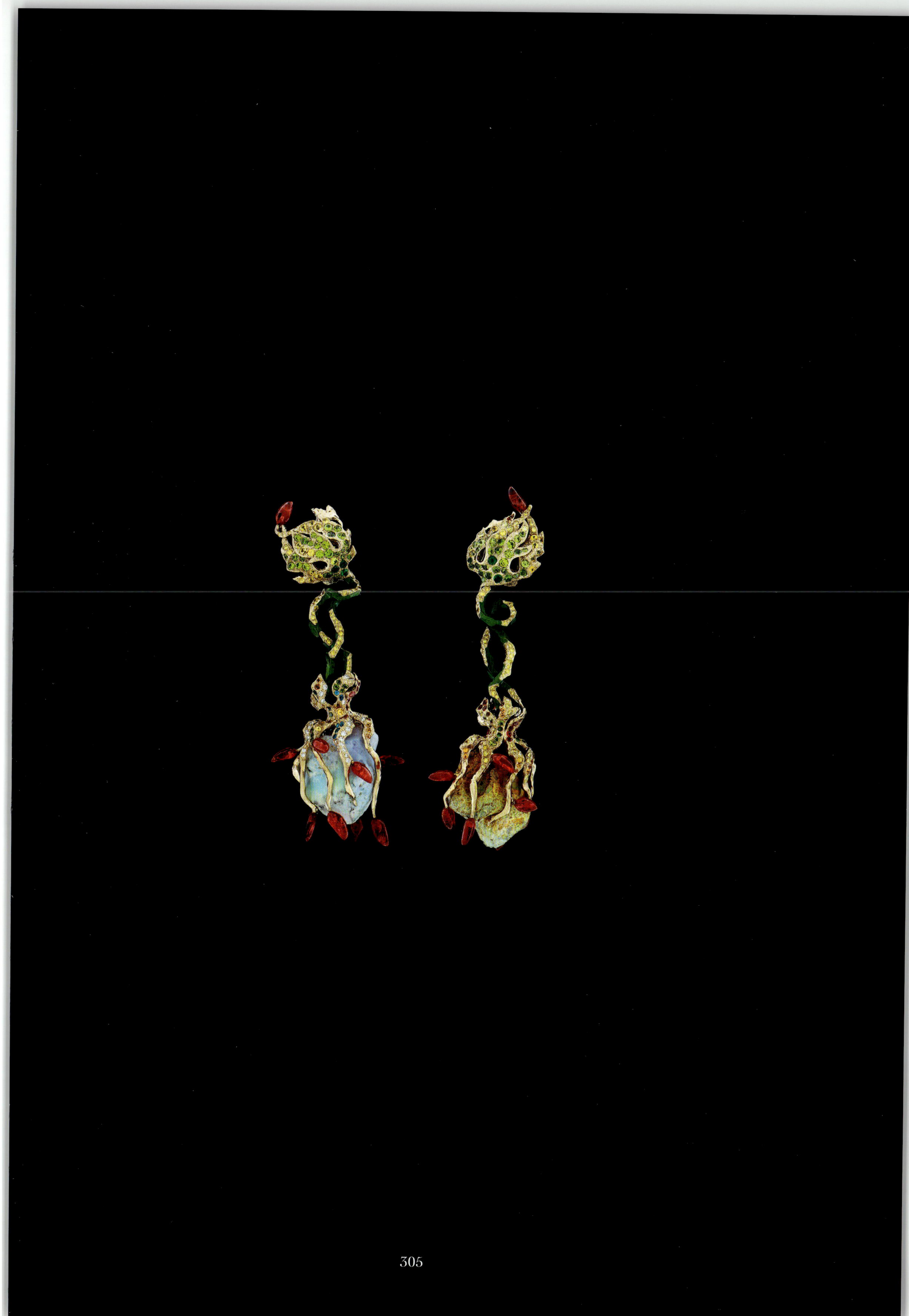

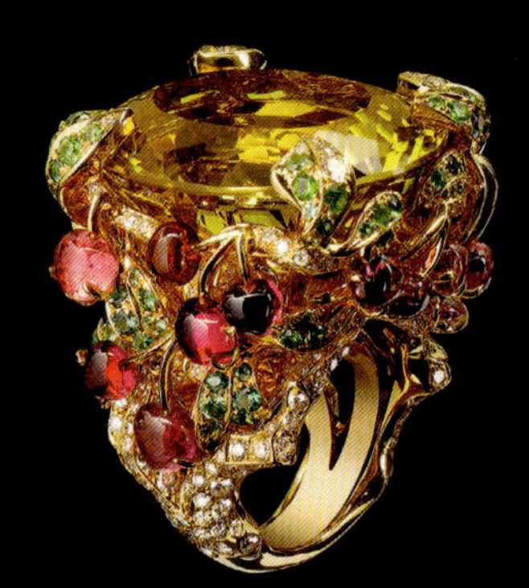

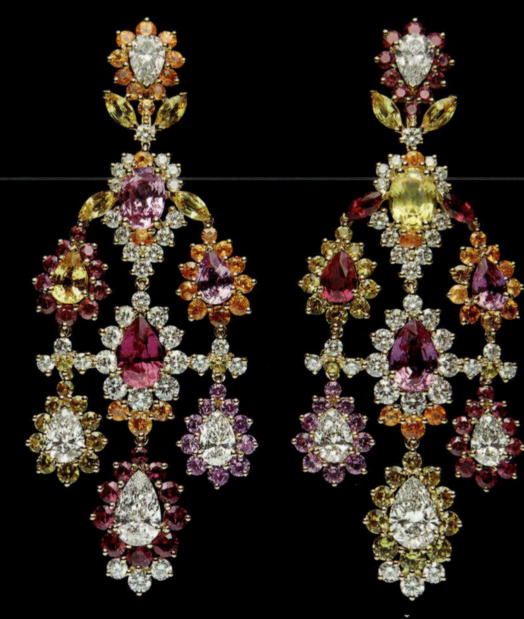

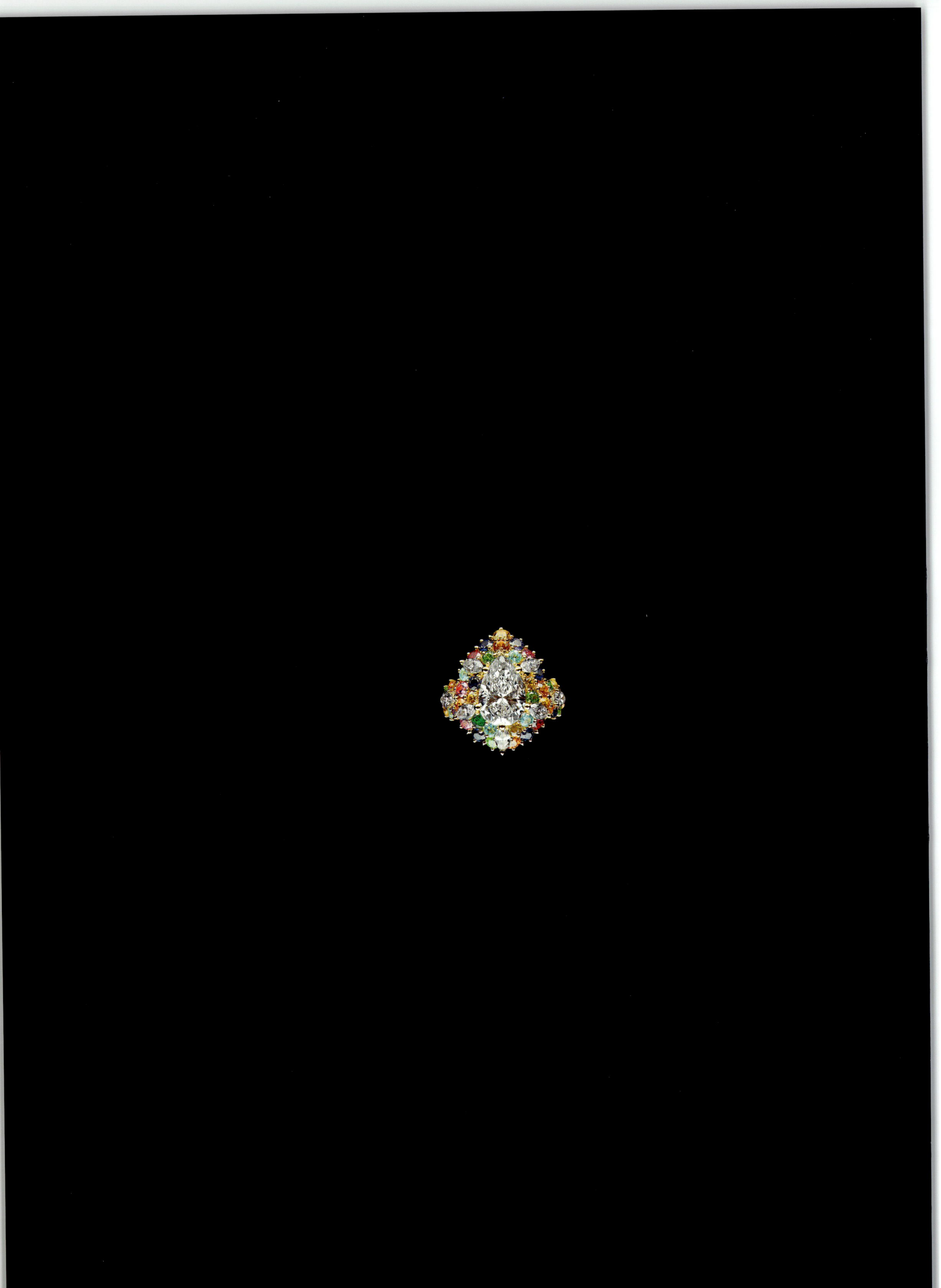

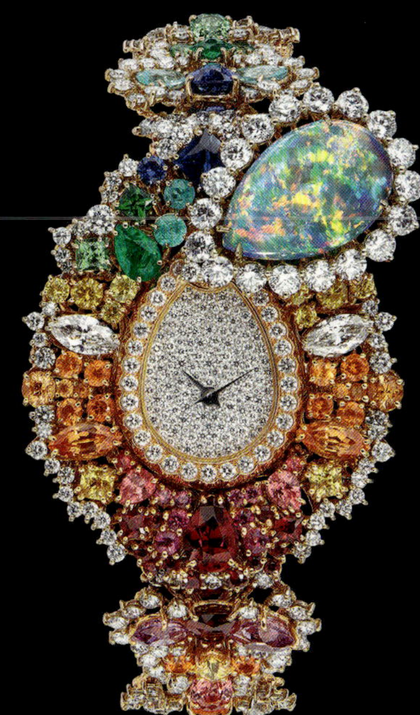

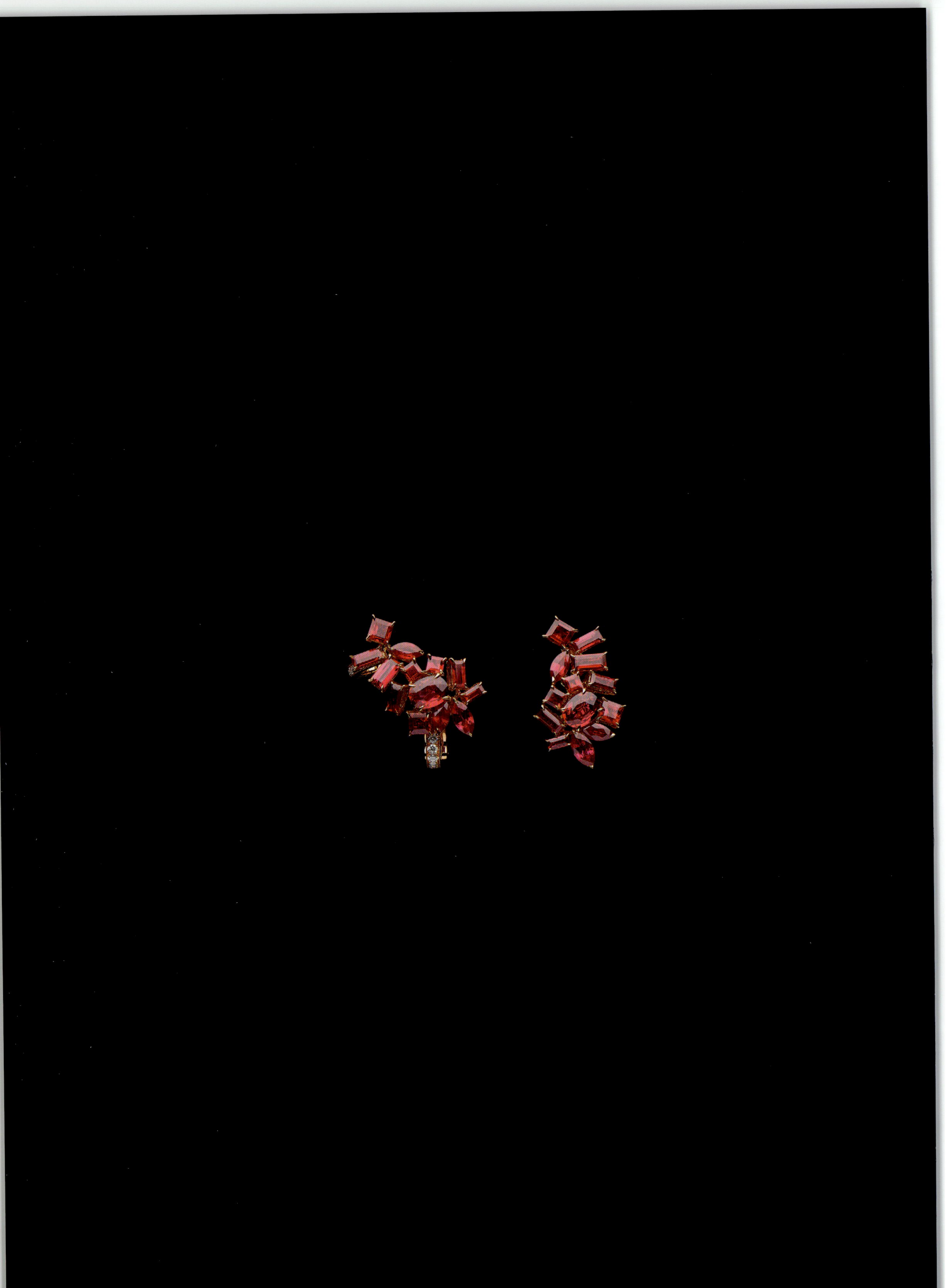

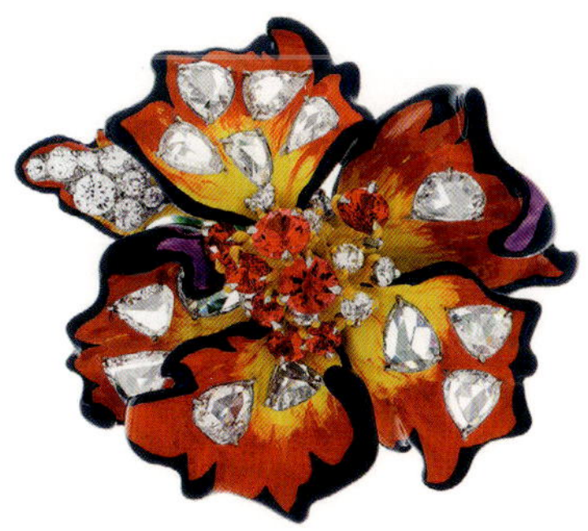

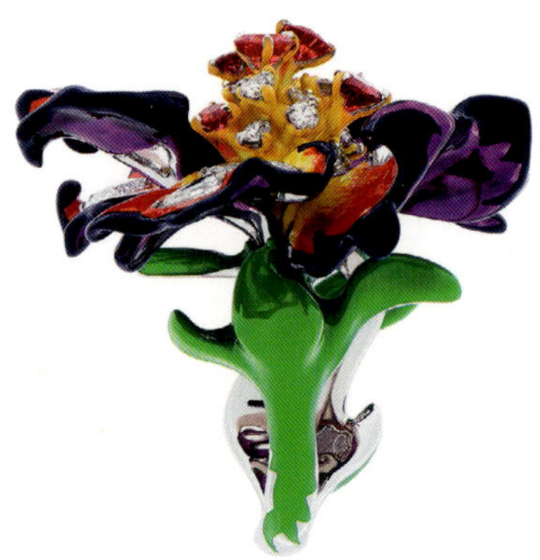

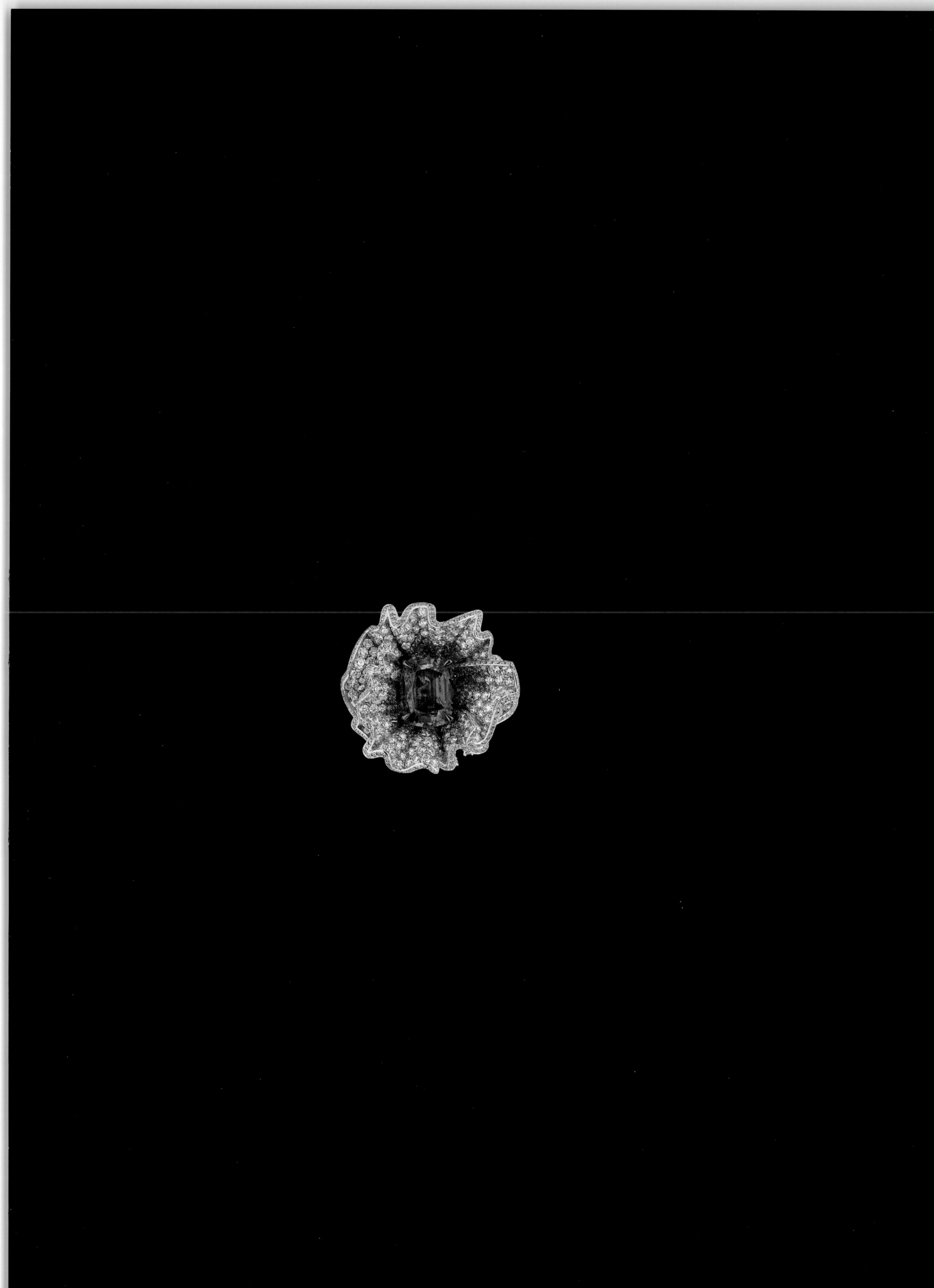

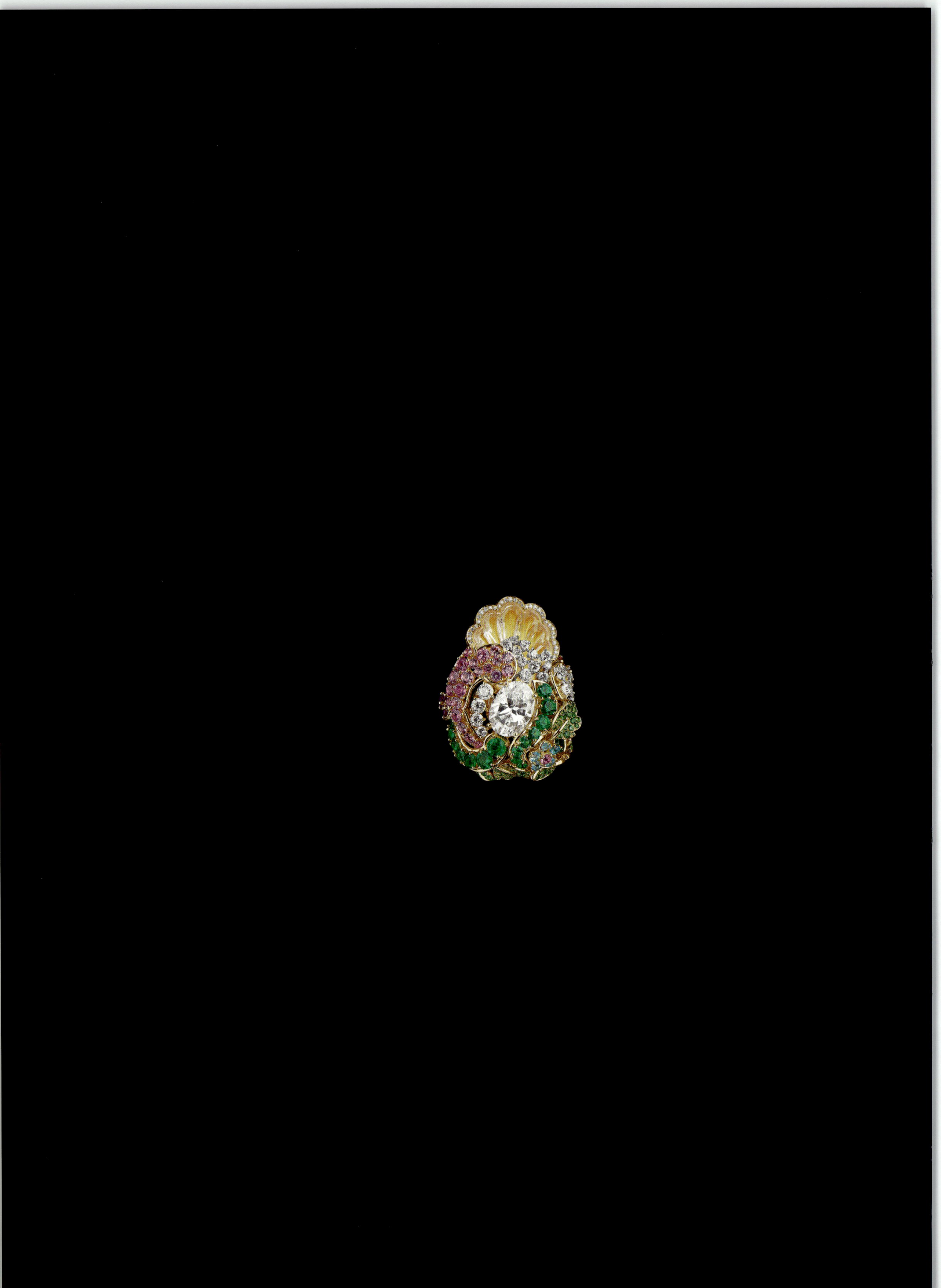

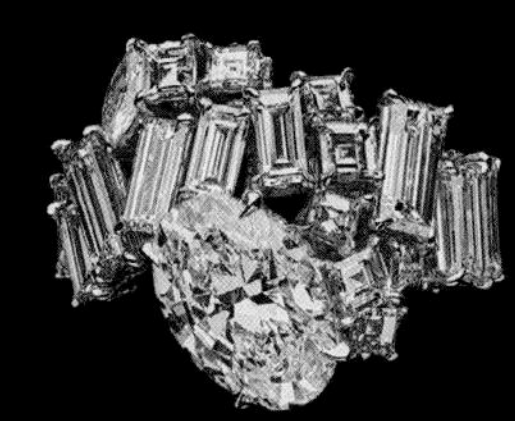

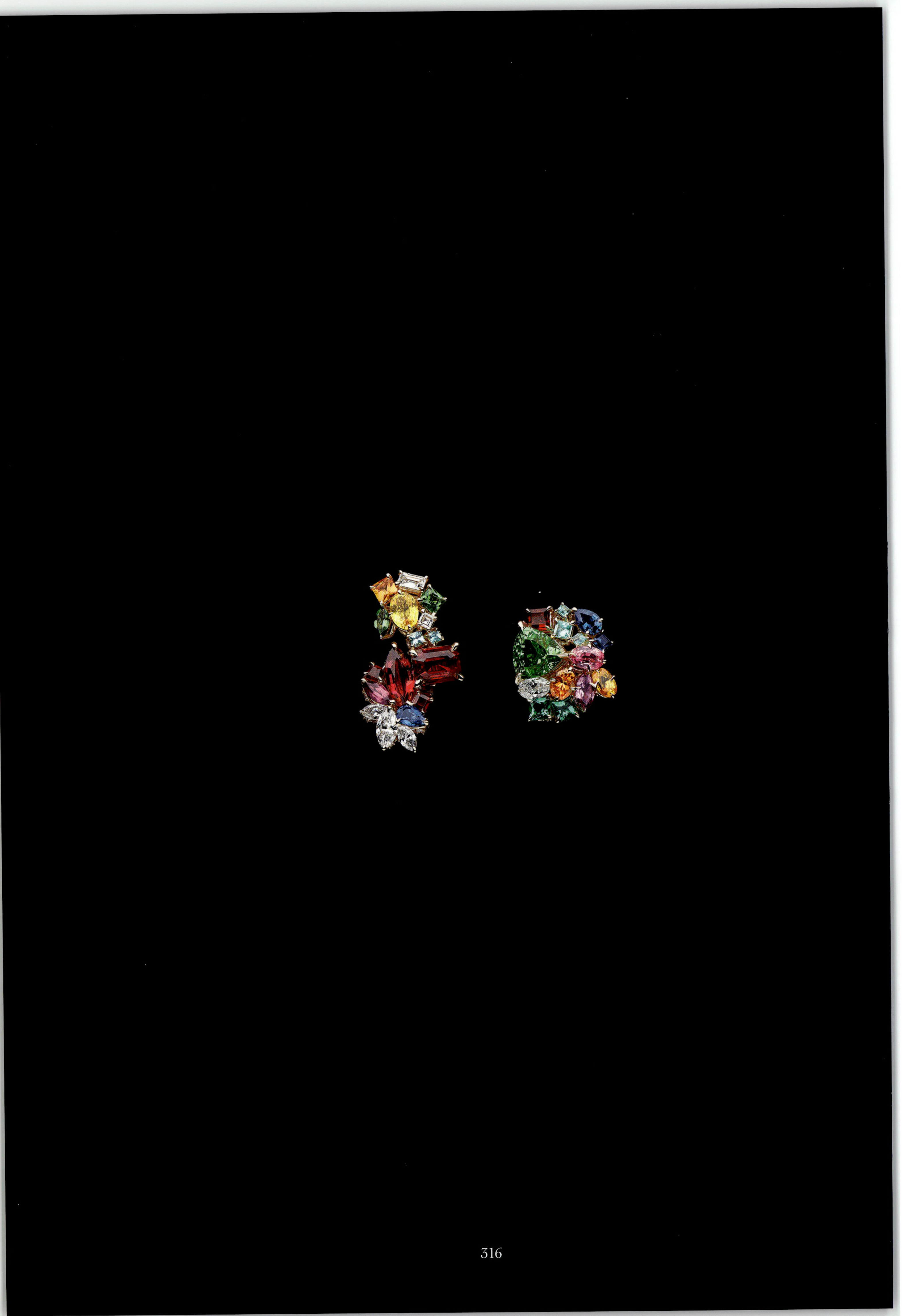

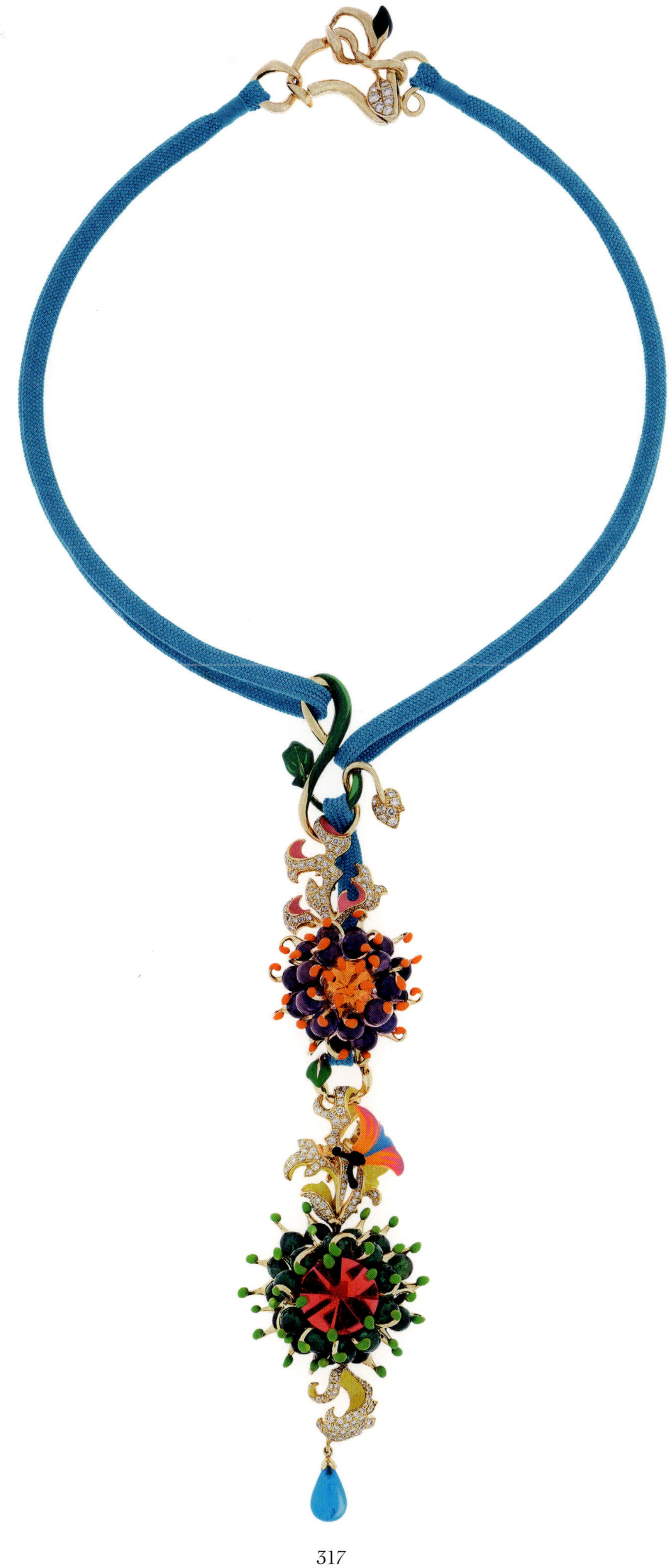

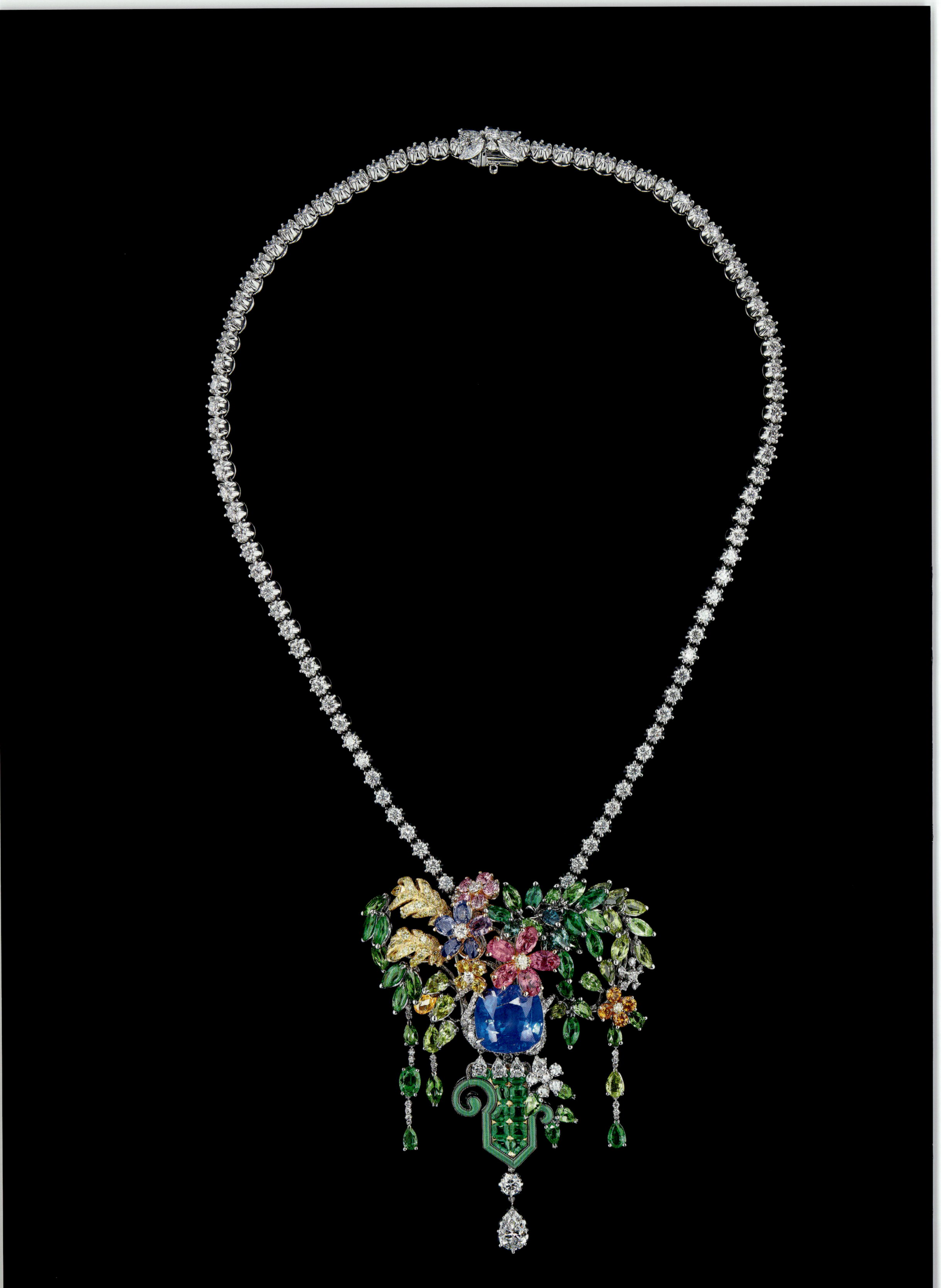

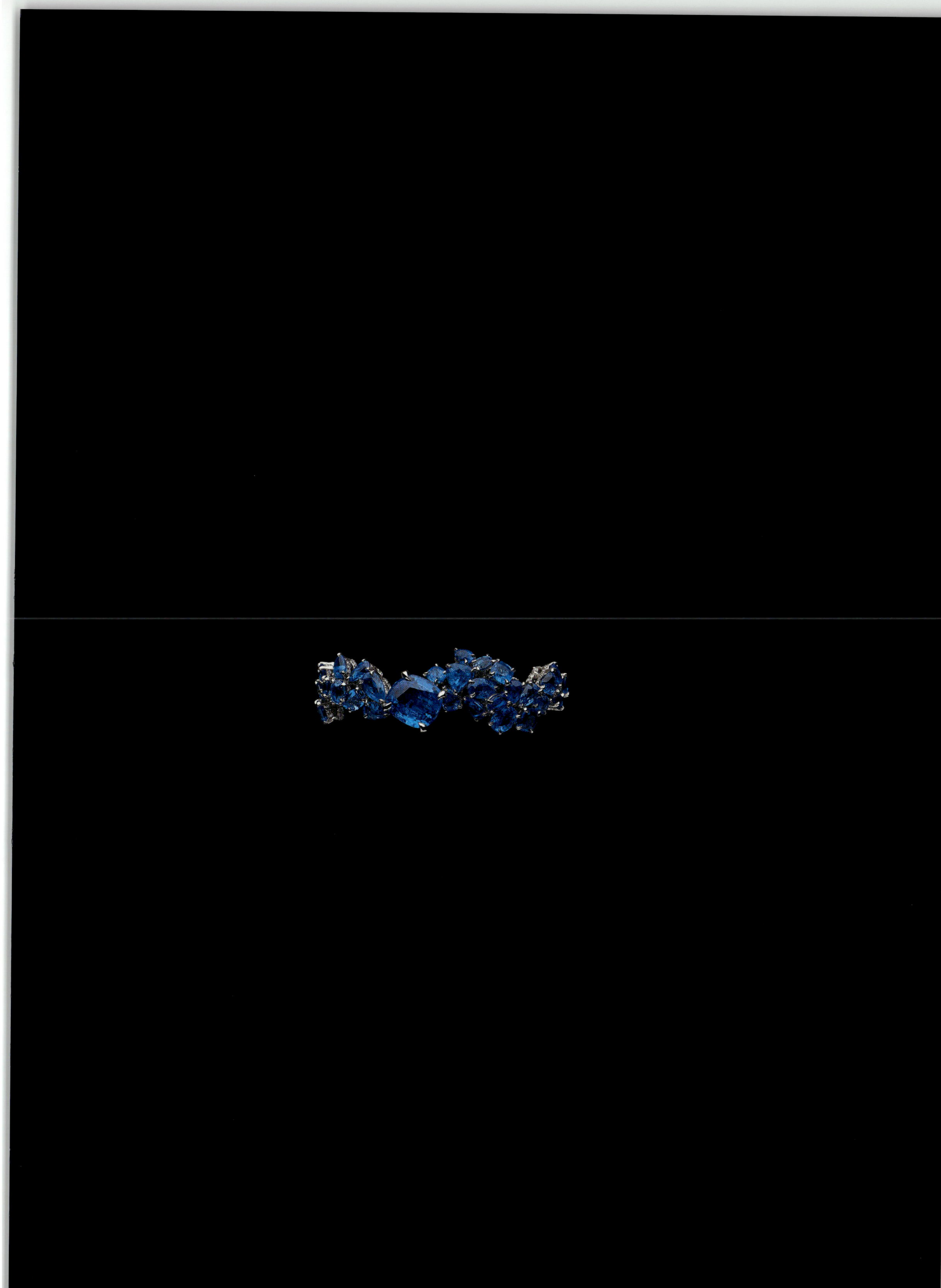

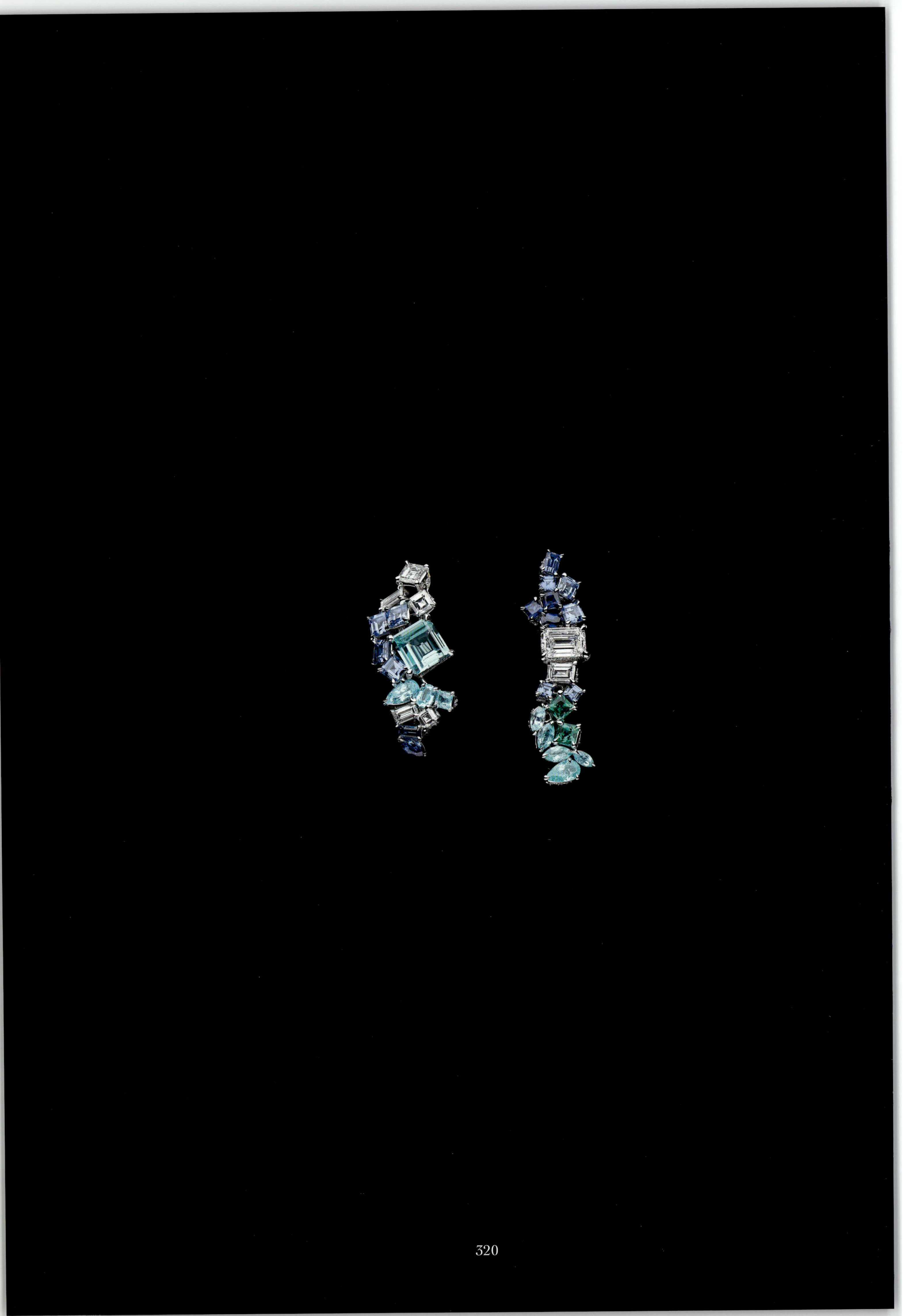

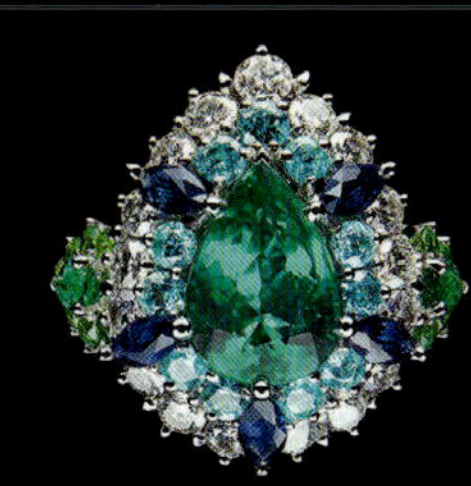

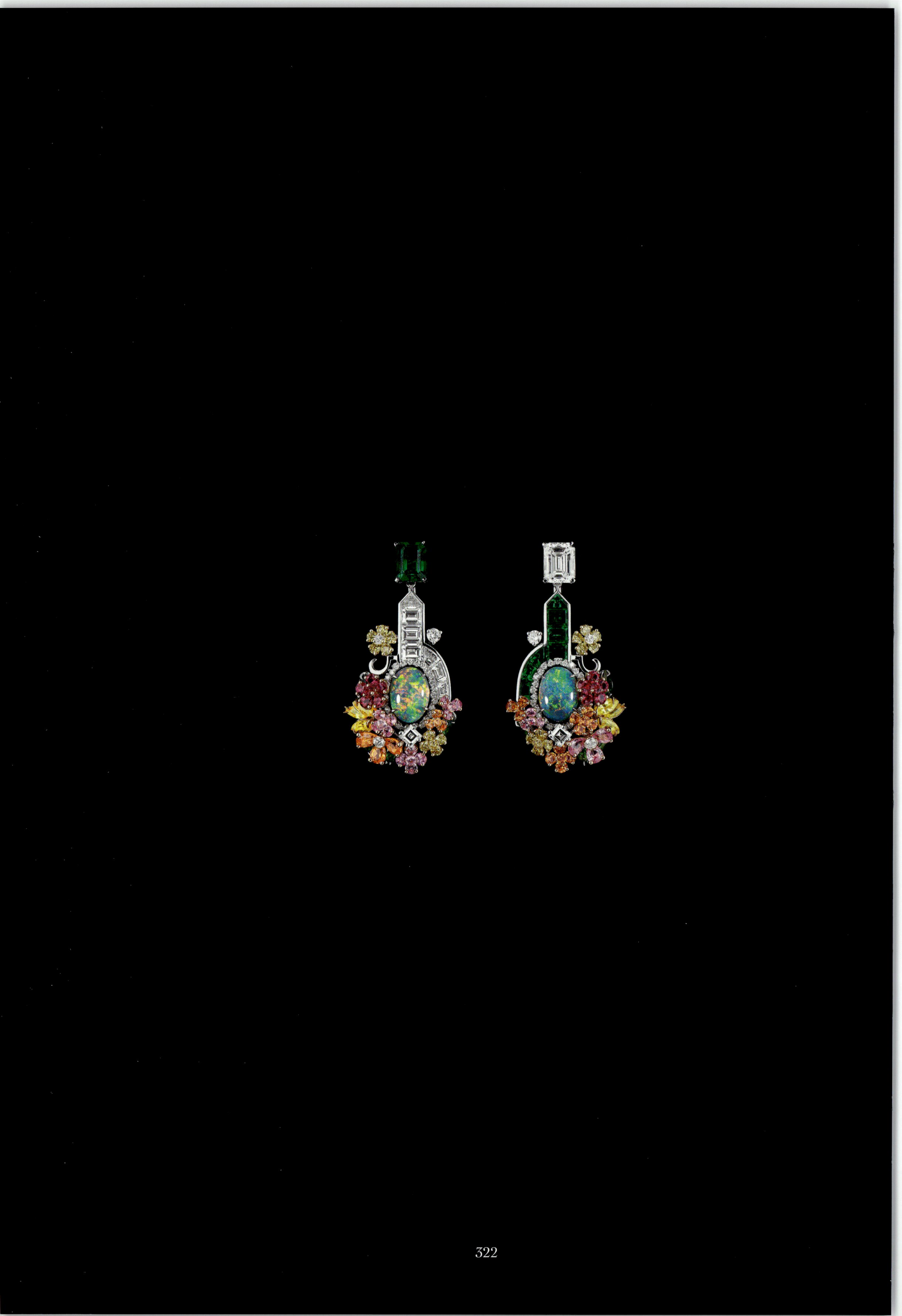

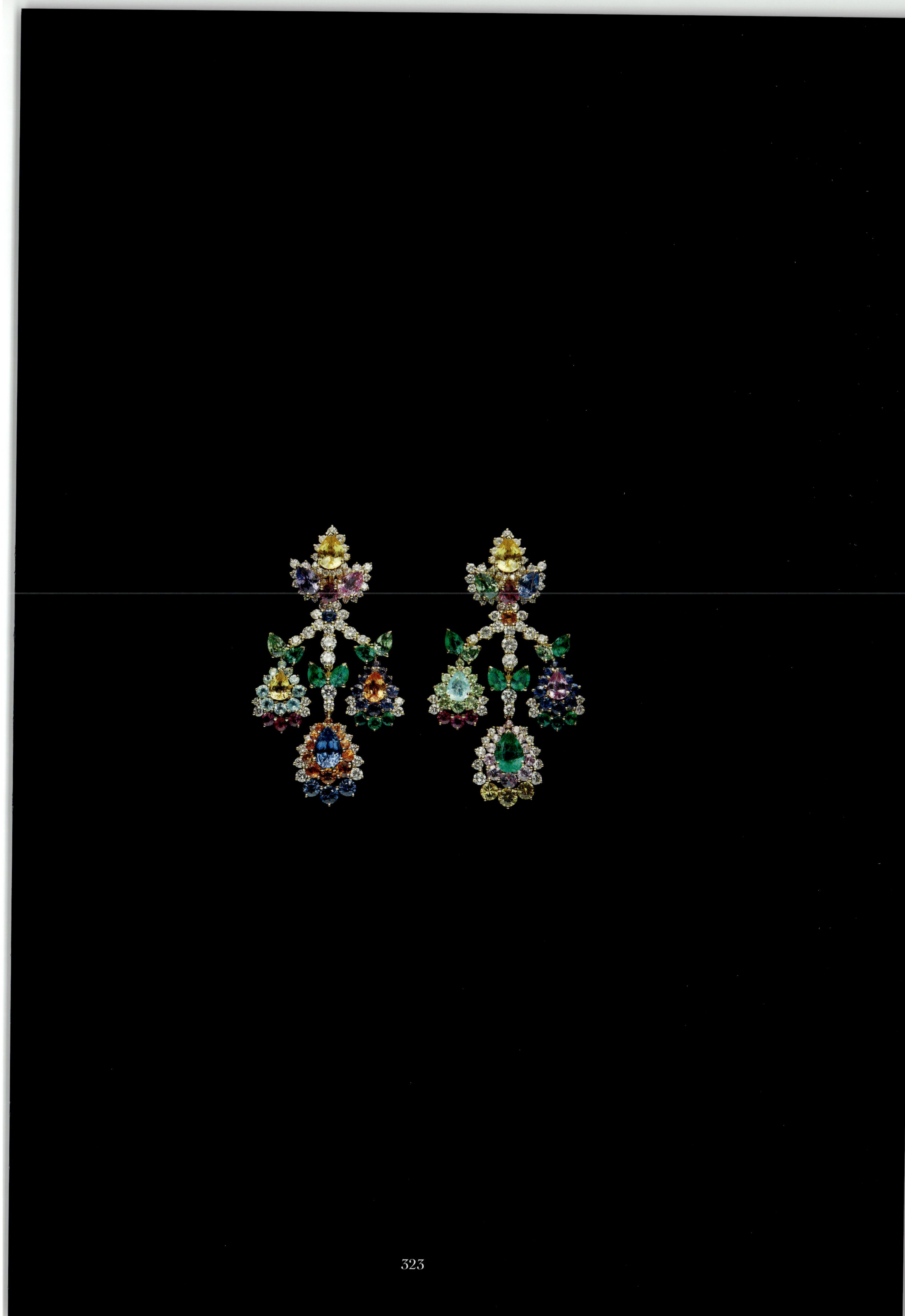

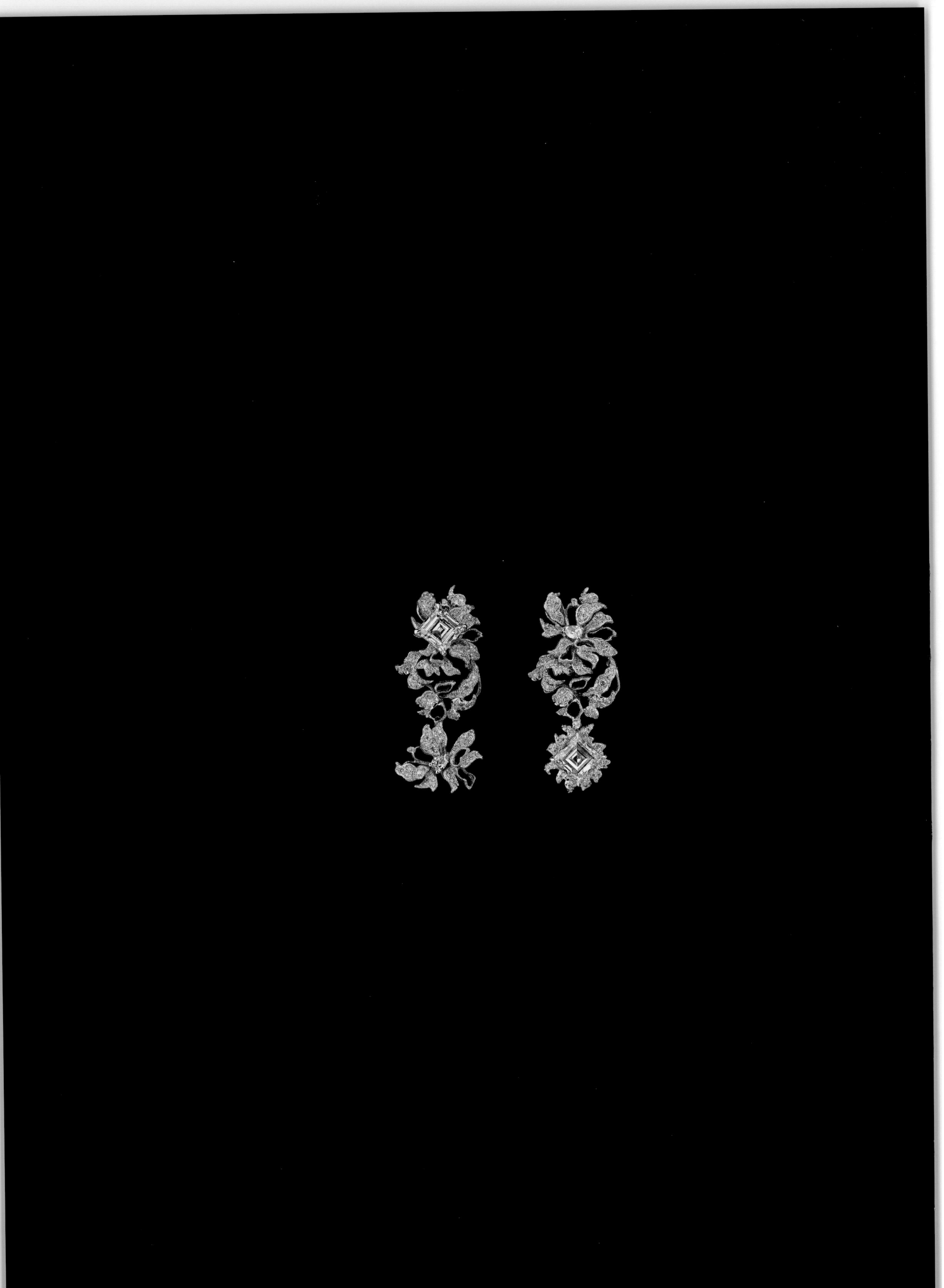

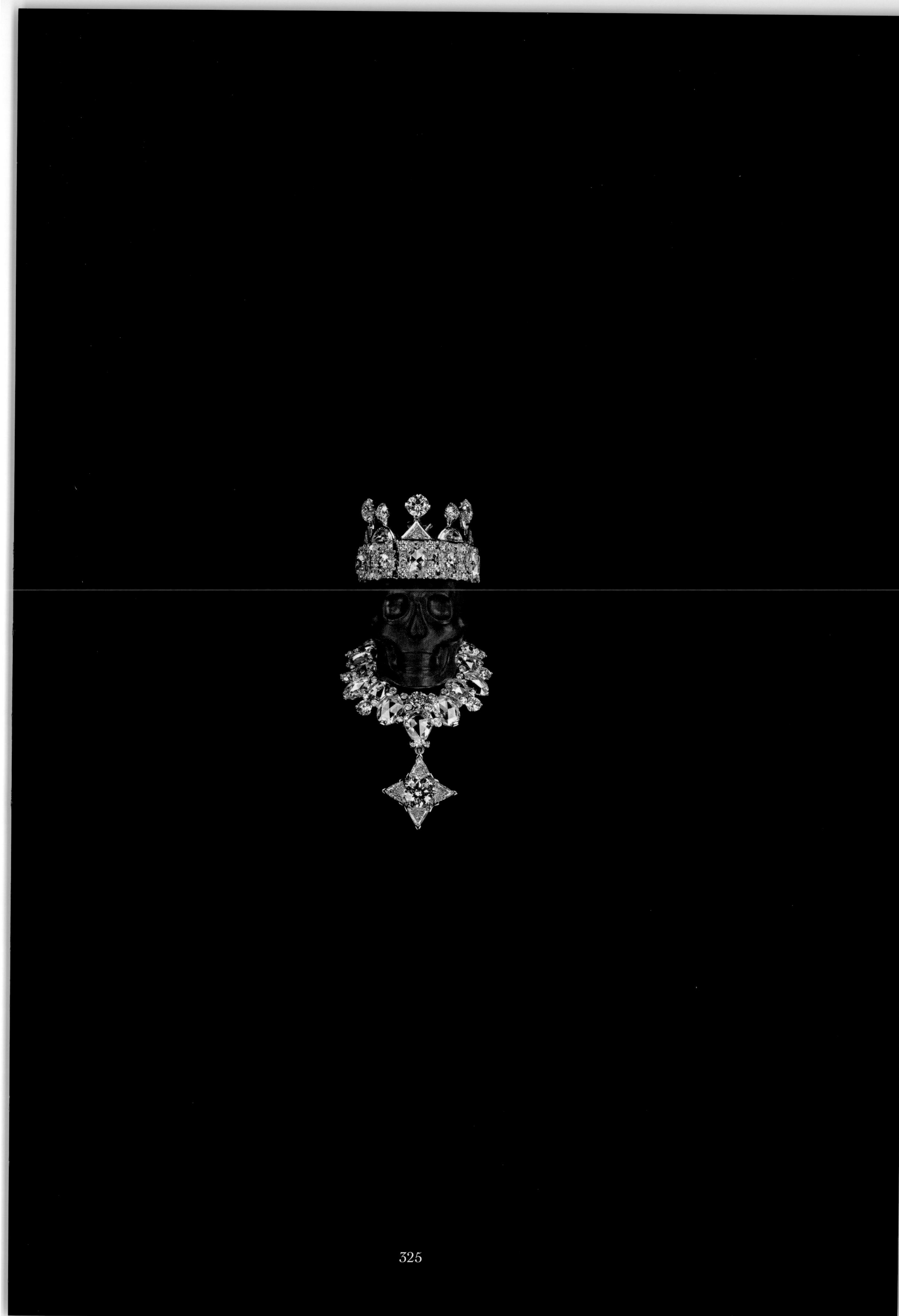

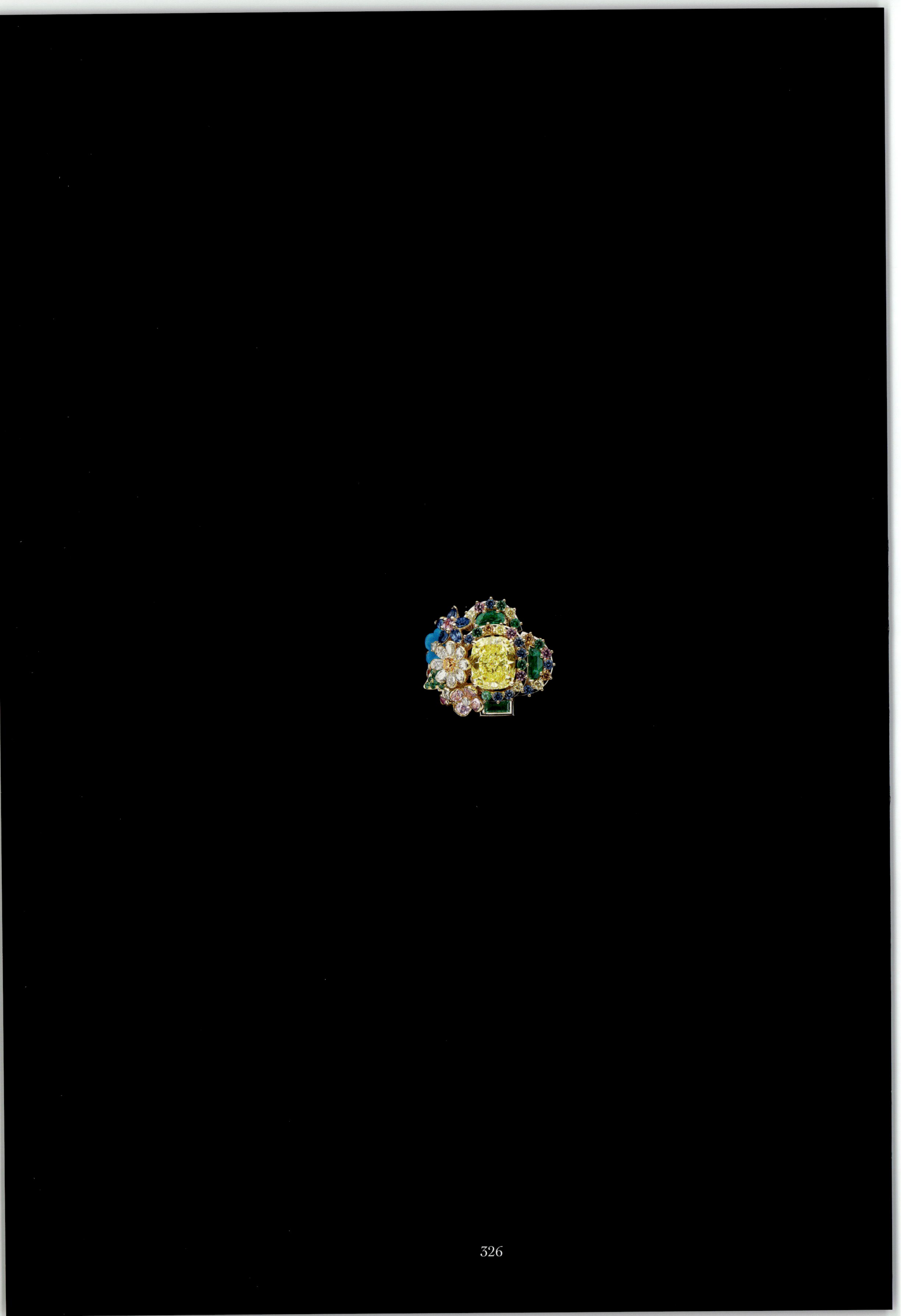

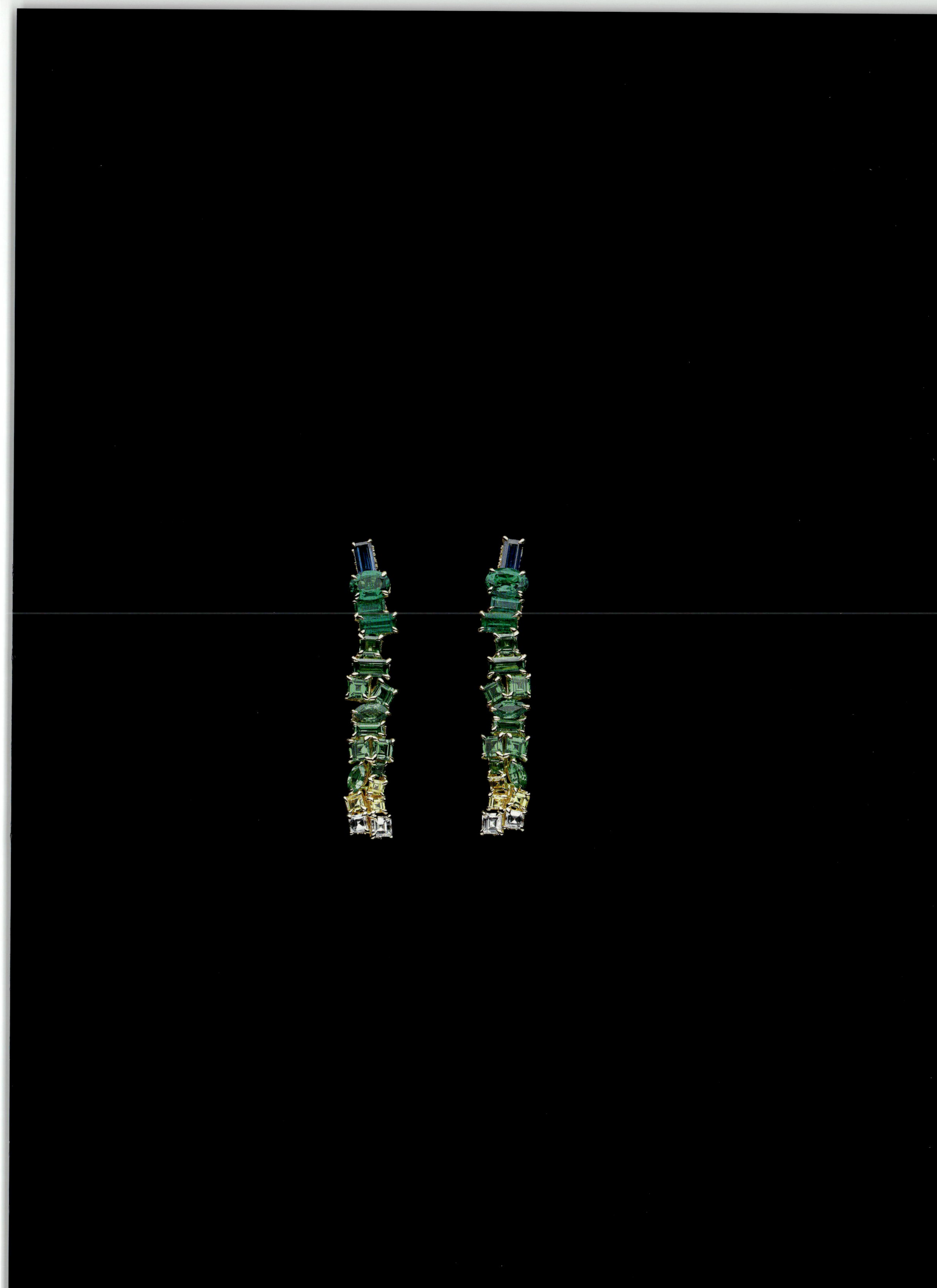

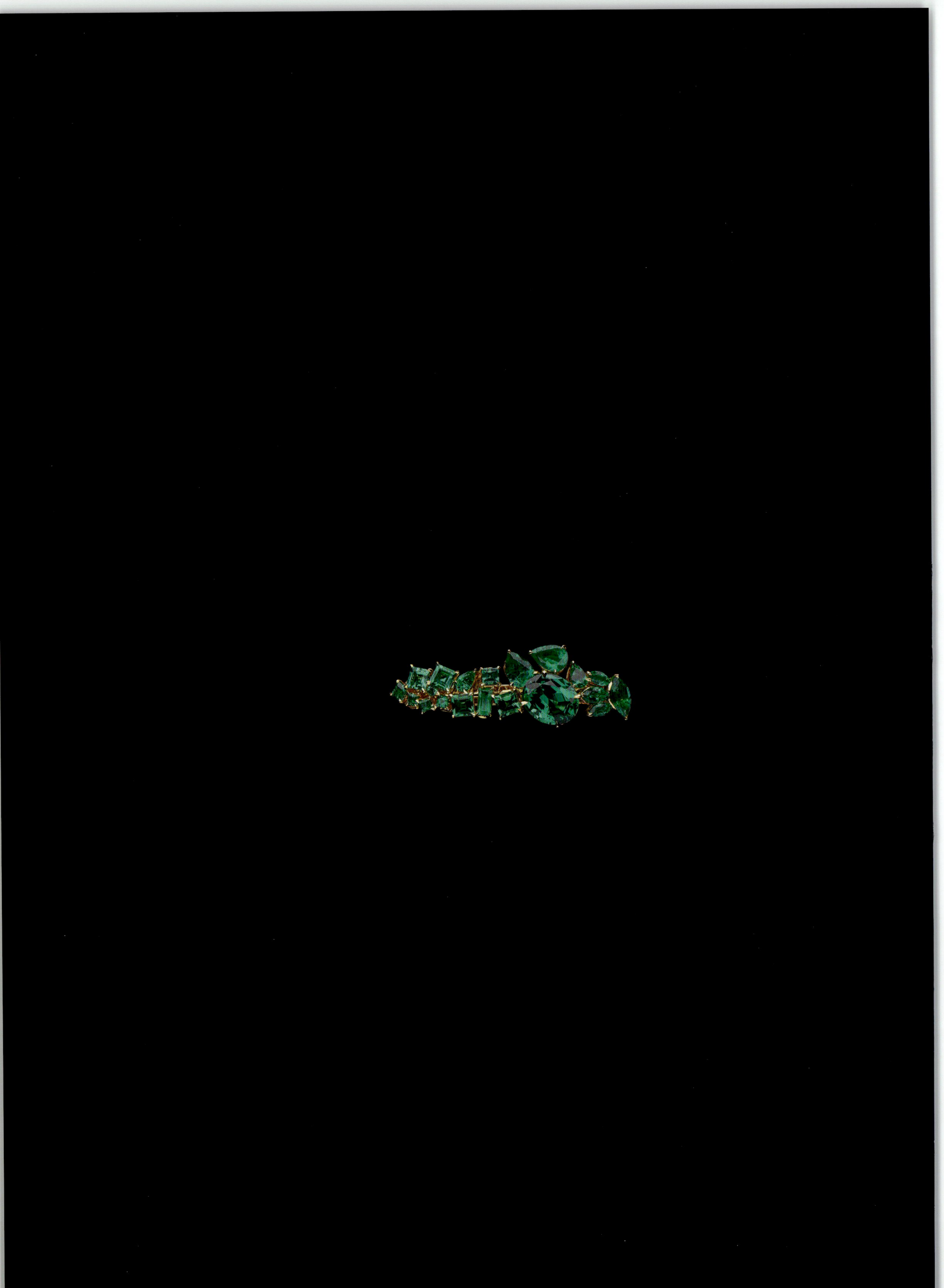

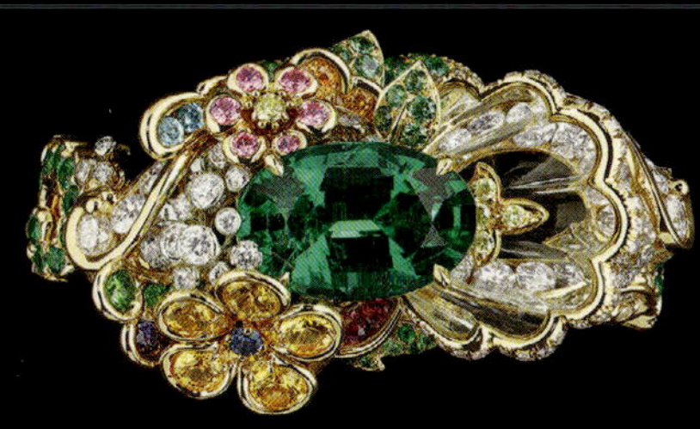

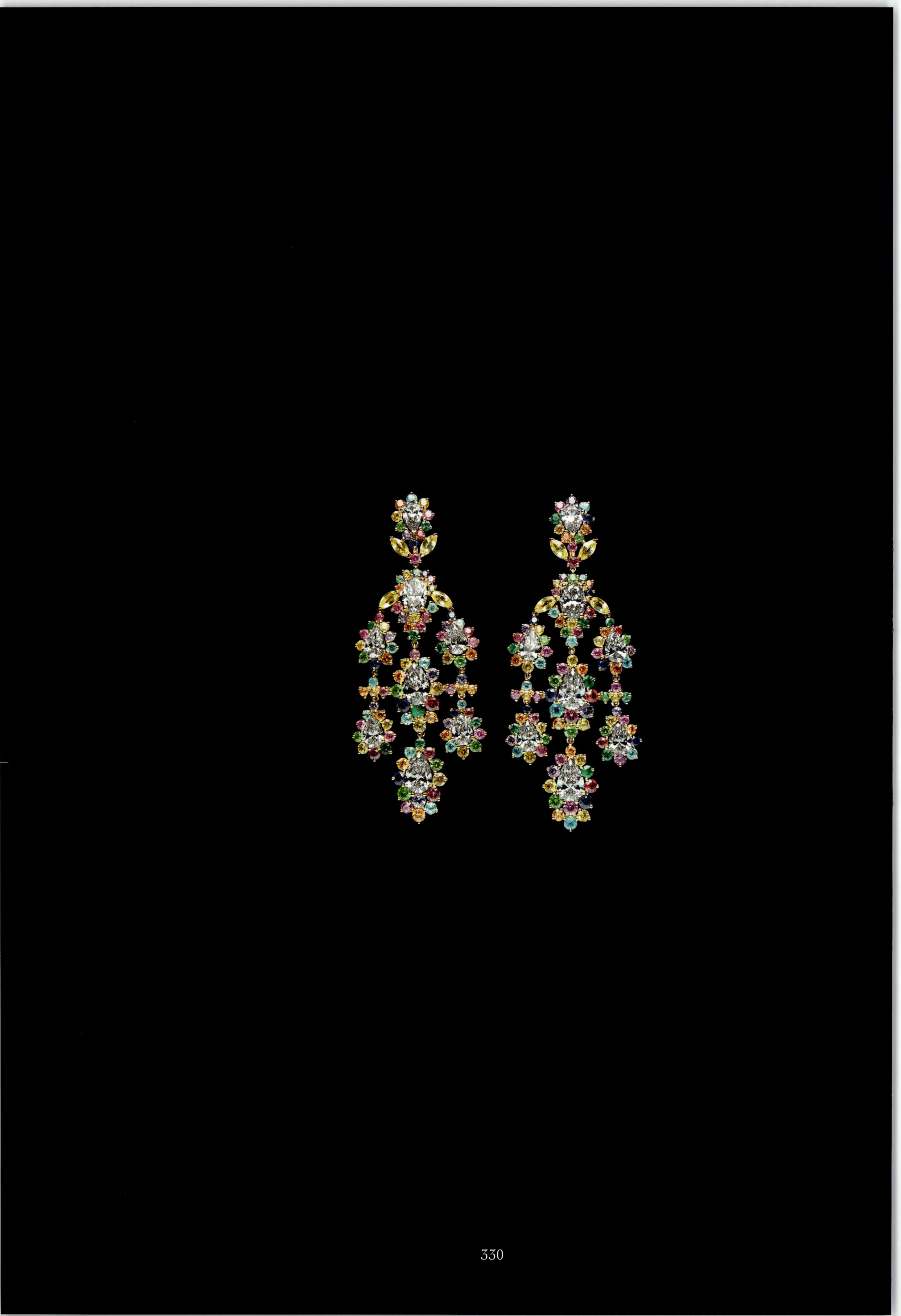

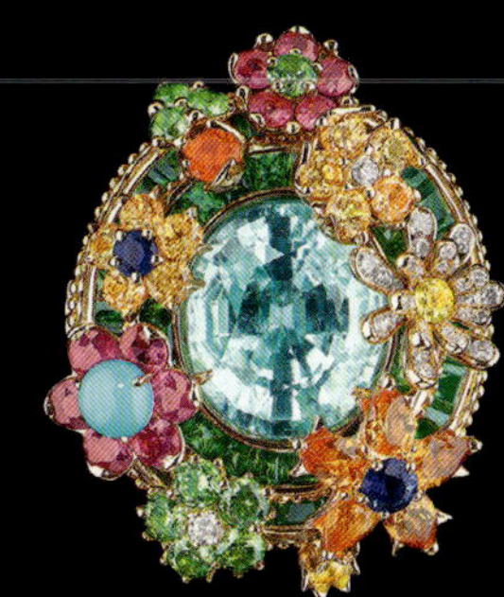

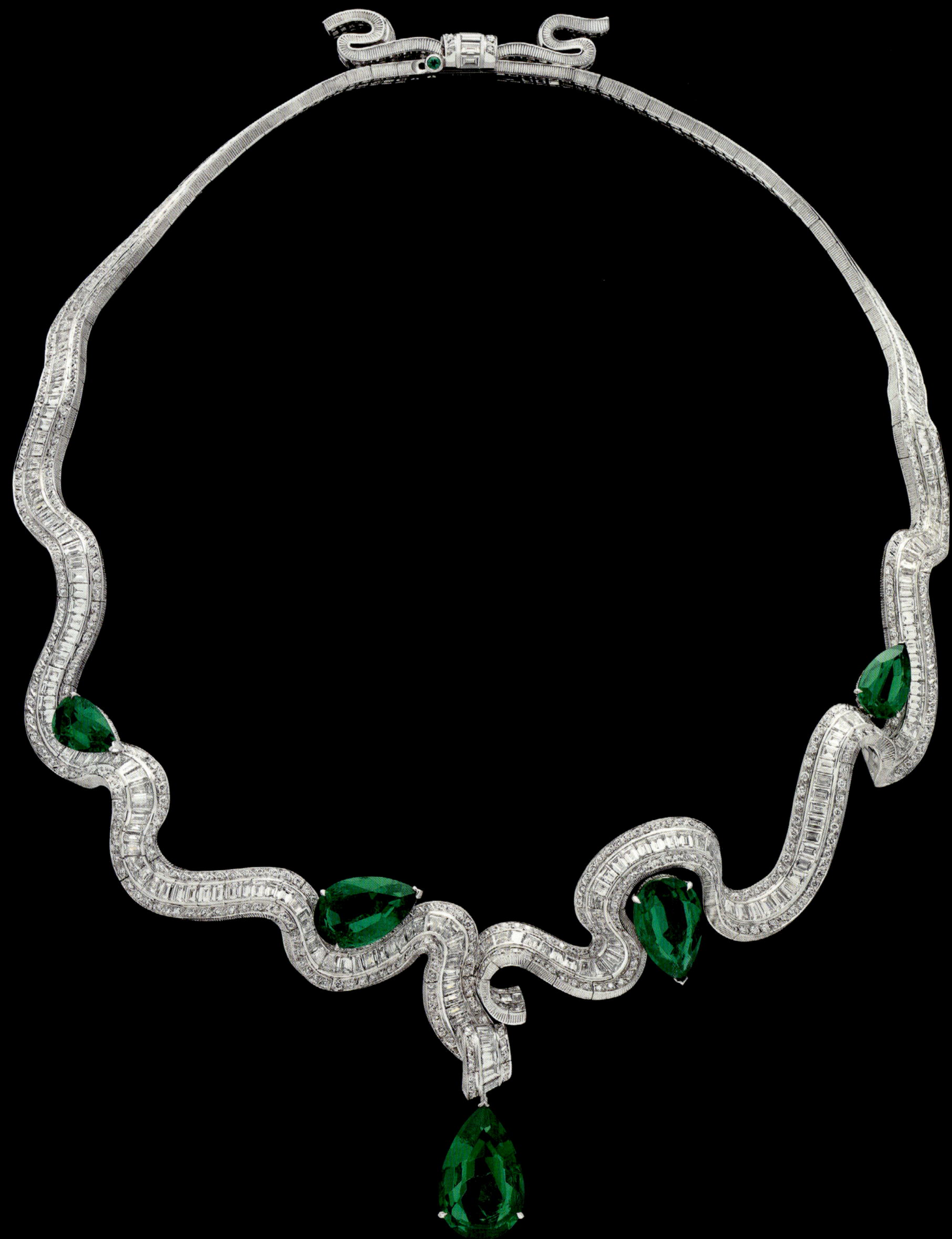

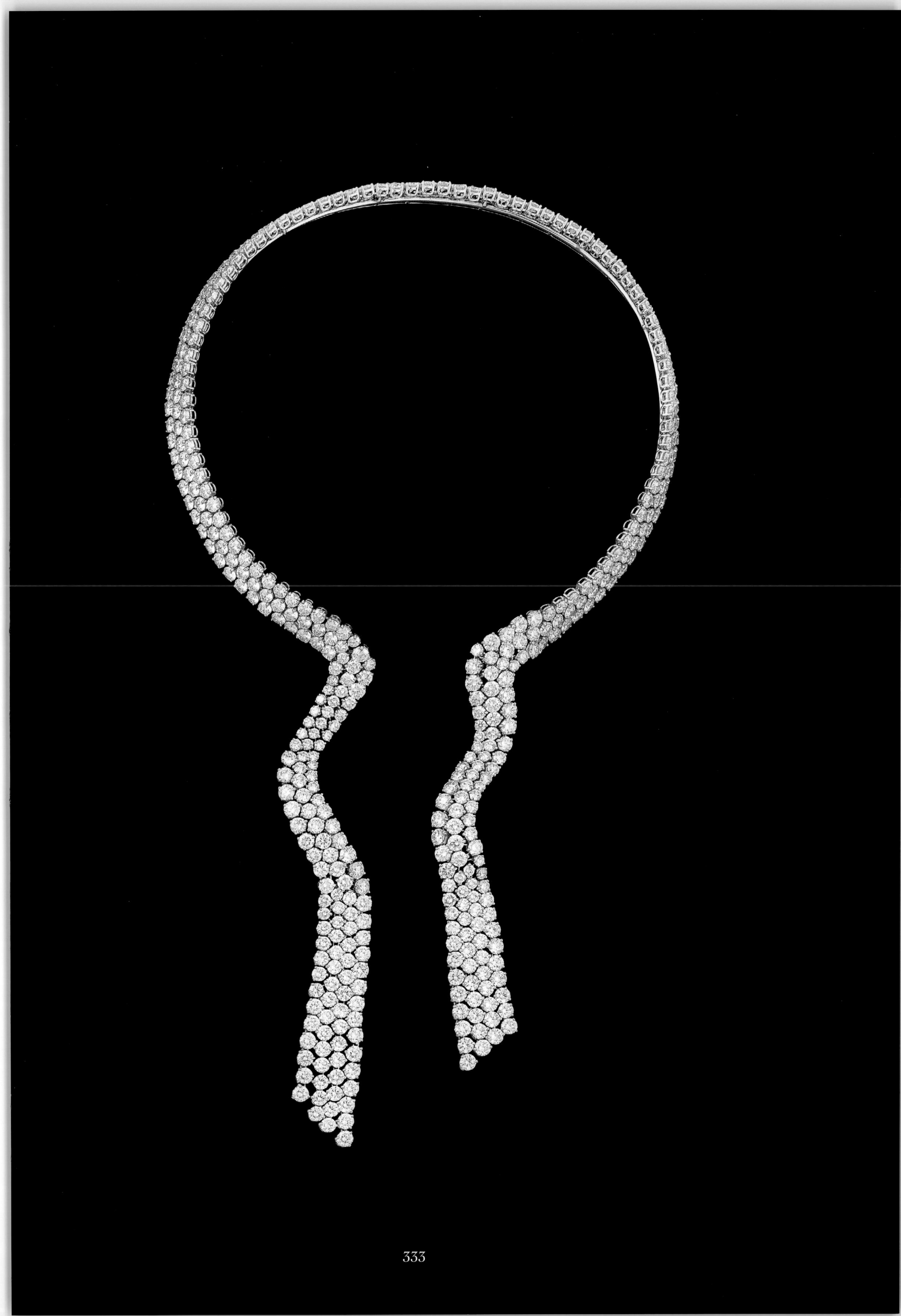

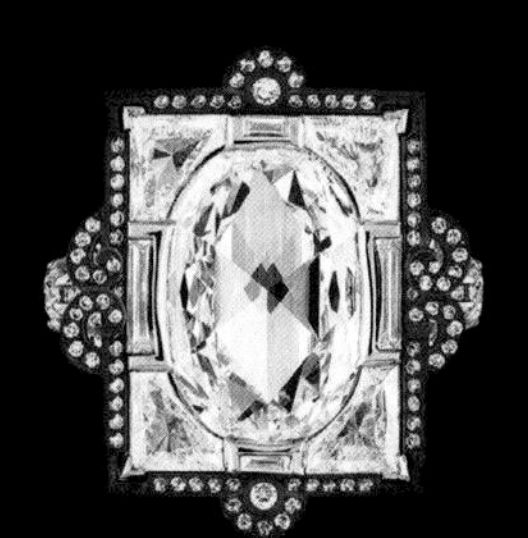

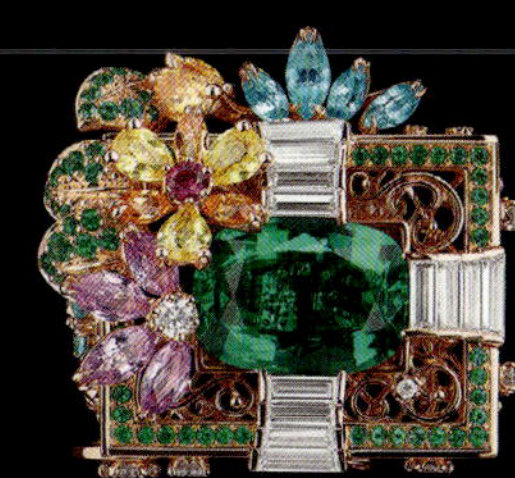

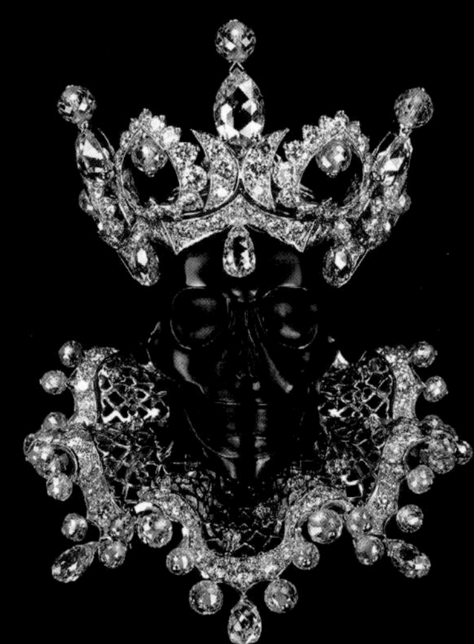

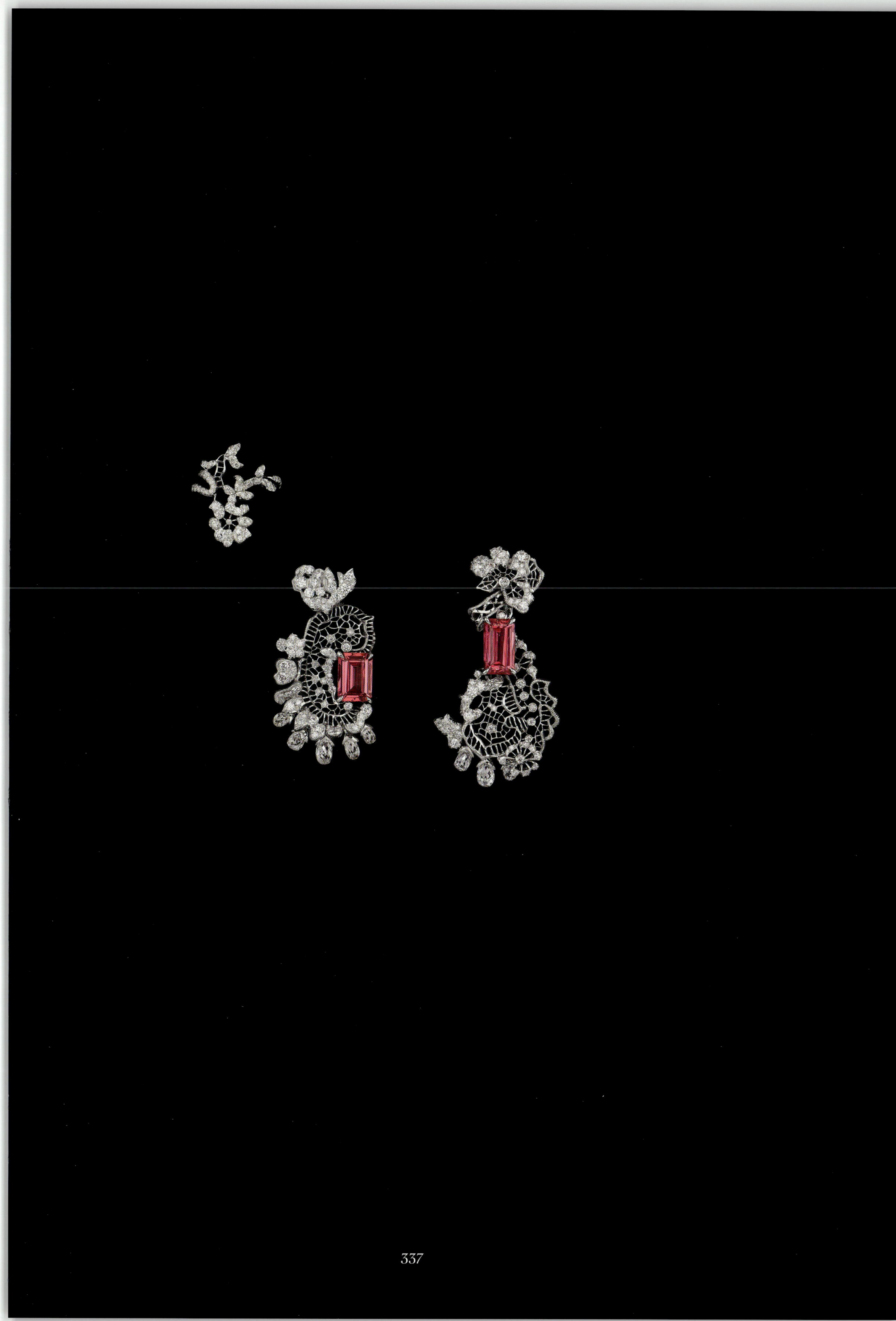

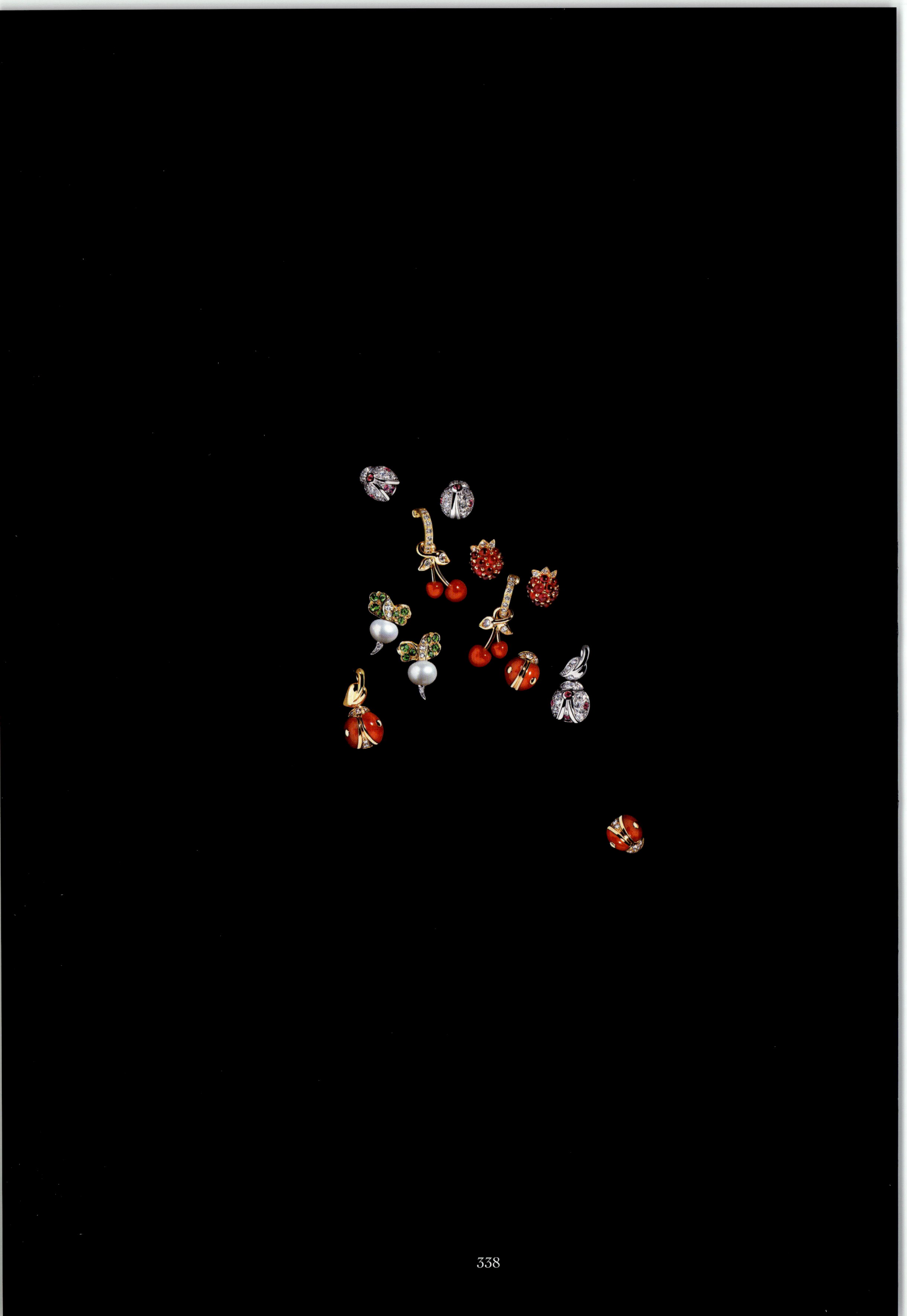

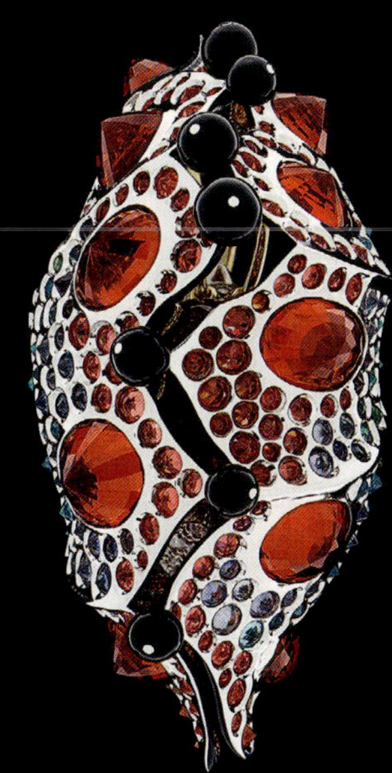

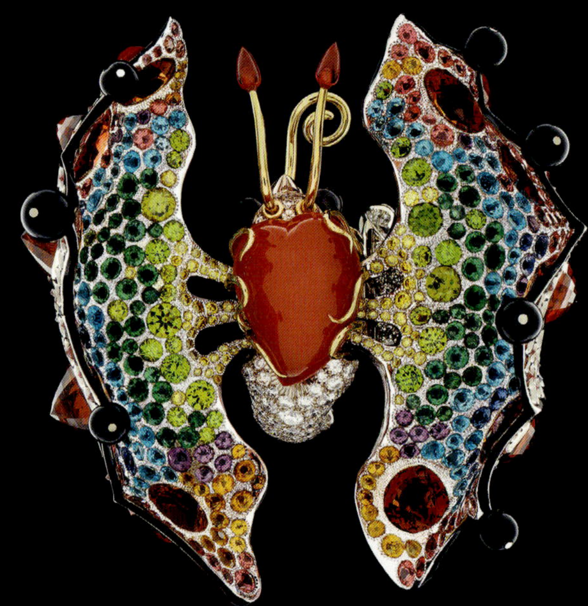

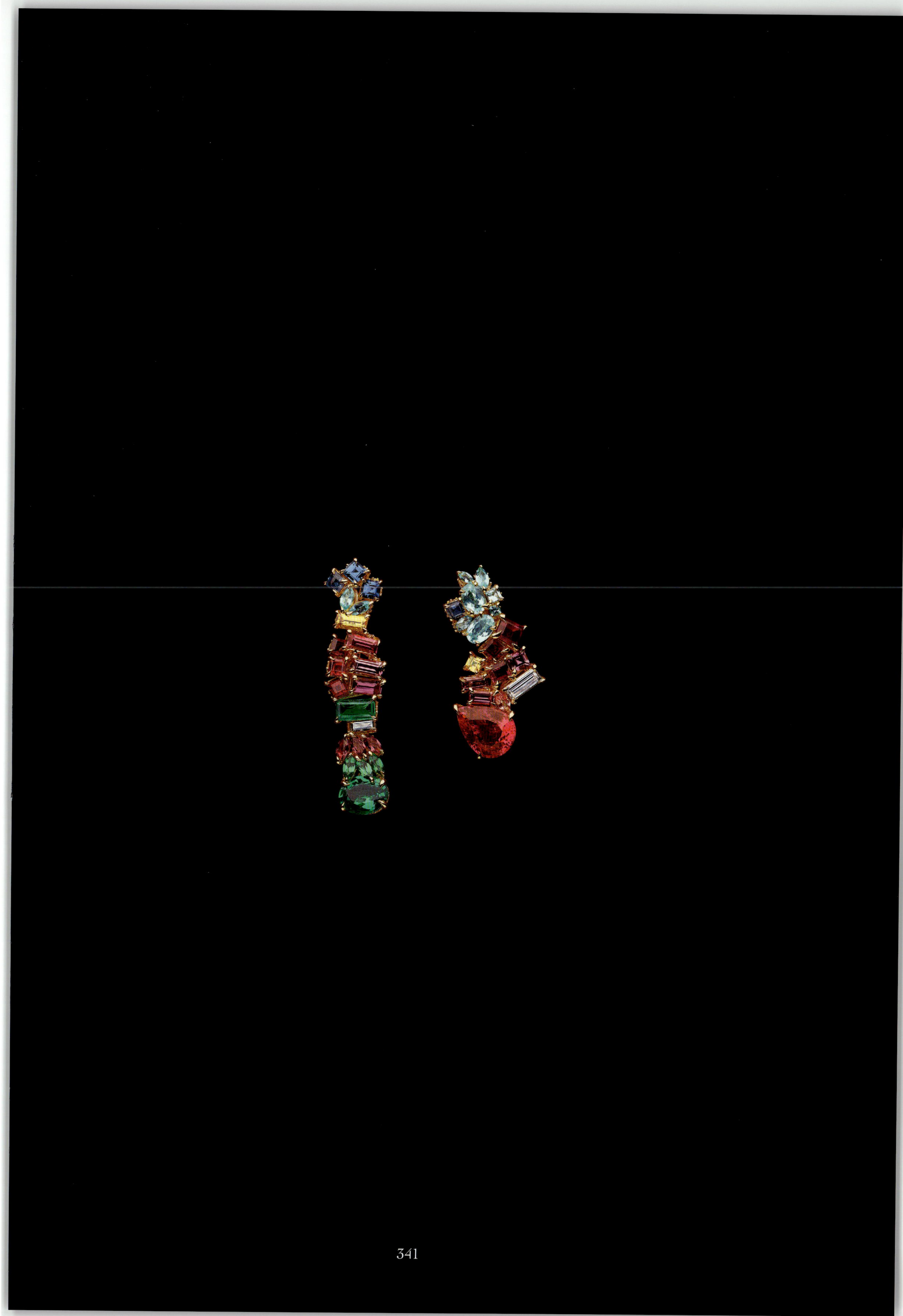

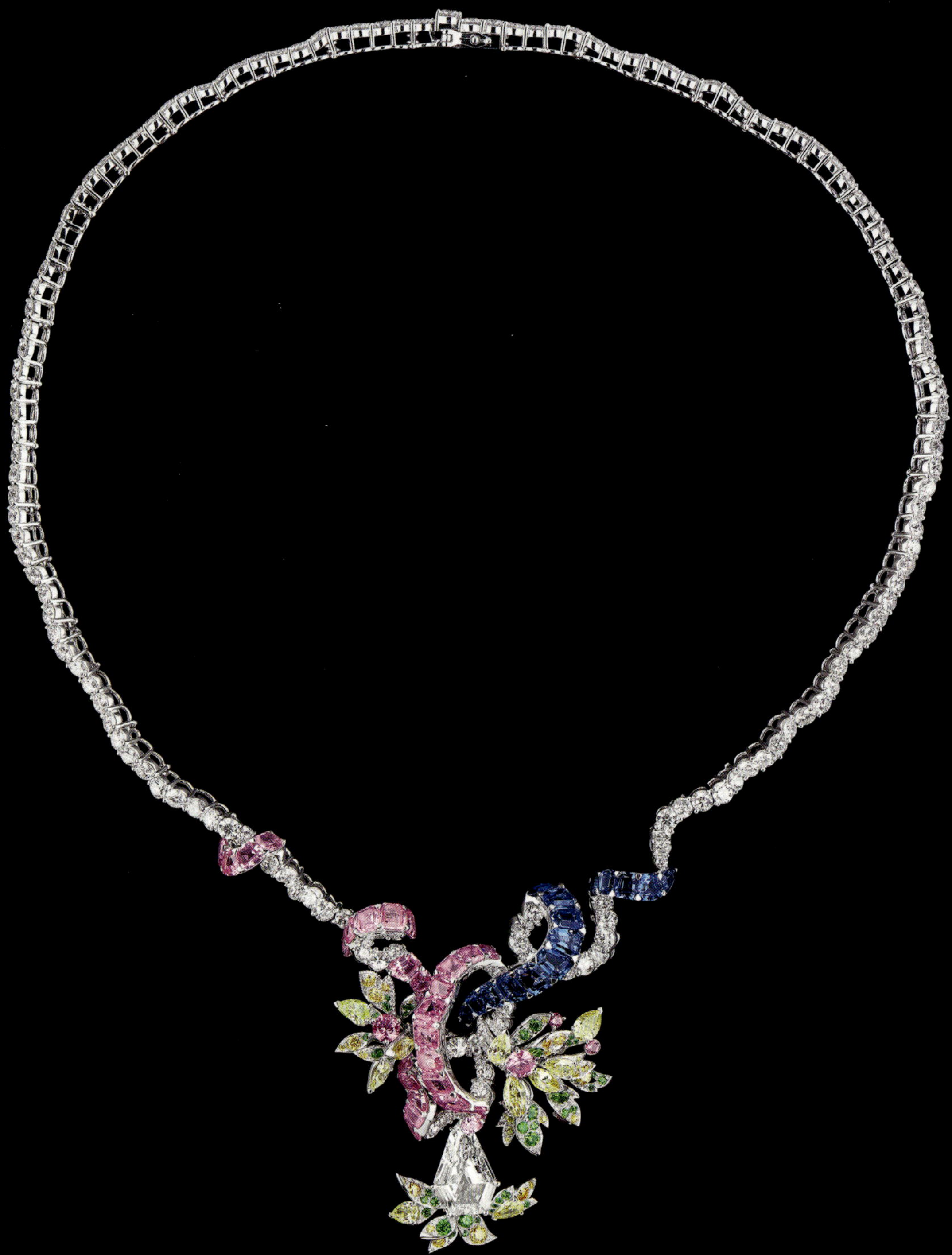

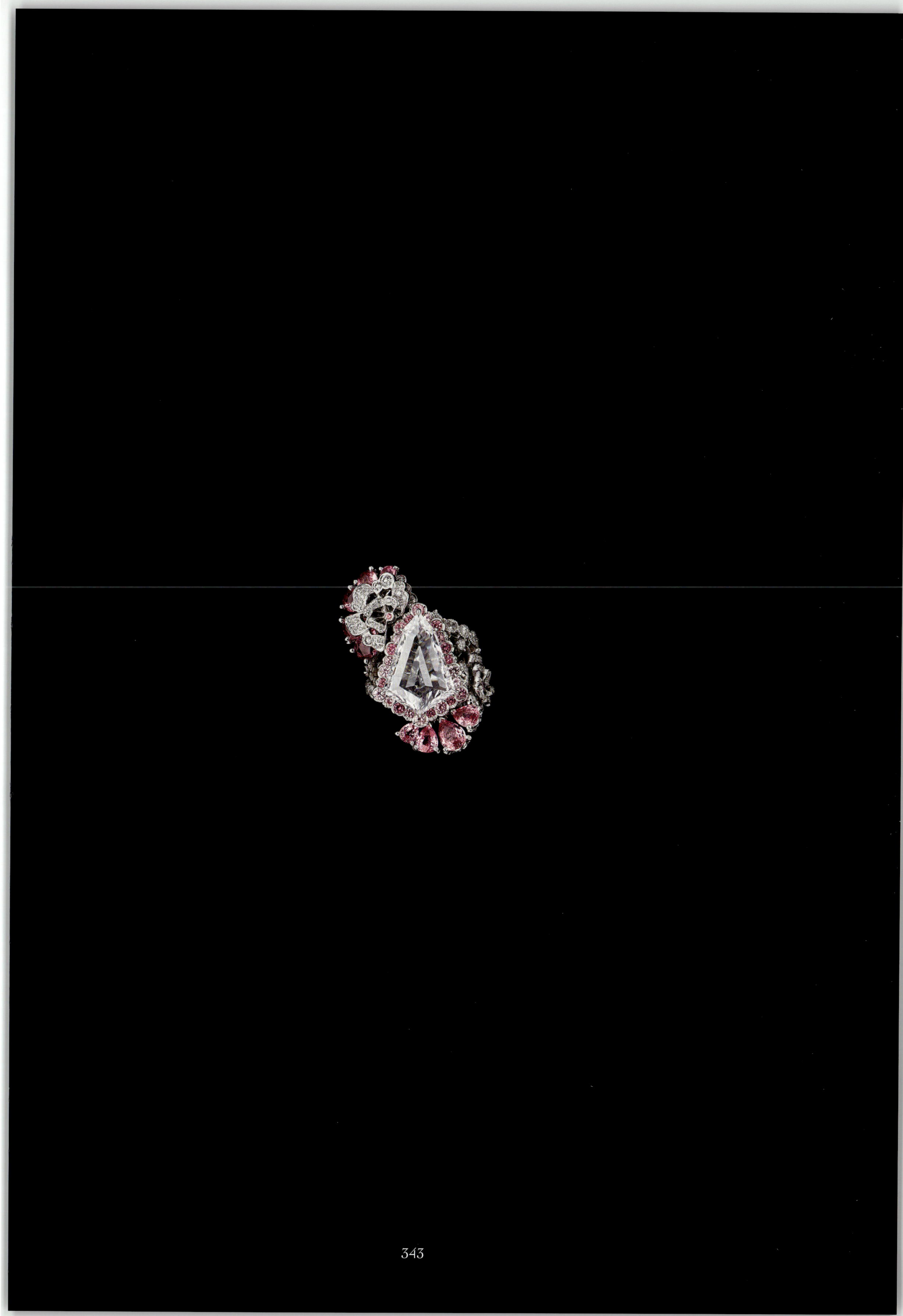

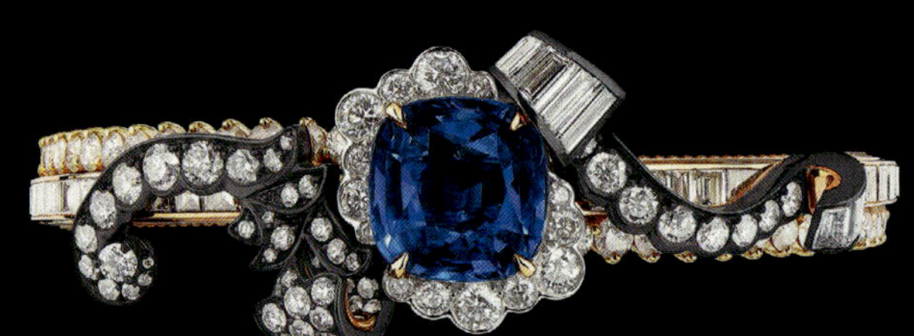

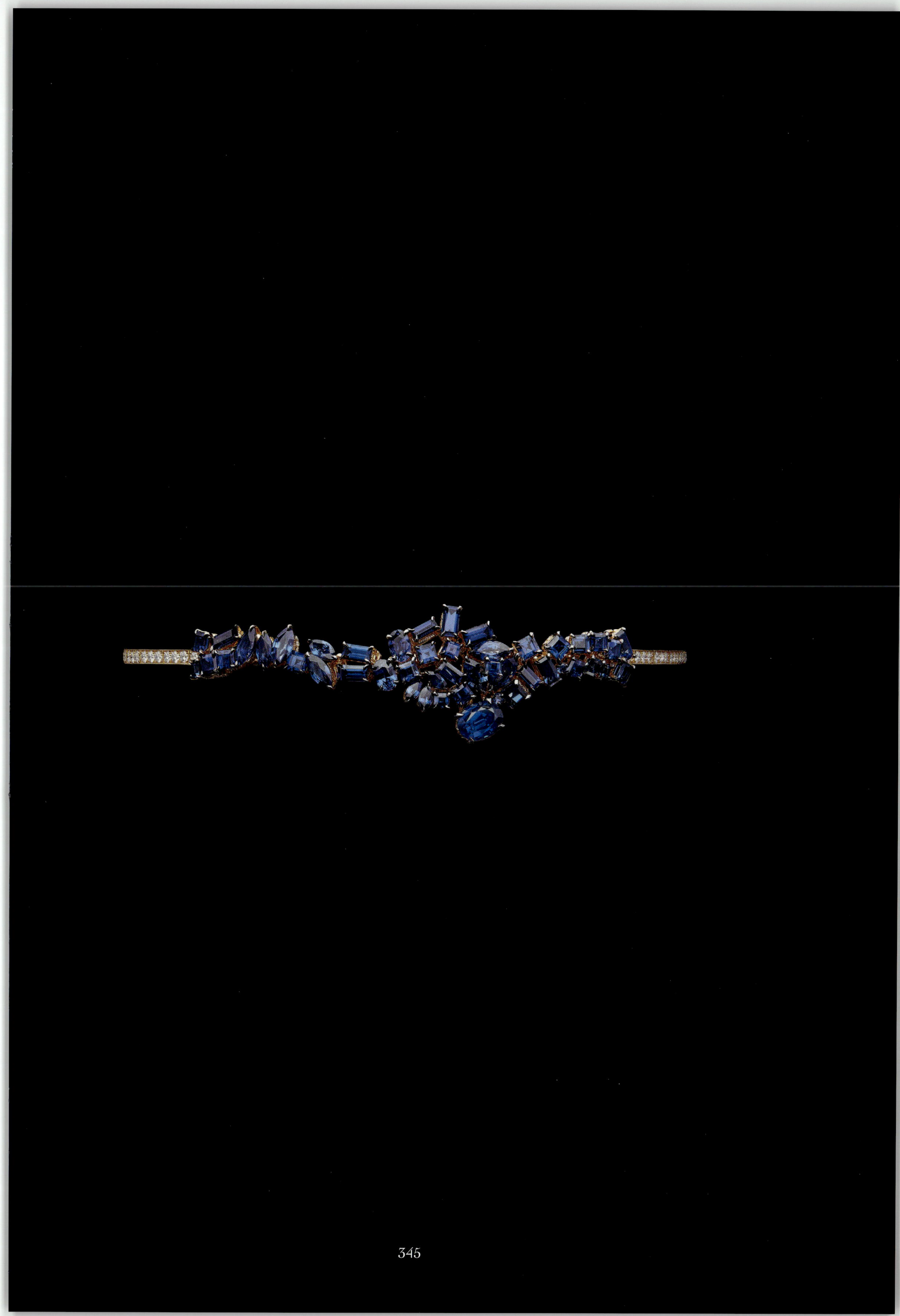

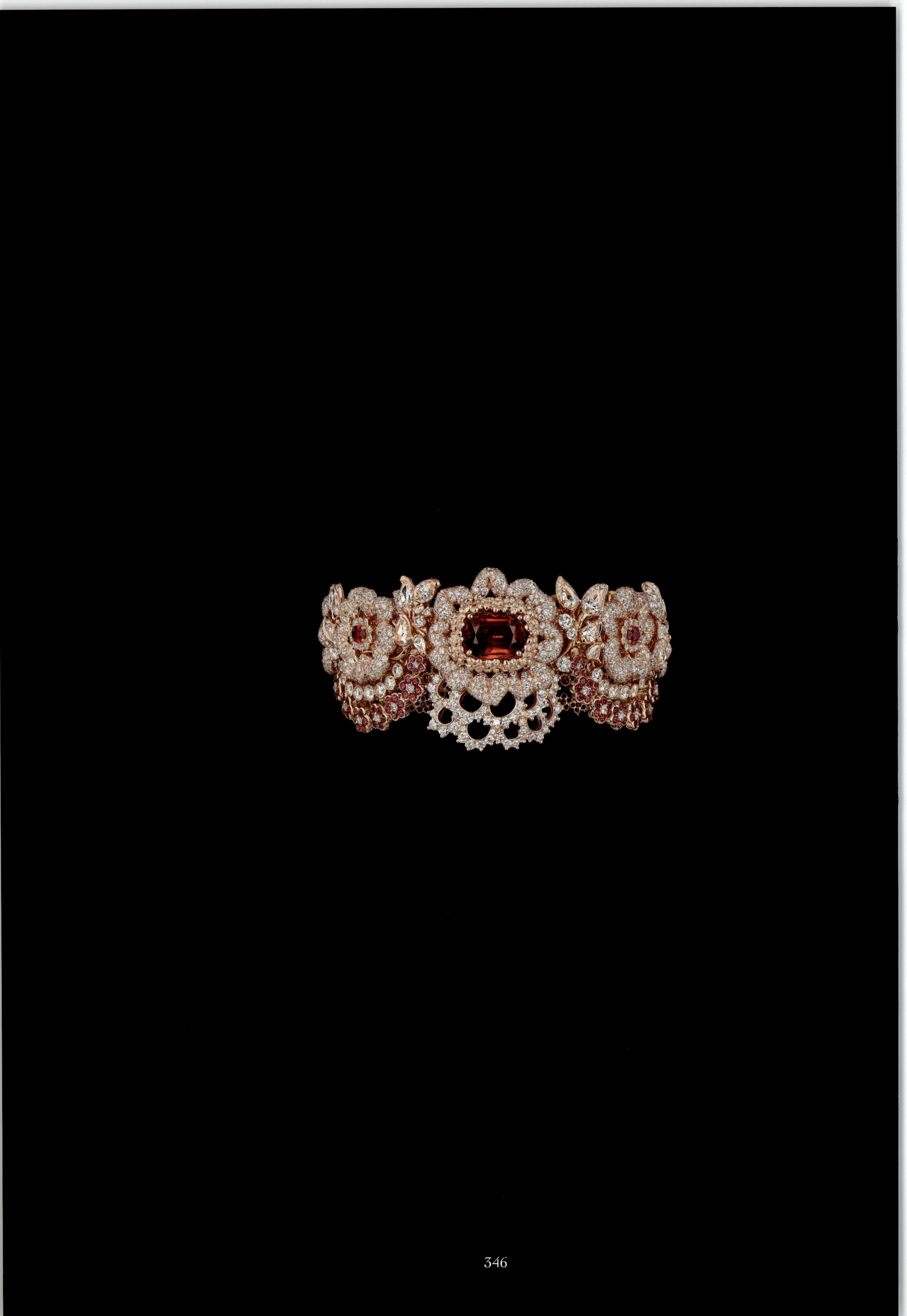

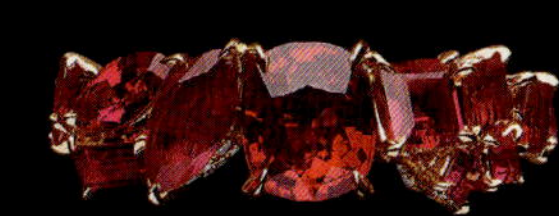

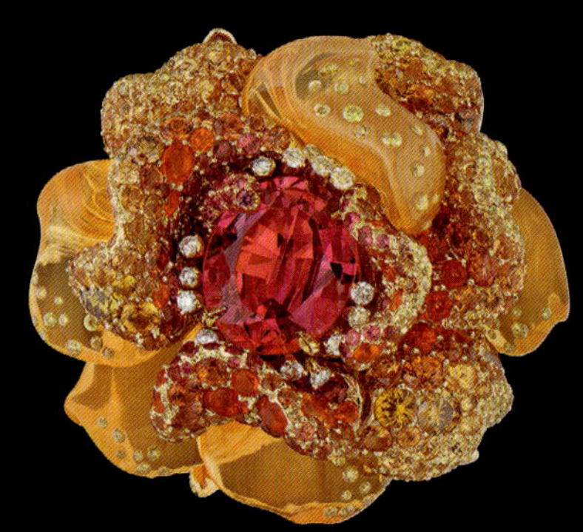

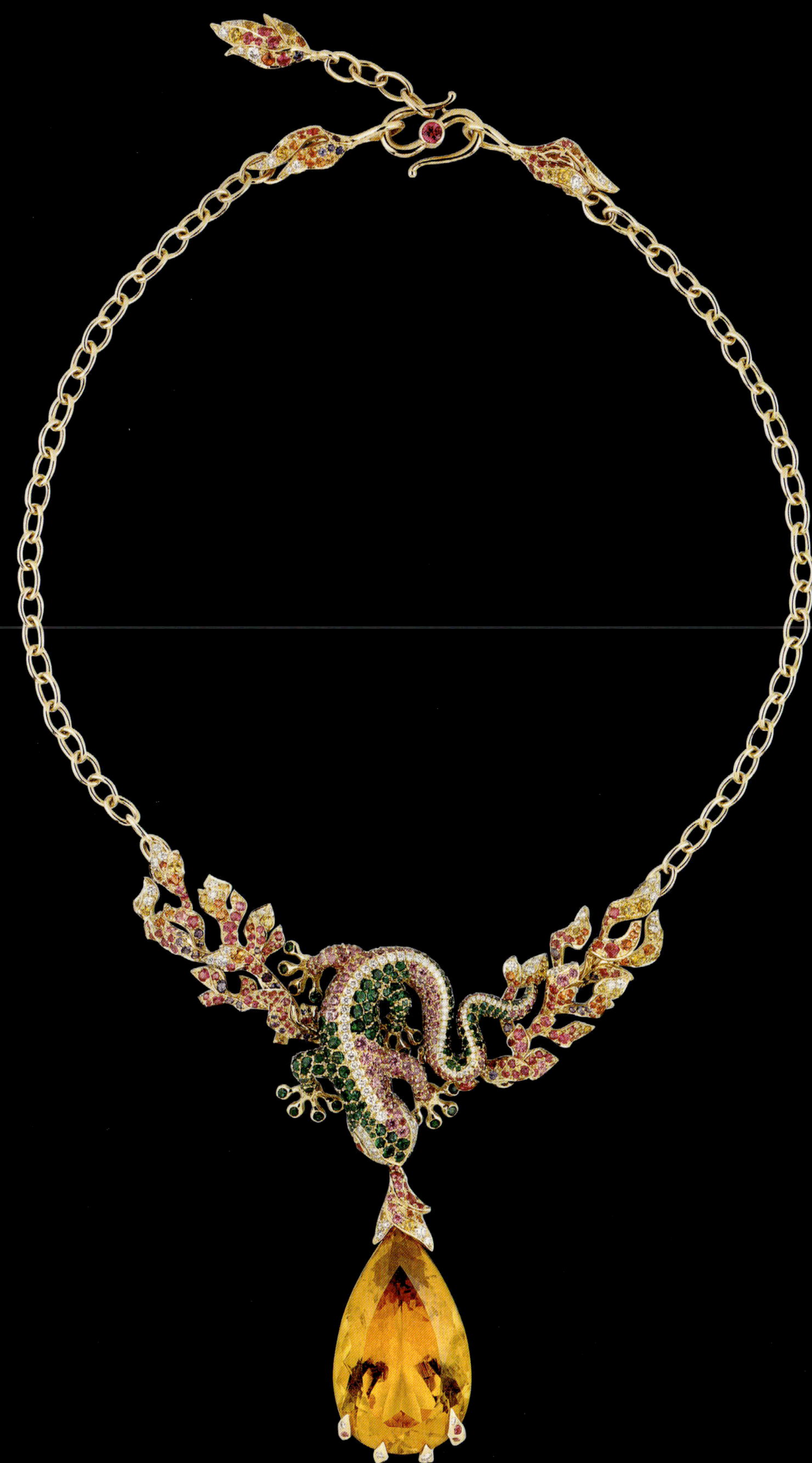

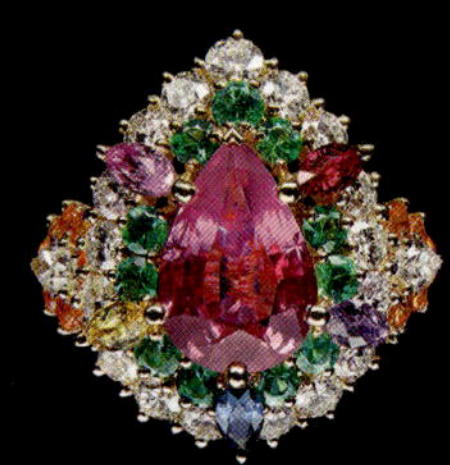

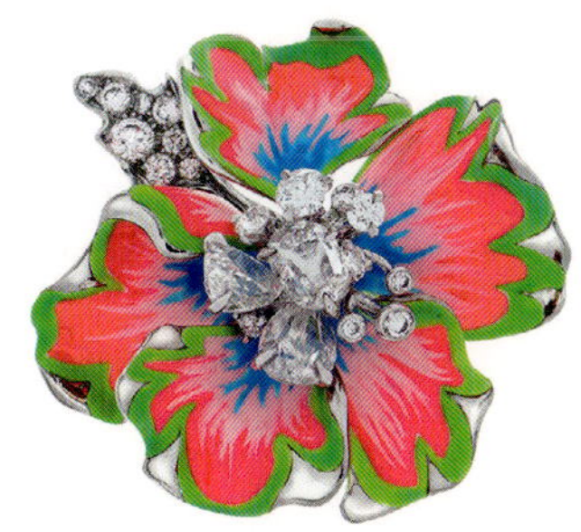

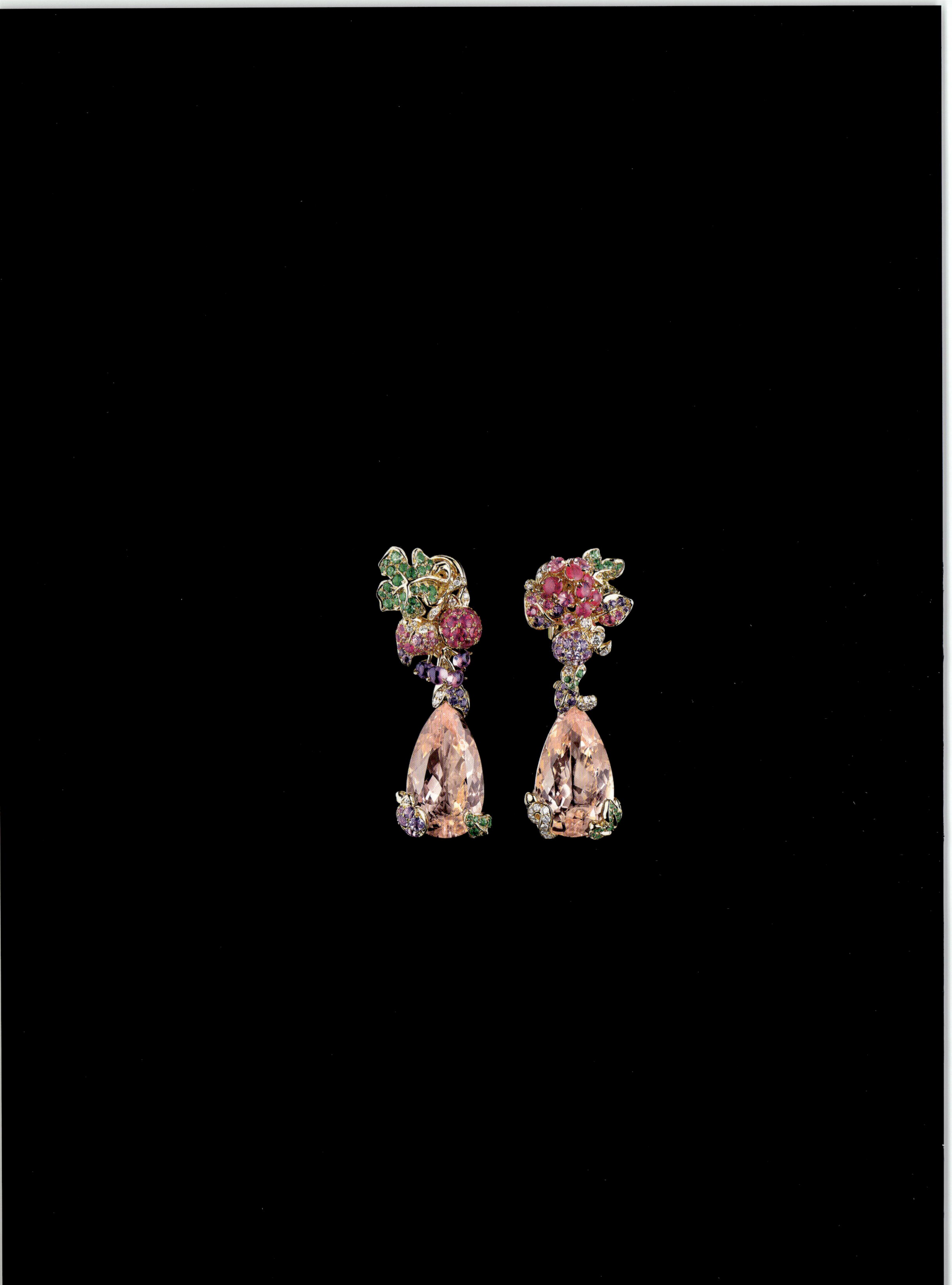

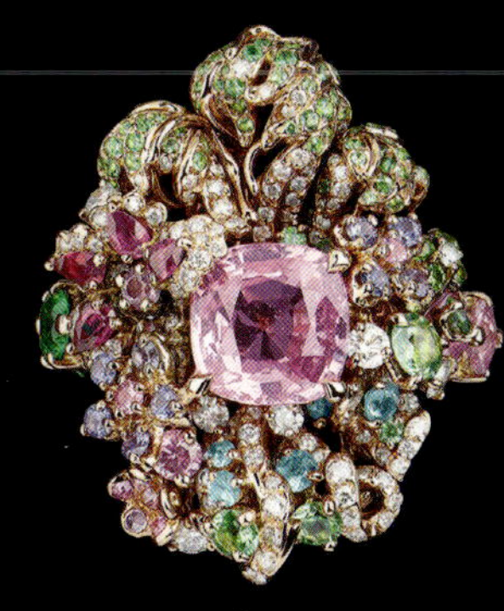

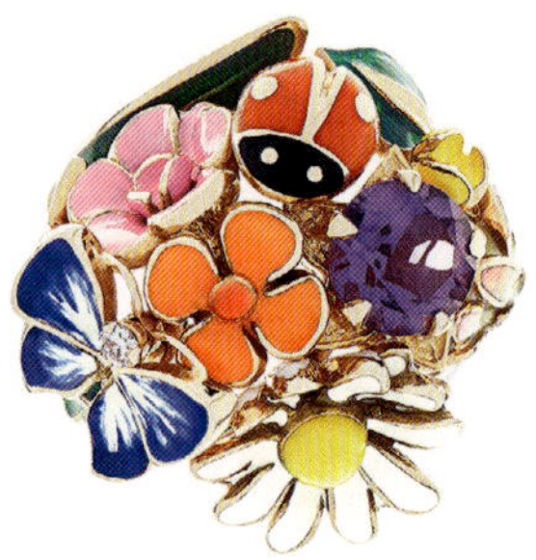

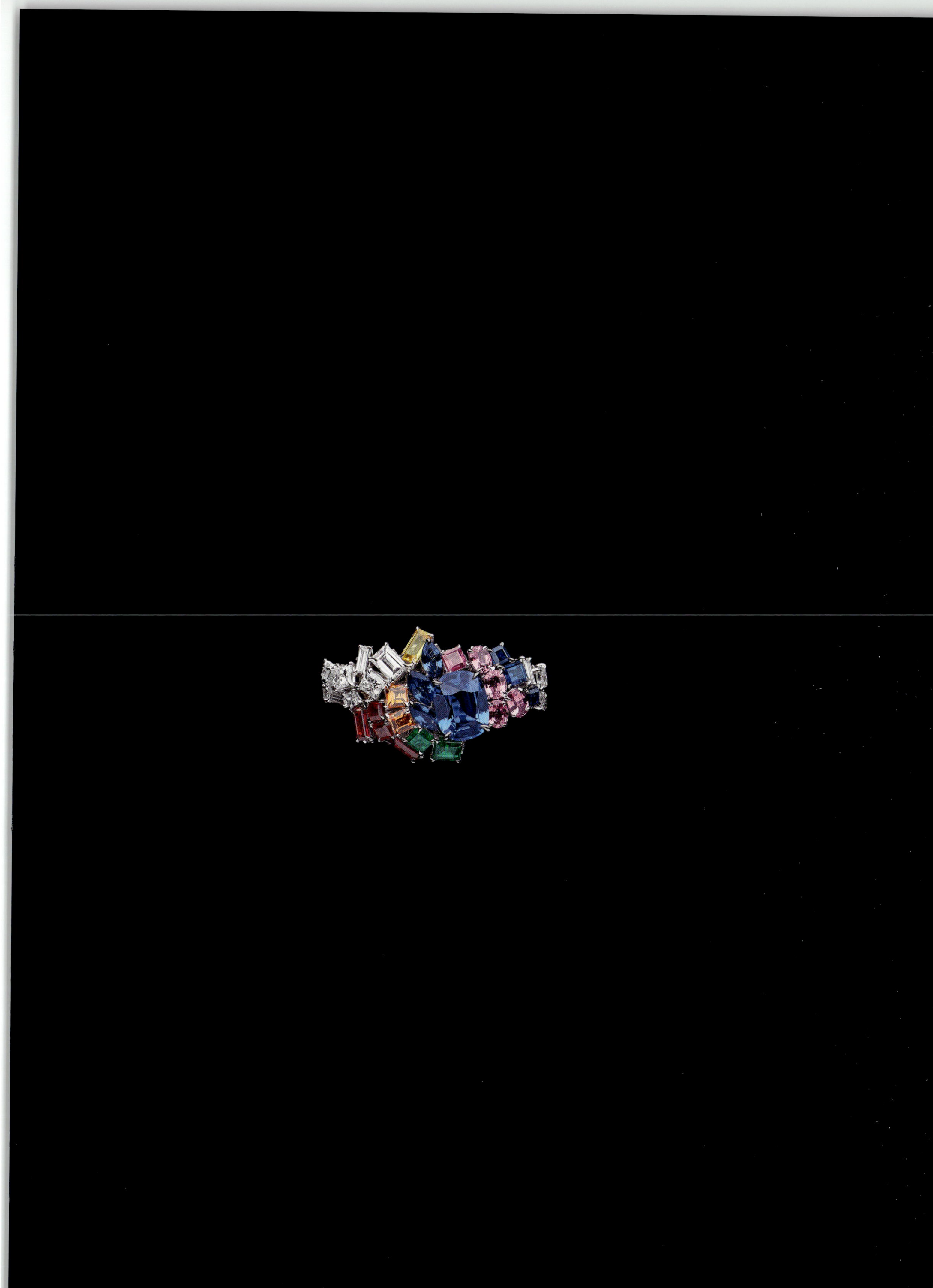

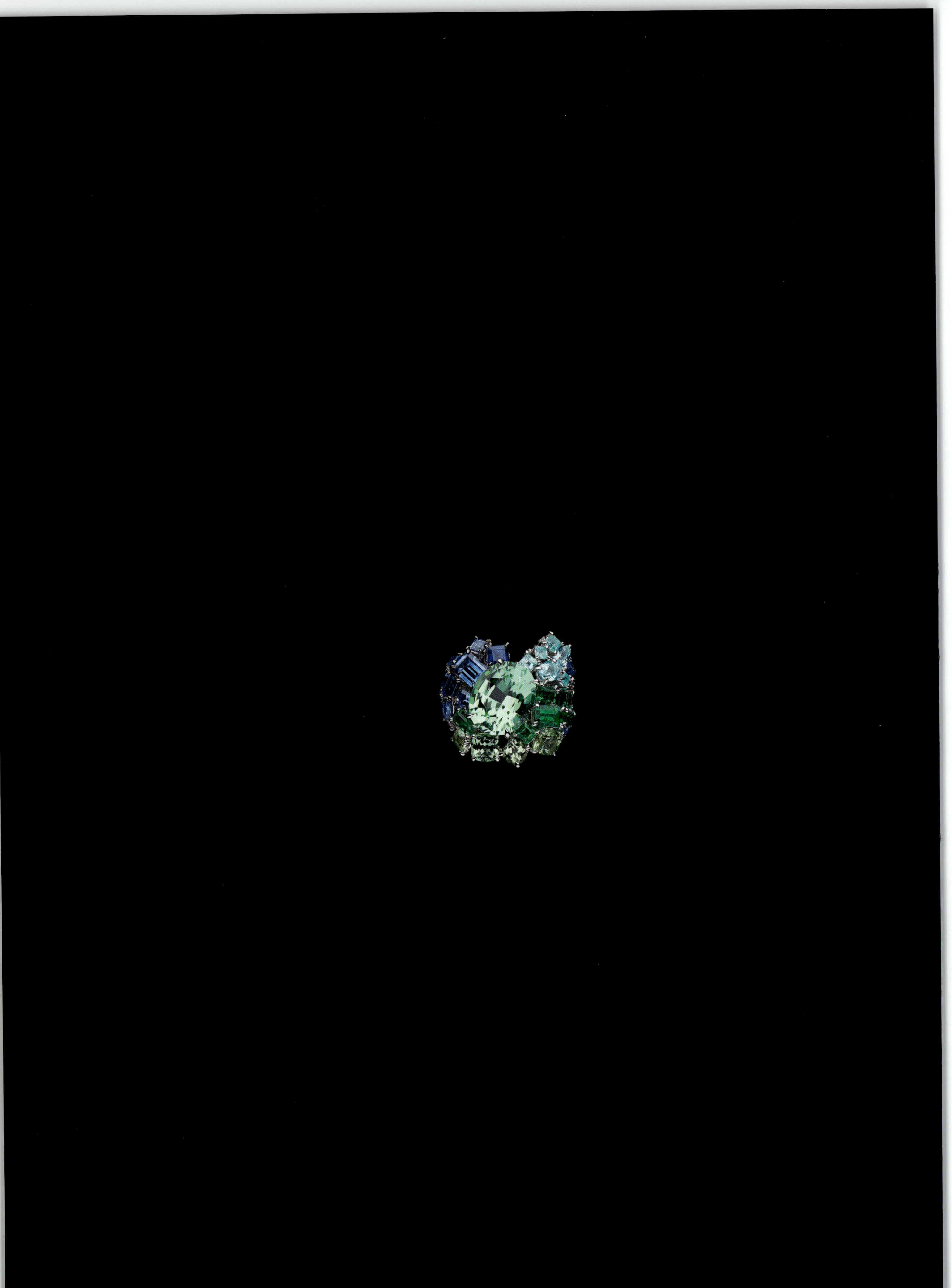

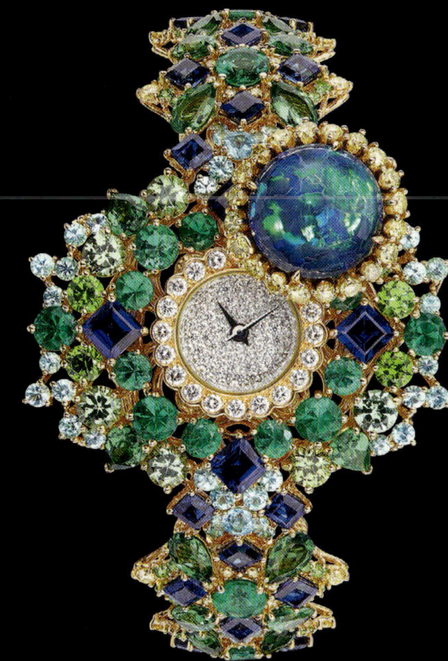

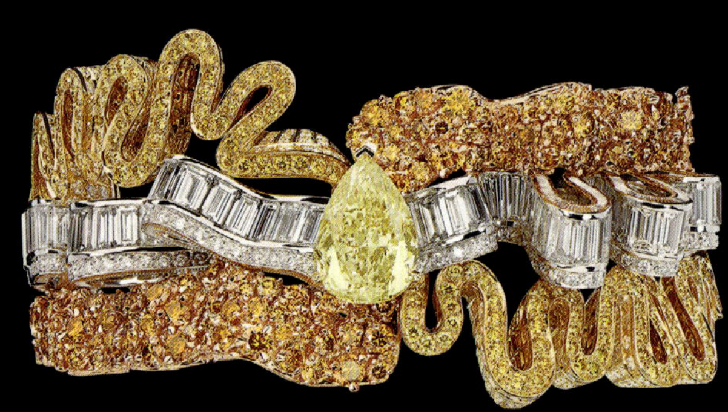

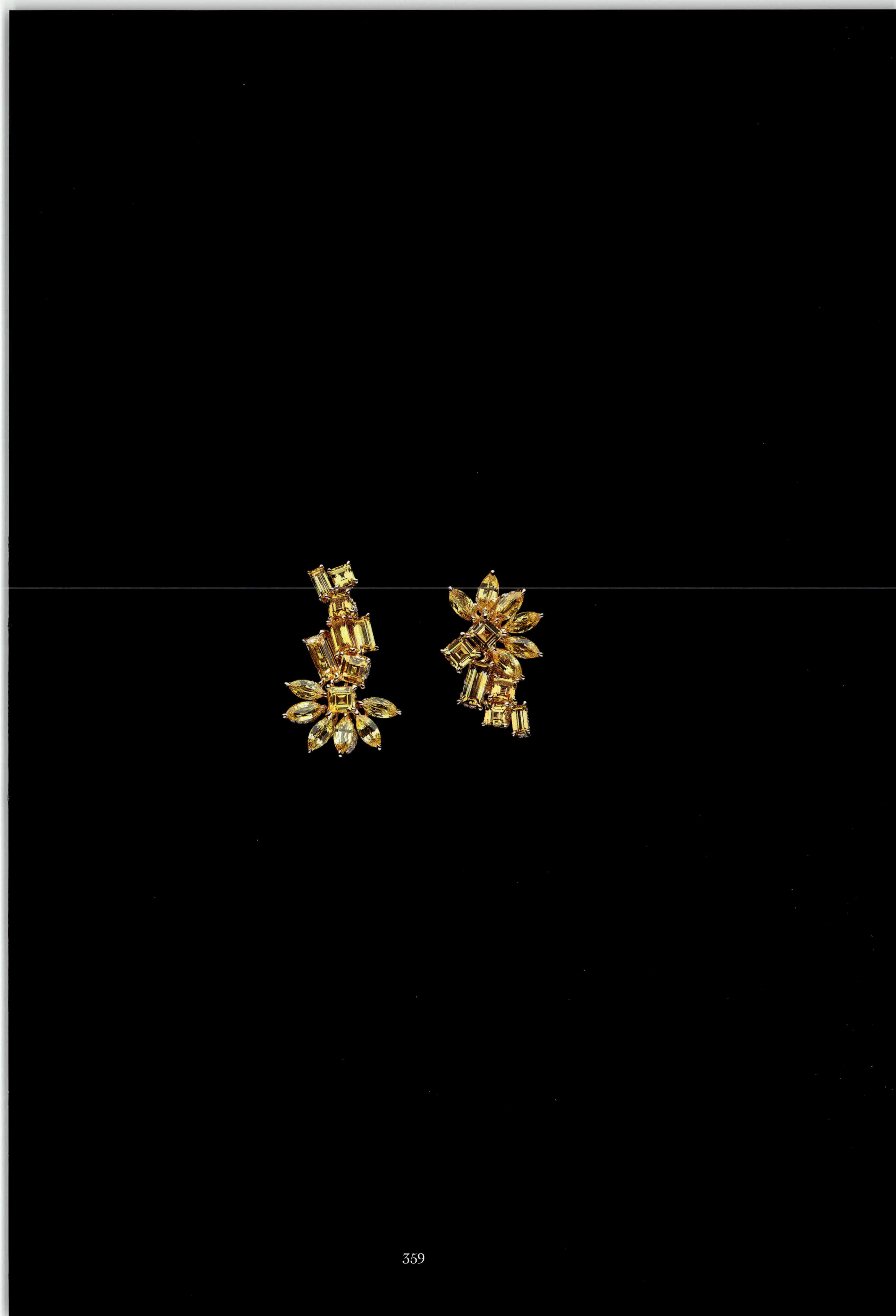

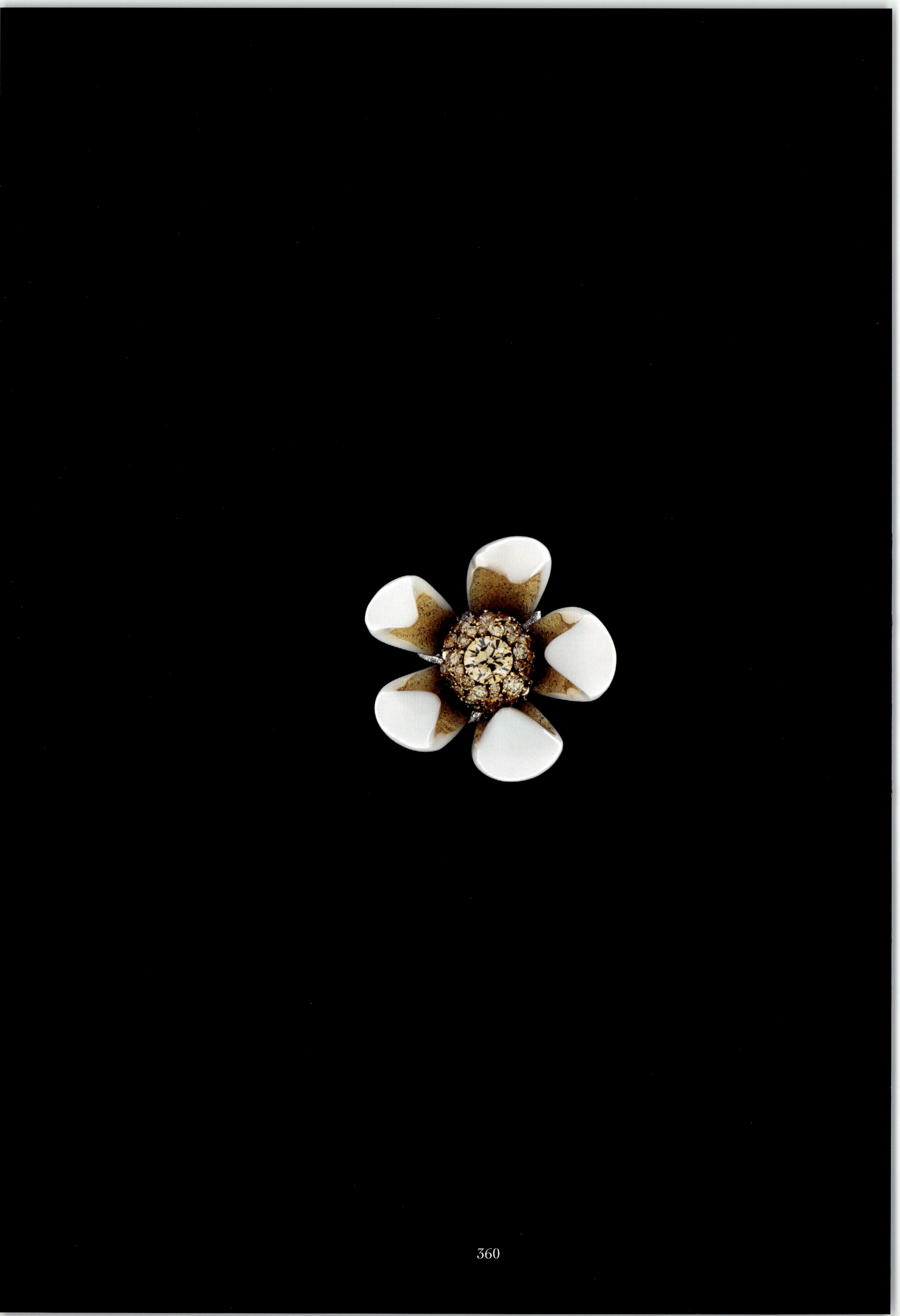

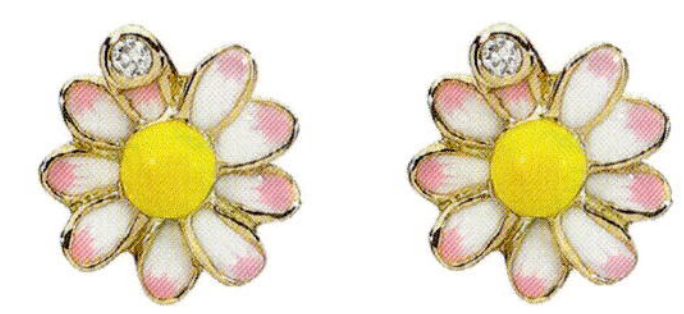

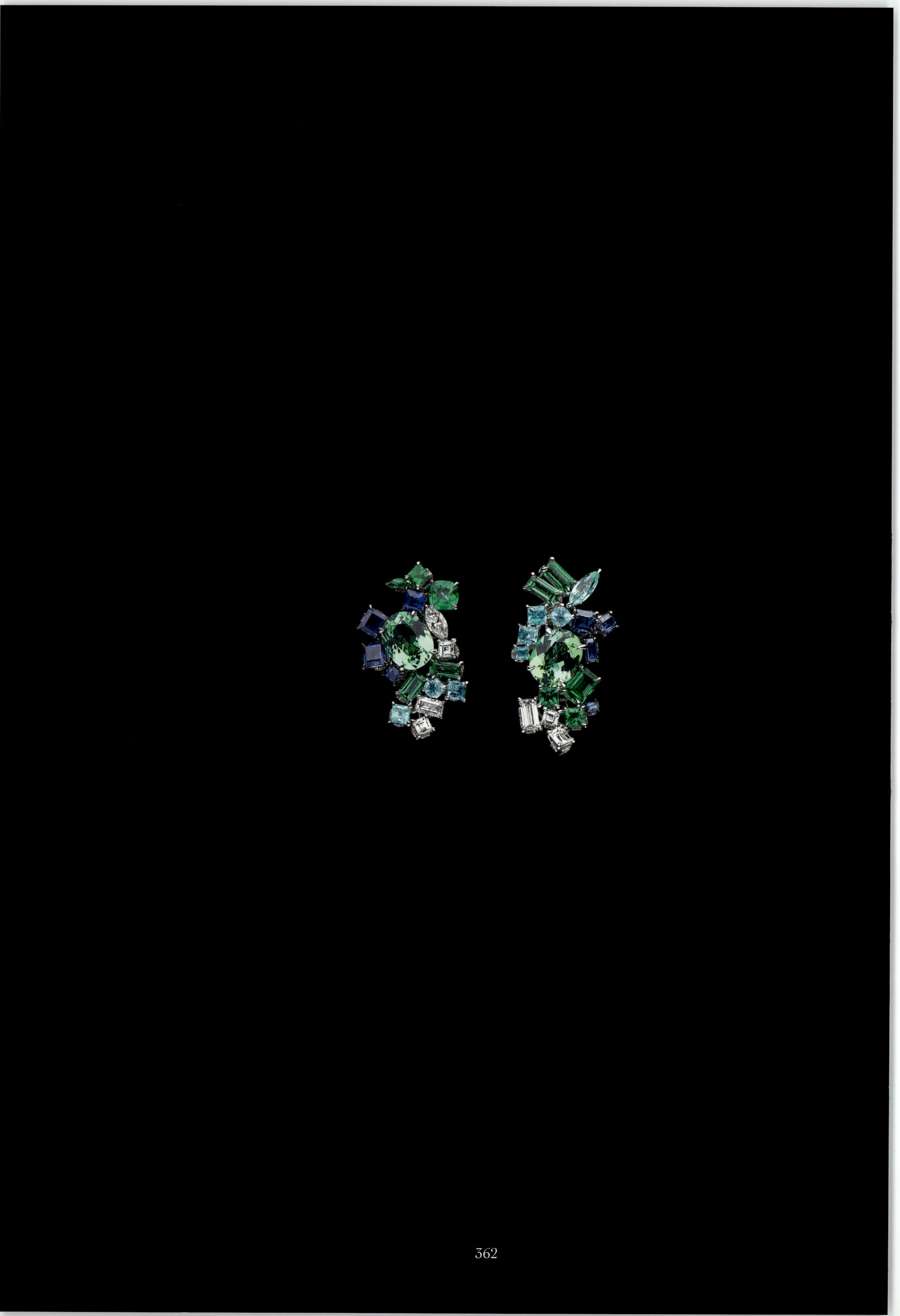

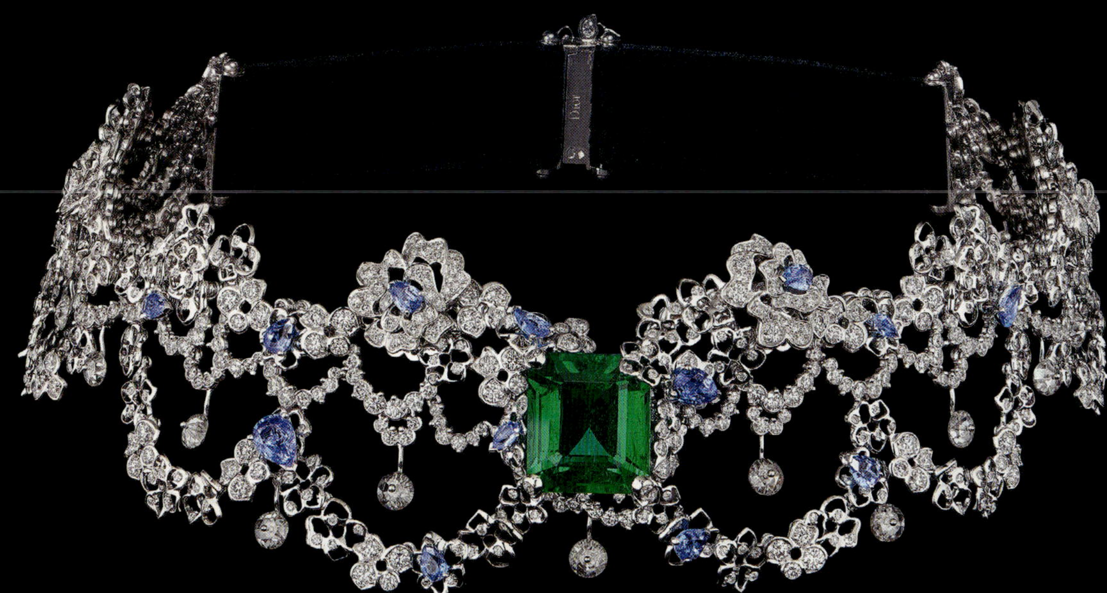

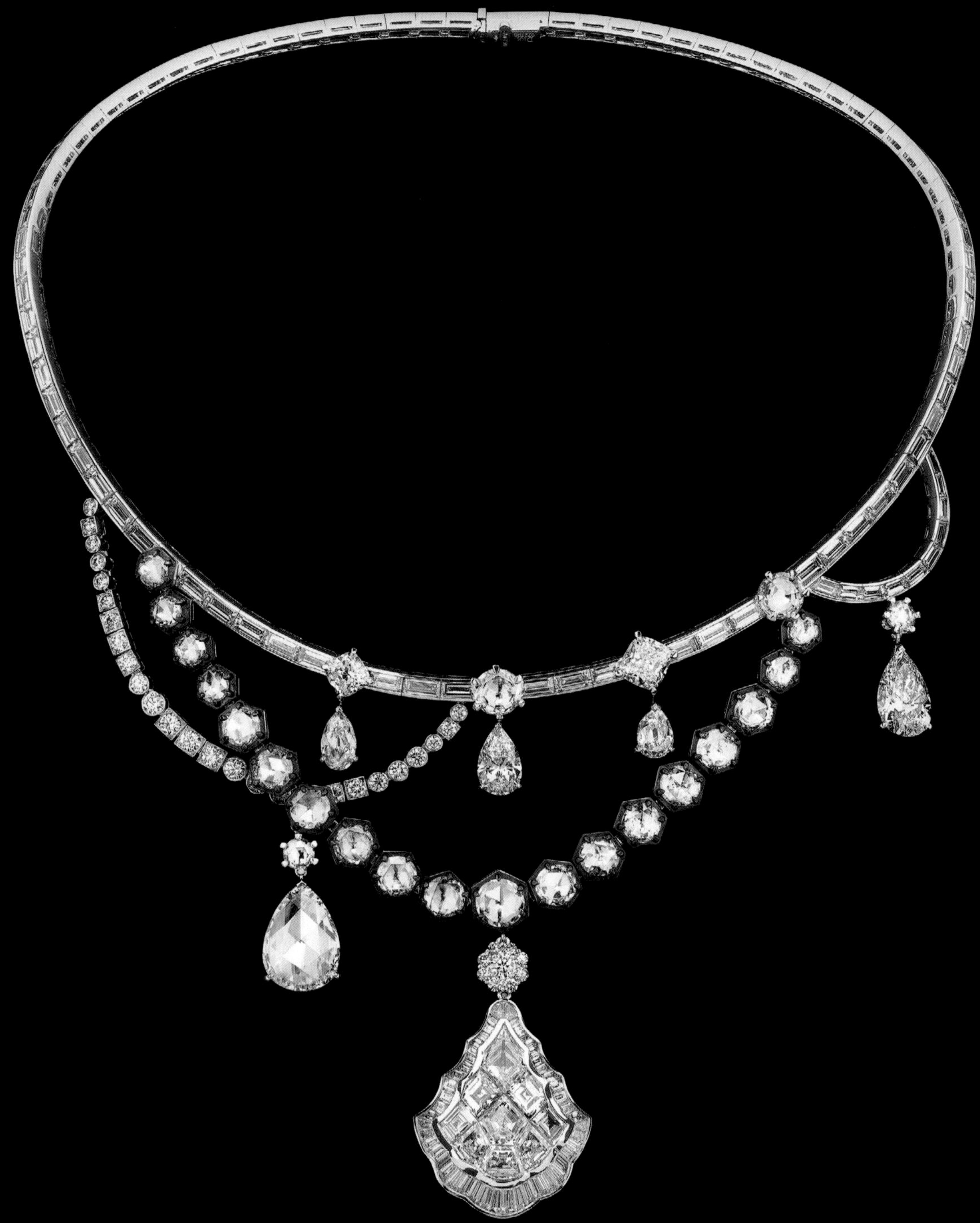

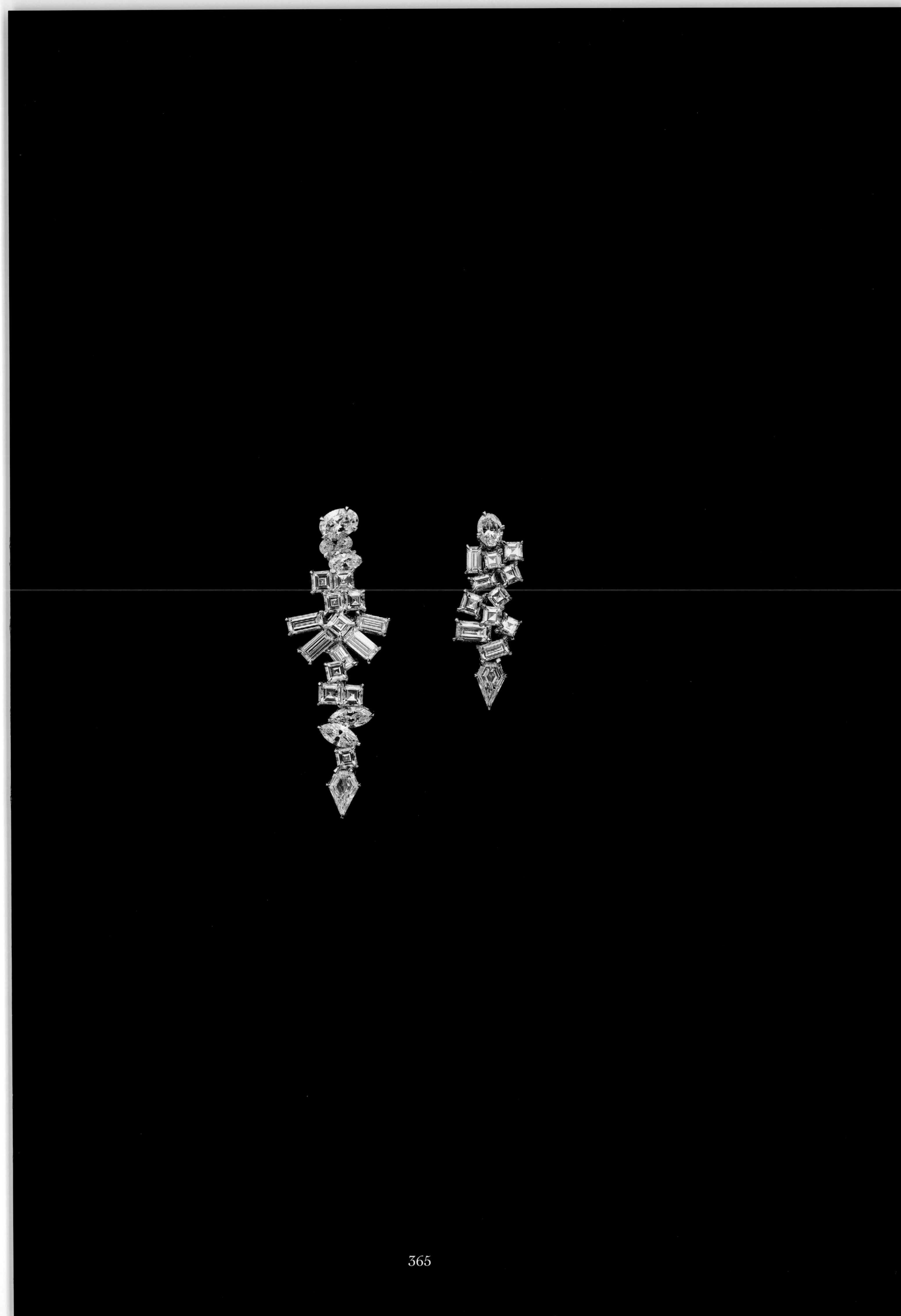

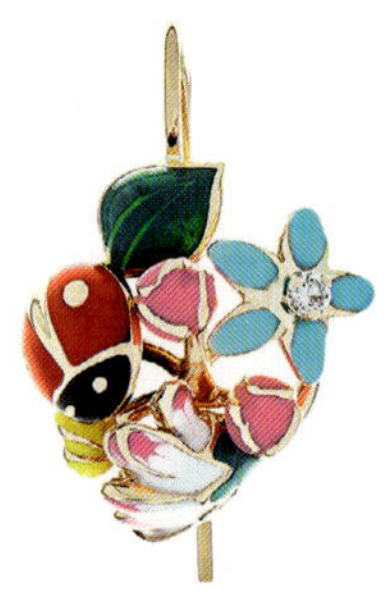
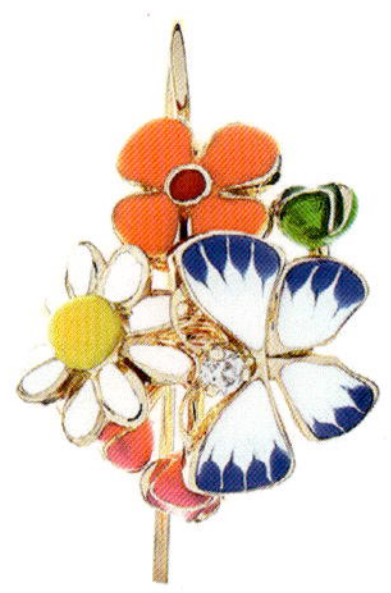

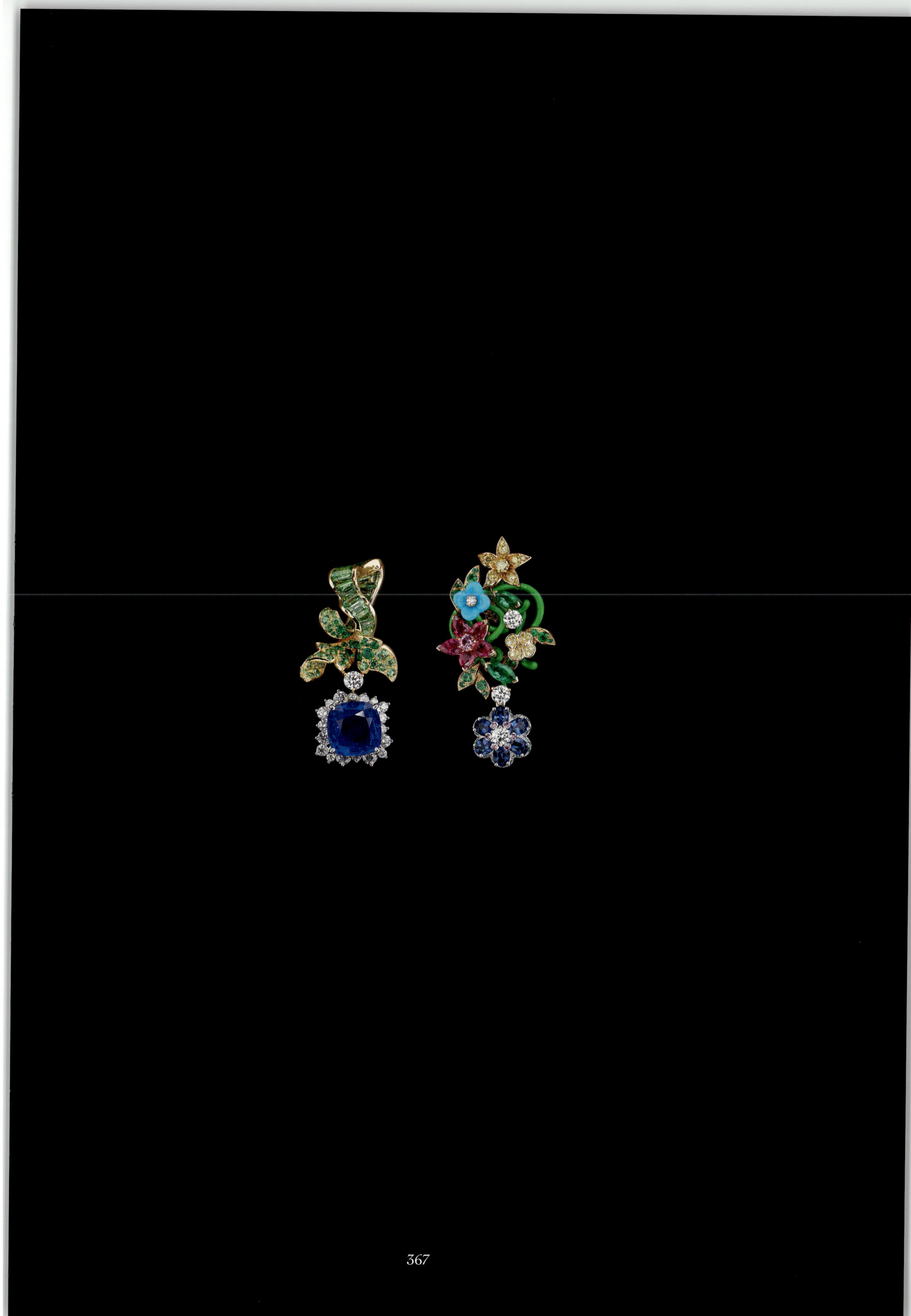

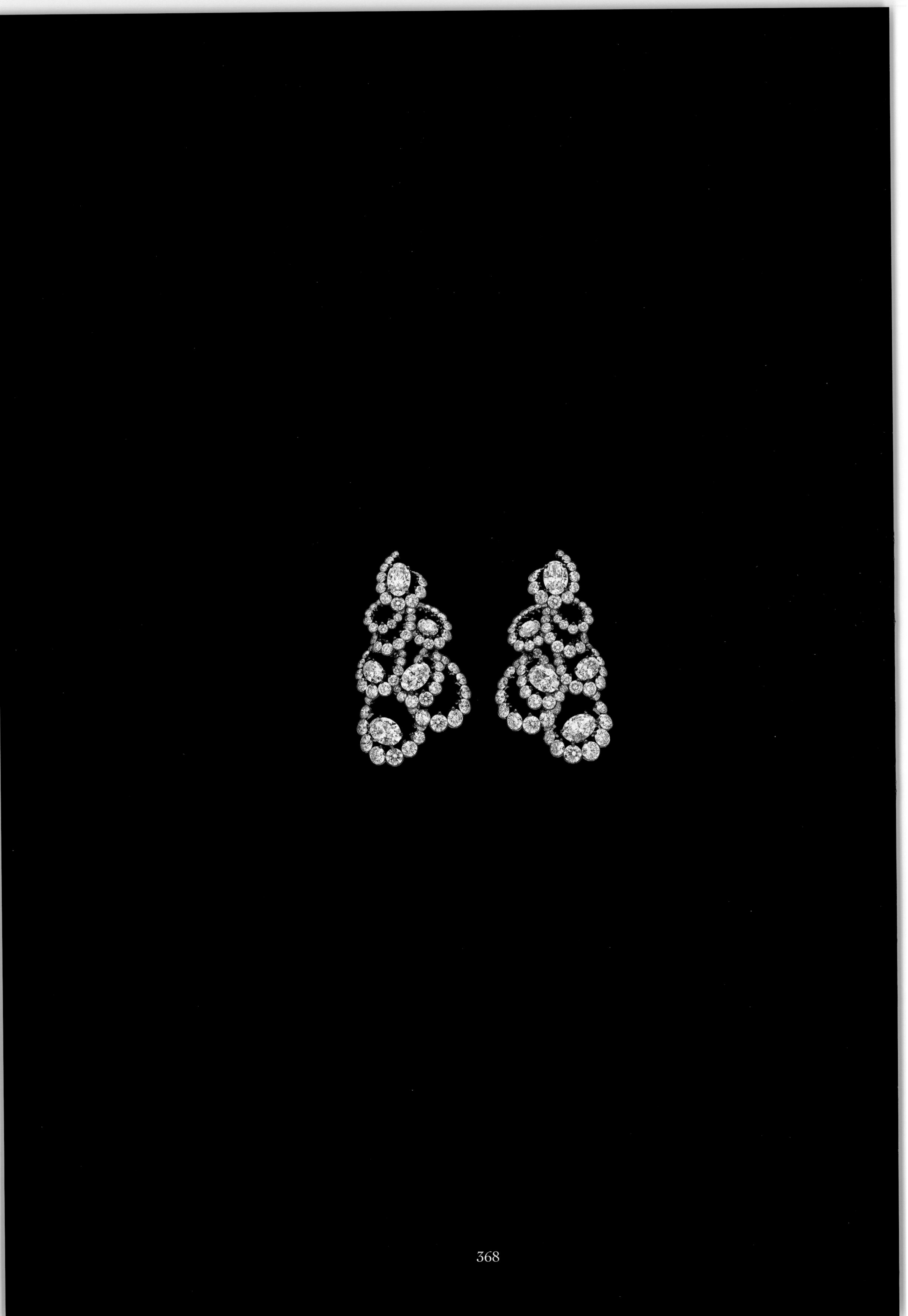

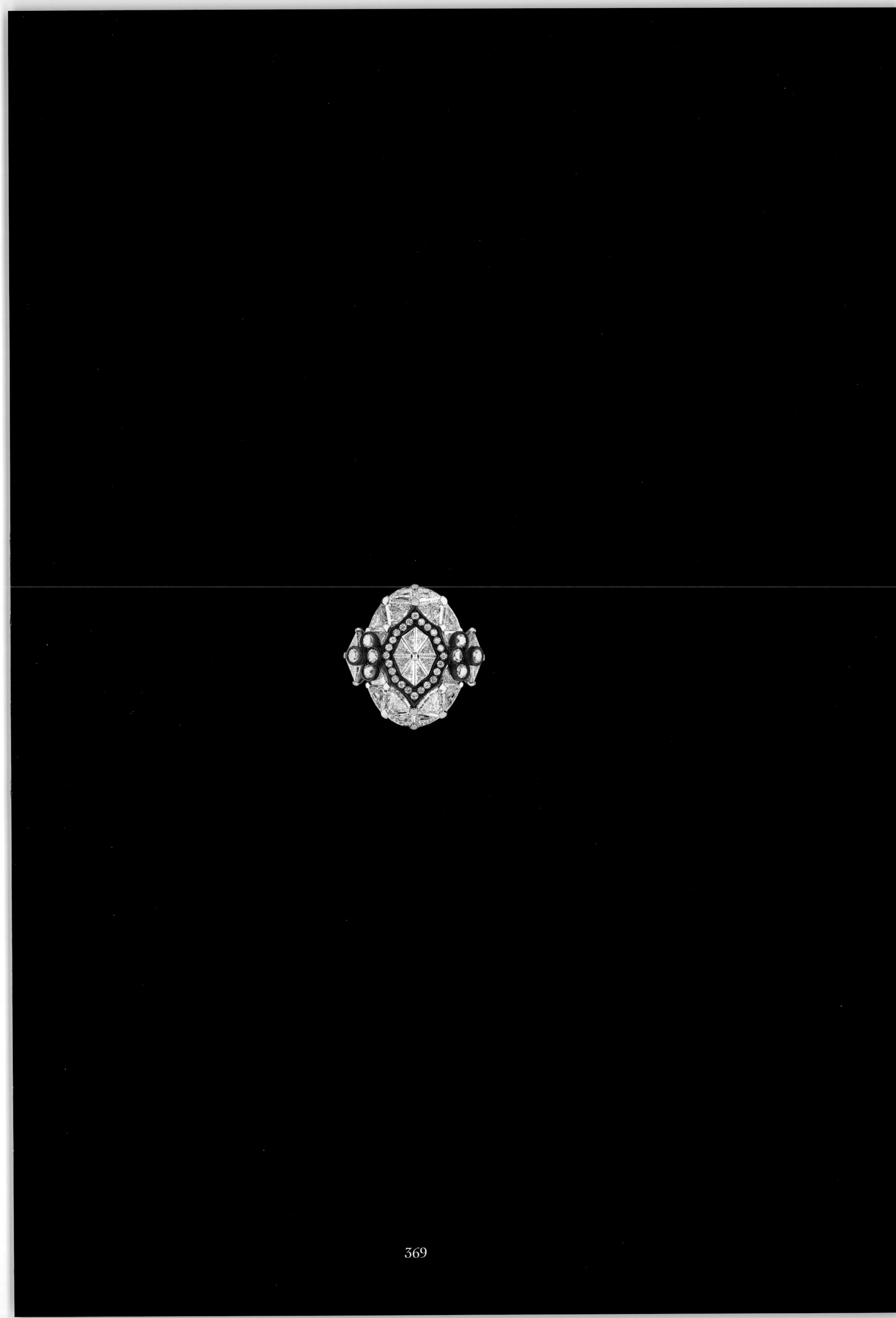

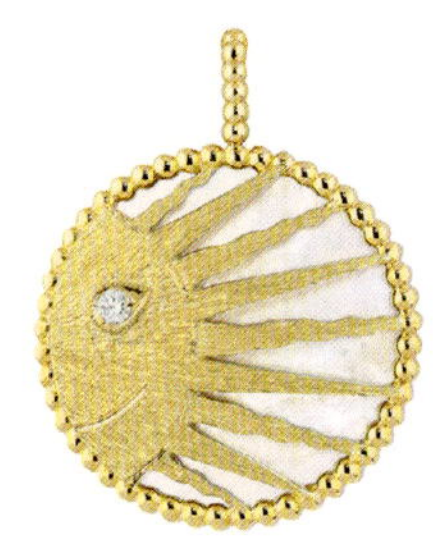

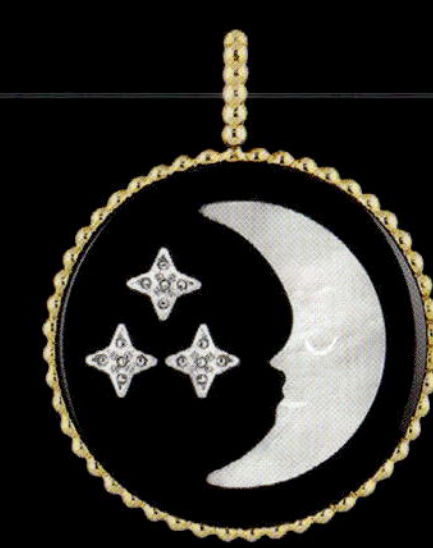

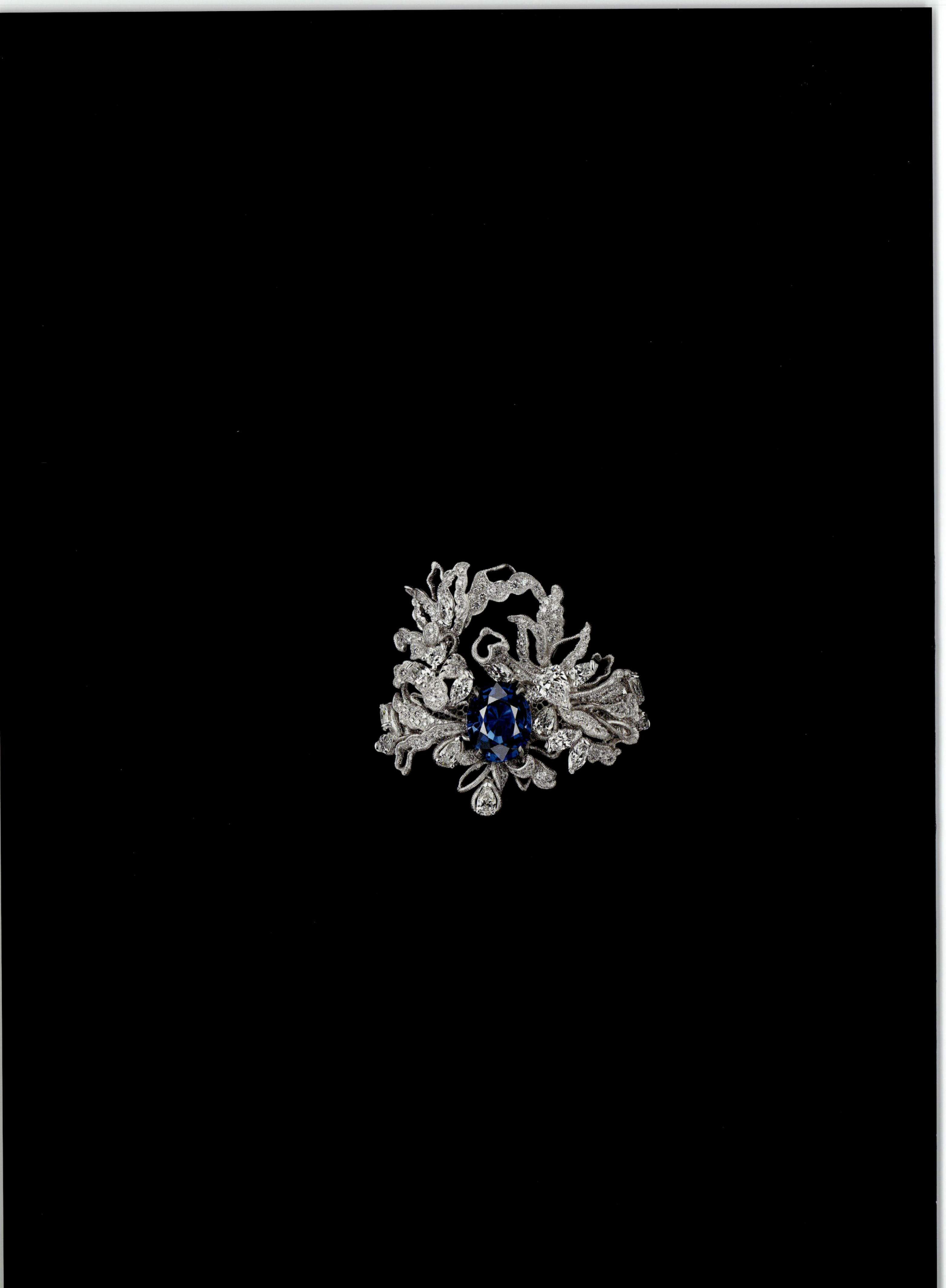

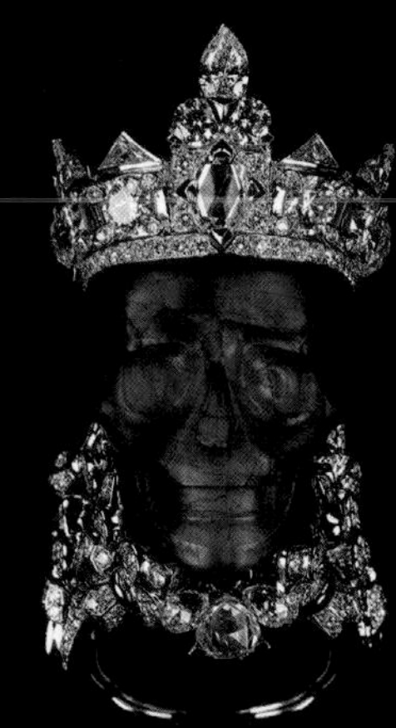

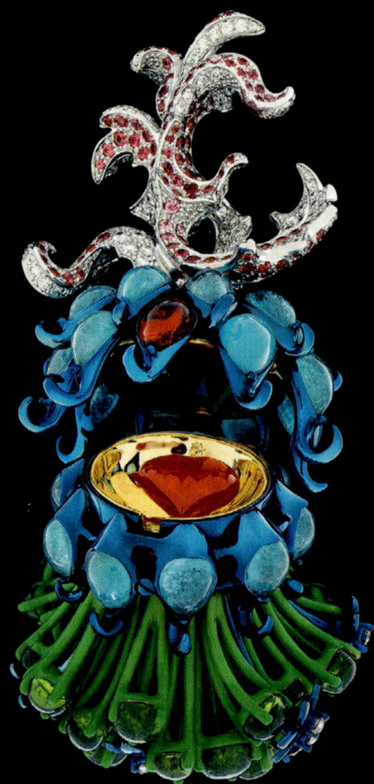

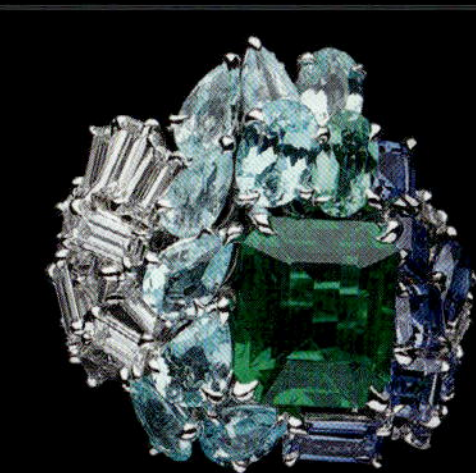

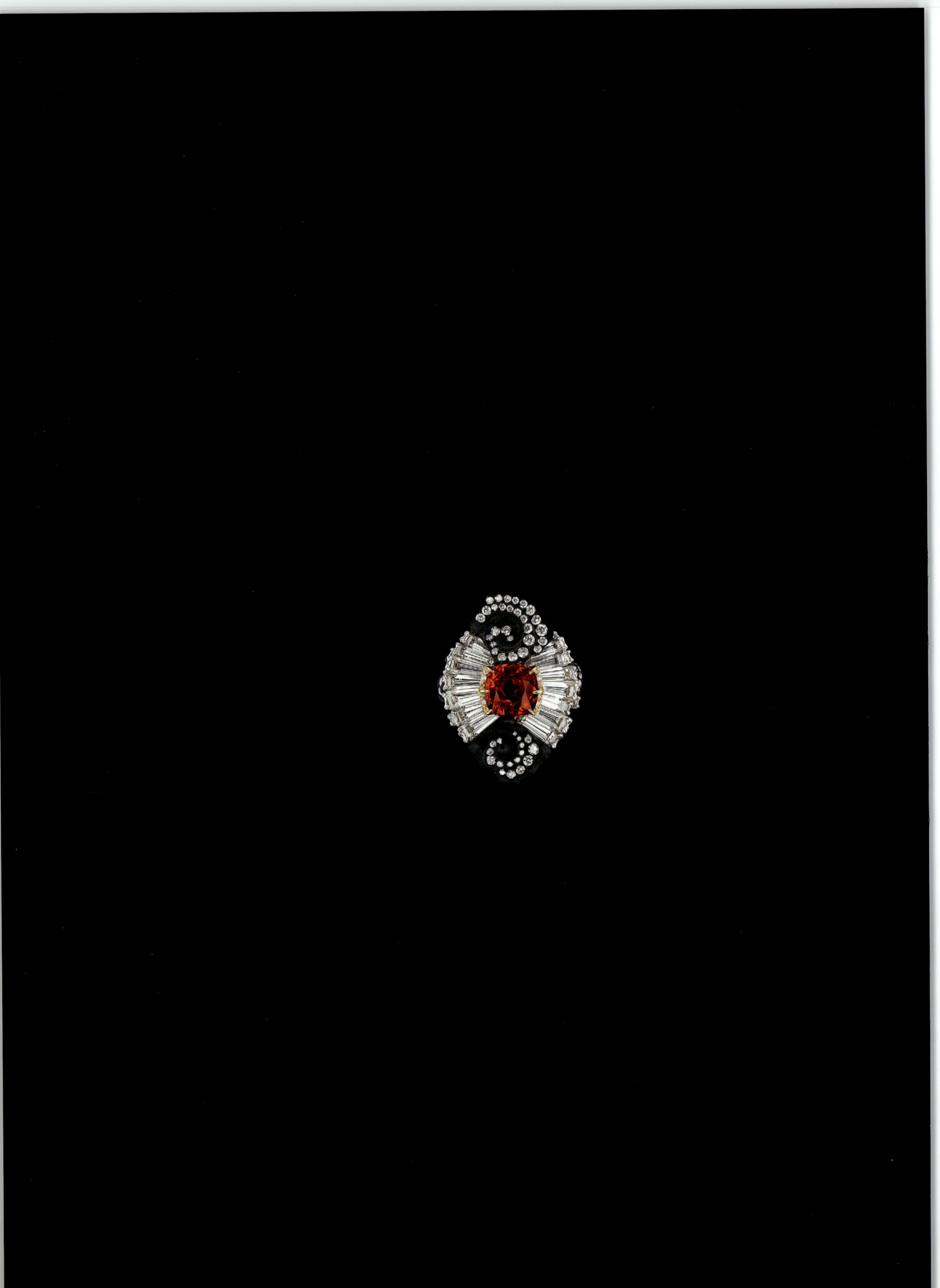

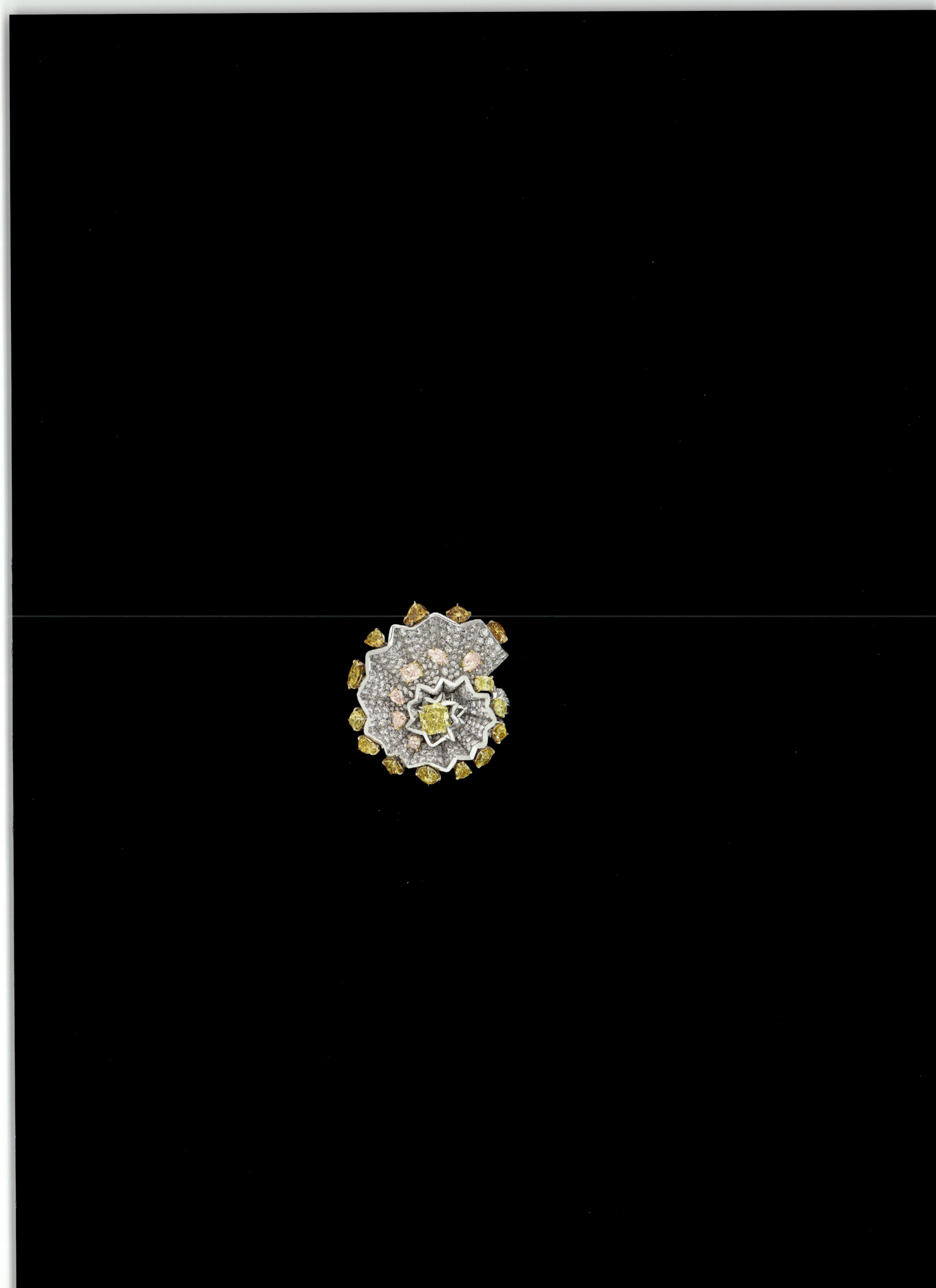

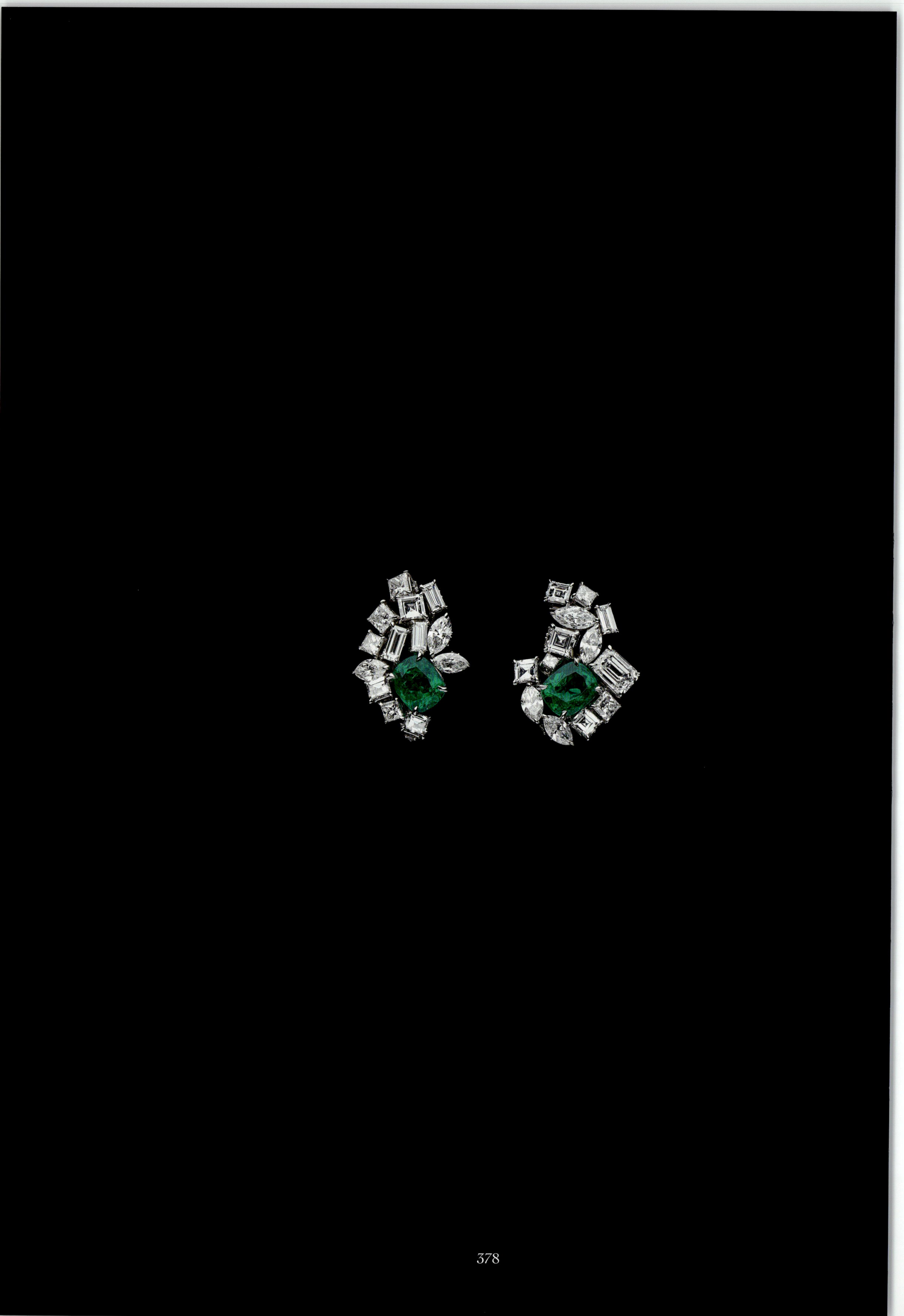

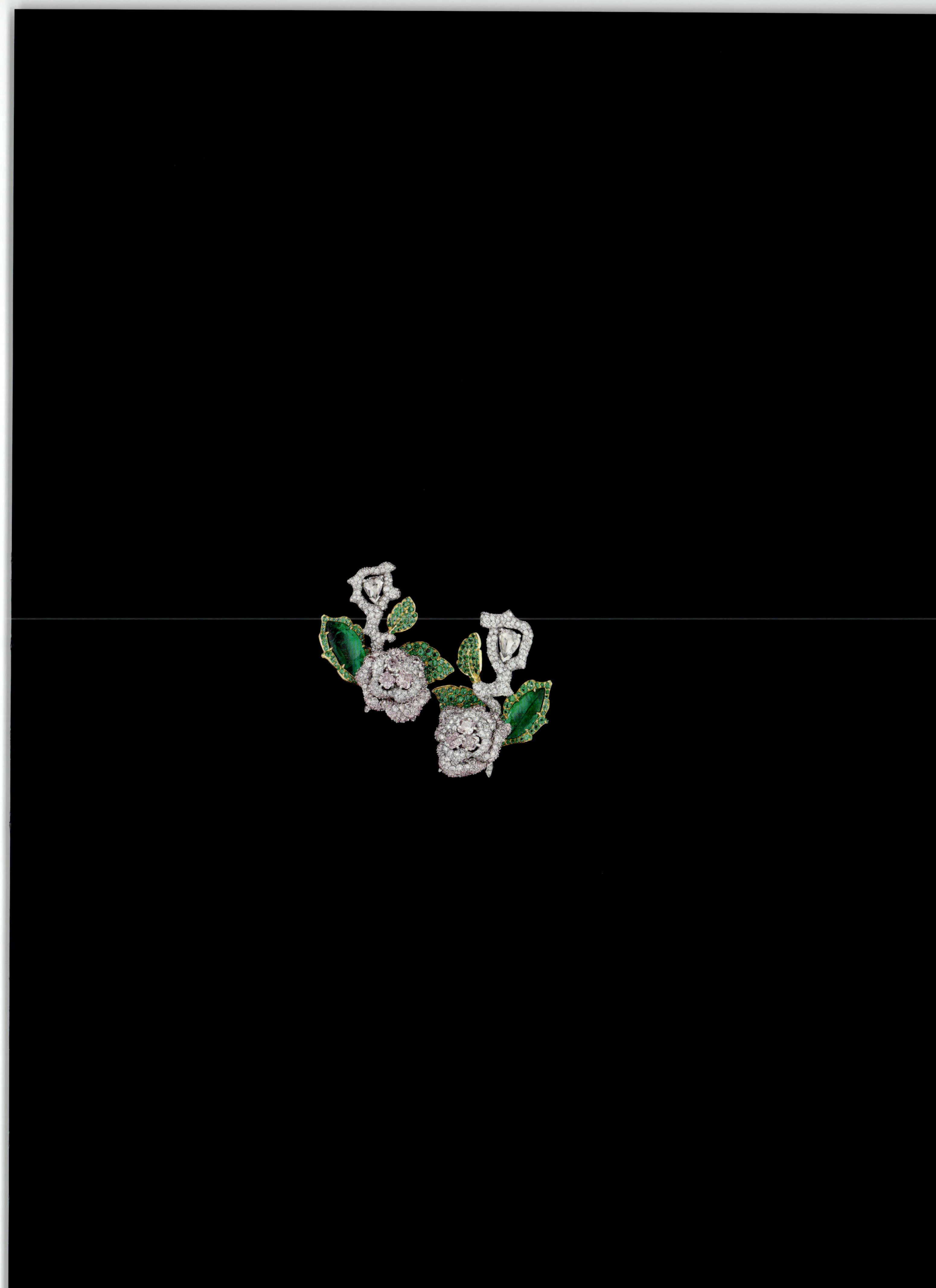

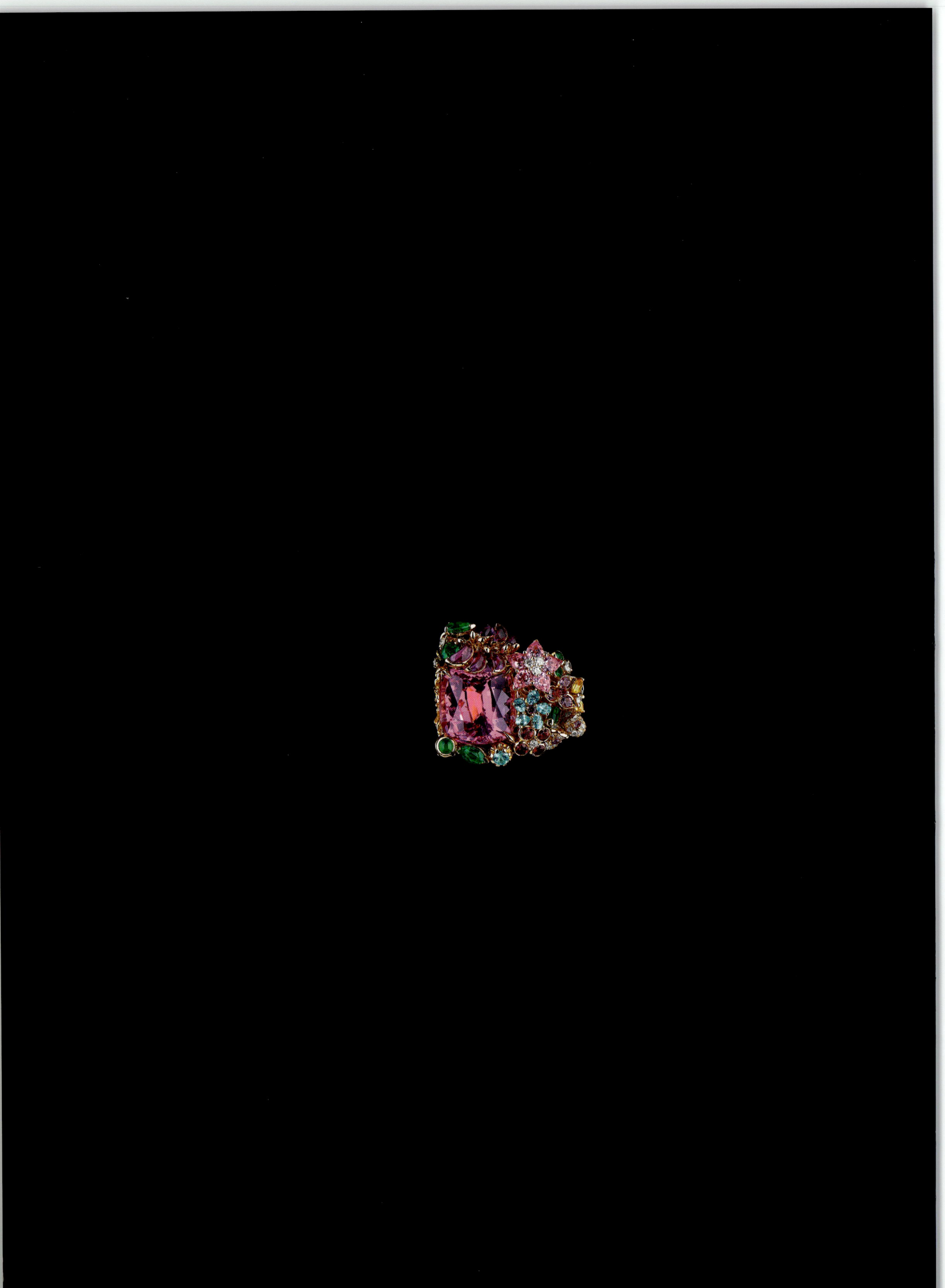

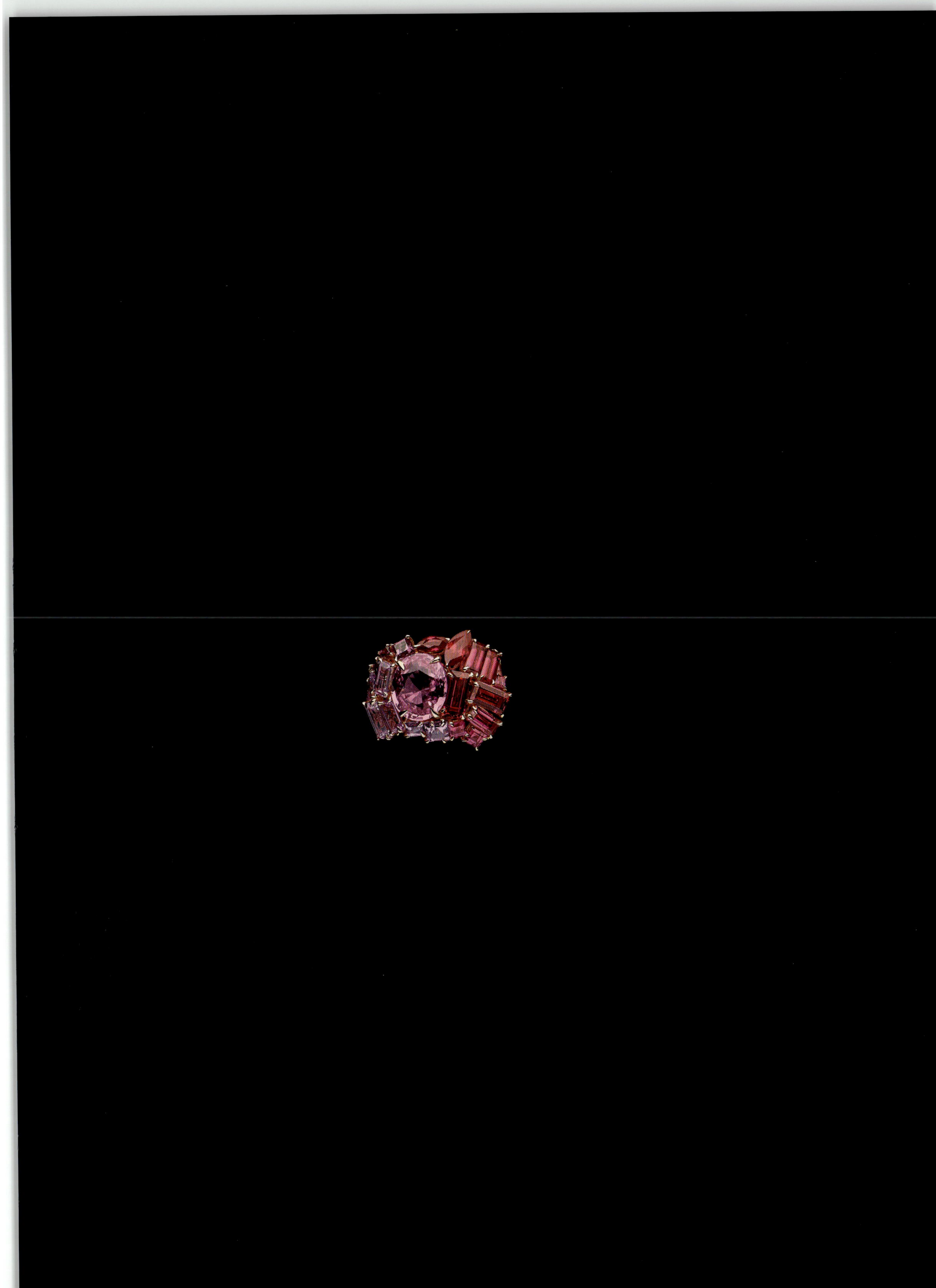

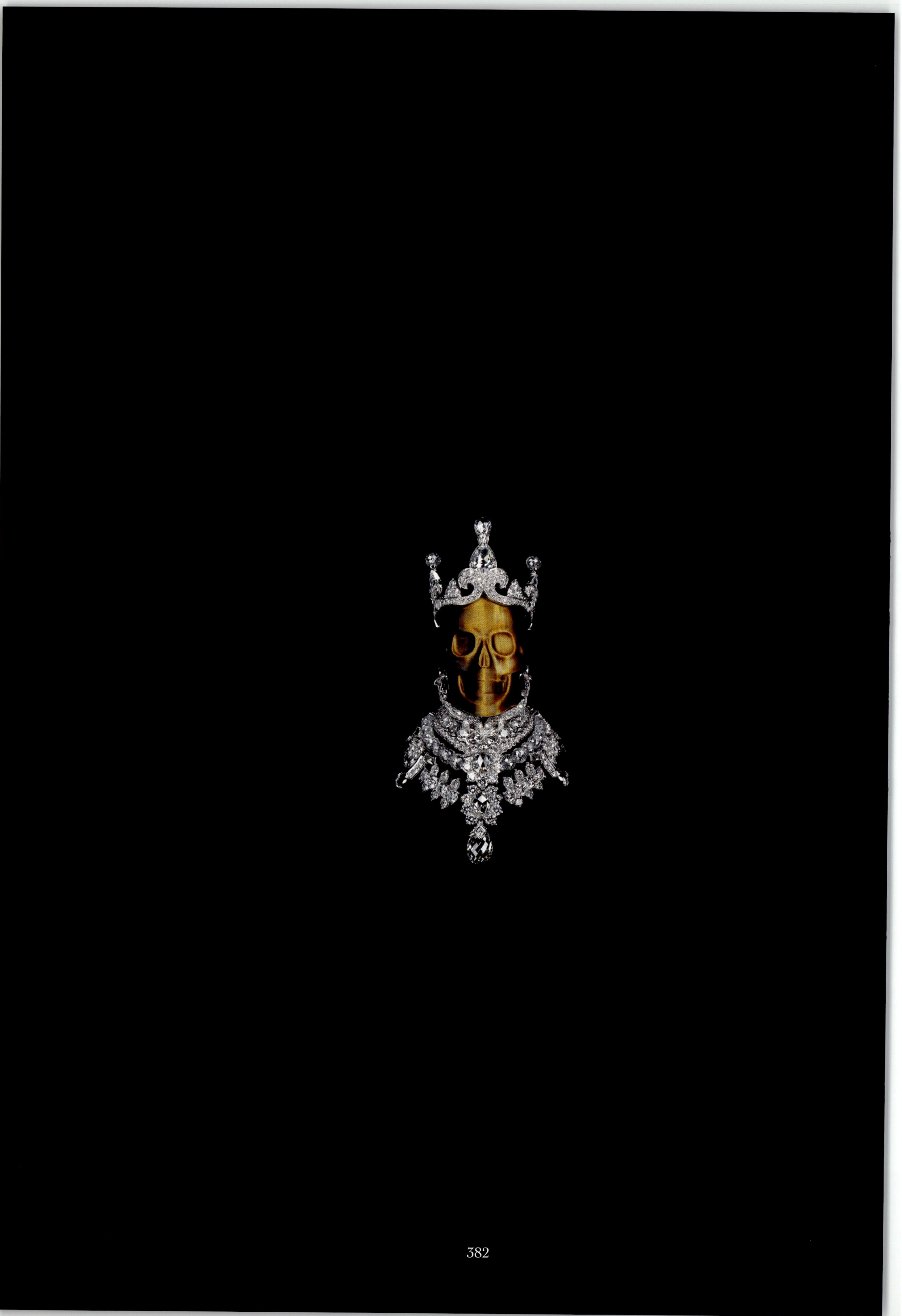

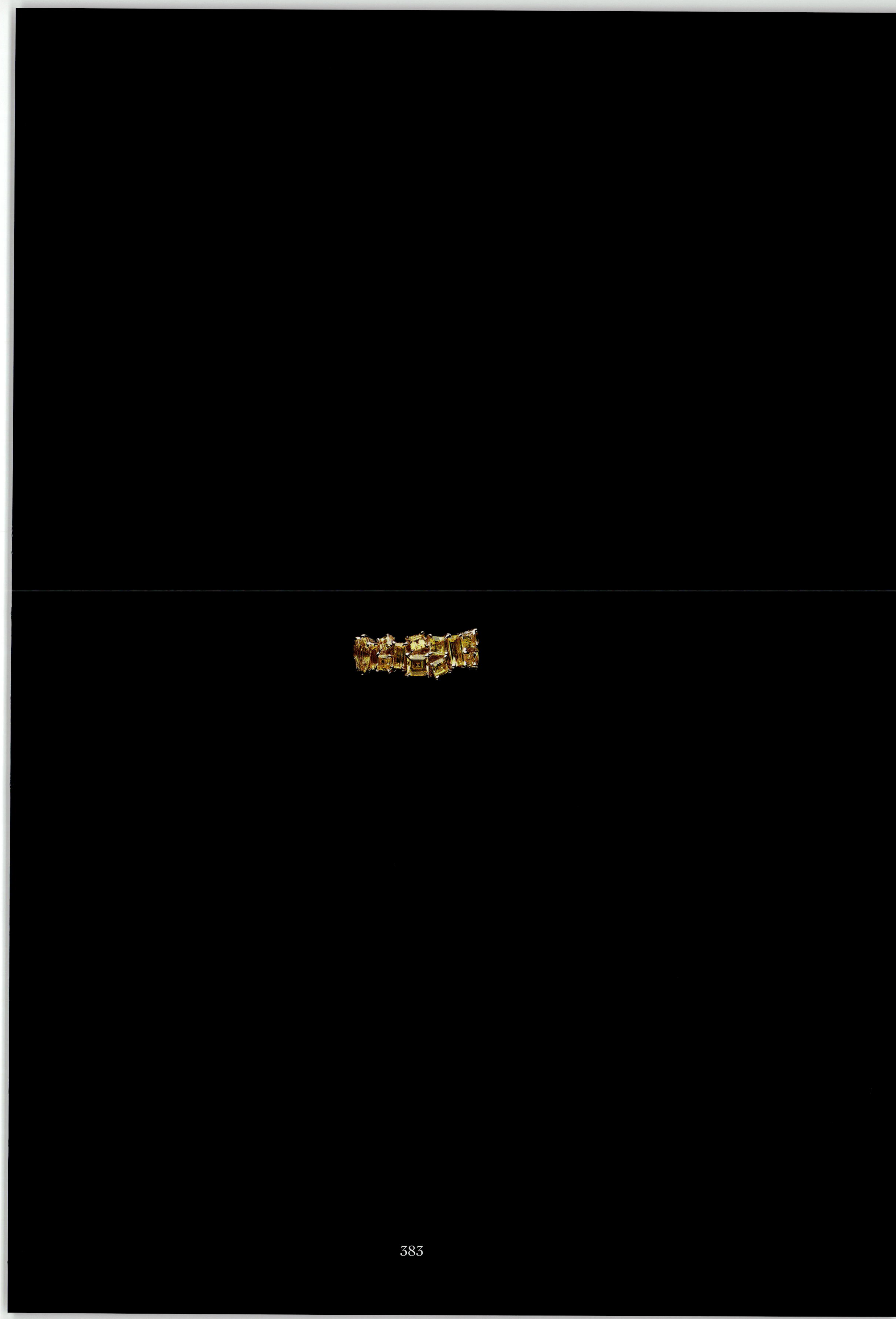

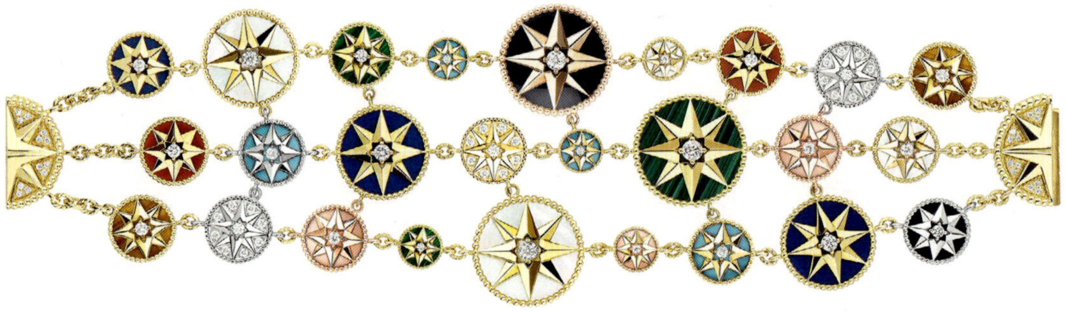

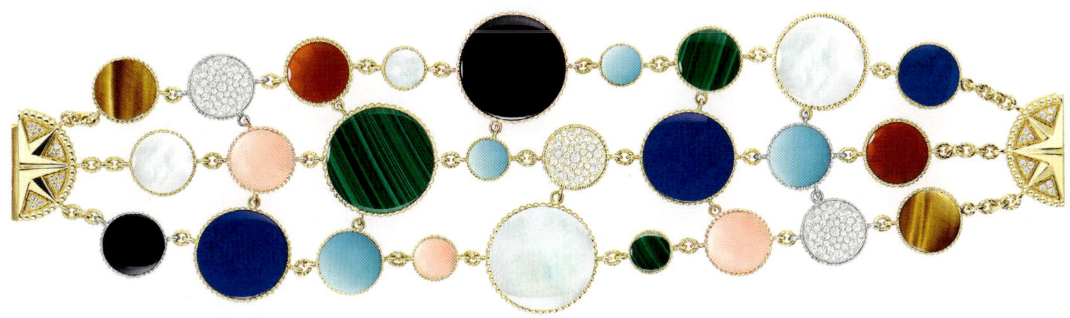

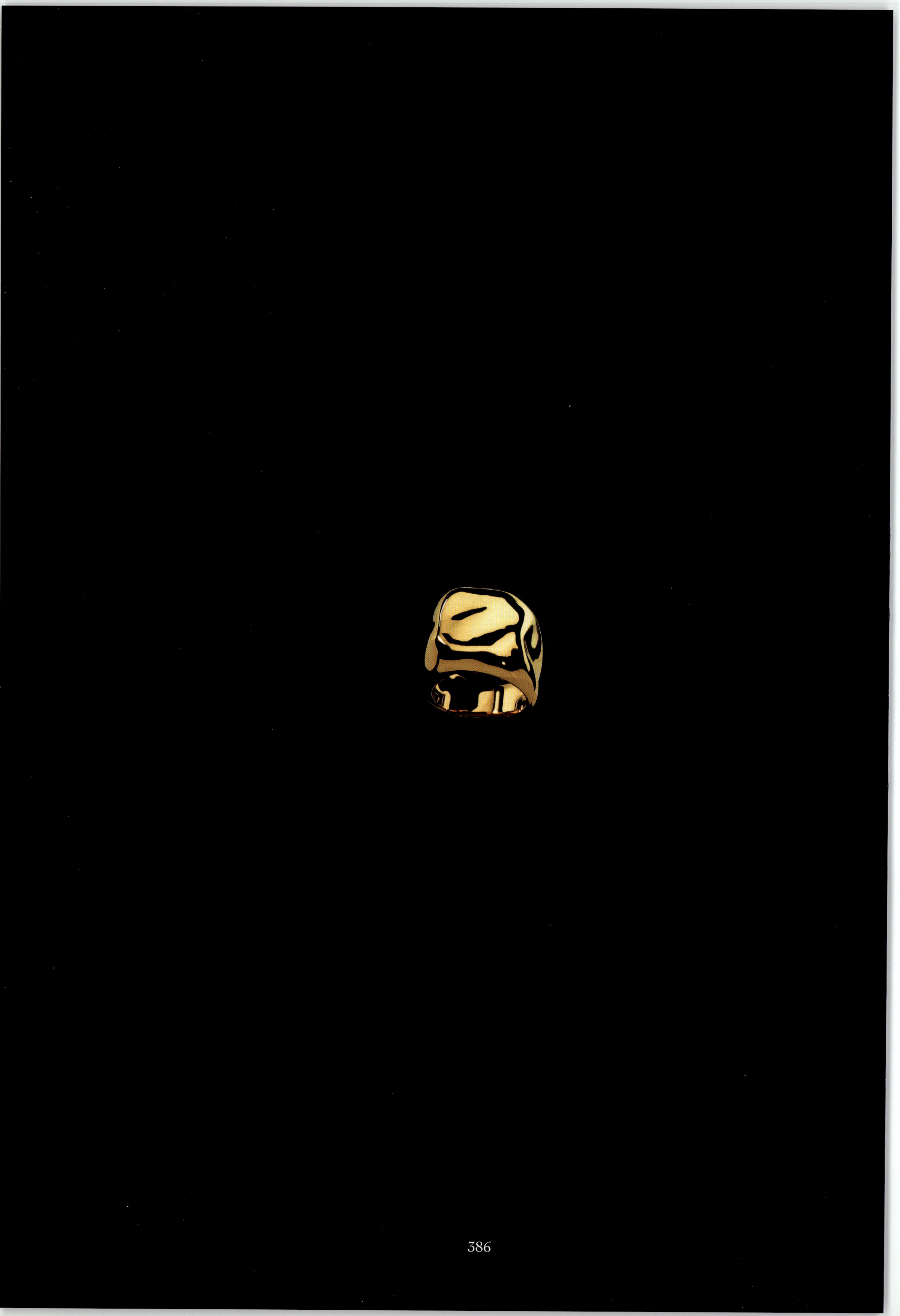

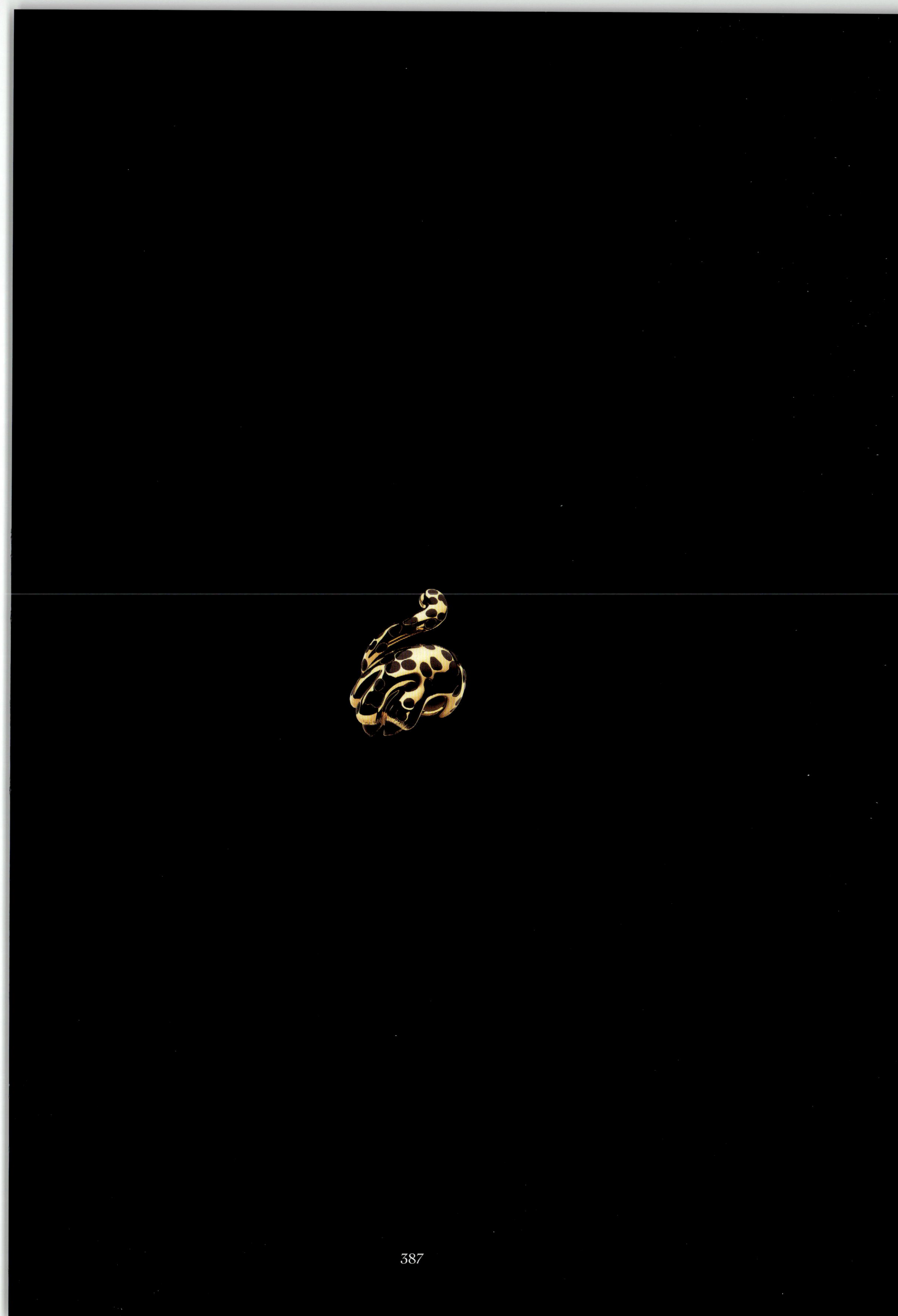

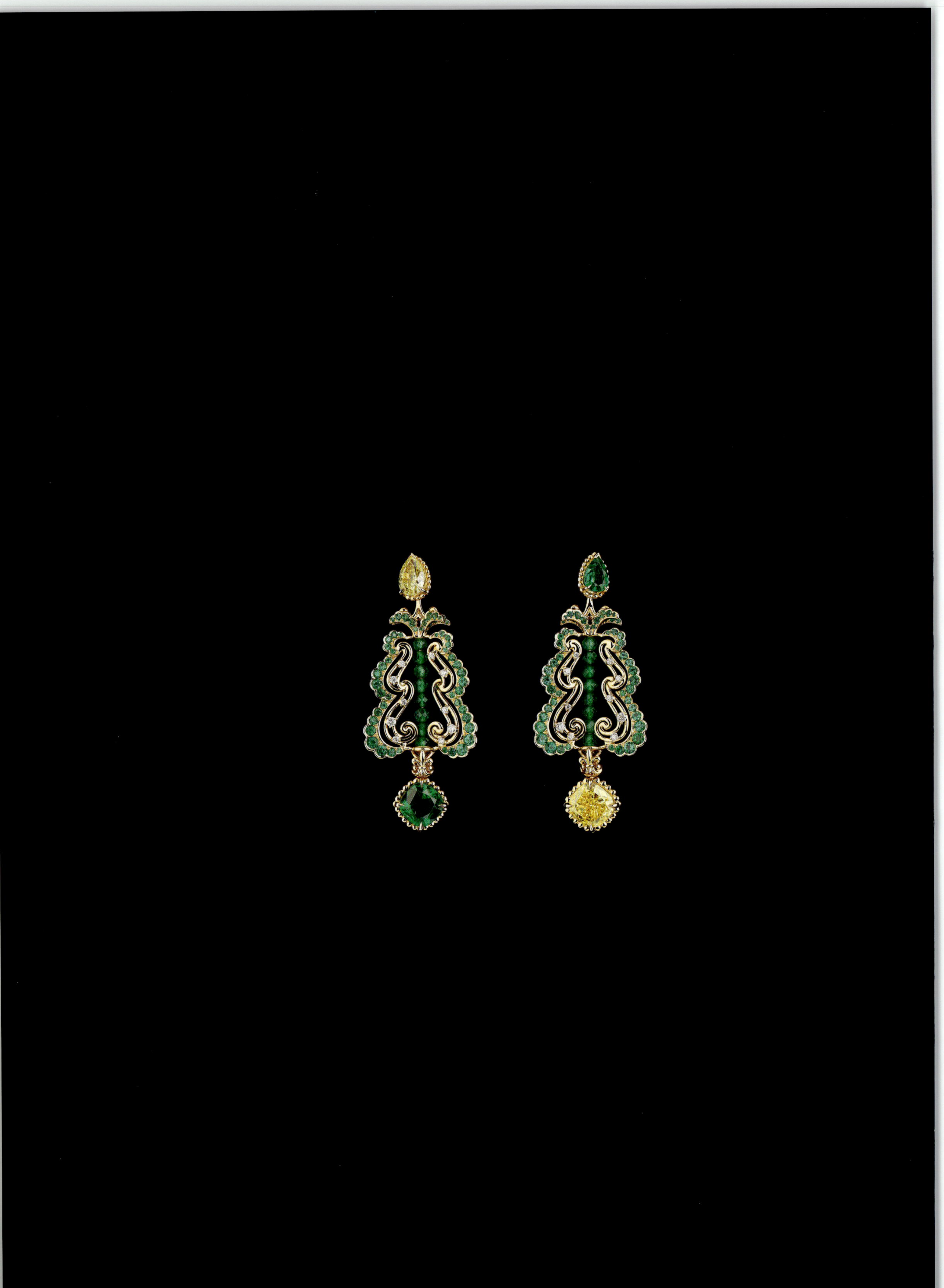

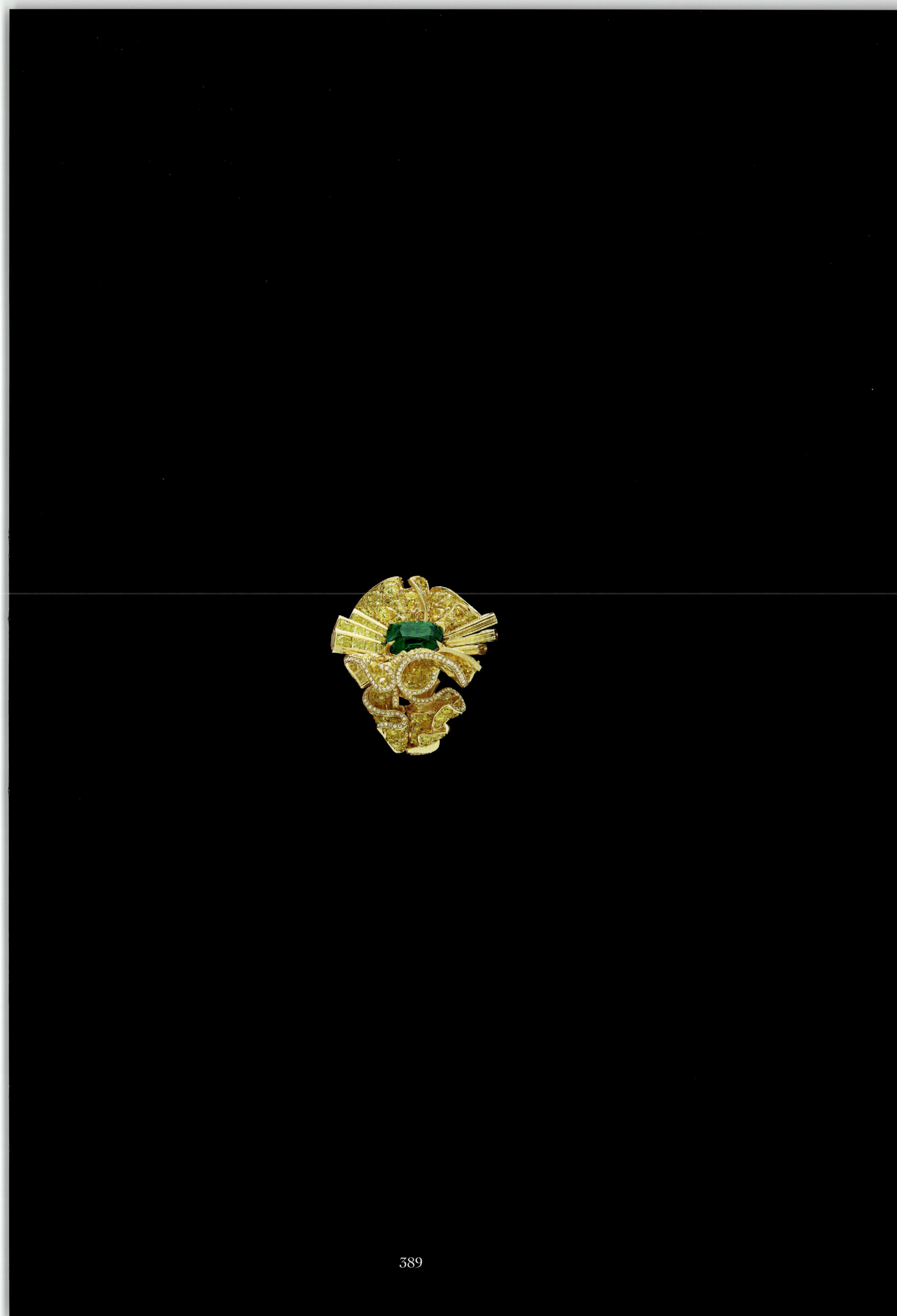

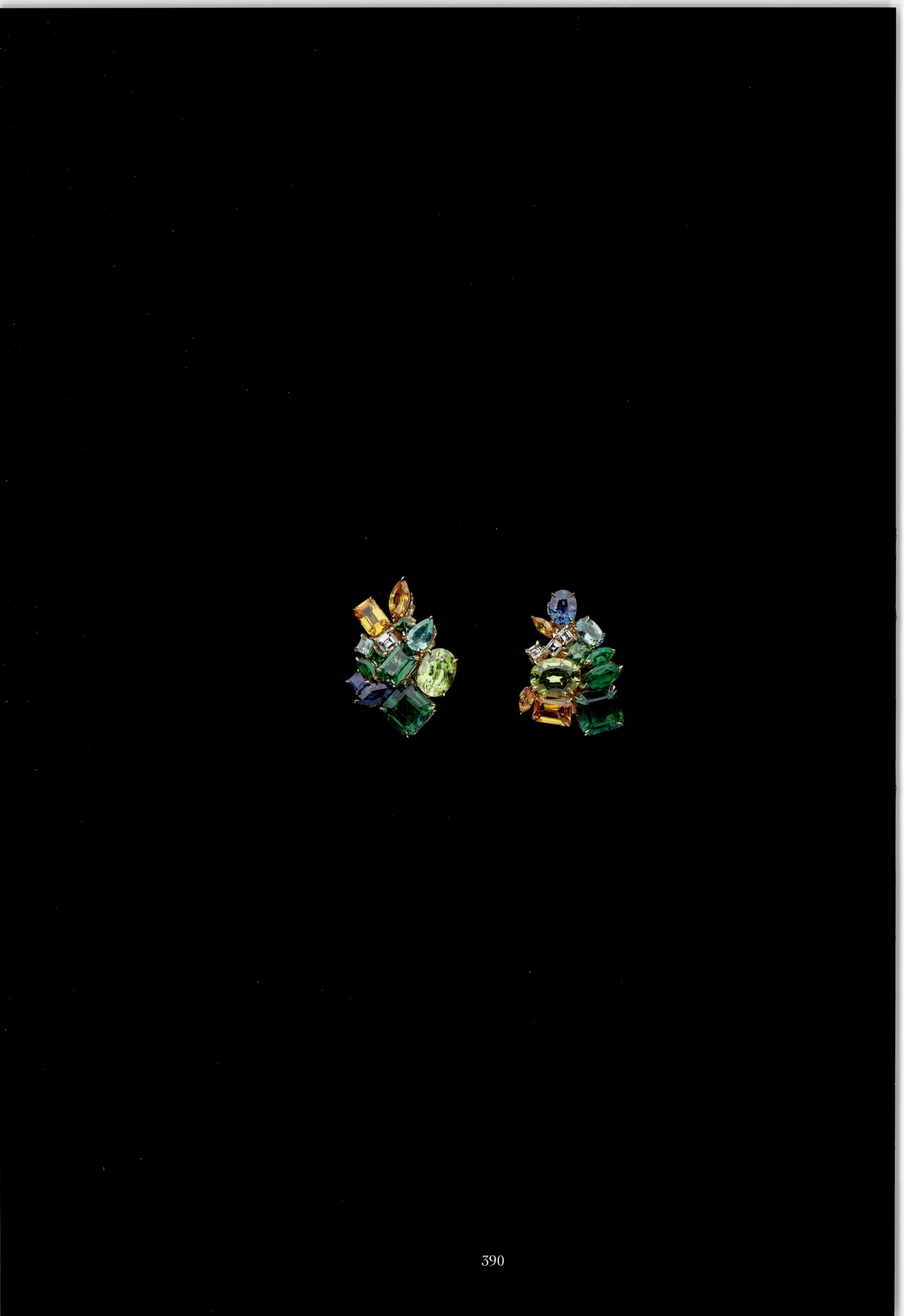

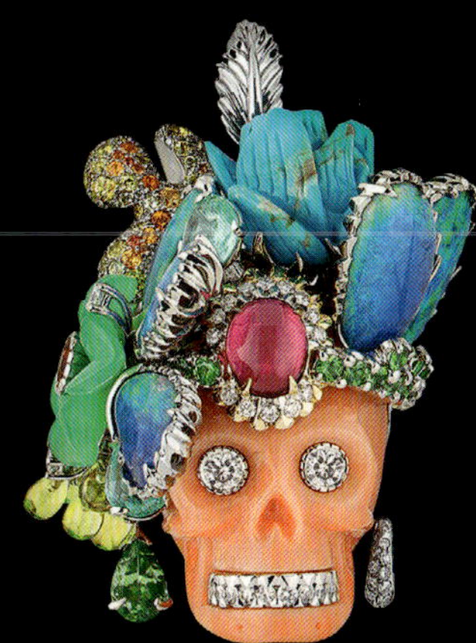

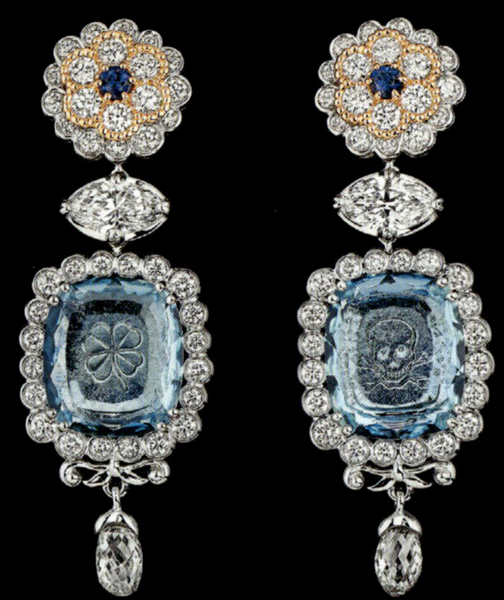

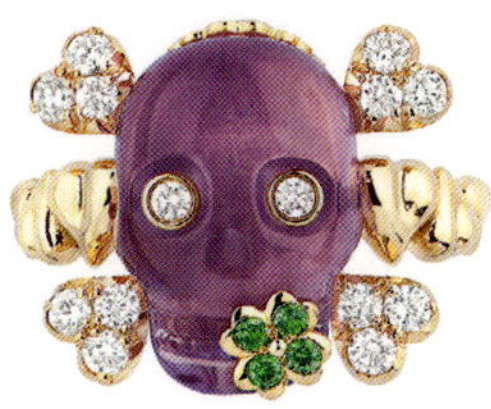

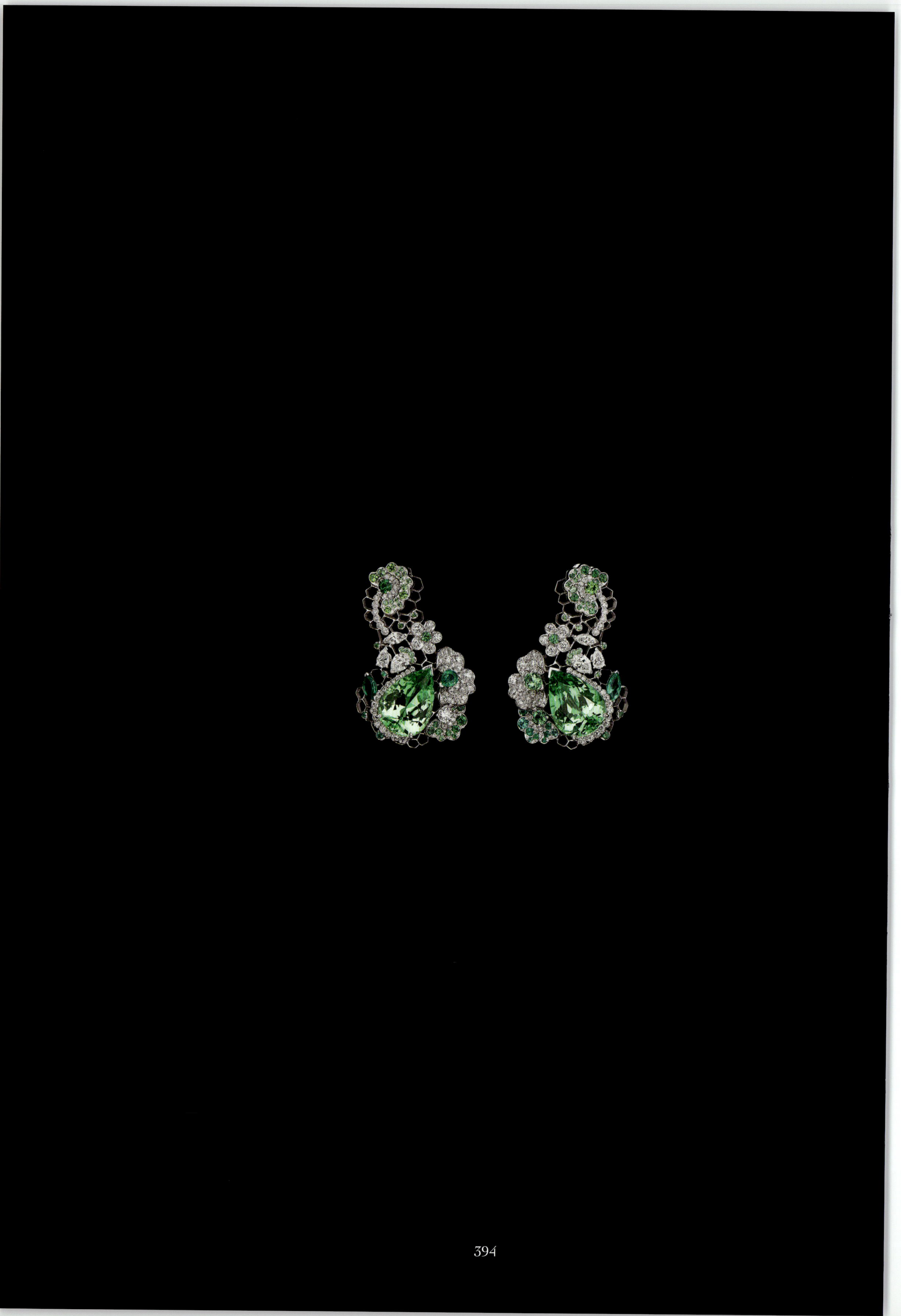

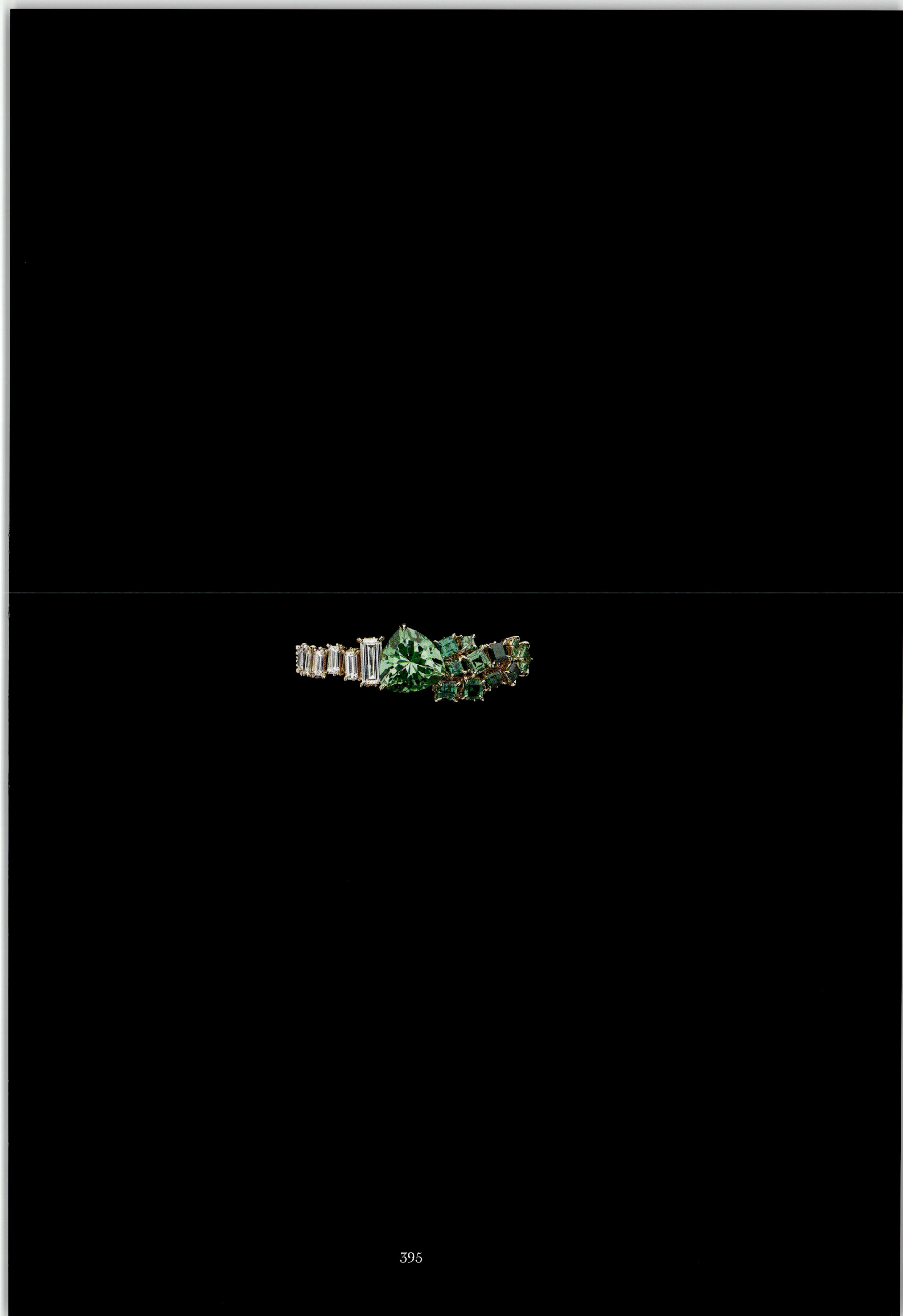

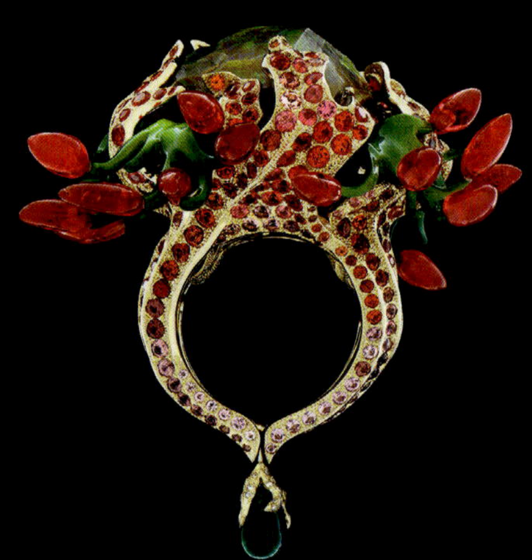

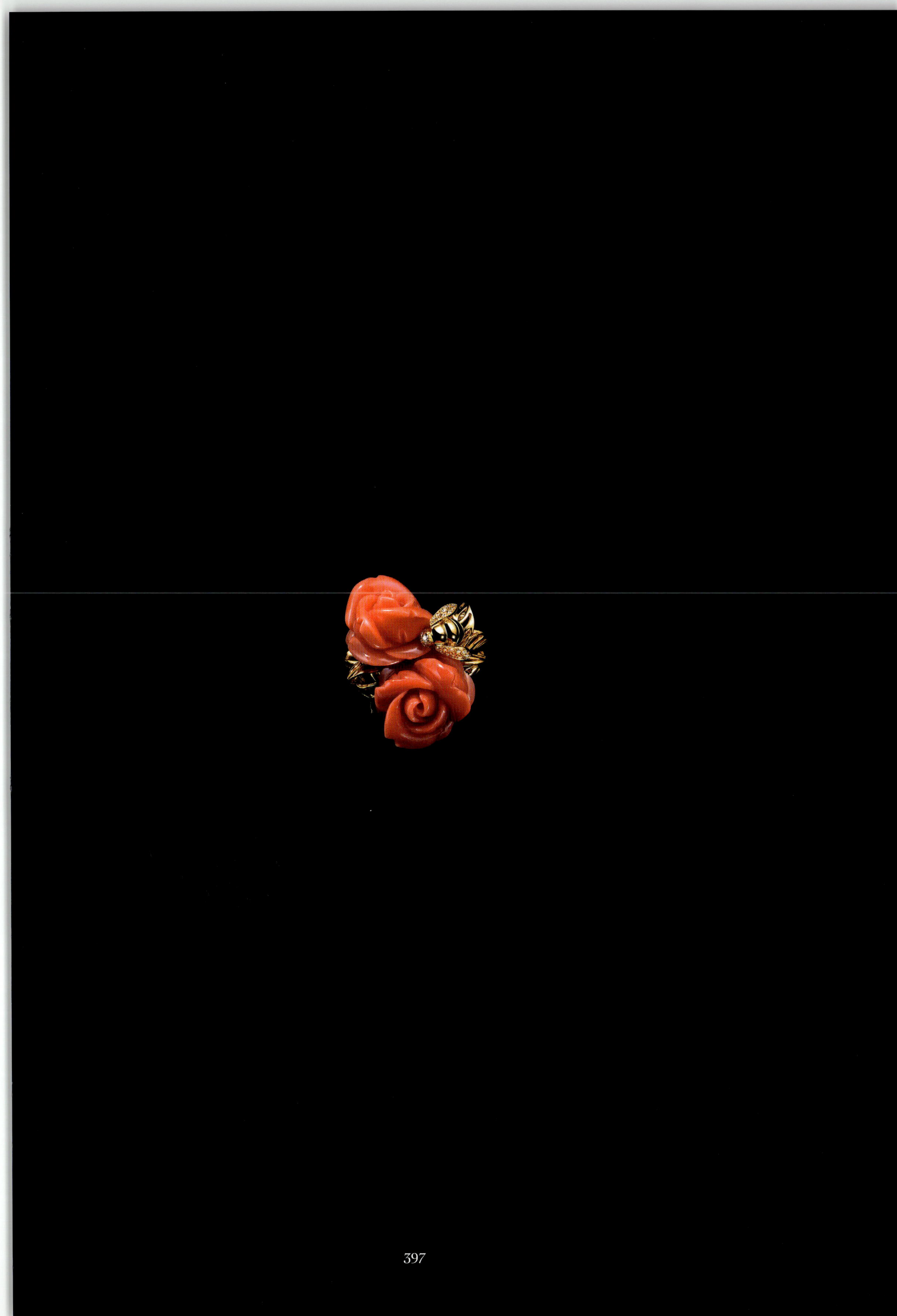

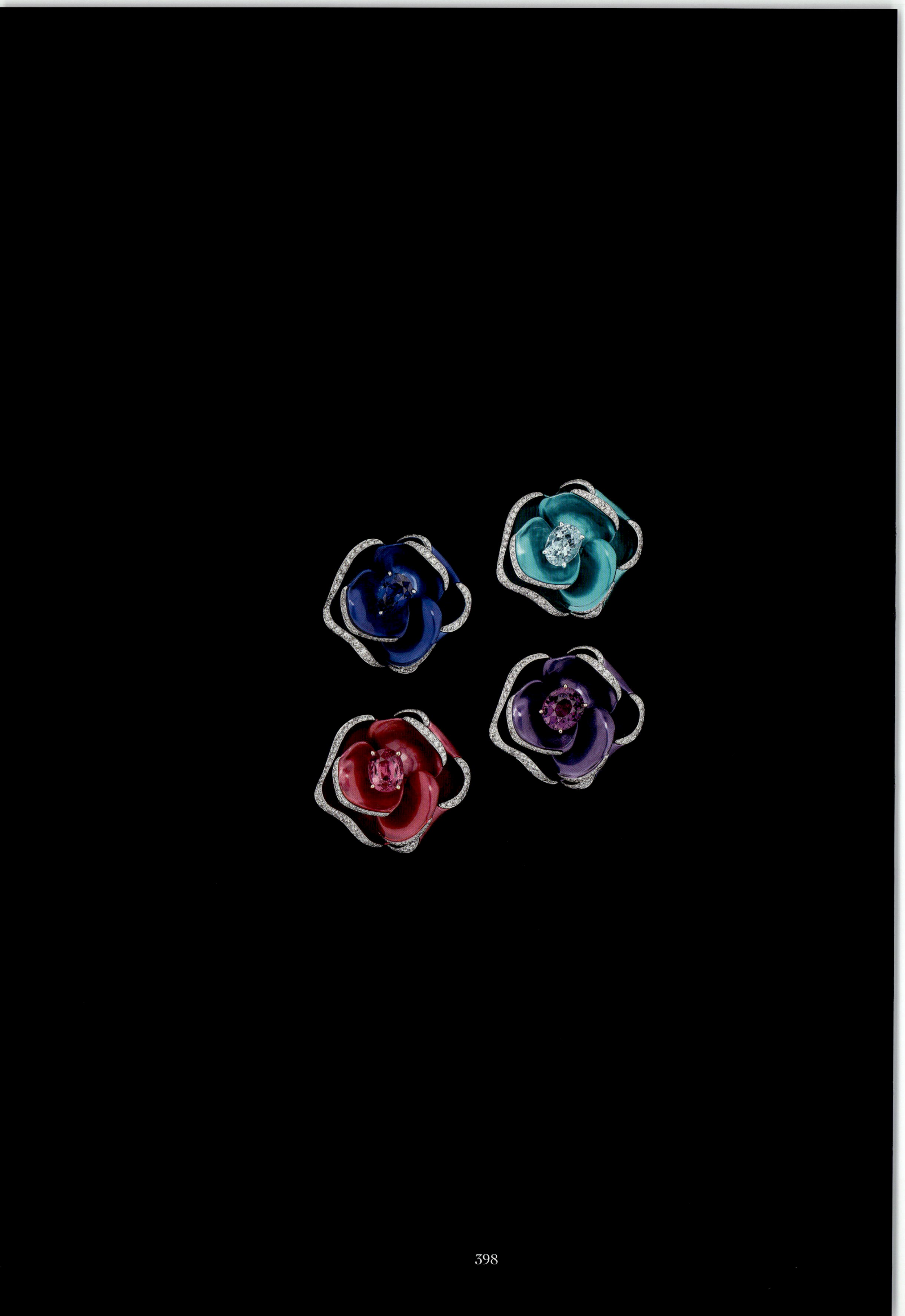

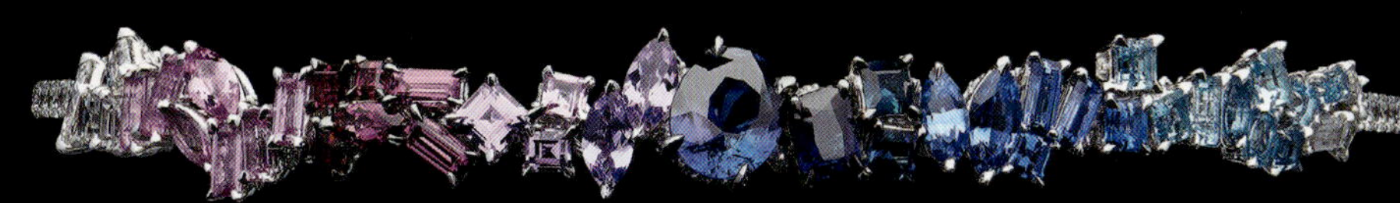

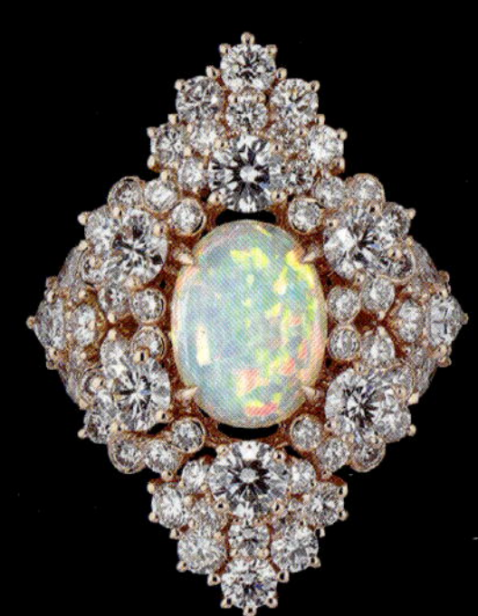

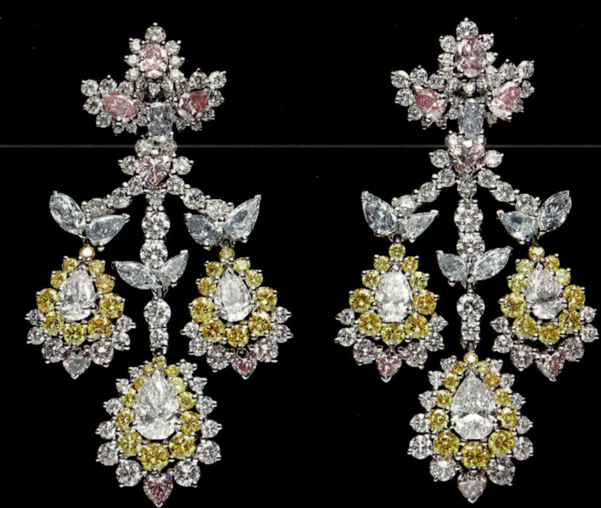

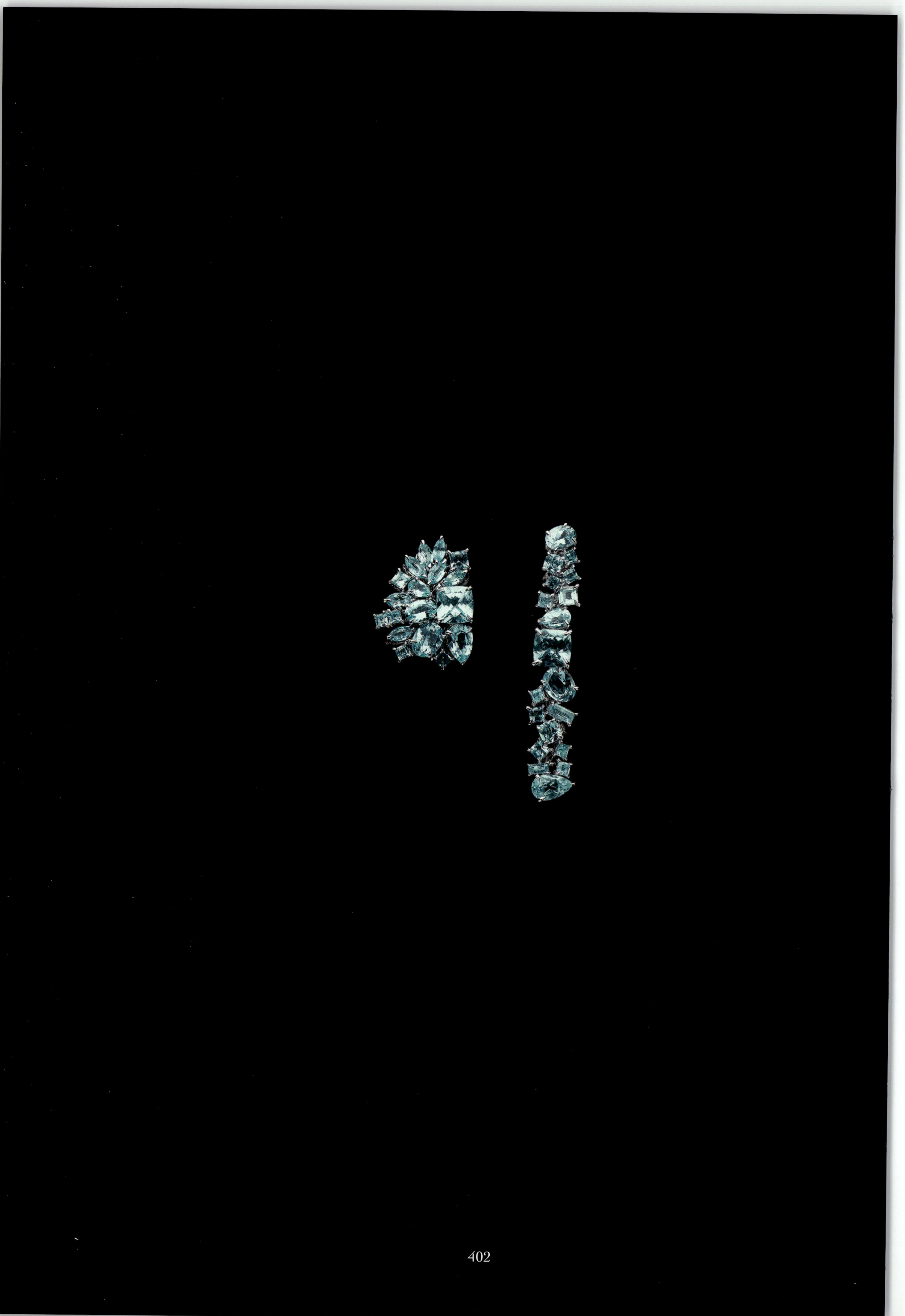

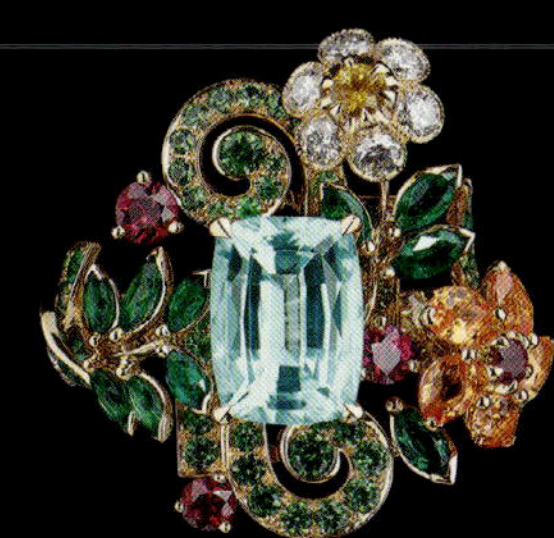

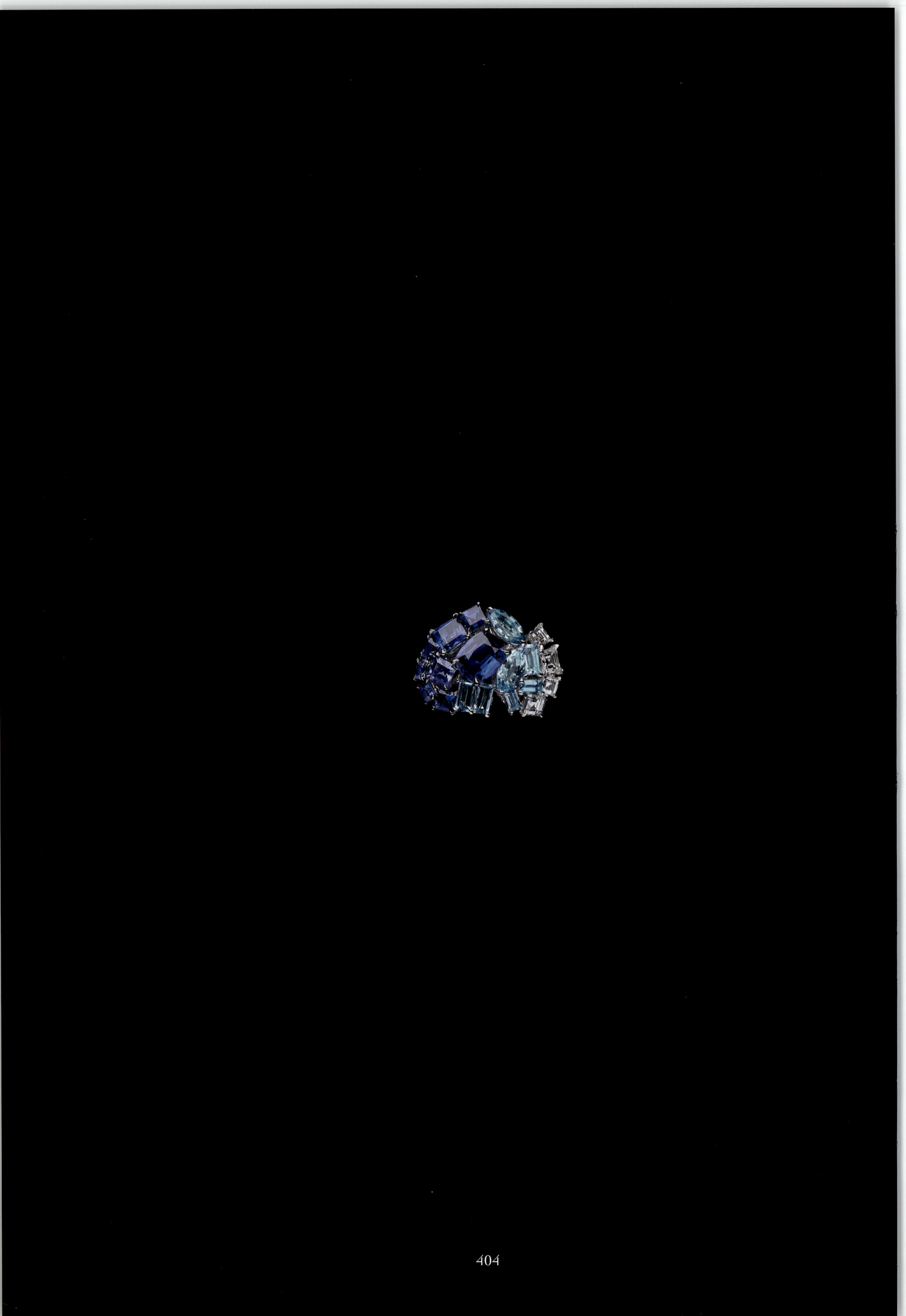

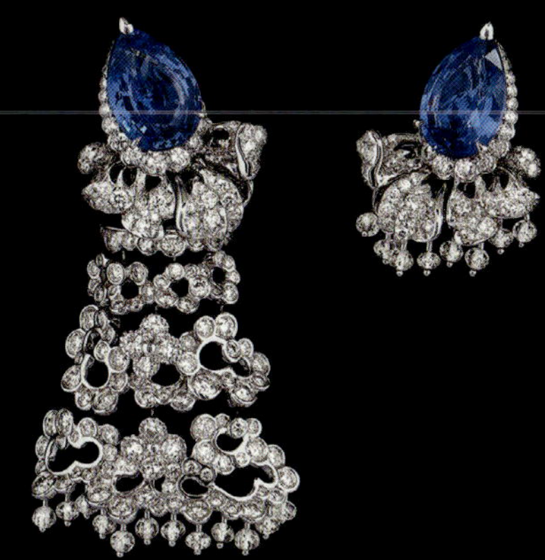

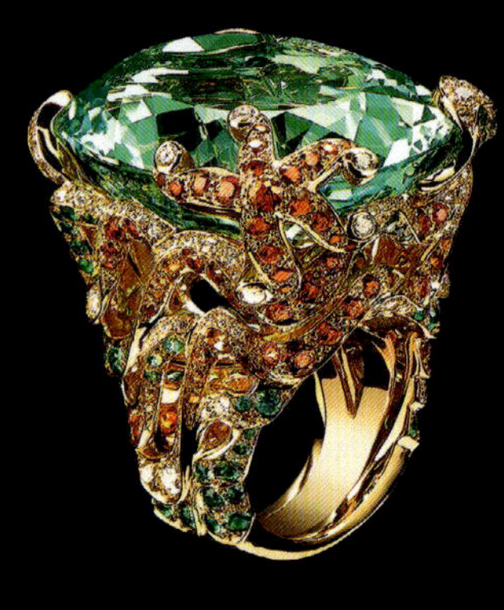

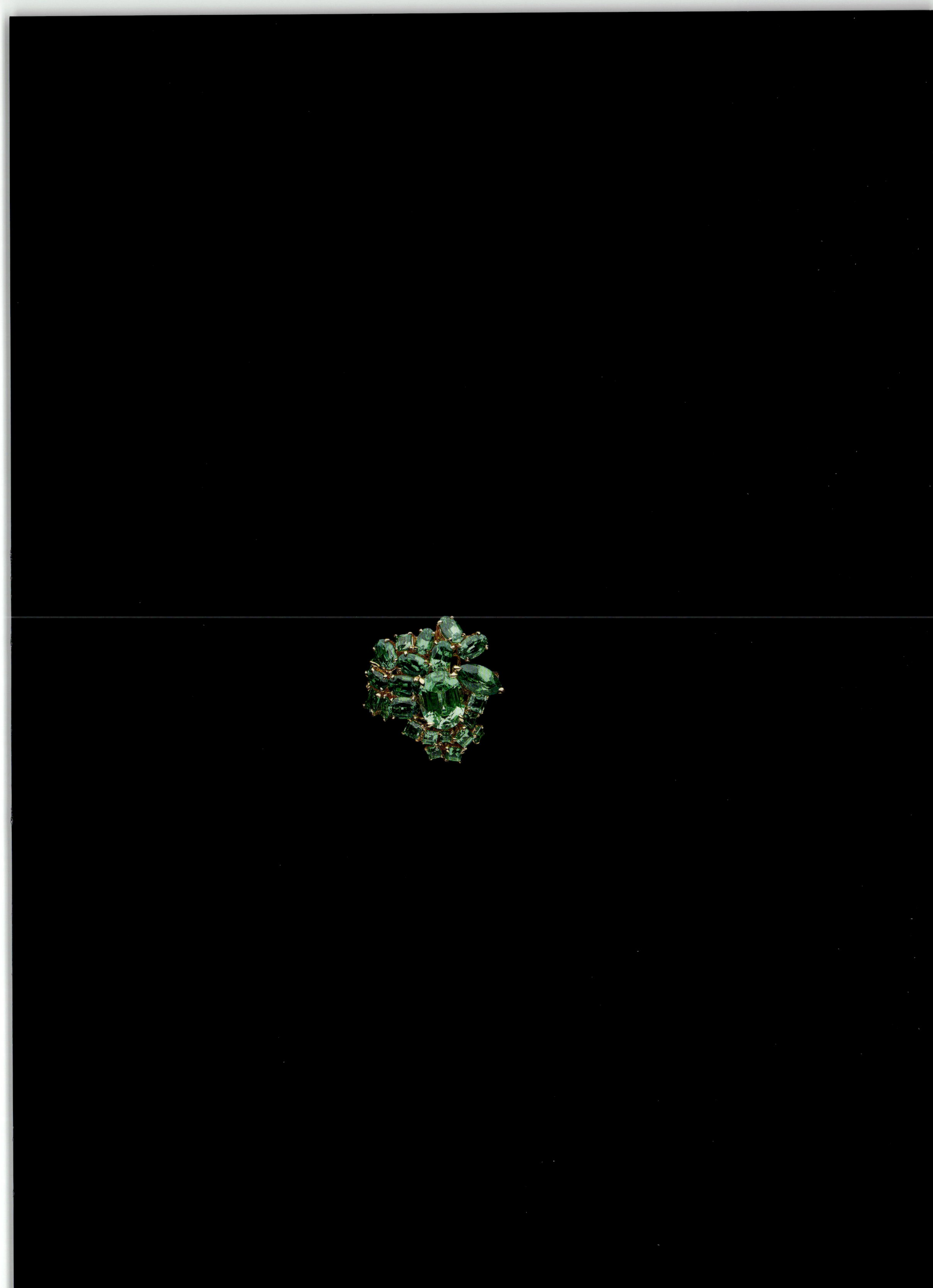

DESCRIPTIONS

105 – 6
Dracula Spinella Devorus ring,
Belladone Island collection, 2007.
White gold, diamonds, micro-crystallized chalcedony, spinels, and sapphires.

107
Salon de Mercure bracelet,
Dior à Versailles collection, 2016.
Pink gold, platinum, darkened silver, diamonds, and ruby.

108
Bosquet de la Salle de Bal Émeraude necklace,
Dior à Versailles, côté Jardins collection, 2017.
Yellow, white, and pink gold, platinum, diamonds, rock crystal, emeralds, pink and yellow sapphires, tsavorite and demantoid garnets, Paraiba-type tourmalines, pink spinels, sapphires, yellow diamonds, hauynes, spessartite garnets, peridots, and lacquer.

109
Vert Prairie Émeraude necklace,
Gem Dior collection, 2019.
Yellow gold, diamonds, emeralds, Paraiba-type tourmalines, tsavorite garnets, sapphires, chrysoberyls, and yellow sapphires.

110
Mimioui ring, *Mimioui* collection, 2001.
Yellow gold and diamond.

111
Roi Soleil necklace,
Roi Soleil collection, 1999.
Yellow gold, diamonds, yellow sapphires, and garnets.

112
Epinosa Verte ring,
Milly Carnivora collection, 2008.
White gold, diamonds, citrine, rubellite, amethyst, sapphires, tsavorite garnets, and lacquer.

113
Parterre du Midi Émeraude
High Jewellery timepiece,
Dior à Versailles, côté Jardins collection, 2017.
White, yellow, and pink gold, diamonds, emeralds, tsavorite garnets, sapphires, pink sapphires, indigolite tourmalines, spessartite garnets, yellow sapphires, rubies, Paraiba-type tourmaline, purple sapphires, peridots, turquoise, and blue chalcedonies. Quartz movement.

114
Bosquet de l'Encelade Opale Noire bracelet,
Dior à Versailles, côté Jardins collection, 2017.
White, pink, and yellow gold, diamonds, rock crystal, black opal, emeralds, spessartite and tsavorite garnets, sapphires, pink spinels, yellow sapphires, red spinels, Paraiba-type tourmalines, yellow diamond, and turquoise.

115
Dentelle Opale d'Orient bracelet,
Dear Dior collection, 2012.
Yellow gold, platinum, diamonds, black opal, pink-red spinels, spessartite and tsavorite garnets, tanzanites, and rubies.

116
Coffret de Victoire ring,
Coffret de Victoire collection, 2003.
White gold, diamonds, coral, cultured pearls, spinels, moonstone, iolites, and Paraiba tourmalines.

117
Rose Jacinthe Rubis earrings,
Gem Dior collection, 2019.
White gold, diamonds,
rubies, and pink sapphires.

118
Arabesque ring,
Dior à Versailles collection, 2016.
Pink and yellow gold, platinum,
darkened silver, diamonds, and emerald.

119
Dénoué Saphir bracelet,
Soie Dior collection, 2015.
White and yellow gold, diamonds,
emeralds, and sapphire.

120
Bosquet de la Salle de Bal Rubis bracelet,
Dior à Versailles, côté Jardins collection, 2017.
Yellow gold, diamonds, rock crystal,
emeralds, rubies, pink sapphires, mandarin
garnets, sapphires, tsavorite garnets, yellow
diamonds, purple and yellow sapphires,
demantoid and spessartite garnets,
turquoise, and lacquer.

121
Multicolore Anglais Rubis ring,
Gem Dior collection, 2019.
Yellow gold, diamonds, ruby, sapphires,
spessartite and tsavorite garnets,
pink sapphires, purple garnets, emeralds,
and yellow sapphire.

122
Rose des Vents bracelet,
Rose des Vents collection, 2015.
Yellow gold, diamond, and mother-of-pearl.

123
Salon d'Apollon bracelet,
Dior à Versailles collection, 2016.
Darkened silver, pink, yellow, and white
gold, diamonds, and yellow diamonds.

124
Rose Fushia Spinelle Rose double ring,
Gem Dior collection, 2019.
White gold, diamonds, and pink spinels.

125
Reina Magnifica Sangria necklace,
Belladone Island collection, 2007.
White gold, diamonds, Paraiba tourmalines,
rubies, demantoid garnets, and lacquer.

126
Bal de Paris ring,
Le Bal des Roses collection, 2011.
White gold, diamonds,
rubies, and white quartz.

127
Noces de Sang necklace,
La Fiancée du Vampire collection, 2002.
White gold, diamonds, and spinels.

128
Vert Sinople Émeraude earrings,
Gem Dior collection, 2019.
Yellow gold, diamonds, and emeralds.

129
Grand Canal Émeraude necklace,
Dior à Versailles, côté Jardins collection, 2017.
White and yellow gold,
diamonds, emeralds, and rubies.

130
Reine de Quartzie ring,
Reines et Rois collection, 2009.
Platinum, pink quartz, and diamonds.

131
Ailée Diamant bracelet,
Archi Dior collection, 2014.
White gold, diamonds, purple
sapphires, sapphires, pink sapphires,
multicolored sapphires, and rubies.

132
Bosquet de la Colonnade Saphir Rose earrings,
Dior à Versailles, côté Jardins collection, 2017.
Yellow, white, and pink gold, diamonds, pink and yellow sapphires, sapphires, yellow tourmalines, Paraiba-type tourmalines, demantoid and tsavorite garnets, emeralds, yellow diamonds, and hauyne.

133
Carnivora Devorus earrings,
Milly Carnivora collection, 2008.
Yellow gold, diamonds, tsavorite garnets, yellow sapphires, Paraiba tourmalines, and lacquer.

134
Dentelle Organza Diamant ring,
Dior Dior Dior collection, 2018.
White gold, diamonds, and pink sapphires.

135
Chambre de la Reine necklace,
Dior à Versailles collection, 2016.
White and pink gold, darkened silver, diamonds, and pink sapphire.

136
Dentelle Médaillon Soleil ring,
Dear Dior collection, 2012.
Yellow gold, fancy yellow diamonds, fancy green diamonds, fancy brown diamonds, and white opal.

137
Dénoué Diamant necklace,
Soie Dior, 2015.
White and yellow gold, diamonds, and yellow diamonds.

138
Bal d'Autrefois ring,
Le Bal des Roses collection, 2011.
White gold, diamonds, emeralds, chrysoprase, green tourmalines, tsavorite garnets, and Paraiba tourmalines.

139
Exquise Emeraude earrings,
Cher Dior collection, 2013.
White gold, diamonds, sapphires, emeralds, demantoid garnets, and Paraiba tourmalines.

140
Carnivora Fluora Eternita bracelet,
Belladone Island collection, 2007.
Yellow and white gold, diamonds, demantoid garnets, Paraiba tourmalines, tsavorite garnets, Sandawana emeralds, rubies, blue tourmalines, rough Ethiopian opal, pink spinels, orange sapphires, amethysts, spessartite garnets, purple sapphires, and lacquer.

141
Idylle à Bornéo bracelet,
Idylle aux Paradis collection, 2009.
Yellow gold, diamonds, boulder opal, orange sapphires, tsavorite garnets, sapphires, yellow sapphires, demantoide garnets, red spinel, emeralds, rubies, and lacquer.

142
Roi de Charoïte pendant,
Reines et Rois collection, 2009.
Platinum, white gold, charoite, and diamonds.

143
Salon d'Apollon brooch,
Dior à Versailles collection, 2016.
White and pink gold, darkened silver, and diamonds.

144
Reine de Jadélénie ring,
Reines et Rois collection, 2009.
Platinum, jadeite jade, and diamonds.

145
Grani Opalia Devorus ring,
Belladone Island collection, 2007.
White gold, diamonds, chrysoprase,
Australian black opal, tsavorites
garnets, spessartite garnets,
pink sapphires, sapphires, and amethysts.

146
Mini Épices earrings,
Harem collection, 2001.
Yellow gold, green tourmaline,
pink tourmalines, citrines, iolites,
and aquamarine.

147
Dentelle Satin Émeraude ring,
Dior Dior Dior collection, 2018.
Yellow gold, diamonds, emeralds, yellow
sapphire, sapphire, ruby, purple and pink
sapphires, and Paraiba-type tourmaline.

148
Tulle Pointillés Colorés ring,
Dear Dior collection, 2012.
Yellow gold, diamonds, pink sapphires,
purple sapphires, spessartite garnets,
red spinels, sapphires, hauynes, yellow
sapphires, emeralds, Paraiba tourmalines,
and demantoid garnets.

149
La D de Dior Color timepiece, 38mm,
La D de Dior collection, 2003.
White gold, diamonds, Paraiba
tourmalines, emeralds, tsavorite garnets,
yellow sapphires, spessartite garnets,
spinels, rubies, pink sapphires, amethysts,
purple sapphires, sapphires, and
black satin strap. Zenith Elite movement.

150
Ancolia Veneinosa Pop ring,
Belladone Island collection, 2007.
Yellow gold, diamonds, fire opal,
yellow, orange, and pink sapphires,
spinels, Ethiopian white opal,
tsavorite garnets, and lacquer.

151
Guipure Framboise Rebrodée ring,
Archi Dior collection, 2014.
Pink and yellow gold, diamonds, red spinels,
yellow sapphires, pink sapphires, purple
sapphires, fire opals, pink tourmalines,
spessartite garnets, pink spinels,
amethysts, rubies, and orange sapphires.

152
Rose Lavande Rubis ring,
Gem Dior collection, 2019.
Pink gold, diamonds, pink sapphires,
rubies, purple spinel, and purple garnets.

153
Chardonus necklace,
Milly Carnivora collection, 2008.
Yellow gold, diamonds, amethysts,
aquamarine, tsavorite garnet, and lacquer.

154
Idylle à la Baie d'Along bracelet,
Idylle aux Paradis collection, 2009.
White gold, diamonds, Australian
white opal, fire opals, spessartite
garnets, emeralds, amethysts, sapphires,
yellow, pink, and orange sapphires,
Paraiba tourmalines, tsavorite garnets,
demantoide garnets, and lacquer.

155
Dentelle Tulle Tourmaline Type Paraïba ring,
Dior Dior Dior collection, 2018.
Yellow and white gold, diamonds,
Paraiba-type tourmalines,
emeralds, tsavorite garnets, pink
sapphires, and spessartite garnets.

156
My Dior ring, *My Dior* collection, 2012.
Yellow gold and diamonds.

157 – 58
Dentelle Chantilly Multicolore earrings,
Cher Dior collection, 2013.
Yellow and pink gold, platinum, diamonds, fancy yellow diamonds, Paraiba tourmalines, pink spinels, fire opals, emeralds, yellow beryls, spessartite garnets, amethysts, demantoid garnets, red spinels, sapphires, and pink sapphires.

159
Coffret de Victoire ring,
Coffret de Victoire collection, 2003.
Yellow gold, diamonds, Aka coral, turquoise, pink tourmalines, citrines, and rubies

160
Multicolore Primevère Saphir Rose earrings,
Gem Dior collection, 2019.
Yellow gold, diamonds, pink sapphires, sapphires, rubies, yellow sapphires, tsavorite garnets, purple garnets, spessartite garnets, emeralds, and Paraiba-type tourmalines.

161
Trianon Diamant necklace,
Dior à Versailles, côté Jardins collection, 2017.
Pink, yellow, and white gold, diamonds, pink sapphires, emeralds, sapphires, tsavorite and spessartite garnets, yellow sapphires, yellow diamonds, turquoise, Paraiba-type tourmalines, and ruby.

162
Organza Brodé Paraïba ring,
Dear Dior collection, 2012.
White, yellow, and pink gold, diamonds, fancy yellow diamonds, bicolor opal, tsavorite garnets, chrysoberyls, yellow sapphires, fire opals, spessartite garnets, tanzanites, Paraiba tourmalines, and peridots.

163
Vert Menthe Émeraude necklace,
Gem Dior collection, 2019.
Yellow gold, diamonds, tsavorite garnets, emeralds, rubies, yellow sapphires, spessartite garnets, and red spinels.

164
Étincelante Diamant ring,
Cher Dior collection, 2013.
White gold, diamonds, sapphires, Paraiba tourmalines, and emeralds.

165
Vert Tilleul Tourmaline Paraïba triple ring,
Gem Dior collection, 2019.
White gold, diamonds, Paraiba-type tourmalines, sapphires, and emeralds.

166
Bar en Corolle Émeraude bracelet,
Archi Dior collection, 2014.
White gold, diamonds, pink sapphires, emeralds, demantoid garnets, purple sapphires, tsavorite garnets, and orange-pink spinels.

167
Bassin des Nymphes Tourmaline Paraïba bracelet,
Dior à Versailles, côté Jardins collection, 2017.
White and yellow gold, diamonds, Paraiba-type tourmalines, rock crystal, pink and purple sapphires, sapphires, emeralds, tsavorite garnets, and yellow diamonds.

168
Dentelle Guipure Diamant Jaune bracelet,
Dior Dior Dior collection, 2018.
Yellow and pink gold, diamonds, and yellow diamonds.

169
My Dior cuff, *My Dior* collection, 2012.
Yellow gold and diamonds.

170
Salon de l'Abondance bracelet,
Dior à Versailles collection, 2016.
Pink, yellow, and white gold, diamonds, orange and yellow diamonds, and pink sapphires.

171
Salon de l'Abondance Diamant Jaune double ring,
Dior à Versailles collection, 2016.
Yellow and pink gold, darkened silver, diamonds, yellow diamonds, and pink sapphires.

172
Bal de Mai necklace,
Le Bal des Roses collection, 2011.
White and yellow gold, diamonds, fancy brown diamond, fancy pink diamonds, fancy lilac diamonds, fancy mauve diamonds, pink opal, and emeralds.

173
Idylle à Valparaiso bracelet,
Idylle aux Paradis collection, 2009.
Pink gold, diamonds, white mother-of-pearl, cultured pearls, white opal, Mediterranean coral, chalcedony, fire opal, pink sapphires, purple sapphires, orange sapphires, tsavorite garnets, red spinels, pink spinels, and lacquer.

174
Soumission necklace,
Soumission collection, 2001.
Yellow gold and diamonds.

175
La D de Dior timepiece, 38 mm,
La D de Dior collection, 2003.
Yellow gold and malachite.
Quartz movement.

176
Egratigna Angélique ring,
Milly Magic Carnivora collection, 2008.
White gold, diamonds, and glittery lacquer.

177
Roi d'Opalie pendant,
Reines et Rois collection, 2009.
Platinum, white gold, pink opal, cultured pearls, and diamonds.

178
Paradisea Coeur Secretus pendant,
Belladone Island collection, 2007.
Yellow gold, diamonds, spinels, amethysts, peridots, pink sapphires, rubies, yellow sapphires, cultured pearl, and lacquer.

179
Incroyables et Merveilleuses Mer earrings,
Incroyables et Merveilleuses collection, 2008.
Yellow gold, diamonds, amethysts, pink sapphires, tsavorite garnets, and purple sapphires.

180
Méduse Évanescente ring,
Le Bestiaire fantastique collection, 2004.
White gold, diamonds, multicolor sapphires, sapphires, black opal, Paraiba tourmalines, and fire opal.

181
Bal Romantique ring,
Le Bal des Roses collection, 2011.
White gold, platinum, diamonds, fancy purple diamonds, fancy pink diamonds, fancy pink purple diamonds, lavender chalcedony, purple sapphires, pink spinels, and pink purple spinels.

182
Reina Magnifica Sangria ring,
Belladone Island collection, 2007.
White gold, diamonds,
Paraiba tourmalines, and lacquer.

183
Egratigna Angélique earrings,
Milly Carnivora collection, 2008.
White gold, diamonds, and lacquer.

184
Coffret de Victoire ring,
Coffret de Victoire collection, 2003.
White gold, diamonds, mother-of-pearl,
Paraiba tourmalines, doublet opals, pink
sapphires, red spinels, spessartite garnets,
yellow sapphires, and tsavorite garnets.

185
Manga ring, special creation, 2008.
White gold, diamonds, jaspe,
black opal, purple sapphires, orange
sapphires, tsavorite garnets,
pink sapphires, yellow sapphires,
and Paraiba tourmalines.

186
Alcove ring, *Dior à Versailles* collection, 2016.
Yellow, white, and pink gold, darkened
silver, diamonds, and sapphire.

187
Reine de Calcédonia ring,
Reines et Rois collection, 2009.
Platinum, white gold, blue
chalcedony, and diamonds.

188
Coffret de Victoire ring,
Coffret de Victoire collection, 2003.
Yellow gold, diamonds, fire opal,
pink tourmaline, demantoid garnets, orange
sapphires, and yellow sapphires.

189 – 90
Ancolia ring,
Milly Carnivora collection, 2008.
Yellow gold, diamonds, yellow
tourmalines, rubellite, and lacquer.

191
Salon de Mars Pampille earrings,
Dior à Versailles collection, 2016.
White, pink, and yellow gold,
darkened silver, diamonds, and emeralds.

192
Dénoué Saphir necklace,
Soie Dior collection, 2015.
White and yellow gold,
diamonds, sapphire, and emeralds.

193
Vert Sinople Émeraude earrings,
Gem Dior collection, 2019.
Yellow gold, diamonds, and emeralds.

194
Dentelle Saphir Iris earrings,
Dear Dior collection, 2012.
White gold, diamonds, apatites, sapphires,
Paraiba tourmalines, rubies, and amethysts.

195
Rose Lavande Rubis earrings,
Gem Dior collection, 2019.
Pink gold, diamonds, rubies, sapphires,
pink sapphires, and purple garnets.

196
Rose Jacinthe Rubis ring,
Gem Dior collection, 2019.
White gold, diamonds,
rubies, and pink sapphires.

197
Bal de l'Opéra necklace,
Le Bal des Roses collection, 2011.
White and pink gold, diamonds, pink
spinels, red spinels, rubies, and rubellites.

198
Bal Champêtre ring,
Le Bal des Roses collection, 2011.
Yellow gold, diamonds, fancy yellow diamonds, fancy green diamonds, fancy green yellow diamonds, tsavorite garnets, demantoide garnets, and chrysophrase.

199
Bois de Rose ring, *Bois de Rose* collection, 2010.
Yellow gold.

200
Vert Prairie Émeraude double ring,
Gem Dior collection, 2019.
Yellow gold, diamonds, emeralds, chrysoberyls, Paraiba-type tourmalines, sapphires, tsavorite garnets, and yellow sapphires.

201
Plaisir Champêtre brooch,
Dior à Versailles, côté Jardins collection, 2017.
Yellow, white, and pink gold, diamonds, tsavorite garnets, pink sapphires, emeralds, yellow sapphires, rubies, yellow diamond, Paraiba-type tourmalines, and sapphires.

202
Je t'aime earrings, *Oui* collection, 2005.
Yellow gold and diamonds.

Toi Moi earrings, *Oui* collection, 2005.
Yellow gold and diamonds.

Oui earring, *Oui* collection, 2005.
Yellow gold and diamond.

203
Carnivora Fluora Eternita bracelet,
Belladone Island collection, 2007.
Yellow and white gold, diamonds, and lacquer.

204
Majestueuse Opale High Jewellery timepiece,
Dior et d'Opales collection, 2017.
Yellow and white gold, diamonds, black opal, pink sapphires, spessartite and tsavorite garnets, emeralds, yellow sapphires, amethysts, rubies, and sapphires.
Quartz movement.

205
Majestueuse Multicolore necklace,
Cher Dior collection, 2013.
Yellow gold, diamonds, pink sapphires, yellow sapphires, sapphires, emeralds, demantoid garnets, spessartite garnets, Paraiba tourmalines, purple sapphires, and ruby.

206
Phoenix Arc-en-Ciel necklace,
Dragon collection, 2007.
Yellow gold, diamonds, black opals, emeralds, spessartite garnets, pink sapphires, Paraiba tourmalines, tsavorite garnets, orange sapphires, and lacquer.

207
Chardonus Kiwi Mangue necklace,
Milly Carnivora collection, 2008.
Yellow and white gold, diamonds, mandarin garnets, peridot, emerald, tanzanites, and lacquer.

208
Pli Plat Saphir Rose bracelet,
Soie Dior collection, 2015.
Yellow gold, diamonds, yellow diamonds, pink sapphire, and emeralds.

209
Multicolore Framboise Rubellite ring,
Gem Dior collection, 2019.
Yellow gold, diamonds, rubellite, spessartite garnets, sapphires, tsavorite garnets, yellow sapphires, Paraiba-type tourmalines, and emerald.

210
Dentelle Médaillon Soleil earrings,
Dear Dior collection, 2012.
Yellow gold, diamonds, fancy yellow diamonds, fancy green diamonds, fancy brown diamonds, and sphenes.

211
Bal d'Été ring,
Le Bal des Roses collection, 2011.
Yellow and white gold, diamonds, fancy yellow diamonds, fancy orange diamonds, and golden opal.

212
Fiancée du Vampire pendant,
La Fiancée du Vampire collection, 2002.
White gold and diamonds.

213
Roi de Crocidolia pendant,
Reines et Rois collection, 2009.
Platinum, white gold, green crocidolite, and diamonds.

214
Bosquet de la Reine Tourmaline Paraïba earrings,
Dior à Versailles, côté Jardins collection, 2017.
White, yellow, and pink gold, diamonds, Paraiba-type tourmalines, emeralds, pink sapphires, and lacquer.

215
Multicolore Printemps Émeraude double ring,
Gem Dior collection, 2019.
Yellow gold, diamonds, emerald, tsavorite garnet, rubies, sapphires, purple garnets, pink sapphire, yellow sapphires, Paraiba-type tourmalines, and spessartite garnet.

216
Rose Azalée Saphir Rose ring,
Gem Dior collection, 2019.
White gold, diamonds, and pink sapphire.

217
Dentelle Guipure Saphir Rose necklace,
Dior Dior Dior collection, 2018.
White gold, diamonds, and pink sapphire.

218
Carnivora Devorus ring,
Milly Carnivora collection, 2008.
Yellow gold, diamonds, Paraiba tourmalines, pink sapphires, yellow sapphires, tsavorite garnets, and lacquer.

219
Dentelle Chantilly Multicolore ring,
Dear Dior collection, 2012.
Yellow and white gold, diamonds, fancy yellow diamonds, Paraiba tourmalines, emeralds, pink spinels, red spinels, fire opals, amethysts, sapphires, yellow sapphires, hauynes, pink sapphires, demantoid garnets, and spessartite garnet.

220
Roi de Quartznoir pendant,
Reines et Rois collection, 2009.
Platinum, white gold, black rutile quartz, and diamonds.

221
Tête de Mort pendant,
La Fiancée du Vampire collection, 2002.
White gold and diamonds.

222
Organza Brodé Paraïba ring,
Dear Dior collection, 2012.
White, yellow, and pink gold, diamonds, fancy yellow diamonds, bicolor opal, tsavorite garnets, chrysoberyls, yellow sapphires, fire opals, spessartite garnets, tanzanites, Paraiba tourmalines, and peridots.

223
Fascinante Opale ring,
Dior et d'Opales collection, 2017.
White gold, diamonds, and black opal.

224
Dentelle Opale d'Orient ring,
Dear Dior collection, 2012.
Yellow gold, platinum, diamonds, black opal, spessartite garnets, pink-red spinels, tanzanites, tsavorite garnets, and rubies.

225
Coffret de Victoire pendant,
Coffret de Victoire collection, 2003.
Yellow gold, diamonds, coral, pink sapphires, peridots, aquamarines, iolites, and pink tourmalines.

226
Poisonus necklace,
Milly Carnivora collection, 2008.
White gold, diamonds,
tsavorite garnets, rubellites, and lacquer.

227
Poisonus necklace,
Milly Magic Carnivora collection, 2008.
White gold, diamonds, and glittery lacquer.

228
Roi de Rutilie pendant,
Reines et Rois collection, 2009.
Platinum, white gold,
orange rutile quartz, and diamonds.

229
Orange Safran Grenat Spessartite hand jewel,
Gem Dior collection, 2019.
Pink gold, diamonds,
and spessartite garnets.

230
Parterre de Latone Saphir bracelet,
Dior à Versailles, côté Jardins collection, 2017.
Yellow gold, diamonds, chrysoprases, emeralds, sapphire, and turquoise.

231
Organza Brodé Paraïba bracelet,
Dear Dior collection, 2012.
Platinum, yellow and white gold, diamonds, Paraiba tourmalines, emeralds, demantoid garnets, green tourmalines, tsavorite garnets, and chrysoberyls.

232
Salon de Diane necklace,
Dior à Versailles collection, 2016.
White, pink, and yellow gold,
darkened silver, diamonds, and emerald.

233
Vert Impérial Émeraude ring,
Gem Dior collection, 2019.
Platinum, diamonds, and emeralds.

234
Paradisea Cœur Secretus ring,
Belladone Island collection, 2007.
White and yellow gold, diamonds, Paraiba tourmalines, pink spinels, pink sapphires, ruby, and lacquer.

235
Dentelle Saphir Iris ring,
Dear Dior collection, 2012.
White gold, diamonds, sapphires, rubies, apatites, Paraiba tourmalines, purple sapphires, and amethysts.

236
Ancolia earrings,
Milly Carnivora collection, 2008.
Yellow gold, diamonds, yellow tourmalines, rubellites, and lacquer.

237
Ancolia Veneinosa Pop earrings,
Belladone Island collection, 2007.
Yellow gold, diamonds, fancy yellow diamonds, yellow, orange, and pink sapphires, fire opals, spinels, tsavorites, demantoid garnets, and lacquer.

238
Orangerie Tanzanite bracelet,
Dior à Versailles, côté Jardins collection, 2017.
White, yellow and pink gold, diamonds, tsavorite garnets, tanzanite, emeralds, pink, and purple sapphires, sapphires, yellow sapphires, turquoise, yellow diamonds, and ruby.

239
Multicolore Nuit Saphir double ring,
Gem Dior collection, 2019.
White gold, diamonds, sapphire, rubies, emeralds, pink sapphire, tsavorite garnets, yellow sapphire, spessartite garnet, Paraiba-type tourmaline, and purple sapphire.

240
Trompe-L'Œil Diamant Jaune ring,
Archi Dior collection, 2014.
Yellow and pink gold, diamonds, fancy yellow diamonds, spessartite garnets, and pink sapphires.

241
Orange Tangerine Grenat Spessartite ring,
Gem Dior collection, 2019.
Pink gold, diamonds, spessartite garnets, pink sapphires, and yellow sapphires.

242
Guipure Framboise Rebrodée ring,
Dear Dior collection, 2012.
Pink and yellow gold, diamonds, red spinels, yellow sapphires, pink sapphires, purple sapphires, fire opals, pink tourmalines, spessartite garnets, pink spinels, amethysts, rubies, and orange sapphires.

243
Idylle à Oulan-Bator bracelet,
Idylle aux Paradis collection, 2009.
Yellow and white gold, silver, diamonds, ammolites, Ethiopian opal, emeralds, and lacquer.

244
Multicolore Persan Tourmaline Paraïba double ring,
Gem Dior collection, 2019.
White gold, diamonds, Paraiba-type tourmalines, sapphires, rubies, tsavorite garnets, yellow and pink sapphires, emeralds, and spessartite garnet.

245
Orangerie Diamant earrings,
Dior à Versailles, côté Jardins collection, 2017.
White and pink gold, diamonds, pink sapphires, emeralds, Paraiba-type tourmalines, sapphires, and demantoid garnets.

246
Incroyables et Merveilleuses Papillon ring,
Incroyables et Merveilleuses collection, 1999.
Yellow gold, diamonds, citrine, pink sapphires, orange sapphires, and emeralds.

247
Mangatus Orange Réglisse ring,
Milly Carnivora collection, 2008.
White gold, diamonds, tsavorite garnets, and lacquer.

248
Coffret de Victoire ring,
Coffret de Victoire collection, 2003.
Yellow gold, diamonds, fancy yellow diamonds, amethyst, tsavorite garnets, sapphires, demantoid garnets, Paraiba tourmalines, aquamarines, orange sapphires, and lacquer.

249
Guirlande de Fleurs Rubis double ring,
Dior à Versailles, côté Jardins collection, 2017.
Yellow gold, diamonds, rubies, spessartite garnets, turquoise, pink sapphires, tsavorite garnets, emeralds, and yellow sapphire.

250
Chambre du Roi necklace,
Dior à Versailles collection, 2016.
White, pink, and yellow gold, darkened silver, diamonds, and sapphire.

251
Roi de Sugilie pendant,
Reines et Rois collection, 2009.
Platinum, white gold, sugilite, and diamonds.

252
Rose Bonbon Saphir Rose ring,
Gem Dior collection, 2019.
Pink gold, diamonds, and pink sapphires.

253
Mimirose bracelet, *Mimirose* collection, 2019.
Pink gold and pink sapphires.

254
Carnivora Devorus necklace,
Milly Carnivora collection, 2008.
Yellow gold, diamonds, Paraiba tourmalines, pink sapphires, yellow sapphires, tsavorite garnets, orange sapphires, and lacquer.

255
Diorette ring, *Diorette* collection, 2006.
Yellow gold, diamond, amethyst, mandarin garnets, pink sapphire, tsavorite garnet, and lacquer.

256
Fleuro Poisonus Spinella ring,
Belladone Island collection, 2007.
White gold, diamonds, yellow diamonds, pink sapphires, orange spinels, tsavorites garnets, demantoid garnets, and lacquer.

257
Roi de Crocidolite pendant,
Reines et Rois collection, 2009.
Platinum, white gold, blue crocidolite, and diamonds.

258
Baguette earrings,
Dior à Versailles collection, 2016.
White, yellow and pink gold, darkened silver, platinum, diamonds, and emeralds.

259
Dentelle Guipure Émeraude ring,
Dior Dior Dior collection, 2018.
Yellow gold, diamonds, and emerald.

260
Idylle à Moyobamba bracelet,
Idylle aux Paradis collection, 2009.
Platinum, yellow and white gold, silver, diamonds, pink shell, turquoise, aquamarine, amethyst, yellow orange sapphires, citrine, yellow tourmalines, emeralds, demantoide garnets, doublet opal, pink sapphires, pink spinels, purple sapphires, tsavorite garnets, fire opals, pink tourmaline "Eye of the Falcon" quartz, and lacquer.

261
Rose des Vents bracelet,
Rose des Vents collection, 2015.
Pink gold, diamond, malachite, and pink opal.

262
Incroyables et Merveilleuses Fleurs earrings,
Incroyables et Merveilleuses collection, 1999.
Yellow gold, diamonds, amethysts, cultured pearls, tsavorite garnets, yellow sapphires, sapphires, and emeralds.

263
Résille Bouquet d'Opales ring,
Dear Dior collection, 2012.
Yellow gold, platinum, diamonds,
black opals, turquoises, demantoid garnets,
amethysts, emeralds, and sapphires.

264
Chardonus earrings,
Milly Carnivora collection, 2008.
Yellow gold, diamonds,
amethysts, yellow beryls, rubellite,
tsavorite garnet, tanzanites,
pink sapphires, and lacquer.

265
Dragon du Ciel pendant,
Dragon collection, 2007.
White gold, diamonds, Australian
black opals, sapphires, purple sapphires,
rubies, and lacquer.

266
Bleu Azur Saphir double ring,
Gem Dior collection, 2019.
White gold, diamonds,
sapphires, and aquamarines.

267
Dentelle Tulle Saphir necklace,
Dior Dior Dior collection, 2018.
White gold, diamonds, and sapphire.

268
Premier Bal necklace,
Premier Bal collection, 1999.
White gold, platinum, diamonds, and rubies.

269
Gros Grain Saphir Rose bracelet,
Soie Dior collection, 2015.
White gold, diamonds, and pink sapphires.

270
Reina Magnifica Sangria earrings,
Belladone Island collection, 2007.
White gold, diamonds, ruby,
Paraiba tourmalines, and lacquer.

271
Mangatus Pistache Fraise ring,
Milly Carnivora collection, 2008.
Yellow gold, diamonds,
orange sapphires, and lacquer.

272
Blanc Titane Diamant ring,
Gem Dior collection, 2019.
White gold and diamonds.

273
Précieuses Rose necklace,
Précieuses Roses collection, 2010.
White gold and diamonds.

274
Rose Dior Bagatelle ring,
Rose Dior Bagatelle collection, 2000.
Yellow gold, diamonds,
rubies, and emeralds.

Rose Dior Bagatelle ring,
Rose Dior Bagatelle collection, 2000.
White gold, diamonds, pink sapphires,
and emeralds.

Rose Dior Bagatelle ring,
Rose Dior Bagatelle collection, 2000.
White gold and diamonds.

Rose Dior Bagatelle ring,
Rose Dior Bagatelle collection, 2000.
White and yellow gold, diamonds,
fancy yellow diamonds, and tsavorite garnets.

275
Mimirose ring, *Mimirose* collection, 2019.
Pink gold and ruby.

Mimirose ring, *Mimirose* collection, 2019.
Pink gold and pink sapphire.

Mimirose ring, *Mimirose* collection, 2019.
Yellow gold and diamond.

Mimirose ring, *Mimirose* collection, 2019.
Yellow gold and emerald.

276
Noué Émeraude bracelet,
Soie Dior collection, 2015.
White gold, diamonds, and emerald.

277
Trianon Émeraude earrings,
Dior à Versailles, côté Jardins collection, 2017.
White and pink gold, diamonds, emeralds, yellow diamonds, onyx, and pink sapphires.

278
Bal Romantique earrings,
Le Bal des Roses collection, 2011.
White gold, diamonds, and mauve sapphires.

279
Chardonus necklace,
Milly Magic Carnivora collection, 2008.
White gold, diamonds, and glittery lacquer.

280
Résille Bouquet d'Opales earrings,
Dear Dior collection, 2012.
Yellow and pink gold, platinum, diamonds, black opals, emeralds, amethysts, turquoise, demantoid garnets, and sapphires.

281
Fascinante Opale earrings,
Dior et d'Opales collection, 2017.
White gold, diamonds, and black opals.

282
Salon de Vénus bracelet,
Dior à Versailles collection, 2016.
White gold, darkened silver, diamonds, and pink sapphire.

283
Rose Azalée Saphir Rose necklace,
Gem Dior collection, 2019.
White gold, diamonds, and pink sapphire.

284
Coffret de Victoire ring,
Coffret de Victoire collection, 2003.
Yellow gold, diamonds, cultured pearls, turquoise, red spinels, pink tourmalines, and green tourmalines.

285
Dentelle Tourmaline Rebrodée ring,
Dear Dior collection, 2012.
Yellow gold, diamonds, fancy yellow diamonds, Paraiba tourmalines, chrysoberyls, peridots, demantoid garnets, emeralds, fire opals, and hauynes.

286
Blanc Neige Diamant ring,
Gem Dior collection, 2019.
White gold and diamonds.

287
Cour de Marbre bracelet,
Dior à Versailles collection, 2016.
White and pink gold, darkened silver, and diamonds.

288
Gros Grain Saphir bracelet,
Soie Dior collection, 2015.
White gold, diamonds, and sapphires.

289
Hameau de la Reine Diamant ring,
Dior à Versailles, côté Jardins collection, 2017.
Yellow, white, and pink gold, diamonds, tsavorite and demantoid garnets, sapphires, purple and pink sapphires, pink diamonds, Paraiba-type tourmalines, and lacquer.

290
Salon d'Apollon necklace,
Dior à Versailles collection, 2016.
White, pink, and yellow gold, darkened silver, diamonds, and yellow diamonds.

291
J'adore special edition
by Victoire de Castellane
with Baccarat crystal and a neck
decorated with a Fontanges knot,
pink gold, silver, and diamonds,
Christian Dior Parfums, Paris, 2017.

292
Mimirose necklace, *Mimirose* collection, 2019.
Yellow gold and diamonds.

293
Gourmette de Dior ring,
Gourmette de Dior collection, 2004.
Yellow gold.

294
Exquise Rubis ring,
Cher Dior collection, 2013.
Yellow gold, diamonds, ruby, yellow sapphires, spessartite garnets, and pink sapphires.

295
Rouge Coquelicot Rubis pendant earrings,
Gem Dior collection, 2019.
Pink gold, diamonds, rubies, spessartite garnets, yellow sapphires, and red spinels.

296
Guirlande de Fleurs Diamant earrings,
Dior à Versailles, côté Jardins collection, 2017.
Yellow and white gold, diamonds, mandarin garnets, emeralds, cultured pearls, pink sapphires, Paraiba-type tourmalines, pink spinels, pink tourmalines, red spinel, sapphires, turquoise, fire opals, hauynes, tsavorite and spessartite garnets, amethyst, ruby, and yellow diamond.

297
Epinosa Vertes earrings,
Milly Carnivora collection, 2008.
White gold, diamonds, rubellites, citrines, amethyst, sapphires, pink sapphires, tsavorite garnets, and lacquer.

298
Fascinante Opale bracelet,
Dior et d'Opales collection, 2017.
White gold, diamonds, and black opal.

299
Bleu Cyan Tourmaline Paraïba ring,
Gem Dior collection, 2019.
White gold, diamonds, and Paraiba-type tourmalines.

300
Bal Bleu Nuit ring,
Le Bal des Roses collection, 2011.
White and yellow gold, diamonds, gray diamonds, sapphires, blue chalcedony, and tanzanite.

301
Egratina Chipie ring,
Milly Magic Carnivora collection, 2008.
White gold, diamonds and glittery lacquer.

302
Carnivo Papidevorus earrings,
Belladone Island collection, 2007.
White and yellow gold, diamonds, fancy yellow diamonds, black spinels, rubies, tsavorite garnets, spinels, pink spinels, Paraiba tourmalines, sapphires, demantoid garnets, emeralds, spessartite garnets, and lacquer.

303
Diorette Papillon earrings,
Diorette collection, 2006.
White gold, diamonds, and lacquer.

304
Incroyables et Merveilleuses Champêtre earrings,
Incroyables et Merveilleuses collection, 1999.
Yellow gold, diamonds, black diamond, aquamarines, emeralds, orange sapphires, tsavorite garnets, and yellow sapphires.

305
Poisono Misterius Green Epicea earrings,
Belladone Island collection, 2007.
White gold, diamonds, fancy yellow and orange diamonds, rubies, rough Ethiopian opal, orange and yellow sapphires, demantoid garnets, Paraiba tourmalines, tsavorites and spessartite garnets, Sandawana emeralds, purple and pink spinels, and lacquer.

306
Incroyables et Merveilleuses Cerise ring,
Incroyables et Merveilleuses collection, 1999.
Yellow gold, diamonds, heliodor, pink tourmalines, tsavorite garnets, and demantoid garnets.

307
Exquise Rubis earrings,
Cher Dior collection, 2013.
Yellow gold, diamonds, yellow sapphires, rubies, pink sapphires, and spessartite garnets.

308
Exquise Diamant ring,
Cher Dior collection, 2013.
Yellow gold, diamonds, spessartite garnets, yellow sapphires, sapphires, Paraiba tourmalines, pink sapphires, demantoid garnets, rubies, purple sapphires, and emeralds.

309
Flamboyante Opale High Jewellery timepiece,
Dior et d'Opales collection, 2017.
Pink, white, and yellow gold, diamonds, black opal, sapphires, spessartite garnets, rubies, yellow sapphires, tsavorite garnets, pink sapphires, Paraiba-type tourmalines, emeralds, and pink spinels.
Quartz movement.

310
Rouge Vermillon Rubis ring,
Gem Dior collection, 2019.
Pink gold, diamonds, and rubies.

311 – 12
Egratigna Chipie ring,
Milly Carnivora collection, 2008.
White gold, diamonds, spinels, and lacquer.

313
Volant Émeraude ring,
Soie Dior collection, 2015.
White gold, diamonds, emerald, and sapphires.

314
Bosquet de la Salle de Bal Diamant ring,
Dior à Versailles, côté Jardins collection, 2017.
Yellow gold, diamonds, rock crystal, emeralds, pink sapphires, tsavorite garnets, rubies, spessartite garnets, and Paraiba-type tourmalines.

315
Blanc Flocon Diamant ring,
Gem Dior collection, 2019.
White gold and diamonds.

316
Multicolore Anglais Rubis earrings,
Gem Dior collection, 2019.
Yellow gold, diamonds, rubies, tsavorite garnets, yellow sapphires, sapphires, spessartite garnets, pink sapphire, emeralds, purple garnet, purple sapphire, and Paraiba-type tourmalines.

317
Chardonus Myrtille Passion Menthe necklace,
Milly Carnivora collection, 2008.
Yellow gold, diamonds, tanzanites, emeralds, rubellite, Paraiba tourmaline, spessartite garnet, and lacquer.

318
Bosquet de l'Encelade Saphir bodice jewel,
Dior à Versailles, côté Jardins collection, 2017.
White, yellow and pink gold, diamonds, sapphire, emeralds, tsavorite garnets, peridots, pink tourmalines, purple sapphires, demantoid and spessartite garnets, yellow diamonds, alexandrites, pink sapphires, chrysoprases, and yellow sapphires.

319
Bleu Cobalt Spinelle double ring,
Gem Dior collection, 2019.
White gold, diamonds, and cobalt spinels.

320
Bleu Égyptien Tourmaline Bleue earrings,
Gem Dior collection, 2019.
White gold, diamonds, sapphires, blue tourmaline, Paraiba-type tourmalines, and emeralds.

321
Exquise Émeraude ring,
Cher Dior collection, 2013.
White gold, diamonds, emeralds, Paraiba tourmalines, demantoid garnets, and sapphires.

322
Bosquet de la Girandole Opale Claire earrings,
Dior à Versailles, côté Jardins collection, 2017.
White, pink, and yellow gold, platinum, diamonds, emeralds, light opals, spessartite garnets, pink sapphires, tsavorite garnets, yellow diamonds, yellow sapphires, and rubies.

323
Majestueuse Multicolore earrings,
Cher Dior collection, 2013.
Yellow gold, diamonds, sapphires, yellow sapphires, emeralds, pink sapphires, demantoid garnets, spessartite garnets, purple sapphires, and Paraiba tourmalines.

324
Dentelle Guipure Diamant earrings,
Dior Dior Dior collection, 2018.
White gold and diamonds.

325
Roi d'Osumilie pendant,
Reines et Rois collection, 2009.
Platinum, white gold, sugilite, and diamonds.

326
Hameau de la Reine Diamant Jaune ring,
Dior à Versailles, côté Jardins collection, 2017.
Yellow, white, and pink gold, diamonds, yellow diamonds, emeralds, sapphires, pink sapphires, turquoise, spessartite garnets, and rubies.

327
Vert Menthe Émeraude pendant earrings,
Gem Dior collection, 2019.
Yellow gold, diamonds, tsavorite garnets, emeralds, sapphires, and yellow sapphires.

328
Vert Gazon Émeraude double ring,
Gem Dior collection, 2019.
Yellow gold, diamonds, and emeralds.

329
Bosquet de la Salle de Bal Émeraude ring,
Dior à Versailles, côté Jardins collection, 2017.
Yellow gold, diamonds, emeralds, rock crystal, tsavorite garnets, yellow sapphires, rubies, pink sapphires, yellow diamonds, amethysts, Paraiba-type tourmalines, demantoid and mandarin garnets, and purple sapphire.

330
Exquise Diamant earrings,
Cher Dior collection, 2013.
Yellow gold, diamonds, yellow sapphires, pink sapphires, spessartite garnets, demantoid garnets, Paraiba tourmalines, purple sapphires, rubies, sapphires, and emeralds.

331
Bosquet de la Girandole Tourmaline Paraïba ring,
Dior à Versailles, côté Jardins collection, 2017.
Yellow gold, diamonds, amazonite, Paraiba-type tourmaline, tsavorite garnets, pink sapphires, mandarin and demantoid garnets, turquoise, sapphires, yellow tourmalines, and fire opal.

332
Corolle Jour Émeraude necklace,
Archi Dior collection, 2014.
White gold, diamonds, and emeralds.

333
Nuit Blanche necklace,
Nuit Blanche collection, 1999.
White gold, platinum, diamonds, and rubies.

334
Cassette ring,
Dior à Versailles collection, 2016.
Yellow and pink gold, platinum, darkened silver, and diamonds.

335
Bosquet de la Reine Émeraude ring,
Dior à Versailles, côté Jardins collection, 2017.
Pink gold, diamonds, emeralds, Paraiba-type tourmalines, orange, yellow, and pink sapphires, spessartite garnets, yellow diamonds, and ruby.

336
Roi d'Obsidienne pendant,
Reines et Rois collection, 2009.
Platinum, white gold, rainbow obsidian, and diamonds.

337
Dentelle Guipure Spinelle Rose earrings,
Dior Dior Dior collection, 2018.
White gold, diamonds, and pink spinels.

338
Coccinelle de Jour earrings,
Milly-la-Forêt collection, 1999.
Yellow gold, diamonds, and coral.

Cerise earrings,
Milly-la-Forêt collection, 1999.
Yellow gold, diamonds, and coral.

Coccinelle de Jour pendant,
Milly-la-Forêt collection, 1999.
Yellow gold, diamonds, and coral.

Navet earrings,
Milly-la-Forêt collection, 1999.
Yellow gold, diamonds, tsavorites, and cultured pearls.

Coccinelle de Nuit pendant,
Milly-la-Forêt collection, 1999.
White gold, diamonds, and pink sapphires.

Coccinelle de Nuit earrings,
Milly-la-Forêt collection, 1999.
White gold, diamonds, and pink sapphires.

Framboise earrings,
Milly-la-Forêt collection, 1999.
Yellow gold, diamonds, and rubies.

339 – 40
Carnivo Papidevorus ring,
Belladone Island collection, 2007.
White and yellow gold, diamonds, fancy yellow diamonds, spinels, rubies, black spinels, pink spinels, emeralds, Paraiba tourmalines, demantoid garnets, spessartite garnets, amethysts, sapphires, pink sapphires, and lacquer.

341
Multicolore Printemps Spinelle Rose earrings,
Gem Dior collection, 2019.
Yellow gold, diamonds, pink spinel, rubies, emeralds, pink sapphires, Paraiba-type tourmalines, sapphires, purple garnets, tsavorite garnets, yellow sapphire, and spessartite garnet.

342
Bosquet des Dômes Diamant necklace,
Dior à Versailles, côté Jardins collection, 2017.
White gold, diamonds, pink sapphires, sapphires, yellow diamonds, and demantoid, and tsavorite garnets.

343
Dentelle Organza Diamant ring,
Dior Dior Dior collection, 2018.
White gold, diamonds and pink sapphires.

344
Boiserie Saphir ring,
Dior à Versailles collection, 2016.
Pink, white, and yellow gold, platinum, diamonds and sapphire.

345
Bleu Outremer Saphir necklace,
Gem Dior collection, 2019.
Yellow gold, diamonds, and sapphires.

346
Dentelle Satin Rubis bracelet,
Dior Dior Dior collection, 2018.
Pink gold, diamonds, and rubies.

347
Rouge Vermillon Rubis ring,
Gem Dior collection, 2019.
Pink gold, diamonds, and rubies.

348
Bal Vénitien ring,
Le Bal des Roses collection, 2011.
Yellow gold, diamonds, fancy brown diamonds, fancy orange yellow diamonds, pink spinel, fire oppals, spessartite garnets, and pink sapphires.

349
Special order necklace, 2008.
Yellow gold, diamonds, yellow beryl, pink sapphires, emeralds, yellow sapphires, orange sapphires, purple sapphires, and rubies.

350
Exquise Saphir Rose ring,
Cher Dior collection, 2013.
Yellow gold, diamonds,
pink sapphires, yellow sapphires,
spessartite garnets, emeralds,
ruby, purple sapphire, and sapphire.

351
Egratigna Angélique ring,
Milly Carnivora collection, 2008.
White gold, diamonds, and lacquer.

352
Incroyables et Merveilleuses Fruits earrings,
Incroyables et Merveilleuses collection, 1999.
Yellow gold, diamonds, morganites,
purple sapphires, tsavorite garnets,
pink sapphires, and emeralds.

353
Bassin des Nymphes Saphir Rose ring,
Dior à Versailles, côté Jardins collection, 2017.
Pink gold, diamonds, pink sapphires,
tsavorite garnets, emeralds, purple
sapphires, Paraiba-type tourmalines,
and demantoid garnets.

354
Diorette ring,
Diorette collection, 2006.
Yellow gold, diamond, amethyst, and lacquer.

355
Multicolore Marine Saphir double ring,
Gem Dior collection, 2019.
White gold, diamonds, sapphires,
pink sapphires, rubies, spessartite garnets,
yellow sapphire, and emeralds.

356
Vert Tilleul Tourmaline Paraïba ring,
Gem Dior collection, 2019.
White gold, diamonds, Paraiba-type
tourmalines, sapphires, and emeralds.

357
Captivente Opale High Jewellery timepiece,
Dior et d'Opales collection, 2017.
Yellow and white gold, diamonds,
tsavorite garnets, sapphires, emeralds, black
opal, demantoid garnets, Paraiba-type
tourmalines, and yellow diamonds.
Quartz movement.

358
Smock Diamant Jaune bracelet,
Soie Dior collection, 2015.
Yellow, white and pink gold, diamonds,
and yellow, and orange diamonds.

359
Jaune Jonquille Saphir Jaune ring,
Gem Dior collection, 2019.
Yellow gold, diamonds, and yellow sapphires.

360
Manga ring, special creation, 2008.
White and pink gold, diamonds,
fancy brown diamonds, fancy colored
diamond, agate, and ruby.

361
Diorette earrings,
Diorette collection, 2006.
White gold, diamonds, and lacquer.

362
Vert Tilleul Tourmaline Verte earrings,
Gem Dior collection, 2019.
White gold, diamonds, green
tourmalines, emeralds, sapphires,
and Paraiba-type tourmalines.

363
Dentelle Velours Émeraude necklace,
Dior Dior Dior collection, 2018.
White gold, diamonds,
emerald, and blue spinels.

364
Galerie des Glaces necklace,
Dior à Versailles collection, 2016.
White and pink gold, platinum,
darkened silver, and diamonds.

365
Blanc Titane Diamant earrings,
Gem Dior collection, 2019.
White gold and diamonds.

366
Diorette earrings,
Diorette collection, 2006.
White gold, diamonds, and lacquer.

367
Plaisir Champêtre Saphir earrings,
Dior à Versailles, côté Jardins collection, 2017.
Yellow and white gold, diamonds,
sapphires, tsavorite garnets, pink sapphires,
emeralds, turquoise, yellow diamonds,
Paraiba-type tourmalines, and lacquer.

368
Milieu du Siècle Diamant earrings,
Archi Dior collection, 2014.
White gold plated, black gold, and diamonds.

369
Galerie des Glaces ring,
Dior à Versailles collection, 2016.
White and pink gold,
darkened silver, and diamonds.

370
Rose Céleste pendant,
Rose des Vents collection, 2015.
Yellow gold, diamond,
and white mother-of-pearl.

371
Rose Céleste pendant,
Rose des Vents collection, 2015.
White and yellow gold,
white mother-of-pearl, and onyx.

372
Dentelle Guipure Saphir double ring,
Dior Dior Dior collection, 2018.
White gold, diamonds, and sapphire.

373
Reine de Labradorie ring,
Reines et Rois collection, 2009.
Platinum, white gold,
labradorite, and diamonds.

374
Paradisea Coeur Secretus pendant,
Belladone Island collection, 2007.
Yellow gold, diamonds, spinels, amethysts,
peridots, pink sapphires, rubies,
yellow sapphires, cultured pearl, and lacquer.

375
Bleu Égyptien Emerald ring,
Gem Dior collection, 2019.
White gold, diamonds,
Paraiba-type tourmalines,
emerald, and sapphires.

376
Marqueterie ring,
Dior à Versailles collection, 2016.
Yellow, white, and pink gold,
darkened silver, diamonds, and ruby.

377
Verticale Plissée Diamant Jaune ring,
Archi Dior collection, 2014.
White, yellow, and pink gold,
diamonds, fancy yellow diamonds,
fancy orange diamonds,
and fancy pink diamonds.

378
Vert Imperial Émeraude earrings,
Gem Dior collection, 2019.
Platinum, diamonds, and emeralds.

379
Bal de Mai earrings,
Le Bal des Roses collection, 2011.
White and yellow gold, diamonds,
fancy pink, mauve diamonds and emeralds.

380
Hameau de la Reine Spinelle Rose ring,
Dior à Versailles, côté Jardins collection, 2017.
Pink, yellow, and white gold,
diamonds, pink spinels, pink sapphires,
emeralds, Paraiba-type tourmalines,
rubies, and yellow sapphires.

381
Rose Antique Sapphire Rose ring,
Le Bal des Roses collection, 2011.
Pink gold, diamonds,
pink sapphires, and rubies.

382
Roi de Crocidolior pendant,
Reines et Rois collection, 2009.
Platinum, white gold, eye of the tiger,
quartz, and diamonds.

383
Jaune Jonquille Saphir Jaune ring,
Gem Dior collection, 2019.
Yellow gold, diamonds,
and yellow sapphires.

384 – 85
Rose des Vents cuff,
Rose des Vents collection, 2015.
Yellow, white and pink gold,
diamonds, mother-of-pearl, lapis lazuli,
malachite, turquoise, onyx,
Tiger Eye, carnelian, and pink opal.

386
Nougat ring,
Nougat collection, 2003.
Yellow gold.

387
Mitza ring,
Mitza collection, 2003.
Yellow gold, brown and black lacquer.

388
Bosquet du Théâtre d'Eau Diamant jaune earrings,
Dior à Versailles, côté Jardins collection, 2017.
Yellow gold, diamonds,
emeralds and yellow diamonds.

389
Envol Drapé Émeraude ring,
Archi Dior collection, 2014.
Yellow gold, diamonds,
fancy yellow diamonds and emeralds.

390
Vert Prairie Émeraude earrings,
Gem Dior collection, 2019.
Yellow gold, diamonds, emeralds,
chrysoberyls, yellow sapphires,
sapphires, Paraiba-type tourmalines
and tsavorite garnets.

391
Coffret de Victoire pendant,
Coffret de Victoire collection, 2003.
Platinum, diamonds, coral,
doublet opals, chrysoprase, peridots,
Paraiba tourmalines, rubellite,
green tourmaline, tsavorite garnet
and yellow tourmalines.

392
Volupté Aigue-Marine earrings,
Dior à Versailles, Pièces Secrètes collection, 2018.
White and pink gold, diamonds,
aquamarines and sapphires.

393
Tête de Mort ring,
Tête de Mort collection, 2018.
Yellow gold, diamonds,
amethyst and tsavorite garnets.

394
Dentelle Organza Grenat Tsavorite earrings,
Dior Dior Dior collection, 2018.
White gold, diamonds, tsavorite
garnets, emeralds, and demantoid garnets.

395
Vert Pistache Grenat Tsavorite double ring,
Gem Dior collection, 2019.
Yellow gold, diamonds,
tsavorite garnets, and emeralds.

396
Poisono Misterius Green Epicea ring,
Belladone Island collection, 2007.
White gold, diamonds, rubies,
Ethiopian opal, pink spinels, purple
spinels, spinels, tsavorite garnet,
orange sapphires, orange spinels,
purple sapphires, and lacquer.

397
Rose Dior Pré Catelan ring,
Rose Dior Pré Catelan collection, 2000.
Yellow gold, diamonds, and red coral.

398
Rose Dior Pop ring,
Rose Dior Pop collection, 2019.
White and pink gold, diamonds,
sapphire, and blue lacquer.

Rose Dior Pop ring,
Rose Dior Pop collection, 2019.
White and pink gold, diamonds,
Paraiba-type tourmaline, and blue lacquer.

Rose Dior Pop ring,
Rose Dior Pop collection, 2019.
White and pink gold, diamonds,
pink sapphire, and pink lacquer.

Rose Dior Pop ring,
Rose Dior Pop collection, 2019.
White and pink gold, diamonds,
purple garnet, and purple lacquer.

399
Bleu Azur Saphir necklace,
Gem Dior collection, 2019.
White gold, diamonds, sapphires,
purple sapphires, pink sapphires,
aquamarines, and purple garnets.

400
Étincelante Opale ring,
Dior et d'Opales collection, 2017.
Pink gold, diamonds, and light opal.

401
Majestueuse Diamant Pastel earrings,
Cher Dior collection, 2013.
White gold, diamonds, fancy yellow
diamonds, fancy pink diamonds, and
fancy blue-gray diamonds.

402
Bleu Cyan Tourmaline Paraïba earrings,
Gem Dior collection, 2013.
White gold, diamonds, and
Paraiba-type tourmalines.

403
Hameau de la Reine Diamant ring,
Dior à Versailles, côté Jardins collection, 2017.
Yellow, white and pink gold, diamonds,
tsavorite and demantoid garnets, sapphires,
purple and pink sapphires, pink diamonds,
Paraiba-type tourmalines, and lacquer.

404
Bleu Azur Saphir ring,
Gem Dior collection, 2019.
White gold, diamonds,
sapphires, and aquamarines.

405
Dentelle Satin Sapphire earrings,
Dior Dior Dior collection, 2018.
White gold, diamonds, and sapphires.

406
Incroyables et Merveilleuses Étoile de Mer ring,
Incroyables et Merveilleuses collection, 1999.
Yellow gold, diamonds, green beryl,
tsavorite garnets, orange sapphires,
and spinels.

407
Vert Pomme Grenat Tsavorite ring,
Gem Dior collection, 2019.
Yellow gold, diamonds, and
tsavorite garnets.

CHRONOLOGY OF THE COLLECTIONS

1999
Milly-la-Forêt
Incroyables et Merveilleuses
Nuit Blanche
Premier Bal
Roi Soleil

2000
Rose Dior Pré Catelan
Rose Dior Bagatelle

2001
Mimioui
Soumission

2002
La Fiancée du Vampire

2003
Mitza
La D de Dior
Nougat
Coffret de Victoire

2004
Gourmette de Dior
Le Bestiaire fantastique

2005
Oui

2006
Précieuses
Diorette

2007
Belladone Island
Dragon

2008
Milly Carnivora
Milly Magic Carnivora

2009
Reines et Rois
Idylle aux Paradis

2010
Bois de Rose
Précieuses roses

2011
Le Bal des Roses

2012
My Dior
Dear Dior

2013
Cher Dior

2014
Archi Dior

2015
Diorama précieuse
Rose des Vents
Soie Dior

2016
Dior à Versailles
Archi Dior, Milieu du Siècle line

2017
Dior et d'Opales
Dior à Versailles, côté Jardins

2018
Dior Dior Dior
Dior à Versailles, Pièces Secrètes

2019
Mimirose
Gem Dior
Rose Dior Pop

These pieces are made in 750/1000 gold and 950/1000 platinum.
They are not all reproduced at actual size.

These models are the property of Christian Dior Couture.
Any infringement of any of the trademarks, tradenames or copyrights of Christian Dior will be prosecuted to the full extent of the law.

Photographic Credits

Frederike Helwig p. 5. Guido Mocafico p. 105, 106, 111, 125, 130, 140, 142, 144, 145, 150, 177, 182, 185, 187, 203, 213, 220, 228, 234, 237, 251, 256, 257, 305, 325, 336, 339, 340, 373, 374, 382, 387, 396. Anna Leroy p. 107 – 109, 112 – 124, 128, 129, 132 – 135, 137, 141, 147, 149, 152 – 156, 159 – 161, 163, 165, 167 – 171, 173, 176, 183, 184, 186, 189 – 193, 195, 196, 199 – 202, 204, 207– 209, 214 – 218, 221, 223, 226, 227, 229, 230, 232, 233, 236, 238, 239, 241, 243 – 250, 252 – 255, 258, 259, 261, 264, 266, 267, 269 – 278, 279, 281 – 290, 292, 295 – 297, 299, 301, 304, 308 – 321, 324, 326 – 329, 331, 334, 335, 337, 341 – 347, 351 – 359, 362 – 367, 369 – 372, 375 – 378, 380, 381, 383 – 385, 388 – 395, 398 – 400, 402 – 407. Thomas Hugues p. 110, 127, 146, 174, 175, 212, 217, 386, 397. Lenthal p. 115, 131, 136, 148, 151, 157, 162, 166, 194, 210, 219, 222, 224, 231, 235, 240, 242, 263, 280, 332, 368. Erwan Frotin p. 126, 138, 172, 181, 197, 198, 211, 278, 300, 348, 349, 379. Damien Ropero p. 139, 164, 178, 179, 184, 205, 294, 307, 321, 323, 330, 350, 401. Nicolas Bluche p. 180. Dominique Dubois p. 206, 262, 265, 306. All rights reserved. Courtesy of Dior p. 256. Art Go p. 268, 333. Eric Maillet and Nicolas Bluche p. 289. Iris Velghe p. 291. Studio 36 p. 303, 361. Albert Giordan p. 338.

The A to Z of Victoire de Castellane
Dior Joaillerie

First published in the United States of America in 2019 by
Rizzoli International Publications, Inc.
300 Park Avenue South
New York, NY 10010
www.rizzoliusa.com

© 2019 Christian Dior Couture

Texts: Olivier Gabet
Illustrations: Victoire de Castellane

Art Direction: Lenthal

Cover: Erwan Frotin

Publisher: Charles Miers
Editorial Director: Catherine Bonifassi
Editor: Victorine Lamothe
Production Director: Maria Pia Gramaglia
Managing Editor: Lynn Scrabis

Editorial Coordination:
Cassi Edition
Vanessa Blondel, Emma Sroussi

All rights reserved. No part of this publication may be reproduced,
stored in a retrieval system, or transmitted in any form
or by any means, electronic, mechanical, photocopying,
recording, or otherwise, without prior consent of the author.

ISBN: 978-0-8478-6336-5
Library of Congress Control Number: 2019952087
Printed in Italy

Visit us online: Facebook.com/RizzoliNewYork
Twitter: @Rizzoli_Books
Instagram.com/RizzoliBooks
Pinterest.com/RizzoliBooks
Youtube.com/RizzoliNY
Issuu.com/Rizzoli